MAJOR GOVERNMENTS OF ASIA

MAJOR GOVERNMENTS

OF ASIA *By Harold C. Hinton,*

Nobutaka Ike, Norman D. Palmer,

Keith Callard, George McT. Kahin

EDITED BY GEORGE McTURNAN KAHIN

♦♦♦

Cornell University Press, Ithaca, New York

Preface

THIS is the first study in comparative government devoted to the five major states of Asia. It deals with China, India, Japan, Indonesia, and Pakistan, which in population rank respectively as first, second, fifth, sixth, and seventh among the nations of the world. In Asia their stature sets them clearly apart, Pakistan having a population nearly four times that of Turkey, the Asian state next in size.

Comparative government is, of course, a field which has been concerned primarily with the political experience of the West. Its premises, concepts, and principles are largely grounded in that experience, and few scholarly efforts have been made to apply them to Asia. This has been the case with all five of its major states—but especially India, Pakistan, and Indonesia. These three states have, after all, existed for only about a decade, and it is understandable that until quite recently political scientists have been little concerned with them. Their lack of attention to all five countries may reflect an uncertainty as to the extent a discipline so predominantly rooted in Western experience can, at least in its present form, properly be applied to analysis of the widely ranging social and political patterns of the Asian continent.

Whatever the case, there is a serious lack of scholarly studies on the major governments of Asia, particularly the three youngest. Undoubtedly because of this there has been a reluctance to undertake general

v

surveys designed to serve as broad, but solidly based, introductions to Asian government. Until a more substantial foundation of scholarly studies of the particular Asian governments and their principal component elements has been built, it will be difficult for any one man to produce such a survey. Presumably at this stage the best way to achieve a reasonably sound coverage is to assemble a group of specialists, each of whom has already done extensive research and writing on one of these countries—and that is the basis of this book.

The editor suggested a plan of organization, but it has been up to each contributor to decide for himself to what extent it was feasible to follow this. Thus, although among the contributions there is a fair congruence of treatment, the extent of this varies. It is hoped, however, that there is sufficient similarity to help the reader in understanding the material presented and in comparing certain aspects of government and politics in these five major Asian countries.

The authors have all, in varying degrees, presented considerable new and hitherto unavailable data and analyses which it is hoped will interest specialists as well as increase the book's effectiveness as an introductory guide for students and the general reader. In addition, each has prepared an extensive and in general annotated reading list to provide guidance to readers who wish to go more deeply into various aspects of the subjects treated.

For their reading of the manuscripts and their helpful suggestions the contributors wish to acknowledge their indebtedness to their wives —Virginia S. Hinton, Tai Ike, Evelyn K. Palmer, and Maggie McF. Kahin.

The editor desires to express his appreciation to Evelyn Boyce, associate editor of the Cornell University Press, for her assistance in preparing the manuscripts for the printer and for her patience and good humor throughout this long process.

G. McT. Kahin

Cornell University
June 1958

Contents

x *Contents*

Part Four: PAKISTAN *By Keith Callard*

Part Five: INDONESIA By George McT. Kahin

       Indonesia 531

       Formation of a Federal Government 532
       The Unitarian Movement and Creation of a Unitary Govern-
       ment 535
       Soekarno and the Presidency 539
       Hatta and the Vice-Presidency 545
       Cabinet and Parliament 546
       Political Parties 549
       Political Developments, 1950–1958 559

XXIII Some Major Problems 573

       Representative Government 573
       National Unity and Decentralization 574
       The Army 575
       Economic Development 576
       Foreign Relations 578

       Suggested Reading 583

       Index 593

Maps and Charts

xiii

PART ONE : CHINA

By Harold C. Hinton

· I ·

The Historical Background

"CHINA," Napoleon Bonaparte is supposed to have remarked, "there lies a sleeping giant. Let him sleep, for when he wakes he will shake the world." Napoleon's fellow Europeans proceeded to ignore his prophetic advice and to intrude themselves insistently on what he had taken for China's slumber, but what was in reality only its traditional self-containment and self-satisfaction. Within a century after Napoleon's death, China began to awaken, and its awakening, for good or ill, has indeed shaken the world.

China today demands the attention of thinking persons everywhere in the world, and of none more than of Americans. It ranks easily first among the nations of the world in population; the total given by the Communist census of 1953–1954 was 583 million people then living under Chinese Communist rule, and there are no compelling reasons to doubt the essential accuracy or good faith of this figure. China is also among the largest political units in the world in area. It contains quantities of raw materials which may prove large enough to make it in time a major industrial and military power, provided the present Communist policy of putting the might of the state ahead of the satisfaction of consumer needs continues. Since 1949 China has been led by a strong and able leadership operating in close affiliation with, though not subservience to, the international Communist movement. This leadership wields an enormous influence throughout the under-

3

developed areas of the world, and especially in Asia, by virtue of the
fear and the admiration which it inspires. An able and influential, but
perhaps too imaginative, German writer has gone so far as to predict
the emergence of China as a third world power even stronger than
the Soviet Union.[1] An ignorance of the nature and aims of this rising
colossus, regardless of the attitude taken toward it, is a serious chink
in anyone's intellectual armor.

The pages that follow will discuss the place of Communist China
within the Soviet bloc as well as its relationship with pre-Communist
China. Necessary also, for clearer understanding, is some knowledge
of how the Chinese Communists came to power and of what China
was like during its long pre-Communist history.

Ancient China

The prehistory of China is something of a mystery. Archaeology
shows neolithic cultures which existed in parts of North China about
2000 B.C., but it has yet to show how there happened to emerge among
them, by about 1500 B.C., a very highly developed Bronze Age culture
centered in the middle Yellow River Valley. This apparent sudden
bound of the early Chinese into civilization and the strikingly different qualities which that civilization displayed as compared with
any other known early civilization are probably related to one of the
basic and determining facts of China's geography and history, its
isolation.

Bounded as it is on the west and south by deserts and mountains
and on the east by an interminable expanse of water, China has been
throughout its long history the most nearly isolated of all the great
ancient cultural centers. Largely for the same reason, China's power
to transmit its civilization to other lands has been limited to Korea,
Japan, northern Indochina, and parts of Central Asia. Since the Chinese
had close contact with no other civilization which was the equal of
theirs, they early developed a huge cultural superiority complex which
led them to think of China as the Middle Kingdom, or in other words
as the only truly civilized state on earth, and as one to which all other
peoples ought to pay respect and obedience.

From about 1000 B.C. until the foundation of the First Empire in
221 B.C., the Chinese people and Chinese culture were confined to

[1] Wilhelm Starlinger, *Grenzen der Sowjetmacht* (Würzburg: Holzner-Verlag,
1955), pp. 115–122. A summary English translation was published in *U.S. News
and World Report,* Nov. 4, 1955.

an area roughly extending from the Yangtze River to the Great Wall. Over this area there reigned, with an authority that grew weaker as time passed, the Chou dynasty. The center of its power, as with all major Chinese dynasties until the twelfth century A.D., lay in the valley of the Yellow River, an area whose soil is easily workable with simple agricultural implements and one which has a favorable strategic location. During the last several centuries of the Chou period China, from the Great Wall to the Yangtze Valley, was organized in a way that for want of a better term can be called feudal. Both political power and social life were graded in an elaborate but decentralized fashion reminiscent of medieval Europe.

The most powerful of the various states under the increasingly nominal suzerainty of the Chou kings was that of Ch'in, located in Northwest China with its center in what is today the province of Shensi. In the fourth century B.C. the rulers of this state adopted a political philosophy of an almost totalitarian type, known as Legalism, and militarized their state in a way suggesting that of ancient Sparta. By 221 B.C. they had eliminated the Chou kings and conquered all their former vassals. The Ch'in ruler of that period then took the title Ch'in Shih Huang Ti, meaning First Emperor of the Ch'in Dynasty. The Chinese empire, which was to endure until A.D. 1911, had begun.

Imperial China

There is need here for only the briefest summary of the history of imperial China. Its most important feature was the gradual but relentless expansion of the Chinese people into South and Southwest China. This process, which got under way on a large scale about the fourth century A.D., when North China was invaded by alien barbarians, eventually left the prolific and hard-working Chinese peasant in possession of nearly all the cultivable land in the whole of China. The former aboriginal inhabitants, whose descendants still survive in South and Southwest China, were steadily pushed back into the forests and mountains to make room for the energetic Chinese rice farmer, backed by the officials and troops sent by his government.

The southward expansion of the Chinese, combined with an eastward pressure then being exerted by the Tibetans, was responsible for displacing the Thai (Siamese) and the Burmans about a thousand years ago from their original homes in Southwest China and Eastern Tibet respectively into the areas they now inhabit and for pushing the Vietnamese more than a thousand years earlier still from South China

into North Vietnam. Gradual penetration by Chinese merchants into
Southeast Asia had begun before the beginning of the Christian era.
In the late nineteenth and early twentieth centuries a large-scale mi-
gration of South Chinese to Southeast Asia took place, with the result

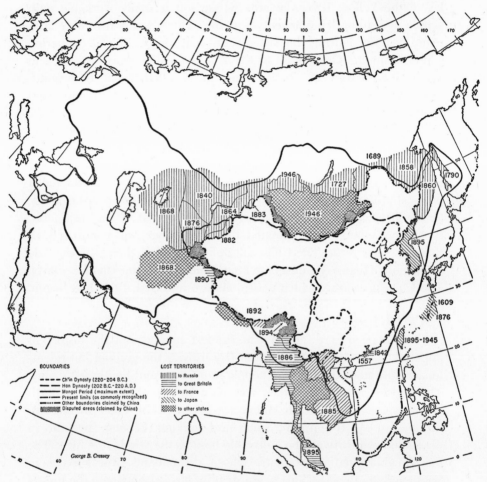

Map 2. Changing China. (By permission from *Land of the 500 Million,*
by G. B. Cressey, copyright 1955, McGraw-Hill Book Co., Inc.)

that there are today at least 10 million and perhaps as many as 13
million Chinese in that region, where they hold a tremendously powerful economic position. A similar migration into Manchuria and Inner
Mongolia has occurred during the past half century.

On this basic theme of Chinese history the rise and fall of dynasties
is superimposed like the comparatively nonessential superstructure of

a ship. During the short-lived but momentous Ch'in dynasty (221–206 B.C.) China was given a very considerable degree of political unity, many of its imperial political institutions, a uniform writing system, and reasonably good communications. Under the next dynasty, the Han (202 B.C.–A.D. 220), this imperial unity was enhanced and solidified, so that the Chinese have ever since believed that all Chinese—that is, all persons of whatever race who are Chinese by culture—ought to be as united politically under a common government as, largely through the medium of the ideographic and comparatively unchanging written language, they are in the cultural realm. China in the great days of the Han (especially the second century B.C. and the first century A.D.) was a mighty empire stretching westward as far as the T'ien Shan mountains, which divide Chinese from Russian Turkestan, and was certainly the equal in power and wealth of the Roman empire, with which it had some indirect cultural and commercial contacts.

Like other Chinese dynasties after them, the Han went through a life cycle usually known as the dynastic cycle. In the first phase of this process, a given dynasty was generally governed by able and martial emperors, who in turn entrusted the tasks of administration to able ministers. These were drawn for the most part from the educated class, often known as the gentry or literati, which nearly monopolized the knowledge, enlargement, and transmission of China's rich and complex literary culture and was hence indispensable to any stable dynasty.

After a few generations, however, the character and ability of the rulers tended to decline, partly at least because of the unwholesome effects of childhood and life in the environment of an Asiatic court, with its harem and eunuchs. Nor were the Chinese emperors exempt from the operation of Lord Acton's profound observation that "power tends to corrupt, and absolute power corrupts absolutely." As emperors began to fight costlier wars and build costlier palaces for their own glorification, they necessarily had to impose increasingly heavy taxes on the peasants who made up the vast majority of their subjects. At the same time, the standards of behavior of ministers, officials, and landowners throughout the empire tended to decline correspondingly. Wealthy and powerful landowners often bribed or browbeat local officials into leaving their lands off the tax registers, so that a proportionately heavier part of the mounting tax burden fell on the shoulders of the peasants and small proprietors, who were least able to pay.

Thus in the last phases of a dynasty China tended to approach, although it never reached, the state of Bourbon France before the Revolution, where the first two estates were exempt from taxes and the third estate and the poor paid instead. When the peasantry had passed the limits of endurance they generally rose in revolt, and the dynasty collapsed in a welter of civil war, and sometimes also foreign invasion, to be succeeded by yet another.

The fall of the Han was followed by a period of about two and one-half centuries during which North China was divided among a number of kingdoms ruled by invading Turks, Mongols, and Tibetans, while South China remained under weak Chinese dynasties. In addition to accelerating the movement of Chinese southward, the turbulence of this period fostered the spread of Buddhism, which became for a time almost the national religion of China. After the restoration of imperial unity, however, Buddhism gave ground before the hostility of the Confucian literati, occasional official persecutions, and the advance of Islam in Central Asia, so that by about the year 1000 Buddhism had ceased to be an important force in Chinese life. It received its final blow from Neo-Confucianism, an eclectic philosophy formulated during the eleventh and twelfth centuries, which grafted elements of Buddhist thought onto the Confucian trunk, stole Buddhism's thunder in this way, and became the official philosophy of the Chinese empire for the rest of its days.

The reunifier of China and founder of the Second Empire was the Sui dynasty (581–617), which like the Ch'in was short-lived and violent. The counterpart of the Han was the glorious T'ang dynasty (618–907), which has a strong claim to being the greatest in the history of all Asia. Once again China ruled Central Asia as far west as the T'ien Shan. So efficient and powerful was China's government and so brilliant was its culture that the Chinese were admired by all other Asian peoples who knew them, and the Japanese consciously and systematically introduced at least the externals of Chinese culture into their own country.

After a short interval of disunion, following the fall of the T'ang, China came under the rule of the Northern Sung dynasty (960–1125). Being peacefully inclined and militarily weak as compared with the T'ang, this dynasty steadily lost control over its northern marches to a people of Mongolian stock, the Khitan. Turning their attention instead toward the sea, the Sung became a great naval and commercial power. The Sung period was also great in art, philosophy, and commercial prosperity and appears to have seen the beginning of a steady growth in China's population which has continued with no significant interruptions down to the present.

In 1125 the Sung lost control of North China to the Juchen tribesmen of Manchuria, with whom they had foolishly allied to crush the Khitan. They are therefore known from then on as the Southern Sung (1127–1279) and soon were confronted with a menace far graver than the Juchen, in the shape of the Mongols. These fierce and extremely mobile nomad cavalrymen had been welded into an empire by the great conqueror Chinggis Khan (ca. 1165–1227; often misspelled Genghis or Jenghiz), who subdued most of North China and Central Asia but did not live to see his horsemen overrun Russia, Persia, and China. It is interesting that the Sung, a weak dynasty by Chinese standards, held out longer against the Mongols than any of these others, so mighty was China even in its time of weakness.

The conquest of the Sung was completed by Chinggis' famous grandson Khubilai, who thereupon founded the Yuan (Mongol) dynasty (1280–1368). The Mongols made few concessions to the Chinese viewpoint. Between them and most Central Asian peoples on the one hand and the Chinese on the other a great cultural gulf is fixed, far wider than divides the Chinese from most of the peoples of Southeast Asia. The Central Asian peoples are nomadic by necessity and warlike by preference, whereas the Chinese can fight when necessary, but generally prefer not to, and get their food from agriculture rather than from herding. In view of this absence of compatibility, the Chinese have regarded the nomads as barbarous and as a serious military problem against which precautions must be taken.

The Yuan dynastry was expelled from China by a national upsurge of Chinese patriotism and xenophobia in 1368, after a comparatively short rule. It was succeeded by a major Chinese dynasty, the Ming (1368–1644). During this period the growing wealth of South China, which had begun to outstrip that of the North during the T'ang period, found its logical reflection in the political sphere. Beginning with the Ming dynasty every major Chinese political movement, including in recent times the Chinese Communist Party, has been led mainly by South Chinese. During their early vigorous years the Ming sent out a series of seven large naval expeditions (1405–1433) which explored the shores and islands of Southeast Asia, penetrated the Indian Ocean, and even went as far west as the Red Sea, trading and enrolling local rulers in the ranks of nominal vassals of the Chinese Emperor. If these expeditions had been followed up, they might have led to the establishment of a Chinese empire in Southeast Asia and materially altered history by excluding the Europeans who came later. But they were not, mainly because of the aversion of the Confucian literati to overseas adventures and unnecessary expenditure. Instead, the Ming tended to lapse into military weakness, corruption, and conservatism, so that in the sixteenth century their northern frontiers were harassed by Mongol armies and their coasts by Japanese pirates.

It was neither of these who finally replaced the Ming, however, but the forest-dwelling Manchus to the north of the Great Wall. By the time of his death in 1626, the great Manchu leader Nurhaci had welded his people into a formidable military and political force. One of his last acts was to fix his capital at Mukden, in a fertile area farmed by Chinese colonists, where under his successors the Manchus rapidly improved their knowledge of Chinese culture and the Chinese way of governing.

Within a decade of Nurhaci's death the tribes of Inner Mongolia and the Korean kingdom had both became vassals of the Manchus, whose flanks were thereby rendered safe for a southward advance against the Ming. In 1644, when the Ming had already been overthrown by domestic rebellions, the Manchus crossed the Great Wall and began the conquest of China. They had already taken the dynastic title Ch'ing (Pure), under which they ruled until 1912.

The further conquests by which the Manchus rounded out their empire may be briefly mentioned. In 1683 Taiwan (Formosa) fell to them, and by the end of the seventeenth century most of the Outer Mongolian tribes had acknowledged themselves vassals. Tibet also became a vassal during the first half of the eighteenth century, and Sinkiang (Chinese Turkestan) was conquered in 1755–1758. The areas so far mentioned, except Korea, constituted the Manchu empire properly speaking. Around the empire lay a fringe of tributary states, of which Korea and Annam (more correctly known as Vietnam after 1803) were the most faithful because the most Sinicized.

The zenith of the Ch'ing dynasty was unquestionably the reign of the wise and vigorous K'ang-hsi Emperor (1661–1722), which was the last golden age of traditional China. Under his able but warlike and arbitrary grandson, the Ch'ien-lung Emperor (1736–1795), the state and society began to groan under the burden of extravagance, growing official corruption, intolerance of unorthodox ideas, and domestic and foreign wars. The empire was still wealthy and powerful, but its foundations were being sapped. Even if its problems had not been further complicated by the intrusion of Western influences, it would have declined and perhaps fallen in the nineteenth century.

The economy of traditional China rested squarely on the production of cereal grains, especially rice, which was grown by countless peasant households using intensive methods of hand cultivation. Above the family, which was the basic economic as well as the basic social unit, the next important entity was the village, in which the peasants lived and from which they went out to tend their scattered plots of land. The village was nearly self-sufficient, except for certain commodities and implements which its residents had to buy from the nearest market town, and its near self-sufficiency imparted to traditional China something of the quality of a modern ship with its watertight compartments; a leak in one or more compartments, such as a local or regional plague or famine, did not necessarily impair the condition of neighboring compartments or the ability of the ship of state to navigate. Higher still there were cities, the imperial capital in particular, in which arts and crafts were highly developed and merchant guilds dealt in such important traditional commodities as tea, silk, porcelain, salt, and copper. These cities never developed the political power and local self-government characteristic of many medieval European cities.

Social classes in traditional China, the barriers between which were much less difficult to cross than in traditional India, were divided into two main groups, the privileged and the unprivileged, their most important representatives being the gentry and the peasantry respectively. The gentry dominated, though it never quite monopolized, the three important fields of literary activity, government service, and land ownership. It was the true elite, and its support or defection was often enough to ensure the survival or fall of a dynasty. Though respected in theory as the basis of society and the producers of food, the peasants in practice enjoyed very few legal or social rights and were usually heavily taxed. They relied mainly on local custom, official inertia, and the implied or actual threat of rebellion to protect them from excessive oppression.

Two other classes, both unprivileged in theory if not always in fact, also deserve mention—the merchants and the soldiers. The Chinese are good businessmen and have always produced energetic and wealthy merchants, but the latter have generally operated under a cloud of social disapproval and have seldom exerted much political influence. Still more despised were the soldiers, who were generally conscripted peasants or semireconstructed bandits. It would be a serious mistake to conclude from this that warfare has not played an important part in Chinese history or that the Chinese are by nature more pacifistic than other peoples. They have produced many fine generals and have fought as successfully and ruthlessly as anyone else when the occasion demanded, but they have always rated the arts of peace above those of war.

For practical purposes, traditional Chinese political thought was dominated by two main philosophic schools, the Confucians and the Legalists. The Confucians succeeded in setting the tone of Chinese social and cultural life and political institutions. They preached respect for tradition (as interpreted by Confucian scholars), for conventional social relationships (including the rites in honor of deceased male ancestors which are inaccurately known as "ancestor worship"), for rule by benevolence and moral example rather than by force, for learning, and for outward proprieties. The Confucian emphasis on loyalty and conformity commended their system to the Han and later emperors, who, however, often violated the Confucian injunction to rule benevolently. When a dynasty governed well, it was considered by both the Confucians and the people to hold the "mandate of heaven," which it could lose, however, through misgovernment. The people were believed to be entitled under this theory to revolt against a dynasty which had lost the mandate, but there was no idea of doing anything more revolutionary than installing a new dynasty.

The actual conduct of public affairs in imperial China was often more reminiscent of Legalism than of Confucianism. Legalism, which was espoused by the state of Ch'in in the fourth century B.C. and extended after 221 B.C. to all of what was then China, was a brutally statist philosophy. Subjects exist only for the benefit of the ruler, and those who benefit him the most are the farmers and the soldiers. All subjects must be kept in line by stringent laws and harsh punishments.

The political institutions of imperial China may be regarded as embodying a subtle and shifting blend of Confucian theory and Legalist practice. At the top of the edifice stood the Emperor, the Son of Heaven, who mediated between the people and their vaguely conceived deities. His power over his subjects was theoretically absolute and tended in practice to grow greater with the passage of time, but it was also considerably limited by precedent and by the "countervailing power" of the nobility and the gentry. Although his approval was necessary for nearly all measures and his work load was therefore enormous, his part in government was usually passive. Barring an exceptional Emperor or an abnormal situation, he generally waited for others to bring matters to his attention much as a modern judge does.

The Emperor was surrounded by an elaborate court, but he depended for the execution of his directives on a quite distinct group, the bureaucracy. This was recruited largely from the gentry class, more particularly from men who had passed a series of difficult civil service examinations testing their knowledge of the classical Confucian philosophical literature. These men had a common body of knowledge, a common standard of behavior, and a common tradition. In the last analysis, the bureaucracy governed the empire, though the total number of its career members at any given time probably never exceeded 10,000. They held the professional positions in the administrative boards (Rites, Civil Office, War, Revenue, Punishments, and Works) and other agencies at the imperial capital, as well as corresponding posts at the provincial and other local levels down through the *hsien* (rural district, or county). The *hsien* magistrate was the lowest ranking official to be appointed directly from the imperial capital. Since he was by usage not appointed to his own native province, he was dependent in many ways on the favor and co-operation of the local gentry and his own locally recruited staff of tax collectors, police, clerks, messengers, and the like. The people themselves were usually more affected by the actions of these subordinates than by those of the magistrate himself.

This far-flung bureaucratic system, reinforced at strategic points by garrisons of imperial troops or local levies, was held together, especially under the non-Chinese Yuan and Ch'ing dynasties, by an elaborate system of postal communications. This system permitted documents to travel in both directions between the capital and the outlying administrative centers by horse or on foot, at a speed proportional to the urgency of the document in question.

Another important bit of cement which contributed to holding the empire together was the censorate, a body of officials empowered to investigate and report abuses on the part of anyone up to and including, at least theoretically, the Emperor himself.

The revenues which nourished the system were derived from four major sources. The first and most important was the land tax, levied on all agricultural land. The second was the grain tribute, levied only in certain provinces and shipped annually up the Grand Canal to feed the bureaucracy and garrison in and near the imperial capital. The third was the salt monopoly, under which the right to deal in salt was sold to private merchants for high fees. The fourth was the "native" (or traditional) customs, imposed on foreign goods or any goods passing certain customs stations. Payment of the first two types of tax, which bore on the peasantry, was generally remitted or postponed in times of distress. On the other hand, the actual tax burden on the people was often greatly increased by corruption and extortion in various forms.

The main traditional categories of governmental expenditure were the maintenance of the court, army, and bureaucracy, the building and repair of public works (such as the dikes along the Yellow River and the Grand Canal), and the giving of relief to the suffering in time of disaster.

It should be clear that the traditional structure of government in China, given the limited bureaucratic and financial resources at its disposal, rested fairly lightly in ordinary times on the people. The only governmental activities which normally and directly concerned them were the collection of taxes, the maintenance of order, and the conscription of men for the army and for labor on public works. The village, under a headman of its own choosing, was almost as autonomous in its political life as it was self-sufficient in its economic life. Where severe oppression existed, it was more likely to be the result of some local or temporary malfunctioning of the system or abuse of authority than of the nature of the system itself. The system was not perfect, its main defect being a tendency toward rigidity resulting from the enormous weight of China's cultural tradition and resistance of the privileged classes to change, but it had the great virtue of stability.

Something remains to be said about traditional China's foreign relations. Not only were the Chinese convinced that all other peoples ought to admire what the Chinese regarded as their superior culture, but they tended to believe that their culture actually was so admired. In fact, the Chinese are admired and respected by their neighbors for their high culture, but they are also hated and feared for their tendency toward demographic expansion and their tremendous actual or potential military and political power. The traditional tributary relationship, already referred to, between China and many of its neighbors institutionalized these ambivalent mutual feelings. It soothed the cultural pride of the Chinese to see those they regarded as barbarians coming to the imperial capital to acknowledge a largely nominal suzerainty of the Chinese Emperor over their own rulers. For this euphoria the Chinese paid the barbarians well with rich gifts and empty titles and occasionally with more valuable protection against foreign and domestic enemies. The tributary states, for their part, derived some cultural and commercial benefit from this client relationship but (except probably in the case of Korea) felt little genuine enthusiasm for the Chinese claim to cultural superiority.

The Western Impact

The Western impact on China has been one of the most important facets of what is perhaps the salient feature of the whole of modern history, the expansion of Europe. Unlike many other areas so affected, China was not transformed into a European political dependency. It was, however, confronted with a challenge too severe for its traditional ideas and institutions to cope with.

Until the end of the nineteenth century, Western influences came to China mainly in the baggage of the Western merchant and the Western missionary. Broadly speaking, the former brought with him Western commodities and technology, and the latter Christianity and European culture.

Portuguese merchants began to come to China in limited numbers in the sixteenth century, and they were followed in the subsequent century by Dutch, French, British, and Russian rivals. China at that time was in advance of Europe in most material respects; Chinese goods, especially tea, silk, and porcelain, were in great demand in Europe, but there was no corresponding demand in China for European goods. The foreigners were therefore faced with a serious payments problem, which they solved by importing silver bullion and coins. The situation was greatly eased by the British discovery in the late eighteenth century that opium grown in the newly acquired British territories in India could be sold at handsome prices in China.

According to the official attitude of the Chinese government during this early period foreign trade was considered a minor nuisance which should be tolerated but not encouraged. By about 1760, however, the Ch'ien-lung Emperor had banned trade with the Western nations except at the port of Canton, and even there it was subjected to very strict regulation.

By the beginning of the seventeenth century a group of Jesuit missionaries had begun to gain acceptance at the Chinese court as a first step toward converting China. They even hoped, very unrealistically, to convert the Emperor himself and thus create a Chinese

Constantine. Unfortunately for them and their cause, the Jesuits aroused the jealousy of other Catholic missionary orders by their successes in China and by certain concessions they made to Chinese culture, such as allowing their converts to continue to perform the rites of "ancestor worship." When it became clear that the Holy See was inclining against the Jesuit position in the so-called Rites Controversy, the K'ang-hsi Emperor in 1706 decreed that only those missionaries would be allowed to preach in China who adhered to the Jesuit view on the questions in dispute. After 1742, when the Jesuit position was officially condemned at Rome, this edict had the effect of putting a virtual end to Catholic missions in China for the time being.

China's contacts with both the foreign merchant and the foreign missionary entered a new phase in the early nineteenth century. China's foreign trade was transformed during that period by two new features. The first was the growing trade in opium, which was smuggled into China and adversely affected not only the health but the finances of the coastal population of South China. The second was the industrialization of Britain, which rendered British manufacturers and exporters anxious to sell their goods, especially textiles, on the supposedly limitless Chinese market. In 1833 Parliament abolished the British East India Company's monopoly on British trade with China. The company had not taken part in the opium trade directly and had tended to act as a check valve on Sino-British trade in general. With its removal, China began to feel the full impact of British goods and British pressure for expanded trade.

The so-called Opium War (1839–1842) between Britain and China resulted from China's refusal to permit normal diplomatic relations and free trade between the European nations and itself, from the Chinese insistence on subjecting foreign nationals accused of crimes to the brutalities of Chinese criminal procedure, and from a determined Chinese effort to put an end to the opium trade. The decayed might of the Manchu empire proved no match for the small British expeditionary force sent against it. The Treaty of Nanking, imposed by the British in 1842, set the pattern for a long series of what the Chinese came to call "unequal treaties."

Under these treaties, which China was compelled to sign with all principal foreign powers including the United States and Japan, China lost much of its sovereignty. It could no longer try foreigners on its soil, but had to allow them to be tried by their own courts and under their own law. It could no longer fix its own tariffs on foreign goods entering its ports; these were set by treaty at a very low rate. It was compelled to establish conventional diplomatic relations with the treaty powers. It was forced to open numerous "treaty ports" to foreign trade and allow the establishment in them of foreign concessions, in which foreigners could lease land and carry on business and which were not subject to Chinese administration. It was made to legalize the importation of opium, to allow the establishment of foreign-owned factories in the treaty ports, and to open its inland waterways to foreign shipping.

The advantages which these treaties gave to foreign manufacturers and merchants were considerable. Foreign goods, especially opium and cotton textiles, entered in increasing quantities and tended to disrupt the Chinese economy by creating an unfavorable trade balance and wiping out local handicrafts. China's two major traditional exports, tea and silk, were almost driven off the world market about the end of the nineteenth century by British and Japanese competition respectively.

The nineteenth-century Western impact began to undermine not only China's economic self-sufficiency but also its cultural self-confidence. About the middle of the century, under the protection of the "unequal treaties," Christian missionaries both Catholic and Protestant came to China in sizable numbers and made steady but not spectacular progress in the field of conversions. They also set up schools, hospitals, and orphanages, which helped to acquaint the Chinese with Western ethics and culture. They waged war on Chinese superstitions and on cruel customs such as the binding of the feet of upper-class girls. Less tolerant than the earlier Jesuits, they denounced the Confucian basis of Chinese culture and thus sowed doubt in the minds of some and resentment in the minds of others.

In 1898 some of the powers began to establish "spheres of influence" for themselves in China: a Russian sphere in Manchuria (the southern third of which was taken over by the Japanese after the Russo-Japanese War of 1904–1905), a German sphere in Shantung, a British sphere in the Yangtze Valley, a Japanese sphere in Fukien, and a French sphere in Southwest China. Within each sphere the power in question held a near monopoly on investment and the development of communications. The fact that this trend did not lead to an outright partition of China into a number of foreign possessions was due to two main causes: the first and more important was the rivalry among the powers themselves, which culminated in the First World War and which preserved a precarious balance among their interests in China; the second was the policy of the United States.

The United States was reluctant to see China partitioned into Western spheres of influence or outright colonies. This reluctance found expression in Secretary of State John Hay's two famous Open Door notes, the first (1899) of which attempted to secure equality of opportunity for American trade within the newly created foreign spheres of influence and the second (1900) of which requested the other powers to respect the "territorial and administrative entity" of China. The Open Door Policy had a slight, but only a slight, effect in checking foreign pressures on China; it would have had more effect if there had been any reason to think that the United States would fight to enforce it.

The Chinese response to the challenge posed by the Western impact in the nineteenth century was slow, uncertain, and much less impressive and effective than Japan's contemporary response to the same challenge. The Chinese were handicapped from the outset by their complacency and cultural superiority complex, as well as by their abysmal and comic ignorance of the West and of its true strength. Few Chinese could deny after 1842, however, that Western armies and navies were stronger than those of China. During the terrible Taiping Rebellion (1850–1864), which if it had not been suppressed would have resulted in the overthrow of the Ch'ing dynasty by a pseudo-Christian successor dynasty, both sides made some use of Western weapons and military techniques. The years after the rebellion, known to the Chinese as the T'ung-chih Restoration (1861–1874), saw the building of a limited number of modern arsenals and dockyards with the help of foreign technicians, the translation of some Western technical treatises into Chinese, the training of a few young Chinese in Western languages and studies, and the beginnings of conventional diplomatic relations between China and the major foreign powers. These essentially technical innovations continued, at a moderate pace which was far from adequate to the need, during the remainder of the nineteenth century.

The early Chinese modernizers responsible for these innovations were mainly officials committed to the traditional values of Chinese culture, though they made use of foreign advisers and Chinese compradors (agents for foreign firms doing business in the treaty ports). The aim of these officials was not to abandon or even modify the essentials of Chinese culture, but rather to preserve them by arming them with efficient modern military and economic techniques.

Toward the end of the nineteenth century it became clear to a growing number of Chinese, though not yet to the dynasty itself, that this formula was not good enough. Western technology would not flower in China unless some of the institutional soil in which it thrived at home were transplanted as well. The earliest convincing demonstration of this truth was the Sino-Japanese War (1894–1895), in which China was roundly defeated by another Asian power which had modernized far more effectively than China and had adopted not only Western techniques but also some Western institutions, such as a constitution and a parliament. The next demonstration was the "Scramble for Concessions" of 1898, which showed the Chinese how weak they still were and how close China had come to being partitioned by the powers.

The seriousness of the situation lent force to the arguments of a rising group of Chinese who favored the institutional as well as technical modernization of China under a constitutional monarchy of either the authoritarian Japanese or the liberal British type. The leaders of this group were two prominent intellectuals named K'ang Yu-wei and Liang Ch'i-ch'ao. In the spring of 1898 they gained the confidence of the young and well-meaning Kuang-hsü Emperor (1875–1908) and persuaded him to implement their program. There ensued the so-called Hundred Days Reform (June–September 1898), during which the Emperor promulgated a series of decrees aimed at modernizing the armed forces, the bureaucracy, the legal and educational system, and the economy. The people remained apathetic, however, and the bureaucracy was strongly hostile to the reforms. These reforms were nearly all canceled when the Empress Dowager Tz'u-hsi, the Emperor's aunt, who had dominated the court in her capacity of regent during most of the period from 1861 to 1889, resumed power and overthrew the reformers.

Even the Empress Dowager, however, became convinced of the urgent necessity for reform as a result of the Boxer Rebellion (1899–1900). This was an antiforeign, and especially anti-Christian, rising of lower-class Chinese in the northern provinces. The Empress Dowager lent the movement encouragement and support and even went so far as to declare war on the foreign powers (June 1900) and besiege the Legation Quarter in Peking. In mid-August, however, an international relief expedition moved up from Tientsin, took Peking, and drove the Empress Dowager and court into exile. The dynasty then had to put its seal on a humiliating peace treaty which included a large indemnity.

Convinced too late of the need for modernization, the Empress Dowager proceeded to put into effect a reform program basically similar to the abortive one attempted by the Emperor in 1898. Usually known as the Manchu Reform Movement, this program showed some genuine if inadequate progress until the Empress Dowager's death in 1908, but thereafter tended to flounder for lack of strong leadership. The most concrete success was the almost complete eradication of opium production in China and a simultaneous agreement by the powers to eliminate gradually the importation of opium into China from abroad. Others were the creation of a modernized model army of six divisions under the able but unscrupulous official Yuan Shih-kai, a partial modernization of the bureaucracy, the promulgation of a monarchical but parliamentary constitution modeled largely on the Japanese, the construction of a sizable mileage of railways by foreign firms and groups of provincial gentry, and the drawing up of modernized legal codes.

But this official program of reform, like the private one led by K'ang Yu-wei and Liang Ch'i-ch'ao, bore the stamp of too little and too late. China was growing ripe for revolution.

The Revolutionary Movement

The cause of revolution in China, like that of reform, received its first major stimulus from the Japanese defeat of China in 1894–1895. The Japanese defeat of Russia in 1904–1905 gave further impetus to the revolutionary movement, especially in view of the contrast between Japan's strength and the miserable weakness which China had displayed at the time of the "Scramble for Concessions" and the Boxer Rebellion. Japan appeared to Chinese, Indians, and other Asians, suffering in varying degrees from the effects of the Western impact, as the light of Asia. Attracted also by the comparative nearness and cheapness of the Japanese schools and universities, Chinese and other Asian students flocked there in the early years of the twentieth century. Some were sent on scholarships provided by the Ch'ing dynasty, but regardless of the source of their support most of these students were extremely nationalistic, anti-Manchu, and susceptible to the propaganda of revolutionaries.

There is space here only for an account of the most important of these revolutionaries, Sun Yat-sen. Born near Canton in 1866, into a poor family, Sun received a secondary and advanced education of the Western type in Hawaii and Hong Kong. About 1885 he became a revolutionary, and in 1895 he founded the first of a series of secret organizations dedicated to the overthrow of the Manchus. Between then and the Revolution of 1911 he launched around ten risings, some comic, some tragic, and all unsuccessful. In the intervals he spent most of his time traveling in America, Europe, and the Far East, soliciting funds and support for his movement from among overseas Chinese. These he received, but the movement was doomed to frustration by its limited membership and conspiratorial methods. This political ineffectiveness acted as a check on the influence of Sun's political ideas, which had begun to take shape by about 1905.

By 1911 both the finances and the prestige of the Ch'ing dynasty had reached an extremely low point. On October 10 of that year a mutiny began in a government garrison at Wuchang, near Hankow, among troops who had been infected by revolutionary propaganda. This mutiny rapidly grew into a revolt which by the end of the year swept most of South China clear of Manchu authority. Representatives of the revolutionary groups met at Nanking in December, proclaimed the Republic of China, and elected Sun Yat-sen, then returning from the United States, its provisional President.

Meanwhile the Ch'ing government, under pressure of the crisis and at the insistence of its own National Assembly, had appointed Yuan Shih-kai Premier with dictatorial powers and the mission of suppressing the revolt. He had other ideas, however, and after inflicting some sharp defeats on the insurgents he opened secret negotiations with them in December 1911. The outcome was a celebrated agreement between Yuan and Sun Yat-sen in January 1912, under whose terms Sun resigned the provisional presidency in Yuan's favor and Yuan on his part agreed to compel the Manchu boy Emperor to abdicate and thereby to extend the authority of the revolutionary government to North China. This Yuan did in February, but he violated other commitments to the revolutionaries by removing the capital from Nanking to Peking and negotiating for a foreign loan to render him financially independent of them. It was clear that Yuan intended to dominate, and perhaps even to overthrow, the infant republic.

In preparation for the parliamentary elections scheduled for the winter of 1912–1913, a number of new political parties arose. Among these was the Kuomintang (National People's Party), which though led by Sun Yat-sen and composed of his followers was so reorganized and revitalized at that time by Sun's leading lieutenant, Sung Chiao-jen, that it may be regarded as virtually a new party. The Kuomintang won a plurality in both houses of parliament in the elections, and Sung would probably have become Premier if he had not been assassinated at Yuan Shih-kai's instigation in March 1913. Revolts, in which the Kuomintang was heavily implicated, broke out in some southern provinces during the following summer, but Yuan suppressed them without much difficulty.

He then dissolved the parliament, outlawed the Kuomintang (most of whose leaders fled to Japan), and proceeded to promulgate a constitution under which he, as President, became a virtual dictator. He ruled with an iron hand and gave China the most orderly and oppressive government it had known for more than a century. He was soon ruined, however, by Japanese enmity and his own ambition.

The Japanese government was opposed on principle to the unification of China under a strong leader, which would render China less susceptible to Japanese influence. Yuan seemed to be such a leader, and he had earned additional hatred from the Japanese by opposing their encroachments in Korea during the decade preceding the Sino-Japanese War. In August 1914 the Japanese government entered the First World War on the Allied side, primarily in order to acquire German holdings in the Pacific. Having seized the former German sphere of influence in Shantung, the Japanese presented Yuan Shih-kai in the spring of 1915 with the notorious Twenty-one Demands, which if accepted in their entirety would have transformed China into a virtual protectorate of Japan. Backed by world opinion, Yuan was able to secure a considerable modification of these demands, but he had to acquiesce in the Japanese position in Shantung.

The final Japanese blow to Yuan was delivered in connection with his plans to make himself Emperor. Late in 1915 he manipulated a show of popular support for his plans and announced that he would establish a new dynasty. This step aroused widespread opposition and even revolts in China, and the Japanese and other governments added their disapproval of the scheme. Yuan abandoned his imperial ambitions, and in June 1916 he died, while trying vainly to suppress the revolts which his announcement had touched off.

After Yuan's death the constitution and parliament of 1913 were restored. Within about a year, however, the republic was gravely weakened by the defection of the Kuomintang (which proceeded to set up a rival regime at Canton) and by widespread opposition to the government's action in taking China into the First World War on the Allied side. This it did at American insistence and mainly in order to secure a seat at the peace conference, from which it could press for abrogation of Japan's position in Shantung.

In fact, the republic soon degenerated into a dismal farce, which did much to disillusion Chinese intellectuals with Western parliamentary institutions, as embodied in the half-dozen constitutions drawn up in China between 1912 and 1928, and to pave the way for avowedly authoritarian alternatives. The recognized government at Peking became the plaything of shifting combinations of disreputable generals usually referred to as warlords. The typical warlord was a man of humble birth who had acquired at least the rudiments of a modern military education either in China or abroad and who after the Revolution of 1911 had become military governor of a province. Controlling the armed forces of the province, he also dominated its political life. He fought frequently with nearby rivals and generally treated the province as his private preserve, taxing the population almost beyond endurance. A few particularly powerful generals, who could be called superwarlords, controlled entire regions such as Manchuria (Chang Tso-lin) and Northwest China (Feng Yü-hsiang). Though often colorful and not always vicious, these warlords had a bad effect on China. Militarism and Western imperialism came to rank in the eyes of Chinese revolutionaries as the two major evils which must be eliminated if China was to progress. Nevertheless, warlordism, or regional militarism, survived the fall of the republic in 1928 and continued to plague China until at least as late as 1949.

There are several important trends operating during the period from 1912 to 1928 which need to be mentioned before discussion of the republic and the warlords is concluded and the rise of the Kuomintang is considered. One was the tendency of the major parts of the former Manchu empire to separate themselves from China after 1912 and go their separate ways. The peoples of Outer Mongolia, Sinkiang, and Tibet had regarded themselves as subjects of the Manchus, not of the Chinese. Some of them had, furthermore, been antagonized by Chinese immigration into their territories, which the Manchus had encouraged after about 1900 as a precaution against absorption of the regions by Russia or Japan. After the Revolution, Outer Mongolia became independent of China in all but name and came under Soviet domination after 1921; Sinkiang fell under a succession of local Chinese warlords and was subject to powerful Soviet economic and political penetration from 1932 to 1943; and Tibet remained largely free of Chinese influence until the Chinese Communists overran it in 1950–1951.

The tendency toward gradual economic modernization, especially in the coastal regions of China, which was noted in the nineteenth century, continued to operate during the republican period. Western commodities came increasingly into use, except in the most remote regions, and the growing of cash crops such as cotton or tobacco partially replaced subsistence farming in some coastal areas. On the whole, however, the peasant was more affected during this period by domestic political disorder than by foreign economic influences. No important change occurred in his agricultural techniques or in the trend toward more widespread tenancy. This trend was especially prevalent near the coastal cities and was the result primarily of the growth of population and the traditional preference of Chinese investors for land as the safest and most respectable outlet for their capital. Modern enterprises, both Chinese and foreign in ownership, continued to grow in the cities, but they were still far too few to make much of an impression on China's poverty and backwardness. China remained an overwhelmingly agrarian country, and the living standards of its people tended on the whole to get worse rather than better.

The most important trend of all was the growth of Chinese nationalism, in protest against both foreign imperialism and domestic militarism. One aspect of this trend was cultural and is usually known as the Chinese Renaissance. The two main leaders were Hu Shih, who had studied at Columbia University in New York, and Ch'en Tu-hsiu, a professor who later became a founder of the Chinese Communist Party. Both men, and especially Ch'en, favored an almost complete scrapping of traditional Chinese culture and the substitution of Western culture in its materialistic and scientific aspects; Hu also led an ultimately successfully campaign for the use of *pai-hua* (the spoken vernacular) in literature, instead of classical Chinese.

Still more important were the political manifestations of nationalism, which may be said to have begun to affect the intellectuals about 1895, the merchants a few years later, the small but growing industrial working class about 1918, and the peasants about 1925. The decision of the Versailles Conference in 1919 awarding the former German sphere in Shantung to Japan and the willingness of the pro-Japanese clique then in control of the Peking government to accept that award promptly touched off the first major manifestation of modern Chinese nationalism, the so-called May Fourth Movement. This movement, which began with student demonstrations in Peking and spread from there to other parts of the country, had the effect of preventing Chinese adherence to the Treaty of Versailles and of raising nationalist feeling to new heights. It later rose to fever pitch at the time of the May Thirtieth Movement of 1925, which was precipitated by the shooting of Chinese demonstrators by British-officered police in the International Settlement at Shanghai. For the next two years antiforeignism in China raged unchecked, and many Christian missionaries found it wise to leave their mission stations for safer places.

This upsurge of Chinese nationalism, combined with a rising feeling in foreign countries that China had been unjustly treated and that Japan must be checked, led to some improvements in China's international position. At the Washington Conference (1921–1922), Japan agreed to evacuate Shantung, the Open Door Policy was written into treaty form for the first time (the Nine Power Pact), and it was agreed in principle that the obnoxious features of the "unequal treaties" ought to be abrogated. Lenin's Bolshevik government made a very favorable impression in China by issuing in 1919 a ringing renunciation of former tsarist special privileges in China, though it was careful to regain in 1924 the right to operate the Chinese Eastern Railway through Manchuria to Vladivostok.

From 1913 to 1923 Sun Yat-sen's position was pathetic. His party was weak and ineffective, and he was largely dependent for what power he had on temporary alliances with unreliable warlords or other revolutionary factions. His futility was to a great extent the result of his own character, which was unselfish, patriotic, and sincere, but also impulsive, vacillating, and naïve. Even his political philosophy was not especially remarkable, but since it later became the official philosophy of China it deserves some attention.

Sun held that China could and should be transformed through the implementation of what he called the Three Principles of the People (San Min Chu I). Sun had advocated these principles as early as 1905, but they did not take final form until 1924, by which time Sun had become disillusioned with the Western democracies and favorably impressed by some aspects of Bolshevism.

The first was Nationalism, which meant the elimination of foreign imperialism and domestic militarism from China and the creation of a united but not aggressive national state embracing not only the

Chinese but also the Manchus, the Mongols, the Moslems of North-west China and Chinese Central Asia, and the Tibetans.

The second principle was Democracy, by which Sun meant a form of government in which the people should exercise the rights of election, recall, initiative, and referendum, but in which only educated and qualified persons should be admitted to the civil service. The government was to be divided into five branches corresponding to what Sun considered the major functions of government: executive, legislative, judicial, examination (roughly equivalent to the imperial civil service examination system), and control (roughly equivalent to the imperial censorate). Democracy as Sun defined it, however, was to be attained only in the last of three constitutional stages. During the first stage, the Kuomintang would unify China by force of arms. In the second, known as the period of Political Tutelage, the Kuomintang would exercise a monopoly of political power but use that power to train the people in the arts of self-government, so as to make possible the establishment of democracy and constitutional government.

The third principle was People's Livelihood, meaning the redistribution of land among the actual cultivators and state control of communications and heavy industry, all for the public benefit. As the comparative mildness of this program shows, Sun was far from being a Marxist.

It hardly seems necessary to comment on the vagueness and naïveté of these principles, except to emphasize Sun's unrealism in expecting a party once entrenched in dictatorial power to work for the abolition of its own dictatorship.

Sun's political ideas would not warrant even this brief summary if he had not found an ally to help him implement them. At that time Lenin and the Comintern (Third International) were casting about for Asian nationalist movements with which they might ally themselves in a joint struggle against the position of the Western powers in Asia. In 1922 they fixed on the Kuomintang as the most likely prospect in China, and a fateful alliance was accordingly concluded in 1923.

Under the terms of this alliance, the Comintern and the Soviet government provided the Kuomintang with arms, funds, and a staff of military and political advisers. The advisers reorganized the Kuomintang from top to bottom along the "democratic centralist" lines of the Soviet Communist Party and thereby transformed it for the first time into an effective political instrument. The Kuomintang also began to acquire something else it had lacked before—a reliable and effective army, which was built around an officer corps trained at the newly founded Whampoa Military Academy, near Canton.

There was another important aspect to the Kuomintang-Comintern alliance, namely, a coalition between the Kuomintang and the young and far weaker Chinese Communist Party. Sun Yat-sen insisted that Communists could enter the Kuomintang only as individuals, not as a bloc, and that they must abide by the usual conditions of membership, including party discipline. The Comintern compelled the Chinese Communists, against the better judgment of their leaders, to comply. They did so with the aim of using the Kuomintang for their own purposes, if possible.

The alliance between the Kuomintang on the one hand and the Comintern and the Chinese Communist Party on the other conferred during its brief existence considerable benefits on all the parties, but most of all on the Kuomintang. It gave the Kuomintang not only efficient party and military machinery, but also a revolutionary zeal and a corps of agitators and propagandists, mostly Communists, who were of inestimable value in forming labor and peasant unions and in undermining the will of warlord armies to resist. The alliance, however, was an unstable one, because the two parties to it had incompatible aims and distrusted each other.

The alliance began to show signs of strain not long after the death of Sun Yat-sen in March 1925. A year later General Chiang Kai-shek, the Kuomintang's leading military figure, brought off a coup which severely limited the power of the Soviet advisers and the Communists over party affairs. Stalin and the Comintern, however, decided to ignore the challenge, on the theory that everything must be subordinated to the success of the Northern Expedition, as the projected military campaign for the unification of China was called. Later, as Stalin put it, Chiang Kai-shek could be cast aside, like a squeezed lemon.

The Northern Expedition accordingly got under way in the summer of 1926 and from the beginning won brilliant successes. The rabble armies of provincial militarists melted away before the advance of the Kuomintang forces and their accompanying agitators. By the end of 1926 most of South China and the Yangtze Valley had been conquered, and the capital of the Kuomintang revolutionary regime and its party headquarters were transferred from Canton to Hankow. There they fell under the virtually complete control of the Soviet ad-

visers, the Communists, and those elements within the Kuomintang
which favored a leftist orientation for the party.

Chiang Kai-shek, whose forces were advancing farther to the east, in
the lower Yangtze Valley, noted this trend with disapproval. To protect his own position and prevent the Bolshevization of the Kuomintang, he prepared to strike. Against his blow his leftist opponents took
no adequate steps to protect themselves, mainly because of Stalin's
insistence that everything possible must be done to avoid giving offense
to Chiang Kai-shek. Having entered Shanghai with the active and
effective co-operation of the Communist-led labor unions of that city,
Chiang turned on them suddenly on April 12, 1927, and crushed them.
He then set up a rival capital at Nanking in opposition to the one at
Hankow.

Stalin now had to admit that Chiang Kai-shek had betrayed the
common cause, but he still would not allow the Chinese Communists
to break off their alliance with the Kuomintang. On the contrary, he
sent them directives instructing them to seize control of the Kuomintang's party machinery and embark on a program of revolutionary
class warfare. Having learned of this policy, however, the Left Kuomintang at Hankow broke with its dangerous allies on July 15, 1927, and
expelled the Communists and the Soviet advisers. Soon afterward most
of the Left Kuomintang leaders submitted to Chiang Kai-shek.

By the spring of 1928 Chiang had consolidated his position within
the party sufficiently to resume the Northern Expedition. In spite of
a Japanese attempt to block the advance of his armies by sending
troops back to Shantung, he took Peking in June 1928. The Kuomintang
thereupon transferred the capital of China from Peking (which was
then renamed Peiping) to Nanking and officially proclaimed the military unification of China to be complete. The second of Sun Yat-sen's
three constitutional stages, that of Political Tutelage, had begun.

The Kuomintang in Power (1928–1937)

The unity achieved in 1928 was much more nominal than real. The
new government at Nanking controlled little more than the eastern
provinces; elsewhere, especially in Southwest and Northwest China,
provincial or regional militarists still exercised effective power. The
Kuomintang was never able to subdue some of these militarists; instead, it generally followed a policy of giving them high military and
political posts in their own provinces or regions, in the hope of thereby
securing their loyalty. The support purchased in this way resulted in

little of actual value, for some of these generals proved unreliable against the Japanese and still later proved unreliable against the Communists. Their loyalty lasted only as long as the Kuomintang's power lasted.

After the failure of a disarmament conference in 1929 showed how unwilling the regional militarists were to subordinate themselves in fact to the National Government, there occurred a series of revolts against the power and policies of Chiang Kai-shek. Only the most serious of these need be mentioned. In 1929 there was a revolt by the so-called Kwangsi Clique led by Li Tsung-jen and Pai Chung-hsi; in 1930, one by a formidable combination of Feng Yü-hsiang, Yen Hsi-shan (the warlord of Shansi), and Wang Ching-wei (a prominent Left Kuomintang leader); in 1931, one by a group of Left Kuomintang politicians at Canton; in 1933, one by (non-Communist) Left Kuomintang generals and politicians in Fukien; and in 1936, another by the Kwangsi Clique. Chiang overcame all these revolts by force or diplomacy. His army, trained by German advisers, was easily the strongest in China, although it could not eliminate Chiang's most dangerous and elusive enemies, the Communists.

From having been a decidedly revolutionary party under Sun Yat-sen as well as during the brief life of its alliance with the Communists, the Kuomintang after 1927 rapidly turned into a conservative and even reactionary party. Under Chiang Kai-shek's stultifying influence it ceased to produce able, prominent, and original political thinkers, and it therefore had no choice but to deify Sun Yat-sen and his ideas and parrot them without developing them further. Since Sun's political ideas had serious weaknesses, the uncritical propagation of them, combined with a rejection of the generous spirit which had been behind Sun's ideas, imparted to the Kuomintang a rigid and unattractive quality which tended to minimize popular support for it. Chiang Kai-shek and other prominent Kuomintang figures began to preach a return to the ancient Confucian virtues of loyalty, propriety, and the like, ideas which no longer held compelling appeal for a people becoming increasingly convinced of the possibility of and necessity for progress and modernization. One of the least attractive features of official Kuomintang thinking was its strong tendency toward xenophobia; in Chiang Kai-shek's famous tract, *China's Destiny* (published in 1943), for example, almost all China's ills and problems are attributed to Western influence. This strong anti-Western feeling, although to some extent justified, had the effect of making the Western powers less enthusiastic than they would otherwise have been about supporting the National Government against Japanese encroachments.

Another source of weakness was the fact that, although it retained the "democratic centralist" organization imparted to it during the period of the Communist alliance, the Kuomintang was never truly a "monolithic" party of the Communist type. On the contrary, it was ridden with competing cliques whose selfish interests generally outweighed whatever loyalty to a common ideology, common party organization, and common cause they may have had. Basically, the Kuomintang was an unstable coalition of military leaders, businessmen, and rural landlords. More precisely, it was composed of the following major cliques.

On the extreme right stood the CC (or Organization) Clique, so called because it was controlled by the Ch'en brothers. The elder, Ch'en Kuo-fu, was the leading specialist in party organization and controlled most of the local party branches. He was therefore always in a strong position at the rather infrequent party congresses (there were six between 1924 and 1945), whose membership was elected by the local party organs. His younger brother, Ch'en Li-fu, was a leading party ideologist and specialist in education and public indoctrination. He preached a strange philosophy called Vitalism, which represented a blend of Confucianism with nineteenth-century European idealism and enjoyed a decidedly limited popularity. The CC Clique was strongly anti-Communist, dominant in the secret police, and very conservative in its views on social and economic questions.

Slightly less to the right stood the so-called Whampoa (or Military) Clique, whose leader was Chiang Kai-shek. Although also conservative and anti-Communist, this group was more concerned with problems of power than with party organization or ideology. Being specialists in force, the group generally held the balance of power in, though it did not entirely dominate, the party.

Another faction was the Political Science Clique. It was composed largely of bureaucrats and intellectuals devoted to the goal of modern and efficient administration, but without any clearly defined political program.

Apart from these cliques, there were two other groups worth mentioning, though they were not well organized or very influential. The first was a handful of Left Kuomintang politicians, of whom Wang Ching-wei and Sun Yat-sen's son, Sun Fo, were the most prominent. The other group comprised a number of wealthy businessmen, Chiang

Kai-shek's able but temperamental brother-in-law T. V. Soong being the best known.

The keystone in the entire arch of Kuomintang power was Chiang Kai-shek himself. He was by no means all-powerful or universally respected within the party, yet he alone commanded both enough power and enough loyalty to lead the party over a long period of time. Of humble origin, having close connections with the Shanghai underworld, militaristic by training and background, conservative by inclination, and intensely patriotic in a way which led him to consider the maintenance of his own power as essential to the good of the country, Chiang personified both the strengths and the weaknesses of the Kuomintang. A strong man himself, he could not tolerate disagreement from other strong men and preferred to surround himself with sycophants. Personally honest, he refused to credit, or at any rate to punish, the widespread and increasing corruption among his associates and subordinates. Even more addicted than other Kuomintang leaders to multiple officeholding, he held a list of posts in the party, government, and armed forces so long that it would be tedious to reproduce it. If he lacked both the dictatorial power and the charismatic appeal of a Hitler, he was nevertheless a powerful party boss with a secret police force and an army at his disposal.

During the period under consideration, China's constitutional structure, like its political life, reflected the official view that the Kuomintang enjoyed a monopoly of legal political power. As early as 1928 the Kuomintang set up a central government containing five Yuan (branches) corresponding to the five envisioned by Sun Yat-sen: Executive, Legislative, Judicial, Examination, and Control. This was a departure from Sun Yat-sen's program, for Sun had intended the fivefold governmental structure to be introduced at the end, not at the beginning, of the period of Political Tutelage. In most other respects the regime established in 1928 conformed to Sun's plan. The officials of the five Yuan were appointed Kuomintang members whose work was supervised by the Central Executive Committee of the Kuomintang through one of its agencies, the Political Council. Among the Yuan themselves, the executive was by far the most important, though of course it was still bound by party directives. At the top of the governmental structure, though also subject to control by the Kuomintang, stood the State Council, whose chairman was the nearest thing China had to a chief of state. Provincial and local offices were appointive and controlled by the central government and the Kuomintang.

In 1931 a semblance of greater constitutionality was conferred on the National Government through the adoption, by a National People's Convention whose membership had been hand-picked by the Kuomintang, of a provisional constitution. The main change which this constitution made in the pre-existing situation was that it decreased the powers of the chairman of the State Council, which post Chiang Kaishek had just given up as a sop to his opponents, who were then very vocal. He continued, however, to be very powerful in the government, in the party, and (through his chairmanship of the Military Affairs Commission) in the armed forces. The provisional constitution contained no provision for its own amendment and vested the important power of constitutional interpretation in the Central Executive Committee of the Kuomintang. It was, in short, a legalization of Political Tutelage.

With amazing optimism the Kuomintang had promised in 1929 to complete the tasks of Political Tutelage within six years, and accordingly as early as 1933 it began work on a draft constitution for the last stage, that of constitutional government. After numerous revisions the draft was published with the party's blessing in May 1936. Unfortunately, it had several serious defects. The Executive Yuan was to be responsible, not to the Legislative Yuan in the British manner, but to a large and infrequently convened National Assembly. The powers of the President of the Republic, the chief of state, who was to be elected by the National Assembly, were so broad that it seemed likely that he would dominate the five Yuan and their respective presidents. The powers of the provincial and local governments were insufficiently protected from possible encroachments by the central government, and civil liberties were subject to restriction by legislation. It was very probable that under this constitution the Kuomintang would continue to dominate the political life of the country. It did in fact dominate elections held in 1936 for the members of a National Assembly to which the draft constitution was to be submitted for consideration; the convening of the Assembly, however, was prevented by the outbreak of war with Japan in July 1937.

The question of how the National Government of China functioned in practice during the period from 1928 to 1937 is a very important one, for it was then that the Kuomintang had its best chance to show what it could do for China. It is true that the Kuomintang was faced with enormous obstacles, such as a backward economy, domestic insurrections, and continuous Japanese pressure after 1931, but even when allowance is made for these difficulties its record remains far from impressive.

By 1937, and for that matter as late as 1949, not a single one of the 2,000-odd *hsien* in China had attained the state of local self-government which Sun Yat-sen had considered a prerequisite to the establishment of self-government on the provincial and national scales. Nor was the mere absence of self-government the worst feature of Political Tutelage. The latter also carried with it a rigorous punitive censorship of the press, a large network of secret police and prisons, and a massive "white terror" flourishing in the cities and towns and directed not only against real or suspected Communists but also against others to whose actions or statements the Kuomintang objected. In some rural areas, especially those reconquered from the Communists, the National Government introduced after the mid-1930s the oppressive *pao-chia* system of collective responsibility for the crimes of individuals. To propagandize its official ideals of obedience and propriety, the Kuomintang inaugurated in 1934 a so-called New Life Movement, which was, however, perhaps more comic than oppressive in its actual working.

Unfortunately, the absence of freedom was not compensated by any significant increase in efficiency or mitigated by any noteworthy progress in the social and economic fields. Much praiseworthy legislation was promulgated, but it remained largely on paper. This was true, for example, of a law of 1930 fixing maximum rents on agricultural land at three-eighths of the annual crop. The unfortunate effects of the Depression, which included an outflow of silver, led to the introduction of a managed currency in 1935, under which the right of note issue was profitably confined to four central banks controlled respectively by T. V. Soong, H. H. Kung, the Ch'en brothers, and Chiang Kai-shek. The Kuomintang's approach to economic questions, at least in practice, was essentially one of dipping its hand as often as possible into a stagnant pool of wealth rather than one of trying to stir up the pool and increase its size.

In the field of foreign affairs the Kuomintang was only slightly more successful. By 1931 it had successfully asserted its right to fix its own tariff rates and was on the way to abolishing the extraterritorial rights of citizens of all but the major foreign powers (the United States, Great Britain, and Japan). But these successes were dearly won, for the extreme antiforeignism of the Kuomintang tended to alienate the Western powers and render them less sympathetic to China's case against its major enemy, Japan, than they might otherwise have been.

At the hands of Japan the Kuomintang suffered a long series of injuries and humiliations: the conquest of Manchuria in 1931–1932, an attack by the Japanese navy on the "native" city of Shanghai in 1932, the occupation of Jehol province and the forced demilitarization of the Peiping-Tientsin area in 1933, an unsuccessful attempt in 1935 to make five provinces of North China and Inner Mongolia "autonomous" and thus more susceptible to Japanese penetration, and an extraordinary set of demands in 1936 which if accepted would have transformed Nationalist China into a virtual Japanese protectorate.

Until 1936 the National Government's response to these outrages was one of temporizing, for it feared the power of the Japanese and in any case was more interested in trying to suppress the Communists. This negative policy served only to whet the Japanese appetite and to arouse further the indignation of the articulate Chinese public. In 1935 the chorus of protest, to which the Communists contributed a share but only a share, reached fever heat. Thereafter the Kuomintang was under almost irresistible pressure to stop fighting the Communists and ally with them to resist the Japanese.

The Chinese Communist Movement (1921–1937)

Until 1917 Marxism enjoyed in China merely the position of one of the least influential intellectual currents which had entered from the West. It would probably have remained in this state if other political movements, notably the Kuomintang, had not failed to provide any quick and spectacular answer to China's difficult and humiliating problems and if a Marxist party had not come to power in Russia in 1917. The Bolshevik Revolution was an event of incalculable importance for China. It provided China and all Asia with the spectacle of a backward nation trying energetically, if brutally, to transform itself into a modern one almost overnight through planned effort. It enabled the Soviet government to pose as a benevolent and nonimperialist friend of China in contrast to the admittedly self-interested nations of the West. It led to the formation of a Chinese Communist Party and provided that party with a powerful, often too powerful, leader and guide.

Shortly after the Bolshevik Revolution, Marxist study groups began to be formed among Chinese students and intellectuals in various cities of China and among groups of Chinese students abroad. By 1920 the respected intellectual Ch'en Tu-hsiu and some of his colleagues had become converts to Marxism-Leninism and had made contact with agents of the Comintern (the Third International). On July 1, 1921, the Chinese Communist Party (CCP) convened its First Congress and formally established itself, with Ch'en Tu-hsiu as its secretary-general. Naturally enough, the party's first major activities lay in the field of labor organization and agitation, in which it achieved considerable success. At its Second Congress, held in 1922, the party took another logical step in affiliating itself with the Comintern.

As yet the CCP was small and composed largely of intellectuals without political power or popular support. For this reason the Comintern in 1922–1923 chose the Kuomintang, rather than the CCP, as its major instrument in China and compelled the CCP to enter into its ill-fated alliance with the Kuomintang, the results of which have already been described. The CCP was nearly ruined in its infancy by Stalin's blind conviction that he could control an explosive and far-away revolutionary situation of whose power relations he actually understood very little. In spite of this disastrous error of judgment, Stalin's control over the central machinery of the CCP remained substantially unimpaired until the rise of a more independently minded CCP leadership under Mao Tse-tung about 1935.

The first reaction of Stalin and the Comintern to the disasters of 1927 was to blame Ch'en Tu-hsiu for them, to remove him from power, and to order a program of armed risings. The most important of these —the Nanchang Rising of August 1, among Communist-led units of the Kuomintang Fourth Army; the Autumn Harvest Rising, led by Mao Tse-tung in Hunan; and the bloody and short-lived Canton Commune of December 11–13—were more or less disastrous failures, but they did leave behind the nucleus of a Red Army which in turn made possible the creation of a number of local soviets in the rural areas of Central and South China.

Rural activity of this kind offered the only prospect for the CCP, for the cities were firmly in the control of the Kuomintang or other anti-Communist factions. Furthermore, the urban labor unions, on which the CCP had placed its main reliance, were disgusted with Communist manipulation and were coming rapidly under Kuomintang control. Accordingly, the Sixth Congress of the CCP, held at Moscow in July 1928, gave permission for peasant organization and guerrilla warfare while still insisting that the main task of the CCP was to recapture leadership of the urban labor movement. The congress also confirmed the downfall of Ch'ü Ch'iu-pai, who had succeeded Ch'en Tu-hsiu as secretary-general but had been purged after the failure of the risings of 1927.

Leadership then passed into the hands of the energetic and over-bearing labor organizer Li Li-san and his lieutenant Chou En-lai. Li was under almost constant pressure from the Comintern for spectacular accomplishments in order to erase the defeats of 1927. He soon found that it was impossible to capture cities by means of proletarian risings, and his only alternative was therefore to turn to the Red Army, the most important section of which was under the control of Mao Tse-tung, and attempt to capture cities from without rather than from within. This policy, to which the Comintern gave its approval in July 1930, also failed, for a Red Army force was driven out of the city of Changsha early in August after an occupation of about a week.

At first Li Li-san withstood the efforts of his opponents within the party to unseat him because of this failure, but in November 1930 he was condemned by the Comintern and thereupon resigned his posts and went into exile in Moscow. Leadership then passed into the hands of a group of young men just returned from study in Moscow and usually known as the Returned Students, or sometimes ironically as the Twenty-eight Bolsheviks. The unusually adaptable Chou En-lai managed to make himself indispensable to this new leadership, as he had to its predecessor. In their outlook and policies the Returned Students differed in no essential way from Li Li-san, except that they enjoyed greater personal favor from Stalin; they too were doctrinaire, impatient, oriented toward the cities, and subservient to the Comintern. They established the central machinery of the party briefly in Shanghai, but by the beginning of 1933 they had felt compelled to transfer it to Juichin, the capital of the central soviet government, partly as a result of Kuomintang police pressure in Shanghai and partly in order to contest with Mao Tse-tung the control of the central soviet government.

After the failure of his Autumn Harvest Rising in 1927, Mao had retreated southward with a handful of followers and set up a small soviet in the rugged terrain along the border between Hunan and Kiangsi. There he was joined by a stronger force under Chu Teh early in 1928. Together the two men began to organize a force capable of effective guerrilla warfare and to implement a program of land redistribution and peasant organization. Mao's rural orientation was not primarily attributable to his peasant origin, but rather to the impression made on him by the upsurge of antiforeignism and antilandlordism on the part of the peasants in his native province of Hunan in 1925. Mao's emphasis on the revolutionary role of the peasantry earned him the disfavor of the successive leaderships of the CCP already mentioned, by whom he was deprecated as a "local Communist" who had never studied in Moscow and therefore had little understanding of pure Marxism-Leninism.

Nevertheless, Mao's soviet, which he transferred to Kiangsi in 1928 and thereafter steadily expanded, was the most important soviet in China, and these soviets were virtually the only concrete success to which the CCP could point at the end of its first decade of existence. First Li Li-san, and later the Returned Students, attempted to take control of Mao's soviet away from him. Li's effort was comparatively ineffective and fairly easily resisted, but against the Returned Students Mao had less success. His principal opponents among the Returned Students were Po Ku (secretary-general, 1932–1934), Chou En-lai, and Wang Ming (secretary-general, 1931–1932; principal CCP representative to the Comintern, 1932–1937).

Mao was elected chairman of the central soviet government (controlling in theory all soviets in China) at the First All-China Congress of Soviets held at Juichin, Kiangsi, in November 1931. Nevertheless, his actual control over the party machinery and armed forces in that area was steadily usurped by Chou En-lai and the Returned Students and their appointees. The Returned Students showed much more responsiveness to direction from the Comintern, favored a more radical and violent program of "land reform," and placed much more emphasis on regular as opposed to guerrilla warfare than did Mao.

At the end of 1930, alarmed by Li Li-san's attempt to capture Changsha, Chiang Kai-shek launched a series of so-called Annihilation Campaigns aimed at wiping out the soviets in Central China, especially the one in Kiangsi. All but the last of these campaigns were defeated by the Red Army, though with great effort and at considerable cost, by means of skillfully conducted guerrilla warfare. For the last campaign, however, which began in the summer of 1933, Chiang Kai-shek assembled an enormous army and adopted a strategy of complete blockade and steady pressure which would probably have overwhelmed the weaker Red Army in the end regardless of the method of defense employed. It is therefore not necessary to attach complete validity to Mao Tse-tung's statement,[2] made not long afterward, in

[2] Edgar Snow, *Red Star over China* (New York: Random House, 1944), p. 186.

which he named the adoption of positional warfare instead of guerrilla warfare as one of the two major reasons for the destruction of the Kiangsi soviet and by implication blamed the Returned Students for this alleged error.[3]

Nor is it wise to take at face value the other reason advanced by Mao, a failure to co-operate with a Left Kuomintang revolt against Chiang Kai-shek which occurred in nearby Fukien in November 1933 but was suppressed by National Government troops in January 1934.[4] There is fairly convincing evidence that the Returned Students favored active and prompt co-operation with the Fukien rebels, but that Mao advocated a more cautious policy, and that as a result of the ensuing indecision Chiang Kai-shek was enabled to move in and administer the *coup de grâce* to the rebellion.[5] According to the same source, Mao was thereupon not entirely unjustly made the scapegoat by the Comintern and the Returned Students for this disaster, which placed an implacably hostile army on the coastal flank of the Kiangsi soviet. At the Second All-China Congress of Soviets (January 1934), or shortly afterward, Mao was apparently stripped of virtually all his remaining power and sent out of Juichin. He was therefore not a party to the crucial decisions which had to be made during the ensuing months.[6]

By that time the CCP was confronted with a choice between being destroyed or attempting to break through the Kuomintang blockade and find safety elsewhere. The decision was in favor of the second course. On the night of October 15–16 the First Front Army—which had been built up by Mao Tse-tung and Chu Teh but was now largely under the control of the Returned Students and their military adviser from the Comintern, a German Communist invariably known by his Chinese name Li Teh (or Li T'e)—set out in a general westerly direction accompanied by about 30,000 civilians, mainly party functionaries.

[3] This imputation of blame has since been made explicit (e.g., Resolution on Some Questions in the History of Our Party, 1945, in *Selected Works of Mao Tse-tung* [New York: International Publishers, 1954–], IV, 196).

[4] This earlier claim is contradicted by Mao's later statement that the CCP "formed an alliance with the People's Government in Fukien" (*Selected Works*, IV, 192).

[5] Kung Ch'u (a former general in the Chinese Red Army), *Wo yü Hung Chün* [The Red Army and I] (Hong Kong: South Wind Publishing Company, 1954), pp. 362–367.

[6] *Ibid.*, pp. 395–400. See also statement by Chang Kuo-t'ao in Robert C. North, "The Rise of Mao Tse-tung," *Far Eastern Quarterly*, Feb. 1952, p. 141.

During the first part of the Long March, as it came to be called, the Red Army followed a fairly straight and predictable course and therefore suffered heavy casualties. Indeed, there were several occasions on the Long March when the Kuomintang, with better generalship and greater energy, could have annihilated the First Front Army and thereby dealt a heavy, perhaps fatal, blow to the prospects of communism in China. The military incapacity of the Returned Students, both in Kiangsi and now on the Long March, cost them the confidence of many of the Red Army commanders.

Skillfully utilizing this discontent and the support of some of his fellow Hunanese in the party hierarchy, Mao Tse-tung was able to seize control of the central party and military machinery of the CCP at a crucial conference held at Tsunyi, in Kweichow, in December 1934–January 1935. His triumph received a partial and probably grudging endorsement from the Comintern later in 1935. Thereafter Mao's pre-eminent position within the CCP, which never approached the iron dictatorship exercised by Stalin over his own party, was not seriously threatened although it was occasionally challenged.

Another important conference was held at Maoerhkai, in northwestern Szechuan, in July 1935. This time the principal antagonists were Mao and Chang Kuo-t'ao, Mao's last remaining serious rival for power within the party. Chang considered rural soviets unsuitable for China and favored moving out of China proper, to eastern Tibet or Sinkiang; according to his own later account, he was supported in his views by the Comintern. Mao, on the other hand, upheld the suitability of soviets and refused to leave China proper, and advocated going to Shensi, where a soviet had been set up in 1930. As a result the two men separated. Chang with his Fourth Front Army and some party functionaries who agreed with him retired to Sikang, in eastern Tibet, where they set up a central party apparatus in rivalry with that of Mao Tse-tung. Chu Teh accompanied them, for somewhat obscure reasons, and they were later joined by the Second Front Army under Ho Lung. After an unsuccessful attempt to reach Sinkiang, they finally came to Shensi to join Mao Tse-tung in October 1936.

Meanwhile, Mao and the First Front Red Army had proceeded northward through eastern Tibet into Kansu and thence into Shensi, where they arrived in October 1935 after a year on the road. The Long March had been a terrible ordeal and a tremendous feat of military and physical endurance, which left the participants in it decimated and physically weakened but with enormous prestige and determination. Since that time, to have taken part in the Long March has been re- garded in the CCP as a major honor.

In northern Shensi, Mao Tse-tung re-established the central soviet government and proceeded to implement the moderate policies, by Communist standards, whose realization in Kiangsi had been hampered by the Returned Students. His troubles with Chang Kuo-t'ao were not over, however. Chang reached Shensi in October 1936, his position greatly weakened by military defeats suffered en route, and he evi- dently had further disputes with Mao over matters of power and policy. In 1937 the two men split openly on the question of the proper policy to be pursued toward the Kuomintang during the war against Japan. Chang favored sincere co-operation with the Kuomintang against the common enemy, Mao a policy of struggling against both simultaneously under cover of a purely nominal alliance with the Kuo- mintang. Mao prevailed, and in 1938 Chang was expelled from the CCP with the sanction of the Comintern.

Ever since the Japanese invasion of Manchuria in September 1931, the problem of Japanese aggression had been prominent in the minds of the Chinese Communists as it had in those of other Chinese. In April 1932 the central soviet government in Kiangsi declared war on Japan for propaganda effect. For the next three years the Comintern and the CCP repeatedly called for the overthrow of the Kuomintang and the formation of a united front, from which the Kuomintang as such would presumably be excluded, against Japan. By the time of the Seventh World Congress of the Comintern in August 1935, how- ever, Stalin had concluded that this policy of a "united front from below" was futile. A united front against Japan must be one "from above"; in other words, it required the participation of the Kuomin- tang and even the leadership of Chiang Kai-shek. This view did not prevail with the CCP until reinforced by the logic of events in China.

As yet Chiang Kai-shek and the Kuomintang had given no sign of any willingness to establish a united front with the CCP. On the con- trary, Chiang blockaded the soviet in Shensi as he had that in Kiangsi, though less effectively. His own blockade commanders became con- vinced of the futility of civil war and the desirability of united re- sistance to Japan. When Chiang flew to the headquarters at Sian to urge his commanders on against the Communists, they arrested him on December 12, 1936, and held him prisoner for a fortnight. They pressed him, at first without result, to form a united front with the Communists and invited a CCP delegation led by Chou En-lai to take part in the discussions. Chou abandoned any reluctance the CCP may have felt earlier about dealing with Chiang Kai-shek and, acting on instructions from the Comintern, even intervened in Chiang's favor with his now-infuriated generals.

As a result, Chiang was released, apparently unconditionally, but in reality he had agreed reluctantly to a united front with the Communists. During the next several months its details were worked out, with much maneuvering and many propaganda blasts on both sides. On their part the Kuomintang and the National Government gave up their campaign against the Shensi soviet and relaxed their blockade considerably, lightened police controls and censorship of the press in Nationalist China, and agreed to resist the Japanese. On its side the CCP agreed to abandon land redistribution and other manifestations of class warfare, cease its propaganda against the Kuomintang, and subordinate its government (renamed the Shensi-Kansu-Ningsia Border Region Government) and armed forces (renamed the Eighth Route Army) to those of the central government.

Neither side made these commitments in good faith. Nevertheless, for a short time, until nearly the end of 1938, both sides observed at least the letter of their agreement fairly faithfully, and an appreciable increase in China's unity resulted. Alarmed by this trend, the Japanese army began full-scale war against China on July 7, 1937.

The War against Japan (1937–1945)

To understand the course of the war it is necessary to recognize that the Japanese high command did not seriously intend to conquer all of China; this would probably have been impossible, and in any case not worth the effort. All that was needed was to seize and hold the major cities and lines of communication in eastern China and to integrate the raw materials and manpower of that area into the economy of the Japanese empire. This was done, with at least partial success, for about eight years (1937–1945). In addition, China was used as a gigantic training ground on which Japanese troops were prepared to meet more formidable enemies elsewhere. Since the Japanese did not make their main military effort in China, at least after 1941, the strength or weakness of Chinese resistance had little effect on Japan's ultimate collapse, which can be attributed exclusively to the

efforts of the United States. Japan's adventure in China was not the
drain on its strength that the campaign in Russia proved to be for Nazi
Germany.

As in other Asian countries, the Japanese in China were able to
find Chinese, though not very many, who were willing to collaborate
with them; some did so out of sincere if misguided patriotism, some
out of opportunism, and some out of a mixture of both. The leading
collaborator was Wang Ching-wei, a brilliant but unstable Kuomintang
politician who felt a personal jealousy toward the more powerful
Chiang Kai-shek and sincerely believed that China's interests would
be best served by co-operating with Japan rather than fighting it. In
1938 Wang went over to the Japanese and two years later was set
up by them at the head of a powerless puppet government in Nanking.
The puppet troops under his command became the weakest and least
active of the four contestants in an extraordinarily complex military
and political struggle, aptly known as a "war within a war," in which
the others were the Japanese themselves, the Kuomintang, and the
CCP.

Before the roles of the last two of these four opponents are considered, it would be well to summarize the major military operations
of the war. The Japanese overran the North China Plain with very
little difficulty, and the scene of hostilities shifted to the Yangtze Valley. After committing and losing many of his best troops in a brave
but futile defense of Shanghai, Chiang Kai-shek also was forced in
December 1937 to abandon his capital city of Nanking to Japanese
pillaging. The Nationalist capital was then moved to Hankow, and
when Hankow fell to the Japanese in October 1938 it was transferred
to Chungking, in the fertile but remote province of Szechuan. At about
the same time as the capture of Hankow, the Japanese also launched
an amphibious assault on Canton which left them in possession of
that city and a sizable beachhead around it.

By the end of 1938 the front had become nearly stable. In broad
terms, it ran almost due north and south, from a point a little west of
Peiping through a point a little west of Hankow to a point a little
west of Canton. The Japanese were very far from controlling all the
territory to the east of that line, but they controlled the cities and the
principal lines of communication. To the east of the line Chinese irregular and even regular forces, mainly Communist rather than Nationalist, operated in pockets between the points held by the Japanese.
In 1943, foreseeing a military crisis, the Japanese began to withdraw

their troops into the cities and leave the garrisoning of outlying areas to puppet forces. In the summer of 1944 the strongest offensive since 1938 was launched by the Japanese in a successful attack on Chinese ground units and American air bases in Hunan and Kwangsi.

During the first year or two of the war, in spite of defeats suffered in the field, the position of the National Government and the Kuomintang was in some ways a strong one. The Japanese invasion and Japanese atrocities tended to rally the Chinese people behind the government. The united front with the CCP was still a reality. A consultative body known as the People's Political Council, in which all major Chinese parties and groups were represented, was appointed by the National Government and functioned fairly effectively. Limited but still useful military and economic aid flowed in from the Soviet Union, Great Britain, and the United States via Outer Mongolia, Sinkiang, and the newly constructed Burma Road. There was a massive movement of factories, universities, and people out of areas threatened by the Japanese and into Free China, as it was then called.

After the removal of the capital to Chungking at the end of 1938, however, the Nationalist position started to deteriorate alarmingly. The terrible strain of the war began to tell, and the virtual isolation of the government in rural and backward Southwest China tended to promote an increase in the influence within the Kuomintang of the reactionary rural landlord element and of the CC Clique. Relations with the CCP showed signs of decline in 1939, the blame being attributable more to the CCP than the Nationalists. The Kuomintang reimposed a military blockade on the CCP-controlled areas in Northwest China, and in 1941 a semiconcealed civil war began between the two sides. Rampant inflation set in after 1941 in the Nationalist areas, and it was aggravated by growing corruption at all levels in the government, party, and armed forces of Nationalist China. Despite a substantial volume of American military aid and advice, the Nationalist war effort against the Japanese became, with local and temporary exceptions, almost negligible. The effects of the war on the Nationalists and their government were in fact disastrous, although their seriousness was not generally understood at the time, and it has been said with much truth that the Japanese in the name of anticommunism delivered China to the Communists.

The Communists enjoyed throughout the war several unspectacular but solid advantages over the Nationalists. They did not have to maintain a formal government or foreign relations. Partly for that reason, they stood to gain by chaos, not lose by it. They controlled no major cities and therefore had to feed none. They had comparatively little trouble with inflation. Their elaborate ideology, their sense of being part of an irresistible world movement centering in a powerful neighbor, and their disciplined party organization gave them a morale and staying power largely absent in the case of the Kuomintang. By temperament and training they were well suited to organizing peasant guerrilla forces—an activity from which the Kuomintang generally preferred to abstain—in order to supplement the efforts of their regular forces, which were by no means negligible. Although they are not known to have received any military or economic aid from the Soviet Union, they maintained communication and liaison with it throughout the war; for example, Chou En-lai, the CCP's leading expert on external relations, spent six months (September 1939–March 1940) in the Soviet Union immediately after the outbreak of war in Europe.[7]

Another important advantage of the CCP over the Kuomintang, which it has held at all times since about 1935, was that of superior leadership. After the expulsion of Chang Kuo-t'ao from the CCP in 1938, Mao Tse-tung remained without any serious rival for control of the party. By that time he had already elaborated a basic strategy against both the Japanese and the Kuomintang which later brought the CCP out of the war against Japan far stronger than when it had entered. His plan was to use mobile warfare conducted by regular troops and guerrilla warfare conducted by irregular forces, but seldom positional warfare. In the case of the Kuomintang the struggle was to be masked behind a propaganda calculated to appeal to non-Communist Chinese public opinion by emphasizing resistance to Japan and short-term rather than long-term Communist goals.

During this period Mao was clearly moving closer to Stalin and the Soviet Communist Party, both of whom appear earlier to have regarded Mao's rise to power with some disfavor and were in return regarded by Mao as largely extraneous to his own problems and those of the CCP as he saw them. By at least as early as 1939, however, Mao had become a fairly close student of Stalin's writings and had accepted at least the essentials of Stalin's domestic program (collectivization of agriculture, state-controlled industrialization, and totalitarian police controls) as necessary for China once the CCP gained power. The major reasons for this *rapprochement* were probably three: Mao was beginning to publish his program for the exercise of power, which

[7] See *New York Times*, Sept. 17, 1939, March 26, 1940.

owed almost as much to Stalin as his strategy for the seizure of power did to Lenin; Mao was being forced by the outbreak of the Second World War to pay more attention to international affairs, to which Stalin seemed a useful guide; and Mao was preparing to apply at least some of Stalin's techniques of party control to his own party. This he did in the so-called Cheng Feng (Rectification of Working Style) Movement of 1942, a purge of ideas rather than of individuals. To guard against a relaxation of party discipline and a dissipation of party ideology in the course of the struggle against Japan, both high-ranking and low-ranking CCP members were lectured against various failings ("subjectivism," "sectarianism," and "formalism") which seemed likely to lead to such a result. The movement appears to have had the desired effect.

Mao Tse-tung's revolutionary strategy, which he perfected during the war against Japan, resembled Stalin's formula for China somewhat, but this was mainly because the ideas of both were derived from a common Leninist base. Where Mao improved on Stalin was mainly in his keen understanding of Chinese conditions and of the consequent necessity for adaptations and flexibility. Mao himself described his strategy in 1939 as follows:

The united front and the armed struggle are the two chief weapons for defeating the enemy. The united front is a united front for carrying on the armed struggle. And the [Communist] Party organisation is the heroic fighter who wields the two weapons, the united front and the armed struggle, to storm and shatter the positions of the enemy.[8]

Mao's formula for employing these two main weapons of armed struggle and the united front was to base himself on the peasantry rather than on the proletariat (while still paying verbal tributes to the revolutionary role of the latter), in order to "encircle the cities from the countryside"; to establish local soviet governments as nuclei of further expansion; to build up a Red Army skilled at mobile and guerrilla warfare; and to isolate the Kuomintang politically and appeal to middle-of-the-road opinion by calling for a united front or "four class bloc" composed of the proletariat, the peasantry, the national (big but patriotic) bourgeoisie, and the petty bourgeoisie (including intellectuals).

By 1945 skillful application of Mao's formula and steady expansion at the expense of both the Japanese and the Kuomintang had resulted

[8] *Selected Works*, III, 65.

in the establishment of some twenty "liberated areas" under the control of the CCP and scattered from Manchuria to Hainan and in an enormous expansion of the Red Army and of the population ruled by the CCP, to about 1 million and 85 million respectively.

Probably for this reason, the CCP had begun in 1944 to put forward a demand for the formation of a coalition government in which the CCP, as well as the Kuomintang and certain minor middle-of-the-road parties, would participate. Although several American officials then in China, including Ambassador Hurley, inclined toward this proposal, the Kuomintang rejected it and advocated instead the convening of the National Assembly elected in 1936, with the addition of representatives of the CCP and the minor parties. Whether the CCP seriously expected its demand for a coalition government to be accepted is impossible to say, but there is no doubt that effective propaganda was made out of it. *On Coalition Government* was the title of Mao Tse-tung's report to the Seventh Congress of the CCP, which met at Yenan (Shensi), the capital of the Shensi-Kansu-Ningsia Border Region, in April–June 1945.

The congress clearly legitimated the ascendancy of Mao Tse-tung within the CCP, which he had won since the time of the Sixth Congress in 1928. The alleged errors committed by Mao's predecessors in the party leadership were excoriated, yet three of them (Wang Ming, Po Ku, and Li Li-san) were elected to the new Central Committee in a gesture toward party harmony. A new party constitution, confirming Mao's control over the major central organs of the party and emphasizing his importance as a theorist, was adopted. The proceedings of the congress reflected an expectation of an early end to the war with Japan and of a possible outbreak of full-scale civil war with the Kuomintang.

Civil War (1945–1949)

The Japanese surrender on August 15, 1945, took both the CCP and the Kuomintang by surprise. From their comparatively nearby bases in Southwest China and with important American help in the form of transport, Nationalist forces had little difficulty in occupying the cities in the Yangtze Valley and to the south of it which had been held by the Japanese; the CCP's New Fourth Army, which had operated in the lower Yangtze Valley since the beginning of the war, evacuated this area and moved northward, part of it going to Manchuria.

In North China it was another story. Here the Red Army had long had powerful bases, especially in Shantung. The best the Nationalists could do, again with American help, was to occupy the coastal cities and the lines of communication between them.

Still more difficult was the situation in Manchuria, which both sides regarded as the major prize at stake. Soviet forces were in occupation of the entire region, and the National Government had no choice but to ratify, in a Sino-Soviet treaty signed on August 14, 1945, the right to use the principal Manchurian ports and railways which had been granted to the Soviet Union at Yalta and confirmed at Potsdam. While in occupation the Soviet forces made entry as difficult as possible for Nationalist troops, so that the latter were never able to occupy more than the major cities and rail lines from Changchun south. In violation of the Soviet government's pledge to deal only with the National Government, Soviet forces permitted CCP military units to enter Manchuria overland from Inner Mongolia and by sea from Shantung and made stocks of captured Japanese weapons available to them. A large amount of industrial equipment of Japanese origin was also shipped out of Manchuria to the Soviet Union to help restore the battered Soviet economy.

The net effect of these Soviet actions was undoubtedly to make things easier for the CCP in Manchuria. In any event the CCP was determined to control Manchuria, both because of its industrial facilities and because the CCP would then have direct contact with the Soviet Union and a base with a secure rear from which it could drive southward. The Kuomintang too was determined to control Manchuria if it could, even though its control over North China was far from secure. Against American advice, but with the aid of American transport, the Kuomintang threw its best troops into the ill-fated struggle for Manchuria.

It was clear that the rapidly developing race for control of areas formerly occupied by the Japanese, and of Manchuria in particular, threatened with civil war a country which had known little peace since the collapse of the Manchus, and none at all since 1937. This possibility was extremely unwelcome to Chinese public opinion and only slightly less so to the United States government, which during the Second World War had insisted on treating China as a major and essential ally. The pressure for peace from these two directions sufficed to delay, but not to prevent, the outbreak of civil war.

In December 1945 General George C. Marshall arrived in China as President Truman's special representative with instructions to urge the National Government to call "a national conference of representatives of major political elements" and to advocate a modification of the Kuomintang's dictatorship, the formation of a coalition government representing all major parties, and the establishment of a unified national army. This program corresponded fairly closely with the one which the CCP had been advocating since 1944, but the United States government proposed it not for this reason but because it appeared to offer the only alternative to civil war.

In January–February 1946 General Marshall was able to arrange a cease-fire agreement between the two sides. Thereupon a multiparty Political Consultative Conference met and agreed on the convening of a National Assembly in May 1946, the formation of an interim coalition government, and the creation of a national army with a five-to-one ratio of divisions as between the Kuomintang and the CCP. The conference also appointed a committee to draw up a draft constitution for submission to the National Assembly; this document when completed proved to be considerably more democratic than the draft which the Kuomintang had published in 1936.

Both sides soon began to violate both the spirit and the letter of the cease-fire agreement and the resolutions voted by the Political Consultative Conference, which therefore never went into effect. General Marshall tried to enforce their observance, but in vain. He could apply sanctions only to the Kuomintang, for the CCP was beyond his reach, and he actually embargoed arms shipments to the National Government from the United States for one year (1946–1947). In the summer of 1946 fighting broke out in Manchuria, and in October the National Government further decreased the chances of peace by re-instituting conscription and announcing that it would convene the National Assembly, which the CCP and several of the minor parties had already announced they would boycott, in November. Convinced that his mission had failed, General Marshall returned to the United States in January 1947. After that the United States shifted from a policy of mediation to one of limited but still significant support for the National Government, combined with entreaties to it to reform itself.

These were to no avail; the Kuomintang continued on the same suicidal course on which it had embarked at least as early as 1941, and by 1945 it was probably past saving. The influence of the extreme right wing within the party increased steadily, and so did oppression and corruption. High-ranking officials rushed to gain control of former

Japanese assets and exploit them for private profit. The territories re-occupied from the Japanese were lamentably misgoverned, and in one such area, Taiwan, there were serious popular risings against the Kuomintang beginning on February 28, 1947. Despite the adoption of a reasonably democratic permanent constitution by the National Assembly in December 1946 and its inauguration a year later, the grip of the Kuomintang on the governmental machinery remained unbroken. Inflation continued to mount at an almost geometric rate, and the government's last effort to check it and save the national currency, by introducing in August 1948 a currency backed by gold, was a miserable failure. The intellectuals and students were increasingly alienated from the Kuomintang by its police terror and its denial of freedom of expression. Small businessmen were disgusted at speculation by high officials and ruined by inflation. The peasants were more than ever indifferent, if not actually hostile, to a regime which showed no interest in their welfare and left them to be exploited by their landlords and local officials or organized and propagandized by the Communists. Since the Kuomintang's dictatorship had always inhibited the growth of middle-of-the-road parties, those who were disillusioned with the Kuomintang had in effect nowhere else to go except to the Communists, to whom many of them turned as a possible lesser evil rather than as a positive good.

Given these conditions, there is nothing surprising in the fact that the Kuomintang suffered almost continuous defeats in the field at the hands of the Communists. That these defeats were the result rather than the cause of the conditions just described can be easily shown. The National Government entered the civil war in 1946 with roughly a three-to-one advantage in population, territory, and troops under arms and an even greater superiority in industrial potential. It also enjoyed considerable, though by no means total, diplomatic, economic, and military support from the United States, whereas the CCP is not known to have received any important aid from the Soviet Union during the civil war apart from the Soviet actions in Manchuria already mentioned. Even there, the Japanese weapons which the CCP acquired were more than counterbalanced by Japanese weapons surrendered to Nationalist forces in China proper.

On paper, then, the Kuomintang was vastly superior and ought to have won, but the loyalty of its commanders and the morale of its troops were progressively undermined by inept strategic decisions taken above them and by the deterioration of the home front behind them. Provincial warlords serving in the governmental forces, never much more than nominally loyal to the National Government, often deserted when the military pressure from the Communists increased.

The Communists took full advantage of their enemy's weaknesses by means of skillful organization, training, propaganda, strategy, and tactics. Until 1947 they waged a largely defensive war of maneuver and under its cover began a reorganization of their forces into larger and more powerful units which became known after 1948 as field armies. In 1947 they opened a powerful offensive in the Yellow River area from their bases in Shantung. The next year another such offensive, led by their outstanding field commander Lin Piao, completed the conquest of Manchuria and thereby deprived the National Goverment of most its best troops. At the beginning of 1949 the Communists took Peiping, Tientsin, and the important rail junction of Hsuchow not far north of Nanking. In April and May the Yangtze Valley cities, including Nanking and Shanghai, fell to the People's Liberation Army, as it was now officially called. The Nationalist capital was moved successively to Canton, Chungking, and Chengtu, as each city fell before the advancing Communists. By the end of 1949 the Kuomintang had transferred most of its party and governmental apparatus to Taiwan, and the CCP controlled all of China proper and the outlying regions except Taiwan itself and Tibet.

The speed with which the civil war on the Chinese mainland came to an end was probably a surprise to nearly everyone concerned. It seems likely that Stalin was one of the most surprised of all, for he had given signs that he did not take the Chinese Communists or their prospects very seriously. For good or ill, the CCP had now become of necessity a major factor in the calculations of all other powers, Communist and non-Communist alike. The most significant reasons for its triumph, in descending order of probable importance, appear to have been the Japanese invasion of China, the shortcomings of the Kuomintang, and the revolutionary strategy of Mao Tse-tung.

The CCP gave several indications during 1949 of the course it would pursue after completing the seizure of power in China. In March its Central Committee announced that the center of gravity of party work had shifted from the countryside to the cities and exhorted all party members to devote themselves to economic reconstruction. In his important work *On the People's Democratic Dictatorship,* published on July 1, Mao Tse-tung clearly stated his intention to introduce into China the essentials of Stalinism: collectivized agriculture, the development of heavy industry to the comparative neglect of light industry, and a police state equipped to suppress "counterrevolutionaries." He also announced that the "new" China would "lean to one side," toward the Soviet Union, and denied forcefully that China or any other country could remain neutral as between the Soviet and American "camps." This essentially uncompromising program Mao softened somewhat by elaborating the fiction that the new state would not be a pure Communist dictatorship or a "dictatorship of the proletariat" but would be a multiclass dictatorship "of the people," led by the CCP and exercised by the workers, the peasants, the national bourgeoisie, and the petty bourgeoisie. Minor "democratic" parties would be allowed to exist within the framework of a "united front" led by the CCP. Both the essential sternness and the superficial reasonableness of this pronouncement were to mark the history of the regime which the CCP proceeded to establish in the autumn of 1949.

· II ·

China since 1949

COMMUNIST China since the "Liberation" of 1949 is a phenomenon unique in the contemporary world. It is a Communist regime which came to power in the most populous country on earth after a generation of armed struggle against domestic and foreign enemies and with the active or passive support of a considerable section of the Chinese people. Abroad, the impact of this phenomenon on the rest of Asia has been even greater than that of the Bolshevik Revolution, because it is closer to home. Domestically, the Chinese Communists have been able to consolidate their power more rapidly and thoroughly than the Bolsheviks in Russia were able to do during the first few years after their seizure of power in 1917. The Bolsheviks had to fight a civil war after seizing power whereas in China the civil war came first.

If knowledge of China's history before 1949 is necessary to adequate understanding of Chinese government and politics since 1949, so is knowledge of the main events in China's history since the "Liberation."

Historical Summary

The People's Republic of China (PRC) was officially proclaimed at Peking, which became its capital, on October 1, 1949. The necessary preliminaries had been managed by the Chinese People's Political Consultative Conference, a large body nominated by the CCP to represent

Map 3. Communist China in 1958. (From Communist China Today, b...

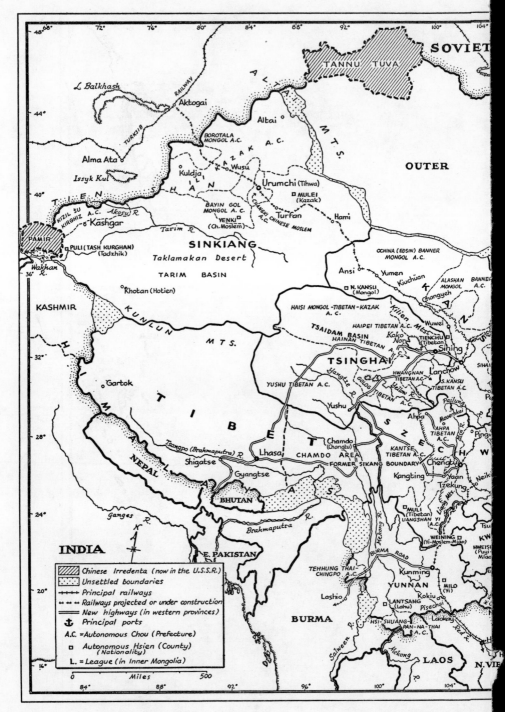

Map 3. Communist China in 1956. (From *Communist China Today*, b

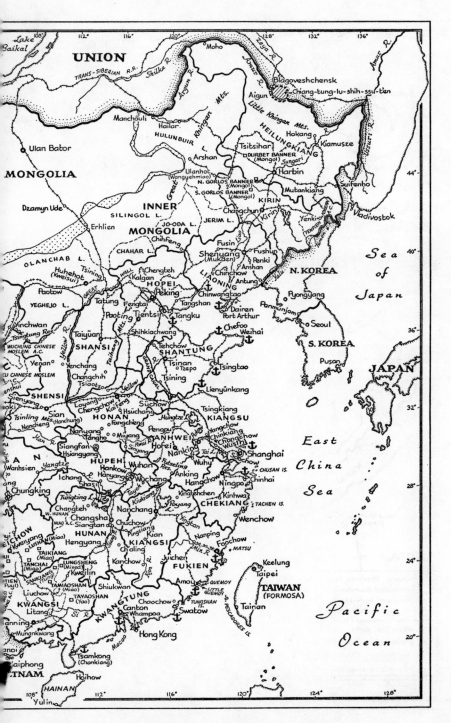

various elements in the "united front" such as the CCP itself, the "democratic" political parties, various occupational groups, national minorities, and the like. This body, which met at Peking from September 21 to September 30, was of course entirely controlled by the CCP. It elected a Central People's Government Council, the highest governmental body under the new regime, designated Peking as the capital, and approved a new flag and a national anthem. It also adopted two important semiconstitutional documents: the Common Program, a statement purporting to represent the aims of the "united front" but actually elaborating some of the principles set forth by Mao Tse-tung in *On the People's Democratic Dictatorship*, and the Organic Law, which specified the organization of the Central People's Government.

Having set up this regime, the CCP next had to regulate its relations with Big Brother. This was a difficult task, for Stalin clearly would have liked to receive from the CCP the same subservience he had imposed on the Communist parties and regimes of Eastern Europe. To accomplish his task, Mao Tse-tung, acting officially as Chairman of the Central People's Government rather than as leader of the CCP, took his first trip outside his native country, arriving in Moscow in time to help Stalin celebrate his seventieth birthday on December 21, 1949. Later Mao and his delegation were reinforced by the arrival of Premier and Foreign Minister Chou En-lai, an able negotiator whom Stalin admired greatly.

Weeks of secret and probably hard bargaining preceded the signing of a treaty on February 14, 1950. The core of this treaty was a thirty-year defensive alliance directed against Japan or "any state allied with Japan," meaning the United States. The relationship between the Soviet Union and the PRC was proclaimed to be one of friendship based on a set of principles very similar to those which later came to be known as the Five Principles of Peaceful Coexistence. A supplementary agreement provided that the Soviet Union should continue to share in the use of the principal Manchurian railways (known collectively as the Chinese Changchun Railway) and the naval base of Port Arthur until the conclusion of a peace treaty with Japan or the end of 1952, whichever came earlier, but should immediately turn over to the PRC all its property in the nearby commercial port of Dairen. Another agreement committed the Soviet Union to lend the PRC $300 million; the loan was to be used to buy industrial equipment from the Soviet Union and was to be repaid in raw materials and currency beginning no later than the end of 1954. This scarcely constituted an act of princely generosity on Stalin's part. Such were the major published terms of the treaty, but there were numerous reports, some of them fantastic, of additional secret clauses.

Of the large number of Sino-Soviet cultural and economic agreements signed in the wake of the treaty of February 14, 1950, the most important was a series of agreements signed on March 27 providing for the sending of Soviet military and economic advisers to China and creating four Sino-Soviet "joint-stock" companies. One was to operate a civil air line between the two countries; another was to extract nonferrous and rare minerals (probably including uranium) in Sinkiang; a third was to extract and refine petroleum in Sinkiang; and the fourth was to build and repair ships at Dairen. Although nominally operated on a footing of equality between the two partners, these companies were strongly reminiscent of the notorious joint companies through which the Soviet Union was draining the economies of the Eastern European satellites and constituted a serious threat to Chinese sovereignty, especially in Sinkiang. Such was the price, or at least part of the price, which the PRC had to pay for military and economic aid from the Soviet Union.

By 1949 war and inflation had nearly ruined the Chinese economy and brought production almost to a standstill. The most urgent initial task of the CCP was to rehabilitate the economy by checking inflation and restoring production. To these tasks it devoted most of its energy during 1950, and with considerable success. It was able to check inflation after a time by bringing the whole economy under control and by the simple but effective method of computing the value of bank deposits in terms of the prices of essential commodities; thus the value of a deposit would increase in proportion to any subsequent rise in prices. The restoration of production was more difficult, and it was not until about 1952 that the output of the economy reached a level roughly equivalent to the highest achieved before 1949. In this field the major effort was made in Manchuria, which in spite of its partial sacking by the Soviet Army was still the most highly industrialized region in China.

Like the Bolsheviks in revolutionary Russia, the CCP was faced with the difficult problem of controlling the countryside so as to ensure a reasonably adequate supply of food for the cities. To do this and break the power of the potentially dangerous landlord class, the CCP undertook a nation-wide program of "agrarian reform." In line with the views of Lenin, the CCP had long divided the rural population into the following major categories, on the basis of type of labor performed and relationship to the land: landlords, rich peasants, middle peasants, poor peasants, and landless peasants or "rural proletariat." Except for an interval of about a decade after the outbreak of war with Japan, the CCP had generally pursued a policy of confiscating landlords' land without compensation and redistributing it among poor and landless peasants. This was not in the main done out of benevolence, but rather to break the power of anti-CCP elements in the countryside, gain support for the CCP and recruits for the Red Army from among the poorer groups, and bring the rural areas under firm Communist control.

The same basic principles inspired the Agrarian Reform Act of June 30, 1950, which provided for the confiscation and redistribution of land belonging to landlords, but not of land belonging to rich peasants. This policy was implemented with great brutality during 1950–1952 in all major agricultural regions of China except those inhabited by national minorities. In the course of the "reform," CCP cadres (fieldworkers) put into the landlord classification and accordingly "liquidated," economically or physically, many thousands of individuals who were actually not landlords at all, or at any rate had not been exploiters.

On this bloodbath others were superimposed after China's intervention in the Korean War. The most spectacular was a campaign against "counterrevolutionaries," during which hundreds of thousands of persons accused of disloyalty to the regime and to "the people" were tried and imprisoned or executed in the presence of howling mobs. Two similar but distinct campaigns also conducted during 1951–1952 were the San Fan [1] campaign against corruption on the part of governmental personnel and the Wu Fan [2] campaign against alleged similar offenses on the part of private businessmen. The Wu Fan campaign, which resulted in the fining or imprisonment of many businessmen and the suicide of some, was probably prompted by the weak state of the PRC's budget and by a desire to break the power of the bourgeoisie and netted the regime perhaps as much as US$2.2 billion.

[1] That is, "Three Anti," so called because directed against corruption, waste, and bureaucratism.

[2] "Five Anti," so called because directed against bribery, tax evasion, fraud, theft of state property, and divulgence of state economic secrets.

The CCP was keenly aware that two regions, Taiwan and Tibet, remained to be "liberated." At the end of 1949, accordingly, it began preparations for an amphibious assault on Taiwan. It was frustrated by its own unpreparedness for such an ambitious operation and by an epidemic of liver-fluke disease among the troops involved, most of whom were North Chinese unaccustomed to the unhealthy conditions of South China. Soon an invasion of Taiwan was rendered impossible by the outbreak of war in Korea, which led to the interposition of the United States Seventh Fleet between Taiwan and the mainland. No such obstacle prevented the conquest of Tibet, which was invaded from the east in October 1950 by troops of the Second Field Army. The completion of the campaign required about a year, during which Tibetan forces offered spirited but hopeless guerrilla resistance and the Chinese troops suffered severely from the weather and food shortages. The "liberation" of Tibet from the fiction of "Anglo-American imperialism" and its incorporation into Communist China were officially proclaimed on May 23, 1951.

By far the most serious crisis faced by the PRC up to the present was the Korean War. The leaders of the CCP probably had at least a general foreknowledge that such a war was in the offing, but whether they took any real part in planning it seems doubtful. The Soviet Union was much more deeply involved, for North Korea was a Soviet rather than a Chinese satellite. Almost certainly no one on the Communist side expected the United States to react as it did; otherwise the Soviet delegation would not have been boycotting the United Nations Security Council in protest against the presence of Chinese Nationalist delegates when the war began on June 25, 1950.

Almost immediately afterward the CCP began to concentrate troops in Manchuria, many of them withdrawn from the Formosa Strait, and to whip up anti-American feeling over the Korean crisis. These dispositions, combined with the military aid and advice which the People's Liberation Army (PLA) had already begun to receive from the Soviet Union, placed the PLA in a position to intervene in Korea if necessary. It is probable that the CCP co-ordinated its military plans with the Soviet Union even earlier than October 1950, when Chou En-lai first announced that the CCP would not tolerate a northward crossing of the 38th parallel by United Nations forces in Korea. It is possible that Stalin urged the CCP to intervene, and yet there were valid reasons why the CCP should have felt an interest in keeping a potentially hostile force away from its Manchurian frontier and in preventing the destruction of another Communist state; in 1593 another Chinese army had intervened similarly to save a client Korean state from Japanese conquest.

In Korea the Chinese People's Volunteers, as the PLA expeditionary force formed on October 25, 1950, was officially called in order to avoid the possible consequences of formal involvement in a war, won striking initial successes by using the methods of mobile warfare to which they were accustomed. After the disastrous failure of the two great Chinese thrusts toward Seoul in the spring of 1951 and the subsequent respite gained through the initiation of truce talks, the front became nearly stationary and all possibility of a breakthrough by either side soon disappeared.

The war imposed a terrible strain on Communist China. In addition to the heavy losses of men and matériel at the front, there were heavy payments to the Soviet Union for needed military equipment. The entire country was put under a virtual state of siege and racked with the bloody campaigns already mentioned. Forced donations under the guise of voluntary "contributions" were extracted from the public. Many hundreds of thousands of people were mobilized for compulsory labor, especially in Manchuria, including service as ammunition carriers at the front. For this strain the regime, if not the people, was compensated to some extent by more effective control over the country and a great increase in international prestige, especially elsewhere in Asia, as a result of the very respectable showing which the Chinese People's Volunteers made against a technically superior opponent in Korea.

The history of the tedious armistice negotiations in Korea conveys a strong impression that the CCP would have been willing to make peace in the autumn of 1952 on the basis of the compromise Indian resolution on the last major question in dispute—the disposition of prisoners of war who were unwilling to be repatriated—but that Stalin vetoed the idea. Within less than a month after his death on March 5, 1953, the CCP had announced its willingness to reopen negotiations, and a truce agreement was accordingly concluded on July 27, 1953. The truce left a large Chinese force in Korea and was followed by a great increase in Chinese influence at the expense of Soviet influence on the North Korean Communist regime.

Meanwhile a less overt but equally important Chinese intervention had been taking place in another direction, in Indochina. There a Communist-led guerrilla war against the French had been in progress since 1946. Unlike their North Korean colleagues, the Vietnamese Communists were never threatened with military extinction, nor was there any threat to Chinese territory; full-scale Chinese intervention was therefore both unnecessary and undesired by the Vietnamese. After the end of 1949, however, when the CCP extended its control to the border of Indochina, it began to give military aid and advice and send technicians to the Vietminh rebels under Ho Chi Minh. Without this aid the Vietminh would probably not have been able to defeat the French and expel them from North Vietnam.

Even before the disastrous siege of Dienbienphu in the spring of 1954 it was clear that the French had been beaten. Accordingly, a major international conference met at Geneva in the spring and early summer of 1954 to deal with both the Korean and the Indochinese questions. For the first time the PRC took part in a major international conference, the other participants being the Soviet Union, the United Kingdom, France, the (Communist) Democratic Republic of Vietnam, the three (non-Communist) Associated States of Indochina, and to a limited extent the United States. Although nothing significant was decided concerning Korea, an agreement was reached on Indochina whose most important features were as desired by Chou En-lai, the PRC representative. The essence was that Vietnam was divided at the 17th parallel, instead of at about the 14th as the military situation would have indicated. This constituted a serious setback for Ho Chi Minh at the hands of the CCP, which apparently wanted to prevent him from growing too strong and also to enhance its own international standing as a champion of "peaceful coexistence." [3] The PRC emerged from the Geneva Conference with its prestige considerably increased.

It won another striking triumph at the Asian-African Conference at Bandung, Java, held in April 1955. Here, as at Geneva, the PRC was represented mainly by Chou En-lai, who again performed brilliantly. He succeeded in allaying at least some of the fear and suspicion with which the PRC was regarded by its non-Communist Asian neighbors because of its domestic dictatorship, its antireligious policies, its

[3] The CCP probably expected South Vietnam to fall without war as a result of the nation-wide elections scheduled to be held, under the terms of the Geneva agreements, by July 20, 1956. These elections were never held, however, because the Diem government in South Vietnam was strongly opposed to them and because early in 1956 the Soviet government accepted the British government's contention that the holding of elections was less important than the preservation of peace in Vietnam. The indefinite postponement of the elections must have been a serious disappointment to both the Vietnamese Communists and the CCP.

manipulation of overseas Chinese communities, its tendency to pick boundary disputes with its neighbors, and its maintenance of a very large army. Chou appears to have returned from Bandung more than ever convinced that the policy, which the CCP had been urging on the Soviet Union even before the death of Stalin and which it had been implementing increasingly since 1954, of stressing "peaceful coexistence" in its relations with non-Communist states was the right one.

Even if such a policy had not seemed advantageous to the PRC's long-range interests in the field of foreign policy, it would still have been rendered advisable by the strain of the Korean War and the CCP's decision to devote itself to intensive internal economic development. By 1952 the CCP considered that it had sufficiently rehabilitated the economy to prepare for the launching of a Five Year Plan similar to the one inaugurated in the Soviet Union by Stalin in 1928. The Chinese plan, which was not put into final shape until about the beginning of 1955, envisaged a strenuous program of industrialization, with strong emphasis on heavy industry, and the beginning of "socialization" (collectivization, nationalization) of agriculture, handicrafts, and commerce. This Stalinist program signaled the end of the New Democracy period (1949–1952) and the beginning of the "transition to Socialism." The shift was regarded as releasing the CCP from Mao's promise, given in "On New Democracy," not to collectivize agriculture during New Democracy.[4] Collectivization, foreshadowed in *On the People's Democratic Dictatorship,* was regarded not as an end in itself but as a necessary means to control of the countryside and an indispensable adjunct to rapid industrialization of the country.

In November 1952 the Central People's Government announced the establishment of a State Planning Committee to draw up and supervise the First Five Year Plan. The committee was headed by Kao Kang, a member of the CCP's Politburo and the powerful regional satrap of Manchuria.

The First Five Year Plan encountered serious difficulties from the start. It appears to have been drawn up on the assumption that a very substantial volume of aid would be forthcoming from the Soviet Union. Yet prolonged Sino-Soviet economic negotiations in Moscow

[4] See Mao's "On New Democracy," reproduced in Conrad Brandt, Benjamin Schwartz, and John K. Fairbank, *A Documentary History of Chinese Communism* (Cambridge, Mass.: Harvard University Press, 1952), p. 268. Mao's promise in the latest version of this document (*Selected Works of Mao Tse-tung* [New York: International Publishers, 1954–], III, 122) has been reworded to make it appear much less categorical.

(August 1952–June 1953) produced no results sufficient to justify this optimism. When the results of the negotiations were finally announced in Peking on September 15, 1953, it developed that the Soviet Union had agreed, for a consideration, to help with equipment and technicians in the building or reconstruction of 141 industrial enterprises, of which 50 had been contracted for before Stalin's death. Again the Soviet Union had demonstrated its inability or unwillingness, or both, to contribute to China's modernization on a scale commensurate with the need and with what the CCP probably wanted.

The insufficiency of Soviet aid led to some downward revisions in the Plan and may have shaken the position of Kao Kang. In addition to his misfortune in the industrial field, Kao had also made the mistake of adopting a comparatively moderate viewpoint on agriculture by advocating the mechanization of agriculture before collectivization, whereas in 1953 the CCP clearly demonstrated its preference for the reverse order of priorities. Worse still, Kao and his ally Jao Shu-shih, the regional satrap of East China, attempted to gain for Kao a position in the CCP hierarchy second only to that of Mao Tse-tung. This was evidently done about the beginning of 1954, when Mao was seriously ill. If Kao had succeeded, he would have moved over the heads of Liu Shao-ch'i and Chou En-lai, who accordingly combined against him. Kao and Jao were sternly warned in February 1954 to give up their errors and submit to party discipline. When they refused they were crushed in the ensuing spring, Kao allegedly committing suicide and Jao suffering some unannounced fate. The CCP's official statement on their case was not published until April 5, 1955, nearly a year later. It was also strongly implied in the April statement and others issued at the same time that the Five Year Plan had run into difficulties.

Determined to eliminate regional power from its supposedly "monolithic" regime, the CCP leadership proceeded during the summer and autumn of 1954 to abolish the regional organs in the three main systems of power: the party (the regional committees of the CCP Central Committee), the government (the regional governments or Major Administrative Committees), and the armed forces (the field armies).[5] This program of centralization was legitimated, at least in the governmental sphere, in a formal constitution adopted in September 1954.

The major use to which the authorities at the center put their in-

[5] The dissolution of the field armies had probably begun in 1953.

creased power over the provinces was to accelerate the socialization
of the economy along lines which did not require massive Soviet aid.
One of these was a faster collectivization of agriculture, a program intensely unpopular with at least many peasants and opposed by many
within the CCP. Overriding all objections, Mao Tse-tung delivered a
speech on July 31, 1955 (not published until October 16 in order not
to disrupt the gathering of the autumn harvest), in which he urged an
acceleration of collectivization to bring some 43 per cent of all peasant households into semisocialist "co-operatives" by 1957. At the Sixth
Plenary Session of the CCP Central Committee in October 1955, this
percentage was raised to 70–80.

About the same time Mao launched a program to "transform" private
businesses into "joint state-private enterprises" which would be state-
controlled and from which the former owners would receive a modest
rate of interest on their investments in lieu of profits; this program
was virtually completed during 1956. At a Supreme State Conference held in January 1956 it was decided to attain "Socialism" by the
beginning of 1959 and more particularly to complete the collectivization of agriculture in 1957, thus bringing all peasants into "fully Socialist co-operatives" (i.e., collective farms). By the end of 1956, 83
per cent of all Chinese peasant families were in collective farms.

This acceleration of socialization coincided with important trends
in Sino-Soviet relations. It would probably be true to say that the PRC
was becoming more Stalinist, whereas the Soviet Union since Stalin's
death had been becoming somewhat less Stalinist. This divergence
was only partly counteracted by the fact that the CCP was able to
extract rather more economic aid from Stalin's successors than from
Stalin himself. In October 1954 a very high-ranking Soviet delegation
came to Peking in an effort to improve the unsatisfactory state of Sino-
Soviet relations. It agreed to dissolve the four joint-stock companies
mentioned earlier, to evacuate Port Arthur, to co-operate in the construction of one Sino-Soviet railway through Outer Mongolia and
another through Sinkiang, and to grant the PRC an additional 400
million rubles' worth of economic aid to be used, among other things,
for the construction of 15 additional industrial enterprises. It also
made a concession to the CCP's views on foreign policy by subscribing to the Five Principles of Peaceful Coexistence and joining in a
conciliatory declaration of willingness to establish "normal" relations
with Japan. There can be no doubt that this agreement, and the fact

that it was signed in Peking rather than in Moscow, represented a very substantial gain for the CCP leadership, which was now senior in some respects to that of the Soviet Communist Party.

A problem much less easy of solution was posed by Krushchev's heated secret denunciation of Stalin at the Twentieth Congress of the Soviet Communist Party in February 1956. After an ominous silence of six weeks, the CCP published on April 5, 1956, a statement agreeing that Stalin had been guilty of conceit, "subjectivism," and certain errors of policy, but defending the essentials of the system which he had imposed on the Soviet Union (and which, indeed, Khrushchev had not attacked). Peking probably feared that a denigration of one link in the chain of Marxist-Leninist ideological succession—and Mao Tse-tung was agreed in both countries to be another such link—might lead to attacks on others, and it may also have foreseen the disorders which usually follow a relaxation of dictatorial controls.[6]

These were not long in coming. In the summer of 1956 disturbances began in Poland, and by the second half of October they had reached the proportions of a national anti-Soviet rising. The CCP appears to have given the Polish Communists some encouragement beforehand to assert themselves against Moscow, and the CCP may well have interceded to prevent the suppression of the movement by Soviet troops which at one time seemed imminent. From Poland the contagion soon spread to Hungary, where it assumed still more dramatic proportions. On November 1, in its first important public statement on the crisis, the CCP indicated a considerable measure of sympathy with both the Polish and the Hungarian insurgents. Two days later, outraged by Nagy's attempt to take Hungary out of the Soviet bloc, it began to support, at least in public, the brutal Soviet military intervention. Its determination was presumably strengthened by an ominous event much nearer home, a rising of peasants in North Vietnam on November 5 in protest against the enforcement of collectivization in the Chinese Communist manner.

On December 29, while Chou En-lai was touring South and South-

[6] This document had an interesting sequel. Within two days Mikoyan had arrived in Peking and concluded the largest Sino-Soviet economic aid agreement to be signed during 1956. This sequence of events is an example of one of the outstanding trends in Sino-Soviet relations, a tendency for limited economic aid to be exchanged for partial ideological support. In the case in question, a further part of the bargain came to light in mid-April, when the biography of Kao Kang, which inaccurately described him as mainly responsible for the "liberation" of Manchuria in 1948, was belatedly ordered deleted from the *Great Soviet Encyclopedia*.

east Asia in an effort to repair the damage done to the Soviet bloc's standing in that area by recent events, the CCP published a definitive interpretation of the Stalin question. The main points of this document were that "Stalin's mistakes take second place to his achievements," that in any case disputes over Stalin must not be allowed to impair the relations among Communist parties, and that those relations ought to be characterized by essential equality and ideological solidarity with the Soviet Union, rather than by "great-nation chauvinism."

In January 1957, after a brief visit to Peking, Chou En-lai spent two weeks in the Soviet Union and Eastern Europe, attempting to heal the wounds inflicted by the Polish and Hungarian crises. He seems to have had some success, for all parties concerned were apparently anxious not to let such a thing happen again.

The main lesson which the Polish and Hungarian crises would convey to a Communist mind, that "de-Stalinization" is necessary but must be carefully controlled, the CCP had already absorbed. After attributing popular dissatisfaction and unrest during 1955 to "counterrevolutionaries" and trying to suppress them by terror, the CCP in the spring of 1956 began to make some concessions. It promised to allow greater freedom of debate, to pay more attention to the production of consumer goods, to increase wages and introduce the eight-hour day, to pay higher interest rates to businessmen whose enterprises had been "transformed," and to allow some private retail trade in food and other basic commodities; and some steps were taken toward implementing these pledges. The CCP did nothing, however, to abandon or modify its control over the government and over the whole of public life; it merely relaxed that control a little. Indeed, 1956 was a year of industrial overexpansion, which, combined with poor harvests, necessitated a general retrenchment in 1957.

For this real if slight "de-Stalinization" a theoretical justification had to be found. Mao Tse-tung, citing earlier writings by Lenin and himself, told a Supreme State Conference which met on February 27, 1957, that "contradictions" can and do exist even in a "Socialist" society. They exist, he said, both within the ranks of "the people" and between "the people" and the Communist Party, and they are legitimate as long as they do not worsen into "antagonisms." In other words, it is not necessary or right automatically to label anyone who criticizes the Communist Party or its regime a "counterrevolutionary." The "contradiction" which gives rise to his criticism needs to be removed if his criticism is valid. If not, the critic should be "countercriticized"

and convinced of his error, but not abused. This doctrine of "contradictions" has little theoretical originality but considerable practical
importance. It has been well received in Eastern Europe, especially in
Poland and in Yugoslavia. Although Khrushchev has denied that any
"contradictions" exist in the Soviet Union, the doctrine has since been
outwardly accepted there as applicable at least in China.

Following Mao's speech, a "rectification" campaign was launched
within the CCP, and prominent non-Communists were invited to
criticize it and the government. After much encouragement some of
them decided that it was safe to do so and proceeded to denounce
the CCP, with considerable boldness, for the severity of its dictatorship. This plain speaking shocked the CCP, some of whose leaders
seem to have been doubtful all along of the wisdom of Mao's speech
of February 27. Early in June 1957 the CCP struck back with a campaign of "countercriticism," in which manipulated public denunciations of the "rightist" critics, and thinly veiled hints that they were on
the verge of aggravating "contradictions" into "antagonisms" and
might therefore be treated as counterrevolutionaries, sufficed to wring
public confessions and retractions from most of them. On June 18 Mao
Tse-tung's speech of February 27 was published for the first time, in
an edited version which stated that criticism must not go so far as to
challenge the "leadership" of the CCP or the validity of its version of
"Socialism." If this warning had been in the original, the "rightists"
would almost certainly not have spoken out as they did.

In fact, the affair destroyed what slight reality the "united front"
in Communist China had, but of course the CCP did not admit this.
It tried to picture itself as being in real danger from the "rightists" in
order to rally public support. In the summer of 1957 it embarked on
a program of intensified indoctrination of the entire population, including the peasants, many of whom were clearly discontented. The
nonexistence of the "united front" was to be compensated by making
everyone pretend that popular support for the CCP was greater than
ever. The "rectification" campaign mounted in intensity; it combined
the reform of certain obvious abuses, such as administrative over-
centralization, with increased pressure on the public to conform.

From the events of 1957 the CCP concluded that while the economic
foundations of socialism had been laid, the ideological foundations had
not. It therefore insisted in 1958 that, as a necessary precondition to
the "socialist leap forward" which China must take in order to attain
socialism on schedule at the beginning of 1959, intellectuals must

become "Red as well as expert." Evidently the relations between the CCP and the Chinese intelligentsia are characterized by considerable mutual distrust.

The Chinese Communist Party

As with other Communist parties in power, the control which the CCP exercises over China rests on four main foundations: Marxist-Leninist ideology, which links it to the Soviet Union, points out at least the general direction of the path ahead, and gives it a fortifying conviction that it represents the "wave of the future"; organization, which blankets the entire country with party, governmental, and public bodies (see Chart 1) all responsive to the direction of the CCP leadership; propaganda, which constantly upholds the rightness of the CCP's domestic and foreign policies and insists that it is folly to oppose them; and terror, which protects the CCP from internal and external enemies when ideology, organization, and propaganda fail.

Again like other Communist parties, the CCP is organized on the principle of "democratic centralism." The adjective "democratic," which is much the less important of the two words, refers to the principle that at least in theory the membership of party organs is elected by the organs at the next lower level. Furthermore, local party organs elect periodically a National Party Congress which in turn elects the Central Committee and theoretically discusses and ratifies major party policies, as well as adopts a party constitution. The word "centralism" refers to the principle that a decision, once taken by an appropriate party organ, becomes absolutely binding on lower organs under its jurisdiction.

From 1945 to 1956 the party operated under the constitution adopted at the Seventh Congress. This constitution, which was mainly the work of Liu Shao-ch'i, stressed "the thought of Mao Tse-tung" and made the chairman of the Central Committee (Mao) ex officio also chairman of the other two most important party bodies, the Political Bureau (or Politburo) of the Central Committee and the Central Party Secretariat. The constitution presented by Teng Hsiao-p'ing and adopted by the Eighth Congress in September 1956 introduced several changes and innovations. In keeping with recent trends in the Soviet Union, it contains no reference to "the thought of Mao Tse-tung" and lays great stress on "collective leadership," although it does not follow the Soviet example set in 1952 by abolishing the Politburo and the Central Secretariat and replacing them with a Presidium. The post of honorary

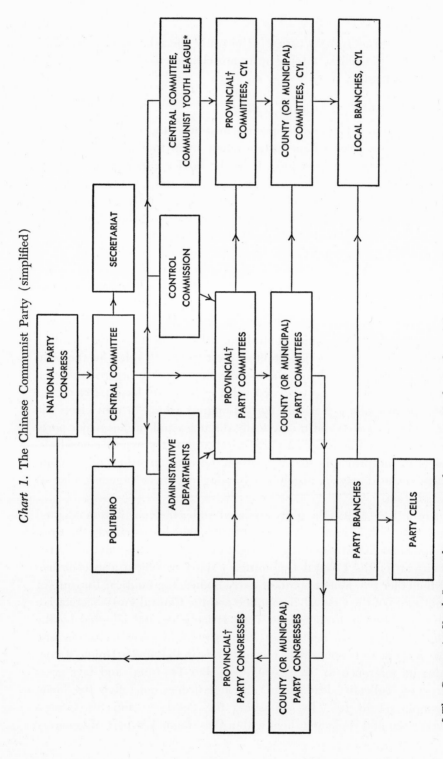

Chart 1. The Chinese Communist Party (simplified)

NATIONAL PARTY CONGRESS

POLITBURO

CENTRAL COMMITTEE

SECRETARIAT

ADMINISTRATIVE DEPARTMENTS

CONTROL COMMISSION

CENTRAL COMMITTEE, COMMUNIST YOUTH LEAGUE*

PROVINCIAL† PARTY COMMITTEES

COUNTY (OR MUNICIPAL) PARTY COMMITTEES

PROVINCIAL† COMMITTEES, CYL

COUNTY (OR MUNICIPAL) COMMITTEES, CYL

LOCAL BRANCHES, CYL

PARTY BRANCHES

PARTY CELLS

PROVINCIAL† PARTY CONGRESSES

COUNTY (OR MUNICIPAL) PARTY CONGRESSES

* The Communist Youth League has a system of congresses similar to that of the Chinese Communist Party.
† Or Special Municipality or Autonomous Region.

chairman of the party is created against the day when Mao may be forced by age or health to retire. The chairman of the Central Committee still serves as chairman of the Politburo, but no longer necessarily as chairman of the Secretariat, which is now known as the Secretariat of the Central Committee and appears much less powerful than the former Central Secretariat. Real power within the party seems to be vested in a Standing Committee of the Politburo. Unlike the 1945 constitution, that of 1956 makes no provision for party conferences to be held in the intervals between plenary sessions of the Central Committee. On the other hand, it calls for party congresses to be held at all levels every year, instead of every three years at the central level and every two years at lower levels, as in theory was the case before.[7] The former new Democratic Youth League is renamed the Communist Youth League and admitted to be affiliated with the party. Some provision is made for party members to get a fair hearing if accused of breaches of discipline and to hold (though not necessarily to express) their own views even if they happen to conflict with those of the party leadership. In spite of these concessions, the new constitution is still clearly much more "centralist" than "democratic."

The organization of the CCP is based firmly on the territorial principle. In other words, anyone whose permanent residence is considered to be in any part of the PRC can join no Communist Party other than the Chinese, no matter what his race; there are no special parties or branches for Mongols, Tibetans, or other non-Chinese living within the PRC. The situation in the overseas Chinese communities is more obscure, but it appears that the same principle usually holds. That is to say, a Chinese in Malaya may join the Malayan Communist Party, which is open to any qualified resident of Malaya; there appears to be no branch of the CCP there, and no branch of the MCP reserved for Chinese.

The highest organ through which the CCP exercises jurisdiction over all Communists living within the PRC is its Central Committee. The current or Eighth Central Committee, elected at the Eighth Congress in September 1956, consists of 97 regular and 73 alternate members. These are all ranked in descending order according to number of votes received at the congress, and it is probable that this order reflects a combination of relative popularity with the rank and file of the party and relative standing in the eyes of the party leadership. The elections were conducted in a carefully controlled fashion which,

[7] No National Party Congress was held during 1957, however.

however, did allow for a limited freedom of nomination on the part of the delegations to the congress.

The bodies whose membership was elected by the Central Committee at its first Plenary Session shortly after its own election are the Politburo (17 regular, 6 alternate members); the Secretariat of the Central Committee (6 regular, 3 alternate members); the Control Commission of the Central Committee, which maintains party discipline (17 regular, 4 alternate members); and the Secretariat of the Control Commission (one secretary and 5 deputies). As already mentioned, there is also a Standing Committee of the Politburo, which appears to exercise supreme power within the party and is composed of Mao Tse-tung, Liu Shao-ch'i, Chou En-lai, Chu Teh, Ch'en Yün, and Teng Hsiao-p'ing, in that order; they are also respectively the chairman, the four vice chairmen, and the general secretary of the Central Committee and before September 1956 made up the membership of the former Central Secretariat.

It seems likely that the organization of the bureaucratic apparatus under control of the Eighth Central Committee is substantially the same as it was under the Seventh. In that case the principal departments are the Organization Department (headed by Jao Shu-shih before his fall), the Propaganda Department, the United Front Work Department (which handles relations with the non-Communist public), the Social Affairs Department (which has intelligence and espionage functions), the Rural Work Department (a fairly new body which deals with the collectivization of agriculture), the General (or Administrative) Office, and the Control Commission (whose powers were increased in 1955). Each of these has supervisory power over corresponding bodies at lower levels in the party hierarchy.

Since the elimination of the regional bureaus of the Central Committee, the next lower party organ is the Communist Party organization in the province, special municipality, or autonomous region. It is organized as a smaller replica of the central party organization and has a party congress and a party committee. At the next lower level is the county or municipal party organization, which is similar in structure. Below that the most important level is that of the party branch or cell, which usually consists of about 20 party members working in the same factory, farm, and so on. It appears that every CCP member must belong to one of these branches. Although the branch is the lowest formal party organ, there also exist nuclei or fractions, small groups of party members working together within some larger nonparty body.

The CCP has expanded enormously in recent years, until it is now the largest political party in the world. Its approximate total membership was 1.2 million in 1945, 5 million in 1949, 10.7 million at the beginning of 1956, and 12 million at the end of 1956. The membership of the Soviet Communist Party was about 7.25 million in February 1956. Only about 10 per cent of the membership of the CCP are women, and until recently 70 per cent of the total membership were of rural origin. The rural percentage may have altered somewhat recently, for since the beginning of 1956 the CCP has been emphasizing the recruitment of "intellectuals," most of whom are actually technicians, and of workers, in order to reduce the preponderance of peasants. It should be noted that members of the small non-Communist "democratic" political parties are not encouraged, and are probably not even allowed, to join the CCP; they are more useful as window dressing.

Although the CCP constitution of September 1956 allows party members somewhat greater freedom of thought and expression than was the case before, party unity and party discipline are still the overriding goals. Erring individual members can be subjected to a variety of administrative punishments ranging from reprimand to expulsion and in extreme cases to criminal penalties at the hands of the regular courts. For dealing with undesirable tendencies within the party membership as a whole, much of which is opportunistic and insufficiently indoctrinated, the CCP evolved during its days at Yenan a purge or "rectification" technique strikingly different from Stalin's. The latest "rectification" campaign began early in 1957 and appears to be true to form. Little use is made of expulsion, and still less of more drastic penalties. The emphasis is on ideological training and reassignment to other jobs, often involving manual labor and close contact with "the masses." In this way the CCP seems to be able to control and manipulate its rank and file with considerable success.

Attached to the CCP are two important youth organizations. The first, formerly known as the New Democratic Youth League but renamed the Communist Youth League since the Eighth CCP Congress, contains about 20 million youths of both sexes between the ages of 15 and 25. The second, the Young Pioneers, has a membership of at least 8 million boys and girls aged from 9 to 14. The importance of these organizations as recruiting grounds for the CCP and as instruments of control and indoctrination of the rising generation is obvious and great.

The CCP like other Communist parties has also at its disposal many millions of cadres, who act as transmission belts between the party and the public. Cadres are individuals who may be CCP members, probationary CCP members, or simply "activists" anxious to serve the party for one reason or another. They do essential work for the party, usually on a part-time basis, in military units, factories, shops, public and mass organizations, agricultural "co-operatives" and collectives, campaigns to suppress "counterrevolutionaries" or liquidate landlords, campaigns to extract "donations" from the public, and the like. The word cadre is broad and vague in meaning and may include high-ranking party members, but it generally refers to individuals at or near the bottom of the party or even outside it altogether. The cadres as a whole constitute an elite with considerable power and privileges.

Of this huge number of people directly or indirectly at the disposal of the CCP, only a minority are full-time paid party functionaries. We do not know how much such functionaries are paid, but it is probably not much. The rest must earn a difficult living in some other way while giving what time they can spare to the party.

Most of them earn their living by serving in the governmental apparatus, in the numerous economic agencies and enterprises controlled by the government, or in the armed forces. The CCP's tight control over the government and armed forces rests, indeed, largely on the fact that virtually all important positions in both are held by CCP members. This has been true since 1949, but the percentage has become greater since 1954; for example, whereas before 1954 there were 2 non-Communist Vice-Premiers out of 5, today there are none out of 12. A corollary to the same principle is the frequency with which CCP members, and especially high-ranking ones, hold multiple offices in the party, government, and armed forces. To take the most obvious example, Mao Tse-tung holds as his principal posts the chairmanship of the Central Committee of the CCP, the chairmanship of the PRC (i.e., he is chief of state), and the chairmanship of the National Defense Council (nominally the highest body in the military field).

An important facet of the infiltration of governmental organs and military units by CCP members is the existence of party committees composed of CCP members working within such bodies. These have long existed in the People's Liberation Army. In the case of government agencies, their creation was announced in May 1956, but they may have existed earlier. Since about the same time, the establishment of closer control by the CCP over the government has been rendered still more obvious by a tendency for the CCP Central Committee and the State Council (cabinet) to issue joint directives on important domestic matters.

Thus the CCP has its chain of control within the government and armed forces, and there appears to be no way in which this control could be destroyed from within except in the unlikely event of a major conflict within the top ranks of the CCP's leadership.

The statement that a serious conflict is unlikely does not mean that there are no differences over policy and power within the CCP. There are, but they appear to be between men who have long known each other, who have more in common than they have at issue, and who have limited objectives and employ limited means in order not to destroy party unity. To violate these rules of the game is to court the fate of Beria, Kao Kang, and Jao Shu-shih.

If the admittedly incomplete evidence on this obscure but interesting and important subject is assembled, the existence of two major factions within the upper ranks of the CCP seems discernible. One, led by Liu Shao-ch'i, is composed largely of men with comparatively little experience abroad and relatively little interest in events outside China, except for a strong feeling of ideological comradeship with the rest of the Soviet bloc. This faction has the upper hand within the party machinery properly speaking and dominates the CCP's pronouncements on major ideological issues. It has never viewed with favor Soviet influence on the CCP and more recently appears to have been the main driving force behind the modest trend toward "de-Stalinization" already mentioned.

The other faction, led by Chou En-lai, contains more men who have had extensive experience abroad. It is stronger within the government and the armed forces than within the party, but it is by no means negligible there. Although no more loyal to the Soviet Union on a strictly ideological plane than the other faction, it appears the more convinced that the PRC's own interests require a close alignment with the Soviet Union in practical matters. It has a more international and a less China-centered outlook and has been the main driving force behind the effort to base the PRC's foreign relations on at least the semblance of "peaceful coexistence." It is probably the more Stalinist of the two in its domestic policies.

Apart from these differences of background and outlook, the two factions are probably involved in a limited contest for power. It is likely that neither Liu nor Chou aspires to wear Mao's mantle when he lays it down or grow to his stature, let alone to displace him in full career. It is not at all improbable, however, that each man would like to hold the first place in a "collective leadership" after the death of Mao, who is five years older than they. Liu's faction has two important and related advantages: it is stronger within the party, where all important decisions are made, and Mao Tse-tung clearly prefers Liu to Chou as a candidate for the succession. Liu has made his way in the party largely by devotion to Mao, whereas Chou attained a high position in the party earlier than Mao and independently of him and has had some serious disputes with him.

If Liu's faction currently appears the stronger, the two are nevertheless balanced after a fashion, and considerable care is taken to preserve the balance. For example, two new members were elected to the Politburo in 1954 or 1955; one was Teng Hsiao-p'ing, whose background strongly suggests that if he has a personal loyalty to anyone it is to Chou En-lai; the other was Lin Piao, whose background similarly suggests an orientation toward the domestic faction if not necessarily toward Liu Shao-ch'i himself. Again, two new Vice-Premiers were named on November 16, 1956: Nieh Jung-chen, a military man with an international background, and Po I-po, a man without such a background. During Chou En-lai's two recent absences from the country, the acting Premier has been Ch'en Yün, a man on good terms with both factions.

It seems likely that Chou En-lai was the main beneficiary, and therefore also the prime mover, of the downfall of Kao Kang and Jao Shushih. Their regional power threatened the central government more than it did the party, and so did the fact that Kao Kang's State Planning Committee was not under the control of Chou En-lai's cabinet (then known as the State Administration Council). Kao had one common deputy in his major posts, and only one: Li Fu-ch'un, who succeeded Kao at the head of the State Planning Committee, which was then brought under the cabinet, and whose background strongly suggests an affiliation with Chou En-lai. It appears probable that Li had been assigned by Chou to watch Kao and that he took an active part in Kao's overthrow. Chou benefited by gaining at least partial control over the armed forces, through the medium of the newly created Ministry of Defense, as well as over economic planning.

If Chou En-lai seems to have benefited considerably from the fall of Kao Kang and Jao Shu-shih, Liu seems to have suffered correspondingly. Jao Shu-shih, who had succeeded Liu as chairman of the Organization Department in 1953, had been considered a protégé of his. Furthermore, Liu had come close in a speech delivered in September 1954 to aligning himself with Kao Kang's relatively moderate agricultural policy. Between that date and April 1956 Liu made no major published speeches.

If it is likely that Chou gained and Liu lost ground during this period, it is equally likely that the reverse happened in 1956. The CCP's statement of April 5, 1956 (the anniversary of the announcement on the Kao Kang–Jao Shu-shih affair), on the Stalin question appeared to suggest that unnamed CCP members had been guilty of offenses not very different in kind from those of Stalin. Shortly afterward the creation of party committees within government agencies was announced. In June 1956 Chou was severely criticized by members of the National People's Congress for various real or alleged shortcomings of his government in the economic field, and he replied in an unpublished speech—of which the published summary reads very much like a "confession." The major report to the Eighth CCP Congress in September was delivered by Liu Shao-ch'i, who has outranked Chou in the party hierarchy since at least as long ago as 1945. In November, at about the time Chou went abroad, a directive was issued that government agencies must stop expanding. If Liu appears now to be in the ascendant, this does not indicate a probable elimination of Chou, who is much too able, useful, and influential to be dispensed with for any but the weightiest of reasons. In fact, Chou may have gained some ground in 1957 as a result of having correctly anticipated that the invitation to freer public discussion conveyed in Mao Tse-tung's speech of February 27, 1957, on "contradictions" would have unpleasant consequences.

In order to see the question of factional differences within the CCP in true perspective, it must be realized that these differences are less important than the common outlook and background which bind CCP leaders to each other and to a common cause. This will probably remain true at least as long as Mao Tse-tung lives, for he uses his immense prestige to arbitrate between the two factions and keep them working in harness. What will happen after his death is another question.

No discussion of the CCP would be complete without some consideration of the theoretical framework into which it attempts to fit its own present and future position and that of the PRC. Although in a few documents, such as the Common Program of 1949 and the constitution of September 1954, the CCP used the term People's Democracy as a possible label for the state which it controlled, it has generally evaded the efforts of Soviet writers to fasten this label officially upon it. The reason is that the term, as applied to the East European satellites, connotes a dictatorship of the proletariat. The CCP insisted and still insists that the PRC is not a dictatorship of the proletariat alone but one exercised by the whole people, and in particular the "democratic" classes and groups making up the "united front," over the "reactionaries." The CCP has preferred the term People's Democratic Dictatorship to describe the state which it controlled. During the Stalin controversy of 1956, however, by which time Soviet theorists had greatly broadened the meanings of the terms under discussion, the CCP began to accept the term dictatorship of the proletariat as applicable to the PRC. Presumably the term will be considered applicable until after the completion of the "transition to Socialism" (1953–1958) and the attainment of "Socialism" at the beginning of 1959.

Other Public Bodies

Given the importance which the CCP attaches to the maintenance of the outward appearance of a "united front," it is bound to permit the existence of other public bodies besides itself. These bodies are granted direct representation in the Chinese People's Political Consultative Conference, which is the principal institutional expression of the "united front." They are also represented indirectly (i.e., by members who are elected from geographical constituencies) in the National People's Congress, the PRC's nearest equivalent to a parliament. All these bodies are carefully supervised by the United Front Work Department of the CCP Central Committee, and none is known to have given the CCP any serious problems of control. In fact, the CCP often has more trouble in controlling its own membership and persuading it to accept some new policy than it does in controlling the non-Communist organizations, which have no access to the machinery of power. Such organizations are formally bound by the constitution of September 1954 to accept the "leadership" of the CCP.

One category of these non-Communist public bodies comprises the minor parties, or the "democratic" parties as they are officially called.

They are eight in number: the Revolutionary Committee of the Kuomintang (defectors from the Kuomintang), the China Democratic League (those elements of the Democratic League, a former third-force party, which adhered to the CCP), the Democratic National Construction Association (businessmen), the Chinese Peasants and Workers Democratic Party, the China Association for Promoting Democracy, the China Chih Kung Tang (composed largely of overseas Chinese), the Chiu San—September Third—Society (intellectuals), and the Taiwan Democratic Self-Government League. Three more parties have been dissolved by the CCP or amalgamated with other parties since 1949, for reasons which are obscure.

Although as stated earlier the number of non-Communists in high governmental posts has tended to decline since about 1954, this trend does not appear to portend an elimination of the "democratic" parties. On the occasion of the opening of the Eighth CCP Congress, the *People's Daily* (the official organ of the CCP Central Committee) promised that "the Communist Party will carry out the policy of long-term coexistence and mutual supervision with other democratic parties; so long as the Communist Party exists, the other democratic parties will also exist." [8]

From shortly after the "Liberation" until about 1956, the minor parties were forbidden to build up any sort of mass-support or grass-roots organization. In 1956 this ban was relaxed to the extent of allowing them to take in a sizable number of new members. Although they go through the motions of holding periodic and usually simultaneous congresses and electing central committees, the minor parties remain essentially small and powerless groups whose membership is largely middle class and therefore automatically suspect in the eyes of the CCP. Their central committees share a single newspaper, the *Kwangming Daily*. There are CCP members both overt and covert, within the minor parties; presumably they act as spies and exercise a considerable degree of control.

The so-called mass organizations have much larger memberships than do the minor parties, and they make little effort to disguise the fact that the key posts, which are not necessarily the chairmanships, are held by CCP members. The services which these organizations perform for the CCP are legion. They help to create the impression at home and abroad, which is only partially justified, that the CCP enjoys overwhelming popular support. They aid in publicizing and

[8] Broadcast by New China News Agency, Peking, Sept. 15, 1956.

implementing its policies. They take part in its mass campaigns. They participate in international congresses and address communications to similar organizations in other countries.

The first major category of mass organizations consists of those which claim to represent definite and permanent groups or interests within society. Examples are the All-China Federation of Trade Unions, which like similar organizations in all Communist countries is more concerned with regimenting the labor force than in attempting to improve its status; the All-China Federation of Co-operatives; the All-China Federation of Democratic Women; the All-China Federation of Democratic Youth; the Peasants Associations; the All-China Federation of Literary and Art Circles; and the National Committee of the (Christian) Churches in China for the Realization of Self-Administration, which attempts to cut off contacts between Christian bodies in China and their coreligionists outside.

The other major type of mass organization exists more for a specific purpose than as the nominal representative of some group. Examples are the Sino-Soviet Friendship Association, which carries on an enormous volume of propaganda on behalf of the Soviet Union and the Sino-Soviet alliance; the Chinese People's Institute of Foreign Affairs; the Red Cross Society of China; the Chinese People's Committee for World Peace and against American Aggression; and the Asian Solidarity Committee.

The fact that an individual is a member or officer of one of these organizations does not necessarily indicate any real sympathy on his part for its aims. This statement probably applies most forcefully to the Sino-Soviet Friendship Association, which includes many non-Communists who have no reason whatever to love the Soviet Union. The same organization also provided a striking example of the way in which these bodies achieve their impressive membership figures when on November 7, 1951, it inducted all members of the People's Liberation Army simultaneously.

Some of the theoretical implications of the CCP's policy toward these non-Communist organizations, which is usually known as the "mass line," seem worth exploring, and all the more so because they show marked differences from the policy pursued in the Soviet Union. In Bolshevik Russia, where the "dictatorship of the proletariat" was inaugurated in 1917 and "Socialism" officially achieved in 1936, no minor parties have been allowed to exist, and mass organizations have flourished much less luxuriantly than they have in Communist China.

This difference might not seem significant if one could expect the disappearance of at least the minor parties by 1959, when China will have achieved "Socialism," by definition a state in which only two classes, the workers and the peasants, exist, with even this distinction in process of disappearing. But this is not likely to be the case, for the CCP has categorically promised that the minor parties will survive as long as it does. This departure from the Soviet policy toward non-Communist organizations is undoubtedly one of the major reasons why it was not until 1956 that the CCP began to accept, and even then with some reservations, the term dictatorship of the proletariat as applicable to the PRC. The greater outward deference to non-Communist opinion in the PRC, as compared with the Soviet Union, is partly an outgrowth of the distinctive characteristics of the "way of Mao Tse-tung," which proved so successful as a means of seizing power in China, partly an implicit encouragement to other Asian countries to "grow over" into "Socialism" through means short of violence, and partly an intimation to the Chinese Nationalists on Taiwan and to the overseas Chinese that they too may take their place in the "new" China.

Constitutional Structure and Development

As in other countries, the constitutional development of the PRC and the evolution of elected, or nominally elected, bodies have been so closely connected that they ought to be discussed together.

For the first five years of its existence (October 1949–September 1954) the PRC had neither a national legislature nor a formal constitution. Instead it had the Chinese People's Political Consultative Conference (CPPCC), the Common Program, and an Organic Law. The groundwork for the CPPCC had been laid during the summer of 1949, in typical CCP fashion, by the appointment of a Preparatory Committee. This committee, though of course dominated by CCP members, also included members of other parties and nonparty men, so that like the CPPCC itself it nominally represented the "united front" on which the present regime supposedly rests. Similar to other preparatory committees, this one arranged the agenda and procedure for the conference itself and gave the CCP members a chance to explain to the others what was expected of them, so that everything went smoothly.

The CPPCC consisted of 662 delegates representing the various political parties including the CCP, the mass organizations, the geographical regions, the People's Liberation Army, and the overseas Chinese. The delegation representing the CCP was only 16 men strong, but other CCP members were present in the delegations representing other bodies, and no one at the conference publicly questioned the "leadership" of the CCP.

The Common Program is essentially an elaboration of the principles set forth in Mao Tse-tung's *On the People's Democratic Dictatorship*, except that it places less emphasis on socialization of the economy and more on short-term CCP objectives such as "agrarian reform" and it forecast the major domestic policies pursued by the CCP during the first few years after the "Liberation."

The Organic Law prescribes the organization of the government, which will be dealt with later, and provides that pending the convening of an All-China People's Congress elected by universal suffrage the CPPCC shall exercise its functions. Before the All-China People's Congress could be elected, People's Congresses had to be elected at the various lower levels of government. Since the election of these was not immediately feasible, the CCP in the meanwhile appointed local "representative" bodies to fulfill the same functions. Like the People's Government Councils, which were the local executive organs, these "representative" bodies were governed by the principle of "democratic centralism."

In January 1953 preparations were begun for nation-wide elections to the People's Congress which were scheduled to be held before the end of 1953. For reasons not quite clear but probably bearing some relation to the serious domestic difficulties which the CCP was facing at that time, these elections had to be postponed until 1954. In connection with the registration for these elections the authorities conducted a census, which was actually the first in the history of China, whose results as published on November 1, 1954, gave the astounding total of some 583 million people living on the Chinese mainland. The minimum voting age was 18, and about 323 million people were declared eligible to vote.

Of this number 86 per cent actually voted, usually by show of hands, for 5.5 million delegates to People's Congresses at the lowest levels, the rural district (*hsiang*) or town. Each of these then elected delegates to the People's Congresses for the *hsien* (county), and so on up through the provincial to the national level. The National People's Congress, which met in Peking in September 1954, consisted of about 1,200 delegates representing not only geographical constituencies but also the armed forces, overseas Chinese, and national minorities. One of its most important tasks was to discuss and adopt a formal constitution.

The groundwork for the constitution, like that for the National People's Congress itself, had been carefully laid. In November 1952 the Central People's Government Council, the highest government body, had appointed a 33-man committee, heavily weighted with high-ranking CCP members, to draft a constitution. Early in 1953 the CCP Central Committee helpfully submitted a draft of its own, which was never published. It is therefore impossible to say how closely this corresponded with the draft completed by the committee and approved by the Central People's Government Council in June 1954, but it can safely be assumed that the resemblance must have been very great.

After that the accepted draft was published and laid before the public for discussion. This discussion was no random affair, but was carefully organized. The draft was explained, discussed, and voted on at numerous carefully controlled gatherings of public bodies and of the general public. One case is on record in which all these things were done within the space of fifteen minutes. Numerous changes, none of them of any substance, were proposed and later transmitted to the National People's Congress for its consideration, and some were actually adopted.

The constitution, adopted by the National People's Congress on September 20, 1954, makes no very striking changes in the pre-existing situation. The preamble, like that of the Common Program, stresses the concepts of the People's Democratic Dictatorship and the "united front." It describes the PRC as a unified state from which no national minority or other group has any right of secession; this view, first openly admitted by the CCP in 1949, represents a departure from the CCP's propaganda before 1949, which had often promised the minorities the right of secession. The preamble and Chapter I also lay much more emphasis on the socialization of the economy than had the Common Program.

Chapter II of the Constitution deals with the organization of the government, which will be discussed below, and Chapter III with the rights and duties of citizens. The meaning of the term citizen is not defined, but it is clear, both from the CCP's general practice and the fact that overseas Chinese are represented in the National People's Congress, that the term is intended to include all permanent residents of the PRC of whatever race (whether they belong to the ranks of "the people" or to those of the "reactionaries") and all persons of Chinese race living abroad. Citizens of the PRC are guaranteed the usual civil liberties, including freedom of religion. They also have the right to work and to rest, as well as the obligations to pay taxes and perform military service as prescribed by law. Chapter V specifies the national flag, emblem, and capital (Peking).

It would be logical to expect that with the election of the National People's Congress and the adoption of a formal constitution the Chinese People's Political Consultative Conference would cease to exist, but something rather more complicated has happened. Shortly after the adoption of the constitution, the CPPCC was in effect replaced by a body known as the National Committee of the CPPCC, which has roughly twice the membership of the old CPPCC and serves like the latter as the representative organ of the "united front." The National Committee of the CPPCC in turn has a smaller Standing Committee, which corresponds to the Standing Committee of the National People's Congress (see below), although it lacks the latter's constitutional powers, and which is under the chairmanship of Chou En-lai. One possible explanation of these trends is a desire on Chou's part to head a public forum comparable to that possessed by Liu Shao-ch'i as chairman of the Standing Committee of the National People's Congress. Another is a desire to show the Nationalists on Taiwan that the "united front" is a reality in which they too may take part.

Governmental Organization

The constitution of 1954 describes the National People's Congress (see Chart 2) as "the highest organ of state power" and as the national legislature. It is elected for a term of four years and meets at least once a year. It has the power to amend the constitution, elect and remove the highest officials of the government, enact legislation, and decide on important matters (such as treaties) laid before it by the government. It also elects its own Standing Committee.

The Standing Committee of the National People's Congress, whose nearest analogue before September 1954 was the Central People's Government Council, exercises at least in theory a general power of supervision over the government—and in fact exercises most of the powers of the National People's Congress when this body is not in session.

Of the officials elected by the National People's Congress, the high-

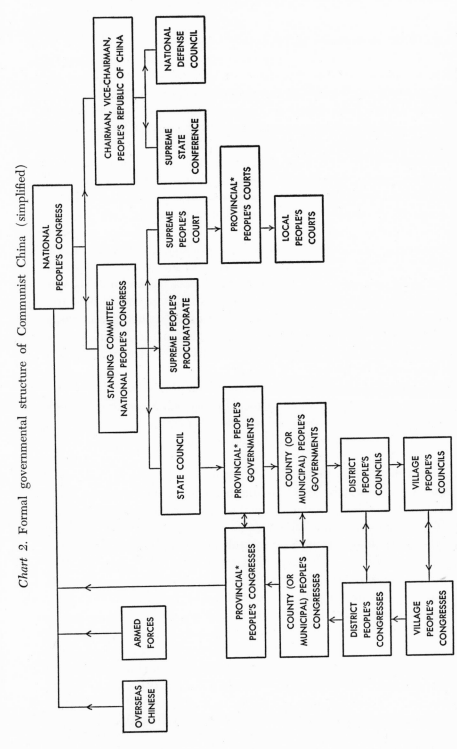

Chart 2. Formal governmental structure of Communist China (simplified)

NATIONAL PEOPLE'S CONGRESS

CHAIRMAN, VICE-CHAIRMAN, PEOPLE'S REPUBLIC OF CHINA

NATIONAL DEFENSE COUNCIL

SUPREME STATE CONFERENCE

STANDING COMMITTEE, NATIONAL PEOPLE'S CONGRESS

SUPREME PEOPLE'S COURT

PROVINCIAL* PEOPLE'S COURTS

LOCAL PEOPLE'S COURTS

SUPREME PEOPLE'S PROCURATORATE

STATE COUNCIL

PROVINCIAL* PEOPLE'S GOVERNMENTS

COUNTY (OR MUNICIPAL) PEOPLE'S GOVERNMENTS

DISTRICT PEOPLE'S COUNCILS

VILLAGE PEOPLE'S COUNCILS

PROVINCIAL* PEOPLE'S CONGRESSES

COUNTY (OR MUNICIPAL) PEOPLE'S CONGRESSES

DISTRICT PEOPLE'S CONGRESSES

VILLAGE PEOPLE'S CONGRESSES

ARMED FORCES

OVERSEAS CHINESE

* Or Special Municipality or Autonomous Region (under each of which the names of the subordinate units are somewhat different from those shown on the chart).

est ranking is the Chairman of the People's Republic of China (Mao Tse-tung). This official exercises the ceremonial functions of a chief of state and also presides over the National Defense Council and the Supreme State Conference. The constitution does not specify whether he is eligible to succeed himself at the end of his four-year term. He is assisted, and in the event of incapacity succeeded, by a Vice-Chairman (Chu Teh).

The constitution says nothing else about the National Defense Council, except that its members are appointed by the Chairman of the PRC and confirmed by the National People's Congress. Its actual membership is much larger (14 vice-chairmen, 80 members) and has a higher proportion of non-Communists than was the case with its predecessor, the People's Revolutionary Military Council, during the 1949–1954 period. The Military Council was an extremely powerful body which actually controlled the armed forces and had military staff sections directly under it. Neither of these things appears to hold true of the National Defense Council, which meets infrequently and seems to share control over the armed forces with the People's Liberation Army General Staff and with the Ministry of Defense within the cabinet.

The Supreme State Conference is an *ad hoc* body composed of the Chairman and Vice-Chairman of the PRC, the chairman of the Standing Committee of the National People's Congress, the premier (or chairman of the State Council), and any other persons whom the Chairman of the PRC sees fit to invite. The Supreme State Conference serves primarily as a personal forum at which the Chairman can put his own views directly before the public. There have been four major sessions of the Supreme State Conference. The first met in January 1956 and approved Mao Tse-tung's program for attaining "Socialism" by the beginning of 1959. The second met in May 1956 to consider the question of "de-Stalinization," with particular reference to intellectuals. The third met in February 1957 to consider Mao's theory of "contradictions." The fourth met in October 1957 to discuss the "rectification" campaign and the agricultural situation.

The ordinary business of government is conducted by the State Council (cabinet), known before 1954 as the Government Administration Council. The governmental reorganization of 1954 added the supervision of economic planning to the cabinet's functions by bringing the State Planning Committee under the State Council (it had formerly been under the Central People's Government Council) and at least partial control over the armed forces by creating a Ministry of Defense within the cabinet. The State Council is responsible to the National People's Congress or to its Standing Committee when the Congress is not in session.

The constitution refrains from specifying the organization of the State Council in any but the most general terms. In addition to the Premier (Chou En-lai, who was also Foreign Minister until 1958), it is headed by twelve Vice-Premiers. Under them are eight general offices and a secretary-general, which co-ordinate administration and are evidently bodies of considerable importance. All the cabinet officials mentioned so far, including the chairmen of the eight general offices, are high-ranking CCP members.

In all there are within the cabinet some forty ministries, commissions, and affiliated agencies, most of them economic in function. The great majority of the ministers and chairmen of commissions are CCP members; those who are not have generally to do with consumer goods and technical problems, and in any event they have Communist vice-ministers under them.[9]

On approximately the same constitutional level with the State Council, though much less powerful in practice, and responsible like it to the National People's Congress and its Standing Committee, are two other bodies. One is the Supreme People's Court, which supervises a hierarchy of People's Courts corresponding to the various levels of the governmental structure. The other is the Supreme People's Procurator's Office, which controls a similar hierarchy of subordinate offices and acts as the public prosecutor in criminal cases.

Before 1954 the next level of government below the central government was the five Major Administrative Committees or regional governments (Northeast, Northwest, East China, Central South, and Southwest) and the North China Administrative Committee. These regional governments, whose powers were considerably curtailed at the end of 1952, were headed by very powerful and high-ranking

---

[9] Readers familiar with Parkinson's Law will realize that the cabinet's large size prevents it from functioning as a coherent unit. The same observation would also apply to the premier, vice-premiers, and chairmen of the general offices taken together. Business is therefore probably transacted by the premier in conjunction with one or another of the chairmen of the general offices and the leading officials of the appropriate ministries and/or chairmen of commissions. Each vice-premier, insofar as his other commitments permit, probably specializes in various branches of governmental work (Nieh Jung-chen, for example, deals with scientific development) and sits in when a meeting is called in which he is especially interested.

CCP officials, who were respectively Kao Kang, P'eng Te-huai, Jao Shu-shih, Lin Piao, Liu Po-ch'eng, and Nieh Jung-chen. These men also held high, but usually not the highest, posts in their regional party organizations. All but two, Kao Kang and Jao Shu-shih, also commanded field armies, and it is probably more than a coincidence that these were the two men purged in 1954. After their elimination the regional governments, along with the regional party organizations and the field armies, were broken up.

Since the time of these changes and the adoption of the constitution of September 1954, the governmental levels directly under the central government have been of three kinds. The first is the special municipality, of which there are 3 (Peking, Tientsin, and Shanghai); before 1954 there were 14. The second is the autonomous region, of which there are 5: the Inner Mongolia Autonomous Region, established in May 1947; the Sinkiang Uighur Autonomous Region, established in September–October 1955; Tibet, which is in the process of receiving its "autonomy"; the Ningsia Hui Autonomous Region; and the Kwangsi Ch'uang Autonomous Region (the creation of the last two was announced in June 1957).[10] The third and most important is the province, of which there are 21.

Below this level the most important units are the rural county (*hsien*) and the municipality (*shih*), both of which come directly under the government of a province or an autonomous region. At the lowest level the most important units are the rural districts (*hsiang*), the urban districts, and the towns.

The governments of all these units are remarkably uniform throughout the country and are organized as smaller replicas of the central government. That is to say, each has a People's Congress and a People's Council, the latter being elected by the former and nominally responsible to it. The chairman of a Provincial People's Council is also referred to as the chairman of the Provincial People's Government of that province or simply as the governor. The corresponding official at the municipal level is also called the mayor.

What has been said so far about governmental organization applies mainly to areas inhabited almost entirely by Han (i.e., racial) Chinese. In addition to the Chinese, there are within the PRC about 35 million members of minority groups, of which the most important are of

[10] The terms Uighur, Hui (Chinese-speaking Moslem), and Ch'uang (Thai) are the names of the principal national minorities inhabiting these regions respectively.

Mongolian, Turkish, Tibetan, or Thai stock. These minorities live for the most part thinly scattered over the western half of the PRC. Like the minorities in the Soviet Union, many of them have kinsmen in other parts of Asia, and the CCP therefore finds it advisable to treat them with an appearance of great consideration. It has followed the general pattern worked out in the Soviet Union by Stalin, the essence of which is to give the minorities their own "autonomous" governments and allow them to enjoy the use of their indigenous language and culture at least for a time, while in reality keeping them tightly under control.

In one respect the minority policy of the CCP is even less liberal than that of the Soviet Union. The sixteen republics of the Soviet Union enjoy a theoretical right of secession, but even this is denied to the minorities in the PRC. The PRC minorities are also explicitly required to accept the "leadership" of the CCP and the central government.

Where a sufficiently large number of people of a single minority group live together in a single area, they are organized into an "autonomous" government of one type or another. There are well over a hundred of these "autonomous" units, some of them situated in the autonomous regions and some in the provinces. In the Inner Mongolia Autonomous Region a concession is made to Mongol tradition by organizing the Mongols into units of local government known by the ancient term league (*meng*) and under them into banners (*ch'i*). "Autonomous" units lying within provinces are of course under the jurisdiction of the appropriate provincial governments. In some cases an "autonomous" government at a lower level belonging to one minority exists as an enclave within a larger "autonomous" government belonging to another. In cases where members of two or more minorities are so intermingled that it is impossible to separate them, a "democratic coalition government" is set up in which all are represented. The result is a patchwork of "autonomous" governments so complex that it would cause serious confusion if it were not for the fact that all are tightly controlled from the center by the CCP and the central government.

Government in Action

There are several ways in which the CCP ensures its control over the governmental machinery, as already mentioned. The first and most significant is the placing of high-ranking CCP members in all really important governmental posts. Another, adopted by the spring of 1956, perhaps in order to ensure implementation by the government of the "de-Stalinization" program, is the establishment of CCP party organizations within governmental agencies. A third, initiated at about the same time, is the custom of issuing important directives on domestic policy jointly in the name of the CCP Central Committee and the State Council, which of course guarantees the Central Committee's prior approval. In reality, even without this device all major administrative measures would in any case be first discussed and approved by the central CCP organs, usually the Politburo or its Standing Committee.

There is still another less obvious way in which control by the CCP over the government is ensured. The constitution of September 1954 vests in the Standing Committee of the National People's Congress the power to supervise, and when necessary to change or annul, actions by all levels of the governmental apparatus. The chairman of the Standing Committee is Liu Shao-ch'i, whose source of power lies mainly within the party machinery and who may be regarded as the symbol of the CCP as distinct from the government and the armed forces. There seems to be no reason to doubt that Liu could carry with him the other members of the Standing Committee, who are all either high-ranking CCP members or respected but powerless figureheads such as the Dalai Lama. On the other hand, the authority of the Standing Committee over the State Council, which is of course headed by Liu's principal rival, Chou En-lai, is not absolute. It can appoint or remove a Vice-Premier, Minister, or secretary-general of the State Council, but not the Premier himself; this can be done only by the full National People's Congress. In this way Chou is given some protection against removal.

The governmental apparatus of the PRC completely lacks any separation of powers; in fact, that concept has been explicitly repudiated by its architects. Just as the CCP dominates the government, so within the government the executive overshadows the other branches, although their personnel seldom overlap. In actuality a legislative branch scarcely exists, for legislative functions are divided among the Politburo of the CCP, the Standing Committee of the National People's Congress, the Congress itself, and the State Council.

The concept of justice, like that of truth, has no meaning to the CCP except insofar as it serves the aims of the party. No pretense is made of administering abstract justice; the courts and laws are designed to serve "the people," whose interests are defined for them by the CCP. The chairman of the Supreme People's Court is Tung Pi-wu, a long-standing member of the CCP Politburo, who has more than once behaved in a fashion unthinkable on the part of a judge in a democratic country by demanding that the police bring the courts more "counter-revolutionaries" to try. The result of this system of party justice is that, as in the Soviet Union, ordinary crimes are often punished no more severely than they deserve, but that political offenses are sternly dealt with on the ground that they are injuries to "the people."

Like the system of justice, elections in the PRC are entirely dominated by the CCP. An election at any given level generally takes place about as follows. The voters are presented with a slate of acceptable candidates which is drawn up by the CCP organization at the next higher level, theoretically after consultation with officials of the minor parties and mass organizations. The only choice the voters have is that they may reject a few candidates as unacceptable and perhaps nominate alternates by petition; they have no way of nominating an entire alternate slate or slates. The same principle applies to the power supposedly exercised by the People's Congresses over their respective People's Councils; they may sometimes challenge the details, but never the essentials, of the policies submitted to them for discussion.

This means that the actual chain of command in the governmental apparatus does not run downward from the National People's Congress through the People's Congresses at the various lower levels and from them to the corresponding People's Councils. It runs downward from the State Council (which appears to be slightly more responsible in practice to its People's Congress than is the case at lower levels) to the People's Councils at the various lower levels.

What has been discussed so far is the main permanent, inherent, and constitutional means by which the CCP dominates the political life of the country through the machinery of the government. There are also a number of other means which are not inherent in the constitutional nature of the system but are equally important in practice.

One is the frequent redrawing of administrative boundaries by the State Council to further the aims of the CCP. In some cases this seems to be done simply to ensure more centralized control. For example, the Manchurian provinces were reduced in number from five to three (Heilungkiang, Kirin, and Liaoning) in the summer of 1954, at the same time that Kao Kang and some of his supporters were purged and many of his Manchurian appointees removed from office.

Another type of redrawing of administrative boundaries has as its aim to divide minority groups and bring them under firmer Chinese control. Here the two main examples are Tibet and the Inner Mongolia Autonomous Region. In October 1955 most of the Nationalist-created province of Sikang, which is inhabited largely by Tibetans, was absorbed into Szechuan; the remainder, the Chamdo area, seems to have some sort of special administrative status. When the Inner Mongolia Autonomous Region was established in May 1947, it was carved out of western Manchuria and the former province of Chahar, and it probably did contain a population of which a majority were Mongols; nevertheless, there were many Mongols living outside its boundaries, for example in Suiyuan. Since then the Inner Mongolia Autonomous Region has grown considerably by absorbing Suiyuan in 1954 and part of Jehol at the end of 1955. It is now believed to have a total population of about 8 million, of whom only about 1 million are Mongols. Another curious fact is that it was not until the absorption of Suiyuan in 1954 that the capital of the region (Huhehot, or Kweisui) lay within its borders.

Propaganda and persuasion are more prominent, and perhaps more important, features of life in Communist China than is force, although they would be much less effective if it were not for the existence of force in the background. Except in the cases of particularly dangerous times or particularly dangerous persons, the CCP seems to operate on the principle that it is better to convince an opponent or doubter of his error and get him to admit it publicly and promise to mend his ways than to liquidate him. This preference stems from the CCP's strong desire to make it appear that it is supported by the overwhelming majority of the public and from its liking for seeming to be always in the right. Since it is not satisfied with mere passive support or neutrality, there is neither freedom of speech nor freedom of silence in Communist China. Everyone is expected to proclaim his loyalty to the regime and his enthusiasm for its basic policies.

The task is made much easier, though still not entirely attainable, by the CCP's monopoly of the educational system and the press. It is thus almost impossible for any idea of which the CCP does not approve, or which it is not at least prepared to tolerate, to find public expression. Other means of communication with the public which the CCP uses, and which it also controls completely, are the radio, wall posters, books and periodicals, and innumerable meetings. The meetings, which are probably the most important of these means, are of various kinds.

One is the organized congress or conference held by some recognized public body. Another is the mass rally of the public in any given place to celebrate some event, listen to some message, or the like. Another is the small discussion group, at which each participant not only listens to the person in charge, who is usually a CCP cadre, but is also expected to say something. If he entertains doubts or objections to CCP policies, or has in the past, he is expected to confess this and accept gratefully the criticisms of the others present; he also criticizes them when his turn comes to do so. Sometimes individuals are required to keep diaries in which they record not only their actions but their thoughts and to produce these for inspection by CCP cadres or police officials. In their most extreme form, when applied intensively to political or military prisoners, these techniques of thought control are commonly known as "brainwashing," but it is important to realize that the entire population is exposed in varying degrees to the same techniques.

There is no doubt that "brainwashing," applied intensively to limited groups of people, can produce not only outward conformity but a great measure of inward conformity as well. Whether it can affect an entire vast population as strongly is more doubtful. The CCP is attempting to revolutionize one of the oldest, toughest, and most deeply rooted cultures in the world. Recent events in Eastern Europe and the Soviet Union lead one to suspect that this culture would tend to reassert itself and that students and intellectuals would begin to demand real freedom, instead of the bogus variety which the CCP has imposed on them, under any one of three conditions: a serious failure on the part of the CCP to modernize the economy and improve living standards, a sudden relaxation of bureaucratic and police controls over the populace, or a massive exposure of the populace in some way or other to objective truth about the situation in the world at large and China's place in it. As a matter of fact, the recent mild "de-Stalinization" campaign produced student disorders in China just as it has in the Soviet Union.

In the event that the method of persuasion, which seems to work fairly well under normal conditions, should fail to work for any reason, there still remains the apparatus of terror. This is presided over mainly by the Ministry of Public Security of the State Council. In June 1951 the ministry, to make things easier for itself, issued a regulation decreeing the disarming of the populace and the confining of firearms to military and governmental personnel. The ministry controls Public

Security Forces about a million men strong. Some of these supplement the ordinary police, in which capacity they have been known at the *hsien* level and below, since the summer of 1955, as the People's Armed Police. There are also Public Security units within the People's Liberation Army which guard frontiers, as well as forced-labor battalions and the like.

At the end of the year 1954, during which there had been serious floods and unrest in the countryside and a "blind influx" of peasants into the cities in search of better conditions, police controls over the populace were considerably tightened. Public Security personnel were empowered to arrest and punish persons accused of offenses against "security" without seeking a regular indictment or court trial. The urban population had already been organized into committees or teams each under the supervision of its own leaders and the police; this system was now tightened, and the regulations governing it were published.

For those who are found guilty of offenses either by the regular courts or by the police, there is a whole range of punishments from reprimand to execution. The most important, and certainly one of the most common, is forced labor or, as the CCP calls it, "reform through labor." It is also the most logical, for idleness is a vice which the CCP detests, and there are many jobs to be done for which it would be impossible or prohibitively expensive to procure machinery. The total number of forced laborers in the PRC, on which there is much less evidence than in the case of the Soviet Union, has been the subject of unrestrained speculation in some quarters. Part of the confusion arises from a failure to make a necessary distinction between true forced laborers, who are prisoners serving sentences, and what the CCP calls "unpaid labor." The latter is an ancient and probably indispensable Chinese institution under which people are conscripted in large numbers, during the agricultural slack season when possible, to perform some necessary task such as building a road or fighting a flood and are released when the job is finished. The writer would estimate—or, to put it more truthfully, guess—that the total number of true forced laborers in the PRC is probably somewhere in the neighborhood of 2 million. One of the most important functions which they perform is to work under the direction of the PLA building roads, railways, and the like in distant and desolate areas such as Tibet and Sinkiang.

A logical place at which to begin a summary of the CCP's policy toward various social groups is its treatment of the intellectuals, a term under which the CCP groups technicians and advanced students as well as artists and professional people. This group has always been very active and influential in Chinese public life, and its progressive defection from the Kuomintang during the 1940s contributed greatly to the latter's downfall. There have been signs that all was not well in the CCP's relations with the intellectuals. One was a series of obviously extorted public "confessions" of alleged ideological errors issued by certain prominent intellectuals in 1952. Another was the furious public denunciation in the CCP press and the disappearance, and presumably imprisonment, of a harmless fellow-traveling writer named Hu Feng in the spring of 1955. His case seems to have symbolized both growing discontent with the CCP's heavyhandedness toward intellectuals and the CCP's determination, at that time, to overwhelm this discontent with force. The airing of the case may have been timed in order to reinforce the impression made by the announcement on the affair of Kao Kang and Jao Shu-shih.

In January 1956 the CCP Central Committee held "heated discussions" (a very strong phrase in the CCP press) on the question of the intellectuals, and shortly afterward Chou En-lai told the National Committee of the CPPCC that some 40 per cent of China's intellectuals were ideologically unreliable and required further training. This seemed to foreshadow a policy of increased sternness, but such was not the outcome. In May 1956, following the first CCP pronouncement on the Stalin question and apparently taking their cue from an unpublished speech delivered by Mao Tse-tung before a Supreme State Conference earlier in the month, the CCP press and officialdom began to advocate freedom of thought and debate, as long as it was "in accordance with the consolidation of the people's regime." This policy has been described with the now-famous official slogan, "Let all flowers bloom together, let diverse schools of thought contend."

This promised increase in intellectual freedom was greeted with some skepticism on the part of adult intellectuals, who were understandably uncertain how far they dared take advantage of it, and with a certain amount of boisterous disorder on the part of students. The cause of the students' dissatisfaction, which seems to be increasing rather than diminishing, is not only the general lack of academic freedom but also the shortage of facilities for advanced and technical training. This shortage has resulted in the wasting of many middle school graduates in unskilled or semiskilled jobs.

In addition to the intellectuals, the other class whose attitude contributed most to the fall of the Kuomintang and the triumph of the CCP comprised the peasants. The CCP's policy of "agrarian reform" or land redistribution, which was the keystone of its agrarian policy until about 1953, might seem well adapted to gain the support of at least the poorer elements among the peasantry. In actual fact, however, the CCP was more interested in mobilizing and using the peasants than it was in benefiting them, and this must have been obvious to many.

The beginning of "co-operativization" (i.e., the herding of peasants into producer co-operatives, which were collective farms in every important respect except that machinery was generally lacking and that title to the land theoretically remained with the original owners) in earnest in 1953 was followed not long afterward by unmistakable signs of peasant unrest, aggravated by the severe floods of 1954. The CCP press admitted, sometimes directly and sometimes indirectly, that many peasants were resisting collectivization, burning crops, and destroying livestock. Peasant discontent was further increased by the inauguration in November 1953 of a system of "planned purchase and supply" of grain and other basic agricultural commodities, under which the peasant was allowed to keep only the grain considered sufficient for himself and his family and was compelled to sell the "surplus" to the state at low prices fixed by the latter. This system was somewhat modified, in favor of the peasant, in 1955. A period of debate within the CCP on agricultural policy was terminated by Mao Tse-tung's decision of July 1955 in favor of accelerating "co-operativization." After the 1955 harvest "fully Socialist co-operatives," which are true collective farms except for the absence of machinery, began to be formed in large numbers, and collectivization was virtually completed in 1957, at least on paper. The peasantry seems to have received fewer benefits from the "de-Stalinization" program than any other class, the main concession granted it being the temporary opening of free markets in certain types of foodstuffs. If peasant discontent should develop to the point of armed resistance, it is uncertain whether the CCP could rely on its overwhelmingly peasant army to suppress it.

The process of collectivization has introduced noteworthy changes into the Chinese countryside. One of the most obvious is that land is now farmed in larger units, and many space-consuming boundaries have been eliminated. A slight increase in grain production (now about 2 pounds per person per day) has occurred, though not necessarily as a result of collectivization. Undoubtedly enormous numbers of CCP cadres and much persuasion and pressure have been needed to work this change, but it seems that actual force has not been necessary in most cases, at least since 1955. Short-term credit is the lifeblood of the Asian countryside, and the CCP's control over the sources of credit has apparently been enough in most cases to bring the farmers to heel.

The workers, who are theoretically the "leading" class in the PRC, have also had a difficult time, although not necessarily worse than in pre-Communist China. On the one hand, some foreign visitors thought that the enthusiasm of the workers was the factor mainly responsible for the CCP's considerable industrial accomplishments in the first years after the "Liberation." On the other hand Lai Jo-yü, the chairman of the All-China Federation of Trade Unions, told the Eighth CCP Congress that "economism," or in other words a desire for better wages and working conditions, had been rampant among the workers during the same period. Whatever the truth may be, there can be no doubt that the workers have been driven very hard, especially so since the inauguration of the First Five Year Plan in 1953. They have been subjected to various speed-up techniques and paid mainly on a piece-work basis, in order to increase production. Their working hours have been long (8–10 hours, plus political classes and meetings), their wages low (about US$10–15 per month), and their housing and working conditions bad. Their unions act as instruments of the state in squeezing maximum production out of the workers, rather than as their agents. Productivity is also kept up by a complex process known as "labor emulation," whose most conspicuous feature is the setting of periodically increased "norms" (production quotas) for the workers as a whole on the basis of the output of the most productive workers. Labor discipline is strict, and no worker can be hired unless he produces a "labor book" in which all his prior employment since 1949 is entered. There is an excessive differential between the wages of skilled and unskilled workers. Safety devices in the factories are scarce, and accidents are common. It is not surprising, under these conditions, that the quality of goods produced is often poor. There are some Chinese whose situation is probably even worse, for the CCP press has repeatedly admitted the existence of a serious problem of urban unemployment.

The workers have been promised certain concessions in the course of the "de-Stalinization" campaign, but it is not clear that these promises have been actually carried out. One is the reduction of the working day to 8 hours, and another is the introduction of "wage reform," meaning payment in money rather than in goods or certificates. There has been no indication that "wage reform" will mean the elimination of piecework. Workers' councils were established in 1956, but they have much less power than their Yugoslav prototypes.

Since the great "transformation" of 1956, the private businessman scarcely exists in the PRC, except as a salaried employee in what was formerly his own enterprise. In the summer of 1956 he was promised that interest payments to him on his investment would be continued at least through the period of the Second Five Year Plan (1958–1962) and that the minimum rate would be 5 per cent instead of 1 per cent as before. But there is still no provision for compensating him for the value of his capital investment in his "transformed" enterprise, which is thus in effect confiscated.

Worst of all, perhaps, is the lot of the national minorities. This is true in spite of the fact that they are outwardly treated with great consideration. In fact, the CCP has shown great skill in using this consideration to mask a reality of tight Chinese control. The key positions in the "autonomous" governments are generally held by Chinese CCP members. Even the cultural autonomy of the minorities, which is less of a fiction than their political autonomy, is manipulated for political purposes. For example, whereas the CCP has generally adopted the Latin alphabet for the minority languages in China proper, it has adopted the Cyrillic (Russian) alphabet for the Mongols of Inner Mongolia and for the Turkish peoples of Sinkiang; this will give them a common writing system, and probably also a common written language, with their kinsmen in Outer Mongolia and in Soviet Central Asia and perhaps facilitate ultimate penetration of those areas by the CCP.

The nomadic minorities of the People's Republic of China are especially unfortunate because the regions in which they live are very sparsely populated, undeveloped, rich in minerals, and close to strategic frontiers. Consequently these regions are receiving an influx of Chinese settlers at the rate of about 700,000 per year. If this flow continues, the minorities will eventually be drowned in a sea of Chinese. Some places in or near areas inhabited by minority groups, such as Paotow in Suiyuan, Lanchow in Kansu, and various places in Sinkiang, are becoming major centers of mining and industry. The trend toward industrialization of the minority areas will play havoc with the traditional cultures and customs of the minorities, to which most of them are passionately attached, and will force many of them into factories as unskilled laborers. For these things the increased number of schools and hospitals and the building of better communications seem poor compensation.

Pressures by the Chinese and the CCP on the national minorities have not failed to evoke resistance. In 1951, for example, a group of Kazakh herdsmen revolted in Sinkiang, and the survivors made their way during the following winter, after suffering terrible hardships, into Kashmir. In Tibet, heavy-handed behavior by the Chinese occupation forces, an influx of Chinese settlers into the Cham region, and the beginning of preparations to grant Tibet "autonomy" were among the main causes of a revolt which broke out in the Cham region in the spring of 1956. This revolt has not yet been suppressed, and it has succeeded in interrupting land communication between Tibet and Szechuan. Another sign of trouble is the fact that it was not until the summer of 1956 that a half-dozen Tibetans joined the CCP, the first since the "Liberation" of 1951. As a concession to the outraged Tibetans, the CCP promised early in 1957 that "democratic reforms" (i.e., redistribution of land, including that of the monasteries) would not be introduced into Tibet during the period of the Second Five Year Plan. There has been a large-scale withdrawal of Chinese cadres from Tibet, as well as some reduction in the PLA garrison. The probable reason for this surprisingly conciliatory policy is a fear on the part of the CCP that repression in Tibet might touch off revolts by other national minorities.

It is clear that by any reasonable definition the governmental system of the PRC is totalitarian. No previous government of China possessed anything like the bureaucratic apparatus, the budgetary resources, the control over local communities, or the will to transform China which the CCP has shown. It is fallacious to reason that "the totalitarian aspect of the Communist regime does not dismay the Chinese people: the Empire was also totalitarian." [11] The old empire was not totalitarian in theory and still less so in practice. Furthermore, it became thoroughly discredited in the late nineteenth and early twentieth centuries, and the CCP could gain little by any resemblance, real or imaginary, which its regime might bear to the empire. This generalization, it should be noted, applies only to the traditional political system. It does not apply to traditional Chinese culture, which has shown considerable resiliency. On the whole, however, the CCP enjoys whatever

[11] C. P. Fitzgerald, *Revolution in China* (New York: Praeger; London: Cresset Press, 1952), p. 117.

popular support it has, not because it promises a return to old and tried ways, but because it promises something better.

But does the CCP enjoy popular support? It is difficult enough to gauge public opinion accurately in free countries and much more so in the case of totalitarian countries. The writer believes that the CCP does enjoy a very considerable measure of passive popular support because it is firmly in control, no ordinary career in Communist China is possible except for one who obeys it, and there is no alternative in sight. The level of active support or of genuine enthusiasm is almost certainly much lower, as the case of the 14,000 Chinese prisoners in Korea who refused to be repatriated shows.

Economic, Social, and Cultural Policies

On the basis of recent CCP statements and in approximate terms, it appears that the CCP expects to make China a major industrial power comparable to Great Britain by about 1973, or after four Five Year Plans have elapsed, but not before. In this period it envisages an approximate doubling of the national income, which at present stands at about US$30 billion per year. The level of new investment, virtually all of it governmental, will be held in the neighborhood of 20 per cent of the national income, and the ratio of investment in heavy industry to investment in light industry (at least in the period of the Second Five Year Plan) will be 7 or 8 to 1. If this program is carried out, and there seems to be no necessary reason why it cannot be carried out, the Chinese industrial system will grow at a rate which is likely to enhance the strong impression already made on the minds of other Asians anxious to develop the economies of their own countries.

Its total control of the economy has enabled the CCP to keep its finances on a fairly sound footing. It probably acquired a large sum in the course of the Wu Fan (Five Anti) campaign. Seemingly any deficit that might appear in one year's budget is disguised by covering it with revenue received during the next year. Needed foreign exchange is acquired not only by legitimate trade but by smuggling narcotics abroad. Nevertheless, the CCP has willingly or unwillingly allowed the emergence of a creeping inflation, euphemistically described as "an excess of demand over supply," in the past few years.

Much can be learned about Chinese Communist public finance and economic policy by studying a typical budget; the adopted budget for 1956 is summarized in Table 1. Both revenue and expenditure are divided between the central and local governments in the ratio of

Table 1. Summary of adopted budget for 1956

Revenue		Yuan *
Surplus from 1955		1,011,038,000
Taxes		13,980,000,000
Industrial and commercial	9,970,000,000	
Agricultural	3,020,000,000	
Customs and salt tax	990,000,000	
Revenue from state enterprises		14,328,144,000
Industrial enterprises	6,688,587,000	
Communications enterprises	2,108,275,000	
Commercial enterprises	4,094,889,000	
Agriculture and forestry	632,440,000	
Others	603,953,000	
Additional payments to government	200,000,000	
Other receipts		1,423,588,000
Total		30,742,770,000
Expenditure		
Economic construction		16,055,206,000
Heavy industry	7,569,103,000	
Light industry	974,979,000	
Agriculture, forestry, water con-		
servancy, meteorology	2,184,894,000	
Communications and transport	2,895,753,000	
Trade (domestic and foreign)	857,182,000	
Capital construction (other		
than industrial)	1,573,295,000	
Social, cultural, and educational		
expenditure		3,915,993,000
National defense		6,141,391,000
Administration		2,410,935,000
Debt retirement		759,227,000
Foreign aid		669,315,000
Reserve		790,703,000
Total		30,742,770,000

* In order to convert yuan approximately into United States dollars, divide by 2.4.

approximately three to one. The most striking features of the budget are the enormous emphasis on heavy industry and the small expenditure on agriculture. The item for national defense (if it is assumed to be honest, and this is not certain) may not seem large by American or Soviet standards, but it is nearly as large as the total annual budget of the Republic of India, central and state governments combined.

It has been indicated that the CCP's agricultural policy is built around collectivization, which is regarded as an essential concomitant to the industrialization and socialization of the industrial sector of the economy and as a necessary instrument of control over the peasantry. One concrete reason for this attitude is the fact that the virtual destruction of the rural landlord class by "agrarian reform" was followed by a drop in the volume of food marketed, since much grain which had formerly gone to the landlord as rent and had been resold by him was now consumed by the peasant. Considerations such as these are even more important to the CCP than is an increase in food production, desirable as that may be. That is why the CCP decided to launch collectivization concurrently with the First Five Year Plan rather than wait until farm machinery became available in sufficient quantity—this will not take place for several more years—to permit the mechanization of agriculture before or during collectivization. Nevertheless, the CCP has been more careful and less violent in implementing its collectivization program than Stalin was in Russia. The reason for this care was probably a hope, which has been largely borne out to date, that the excesses and disasters associated with Stalin's collectivization campaign could be avoided in China.

The present per capita output of grain is insufficient and is now less than half the corresponding figure in the Soviet Union on the eve of Stalin's inauguration of collectivization in 1928. The actual difference is even greater, for grain constitutes a far more important part of the Chinese diet than it does of the Russian. Furthermore, much of China's increase in food production has been brought about by ultimately self-defeating measures, such as farming land which ought to be lying fallow. Investment in the agricultural sector of the economy is inadequate, and the supply of chemical fertilizers is entirely insufficient. Consequently, Communist China is not far above the starvation level, and nearly every year there are local or regional famines or at least the threat of them. The harvests of 1956 and 1957 were bad, and in the autumn of 1957 the CCP decided to reorganize the agricultural "co-operatives" (i.e., collective farms) into smaller units and began to transfer some 3 million cadres, students, and technicians from the cities to work on the farms.

In short, the CCP's agricultural policy is essentially an orthodox Stalinist one, although of course with some variations to suit Chinese conditions, and it is unlikely to keep pace for long with the growth of population. Agriculture is almost certainly the Achilles' heel of the entire Chinese Communist system.

The CCP has unquestionably shown considerable energy and accomplishment in the field of water conservancy. To give only one example, it began in 1955 to tackle the most formidable problem of all in this field—the Yellow River. The plan for this river calls for the construction of small dams on the upper tributaries and the afforestation of the basin in order to check the accumulation of silt in the middle and lower reaches, which causes floods. The biggest failure in this field to date was the inability to prevent serious damage when the Yangtze River flooded in the summer of 1954.

Another field in which the CCP has achieved much is that of communications. The CCP was remarkably successful in getting the major railway lines back into operation after 1949, and from 1952 through 1956 it reconstructed or built about 5,000 kilometers of additional railways. Many of these lines, however, were hastily and badly built. Two of the most important completed in that period were the broad-gauge line from Chining (not far east of Huhehot and Paotow) to Ulan Bator in Outer Mongolia, which in turn is connected with the Transsiberian, and the railway to Amoy (completed on December 9, 1956), which not only will contribute to the development of the previously isolated and backward province of Fukien but puts the Nationalist-held island of Quemoy in a very dangerous position. An important line under construction is that pushing westward from Lanchow toward Sinkiang and scheduled to be linked with the Turksib Railway near Alma Ata about 1960. Another line is to be pushed southward through Tsinghai to Lhasa. Rail connections with North Vietnam have been improved. Many miles of highway have been built, including a road to Lhasa. The PRC is beginning to produce its own aircraft, trucks, and tires. New ports have been opened, such as that at Tsamkong located on the eastern side of the Luichow Peninsula, southernmost point of mainland China. Regular air service links the principal regions of China with each other and with some of the neighboring countries, Burma and North Vietnam, for example. Another development of interest is a Sino-Soviet agreement of August 1956 for joint exploitation of the Amur River, from which the Chinese have until recently been virtually excluded by the Russians.

The PRC's industrial output is expanding steadily. Steel production is expected to reach 7 million tons in 1958, and from 10.5 to 12 million tons in 1962. There has recently been a bottleneck in the coal industry, as there has in certain types of transportation, but it appears that on the whole industrialization in all basic fields is progressing fairly well. The CCP has set out to explore China's geological resources far more thoroughly than any previous government ever did. It has discovered or confirmed the existence of large coal and iron deposits in North and Northwest China and large oil reserves in the Tsaidam Basin in Tsinghai, to mention only a few of the most important. In addition to the large existing industrial center in the Mukden area, the CCP is building others at Paotow, at Tayeh near Hankow, and around Canton. Shanghai will remain the main center of light industry.

In terms of volume and absolute value the foreign trade of the PRC is rather small, but it is thereby enabled to procure important materials otherwise unavailable, such as natural rubber and certain types of machine tools. Between 75 and 80 per cent of the PRC's external trade is done with other nations of the Soviet bloc, mainly the Soviet Union itself. Generally speaking, the PRC sends raw materials, such as foodstuffs and tungsten, to the other Communist countries in exchange for manufactured goods and above all capital equipment. In this exchange the Chinese often receive less than the world price for their exports. The heavy share of the Soviet bloc in China's foreign trade reflects not only the United Nations embargo on shipment of strategic goods to the Chinese mainland but also the CCP's preference for dealing with other "Socialist" regimes, which are similarly organized and ideologically congenial. With Japan and other industrialized non-Communist nations the terms of trade are similar, except for the absence of strategic goods. To nonindustrialized Asian nations the PRC generally exports light manufactured goods in exchange for raw materials such as rubber and rice.

One of the most obvious features of the CCP's social policy is its strenuous effort to pose as the emancipator of Chinese women, who occupied an undeniably inferior position before the "Liberation." The Marriage Law of 1950 granted women full equality with men in marriage, divorce, and ownership of property. If the CCP has emancipated Chinese women from their husbands, however, this was partly in order to subject them to the state. Very few women hold important positions in public life. Women have been driven to work in factories and offices in large numbers, partly by the simple expedient of keeping their husbands' wages too low to support their families unaided. Working mothers have complained in the press that their jobs left them little time or energy for their families. Another irritant is the CCP's generally austere attitude toward feminine finery—lipstick, dresses with slit skirts, and the like being taboo except for a time in 1956. Like men, women generally go swathed in shapeless blue cotton jackets and trousers.

The 1958 population of Communist China probably approximates 640 million, and it is increasing at the rate of about 2 per cent per year. Before publication of the census of 1953–1954 the CCP talked of 475 million Chinese and clung to the orthodox Marxist view that, since labor is the only source of wealth, a larger population means more wealth. The results of the census seem to have led to a change of heart, however. Since the autumn of 1954 there has been a steadily increasing propaganda on the part of CCP officials in favor of birth control, sterilization, and later marriage. The reasons given are usually the difficulty of providing food and schooling for some 12 million people added to the population every year. The CCP would apparently like the population to remain as nearly stationary as possible for a while, but there seems to be no chance of its doing so, for the death rate is being reduced by improved public health measures. A "population explosion" could easily occur in Communist China within the next generation or two on a scale sufficient to threaten not only China itself but the entire Soviet bloc.

Chinese Communist cultural policy has been largely a product of the interaction between the attitude of the CCP toward traditional Chinese culture and the attitude of the Chinese people as a whole. Basically, the CCP dislikes both traditional Chinese culture and the semi-Westernized culture which succeeded it in the early twentieth century. Many aspects of the traditional culture, however, are still firmly rooted among the populace at large and to a lesser extent also among the educated class. Since 1949, therefore, the CCP has been compelled increasingly to modify its plans for introducing a fundamentally modern and "Socialist" culture in order to fit the actual situation.

This means that the CCP's assault on the traditional culture has been considerably less than total. It tolerates, and to some extent even encourages, much of the ancient political tradition (especially the concept of political unity on a cultural basis and an attitude of

superiority toward peoples not of Chinese culture), traditional medicine, much of the traditional etiquette and customs, and much traditional art and literature.

On the other hand, the CCP has proceeded vigorously against traditional religion (especially Taoism) and superstition; traditional political thought, especially Confucianism; most aspects of the traditional
family system, especially parental authority and "ancestor worship";
those aspects of traditional science and technology—except for medicine and some handicrafts—which can be replaced with something
more modern; and the secret societies (with the principal exception
of the powerful Ko Lao Hui, or Elder Brother Society, which may
have been protected to some extent by the fact that one of its members or former members, Ho Lung, sits on the CCP's Politburo).

Thus it appears that the CCP hopes to create a synthetic culture
basically modern and "Socialist" and yet retaining certain elements
of the traditional culture which are either useful to the CCP or too
tenacious to be eliminated.

Although the standard of education in Chinese schools is not very
high, except in certain specialized technical institutes, there have
been great quantitative achievements. In 1956 there were approximately 380,000 students in colleges, universities, and higher technical
schools; 5 million in regular or technical middle schools; and 62
million in primary schools—all these figures representing enormous
increases since 1949. In addition, there are numerous courses for
adults in basic literacy or more advanced subjects. In 1956 the CCP
launched a reform of the writing system by simplifying several hundred of the most complicated written characters and announced a
plan to introduce the Latin alphabet (with a few additional special
symbols) as the standard means of writing Chinese in ten years. During 1957, however, the program was revised in the direction of using
Latin letters mainly as an aid to the study of characters. To overcome
the problem of mutually unintelligible dialects the CCP advocates a
common speech (*p'u-t'ung-hua*) based on the Peking dialect of
Mandarin. The literacy rate, which is about 30 per cent (of the entire
population), probably does not represent a great advance over the
pre-1949 situation.

The PRC generally takes its cue in scientific matters from abroad,
except that it still encourages traditional medicine as a useful and
cheaper supplement to modern medicine. Though unable to dispense
entirely with Japanese and Western scientific writings and discoveries,

the PRC draws when possible on the Soviet Union. Almost all foreign scientific and technical literature published in the PRC is translated from the Russian. It should not be thought that the PRC has no able and original scientists of its own, for it does, but they are few in number and will be some time in training an adequate number of pupils.

In the fields of literature and art Soviet influence is also strong, although less so. Russian people and Russian culture have never been very popular in China, and many Chinese resent being pressed to learn Russian rather than English. There has been something of a revival of interest in China's traditional literature, taking the form of reprints of classical authors and new works done in the traditional manner. On the whole, however, the most common theme of con- temporary art and literature is the glorification of "Socialist construc- tion" in the "new" China.

The CCP is of course thoroughly antireligious, but it recognizes that force is not always the best way to combat the influence of religion on men's minds. Indigenous cults with no foreign affiliations, such as Taoism, have been severely suppressed. On the other hand, Asian religions with important followings abroad, particularly Islam and Buddhism, have been treated with extreme outward deference. The case of Christianity is more complex. Foreign missionaries have been harshly treated, and few are still at their stations. Chinese clergy and converts have been put under severe pressure to cut all ties with their coreligionists abroad; some who refused, like Kung Pin-mei, the Catholic bishop of Shanghai, have been imprisoned on trumped-up charges. Proselytization is strongly discouraged, but religious ob- servances in public are permitted. The hostile attitude of the au- thorities is well known, and it undoubtedly tends to keep many away even in the absence of severe persecution. It seems likely that even under these adverse conditions Christianity will retain a core of de- vout followers in China, but very unlikely that it will grow or flourish as long as the present regime remains in power.

Military Affairs

Armed struggle played an extremely important part in the CCP's rise to power, far more important than in the case of any other Communist Party except that of North Vietnam. "Political power," wrote Mao Tse-tung in 1938, "grows out of the barrel of a gun." [12]

[12] *Selected Works*, II, 272.

In a state founded in this spirit, military affairs are bound to be of the greatest importance.

Since about 1950 the People's Liberation Army (PLA) has been undergoing a considerable degree of technical modernization with the aid of advisers and equipment procured, at a price, from the Soviet Union. Since 1954 it has also been undergoing organizational changes of comparable importance. In 1953–1954 the regional field armies, which had constituted potentially dangerous loci of decentralized power, were abolished and their commanders given posts more directly under the control of the CCP central machinery. The field armies have been replaced by front armies (*fang-mien-chün*), of whose present organization little is known. In addition, the powerful People's Revolutionary Military Council was abolished and was succeeded by a larger and apparently much less powerful body, the National Defense Council. The PLA General Staff was set up as a separate organization, and a Ministry of Defense was created within the cabinet for the first time. The net effect of these changes seems to have been to diffuse military power and render it more easily controllable by the CCP through its Military Committee, a little-known body which appears to be composed of the party's most powerful members.

In 1955 the PLA began to scrap its traditional "voluntary" system of recruitment in favor of a system of universal liability to military service on the part of men of 18 and over, of whom several hundred thousand are inducted per year. A regular system of ranks and decorations was also created for the first time, and 10 veteran commanders were given the rank of marshal.

There are several ways by which the CCP ensures its control over the armed forces. One is the virtual monopoly which CCP members hold of important command and staff positions; furthermore, many civilian CCP officials have had considerable military experience. Each CCP commander down through the company level has a political officer (commissar) who is a CCP member and whose approval of all orders is required except in times of military emergency. Each political officer also supervises a political department or section, whose main function is to ensure the indoctrination of the men. Within most military units there are also party committees led by the chief CCP members within each unit. So closely intertwined are party and armed forces that a conflict between them is almost unthinkable.

The PLA, whose total strength is probably about 3 million, includes not only the army but also the navy, the air force, and Public Security

Forces. The weakest of these services is the navy, which would be useless in any major war in the Far East unless it were reinforced by the powerful Soviet Far Eastern Fleet. The air force is another matter; it is a fairly powerful force which has a sizable number of Soviet jet aircraft. The army is basically an infantry force which is strong and mobile enough to fight with great effect in or near China's territory and even to conduct amphibious operations across nearby waters, but is not equipped for operations far from home. The PRC has a small but growing armaments industry geared mainly to the production of small arms. All or most weapons of heavier caliber have to be imported from other countries of the Soviet bloc.

In addition to the combat and garrison units of the PLA and the Public Security Forces, the PLA can call on the militia (also known as the People's Armed Forces) for replacements or for help in maintaining order. The total strength of the militia is probably between 10 and 15 million. Since it is poorly trained and poorly armed, it is of little use except against bandits or "counterrevolutionaries" or as a source of replacements for the combat forces.

The CCP has a long-standing tradition that its troops perform productive labor in addition to their military duties. PLA units reclaim land, build roads, and even operate factories, especially in desolate frontier regions.

Both the morale of the PLA and its standing in the eyes of the public tend to suffer from the low pay, low cultural level, and harsh conditions in the PLA. To counteract this state of affairs the PLA command has instituted literacy courses for its troops, kept them intensively indoctrinated, and (especially in 1954, when doubt was cast on the PLA's loyalty by some aspects of the Kao Kang–Jao Shu-shih affair) conducted a press campaign to improve the public image of the PLA.

There seems no reason to question that at the present time the PLA is fully controlled by the CCP and that, within unavoidable limitations of a technical nature, it is an effective fighting force on its home ground. It could overrun any adjacent non-Communist country if its leaders were willing to risk a general war.

Foreign Policy and Foreign Relations

In addition to attempting to promote the advance of communism throughout the world, the CCP has demanded a very considerable degree of supervision over Communist movements in Asia. This claim was first asserted by Liu Shao-ch'i in a famous speech before the Asian-Australasian Trade Union Conference on November 16, 1949. Liu stated that the strategy employed by the CCP in gaining power, which he called "the way of Mao Tse-tung," was applicable to all "colonies and semicolonies" or what are often called the underdeveloped areas. This strategy he defined as an "armed struggle" led by the proletariat and the peasantry in co-operation with some sections of the bourgeoisie, with the Communist Party as its "center" and the rural areas largely as the base. He urged the continuance of such a struggle in Vietnam, the Philippines, Burma, Indonesia, and Malaya; in all these countries, plus India, such a struggle had already been launched, in all but the first two in 1948 under the auspices of the Cominform. Thus Liu was setting up a theoretical pattern of revolutionary action very different from that applicable in industrialized countries, where a much stronger leadership by the proletariat is expected. There are reasons for thinking that Liu's formulation of another revolutionary path and his implied claim to a major supervisory role for the CCP in Asia were not welcome in Moscow, and after 1951 the CCP ceased to assert this claim, without necessarily giving it up. Furthermore, armed struggle did not work except in Vietnam, the most thoroughly colonial of the countries named by Liu.

The CCP therefore began to reappraise both the strength of the newly independent nations of South and Southeast Asia and the nature of their ties to the "imperialist" powers. The new outlook began about 1951, partly, it would seem, as a result of the CCP's appreciation of India's disinterested effort to mediate the Korean conflict. From a policy of armed struggle and denunciation the CCP shifted by degrees to a policy of persuasion and attempts at friendship. Other Asian Communist parties also began to emphasize the peaceful aspects of Maoism, such as the concept of a united front consisting of a bloc of four classes, rather than armed struggle. The Soviet Union displayed only limited enthusiasm for the new approach until after Stalin's death.

The first major manifestation of the new policy was embodied in the famous Five Principles of Peaceful Coexistence, which were formulated for the first time in the Sino-Indian treaty of April 29, 1954, on Tibet. The Five Principles are: mutual respect for one another's territorial integrity and sovereignty, nonaggression, noninterference in one another's internal affairs, equality and mutual benefit, and peaceful coexistence. However platitudinous and repetitious they may sound, these principles have fairly deep roots in Asian religion and philosophy, in Communist slogans of the 1930s, and even in the Sino-Soviet treaty of February 14, 1950. Neither their value to the Communist states as propaganda nor the power of their appeal to Asian minds should be underestimated.

Probably the clearest statement of the new Communist approach to non-Communist Asian and Middle Eastern countries has been given by the Russians, who have adopted the Chinese view enthusiastically but with less skill. At the Twentieth Congress of the Soviet Communist Party (February 1956) Deputy Premier Mikoyan stated that when a small non-"Socialist" country is situated near a large "Socialist" one (i.e., the Soviet Union or the PRC) it can undergo a "transition to Socialism" by peaceful means. In other words, it can be gradually persuaded and maneuvered, by means which will be discussed later, into aligning its domestic and foreign policies with those of the Soviet bloc until it is ripe for the final step. Mikoyan added, however, that, if this approach fails, the "Socialist" nations are ready to resort to force, presumably in the form of insurrections by local Communist parties, although the possibility of invasion by foreign Communist armies should not be discounted.

How long the "Socialist" nations are willing to try their technically nonviolent approach before abandoning it is not clear. It is certain, however, that the Chinese Communists are generally quite willing to exercise one of the most difficult of all virtues, patience, in the conduct of their foreign relations. This gives them a great advantage over democratic governments, which are usually anxious for quick results that will impress the voters.

Because of the strength of its power position, the CCP has been able to maintain, without breaking with the Soviet Union, a view of the proper relations among Communist parties which has been impossible, at least until very recently, for the leadership of any other non-Soviet Communist Party except that of Tito—who had to break with Moscow in order to make his position good. This fact became clear to the Communist world, though it was widely misunderstood outside, at the time of the Stalin-Tito controversy. In November 1948 Liu Shao-ch'i published on behalf of the CCP a commentary on the controversy entitled *On Internationalism and Nationalism*. Instead of condemning Tito for a breach of discipline, as Stalin probably would have liked, Liu accused him of an ideological error which he called "bourgeois nationalism." As against this Liu set up the concept of "proletarian internationalism," a Communist cliché capable of various interpretations; Liu interpreted it to mean a "free federation" of Communist parties on an equal and voluntary footing, united in a common ideology and common allegiance (but not subservience) to the Soviet Union. From this basic concept the CCP has never since deviated. Liu's work was not reprinted in the Soviet press until about six weeks later and even then only with some deletions.

The Soviet party recently seems to have abandoned of necessity any overt objections to this view of "proletarian internationalism." The two parties also appeared to be approaching a common middle ground on the knotty question of the dictatorship of the proletariat, at any rate until Mao Tse-tung enunciated his celebrated theory of contradictions at the end of February 1957. Mao's frank admission that "contradictions" can exist in a "Socialist" society, but need not be acute, differs both from Stalin's view that the class struggle necessarily becomes more acute with the passage of time and from Khrushchev's statement of May 28, 1957, via television (since deleted in the Soviet press and elaborately edited in the CCP press) that no "contradictions" exist in the Soviet Union. Mao's theory apparently strikes his Soviet colleagues as excessively liberal, and they probably feel that the disturbances of 1957 in China have proved them right.

There has been a noticeable tendency since roughly the end of 1957 for the Chinese Communists to lay greater emphasis on the pre-eminence of the Soviet Union within the Communist world. The probable reasons are greater Chinese humility engendered by the partial misfiring of the CCP's "de-Stalinization" and "rectification" programs, increased respect for the Soviet Union's technological progress and military power, a need for continued Soviet aid, and the serious concern for the solidarity of the Soviet bloc which the Polish and Hungarian crises and Tito's denunciation of Soviet intervention in Hungary aroused in the CCP. The new emphasis, together with a strong statement of support for Khrushchev's foreign and domestic policies, formed a principal theme of a speech which Mao Tse-tung delivered while attending the celebration in Moscow of the fortieth anniversary of the Bolshevik Revolution on November 7, 1957. The CCP now tends to support the Soviet Union against the Poles, instead of the other way round as in the autumn of 1956. Nevertheless, the CCP apparently opposes Khrushchev's desire to revive the Cominform and would certainly object to any attempt by the Soviet party to dominate the internal affairs of other Communist parties. The Chinese Communist interpretation of "proletarian internationalism," although of course subject to shifts of emphasis to fit changing circumstances, still remains essentially as Liu Shao-ch'i defined it in 1948: substantial internal autonomy for each party, combined with a willing acknowledgment of Soviet priority in ideological matters, of the value to other parties of Soviet historical experience, and of the necessity for supporting the Soviet Union in international affairs.

As for Sino-Soviet economic relations, it has already been indicated that Soviet economic aid to the PRC has been rather niggardly. In his report to the Twentieth Congress of his party Khrushchev put a total value on it, to date, of 5.6 billion rubles (US$1.4 billion at the official exchange rate, or US$392 million at a realistic rate); this presumably did not include the loan made under the terms of the treaty of February 14, 1950. The amount granted since then probably does not exceed 3 billion rubles. In 1956 the CCP received part of the price for its ideological support in the form of economic aid; the CCP's statement of April 5 on the Stalin question, for example, was followed within two days by the conclusion of an economic-aid pact. The CCP has no reason to feel extravagantly grateful for economic aid granted in such meager amounts and subject to repayment.

It is probably in the field of power politics that the most likely source of Sino-Soviet conflict, in the long run, lies. The two countries have a long pre-Communist history of rivalry in Central Asia, and there can be little doubt that the strong Soviet position in Sinkiang during the period from 1950 to 1955 was a serious irritant. Both countries are engaged in populating and developing their Central Asian territories, partly in order to protect them from penetration from across the border and perhaps ultimately to penetrate the territories of the other, a game in which China's larger population would appear to give it an advantage. The Chinese Communists can hardly have forgotten, although they never say it publicly, that much of the Soviet Far East and Soviet Central Asia were carved out of the Manchu empire a century ago. Both countries are engaged in a quiet contest for influence in Outer Mongolia.

For the present, however, the tensions and irritants in Sino-Soviet relations are more than outweighed by forces tending to hold them together. They share a common ideology, however differently they may interpret it at times. They have common enemies, of whose enmity they have a greatly exaggerated idea. Their alliance has already won notable successes and may win more. Given these conditions, each party undoubtedly feels that much more would be lost than gained by a rupture.

Next to the Soviet Union, the PRC's most important relations with Communist states are those with the three others in Asia: the Mongolian People's Republic (Outer Mongolia), the Democratic People's Republic of Korea (North Korea), and the Democratic Republic of Vietnam (North Vietnam). Of these the first two are for the most part Soviet satellites, Soviet influence being considerably greater than Chinese in the first and probably somewhat greater in the second: the third is more nearly independent, with Chinese influence considerably stronger than Soviet. It should be noted that North Vietnam has a common frontier with Communist China but not with the Soviet Union, whereas the other two have a common frontier with both. In all three Chinese influence has tended to increase in recent years, especially since the death of Stalin. For example, their Five Year Plans were co-ordinated after 1953 with those of Communist China, not with those of the Soviet Union, although in 1957 they began to show some signs of being readjusted to the cycle of Soviet plans. In all three there is Sino-Soviet competition, not necessarily hostile in nature, to exercise influence and extend economic aid. The three lesser governments attempt to take advantage of this by playing the two giants against each other.

The PRC's standing with the Communist parties of Eastern Europe is extremely high. It has done what all of them would like to do, namely, to implement a Stalinist domestic program and play a prominent role in the Communist world without accepting dictation from Moscow. Tito has made no secret of his admiration, but it has been only partially reciprocated; in December 1954 the CCP finally agreed to accept Tito's offer of diplomatic relations, but it still regards Tito as something of a troublemaker and rebuked him in May 1958 for "revisionism" and disruption of the Soviet bloc. The Chinese example, and perhaps even Chinese encouragement, played a large part in the Polish Communists' decision to assert themselves against the Kremlin in October 1956. Since the outbreak of the Korean War the PRC has been engaging in increasingly close diplomatic and economic relations with the East European satellites, and this trend seems likely to continue.

Most of what has been said so far about Chinese Communist foreign policy and foreign relations applies mainly to relations with Communist parties in power. Relations with Communist parties not in power, especially those in Asia, are more obscure, because they lack a formal diplomatic aspect. Three bodies through which the CCP appears to maintain liaison with the other Communist parties of Asia, both in and out of power, are the Asia-Australasian Liaison Bureau of the World Federation of Trade Unions (founded in 1949), the Peace Liaison Bureau of the World Peace Council (founded in 1952), and the Asian Solidarity Committee (founded in 1956). Probably more important as channels of communication, however, are the PRC's diplomatic and consular missions in the countries where they exist (i.e., in India, Pakistan, Ceylon, Nepal, Burma, Indonesia, and the three Communist states) and the frequent visits of other Asian Communist leaders to the PRC.

As for the nature of the relationship, it seems that the CCP's influence and prestige are strong but fall short of domination. In effect the CCP and for that matter the Soviet party also have to choose between subordination and effectiveness in the smaller parties. The more subservient and manageable they are, the less effective they are likely to be on the local scene. On the whole, the CCP has tended to choose effectiveness over subordination. The choice has been made easier by the fact that any attempt by the CCP to reduce the other Asian parties to a position of complete subservience would almost certainly meet with serious objections not only from them but from Moscow.

Since at least as long ago as 1954, the CCP's policy toward the neutral nations of Asia has been, at least outwardly, one of the most cordial friendship. Their independence from the "camp of imperialism" is now conceded, and even their neutrality is praised. It hardly needs to be said that the CCP's attitude is neither sincere nor disinterested. The CCP has available a formidable arsenal of instrumentalities for use in exerting influence or pressure on its Asian neighbors, neutral or otherwise. Some are violent in nature and have therefore been largely abandoned for the time being: the fomenting of insurrections (as in Malaya), direct military intervention (as in Korea or, in the summer of 1956, northern Burma), and the sending of military aid (as in North Vietnam, where it still continues). Others are at least technically nonviolent and are very much in use today: "people's diplomacy" (trade and aid, Communist style; exchange of cultural and other missions; and so on); propaganda stressing the themes of peaceful coexistence, alleged traditional friendship, anticolonialism, anti-imperialism, and praise for neutrality; manipulation in various ways of local Communist parties, Communist-infiltrated mass organizations, and overseas Chinese communities, in the hope of bringing about coalition governments which include Communists; the stirring up of controversies over boundary questions, mainly as bargaining weapons; the formation on Chinese soil of "autonomous" areas populated by minorities with kinsmen across the frontier (as in Thailand and Burma); the harboring and manipulation of refugees (usually left wing) from neighboring countries (for example, the Kachin rebel Naw Seng from Burma, the exile Pridi Phanomyong from Thailand, and K. I. Singh, a Nepalese who returned to Nepal in 1955 and later served for one year as Premier); and the clandestine export of Chinese emigrants, mainly to Burma.

By judicious use of these nominally nonviolent means, the CCP hopes to bring its neutral neighbors to "grow over" into "Socialism" in time, without resort to violence. If these methods fail, it is probably prepared to turn to violence once more.

A few special features of the PRC's relations with its neutral neighbors require special comment. The most important aspect of the Sino-Indian treaty of April 29, 1954, on Tibet was not the routine provisions on trade and travel between Tibet and India or even the Indian agreement to give up most Indian consular and other public property in Tibet. The important features were two: the absence of any boundary agreement (the PRC claims large portions of Kashmir and Assam and clearly has little regard for the McMahon Line, the internationally recognized boundary) and the Indian recognition of the legitimacy of the CCP's seizure of Tibet clearly implicit in the designation "the Tibet region of China." [13] The latter concession, which was also made by the Nepalese government in a Sino-Nepalese agreement of September 1956, in effect deprives India of any legal or moral basis for intervening diplomatically in case Tibetan insurgents should appeal for Indian help, as they have done more than once in the past.

Nevertheless, Nehru showed his skill at dealing with the CCP in the following autumn. During a trip to Peking in October 1954 he secured from it two pledges of the utmost importance: the first, that the CCP would not intervene militarily outside its own borders (this act of self-denial would not be construed by either party as necessarily

[13] The Indian government had heatedly protested the Chinese "liberation" of Tibet in 1950–1951, only to be brusquely rebuffed by the CCP.

applying to Taiwan or the offshore islands), and the second, that it would negotiate the vexed question of the citizenship status of overseas Chinese. The CCP has not wholly lived up to the first of these commitments and has fallen very far short of living up to the second, and this failure is likely to count against it, in the long run, in the eyes of neutral Asians.

Probably the dominant aspect of present Sino-Indian relations is the quiet but intensifying contest for influence in the strategic and backward kingdom of Nepal. In border questions such as this India shows a realism which is sometimes absent from its dealings with Communist China on the diplomatic and cultural planes. It appears that at present the Indian position in Nepal is the stronger, but that the Chinese are beginning to narrow the gap.

The Burmese generally entertain fewer illusions about the nature and aims of their Chinese neighbor than do the Indians and have fewer reasons for any illusions. When the Burmese delegate told the General Assembly of the United Nations, with reference to the Soviet intervention in Hungary, "There . . . but for the grace of God, go we," he probably meant to imply that he hoped the United Nations would help Burma if it were faced with a similar danger. Such a danger could come only from Communist China.

Maps published in Nationalist and Communist China since about 1930 and through 1957 have shown large portions of northern and eastern Burma as Chinese territory. In late July 1956 PLA troops actually made an incursion into one of the disputed areas, the Kachin State. The object of this striking departure from the Five Principles of Peaceful Coexistence may have been to put Burma under pressure for a favorable frontier settlement, or—what is more likely—it may have been to cut off, or threaten to cut off, the Tibetan insurgents from one of their major sources of arms, the town of Myitkyina. Under an agreement announced on November 9, 1956, the Chinese agreed, with one important exception, to withdraw their troops from this area and from certain portions of the Shan and Wa states in eastern Burma which they had occupied since 1952. The exception constituted the three border villages of Hpimaw, Kangfang, and Gawlum dominating the entrance to Hpimaw Pass, through which the PLA could easily re-enter Burma at any time. The Chinese also claim the so-called Namwan Assigned Tract, a small area which is on the edge of the Shan State and which dominates the main highway between the Shan and Kachin states. There is no immediate likelihood of a complete or permanent boundary settlement unless Burma is willing to accept a disadvantageous position.

For several years the Chinese have been infiltrating and propagandizing the peoples of the Kachin State, probably in the hope of fostering secessionist and pro-Chinese sentiment among them. So far, however, Chinese Communist pressures on the frontier peoples of Burma have tended to strengthen rather than weaken their loyalty to the Union of Burma. The CCP also dominates and manipulates the Chinese community in Burma, which has grown since the Second World War to a present estimated size of nearly a million, mainly through illegal immigration. When Chou En-lai was in Burma late in 1956, he was roundly scolded by Burmese officials over the border issue. He advised the Chinese community to take Burmese citizenship and learn Burmese, but it is doubtful whether he meant to be taken seriously.

Burma, which is certainly one of the most admirable of the nations of South and Southeast Asia, is unfortunately the one most likely to be subjected to strong, although not necessarily continuous, Chinese pressures. No other single country in those regions combines, from the Chinese Communist standpoint, all the following advantages. It has a geographic location such that it would constitute, in hostile hands, a wedge driven between South and Southeast Asia. It has a long and disputed common frontier with China, across which pressures can easily be exerted. Its government has a strong socialist and neutralist orientation of the kind which Communists currently, although not necessarily correctly, consider to be fairly easily maneuverable into the "camp of Socialism." It has a large rice surplus, which would be very useful to China. It has a large and growing Chinese community in which Communist influence, exerted mainly through the Chinese embassy in Rangoon, is strong. It has an underground Communist movement with a legal and parliamentary wing. All these considerations are strong inducements to the CCP to seek eventual economic domination, though not necessarily political control, in Burma.

The PRC, like the Soviet Union, has been buying limited amounts of rice from Burma and other rice-producing countries of Southeast Asia, generally not at a very good price but at crucial times of surplus. Some of this rice has been sent by both the Communist giants to North Korea and North Vietnam and probably has been used in the process as bargaining weapons in their dealings with these food-deficit areas.

In Indonesia the PRC's diplomatic mission has been active in propagandizing and manipulating the Chinese community, which is large and as elsewhere economically active and important. The most serious issue between the two countries has been that of citizenship, for the CCP has generally claimed all overseas Chinese as citizens of the PRC. This issue was the subject of a treaty which Chou En-lai negotiated with the Indonesian government in April 1955, while he was attending the Bandung Conference. This treaty, the essence of which is that overseas Chinese in Indonesia may choose the citizenship of either country, contained so many offensive provisions that the Indonesian government did not ratify it until December 1957. It contains a clause stipulating that any such person who has not made a formal choice within two years after the treaty goes into effect will take the citizenship of his father; this would mean, except in the cases of a small number of persons born of mixed marriages in which the father was an Indonesian, the citizenship of the PRC. At the same time Chou promised to negotiate similar citizenship agreements with other nations; none has yet been signed, however, except for an agreement with Nepal relating to the citizenship of persons of Nepalese origin now residing in Tibet (September 1956).

The CCP is clearly reluctant to abandon its claim to the citizenship of the overseas Chinese and still more reluctant to give up manipulating them. Liu Shao-ch'i told the Eighth Congress of the CCP: "We must continue to unite with patriotic Chinese living in various places abroad; they too are a component part of the united front."

It should not be thought that in Communist China's relations with the neutral Asian nations it has always gained the upper hand. The Cambodian government under Prince Norodom Sihanouk has made clever use of its neutral position to get considerable economic aid from both the United States and China and has so far been careful not to make dangerous concessions to the latter. Laos, under the cover of a nominally neutral position guaranteed by the Geneva agreements of 1954, receives military aid from France and has extracted a disguised nonaggression pledge from Communist China (August 1956). Its northern provinces, however, are infiltrated by an insurrectionary Pathet Lao movement sponsored by the Democratic Republic of Vietnam, and in October 1957 the Laotian government agreed to the formation of a coalition government in which this movement would be represented, although not very heavily.

The CCP's policy toward the anti-Communist Asian states (Pakistan, Thailand, the Republic of Vietnam, the Federation of Malaya, Singapore, the Philippines, and the Republic of Korea) does not require detailed comment. The CCP tends to express hostility to them to the extent that they align themselves diplomatically and militarily with the United States. The CCP's aim seems to be to convince them of the disadvantages of alignment with the United States and the advantages of neutralism and friendly relations with the PRC. In this way it apparently hopes to persuade them eventually to enter the ranks of neutral nations, which in the Chinese Communist scheme of things are one step closer to "Socialism." In this effort the CCP has had some success, mainly with the educated public (to whom CCP foreign propaganda is primarily addressed) rather than with the governments. For example, there has been some growth of feeling in Pakistan, Thailand, and the Philippines, the only Asian members of the Southeast Asia Treaty Organization, that their alignment with the West has earned them the dangerous enmity of Communist China without necessarily assuring them of compensating protection by the Western powers. It would be very unwise to overlook the possibility of a drift toward neutralism on the part of the presently anti-Communist Asian states.

Japan is a special case, in that from the PRC's standpoint it was an "imperialist" power until 1945 and thereafter occupied by another "imperialist" power, the United States. Like other Communist states, Communist China refused to recognize the Japanese peace treaty of 1951 and therefore appeared to attach no special importance to the end of the Allied occupation in 1952. Nevertheless, the CCP seems to have realized at about that time the futility of an attitude of hostility toward another Asian state which did not necessarily reciprocate that hostility, just as the CCP came to understand the same thing with reference to the neutral nations of South and Southeast Asia. The CCP was able to persuade the Soviet government to accept its point of view; in a joint declaration of October 12, 1954, both governments stated that they favored the establishment of "normal" diplomatic and commercial relations between themselves and Japan. The Soviet Union negotiated an agreement in October 1956 to establish diplomatic relations with Japan, but Communist China has not yet succeeded in doing so. Sino-Japanese trade is limited by the United Nations embargo on the shipment of strategic goods to the Chinese mainland. Nevertheless, the CCP continues to appeal strongly to pacifism, neutralism, and the desire for trade felt in many quarters in Japan. Mao Tse-tung recently told a Japanese Socialist delegation that Communist China has no atomic bombs and neither wishes nor intends to acquire any; whether true or not, this statement can hardly help making a favorable impression in Japan in contrast not only with the atomic policy of the United States and Great Britain but with that of the Soviet Union, which is showering Japan (and probably parts of China also) with radioactive fallout. The indications are that the CCP exerts somewhat less influence on the Japanese Communist Party than does the Soviet Communist Party.

Relations between Communist China and the United States have been dominated by a mutual hostility which on both sides has strong emotional overtones. In addition to refusing diplomatic recognition and opposing its entry into the United Nations Organization, the United States since Communist China's entry into the Korean War, and even since its termination, has imposed a total embargo on all American trade with the China mainland. This goes beyond the corresponding restrictions that the United States imposes on its trade with the European members of the Soviet bloc and far beyond the restrictions imposed by other non-Communist nations on trade with the China mainland, which extend only to strategic goods. The United States also maintains military forces at a distance from Chinese territory which would seriously alarm us if the situation were reversed.

On its side the CCP has always claimed to believe, though whether it does so any longer is doubtful, that the United States is constantly plotting aggression against China. The conviction of American hostility has enabled the CCP to win several propaganda triumphs by offering concessions in the virtual certainty that the United States government would not meet it half way. A case in point is Chou En-lai's dramatic offer at the Bandung Conference to negotiate the Taiwan issue, which was promptly rejected by the Department of State. It is highly unlikely that the CCP was decisively restrained from still more aggressive action by American policy on any of the three occasions on which the United States allegedly went to the "brink of war" with China: in Korea (1953), Indochina (1954), and the offshore islands (1955). Deterrence has been a mutual, not a one-way, phenomenon.

No issue involves greater danger of Sino-American conflict than that of the offshore islands. The United States government encouraged the Chinese Nationalists to hold a chain of these islands, stretching roughly from Shanghai to Amoy, when they were expelled from the mainland in 1949. In February 1955 the United States Seventh Fleet enabled the Nationalists to evacuate one of these island groups, the Tachens, which had become militarily untenable and yet had the greatest strategic importance of any of them, since they lie on the flyway between the Shanghai area and Taiwan. At about the same time the United States negotiated with the Nationalists a treaty which commits us to the defense of Taiwan itself but leaves to the discretion of the President the decision whether to intervene if the offshore islands are attacked. The main islands which the Nationalists still hold are the Matsus off Foochow and the highly vulnerable island of Quemoy, in Amoy harbor. These islands have some psychological value to the Nationalists but not very much military value, since the United States has quietly forbidden the Nationalists to use them as offensive bases even if they so desired—and this in spite of the "unleashing of Chiang Kai-shek" in 1953. The Nationalists would have very great difficulty in defending them against a determined Communist attack, and American air and naval intervention in offshore waters would be dangerous and might possibly touch off a full-scale war.

The establishment of diplomatic relations between the United States and Communist China is inhibited by the attitudes of both governments. The CCP appears to attach no great value to recognition by the United States; if it did, it could have easily done a number of things that it has not done, such as releasing the remaining Americans now in prison in China, which would help to pave the way for recognition. American nonrecognition confers some moral advantages on the CCP, chiefly the sympathy of the neutralist governments of Asia and the Middle East. Nor does the CCP necessarily desire admission to the United Nations enough to pay any sort of price for it, since membership would carry with it the duty to stand up and be counted on the Soviet side in a way which might alienate much neutralist sympathy.

Great Britain occupies a peculiar position in the PRC's foreign relations, being the only major "imperialist" power with whom it has any sort of diplomatic relations. (In addition to the Communist states and the neutral states of Asia and some of the Middle East, Communist China has diplomatic relations, among other European states, with Switzerland, the Netherlands, and the Scandinavian countries.) Great Britain extended its much controverted recognition to Communist China early in 1950 partly in the hope of preserving British trade with

China, British investments in China, and the British position in Hong Kong and partly in the belief that nonrecognition would tend to drive the PRC more closely and unnecessarily into the arms of the Soviet Union, but most of all because of the simple fact that the CCP was in actual control of the Chinese mainland.

Subsequent history has not dealt very kindly with this reasoning. The PRC did not send a diplomatic mission to London or recognize the British mission in Peking until 1954. It does not appear to have been influenced in its policy toward the Soviet Union by British diplomacy or British trade. It has mercilessly squeezed most British trade out of China and has virtually confiscated British investments. Hong Kong has been left largely alone, because its present status benefits both sides, and the Chinese may even be prepared to wait until the lease on most of the mainland portion of the colony expires in 1997 before making any drastic move. Even though the British government may have seemed to many Americans to be treating the PRC with undue consideration, there is no doubt in Peking that in the last analysis Britain is on the "imperialist" side.

A discussion of Communist China's foreign relations ought to include some mention of its relations with Nationalist China. One of Peking's main aims is of course to "liberate" Taiwan. A forcible "liberation" would probably be impossible while the Seventh Fleet is in the way and in any case would probably bring more disadvantages than advantages. A peaceful "liberation," however, would confer enormous benefits on the CCP. It would mean a tremendous political defeat for the United States, which since 1950 has built much of its Far Eastern policy around the Nationalists. It would probably clinch for Peking the allegiance of many of those overseas Chinese who now look to the Nationalists instead. It would probably also clinch a seat in the United Nations for Peking, since no one could then say that it was not, for good or ill, the government of China.

The constant stream of CCP propaganda in favor of a peaceful "liberation" of Taiwan may well be having some effect on the island. This probably does not apply to indigenous Taiwanese or to older Nationalists such as Chiang Kai-shek himself, much of whose careers has been spent in fighting the Chinese Communists and whose earthly problems will soon be solved by death. But there are many somewhat younger Nationalists whom growing homesickness may have rendered receptive to Peking's appeals for a peaceful "liberation" of Taiwan. The riots of May 24, 1957, in Taipei may have been the outcome of some such feeling. There have been unconfirmed reports of secret negotiations at a high level between Peking and Taipei. Even if they have occurred, however, it appears that Chiang Kai-shek has thrown his weight into the scales against an agreement. Channels for possible negotiation have been and are being kept open by both sides. Nevertheless, the intensity of the recent campaign against the "rightists" on the mainland has probably disillusioned, at least for the time being, anyone on Taiwan who hoped for a peaceful reconciliation and a place for himself in the "united front."

Thus in foreign as well as in domestic affairs the CCP has since coming to power shown itself to be inventive, flexible, ruthless, and disposed to wait when necessary. It is ready and willing to use both force and compromise in any combination which seems advantageous at a particular time. Its leadership is one of the most able and powerful, perhaps the ablest and most powerful, in the world. On the whole, and in the long run, the CCP may well prove a more formidable opponent for the non-Communist world than is its Soviet colleague.

Nationalist China since 1949

The beautiful island of Taiwan, to which the Chinese Nationalists transferred their headquarters from the mainland at the end of 1949, lies on the Tropic of Cancer about 120 miles off the coast of Fukien province and has an area of approximately 14,000 square miles. It is roughly comparable in area and topography to Hainan or Ceylon. For fifty years (1895–1945) it was ruled by Japan, which valued it for its rice, sugar, camphor, and its strategic location. The Japanese gave Taiwan an orderly but oppressive government and a high literacy rate, but no preparation for self-government.

As they had been authorized to do at the Cairo Conference (November–December 1943) and by General MacArthur's General Order Number One (August 15, 1945), the Chinese Nationalists promptly occupied the island after the Japanese surrender. Carpetbagging mainlanders proceeded to misgovern it so badly that on February 28, 1947, many of the inhabitants rose in revolt only to be massacred. Soon afterward the National Government removed the governor, Chen Yi (not to be confused with the Chinese Communist general whose name is pronounced and spelled in English in the same way); eventually Chen was shot, but for planning to go over to the Communists rather than for what he had done on Taiwan.

In January 1949 the National Government, foreseeing the possibility

that Taiwan might be needed as a refuge, appointed one of its ablest
and most honorable officials, Ch'en Ch'eng, as governor of the island.
He set about eliminating the worst abuses and instituting a more enlightened administration. In 1950, when Ch'en became Premier, he
was succeeded as governor by K. C. Wu, another official of the highest
type. Beginning in the summer of 1950, municipal and county elections
were held throughout the island; these elections are especially interesting because they were the first genuine local elections ever held in
Nationalist China. Since then elections have also been held for a
provincial assembly, all but one of whose members are Taiwanese.
Most of the members of the appointive Governor's Council are also
Taiwanese. The governor himself is appointed by the central government and is a mainlander. In the various elections at the provincial
level the Kuomintang (which of course includes Taiwanese members)
has won most of the seats, but some have also been won by two minor
parties (the Youth Party and the Democratic Socialist Party) and by
nonparty candidates.

Taiwan supports not only a provincial government but also a government claiming to be that of all China. At this higher level, because
of the impossibility of holding national elections, the trend toward
democratization scarcely applies. The National Assembly has great
difficulty in mustering a quorum, since most of its members are either
dead or live elsewhere. The five Yuan are entirely dominated by the
Kuomintang and by mainland Chinese rather than by Taiwanese.
Chiang Kai-shek as President exercises an arbitrary power which is
nearly absolute when he chooses to make it so and which tends to
increase rather than diminish with time. The Vice-President, Ch'en
Ch'eng, does not have much influence with the middle ranks of the
Kuomintang hierarchy, although he has some with the army high
command, and his chances of inheriting the full measure of Chiang's
power do not appear great. The Generalissimo's elder son, Chiang
Ching-kuo, exercises much power in the secret police, the political
departments of the armed forces, and the Youth Corps and is probably
next to his father the most powerful man on the island. The central
government still keeps on its payroll, though not in positions of real
power, a number of disreputable former warlords who symbolize the
albatross of the past which still tends to hang round the Kuomintang's
neck.

Taiwan, in short, is essentially a police state, though not a fully
totalitarian one. The tendency toward dictatorship is somewhat re-

strained by the need for keeping on good terms with the United States and by the presence of several thousand Americans on the island. Anyone accused of Communist sympathies is harshly dealt with, usually by execution or by imprisonment on Green Island, the Kuomintang's "counterbrainwashing center," and the regime retains its unfortunate tendency to classify any public criticism of itself as the work of Communist sympathizers. The outward conformity produced by such tactics is really hypocrisy rather than loyalty, and government and people do not trust one another. On the mainland a somewhat similar situation is eased by the regime's ability to point to "Socialization" and economic transformation as a worth-while goal and by its position as the symbol of China's growing power. The Kuomintang has no such goal to which it can point except that of reconquest of the mainland—and this makes no appeal to the Taiwanese and is little more than a dream even to the mainlanders on the island.

As the dominant group within the Kuomintang has become more confident of American support, it has also tended to tighten its grip on the island. This can be seen in the cases of two able officials widely respected by Americans. In 1954 Governor K. C. Wu of Taiwan broke with the Kuomintang and came to the United States, charging that Taiwan had been made into a police state. In 1955 the regime sent into disgrace and retirement one of its ablest field commanders, Sun Li-jen, who had objected to the activities of Chiang Ching-kuo's political departments within his units, had often criticized the Generalissimo himself, and had a not very sanguine view of the prospects for a reconquest of the mainland.

It might be thought that the crushing defeat on the mainland would have taught the Kuomintang something; it has, but not enough. The Kuomintang concluded that its defeat had been caused by bad party discipline, corruption, inefficiency, and bad strategy. This was correct, but inadequate, for the Kuomintang's basic nature and philosophy had also been to blame. Both the Central Executive Committee and the Central Supervisory Committee were abolished in 1950 and were replaced by two smaller bodies, the Central Advisory Committee and the Central Reform Committee. The last-named, which was the more important of the two smaller bodies and was headed by the Generalissimo himself, was abolished in its turn in 1952 and succeeded by a Central Committee. There was considerable transfusion of new blood into the middle and upper ranks of the party, but there has been no fundamental change in its official philosophy.

The economic situation is somewhat more encouraging. By virtue of massive American aid Taiwan enjoys close to the highest standard of living in Asia. In fact, it is higher than the island can afford. The government is afraid to risk popular displeasure and a possible growth of pro-Communist feeling by diverting resources from present consumption to investment. Long-term planning and development are also inhibited by heavy military expenditures and the Kuomintang's refusal to treat Taiwan as anything more than a temporary stopping place. This in turn makes the Kuomintang unable to get along without continued massive American aid.

In the field of agrarian reform accomplishment has been noteworthy; the tragedy is that the Kuomintang waited so long to implement legislation much of which had been on the books since 1930 but had never been enforced on the mainland, except for a time by the Communists. Rents were first reduced to a maximum of three-eighths of the annual crop, and some public lands were sold to would-be owner-cultivators; then, beginning in 1953, most landlord-owned land was bought and resold to the tenants on reasonable terms. The former owners were paid largely in industrial securities and thus transformed willy nilly into entrepreneurs, a sensible device. Today tenancy is almost unknown, and land is equitably distributed, but by virtue of the relationship of population to cultivated land the average size of farms is small.

With the help of ample American economic and technical assistance, Taiwanese industry has considerably expanded, especially in the fields of electricity and light industry. The island has a substantial exportable surplus of rice and does a thriving trade with other Asian states, especially Japan.

Nevertheless, all this has been aptly called progress on a treadmill. The population (about 10 million, of whom roughly three-fourths are Taiwanese and the rest mainlanders) is growing at the high rate of 3.6 per cent per year, and no amount of American aid can provide land and jobs for all the surplus. This economic dilemma is worsened by the island's obscure political future.

Since Nationalist China stands or falls by American aid, it is important to understand what the American policy has been. From the end of 1949 to June 1950 the United States government pursued a policy of inaction and was prepared to do nothing to save Taiwan from "liberation." The outbreak of the Korean War sharply upgraded the importance of Taiwan in the eyes of American officialdom, and

the Seventh Fleet was interposed between Taiwan and the mainland
by President Truman with orders to prevent any major military movement in either direction. The Chinese Nationalists then began to receive military and economic aid which amounted by the end of 1956
to about $2 billion. Early in 1953 the Eisenhower administration re-
moved the ban on Nationalist attacks on the mainland and thus theoretically "unleashed Chiang Kai-shek." Nothing happened, for two reasons.
The Nationalist forces, though growing stronger with American help,
were still far too weak to undertake any major operations against the
mainland; and in any event Washington imposed an unpublished
prohibition on any such operations without prior American consent.
The situation was substantially the same as before. Apart from the
offshore-islands crisis of early 1955, which has already been mentioned,
it has remained so ever since, except that the Communist military
and logistical build-up opposite Taiwan is proceeding steadily.

The Kuomintang enjoys some prestige and support among overseas
Chinese, especially in the Philippines, but in general far less than do
the Communists. It is the Communists, after all, who control the
Chinese mainland, from which all overseas Chinese originally came.
There is also a sizable number of overseas Chinese, especially among
those who have had some experience of both regimes, who refuse to
give support to either and long for something better. It also seems
very unlikely that any considerable number of people on the mainland
of China would welcome a substitution of the Kuomintang for the
CCP.

The Nationalists have diplomatic relations with the anti-Communist
nations of Asia (other than Pakistan), as well as with Japan, the
United States, and some other states outside Asia. Among the neutral
Asian nations they have neither diplomatic relations nor respect.
They are regarded as a revolutionary movement which failed, largely
through its own fault, and which will not get another chance.

The international status of Taiwan presents an apparently insoluble
problem. The island was promised to China at the Cairo Conference
in 1943, and to date no government is officially committed to anything
but this solution. The question of course is, to Communist China or
to Nationalist China? The Japanese peace treaty of 1951 divested
Japan of any claim to Taiwan, but it did not settle the actual disposition of the island. Neither Communist China nor Nationalist China
has given the slightest official sign of abandoning its claim, and with
the latter supported by the United States there seems to be no out-

come but eventual war, unless one side or both sides back down.

Ideally, it would be desirable to allow the inhabitants of Taiwan to vote freely as to which of the two regimes they prefer or whether they would like to remain independent. There is an independence movement among the Taiwanese, which finds it wise to maintain its headquarters in Tokyo. But the Kuomintang would not permit such an election, let alone allow itself to be deprived without a struggle of control over the island in favor of an international trusteeship or an independent government.

It is difficult at the present time to imagine any eventual disposition of Taiwan except amalgamation with the mainland, by peaceful means or otherwise. This could be prevented only if the CCP gives up its claim to the island or if the United States protects it indefinitely. But the first of these two possibilities is very unlikely, and as for the second it would be difficult to defend an island if its government did not want to be defended. The only possible alternative to amalgamation appears to be for the Nationalists to settle down as Taiwanese, abandon all thought of going home, and live indefinitely under the protecting wing of the United States. It is very doubtful whether such a situation would be acceptable to the Chinese Communists or to the Chinese Nationalists, and it would place a heavy and continuing burden on the United States.

SUGGESTED READING

I: The Historical Background

GENERAL WORKS

Cressey, George B. *Land of the 500 Million.* New York: McGraw-Hill, 1955. An excellent geography text.

Fairbank, John K. *The United States and China.* Cambridge, Mass.: Harvard University Press, 1948. Contains an excellent treatment of traditional China.

Fitzgerald, C. P. *China: A Short Cultural History.* Rev. ed. New York: Praeger; London: Cresset, 1952. Stimulating; treatment from 18th century is inadequate.

Goodrich, L. C. *A Short History of the Chinese People.* Rev. ed. New York: Harper, 1951. Especially good on the material aspects of Chinese culture.

Hinton, Harold C., and Marius B. Jansen, eds. *Major Topics on China and Japan: A Handbook for Teachers.* New York: Institute of Pacific Relations, 1957. Contains useful reading lists and discussions of important historical topics.

Latourette, Kenneth Scott. *The Chinese: Their History and Culture.* New York: Macmillan, 1934. Useful but dull; good reading lists.

——. *A History of Modern China.* London: Penguin, 1954. A useful brief survey.

Pulleyblank, E. G. *Chinese History and World History.* Cambridge, Eng.: Cambridge University Press, 1955.

Sinor, Denis, ed. *Orientalism and History.* Cambridge, Eng.: Heffer, 1954. Contribution on China by E. G. Pulleyblank is on pp. 57–81; two stimulating, brief interpretations of Chinese history by the professor of Chinese at Cambridge.

Winfield, Gerald F. *China: The Land and the People.* New York: Sloane, 1948. A penetrating discussion of the causes and possible cure of China's economic backwardness and poverty.

ANCIENT CHINA

Creel, H. G. *The Birth of China.* New York: John Day, 1937; Ungar, 1954. A good account based mainly on archaeological evidence.

Maspero, Henri. *La Chine antique.* Rev. ed. Paris: Boccard, 1955. An excellent survey based on literary evidence.

IMPERIAL CHINA

Carter, T. F. *The Invention of Printing in China and Its Spread Westward.* 2d ed., rev. by L. C. Goodrich. New York: Ronald Press, 1955. A standard treatment of an important and interesting aspect of cultural history.

Chi Ch'ao-ting. *Key Economic Areas in Chinese History.* London: Allen and Unwin, 1936. An interesting Marxist interpretation.

Hummel, Arthur W., ed. *Eminent Chinese of the Ch'ing Period, 1644–1912.* 2 vols. Washington, D.C.: U.S. Government Printing Office, 1943–1944. An invaluable and well-indexed biographical dictionary.

Lattimore, Owen. *Inner Asian Frontiers of China.* Rev. ed. New York: American Geographical Society, 1951. A very stimulating and sophisticated treatment of Central Asia and its relations with China; it also contains material on Chinese history, much of which is extraneous and of inferior quality.

Michael, Franz H. *The Origin of Manchu Rule in China.* Baltimore: Johns Hopkins University Press, 1942. Discusses the origins of the Ch'ing dynasty.

Morse, H. B. *The Trade and Administration of China.* Shanghai: Kelly and Walsh, various editions. A useful guide to China in the late 19th century.

Needham, Joseph. *Science and Civilisation in China.* 2 vols. to date. Cambridge, Eng.: Cambridge University Press, 1954–. Contains much interesting and important information but is marred by inadequate Sinological knowledge and a naïve fondness for Taoism and the ideal of collectivism.

Reischauer, Edwin O. *Ennin's Travels in T'ang China*. New York: Ronald Press, 1955. A fascinating account of China in the mid-9th century as viewed by a Japanese Buddhist monk.

Wilbur, C. Martin. *Slavery in China during the Former Han Dynasty*. Chicago: Field Museum of Natural History, 1943. Contains some excellent historical material of a general nature.

Wright, Mary C. *The Last Stand of Chinese Conservatism: The T'ung-chih Restoration, 1862–74*. Stanford: Stanford University Press, 1956. A scholarly and important study.

THE WESTERN IMPACT

Boardman, Eugene P. *Christian Influence upon the Ideology of the Taiping Rebellion*. Madison: University of Wisconsin Press, 1952. The latest major work in a Western language on this interesting subject.

Cameron, Meribeth E. *The Reform Movement in China, 1868–1912*. Stanford: Stanford University Press, 1931. An excellent study of attempts at modernization.

Latourette, Kenneth Scott. *A History of Christian Missions in China*. New York: Macmillan, 1929. A standard account.

Teng, S. Y., and John K. Fairbank. *China's Response to the West: A Documentary Survey, 1839–1923*. Cambridge, Mass.: Harvard University Press, 1954. Translations of important Chinese documents, with valuable commentaries.

THE REVOLUTIONARY MOVEMENT

Holcombe, Arthur N. *The Chinese Revolution*. Cambridge, Mass.: Harvard University Press, 1930. Very perceptive comments on the Kuomintang at the time of its coming to power.

Houn, Franklin W. *Central Government of China, 1912–1928: An Institutional Study*. Madison: University of Wisconsin Press, 1957. A good recent treatment of a neglected subject.

Isaacs, Harold R. *The Tragedy of the Chinese Revolution*. Rev. ed. Stanford: Stanford University Press, 1951. A brilliant left-wing anti-Stalinist account of the fateful Kuomintang-Communist alliance.

Li Chien-nung. *The Political History of China, 1840–1928*. Trans. and ed. by S. Y. Teng and Jeremy Ingalls. New York: Van Nostrand, 1956. A translation of a standard Chinese text, which, however, is rather dull and detailed.

MacNair, Harley F. *China in Revolution*. Chicago: University of Chicago Press, 1931. Especially good on warlord politics.

Sharman, Lyon. *Sun Yat-sen: His Life and Its Meaning*. New York: John Day, 1934. A perceptive, critical, and standard biography.

Sun Yat-sen. *San Min Chu I*. Trans. by Frank Price. Chungking: Ministry of

Information of the Republic of China, 1943. Sun's last and best-known work.

Wen-han Kiang. *The Chinese Student Movement.* New York: King's Crown Press, 1948. A good treatment of intellectual and cultural currents during the late 19th and early 20th centuries.

THE KUOMINTANG IN POWER (1928–1937)

Chiang Kai-shek. *China's Destiny.* Trans. by Wang Chung-hui. New York: Macmillan, 1947. An authorized translation of this celebrated antiforeign diatribe.

Ch'ien, T. S. *The Government and Politics of China,* Cambridge, Mass.: Harvard University Press, 1950. Highly critical; standard and detailed.

China Year Book, The. Articles on the Kuomintang by George Sokolsky, especially in the 1929 volume, are perhaps the best accounts available.

Linebarger, Paul M. A. *The China of Chiang K'ai-shek: A Political Study.* Boston: World Peace Foundation, 1941. Generally favorable.

Liu, F. F. *A Military History of Modern China, 1924–1949.* Princeton: Princeton University Press, 1956. Deals mainly with the Nationalist army.

North, Robert C. *Kuomintang and Chinese Communist Elites.* Stanford: Stanford University Press, 1952. Contains valuable insights into modern Chinese political history.

THE CHINESE COMMUNIST MOVEMENT (1921–1937)

Brandt, Conrad, Benjamin Schwartz, and John K. Fairbank, eds. *A Documentary History of Chinese Communism.* Cambridge, Mass.: Harvard University Press, 1952. A valuable collection of translated documents with commentaries whose main defect is that it does not treat Mao Tse-tung and his revolutionary strategy in enough detail.

North, Robert C. *Moscow and Chinese Communists.* Stanford: Stanford University Press, 1953. A rather poorly organized account of the Chinese Communist movement whose main merit is its utilization of Soviet sources.

Schwartz, Benjamin I. *Chinese Communism and the Rise of Mao.* Cambridge, Mass.: Harvard University Press, 1951. An excellent study which, however, dates the triumph of Mao within the party about three years too early; see corrections set forth in his article, "On the 'Originality' of Mao Tse-tung," *Foreign Affairs,* Oct. 1955, pp. 67–76.

Snow, Edgar, *Red Star over China.* New York: Random House, 1938, 1944. A justly famous journalistic account based on a visit to the Shensi soviet in 1936; this is a primary source which is only slightly marred by the author's enthusiasm for the Chinese Communists.

Whiting, Allen S. *Soviet Policies in China, 1917–1924.* New York: Columbia University Press, 1953. An excellent account based on meticulous research.

THE WAR AGAINST JAPAN (1937–1945)

Chinese Communist Movement, The. (Appendix II to part 7A, Institute of Pacific Relations.) Washington, D.C.: U.S. Government Printing Office, 1952. A valuable but badly organized military intelligence study of the Chinese Communist movement during the war.

Feis, Herbert. *The China Tangle.* Princeton: Princeton University Press, 1953. A good treatment of American policy on and in China during the war.

Rosinger, Lawrence K. *China's Wartime Politics, 1937–1944.* Princeton: Princeton University Press, 1944. Useful commentary with documents.

White, Theodore H., and Annalee Jacoby. *Thunder Out of China.* New York: Sloane, 1956. A brilliant and highly critical account of the Kuomintang during the war.

CIVIL WAR (1945–1949)

Belden, Jack. *China Shakes the World.* New York: Harper, 1949. Highly colored and too receptive to the Communist viewpoint, but informative and interesting.

Liao Kai-lung. *From Yenan to Peking.* Peking: Foreign Languages Press, 1954. A Communist account.

Military Situation in the Far East (the MacArthur hearings). 5 vols. Washington, D.C.: U.S. Government Printing Office, 1951. An important source of information which can be readily exploited by means of the index.

United States Relations with China (the White Paper). Washington, D.C.: U.S. Department of State, 1949. Contains much valuable information but must be interpreted with care.

II: China since 1949

GENERAL WORKS

American Consulate General, Hong Kong. *Current Background* and *Survey of the China Mainland Press.* These important serials are invaluable sources of information on Communist China since 1950 but are unfortunately rather scarce. *Current Background* is an occasional publication with interpretive comment and is especially valuable. The *Survey* consists of translations without commentary; they have been accompanied by a bimonthly index since 1956.

China News Analysis, Hong Kong. A generally valuable and interesting periodical, although not always reliable.

Communist China. In *Current History,* Jan. 1957.

Communist China: A Special Report. In *New Republic,* May 13, 1957.

Communist China in World Politics. In *Journal of International Affairs,* spring 1957.

Fitzgerald, C. P. *Revolution in China.* New York: Praeger; London: Cresset, 1952. Stimulating, but controversial on some points; too receptive to the Communist viewpoint.

Gluckstein, Ygael. *Mao's China: Economic and Political Survey.* Boston: Beacon Press, 1957. Useful, especially on economic aspects; based on considerable research.

Guillain, Robert. *600 Million Chinese.* New York: Criterion Books, 1957. An interesting account by a distinguished correspondent.

Kuo, P. C. *China: New Age and New Outlook.* New York: Knopf, 1956. An interesting interpretation by a Chinese scholar now living in the United States; unsound on some points.

Report on China. In *Annals of the American Academy of Political and Social Science,* Sept. 1951.

Rostow, W. W., and others. *The Prospects for Communist China.* Cambridge: Massachusetts Institute of Technology, 1954. Useful mainly on the economic aspects.

Tang, Peter S. H. *Communist China Today.* New York: Praeger, 1957. Comprehensive, useful, and generally reliable. A supplementary volume of documents was published in 1958. Unfortunately it is a modest effort in relation to the need. CCP speeches, official documents of various kinds, and news releases constitute by far the most important categories of information on Communist China, although they must be interpreted with great care.

Union Research Institute, Hong Kong. *Union Research Service.* Series of translations of the Chinese Communist press, since 1955, with some commentaries. There is not much duplication of coverage between this and the material issued by the American Consulate General.

United States and the Far East, The. New York: Columbia University, American Assembly, 1956. An excellent contribution by A. Doak Barnett is on pp. 105–171.

Walker, Richard L. *China under Communism: The First Five Years.* New Haven: Yale University Press, 1955. Contains much useful information but is propagandistic in tone and often unreliable in interpretation; strongly anti-Communist.

THE CHINESE COMMUNIST PARTY

Chang Kuo-tao. "Mao—A New Portrait by an Old Colleague," *New York Times Magazine,* Aug. 2, 1953. Contains much interesting information about Mao and his principal colleagues.

Hinton, Harold C. "The Eighth Congress of the Chinese Communist Party," *Far Eastern Survey,* Jan. 1957.

"Leadership in the New China," *Economist*, June 19–July 10, 1954. Valuable.

Schwartz, Benjamin. "China and the Soviet Theory of People's Democracy," *Problems of Communism*, Sept.–Oct. 1954, pp. 8–15. Excellent study of some important theoretical problems.

——. "New Trends in Maoism?" *Problems of Communism*, July–Aug. 1957, pp. 1–8. Interesting interpretation of the theoretical aspects of "de-Stalinization."

W., J. F. A. "The September 1956 Congress of the Chinese Communist Party," *World Today*, Nov. 1956, pp. 469–478. This and the Hinton article have useful information on the Eighth Congress.

CONSTITUTIONAL AND GOVERNMENTAL AFFAIRS

Chao Kuo-chün. "How Communist Power Is Organized in China," *Foreign Affairs*, Oct. 1955, pp. 148–153. Useful, but rather weak in interpretation.

Thomas, S. B. *Government and Administration in Communist China*. Rev. ed. New York: Institute of Pacific Relations, 1953. Detailed and objective.

Yu-nan Chang. "The Chinese Communist State System under the Constitution of 1954," *Journal of Politics*, Aug. 1956, pp. 520–546.

ECONOMIC AND SOCIAL AFFAIRS

Adler, Solomon. *The Chinese Economy*. New York: Monthly Review Press, 1957. An interesting but uncritically favorable book by a highly qualified left-wing author.

Barnett, A. Doak. "China's Road to Collectivization," *Journal of Farm Economics*, May 1953, pp. 188–202. Discusses the early phases of this subject.

Hunter, Edward. *Brain-Washing in Red China*. New York: Vanguard Press, 1951. Journalistic and highly colored, but useful.

Lifton, R. J. "Thought Reform of Chinese Intellectuals: A Psychiatric Evaluation," *Journal of Asian Studies*, Nov. 1956, pp. 75–88. A valuable scientific account.

Shabad, Theodore. *China's Changing Map*. New York: Praeger, 1956. Economic geography.

Yuan-li Wu. *An Economic Survey of Communist China*. New York: Bookman Associates, 1956. Useful, detailed.

MILITARY AFFAIRS

Baldwin, Hanson W. "China as a Military Power," *Foreign Affairs*, Oct. 1951, pp. 51–62.

Rigg, Robert B. *Red China's Fighting Hordes*. Harrisburg: Military Service Publishing Company, 1951. Poorly written, but contains much important information.

FOREIGN RELATIONS

Boorman, Howard L., and others. *Moscow-Peking Axis*. New York: Harper, 1957. A rather superficial treatment of Sino-Soviet relations, but the only extended one of any merit at all.

Communist China's Foreign Policy. In *Current History*, Dec. 1957. Useful, but actually deals with foreign relations more than with foreign policy.

Hinton, Harold C. "Dialogue between Giants," *Commonweal*, April 5, 1957. On Sino-Soviet relations.

Kissinger, Henry A. *Nuclear Weapons and Foreign Policy*. New York: Harper, 1957. An excellent discussion of Soviet and Chinese Communist political and military strategy will be found in pp. 255–268 and ch. x of this important book.

Lindsay, Michael. *China and the Cold War*. Melbourne: University of Melbourne Press, 1955. Very stimulating but underestimates the strength of the CCP's consistent commitment to Marxism-Leninism before 1949.

Shen-yu Dai. "Peking and Indochina's Destiny," *Western Political Quarterly*, Sept. 1954, pp. 346–368. A good analysis of the subject through the Geneva Conference.

——. *Peking, Moscow, and the Communist Parties of Colonial Asia*. Cambridge: Massachusetts Institute of Technology, Center for International Studies, 1954. Useful though not very profound.

Swearingen, Rodger. "Techniques of Communist Aggression and the Moscow-Peking Axis," in Philip W. Thayer, ed., *Nationalism and Progress in Free Asia*. Baltimore: Johns Hopkins University Press, 1956. Pages 307–328. An extremely useful discussion of international Communist strategy in South and Southeast Asia.

Trager, Frank N. "Red Shadows on Southeast Asia," *New York Times Magazine*, July 7, 1957. Contains an excellent discussion of Communist China's relations with Southeast Asia.

NATIONALIST CHINA SINCE 1949

Chiang Kai-shek. *Soviet Russia in China: A Summing Up at Seventy*. New York: Farrar, Straus, and Cudahy, 1957. Interesting and informative, but more as a study of its author than of its subject.

Han Lih-wu. *Taiwan Today*. Taipei: Hwa-kuo Publishing Company, 1951. Rather propagandistic.

Riggs, Fred W. *Formosa under Chinese Nationalist Rule*. New York: Macmillan, 1952. Rather critical.

United States and the Far East. New York: Columbia University, American Assembly, 1956. Contribution by Allen S. Whiting is on pp. 173–201.

Whiting, Allen S. "Mystery Man of Formosa," *Saturday Evening Post*, March 12, 1955. On Chiang Ching-kuo.

PART TWO : JAPAN

By Nobutaka Ike

· III ·

The Historical Background

JAPAN lies off the eastern coast of Asia, forming an arc which extends some 1,200 miles. The northern tip of this arc has about the same latitude as Montreal, and the southern tip is parallel to northern Florida. The country consists of four main islands, Honshu, the largest, Kyushu and Shikoku to the south, and Hokkaido to the north, plus numerous smaller islands. In total area, Japan is just under 143,000 square miles, or slightly smaller than the state of California.

The climate in Japan is influenced by the monsoon, a seasonal wind which brings warm moisture-laden air from the southeast in the summer time and cold air from Manchuria and Mongolia in the winter months, and by the ocean currents, particularly the warm Black Current, which originates near the Philippines and flows northward. Abundant rainfall together with a warm growing season makes Japan ideal for the cultivation of rice, the principal agricultural crop.

Because of its mountainous terrain, however, less than 20 per cent of the land can be cultivated. Japan, unlike China, has no great river valleys, but since its rivers are short and swift they have become the source of hydroelectric power. All its large cities have grown up along the coast. Tokyo, the capital and one of the largest cities in the world, is located in the Kanto plain, and the cities of Osaka, Kobe, and Kyoto are in the Kansai plain to the west.

About 90 million people live on these islands, which makes Japan the fifth most populous country in the world. Although the rate of population growth has declined in recent years, the total population is still increasing and is expected to reach 100 million in the 1960s. The problem of feeding and providing employment for an increasing population remains serious since Japan lacks natural resources necessary for an industrial economy. It is necessary to import large quantities of iron, lead, zinc, salt, petroleum, and coal and about 20 per cent of the food supply.

Early History

The first people to settle on the islands were the Ainu, who were probably of early Caucasic stock. The Ainu, however, were displaced and gradually driven northward by successive migrations of Mongoloid peoples who came from Mongolia and Manchuria through Korea and landed in the southern part of the country. There is evidence to suggest that additional migrations of people from the south, perhaps from the coastal areas of southern China, also occurred. In any case, the modern Japanese represent a racial mixture.

It is difficult to disentangle fact from myth in the early history of the Japanese people because the earliest extant writings date to the eighth century A.D. when two official histories, the *Nihon Shoki* and the *Kojiki,* were compiled. In the early period there were numerous clans, each composed of households which claimed a common ancestor and had a common chieftain. These clans, each of which had their own lands, were settled in the area around the Inland Sea and to the south. Eventually there emerged one dominant clan, the head of which ultimately became the Emperor. One of the purposes behind the compilation of the official histories mentioned above was to justify the authority of the imperial clan.

Starting about the fifth century, Japan began to come increasingly under the influence of Chinese civilization, which was much more complex and advanced. Among the more important elements imported from China at this time were Buddhism and a centralized bureaucratic system of government. The chieftain of the leading clan was proclaimed Emperor, and a bureaucracy chosen, in accordance with Chinese practice, on the basis of competitive examinations, was created to assist the Emperor. The ownership of arable land was vested in the Emperor, and land was apportioned among cultivators in allotments varying in size with the family. It was envisioned that land would be realloted from time to time to ensure equal distribution. Cultivators were made responsible for the payment of taxes to the central government, partly in the form of produce and partly in labor or military service.

It was one thing to borrow what must have been for its time a complex political system, but quite another thing to make it work. A centralized monarchy was simply not adapted to conditions as they existed at that time, with the result that the system never functioned effectively. The competitive examination provision was ignored in giving official posts. In time various tax-dodging devices came to be used, and in addition new land which was gradually developed to the north was kept in private hands. The flow of revenue into the imperial capital eventually became a mere trickle, whereas in the outlying areas large landholding families became richer and more powerful than the imperial family. Thus the ground was laid for the development of a feudal system.

Large sections of the country came to be ruled by feudal barons who recruited armed retainers to help protect their domains. These retainers became the samurai, a warrior caste, who received rice stipends from their feudal superiors in return for faithful service. Gradually the warrior caste evolved a code of behavior which emphasized unswerving loyalty to the feudal lord, contempt of death, and intense sensitivity to insult.

In the shift toward a feudal system, the imperial family was rendered politically impotent, but never eliminated from the political scene. Indeed, the feudal lords often struggled to get control of the person of the Emperor because he who controlled him could rule in his name and thus acquire an aura of legitimacy. The decentralization of power also led sometimes to the breakdown of law and order, and there were periods when feudal barons feuded and fought. In the course of civil wars, one or two families usually emerged with enough strength to become dominant, as, for example, in the twelfth century when the Minamoto family succeeded in establishing a military government in Kamakura. But the Minamoto hegemony could not be perpetuated, and the country was again torn by dissension and civil war. Another cycle leading to the re-establishment of some kind of central authority came around the middle of the sixteenth century, when three military leaders, Oda Nobunaga, Toyotomi Hideyoshi, and Tokugawa Iyeyasu, appeared, each carrying on the process of military unification undertaken by his predecessor. Tokugawa Iyeyasu, the last of the triumvirate, won a decisive victory in the year 1600 to become

the most powerful feudal baron in the country. In 1603 he assumed
the title shogun, or "generalissimo," and he set to work to establish a
social and political order designed to preserve the status quo and

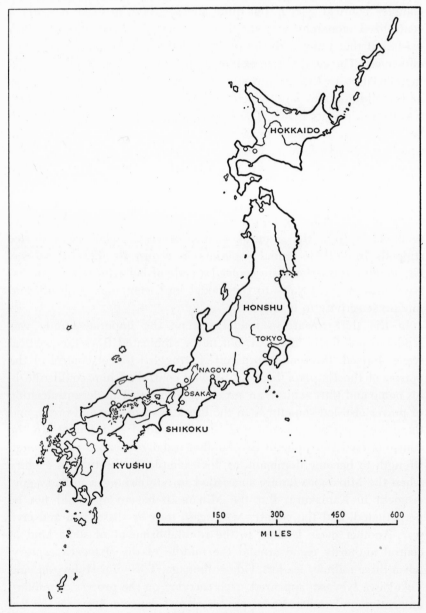

Map 4. Japan.

prevent social change toward the end that he and his descendants would be perpetuated in power.

The Tokugawa Heritage

The British historian, Sir George Sansom, in a delightful book on *The Western World and Japan,* comments that in Asia before modern times, one finds a "common pattern of peasant masses governed by a small class of warriors, priests or officials subsisting on revenue from land." [1] He adds that the aim of government was to maintain, by preventing change, the agrarian economy and the rigid social structure that sustained the ruling class. Moreover, the peasants, being near the margin of subsistence, were mostly concerned with matters that affected their livelihood, a condition which was "not such as to allow, still less to encourage, an interest in the problems of government." [2]

This generalized account provides a fitting introduction to the system of government which prevailed in the Tokugawa period, that is, the period between 1603 and 1867 when the Tokugawa family ruled Japan more or less as military dictators. Historians sometimes describe the political and social system which prevailed under the Tokugawa as "centralized feudalism"; and since, as can be seen, less than a century separates Japan from her feudal past, feudalism is not, as it is in the Western world, a fossilized relic described in textbooks, but in many respects a living thing which affects men's values and behavior. It is useful, therefore, to keep in mind certain salient features of the Japanese feudal system in order better to comprehend the mode of politics that characterizes the modern era.

The Tokugawa directly ruled about one-fourth of the country, and the remainder was divided among some 250 feudal nobles. This resulted in the division of Japan into small political units and the strengthening of local loyalties, particularly since travel between political units was discouraged. But at the same time there was an element of centralization in that administration in the feudal domains tended to be patterned after the Tokugawa administration, and those feudal nobles who had fought against the Tokugawa in the civil wars were required to spend a part of the time in Edo (present-day Tokyo), the capital of the shogunate, and to leave their families behind as hostages when they returned to their domains.

[1] George B. Sansom, *The Western World and Japan* (New York: Knopf, 1950), p. 6.
[2] *Ibid.*, p. 5.

The shogun was the *de facto* ruler of the country. In theory he was subject to the authority of the Emperor, who, together with his court nobles, carried on ritualistic functions in Kyoto, the ancient capital. In practice, however, the Emperor was sealed off from the political life of the nation; and, indeed, it is said that the very existence of the Emperor was unknown to many of the common people.

In governing their domains, the shogun and the feudal nobles were assisted by their samurai retainers. The samurai, who numbered about 5 per cent of the population, were trained as warriors and, together with the feudal nobility, formed the elite of the nation. The privileged position of the samurai vis-à-vis the common people was indicated by the fact that they were subject to their own laws and were tried in their own courts.

The remainder of the population was composed of peasants, artisans, merchants, professional people such as priests and doctors, and the eta, or outcasts. Since the economy was largely agricultural, the peasants were numerically predominant. They provided the chief source of revenue for the ruling elite in the form of a tax, usually paid in rice and amounting to as much as 40–50 per cent of the annual yield. In addition the peasants were subject to numerous taxes on sundry items such as windows and female children and were compelled to provide forced labor on public works.

There were several large cities which served as focal points of commercial activity. In these cities lived artisans and merchants, some of whom succeeded in amassing large fortunes; and there developed, under merchant patronage, a sophisticated urban culture. The *kabuki* theater, for example, was a product of this cultural milieu.

A notable feature of life in the Tokugawa period was the extent to which the ruling authorities concerned themselves with the minute details of daily living and with the morality of the people. Everyone was admonished to be frugal, and sumptuary laws of all kinds sought to regulate the type of clothing that could be worn, the kind of dwelling that could be built, and so on; but as is so often true in matters of this kind, official prohibitions were not always obeyed. Nevertheless, the precedent, if not the habit, of officialdom trying to meddle in the private lives of citizens was established.

In terms of the tasks it set for itself, the Tokugawa administrative structure was relatively simple. At the top of the structure was the shogun, but depending on the ability of the particular individual in office, actual power was sometimes in the hands of a Council of Elders or even in the hands of some palace favorite or high official. The day-to-day tasks of administration were performed by a small corps of officials who saw to it that the taxes were collected, that public morals were not allowed to deteriorate, and that order and security were maintained.

Government at the village level was more or less autonomous. In the Tokugawa period villages were relatively small in size, and they numbered some 60,000 in all the land. In every village there were several officials, generally chosen by a representative of the shogunate from among the wealthiest and long-established landowning families in the village. Their functions were to represent the villagers in any negotiations with high authorities or other villages, to proclaim decrees and injunctions issued by the shogunate, to collect taxes, to adjudicate minor disputes, to keep records, to improve agriculture, and to keep an eye on the villagers' morals. Village leaders were assisted by a village assembly in which the landowning families had a strong voice. An important form of social and political control was the device of mutual responsibility. Groups of five families were organized into a unit; and if, for example, a family in the unit was unable to pay its taxes in full, it was the responsibility of the members of the unit to make up the difference.

The Tokugawa political system enjoyed remarkable longevity, but there was also a price to be paid. For one thing, in the 1630s those who ruled Japan decided to forbid all foreign contacts, except for carefully regulated trade with the Dutch and the Chinese at the port of Nagasaki. The adoption of this policy of national isolation appears to have rested on the fear that Christianity, considered a subversive doctrine, would spread if Europeans were allowed to enter the country and also on the fear that some of the feudal nobles might get powerful enough to challenge Tokugawa hegemony through an alliance with European nations. But by cutting herself off from neighbors in Asia and from Europe, Japan was unable to derive profit from an expanding foreign trade and to benefit from direct contact with Europe which, in the period between 1600 and 1850, underwent a technological and industrial revolution.

Moreover, the passage of time revealed serious stresses and strains within the system. Both the Tokugawa government and the smaller principalities suffered from chronic financial difficulties. Attempts were made repeatedly to overcome such difficulties by resorting to currency debasement, economy measures, higher tax levies, and forced loans, but in the long run no solution was found. Furthermore, with the passage of time, the samurai fell in debt to rice brokers and merchants so that social and political power came to be divorced from wealth. The samurai had social standing but no wealth; the merchants had wealth but no standing.

The coming of peace encouraged the growth of commerce and industry, and marked specialization in the production of goods took place. In the towns and even in the villages, merchants and landowners who had accumulated some capital began to produce goods on the basis of the "putting out" system, so that a kind of nascent capitalism began to develop within the feudal system.

In the meantime, the lot of the small agricultural producer became more wretched. The amount of rice he had to turn over to the tax collector tended to increase. To add to his difficulties there were recurring natural disasters such as floods, and there were periodic famines. Peasant uprisings, varying in scale and intensity, marred the tranquility of the countryside with increasing frequency. By the nineteenth century the "time of troubles" had come.

The travail of the ruling authorities was aggravated by attempts on the part of such countries as Great Britain, Russia, and the United States to force Japan to abandon her traditional policy of national isolation. The Tokugawa rulers were caught in a dilemma. They could not hold off indefinitely the foreign powers who possessed superior military weapons; yet they could not abandon the isolation policy without serious internal repercussions. The political history of Japan from the late 1830s to about 1870 would, if painted in detail, require a broad canvas. It would perhaps be sufficient for our purposes to note merely that the combination of internal difficulties and foreign pressure finally brought the Tokugawa shogunate to an end in 1867. In that year the last Tokugawa shogun resigned and "returned" authority to the youthful occupant of the imperial throne who came to be known as Emperor Meiji. This transfer of power is called the Meiji Restoration; and as the word Meiji, which means "enlightened government," suggests, it opened a new chapter in the political history of Japan.

The Meiji Regime (1867–1912)

There is by no means agreement among scholars as to the interpretation of the Meiji Restoration. But one thing is clear. It was not a social upheaval which brought about a transformation in the basic character of Japanese society, nor, on the other hand, was it a mere palace revolution in which one elite replaced another. Rather the Restoration may be looked upon as a kind of revolution from above in that its leadership was supplied by a small group of young, low-ranking samurai from several principalities in western Japan which were traditionally hostile to the Tokugawa house. In their drive to overthrow the Tokugawa, these samurai had the assistance of nobles from the imperial court, a fact which helped to give this movement an aura of legitimacy, for the ostensible objective was to "restore" the Emperor to his rightful position as the ruler of the country. Funds to finance the movement came from some of the wealthy merchant families in the big cities, and there is evidence to suggest that numerous landowner-entrepreneurs who were producing goods in the towns and villages supplied additional sums and even participated in the brief civil war which followed the resignation of the shogun.

Once in power, the young samurai leaders proceeded to implement a program of modernizing the country. They saw that survival in the modern world necessitated a well-trained army and navy equipped with new-style weapons and backed by industrial power. The national slogan, "Strong army, rich country," summarized the intellectual outlook of those in positions of leadership.

The 1870s and 1880s were a period of intense activity and considerable innovation. Numerous foreign experts and advisers were hired to teach new techniques, and Japanese students were sent abroad to study at government expense. Railroads were built, and a telegraph system was created under government leadership. The government also set up "model" factories and subsidized the development of modern industries. New schools were built and compulsory education was decreed. A modern banking system was established.

In the social field, the legal distinction between samurai and the common people was abolished, and samurai were encouraged to take up useful occupations. Since the state could no longer afford to pay hereditary stipends, these were converted into pensions, and later these pensions were commuted into lump-sum payments. A conscript army replaced the samurai as the fighting force of the nation.

A host of political reforms were made. The feudal principalities were replaced by prefectures which were a part of a centralized administrative structure. A unified coinage system was adopted, and internal trade barriers were eliminated. Eventually a civil service based more or less on the merit system was set up. A legal code and judicial system copied from continental European models were adopted.

The problem of the form of government proved to be a knotty one. Obviously the old feudal system of government was an anachronism and had to be replaced by one more appropriate to the times. It is, therefore, not surprising that considerable interest was shown in Western political thought. Fundamentally, however, Meiji leaders found Western democratic ideas not to their taste. They were convinced that the task of making the country strong and rich in a short span of time called for the concentration of political power at the top. A few people who knew best, they reasoned, should make the decisions for the majority.

The question was whether such an arrangement was acceptable to those who were excluded from power. The Meiji elite soon discovered that it was not. Opposition came from several quarters. Some samurai, refusing to accept the new order, put up sporadic armed resistance, culminating in a rebellion in southwestern Japan in 1877. The rebellion was put down by the new conscript army, bringing to an end attempts to resist the government by the use of force.

Other samurai who had grievances against the government, particularly for its policy of giving a disproportionately large number of government posts to men from Choshu and Satsuma, two principalities in western Japan, organized political opposition to the government. In the beginning they formed small political clubs and societies which included in their membership peasants, especially wealthier peasants, many of whom were also engaged in small-scale rural industry. In agitating against the government, these societies drew heavily on Western political ideas, such as the social contract, natural rights, and utilitarianism. These activities led to the formation in 1881 of the first political party, the Jiyuto or Liberal Party which, according to its program, sought to broaden liberty, protect the people's rights, promote their happiness, reform society, and work for a sound constitutional system. Before long two other parties were organized, the Rikken Kaishinto or Constitutional Progressive Party, composed mostly of ex-bureaucrats, intellectuals, and urban merchants and industrialists, and the Rikken Teiseito or the Constitutional Imperial Party, formed to support the government.

Many of the most ardent adherents of the Liberal Party were landowners who were displeased with the tax policy of the government. Japan was reluctant to borrow foreign capital for fear of compromising her political independence, and hence modernization was financed largely through taxation, internal borrowing, and currency inflation.

The tax burden naturally fell most heavily on the agricultural sector of the economy, since there was no other important source of revenue. But when agriculturalists saw that taxes collected in the countryside were being used to promote industry in the cities, they became vocal in their criticism.

The opponents of the government believed that they could break the hold of the oligarchy and win for themselves a share in the government if a system of representative government could be established. Hence the great issues of the day concerned a demand for the drafting of a written constitution and the establishment of an elected parliament.

The government's answer to the political movement represented by the Liberal Party and to a lesser extent by the Constitutional Progressive Party was suppression on the one hand and compromise on the other. The police frequently censored newspapers, jailed the more outspoken editors, and broke up political meetings. At the same time, in 1881, the government agreed to grant a constitution and to establish a parliament. Later the government dispatched a mission, headed by Ito Hirobumi, a former samurai from Choshu who had become an important figure, to Europe to study constitutions. Ito was much impressed by what he learned in Imperial Germany, and upon his return he and his colleagues, with the help of a Prussian adviser, set to work in strict secrecy to draft a constitution.

The government's concession to the political opposition was more in form than in substance. To be sure, those in power agreed to have a written constitution and to create a parliament, but the vital question was what kind of constitution and what kind of a parliament. The political opposition could not make its influence felt in these matters, partly because the elite was able to keep the situation under control and partly because in the 1880s the popular movement in favor of parliamentary government suffered from internal dissension and hence could not continue to apply pressure on the government in an effort to carry the campaign to its logical conclusion.

In 1889 a constitution, granted, in theory, by the Emperor to his people, was promulgated; and the Imperial Diet, consisting of the House of Peers and the House of Representatives (which is composed of members chosen by a highly restricted electorate), was convened for the first time in 1890.

The constitution reserved broad powers to the Emperor, whereas the authority of the House of Representatives was greatly circumscribed. The civilian government was denied effective control of the military, for the army and navy were considered co-ordinate with the civilian branches, and both were responsible, in theory, to the Emperor. However, despite the dogma of imperial rule enunciated in the constitution and other documents, the Emperor practically never participated in the high-policy decisions of the government. He merely gave formal assent to decisions arrived at by others.

Who were the others? For several decades after the promulgation of the constitution, the "others" were, by and large, the small group of samurai who had participated in the Restoration movement and had worked together to build the Meiji state. These samurai formed an oligarchy, and although there was a certain amount of bickering and dissension among members of the oligarchy, they were held together by the common bond of experiences and values which they shared and by their common determination to prevent popular control of the government. At times some of the members of the oligarchy took the center of the stage and governed as Ministers of State, and at other times they lodged themselves in extralegal institutions such as the "Elder Statesmen" and the Privy Council and manipulated their protégés who occupied the formal offices of government.

The reason the oligarchy was able to maintain control was that the great mass of the population, heirs to the long tradition of Tokugawa rule, was willing to accept this state of affairs. There was, however, always a small minority which refused to accept the status quo, and from the beginning of the twentieth century a small band of socialists were among the dissidents. The socialist doctrine was, of course, anathema to the oligarchy, and so the early socialists were hounded by the police and often put into jail.

The passage of time naturally decimated the ranks of the oligarchy. This was graphically symbolized by the death in 1912 of the Emperor Meiji, who had acceded the throne as a boy and had seen Japan grow into a modernized nation in his lifetime. He was succeeded by his son, Yoshihito, who came to be known as the Emperor Taisho.

The Taisho Era (1912–1926)

The Emperor Taisho, unlike his father who was reportedly energetic and capable, was sickly and toward the end of his reign was because of insanity forced to give way to his son, who was made a regent. Quite clearly the Emperor's illness had little to do with it; nevertheless during his reign some basic changes occurred in the political structure.

It appears in retrospect that the years immediately following the close of the First World War marked a divide in Japanese political history. Prior to that point it had been possible to maintain oligarchic rule; but after that it became increasingly difficult to govern without some reference to the feelings and thoughts of the masses.

One can point to several factors which contributed to this lowering of the political center of gravity. First, compulsory education raised the literacy rate tremendously, paving the way for the growth of mass communications and the diffusion of political ideas. Second, industrialization and urbanization contributed to increased occupational and social mobility, and as people were torn from their old social moorings, they became more receptive to new political values. Third, Japan could not remain isolated from world developments and, like others, felt the ripples of the world-wide spread of democratic ideals following the peace settlement at Versailles.

The Japanese political structure created in the Meiji period was not particularly adapted to meet the problems of the post-1919 age. As has been suggested, the institutional framework blueprinted in the Meiji constitution was not congruent with political practice, especially with regard to the fiction of the Emperor who ruled as well as reigned. The fragmentation inherent in the constitutional structure was latent so long as the Meiji oligarchy was in control, but once they disappeared from the scene, the unity and coherence they had given the government was also removed. The way was now open for one group or another to exercise the power formerly wielded by the members of the oligarchy.

The 1920s were the years when party politicians were in the ascendancy. The Meiji leaders had frowned on political parties, considering them factions which tended to have a divisive effect; but, as already indicated, parties emerged even before the creation of the Imperial Diet, and after 1890 parties had in the House of Representatives a kind of forum from which to make an appeal to the people. The power of the lower house was, to be sure, greatly circumscribed, but still party politicians elected to that body had many an opportunity to harass the government, when they so desired, by asking embarrassing questions and delaying the passage of appropriations bills. Gradually as the members of the oligarchy became older and decreased in numbers, the sphere of action of party leaders was enlarged and they were named increasingly to cabinet posts. It became customary in the 1920s to name the leader of the majority party as Prime Minister, and he brought in prominent men of his party to form the cabinet. In this period, parties enjoyed the financial backing of the industrial combines known as the *zaibatsu* (literally, financial cliques) and the political support of small businessmen and rural landowners. Despite their growing power there were certain sectors of the government which lay beyond the effective control of the parties. The bureaucracy, recruited largely from among the graduates of the law faculty of the Tokyo Imperial University, was jealous of its prerogatives; and the army and navy, with their right of direct access to the throne, brooked no interference from the civilians in the government.

The fact that they lacked clear-cut authority and that certain areas of government were beyond their control was not conducive to the development of a sense of responsibility on the part of the parties. Added to this was the element of political immaturity of party leadership. The result was that corruption became rife, and as scandals were uncovered the public lost confidence in the political parties.

At the time of the death of Emperor Taisho in 1926, Japan was still in the period of party government. The reign of his son, the present Emperor, was designated Showa or "Bright Peace," but ironically forces inimicable to peace were already at work, and before long party government came to an end.

The Showa Era (from 1926)

The samurai background of Meiji leaders as well as national defense needs, particularly in the days following the end of national isolation, assured a certain bias in favor of the military within the framework of government. Under the constitution of 1889 the military achieved a position co-ordinate with the civilian government. Then victories in two major wars, the Sino-Japanese war, 1894–1895, and the Russo-Japanese war, 1904–1905, raised the prestige of the army and navy tremendously. During the 1920s, however, military prestige suffered a setback as part of the revulsion against militarism that occurred almost everywhere throughout the world in this period. There was a reluctance in Japan, as elsewhere, to vote large appropriations for military establishments; the emphasis instead was on peace and disarmament.

The need for retrenchment was something of a blow to the Japanese army because it found itself technologically backward after the end of the First World War. Since funds needed to mechanize the army were not forthcoming, army leaders resorted to a reduction in personnel and used savings thus achieved to acquire new weapons. The reduction of personnel, by creating a feeling of insecurity among career officers and slowing down the rate of promotions, aroused resentment in army circles against the government.

Meanwhile, certain developments on the continent cast their shadow on the Japanese scene. Japan had acquired over several decades special economic and political rights in Manchuria and to a lesser extent in North China. In time many people, particularly in influential positions, came to regard these rights as something both permanent and vital to Japan's well-being. One of the goals of Chinese nationalism, on the other hand, was the elimination of special privileges and the restoration of Chinese sovereignty. It is not surprising that under the circumstances considerable tension was generated between the two countries as the Chinese nationalist revolution went forward, leading to the establishment of the Nationalist government in Nanking in 1928.

A third complicating factor soon entered the picture. This was the world-wide economic depression. The Japanese countryside was especially hard hit by the collapse in commodity prices and there was much suffering.

Some of the younger army officers were sons of farmers, and even those who did not have these connections sensed the gravity of the economic situation as many of the enlisted men under them came from the rural areas. These officers became very restless and thoroughly dissatisfied with the prevailing state of affairs. Much of their resentment came to be directed against the large industrial combines and the men who controlled them. Since these combines were a characteristic feature of Japanese capitalism, pronounced anti-*zaibatsu* sentiment amounted in effect to a crusade against capitalism. The younger officers also leveled sharp attacks against the party politicians, who, in their view, were corrupt and had sold out to the financiers.

There was strong criticism in army circles of the somewhat conciliatory policy pursued by the government toward the rise of Chinese nationalism. Both politicians and financiers were accused of not paying enough attention to national defense and of not using force to protect Japan's privileged position in China.

A concrete manifestation of army discontent and of the urge to resort to action in order to alter the status quo was the formation of secret societies within the army. One of the most important of these societies was the Cherry Blossom Society (Sakurakai), composed mostly of majors and lieutenant colonels. In its prospectus, the Cherry Blossom Society lamented the decline of national power and put the blame on Japan's statesmen who instead of paying attention to spiritual matters were concerned only with gaining personal power and wealth. It pointed to the decadence of political parties, the lack of sympathy for the masses on the part of the capitalistic elite, the responsibility of the mass communications media for bringing about a decline in the national spirit, the lack of patriotism among students, the economic collapse of the farming communities, unemployment, and the economic depression. "People like us," the prospectus read, "yearn for the appearance of a vigorous and clear-cut national policy which would truly rest on the masses and which would be centered on the Emperor."

Groups like the Cherry Blossom Society then began to take matters in their own hands in order to force a change in the composition of government and bring about a policy which would be more to their liking. One of their first steps was to strike in Manchuria where, they believed, the privileged position of Japan was threatened by the successes of the nationalist movement in China.

In the fall of 1931 some army units stationed in Manchuria blew up a section of the tracks of the Japanese-owned South Manchurian Railway. At the time, however, the Japanese accused the Chinese of having perpetrated the deed and, using this as a pretext, quickly took over military control of the whole of Manchuria. It appears that the affair was initiated by units in the field without authorization from the civilian government or even of the supreme command in Tokyo. Once the nation was faced with a *fait accompli*, however, it supported the taking over of Manchuria. An era of militarism and intense nationalism was inaugurated.

Emboldened by their initial success, the younger officers next sought to bring about what they considered a political reformation at home. On May 15, 1932, a group of army and navy officers forced their way into the Prime Minister's residence and killed Prime Minister Inukai Tsuyoshi, a party leader, in cold blood. Other officers attacked a police station and the Bank of Japan and destroyed power stations. If the object of these attacks was to bring about political change, they were successful, for with the death of Inukai, party government came to an end.

There were other acts of violence, and the most important of these was a fairly large-scale army uprising on February 26, 1936. Some 1,400 troops were involved and in the course of the uprising the Finance Minister, the Lord Keeper of the Privy Seal, and the Inspector General of Military Education were killed. The Prime Minister, Admiral Okada Keisuke, narrowly escaped death because the officers shot his brother-in-law, who resembled him, through mistaken identity. The rebels seized some government buildings and held out for three days, after which they surrendered in obedience to an imperial order.

Some civilians were implicated in this uprising, including Kita Ikki, who was the leading theorist of the young officers' movement. Kita's ideas were given in an essay, first written around 1919, called "An Outline Plan for the Reconstruction of Japan," which became the bible of the young officers. In this essay, Kita urged that the parliament, the Privy Council, and other imperial advisers be pushed aside in order that the Emperor, together with all the people, could lay the foundation for the reform of the state, that a limitation be placed on property, including land, to be held by any one family, that large-scale enterprises should be owned and operated by the state, that workers' rights should be protected, including the right to participate in management, and set forth that a state had the right to start a war for self-defense and for the benefit of other states and peoples unjustly oppressed. As the theorist of the movement, Kita was executed along with other leaders of the revolt.

The February uprising turned out to be the last major effort of the young officers to bring their ideas to fruition. It should also be pointed out that the revolt represented not only a struggle between these officers and the civilians, but also the climax of a struggle between two factions in the army. The younger officers belonged mostly to the Imperial Way faction (Kodoha) which, as is evident from an analysis of Kita's views, espoused vague ideas of direct rule by the Emperor together with severe limitations on capitalistic enterprise. They were opposed by the Control faction (Toseiha) made up of the more senior men who were more conservative and less anti–big business. Up to 1936 the Control faction had been rather tolerant of these outbreaks of violence perpetrated by the Imperial Way faction, partly, it would seem, because they were interested in utilizing the unrest to strengthen their hold on the government. But when they saw that the situation might get out of hand, as in the February incident, they took stern measures, and those responsible for the revolt were executed or severely punished.

The assassinations and revolts had the effect of intimidating sufficiently the civilians in the government so that they were more willing to accept the argument that military leaders should be put into positions of responsibility because only they could keep the unruly younger officers under control. In this way the military increased its influence in the government.

The rise of the military led to more stringent censorship and thought control. The schools were compelled to glorify militarism, and in the universities academic freedom was greatly curbed. Liberalism, to say nothing of radical ideas, was considered subversive, and individuals who subscribed to these were subjected to pressure and threats from self-appointed patriots.

In the field of foreign relations the Japanese consolidated their military seizure of Manchuria by creating a puppet state called Manchukuo. China and the Great Powers refused, of course, to recognize Manchukuo, and world opinion was brought to bear against Japan through the League of Nations, which condemned it as an aggressor. Japan then withdrew from the League.

Japanese penetration of China, however, did not end with the creation of Manchukuo. In the mid-1930s the army set up a series of so-called "autonomous" regimes in North China in order to bring the economy of this region into the Japanese economic orbit. Then in the summer of 1937 Japan began the military occupation of North China, and a little later fighting spread to Central China and eventually to South China. Both the Chinese Nationalists and the Chinese Communists resisted Japanese encroachments by resorting to guerrilla operations as well as more conventional methods of warfare. Millions of Japanese troops were sent to China, but they could not bring about the capitulation of the Nationalist government under Chiang Kai-shek. Chinese resistance, moreover, was bolstered by moral support and material aid from the United States and other countries. The prospect of a clear-cut Japanese victory in China was slim, but Japan, on the other hand, could not withdraw without losing face.

As the war in China was prolonged, Japan's economy was put under great strain. In order to secure adequate output of arms, industrial mobilization was undertaken, and the government began to exercise more and more control over the entire economy. Mobilization also occurred on the political front. The parties, as has been indicated, were pushed to the background after the take-over of Manchuria, but they continued to exist and from time to time dared to make guarded criticisms of what the army was trying to do in China and at home. In 1940 the parties were put under pressure to dissolve "voluntarily" and were absorbed into a new organization known as the Imperial Rule Assistance Association (IRAA). Formally organized political parties thus disappeared from the scene.

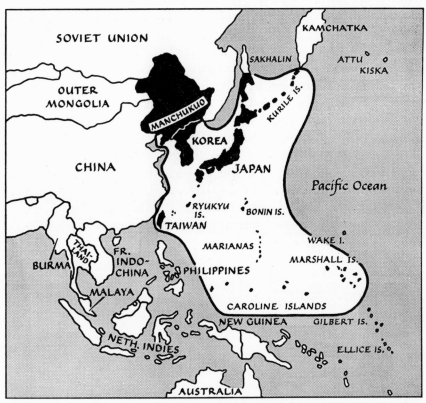

Map 5. The Japanese empire, 1936. (As redrawn from the *New York Times.*)

After Japan's entry into the Second World War, the influence of the military in almost every aspect of life was increased. Japan's initial military victories following the attack on Pearl Harbor, however, apparently generated considerable popular support for the military; but as Japan's fortunes took a turn for the worse, as cities were laid in ruins by bombing attacks, and as severe shortages developed, antagonism toward the military grew.

By 1945 Japan, having fought continuously since 1937, was in no condition to continue the war much longer. It was obvious that Japanese leaders, particularly military leaders, had made fatal miscalculations, but bringing the war to a close was not at all an easy task. There were, however, a few leaders, both civilian and military, who saw that surrender, even unconditional surrender, was preferable to national suicide, and after protracted behind-the-scenes maneuvering they were able to bring about Japan's acceptance of the Potsdam Declaration. Japan, which in less than a century had risen from a small backward nation to a great power, now lay prostrate and faced an uncertain future.

The Allied Occupation of Japan lasted seven years (1945–1952), during which time a host of Occupation-sponsored reforms were attempted. It is interesting to note, however, that in more than one sense the Occupation period was reminiscent of the early years of the Meiji era. First, it was a time when the past stood discredited, when there was widespread willingness to try out new ideas, new institutions, and new ways of doing things. Second, it was, as in the case of the Meiji reforms, a situation in which social change was largely initiated and directed from above. And, third, despite evidence of considerable social change, basic social values and time-honored ways of behavior remained relatively intact.

· IV ·

The Social and

Economic Structure

POLITICAL science is concerned mostly with large and complex associations, such as the state. In this respect it differs from sociology, for example, which is involved more in the study of smaller social groups. It would be unwise, however, for the student of political science to ignore the behavior of man in small groups, or, for that matter, the way in which man creates and distributes goods and services, because both these aspects of social life profoundly affect the character of the state and the distribution of political power within it. The purpose of this chapter is to present a sketch of the social and economic context in which Japanese politics take place.

The Individual and the Group

A common observation in the literature on Japan is that the individual is subordinated to the group. As a general statement this observation is sound. For purposes of political analysis, however, it is useful to go a step farther and inquire into the nature of the group.

First of all, attention should be turned to the family. Everywhere the family plays a vital role in government because, as Professor MacIver says, the family is the "breeding ground of power"; [1] but in Japan the radiating influence of the family extends beyond any-

[1] R. M. MacIver, *The Web of Government* (New York: Macmillan, 1947), ch. ii.

155

thing found in the Western world. In Japan the family rather than the individual was, and is to a considerable extent today, the basic social unit. Very often the Japanese family is larger than the conjugal unit of man and wife and their offspring. It may include, and this is particularly the case in the countryside, the wife and children of the eldest son and his retired father and mother.

When compared to the American family, the Japanese family is as a rule much more closely knit. Emphasis is apt to be put on the welfare of the family as a whole, even if this sometimes involves individual sacrifices. Children are taught to be obedient and respectful, and it used to be said that the obligations which children owe their parents are "deeper than the ocean, higher than the mountain." In important decisions, such as the choice of a vocation or the selection of one's mate, the parents and the other members of the family have much to say. It is generally assumed that sons, particularly eldest sons, have the obligation to support their parents in their old age. Most Japanese value the idea of perpetuating the family line. When a family has no offspring, a distant relative or even someone not kin will generally be adopted, and this person will assume the name of the family into which he has come.

These various obligations binding members of a family are of obvious importance in regulating family life, but they also have, according to some, a wider significance. Many people still believe that filial piety is the basis of all morality. When the postwar constitution, which provides, among other things, for a more democratically oriented family, was being debated in the House of Representatives, a member expressed the view that "after all, I fear that the revision of our Constitution [of 1889] will shake the foundation of the rights of the head of a house and those of parents. What, do you think will follow a revision like this? I fear that this will greatly affect the filial piety which forms the foundation of all morals." The speaker then went on to say that filial piety, which "forms the fundamentals of peace and order in the country," might be destroyed by constitutional revision and that such revision, if not carefully done, "will enable the son to marry a girl against the will of his parents, change his living place, spend money and other property ignoring the wishes of his parents, divorce a respectable wife without the consent of his parents. I fear that these undesirable matters will take place under the new Constitution." [2]

[2] Quoted in Kurt Steiner, "The Revision of the Civil Code in Japan: Provisions Affecting the Family," *Far Eastern Quarterly*, IX (Feb. 1950), 173.

Underlying these fears expressed by the member of the House of Representatives was the assumption that filial piety and political loyalty are fundamentally related. According to the officially prescribed theory of state in the prewar period, the Japanese nation was a large family, headed by the Emperor, who was its patriarchal father. In theory the relationship of the Emperor to his subjects was no different from that of the father to his children. Thus to this very day Japanese of conservative persuasion insist that families must be closely knit by bonds of filial piety and loyalty if the social and political order is to be maintained.

Important as is the family in meeting an individual's social needs, it cannot be all-sufficing. Of necessity families must associate and work with other families. In Japan one finds several or more families coming together to create informal groupings which tend to be hierarchical in structure and relatively long enduring. These informal groupings, which may be looked upon as the "cellular units" of Japanese society, are characterized by face-to-face relationships and a strong sense of personal loyalty among its members. Needless to say, these groupings profoundly affect the values and behavior of its members, for as George Murdock says, "it is mainly through face-to-face relations that a person's behavior is influenced by his fellows— motivated, cued, rewarded, and punished." [3]

The influence of these groupings on the individual is particularly strong in rural areas where many essential tasks are, of necessity, performed through co-operative effort. During the busy season, for instance, families exchange labor, helping each other with transplanting and harvesting. The building and maintenance of roads in the community are done co-operatively. Recreational activities, in the absence of various commercialized forms of recreation, consist of relatives and neighbors getting together to drink, dance, and sing. Families also obtain a kind of social security through the group, for if one's house burns down, or in the case of death in the family, relatives and friends come to render help. There are even forms of co-operative credit where funds are raised to meet emergencies.

The need for co-operation is much less, of course, in urban areas, where life tends to be more impersonal. But even in the cities, there are often informal groupings of kin and nonkin which have the function of providing its members with a sense of security, both psychological and economic, attained through mutual aid.

It is not surprising, given these considerations, that in Japanese

[3] George Peter Murdock, *Social Structure* (New York: Macmillan, 1949), p. 82.

society interpersonal relationships are much more personalized than they are in contemporary America. To be sure, a complex industrialized society such as is found in Japan cannot function without formalized impersonal relationships; yet it is a fact that most Japanese still feel uncomfortable when they cannot deal with their fellow men on a highly personalized basis.

The penchant for personalized relationships has at least two social consequences. First, often the binding cement of many organizations is personal loyalty rather than common objectives, interests, or principles. Since there is a limit to the number of personal ties that individuals can have, such large organizations as political parties and labor unions are almost always torn into factions and cliques, impeding unity and concerted action.

Second, the existence of small cohesive groups has resulted in the growth of what might be called "informal government." There is a tendency to seek solutions to problems within the framework of the small group and to avoid involvement in the formal institutions of government. For example, parties involved in a dispute are likely to avoid taking the case to court and will seek instead settlement within the small group through mediation and compromise.

A particularly important role in "informal government" is played by individuals who belong to certain sections of the middle class in Japan. However, before going into a discussion of this aspect, it is useful to take up the larger question of social stratification.

Social Stratification

Japanese society, like other complex societies, is hierarchical in structure and composed of levels or tiers of social classes. The criteria that go into determining the class to which an individual belongs are varied and, moreover, are changing with the passage of time. In general, education, occupation, income, family lineage, and style of living are important determinants.

Some changes have been produced at the top levels of the social hierarchy as a result of Japan's defeat and subsequent Occupation. As a result of the abolition of the peerage, aristocratic titled families, descended from the old feudal nobility, from the samurai who held important posts in the Meiji government, and from some financial and business families which achieved prominence in the Meiji and Taisho periods, were reduced in prestige and influence. At the same time, government agencies close to the throne, such as the Privy Council, the Imperial Household Ministry, and the Elder Statesmen, and, of course, the House of Peers, through which the nobility had made their power felt, were abolished. Although some of the former peers have found positions in business and government and they still enjoy a vestige of social prestige, it may be said that as a group they are no longer important politically.

Another group that has been removed from the upper levels of the social hierarchy are the top professional soldiers. Many of the officers were of middle-class origin, but had achieved prestige and power when the armed forces were able to push their way into the center of the political stage in the 1930s. As a result of demobilization and the revulsion against militarism, officers lost prestige and status; and although some ex-officers have found posts in business, have been elected to public office, and have become leaders of organizations such as veterans' groups, many have been compelled to take up menial occupations.

The elimination of the nobility and the military has enabled three closely related groups to acquire more power and prestige. They are the top civil servants, leaders of political parties, and executives of large financial institutions and corporations. These social groups have easy access to government bureaus and agencies and are closely allied with the conservative political parties through which they make their political influence felt.

Below the top levels of the social pyramid there is to be found a broad middle class. Compared to the middle class in the United States, the Japanese middle class is proportionately smaller and weaker economically, but undoubtedly it is the most important middle class in all of Asia. For one thing, the growth of capitalist industry has generated the need for occupational skills of all kinds. The complexity of occupations found today is indicated by the fact that a listing of basic occupations published by a Japanese government agency in 1953 contains hundreds of entries.[4]

Among these occupations are those which fall in the white-collar category: professional people such as doctors, writers, and professors; managerial and technical employees in business and government; and clerical workers. As shown in Table 2, a little less than 1 out of 6 in the nation and 3 out of 10 in the big cities are engaged in so-called white-collar occupations.

Another facet of Japanese economic structure worth pointing out is the existence of numerous small "capitalists." Out of a labor force

[4] Gyosei Kanricho, *Nihon Hyojun Sangyo Bunrui* [Standard Classification of Japanese Industries] (Tokyo, 1953).

of 35.5 million in 1950, a little over one-fourth were "self-employed," and an additional one-third were "unpaid family workers." People in these two categories amounted to a little over 11.5 million or about 32 per cent of the total labor force.

Table 2. White-collar workers among gainfully employed, 1950

	National		Six cities	
Occupational groups	Total	%	Total	%
Professional and technicians	1,632,000	4.6	801,000	6.8
Managers and officials	709,000	2.0	440,000	6.0
Clerical and related	3,036,000	8.5	1,784,000	15.2
Total	5,377,000	15.1	3,025,000	28.0

Source: *Japan Statistical Yearbook*, 1951.

The existence of numerous small entrepreneurs is also brought out by classifying establishments in all industries by the size of labor force. An examination of Table 3 shows (1) that establishments employing less than 30 persons accounted for 94.4 per cent of all establishments, but (2) that these establishments were responsible for only 21.7 per cent of the total sales. From the lower part of the table it is found that plants employing 200 or more persons accounted for 0.6 per cent to the total, yet these establishments accounted for 53.1 per cent of the total sales.

These statistics point up the fact that in Japan there are a host of small shops and plants, owned by individuals and operated with

Table 3. Establishments classified by labor force, 1952

No. of operatives	No. of establishments	% of total	% of total sales
Less than 3 persons	230,294	57.8	3.0
4–9 persons	85,439	21.4	5.3
10–19 persons	45,353	11.4	8.0
20–29 persons	15,028	3.8	5.4
30–49 persons	10,837	2.7	7.0
50–99 persons	6,342	1.6	8.9
100–199 persons	2,660	0.7	9.3
200–499 persons	1,625	0.4	15.6
500–999 persons	467	0.1	11.1
1,000 and more persons	358	0.1	26.4
Total	398,403	100.0	100.0

Source: *Kogyo tokei hyo* [Census of Manufactures], vol. I (1952), published by Tsusho Sangyo Daijin Kanbo Chosa Tokeibu.

the help of family labor and a few hired employees. The relationship between employer and employee in these instances is colored by a high degree of paternalism. The employer, like a father, is expected to provide for the welfare of his employee, and the worker is expected not only to perform his tasks but to be loyal and devoted like a son.

As might be surmised, these small enterprises must work with a limited amount of capital, and in many instances they actually operate as subcontractors for large business firms (i.e., the *zaibatsu*). The economic position of small businessmen is usually very precarious because of competition with the large *zaibatsu* firms as well as intense competition among themselves.

Those engaged in white-collar occupations and owners of small enterprises are found everywhere, but they are, of course, proportionately more numerous in the large cities. When attention is turned to the rural areas, the third important component of the Japanese middle class is found, namely, those individuals belonging to the larger landowning families. As a result of the land reform sponsored by the Occupation, the number of those who own land has been increased substantially. Out of a total of a little more than 6 million farm families in 1950, some 3.8 million were "landed" farmers, here defined as those owning 90 per cent or more of the land used for agricultural purposes. It should be added, however, that a little over 70 per cent of all farms were 2.45 acres or less in size. Roughly 1 out of 10 families were operating farms of about 5 acres or more, and these were generally among the top stratum in the rural areas.

Important as it is, property is not the only determinant of social prestige in the farm areas. For a family to enjoy influence, it must be able to claim in addition long residence in the community, good family lineage, education, and connections with local political figures and officials. One may expect to find in every community a few families with these attributes, and these families, even though their members may not hold formal office in local government, are generally consulted on important matters and looked to for local leadership.[5]

The Social Basis of Power

The mode of Japanese politics is affected by its social setting in several ways. As has been indicated, the choice left to the individual

[5] For a more detailed treatment of the social and economic structure see Nobutaka Ike, *Japanese Politics: An Introductory Survey* (New York: Knopf, 1957), chs. ii, v–vii.

is generally highly circumscribed. What a man or woman thinks and, perhaps even more important, how he or she acts both socially and politically are often determined by the social groups to which the individual belongs. Of these groups the family continues to be influential and probably serves as one of the main channels for the transmission of traditional political ideas emphasizing hierarchy and obedience to commands from above. The informal groupings of several or more families bound together by a strong sense of personal loyalty also appear to be instrumental in determining political attitudes and behavior. It is to these groups that an individual turns when he needs guidance or assistance, and this tendency to seek solutions to personal and social problems within the framework of small groups leads to what one might call "informal government."

Among those who often exercise leadership in "informal government" are individuals (and their families) who own property and have some economic reserves, such as owners of small commercial and industrial enterprises and rural landowners. These people make their influence felt partly through economic levers, for example, their position as employers or suppliers of credit, and partly through the social prestige they have in their communities. Other people also playing a part in "informal government" are schoolteachers and priests, who are respected for their specialized training, and such individuals as foremen in factories who are in a position to supervise and train those under them. In terms of political ideology, "informal government" is, of course, tradition-oriented. It rests on the continued acceptance of social hierarchy, authoritarianism, and paternalism, and it represents the carry-over into the twentieth century of older forms of social and political organization. "Informal government" therefore stands on the side of conservatism.

The chief challenge to conservatism comes from urban areas, which have grown tremendously in size since the Meiji Restoration. The city, the university, the office, and the factory represent sources of new ideas and new types of social organization. It is in the city and among the educated that Western influences have been most strongly felt. In the city also more impersonal and formalized social relationships occur with greater frequency. And since the socialist party and the socialist movement essentially represent a break with tradition, it is not surprising that socialists seek and secure support from those urbanized elements of the population most subject to social change.

· V ·

Governmental Organization:

Past and Present

THE organization of government as defined in the constitution and other basic laws reveals something of the allocation of formal authority, the rules governing policy making and execution, the definition of what constitutes legitimate acts of government, and the goals implicit in the constitutional structure. Admittedly, the formal structure seldom gives a complete picture of how a political system works in practice; nevertheless, it does serve as a convenient starting point for an analysis of that system.

The Constitution

THE PREWAR CONSTITUTION

The constitution of 1889 was promulgated by the Emperor as a "gift" to the people. It was issued in response to a popular movement which demanded the adoption of a written constitution and the establishment of a parliament. However, since individuals and groups outside of the government were not consulted during the drafting process, the finished document made little provision for popular control of the government.

The constitution set forth the principle of imperial rule. Thus it was proclaimed in the preamble: "The rights of sovereignty of the state, We [the Emperor] have inherited from our Ancestors, and We shall bequeath them to Our descendants. Neither We nor they shall in future fail to wield them, in accordance with the provisions of the Constitution hereby granted."

Although the constitution established executive, legislative, and judicial departments, there was a high degree of centralization since each of these departments was, in theory, responsible to the Emperor. According to the constitution, "the Emperor exercises the legislative power with the consent of the Imperial Diet"; "the respective Ministers of State shall give their advice to the Emperor, and be responsible for it," and "the Judicature shall be exercised by the Courts of Law according to law, in the name of the Emperor."

In Chapter II entitled "Rights and Duties of Subjects," a series of rights, such as the freedom of religious belief and the liberty of speech, writing, publications, and assembly, were enunciated; but in almost every instance these rights were qualified by such phrases as "within the limits of law" and "except in cases provided for in the law."

In the constitution there was provided no agency to interpret that instrument. In practice it was interpreted by the courts and in some instances by the Privy Council. Amendments to the constitution were to be made only at the initiative of the Emperor. It was necessary that at least two-thirds of the members of each house of the Imperial Diet be present to discuss the proposed amendment; and at least two-thirds of those present had to approve before it could become effective. The fact should be noted that the constitution was never amended.

The Imperial House Law, promulgated at the same time as the constitution, was second in importance only to the constitution. This law, which regulated succession and administration of the imperial family, was deemed to be superior to ordinary legislation and not subject to change by the Imperial Diet. It was to be amended only "by the Emperor, with the advice of the Imperial Family Council and with that of the Privy Council."

THE POSTWAR CONSTITUTION

The theory of imperial rule enunciated in the Meiji constitution was clearly not conducive to democratic rule; and since the prime objective of the Allied Occupation was to destroy Japanese militarism and to remake Japan into a democratic nation, it is not surprising that early attention was given to constitutional reform. During the first months of the Occupation, the Japanese government, on several occasions, was told by General MacArthur of the need for revising the constitution. As a consequence the Japanese government established a committee to study the constitutional problem, and after several months of work this committee completed a draft. This draft made clear that the committee was intent on retaining the basic philosophy of the old constitution and was not disposed to making radical changes; and so it was rejected. The Government Section of MacArthur's headquarters therefore set to work and quickly completed a draft in English. When this document was transmitted to the Japanese government, those in charge were taken aback; however, they realized that they had no alternative but to accede to the wishes of the Occupation authorities. Publicly both sides maintained the fiction that the proposed constitution was a Japanese document. The draft was approved by the cabinet, and after some revision it was submitted to the Diet, where it was debated, amended in certain minor respects, and approved. It became effective on May 3, 1947.

The underlying philosophy of the Meiji constitution and the postwar constitution is vastly different. In keeping with its American origin, the new constitution bears the unmistakable impress of Western liberal thought. The preamble proclaims:

We, the Japanese people, acting through our duly elected representatives in the National Diet, determined that we shall secure for ourselves and our posterity the fruits of peaceful cooperation with all nations and the blessings of liberty throughout this land, and resolved that never again shall we be visited with the horrors of war through the action of government, do proclaim that sovereign power resides with the people and do firmly establish this Constitution.

Quite clearly the theory of imperial rule has been replaced by the doctrine of popular sovereignty.

Another conspicuous feature of the new constitution is the emphasis on civil liberties. Thirty-one articles, out of a total of 103, are contained in Chapter III which is devoted to "Rights and Duties of the People." Article 11 states, "The people shall not be prevented from enjoying any of the fundamental human rights. These fundamental human rights guaranteed to the people by this Constitution shall be conferred upon the people of this and future generations as eternal and inviolate rights." A long series of rights are enumerated: the "right to life, liberty, and the pursuit of happiness," equality under the law, the right to choose public officials, secrecy of the ballot, right of peaceful petition, the right to sue the state or public officials, freedom of thought and conscience, of religion, of assembly and association, of speech and press, academic freedom, equality of the sexes with reference to property rights, choice of spouse, and other matters, the right to "maintain the minimum standards of wholesome and cultural living," the right and obligation to work, the right of workers to organize and bargain collectively, and the right of access to the courts. Protection is also afforded the individual with reference to search and seizure, arrest and detention, the infliction of torture, and being compelled to testify against himself.

A unique feature of the new constitution is Article 9, which has subsequently become a matter of considerable controversy. It reads:

Aspiring sincerely to an international peace based on justice and order, the Japanese people forever renounce war as a sovereign right of the nation and the threat or use of force as a means of settling international disputes.

In order to accomplish the aim of the preceding paragraph, land, sea, and air forces, as well as other war potential, will never be maintained. The rights of belligerency of the state will not be recognized.

The power to interpret the constitution is placed in the Supreme Court, which as a court of last resort determines the "constitutionality of any law, order, regulation or official act." Amendments to the constitution are to be initiated by the Diet, and an affirmative vote of two-thirds or more of all the members of each house is required. The amendment must then be ratified by a majority of all votes cast in a special referendum. Other matters prescribed in the constitution relate to the Emperor, the Diet, the cabinet, the judiciary, finance, local self-government, and the supreme law and supplementary provisions.

Given the circumstances surrounding the drafting and adoption of the constitution, the question remains whether it is likely to become rooted in Japanese political life. Conservatives have openly expressed their desire to amend the present constitution in order to strengthen the position of the Emperor and the cabinet and generally to return, although not all the way, to the old constiution. Liberals and socialists, on the other hand, have supported the constitution and even have argued in favor of strengthening portions of it such as the section on

Chart 3. Structure of the present Japanese government

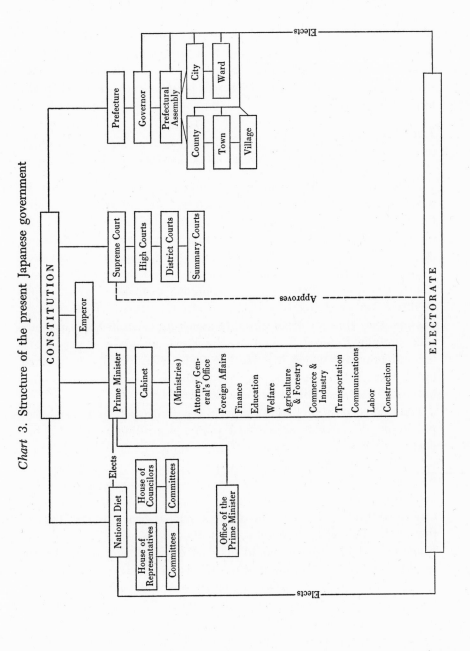

civil liberties. In view of the lack of consensus on this problem and the necessity of obtaining, in order to amend the constitution, a two-thirds majority in the Diet and a majority of the popular vote, it would seem unlikely that the constitution will be drastically changed in the foreseeable future.

The Emperor

THE EMPEROR AS A SYMBOL

From the functional point of view the Japanese Emperor has, in modern times, served as a symbol of national and cultural unity. Since the end of the Tokugawa period, Japanese leaders have used the throne as a counterpoise to decentralizing tendencies and in so doing have developed a kind of Emperor cult. The Emperor, pictured as heaven-descended, divine, sacred, all-wise, and virtuous, was set apart from the nation, and people were forbidden to make of him a topic of discussion or derogatory comment. In the words of Sir George Sansom, the "concept of an absolute monarch, venerated and remote, was carefully fostered throughout the Meiji period by a process of indoctrination for which it is hard to find a close parallel in modern times, though the mass propaganda methods of authoritarian states in recent years resemble it in some respects." [1]

The exalted position of the Emperor was buttressed by the political philosophy of *kokutai* or national polity. According to the *kokutai* doctrine, the Japanese nation is a large family ruled by the Emperor who is its patriarchal father. Consequently, the relationship between the sovereign and his subjects was said to be similar to that existing between father and son, so that filial piety and political loyalty were conceived to be one and the same thing. It was unthinkable, to those who believed in *kokutai,* that the relationship between the Emperor and his subjects could ever be changed, any more than it would be possible for father and son to switch places.

Yet according to the postwar constitutional theory this has happened. Article 1 of the new constitution states, "The Emperor shall be the symbol of the State and of the unity of the people, deriving his position from the will of the people with whom resides sovereign power." The people are now sovereign, and the Emperor derives his position from their will.

[1] George B. Sansom, *The Western World and Japan* (New York: Knopf, 1950), p. 356.

As a result of the shift in the Emperor's constitutional position, at least two important changes have occurred. First, a considerable portion of the taboos which shrouded the imperial institution have been removed. It has become possible to discuss and write openly about the Emperor, both as a person and as an institution, even in a critical vein, without the risk of public censure or arrest. When the Emperor was prevented by his court chamberlains from attending the funeral of his brother, Prince Chichibu, in January 1953, presumably because this would have constituted a departure from tradition, the press condemned this action in no uncertain terms. Such press comments would have been inconceivable before the war.

Second, concerted attempts have been made to "humanize" the Emperor. Previously he had been so exalted that his subjects were required to bow their heads and not to look at his personage when he passed by. After the end of the war, however, the Emperor made many personal appearances, visiting farms, factories, and schools and even attending movie theaters and baseball games. Newspapers and magazines printed stories and pictures to show the daily life of the imperial household, and stories were told of how the Emperor had reduced his standard of living and simplified his daily life in order to share hardships with his subjects.

Prior to the war, many conservatives believed that any tampering with the myth of the Emperor as the exalted father of the nation would weaken the cement holding society together and would lead to social chaos. So far, at least, the conservatives have been proved wrong. Public opinion polls and other surveys, although they are not conclusive, would seem to indicate that the Emperor still enjoys considerable popularity and support, especially among the rural inhabitants and the older segment of the population. The following comment by a 42-year-old lawyer may be regarded as fairly typical:

It is sheer nonsense to think that we ever believed that the Emperor was a real god. I respect him and I support him absolutely as a human being. This is a feeling that is strong within me and one that I am unable to eradicate. I do not support the Emperor as a symbol of Japan, but I do support him completely as the sovereign of our nation. Personally, I think that the word "symbol" is too vague a term to be understood by the people. I feel toward the Emperor much the same deep attachment that a child feels toward its parents.[2]

[2] Quoted in Hugh H. Smythe and Masaharu Watanabe, "Japanese Popular Attitudes toward the Emperor," *Pacific Affairs*, XXVI (Dec. 1953), 341.

THE POLITICAL ROLE OF THE EMPEROR

One reason for the remarkable capacity of the imperial house to survive the vicissitudes of history from the early period down to the present is its noninvolvment in the give-and-take of politics. The political role of the Emperor has been to serve as a symbol, but not to participate in an active way in the formulation and execution of policy. The diaries and other accounts of those individuals close to the throne which have been recently published suggest that the Emperor on occasion asked pointed questions of his ministers and advisers, but seldom if ever took a position contrary to that suggested by them. Clearly the Emperor's role was to give the stamp of formal approval to decisions arrived at by others.

It goes without saying that the Emperor provided a rather convenient shield for the small group which ruled in his name. The Emperor, according to the Meiji constitution, acted on the advice of his ministers, but since the ministers were responsible to the Emperor, they were, in effect, responsible to no one. There were important agencies such as the Imperial Household Ministry, the Privy Council, and the Supreme War Council, the legitimacy of whose actions could not be questioned because of their intimate relation to the throne.

The constitutional position of the Emperor has changed considerably in the postwar period. He is no longer the source of all authority, political and moral; he has been reduced to a "symbol," and sovereignty is now deemed to lie in the people. He has certain ceremonial functions under the constitution, but he has no "powers related to government." Because even before the war the Emperor never took part in political decisions, his present role remains substantially unchanged. The important difference, however, lies in the fact that it is no longer possible for his ministers and advisers to rule in his name. The lines of responsibility are now much more clearly drawn.

The Diet

THE IMPERIAL DIET

Japan has the longest history of parliamentary government in all of Asia. The Imperial Diet, composed of the House of Peers and the House of Representatives, was created in 1890, as a result of a popular movement extending over several decades which called for the establishment of parliamentary government.

The House of Peers was composed of princes of the blood; princes and marquis; counts, viscounts, and barons, elected from among their respective orders for seven-year terms; imperial appointees for life, selected for special service to the state or for distinguished scholarship; representatives of the Imperial Academy; and representatives elected from and by the highest taxpayers of each prefecture. The membership numbered about 400 in the 1930s, having grown by about a hundred since its establishment. It was natural, given its make-up, that the House of Peers was highly conservative; and since its powers were equal to that of the House of Representatives, it served for decades as a bulwark against popular control of the government.

In the beginning the House of Representatives was composed of 300 members, elected for a four-year term and chosen by voters who paid 15 yen or more in direct taxes. Because of the tax qualification, the landed interest was heavily represented in the lower house. With the passage of years, the membership was increased, and tax qualifications were reduced. In 1925 a universal manhood suffrage law was enacted, and under this law the size was set at 466 members. As the size of the electorate was expanded, the proportion of representatives with a background in business, industry, and law was increased substantially, whereas the number of agriculturalists declined.

The relative shortness of its sessions was indicative of the lack of power of the House of Representatives. It was generally convoked every year late in December by the Emperor, and after a recess over the New Year's holidays, it was reconvened, remaining in session until the end of March. The Emperor had the power to prorogue the Diet, but not for more than 15 days at a time, and to dissolve the Diet. In case of dissolution, a new lower house had to be convened within 5 months.

When a bill was passed by a majority of the two houses and approved by the Emperor, it became law. Bills were introduced both by the government and by members, but most legislation was government-sponsored. When a bill was passed by one house, it was sent to the other; and in case one house amended the other's bill and the amendment was not acceptable, it was referred to a committee composed of an equal number of members from each house.

Under the constitution of 1889, the government was empowered in cases of emergency to issue imperial ordinances, but Diet approval in the following session was required if such ordinances were to remain in effect. The approval of the Diet was also necessary in order to amend the constitution; but no amendments were ever made.

A serious weakness of the House of Representatives was its lack of power to exercise firm control over finances. For instance, it had no control over items in the budget for "ordinary expenditures required by the organization of the different branches of the administration and by that of the army and navy, the salaries of all civil and military officers, and expenditures that may be required in consequence of treaties concluded with foreign countries." [3] Moreover, the lower house had no control over expenditures necessitated by the legal obligations of the government, and the expenditures of the imperial household. Finally, in the event that parliament failed to pass a budget bill, the government was authorized under the constitution to "carry out the budget of the preceding year." Thus it is clear that although the prewar Diet could, if it so desired, check the actions of the executive, delay matters, and appeal to public opinion by voicing criticisms of policy, its power was greatly circumscribed.

NATIONAL DIET: ORGANIZATION

The new Diet, established under the constitution of 1947, differs substantially from its predecessor. The intent of the American framers of the constitution was to make the National Diet the core of the government. "The Diet," states the constitution, "shall be the highest organ of state power, and shall be the sole law-making organ of the State."

The present Diet consists of two houses, the House of Representatives and the House of Councilors.

The House of Representatives presently consists of 467 members elected from 118 electoral districts. Each district is represented by 3 to 5 members, but each voter casts his ballot for only one candidate. Members are elected for four-year terms, but the lower house may be dissolved, in which case a new election must be held within 40 days.

The House of Councilors, which replaced the House of Peers, consists of 250 members, 150 of whom are elected from the prefectures and 100 from the nation at large. Each voter casts two votes, one for the prefectural candidate and another for the national candidate. The

[3] Harold S. Quigley, *Japanese Government and Politics* (New York: Century, 1932), pp. 188–189.

members of the House of Councilors, which cannot be dissolved, are chosen for six-year terms, with one-half the membership standing election every three years.

Of the two houses, the House of Representatives is more powerful. All money bills must originate in the House of Representatives. A bill passed by the lower house but voted down by the House of Councilors can become law if it is repassed by the House of Representatives by a majority of two-thirds or more of the members present.

An important innovation is the creation of a standing-committee system. The prewar Diet had 4 or 5 standing committees, but much of the work was done by each house sitting as a committee of the whole. In the National Diet there are some 15 standing committees, one for each major field of legislation, such as foreign affairs, budget, education, labor, agriculture, commerce, transportation, audit, and so on, plus a disciplinary committee and a ways and means committee. Each member of the Diet must be appointed to at least one committee, but no more than three. Committee membership and the chairmanship of committees are allocated on the basis of party strength. From time to time special committees are appointed to deal with problems that cannot be dealt with effectively by the standing committees.

Much of the work of the National Diet is handled by the committees. They deliberate on legislative proposals, and the fate of these proposals is usually determined by their action. As a part of their deliberations on a measure, committees hold public hearings to which witnesses are summoned. Interested individuals and representatives of organizations affected by pending legislation can also appear to make known their views.

Unlike its predecessor, the postwar Diet is empowered to investigate the activities of the executive branch. A special committee on illegal disposal of government property, for example, undertook a lengthy probe of the disappearance of millions of dollars of government property shortly after the surrender. Other committees have looked into such matters as corruption in government and the operations of government agencies.

As is true of other reforms, criticisms have been leveled at the newly created committee system. A common complaint is that committees tend to develop close ties with the ministry whose field of interest is related to it, for example, the agricultural committee and the Ministry of Agriculture and Forestry, and that such ties encourage committees to become special pleaders for the ministries and their clientele.

There are several ways in which the National Diet can exercise authority over the executive branch. First of all, it is the National Diet, rather than the Emperor, who designates the Prime Minister. Moreover, the Diet can force the resignation of the cabinet, or of a cabinet member, by passing a no-confidence resolution. Unlike the prewar Diet, the present Diet enjoys the power of the purse. The budget, submitted by the cabinet, must be passed by the Diet. The Diet also has the power to tax, for no national taxes may be levied or a change made without its approval. The Diet can also exercise control over the conduct of foreign relations through its power to ratify or reject treaties concluded by the cabinet. The power to investigate the conduct of executive agencies has already been mentioned. Finally, the Diet has the authority to impeach judges, by establishing an impeachment court consisting of an equal number of members from each house. Thus it is clear that the powers of the Diet are extensive and go beyond purely legislative matters.

The Cabinet

THE PREWAR CABINET

The cabinet system was established by imperial ordinance in 1885, four years before the promulgation of the constitution. The cabinet, therefore, preceded the creation of the Diet.

The cabinet was not mentioned in the Meiji constitution and therefore was an extraconstitutional body. The constitution provided, however, that the "Ministers of State shall give their advice to the Emperor, and be responsible for it." In constitutional theory, therefore, the cabinet as a body was not responsible collectively to the Emperor. Moreover, since the responsibility of the ministers was upward to the Emperor, the cabinet ministers were very often not even members of the majority party in the Diet.

The Prime Minister was chosen by the Emperor upon the recommendation of his advisers, which included the Elder Statesmen, the Lord Keeper of the Privy Seal, the Minister of the Imperial Household, and others. In the 1920s, the heyday of party government, the leader of the majority party was often named Prime Minister; but if the history of the cabinet between 1885 and 1945 is taken as a whole, it must be said that party cabinets were the exception rather than the rule.

The person designated as Prime Minister selected his ministers, taking into account various factors such as factions within parties, the wishes of the oligarchy, and the views of the armed forces. It was required by custom and law that the Minister of War and the Minister of Navy be career officers of the rank of lieutenant-general or vice-admiral or higher. Since these ministers were chosen by the Prime Minister but appointed by the Emperor on the recommendation of the leading figures in the army and navy, the armed forces were able, if they so desired, to prevent a cabinet from being formed by refusing to nominate a minister or to force the resignation of a cabinet by withdrawing a minister.

There were other ways in which cabinets could fall. Although the cabinet was not responsible to the Diet, severe attacks in the Diet forced the Prime Minister either to dissolve the lower house or to resign. Public criticism of policy, leading to riots and other disturbances, and quarrels with the Privy Council or the House of Peers usually led to resignation. Three cabinets had the support of an absolute majority in the House of Representatives, and in these three instances the prime ministers became targets of assassins, leading to their downfall. An important cause of resignation of cabinets was internal dissension. Although in practice the Prime Minister usually controlled his cabinet, he had no clear-cut authority over his colleagues, for in legal theory the ministers were responsible to the Emperor and not to him.

The power of the prewar cabinet, therefore, was greatly circumscribed both in theory and in practice. Nevertheless, of all the organs of government the cabinet was perhaps most consistently in the public eye; and almost all political figures came to consider appointment as Prime Minister, or even as a cabinet minister, the crowning achievement of their careers.

THE POSTWAR CABINET

The postwar cabinet is markedly different from its prewar predecessor. The new constitution states that "executive power shall be vested in the Cabinet," and it lists its functions in considerable detail. According to the provisions of the constitution the cabinet submits bills, including an annual budget, to the Diet, negotiates and concludes treaties, and in general conducts foreign relations, decides on amnesty, commutation of punishment, and so on, administers the law, directs the civil service, exercises control over the administrative branches of the government, designates the Chief Justice of the Supreme Court and appoints other judges, and issues cabinet orders to carry out the constitution and other laws.

Unlike the prewar cabinet which could function fairly independently of the Diet, the present cabinet is related closely to the legislature. First of all, the Prime Minister is designated from among its members by the National Diet. Although the Prime Minister is empowered by the constitution to appoint and dismiss his ministers, there is a provision that ministers must be civilians and that the majority of ministers must be members of the Diet.

In addition the cabinet is required to report to the Diet on the state of national affairs and foreign relations and on the state of national finances and submit final accounts of expenditures and revenues. The cabinet has the power to dissolve the House of Representatives and to call the House of Councilors in emergency session when the House of Representatives has been dissolved.

In terms of the legal structure, the cabinet would appear to be inferior to the National Diet. In practice, however, it is the cabinet which formulates the legislative program and guides its enactment into law, particularly when the cabinet is backed by a solid majority in the lower house.

To assist the work of the cabinet, there is a Prime Minister's secretariat, headed by a director and two deputy directors. The secretariat arranges the agenda of cabinet meetings, prepares documents, and handles other business matters. Cabinet meetings, which ordinarily take place on Tuesday and Friday mornings in the Prime Minister's official residence, are presided over by the Prime Minister, but in his absence the Vice-Premier takes over the chair. There is no quorum; if decisions are made by a minority of the members, those who were absent may be later asked to sign the documents. Cabinet discussions are secret, and minutes are not published. Cabinet members are warned not to divulge what has transpired, but leaks to the press are not entirely unknown. The section of Article 66 of the constitution which states that "the Cabinet, in the exercise of executive power, shall be collectively responsible to the Diet" is interpreted to mean that cabinet decisions must be unanimous. There have been instances in which ministers have resigned because they could not agree with their colleagues.

A cabinet can stay in power so long as it has the support of the majority of members of the lower house. When it loses such support, however, and the House of Representatives passes a no-confidence resolution or rejects a confidence resolution, the cabinet must either dissolve the lower house within ten days or resign. In the latter event, the presiding officers of both houses are notified in writing by the cabinet, whereupon the Diet begins the process of choosing a new Prime Minister.

The Civil Service

The day-to-day work of the government, whose scope and functions are ever-increasing, falls largely on the thousands of civil servants who staff the ministries and agencies. The average citizen in his relationship with the government comes into contact with the civil servant, and so for him the government is in many ways synonymous with the government official. The bureaucracy of any modern state, therefore, may be regarded as the core of government.

THE PREWAR CIVIL SERVICE

In the early years of the Meiji era, government personnel was drawn largely from the old samurai class and particularly from the geographical areas in western Japan that had provided the leadership of the Restoration movement. But with the passage of years the feeling spread that appointments went to friends of those already in the government and that able men were being kept out of public office. Accordingly, in 1885 the foundations of a modern civil service were laid with the adoption of the principle that appointments to government posts should be based on examinations. The first examinations were held in 1887 for officials of the second and third rank, the first-rank officials being exempt.

The prewar civil service was divided into the higher civil service and the ordinary civil service. Each division was subdivided. The higher civil service consisted of first-rank (*shinnin*) officials, that is, cabinet ministers, ambassadors, highest judicial officers; second-rank (*chokunin*) officials, such as vice-ministers, bureau chiefs, and judges; and third-rank (*sonin*) officials, who held lower-level posts. The higher civil service accounted for less than 5 per cent of the posts in the government. The ordinary civil service consisted of fourth-rank (*hanin*) officials and unclassified (*yatoi*) officials. Between three-fifths and three-fourths of the civil servants were unclassified officials.

Except for technicians, members of the higher civil service were recruited through competitive examinations given anuually in Tokyo. The examinations, largely legal in character, were controlled by a committee, consisting mostly of the members of the law faculty of Tokyo Imperial University, the leading government-supported university which was originally established to train government officials. Those who passed, and they were relatively few in proportion to those who took the examinations, were put on an eligible list from which appointments were made. In making appointments, according to one account, "sons or brothers of leading officials or of those who had influence with the officials received preferential treatment. Letters of recommendation from prominent persons were presented in support of applications, and not infrequently a candidate resorted to the giving of gifts." [4] In the competition for bureaucratic posts, graduates of the Tokyo Imperial University had tremendous advantages, and the higher civil service came to be dominated by men from this university.

The examinations for the ordinary civil service were geared for high school graduates and were given in various localities. Those in the ordinary civil service carried on much of the day-to-day work of administration, but they lacked the prestige and status accorded those in the higher civil service. Officials in the ordinary civil service were seldom promoted to the higher civil service.

In other words, a strong sense of hierarchy pervaded the Japanese civil service. It is said that those who belonged to the higher civil service ate in separate dining rooms; and status within the hierarchy was symbolized by the kind of desk one had and by the number of book shelves and chairs for guests one had in his office.

There was also considerable jealousy among various bureaus, agencies, and ministries, and each was sensitive about its prerogatives. Proposals which required the consent and co-operation of several ministries were often held up. Another result was unnecessary duplication of work. For instance, information and documents assembled by one agency were seldom made available to another agency, so that several agencies were sometimes engaged in collecting similar data.

In its dealings with the public the Japanese bureaucracy acquired the reputation of being arrogant and overbearing. Officials were, in

[4] Maynard Shirven and Joseph L. Speicher, "Examination of Japan's Upper Bureaucracy," *Personnel Administration*, July 1951, p. 49.

theory, responsible to the Emperor, and therefore each official was vested with a segment of imperial authority. In functions at the imperial court, for example, a first-rank official was considered equal to the president of the House of Peers and the Speaker of the House of Representatives, and a second-rank official ranked with the vice-president of the House of Peers and the Vice-Speaker of the lower house. Since officials were deemed to be responsible to the Emperor and not the public, officialdom was never very much concerned with the matter of public relations.

THE POSTWAR CIVIL SERVICE

Of all the branches of the Japanese government, the civil service was probably the least affected by Occupation-sponsored reforms. This resulted partly from the fact that the Occupation avoided direct military government and instead worked through the existing Japanese government and partly from the fact that the bureaucracy was strongly entrenched, making reforms difficult.

This is not to say that no reforms were attempted. On the contrary, considerable changes were made in the institutional structure of the bureaucracy. Late in 1946, the United States Personnel Advisory Mission was sent to Japan to look into the existing system, and in line with its subsequent recommendations a National Public Service Law, providing for service-wide standards of personnel administration, was enacted by the Diet in 1947; and in 1949 a National Personnel Authority, charged with the responsibility of introducing democratic methods, providing scientific personnel management, and creating a job classification system, was established. Moreover, certain provisions affecting public officials were written into the new constitution. Thus Article 15 states in part that "all public officials are servants of the whole community and not any group thereof," and Article 17 provides that "every person may sue for redress as provided by law from the State or a public entity, in case he has suffered damage through illegal act of any public official."

It is doubtful, however, despite these institutional changes, that the Japanese bureaucracy has been altered in its basic orientation. To be sure, graduates from other universities are getting posts in the civil service in larger numbers than formerly; but graduates of the old Tokyo Imperial University are still predominant in many ministries. Since its establishment the power of the National Personnel Authority has been whittled away, and it may eventually lose its status as an independent agency. Despite the new constitution, the Japanese bureaucracy continues to be officious and given to feelings of self-importance.

The Judiciary

THE PREWAR JUDICIAL SYSTEM

The judicial system adopted in the Meiji era was based on French and German models, with modifications to allow for Japanese conditions. The prewar legal system, therefore, was largely Continental, rather than Anglo-Saxon, in outlook.

Before the war, the judiciary was subordinated to the executive. Court administration was under the direct control of the Ministry of Justice; and certain limitations were placed on the power of the courts. The courts had no authority to rule on the constitutionality of laws, nor were they empowered to pass judgment in disputes between the government and citizens.

At the top of the court structure was the Supreme Court, which met in Tokyo. The Supreme Court, consisting of 45 justices, carried on its work in divisions composed of 5 justices each. The Supreme Court heard appeals from the courts of appeals and had exclusive jurisdiction over cases of treason and serious offenses against the imperial family.

Below the Supreme Court were high courts, one in each of the seven districts into which the country was divided. The high courts handled appeals from the lower courts. There were some 50 district courts, at least one being located in each prefecture which had jurisdiction in more serious civil and criminal cases. At the lowest level there were a little under 300 local courts in which minor cases were tried.

In addition to the ordinary courts there was the court of administrative litigation, modeled after the *cours administratives* in Germany and Austria. The administrative court was established on the theory that administrators would be inferior to the judiciary if ordinary courts were permitted to rule on the legality of administrative acts. The court of administrative litigation had authority in such matters as tax cases, disputes over the granting of licenses, cases concerning public works, disputes over boundaries between public and private lands, and cases arising out of police administration.

THE POSTWAR JUDICIAL SYSTEM

Occupation-sponsored reforms in the judicial system were extensive and ranged from changes in the structure of courts and judicial procedure to changes in the underlying philosophy of law and jurisprudence. It is perhaps not surprising, given the nature of the Occupation, that many ideas and practices of Anglo-Saxon origin were incorporated into the judicial system, thereby changing its orientation which was formerly predominantly Continental.

Under the provisions of the new constitution as well as legislation affecting the judicial branch, the courts were made independent of both the executive and the legislature. The Supreme Court, rather than the Ministry of Justice, was placed in charge of the administration of the court system. The separate administrative tribunal was abolished, and all judicial disputes were put under the jurisdiction of the ordinary courts. The courts, moreover, were given the power to pass on the constitutionality of all legislation and administrative action, provided the issue was embodied in a concrete suit of law.

The new Supreme Court consists of 15 justices, 10 of whom must have had long experience in the legal profession. The Chief Justice is appointed by the Emperor upon nomination by the cabinet, and the associate justices are appointed by the cabinet and "attested" by the Emperor. After their appointment, all justices must be approved by the electorate at the first general election of the House of Representatives following their appointment, and they must undergo similar popular review every ten years thereafter. So far in three elections between 1949 and 1955 no Supreme Court justice has been rejected.

The work of the Supreme Court is limited to appeal cases requiring a review of the issues of law. An interesting innovation in procedure is the provision for dissenting opinions. A few cases involving the constitutionality of law or administrative action have come before the Supreme Court. As of the middle of 1957, the court had yet to rule a statute unconstitutional.

Below the Supreme Court there are 8 high courts, which hear appeals from decisions of lower courts. Then there are 49 district courts, which have original jurisdiction over serious crimes and civil suits involving large sums and appellate jurisdiction over cases appealed from the summary courts. The summary courts, numbering 570 and located in principal cities, towns, and villages, try comparatively mild civil and criminal cases. In addition there are 49 family courts, which handle cases involving domestic relations and juvenile delinquency.

Except for the possible removal of Supreme Court justices through a plebiscite, judges enjoy tenure and may not be removed from office except through action taken by the impeachment court, consisting of 14 members, elected equally from the two houses of the National Diet. Reasons for impeachment include neglect of duty and conduct impairing the dignity of the court.

Court procedure in criminal cases has been modified to give more weight to the rights of the individual. Before the war, those accused of crime underwent a preliminary examination by means of questions from the bench in a closed court without the presence of a lawyer. A confession, often extorted by the use of third-degree methods, carried great weight, and in the formal trial the accused had no right to cross-examine witnesses. Moreover, the principle of habeas corpus was not recognized in Japanese law before the war.

As a result of the new constitution and the new code of criminal procedure, the preliminary examination system has been abolished, the cross-examination of witnesses is permitted, and no person may be compelled to give testimony against himself. Confession extracted by torture is not supposed to be accepted as evidence, and the court cannot convict the accused if his confession is the only evidence against him. Finally, the constitution provides that "no person shall be arrested or detained without being at once informed of the charges against him or without the immediate privilege of counsel."

Undoubtedly the intent of the Occupation reformers was to make the judiciary the guardian of the constitution and of human rights by elevating its status and by breathing into it a new philosophy. But in the last analysis, the effectiveness of the courts is dependent only partly on their ability to perform their functions. Popular attitudes toward law and legal institutions must also be taken into account. Here is encountered the unmistakable fact that traditionally people were reluctant to appeal to the courts for the adjudication of disputes and the redress of wrongs and preferred to resort to informal methods of mediation. To be sure, there is a tendency in recent years for more people to take cases to the courts, and organizations such as the Japanese Civil Liberties Committee have taken the lead in getting court action against violations of civil liberties. Nevertheless, it is still true that courts play a relatively minor role. Perhaps the most eloquent testimony is the fact that there are less than 6,000 practicing lawyers out of a total population of some 90 million.

Local Government

PREWAR LOCAL GOVERNMENT

The prewar system of local government originated shortly after the Meiji Restoration when the 250-odd feudal fiefs were consolidated and replaced by prefectures. In this period, too, many new towns and villages were artificially created by government action through the amalgamation of existing towns and villages which had functioned as natural social units. In 1889 and 1890, on the eve of the convocation of the first Imperial Diet, several basic laws pertaining to local government were promulgated in order to prevent the Diet from sharing in the formation of the system of local government.

As may be inferred from this action, the basic philosophy of the Meiji oligarchs was to prevent popular control of local government and to centralize in Tokyo power over local government affairs. A stream of administrative orders flowed from Tokyo to the prefectures. The control of the police and of education was also placed in the hands of the central government. The Ministry of Home Affairs was the most important agency through which central control was exercised. The Home Minister, for example, enjoyed the power to appoint the governor of each prefecture (in 1945 there were 46 prefectures plus Hokkaido and Tokyo-to). Although there was in each prefecture a popularly elected assembly empowered to deliberate and vote on the budget, prefectural taxes, public property, and related matters, the power of the assembly was in fact advisory since the governor either dominated the assembly or could by-pass it if it refused to accede to his wishes.

In the beginning, mayors of towns and cities were selected by the Ministry of Home Affairs, but with the spread of democratic ideals in the 1920s the mayor and his deputies came to be chosen by municipal assemblies. The assemblies, consisting of about 30 members or more, were elected for four-year terms and met about once a month. More frequent meetings were held by the municipal council, made up of 10 to 15 assemblymen elected by the assembly.

There seemed to be a possibility that in the 1920s more local autonomy would be granted, even leading to the popular election of governors; but with the rise of the military to power in the 1930s the trend was reversed, and during the war local government saw its most centralized form with the creation of regional administrative councils and later of regional superintendencies-general, both of which were supraprefectural organizations consisting of prefectural governors, chiefs of police, and other officials.

POSTWAR LOCAL GOVERNMENT

The Occupation authorities believed that the task of democratizing Japan would be aided by drastic changes in the system of local government. They assumed that it would be a good thing if a large measure of local autonomy were granted and that thereby "grass-roots" democracy were fostered. Toward this end the Occupation sponsored a number of institutional changes.

The new constitution enunciates the principle of local autonomy for local public entities, stipulates that local officials shall be elected by direct popular vote, that local government bodies have the right to manage their property, affairs, and administration, and that a special law, applicable only to one local public entity, cannot be enacted by the Diet without the consent of the majority of voters of the local area concerned.

The details of local government structure were set forth in a series of laws, most important among them the lengthy Local Autonomy Law of 1947, which removed the legal power of the central government to control the prefectural government and of the latter to control the municipal governments. Other significant changes included the abolition of the Ministry of Home Affairs, provision for popular election of local officials, including governors of prefectures, creation of a system of recall and initiative, the decentralization of police and education, the creation of a local civil service, and fiscal reforms. The legal foundations of local autonomy, therefore, were laid.

But it cannot be said that as yet Japan has attained local autonomy in practice. The central government continues to exercise extensive influence over local government entities in one way or another. Although the Ministry of Home Affairs was abolished, the Local Autonomy Agency established in 1949 has taken over some of the functions formerly exercised by the Home Ministry. The Local Autonomy Agency issues directives to governors and other officials, summons local officials to meetings in Tokyo, writes model laws which serve as a basis of legislation by prefectural and municipal assemblies, advises on local problems, and exercises indirect influence through semi-official organizations such as the National Association of Governors.

At least four reasons may be cited to explain why, despite legal and institutional changes, local government entities have not in fact achieved more independence. First, the idea of the community is relatively poorly developed, with the result that the level of civic pride is low. This is part of the general problem of political apathy, reference to which will be made later. Second, local officials by tradition and habit are not accustomed to taking the initiative in solving problems at the local level and still prefer to look to Tokyo for leadership. Third, there are many problems—social security, unemployment, economic planning, and so on—which by their nature must be dealt with at the national level. And, fourth, local government lacks the financial resources, given the present tax structure, to support numerous local undertakings and hence must rely on the central government for financial aid in the form of grants-in-aid and subsidies. As is generally true elsewhere, financial aid often leads to controls, direct or indirect.

·VI·

Major Political Forces

ACTION—or lack of action—by the state usually has a marked impact on the economic well-being of diverse groups. Both the flow of revenue into government coffers, at the national and prefectural levels in the form of taxes, license fees, and other imposts, and the services provided by government, including subsidies it gives out, affect every citizen, whether directly or indirectly. In Japan, as in other countries, much political activity is therefore aimed at influencing government agencies in the performance of their tasks; and among those playing an important part in such activities are interest groups.

Interest Groups

BUSINESS ORGANIZATIONS

For understandable reasons, business, labor, and agriculture pay close attention to what government does (or fails to do). Individuals and groups in these sectors of the economy seek to influence government action in several ways. One way is to work through their own organizations, which by a variety of methods make their wants known to the government.

Among the principal business organizations are the Federation of Economic Organizations, the Japan Federation of Employers' Associations, the Chamber of Commerce and Industry, and the Japan Management Association. The Federation of Economic Organizations, organized in 1946, is perhaps the most powerful and is composed of three types of members: (1) federations of business and trade associations, such as the Japan Industrial Council, the Council of Financial Organizations, and the Foreign Trade Association; (2) trade associations; and (3) business firms and businessmen. The Federation of Economic Organizations is mostly concerned with broad economic problems, such as the development of the national economy.

The Japan Federation of Employers' Associations, formed in 1948, is, as the name implies, a grouping of employers' associations which are organized on regional and prefectural levels. Its chief concern is with labor problems and Communist activities affecting labor-management relations. The Chamber of Commerce and Industry traces its history back to 1878 when the Tokyo Chamber of Commerce and Industry was established. In 1890 chambers of commerce and industry were created in various localities by law, and since then chambers of commerce and industry have had quasi-official status. The most recent legislation on them was enacted in 1950. The central chamber of commerce and industry and the local organizations promote business activities, supervise commercial organizations, engage in market research, and provide liaison between business and government. The Japan Management Association, formed in 1946, has branches in the Osaka-Kobe area, Kyushu, and Hokkaido and claims to have more than 8,000 members.

Practically all these business organizations undertake research on economic and labor problems and regularly issue journals, pamphlets, and research reports to keep their members and the business community informed and to influence public opinion indirectly. Another important function of these organizations is to attempt directly to influence public policy. From time to time these organizations issue public statements and resolutions urging the political parties or the government to follow a particular course of action. A more direct method is for the officials of the Federation of Economic Organizations and other groups to meet both formally and informally with leading political figures and personally to present their desiderata for government action.

LABOR ORGANIZATIONS

The basic objective of most labor unions is to endeavor to secure economic benefits for their members in the form of higher wages, security of employment, and improved working conditions. But, like other well-organized groups, labor unions are also endowed with the potentiality of exerting influence in the political arena. In fact, organized labor in Japan devotes considerable time and energy to political activities, but as yet its political effectiveness is not at all commensurate with the large number of workers who have become union members. An important reason for this state of affairs is to be found in the history and structure of Japanese unions.

Historically, the Japanese labor movement began at the turn of the century, but its growth was impeded by, among other things, a hostile atmosphere. Even at a 1936 high point union membership came to a little more than 400,000, and as a result of suppression unions practically ceased to exist during the war period.

Partly because of encouragement given it by the Occupation and partly in response to postwar economic and social conditions, the labor movement gained momentum after the end of the war. Today union membership totals some 6 million distributed among more than 30,000 unions.

A peculiar feature of Japanese unions is the preponderance of "enterprise" unions. The great majority of Japanese unions are organized on an enterprise basis, that is, all permanent employees, including white-collar, skilled, and unskilled workers, of a mine, shop, or factory, or of a company with several factories, are included in one union. Leadership in these unions, moreover, is often provided by white-collar employees who are better educated and more articulate and who often have ambitions of attaining management positions. Because of their structure and leadership, enterprise unions tend to be oriented inward with the result that the development of craft or industrial unions and a working-class ideology are impeded.

Enterprise unions can either remain independent or affiliate with national unions. National unions, in turn, can affiliate with large national federations. Both local and national unions sometimes shift their allegiance from one federation to another, and there are also instances of multiple affiliation.

At present there are two large and several smaller national federations. The General Council of Trade Unions of Japan (Sohyo) claims more than 3 million members and has within it a great variety of unions: those of coal miners, metal workers, automobile workers, communications workers, railway workers, government employees, teachers, seamen, and many others. Its rival, All-Japan Trade Union Congress (Zenro), has about 670,000 members, and two smaller federations, National Federation of Industrial Organizations (Shin San-betsu) and All-Japan Congress of Industrial Unions (Sanbetsu Kaigi), have a little over 40,000 and 10,000 members respectively. In addition there are a number of unaffiliated national unions.

It may be said in general that the attention of the enterprise unions is focused on economic problems while the large national federations, such as the General Council of Trade Unions of Japan, concern them-selves much more with political matters. The General Council's ideol-ogy is unmistakably Marxist in orientation, and its leaders have main-tained close ties with the Socialist Party. The General Council's position on concrete issues, however, varies somewhat from time to time depending on the ideological point of view of those in leader-ship positions. For example, in 1955 the consistently pro-Soviet anti-Western group which had been in power for a number of years in the General Council was displaced by a faction which was more inclined toward a "third-force" neutralist position, and this led to a shift in the political outlook of the federation.

Because of differences in emphasis and interest between the local unions and the large national federations, labor is not nearly so effec-tive politically as might be surmised. As an American observer has noted, "Enterprise unions, affiliated or not, do give a modicum of sup-port to the national organizations simply out of recognition that po-litical achievements favorable to labor serve to fortify their own effectiveness. This support, however, has been sporadic and largely cathartic, but seldom self-sustaining." [1]

FARM ORGANIZATIONS

Agriculture, like business and labor, has its own organizations which seek, among other things, to promote the interests of farmers. In the prewar period the most powerful farm group was the Imperial Agricultural Association (Teikoku Nokai), which evolved from sev-eral earlier farmers' associations created originally under government sponsorship. Established in 1910, the Imperial Agricultural Association was a national federation of agricultural associations organized on village, town, city, and prefectural levels.

The Imperial Agricultural Association acquired the reputation of being a landlord-dominated organization, and, according to a Japa-nese authority on agriculture, landlord influence was stronger at the

[1] Solomon B. Levine, "Labor Patterns and Trends," *Annals of the American Academy of Political and Social Science*, Nov. 1956, pp. 110–111.

higher levels, which were primarily concerned with political matters, and weaker at the lower levels, which were concerned mostly with technical matters involving farm production. Historically, an important function of the association was to help increase agricultural productivity, but it also became concerned with rice prices and disputes between landlords and tenant farmers. Probably its most important function was to serve as a channel of communication between government bureaus interested in farm problems and the agricultural community and as an agency for distributing government subsidies to agriculture.

In the 1920s there also emerged "tenant unions" organized by socialists to defend the interests of tenant farmers against landlords. The Japan Farmers' Union (Nihon Nomin Kumiai), founded in 1922, fought for a reduction in land rents by using such methods as demonstrations, violence, and court action. The effectiveness of the Japan Farmers' Union, however, was reduced by internal dissension, caused in part by a shift in emphasis, which occurred with the passage of time, from rent reduction to the socialization of land and from economic matters to political questions.

Like many other organizations, farm organizations felt an increasing amount of government control with the growth of militarism and the outbreak of the Second World War. In 1943 various farm organizations were combined into the Agricultural Association (Nogyokai). This association, however, was abolished by law in 1947 and was replaced by the Agricultural Co-operative Association (Nogyo Kyodo Kumiai).

This organization consisted in 1952 of some 35,000 local co-operatives with more than 8 million members. Although the Agricultural Co-operative Association primarily acts in matters related to credit, buying and selling, storage, insurance, food processing, and rural welfare, it also has paid some attention to politics. Representatives of the organization, for example, have met and passed resolutions in connection with taxes on farmers.

WOMEN'S ORGANIZATIONS

Women were given the right to vote for the first time under the provisions of the 1947 constitution. The granting of the franchise to women enabled them to become active participants in the political process, and this development was reflected in the formation, in 1948, of the Federation of Housewives (Shufu Rengo Kai), which, as the name implies, is a national federation of women's organizations. In 1955 the federation included some 200 local organizations, mostly in the Tokyo area.

The federation attracted national attention in 1955 by its successful campaign to force dairies to reduce the price of milk. It made arrangements with a small dairy to buy milk at wholesale prices and then it hired students and housewives to deliver the milk to consumers, and in this way it demonstrated to the public that milk could be sold somewhat cheaper. Shortly thereafter the large dairies announced a reduction in the price of milk. Today the federation is so well known that when it sends a delegation to meet with the Prime Minister and other important leaders to present political and economic demands the delegation always gets a hearing.

VETERANS' ORGANIZATIONS

Before the war the Imperial Reservists' Association (Teikoku Zaigo Gunjin Kai), which had branches in practically every city, village, and hamlet, represented a powerful interest group. The association, with its ultranationalistic philosophy, helped mobilize opinion in favor of militarism in the 1930s. With the end of the war, the Imperial Reservists' Association was, of course, abolished; and as a result of the subsequent revulsion against militarism veterans receded into the background.

In recent years, however, there are signs that veterans' groups are again re-forming. In 1952 the National Liaison Association for the Restoration of Pensions for ex-Officers (Kyu Gunjin Kankei Onkyu Fukkatsu Zenkoku Renraku Kai) was organized. By putting pressure on the government it was able to get restored pensions which had been abolished by the Occupation authorities.

There was formed, in 1956, an organization potentially capable of becoming a neo-Imperial Reservists' Association. This group, which calls itself League of Friends from the Same Locality (Kyoyu Remmei), claims to have more than a million members and has established branches in a number of cities, towns, and villages. Its officers are composed largely of ex-generals and admirals. The head of the Defense Agency addressed the League's convention held in Tokyo late in 1956, and it is evident that the Defense Agency looks with favor on the organization.

PRESSURE-GROUP TACTICS

In order to get favorable legislative action and administrative decisions, interest groups resort to various tactics, most of which have a familiar ring to those conversant with American politics. A common maneuver is to resort to organized action. A group trying to apply pressure on the legislature to enact a particular bill might call a mass meeting of its members, pass resolutions, and send delegations with copies of such resolutions to call on the leading members of the government and the Diet. In case the organization has local regional branches, these branches are also likely to be mobilized; the local branches will also hold meetings and send letters or telegrams to Diet members and others.

A less dramatic maneuver, but one which is probably as important in the long run, is to cultivate friendly relations with key personnel in the government. Finally, many interest groups try to educate the public by printing and distributing propaganda pamphlets in order to get public opinion on their side.

Political Parties

PREWAR PARTIES

Political parties differ from pressure groups in that their objective is to get governmental positions for their leaders and in this way achieve control of the government. In Japan the idea of a political party was transplanted from the West, and the early 1870s saw the formation of political clubs and societies. These early political groupings laid the foundations for the creation of the Liberal Party (Jiyuto) in 1881, the Progressive Party (Kaishinto) in 1882, and the Imperial Party (Teiseito), a government-supported party, in 1882.

These parties were more or less voluntarily dissolved in 1885 partly as a result of continued government pressure against them and partly as a consequence of internal divisions, which were particularly acute in the case of the Liberal Party. In 1900 the Association of Political Friends (Seiyukai), which traced its lineage to the Liberal Party, was formed under the leadership of Prince Ito Hirobumi, who had played an important part in the drafting of the Meiji constitution. Like other oligarchs, Ito had been bitterly opposed to the idea of a political party, which to men of his political creed appeared to encourage disunity and weaken Japan in the community of nations. But Ito also recognized that the government needed support in the Diet once a parliament was established. Party leaders, on the other hand, had also come to understand that under the Meiji constitution the power of the Diet was to be greatly circumscribed, and hence they were more willing to compromise with the oligarchs. Those who had been affiliated with the Progressive Party did not regroup to form another party, but were content to join coalitions. Eventually between 1913 and 1915 the Constitutional Association (Kenseikai), which was the descendant of the Progressive Party, was organized.

The political parties reached the zenith of their power in the 1920s, and it appeared for a time that a full-fledged parliamentary form of government might eventually emerge. In June 1924 Kato Takaakira, who had married into the Iwasaki family which controlled the Mitsubishi industrial combine and was president of the Constitutional Association, became Prime Minister, and until the assassination of Prime Minister Inukai Tsuyoshi in May 1932 party leaders headed cabinets, except possibly the one under General Tanaka Giichi. But even in this case, although General Tanaka was a professional soldier and not primarily a politician, he was also at the time president of the Association of Political Friends and hence enjoyed the backing of his party.

In this period the parties worked closely with the *zaibatsu*, who were the prime source of party funds. Large companies contributed liberally to party coffers, some supporting at the same time both the Association of Political Friends and the Constitutional Association in order to have supporters in the government no matter who won the elections. The alliance between the parties and the *zaibatsu* naturally caused the public to be suspicious that the government was partial to the interests of big business, and these suspicions seemed to be confirmed by the frequent charges of bribery and corruption that were aired in the Diet, principally by the party which happened to be in opposition at the moment. It was unfortunate that Japanese parties were forced to operate in an unfriendly atmosphere and with an institutional structure which impeded their attaining maturity.

The problems confronting the parties were accentuated by basic social changes which had taken place with quickened pace since the First World War. The growth of large cities, the beginnings of a labor movement, the creation of a white-collar class, and the spread of education and literacy brought increasing pressure for political participation on the part of those groups which had been denied the ballot. Most of the party leaders as well as the bureaucrats were reluctant to enlarge the electorate for fear that such a step would lead to social instability. But in the face of intense agitation on the part of the press in the large cities, urban intellectuals, and radical political groups, they were forced to enact a law in 1925 granting suffrage to all males 25 years of age and over.

It should be noted, however, that at the same time a Peace Preservation Law was also passed by the Imperial Diet to counteract the granting of suffrage. The Peace Preservation Law provided up to ten years' imprisonment for those convicted of joining societies or organizations advocating a change in the constitution, in the existing form of government, or in the system of ownership of private property. If the established parties hoped to prevent the emergence of radical parties by means of repressive legislation of this sort, they were mistaken, for the law granting universal manhood suffrage paved the way for the emergence of left-wing parties. Socialism had been imported into Japan, along with other social theories, as early as the turn of the century; and numerous socialist and anarchist-syndicalist groups had come and gone over the years. Now that the masses were put in a position of being able to participate in politics, if they so desired, the left-wing forces pushed forward with renewed vigor. However, although those on the left subscribed to Marxism, they were sharply split into several groups because of personal and doctrinal differences. In the 1928 general elections, the first held under the universal manhood suffrage act, four left-wing parties, ranging from the centrist Social Democratic Party (Shakai Minshuto) to the Communist-front organization, the Labor-Farmer Party (Rodo Nominto), ran 88 candidates, but they succeeded in polling only about 500,000 votes, enough to elect 8 representatives to the lower house. In the years that followed, the left remained unable to achieve unity or to enlist significant popular support, and until its demise in the late 1930s, it never gained enough strength to pose a threat to the conservative parties.

The conservative parties were also afflicted by factionalism and general lack of sustained popular support. As has been noted, parties were unable to formulate constructive programs since the institutional structure prevented them from achieving significant control of the government. Moreover, their relative lack of control of the government dulled their sense of responsibility, encouraging party members in the government to engage in corrupt practices. It is therefore not altogether surprising that important sections of the public came to have little respect for political parties; and when the militarists made their bid for power after the invasion of Manchuria in 1931, parties were in a vulnerable position. The fortunes of both conservative and left-wing parties waned in the 1930s, and in 1940 they disappeared from the scene, having been amalgamated into the Imperial Rule Assistance Association (Taisei Yokusankai), a mild Japanese version of a totalitarian party. In the war period, the Imperial Rule Assistance Association was succeeded by the Political Association of Greater Japan.

POSTWAR PARTIES

With the abolition of wartime controls following Japan's surrender, old-line party politicians who had maintained informal groupings throughout the war period were now able to come together openly and reorganize parties. In the beginning literally hundreds of so-called "parties" were formed; but there eventually emerged two major conservative parties, the Liberal Party (Jiyuto) and the Progressive Party (Shimpoto), both of which were led by prewar politicians and both of which traced their lineage back to parties that existed in the 1920s and earlier.

Prewar left-wing leaders were also active in this period, and the non-Communist left succeeded in uniting sufficiently to form the Social Democratic Party (Nihon Shakaito). The Communists, who could not operate legally before 1945, now achieved legal status, and they quickly formed the Japanese Communist Party (Nihon Kyosanto), under the leadership of seasoned Communists who either had been released from jail or had returned from exile abroad. A small Co-operative Party, consisting of rural Diet members and those interested in the co-operative movement, was also formed in this period.

The first national election following the surrender took place in April 1946. The two conservative parties together secured 43 per cent of the vote and 234 seats in the lower house, and the Social Democrats managed to get 17 per cent of the vote and 93 seats. In the second election held one year later, the Social Democrats succeeded in increasing their strength to 143 seats, enough to become the largest single party in the House of Representatives. The two conservative parties, however, still held a combined total of 258 seats. The Social Democrats were therefore able to organize a government only by forming a coalition with the Democratic Party (formerly Progressive Party). As this was the first time in history that they had obtained enough support to install a socialist Prime Minister, the socialists were anxious to carry out their legislative program, which involved nationalization of some industries, but their efforts in this direction were thwarted mostly by the fact that they shared power with one of the conservative parties. The coalition did not last long; and the cabinet was forced to resign in October 1948, giving way to the Liberals (now called Democratic Liberals) who had stayed out of the coalition. Table 4 gives the total votes obtained by the various parties in the five elections that have taken place between 1947 and 1955.

Table 4. Election statistics, House of Representatives, 1947–1955

Party	1947	1949	1952	1953	1955
Democratic	6,839,646	4,812,780	6,429,450 *	9,240,920 †	13,536,044
Liberal	7,356,321	13,402,409	16,938,221	13,476,428	9,849,457
Socialist	7,175,939	4,129,794			
Right-wing			4,108,274	4,677,833	5,129,594
Left-wing			3,398,597	4,516,715	5,683,312
Labor-Farmer	—	606,840	261,190	358,773	357,611
Communist	1,002,903	1,602,496	896,765	655,990	733,121
National Co-operative	1,915,947	1,042,123	—	—	—
Minor parties	1,490,057	2,984,771	949,036	152,050	496,614
Independents	1,580,844	2,011,306	2,355,172	1,523,736	1,229,081

* In 1952 the Democratic Party was called the Progressive Party.

† These figures include the votes cast for the Progressive Party plus the votes cast for the Hatoyama faction of the Liberal Party.

The Liberal Party, under the leadership of Yoshida Shigeru, a former diplomat, went to the electorate in 1949 and won a vote of confidence by securing 264 out of a total of 466 seats. The Liberal Party victory was at the expense of the centrist groups, that is, the Democratic and the Social Democratic parties, whose number was reduced to 69 and 48 seats respectively. There was also a marked show of strength on the far left, for the Communists, who had never won more than 5 seats in any previous election, suddenly found themselves controlling 35 seats in the lower house.

For the six years between January 1949 and February 1955 the Liberal Party held the reins of power, by virtue of its victories in elections held in 1952 and again in 1953. In this period the opposition conservative party, the Democrats, held between 70 and 80 seats. The Social Democrats were weakened by a split into left-wing and right-wing Socialist parties. This split was caused by personal and doctrinal differences which were aggravated by the question of party attitude toward the San Francisco Peace Treaty ending the state of war between Japan and the Allied powers. The right wing favored the signing of a peace agreement even if it excluded Russia, whereas left-wing forces wanted an over-all agreement which would include the Communist countries as well as the free world.

The Liberal Party, like the Social Democratic Party, became torn by dissension with the passage of years. One cause was a growing feeling of antagonism to Yoshida's dictatorial methods. Perhaps an even more important reason was the difficulty which the party experienced in absorbing well-known members who were returning to political life following the rescinding of the purge. Thousands of individuals had been barred from public activities by the Occupation for having contributed to the growth of Japanese militarism; but when Japan regained her independence the purge was rescinded, making it possible for purgees to return to politics. Understandably considerable tension was generated between those already in power in the Liberal Party and those who returned to the party after a period of absence. The upshot of the matter was that a dissident faction opposed to Yoshida bolted under the leadership of Hatoyama Ichiro, one of the founders of the Liberal Party who had been purged and replaced by Yoshida. This faction joined with the Progressive Party to form a new Democratic Party (Minshuto) in 1954. In the February 1955 elections, the newly formed Democratic Party gained 185 seats to become the leading party; the Liberals got 113 seats, the left-wing Socialists 89, and the right-wing Socialists 66 seats. The Communists, whose popularity had rapidly declined since the Cominform criticism of the party in 1950, secured 2 seats. Thus in 1955 the 467 seats in the House of Representatives were divided among two conservative parties, which together controlled the majority, and two socialist parties, which between them had slightly more than one-third of the seats, sufficient to block amendments to the constitution.

The logic of the situation suggested that the two conservative parties and the two socialist parties combine to form a large conservative party and an opposition socialist party. Negotiations had been going on among the socialists for some time to heal the breach between the left and right wings, but the two factions could not easily agree on a common platform. Finally, however, after lengthy conversations, a compromise was arranged and a unified socialist party was formed in the fall of 1956.

Socialist unity spurred the conservatives to settle their disagreements and create a single party that would compete with the left. Personal differences were particularly acute in the conservative camp, but after much wrangling the Democratic and the Liberal parties merged in November 1956 to form the Liberal Democratic Party, with Hatoyama Ichiro, who at the time held the post of Prime Minister, as its leader. Thus for the first time a "two-party system" emerged.

As the foregoing historical sketch shows, parties have been formed, dissolved, and reorganized on numerous occasions in the short period after the end of the war. However, despite these changes the conservatives, except for one occasion, have remained at the helm. Why is it that in the competition for votes the conservatives have been relatively more successful? There are several reasons; and one of these is that the conservative political ideology appeals to more people.

The platform and other public pronouncements of the Liberal Democratic Party pay homage to democracy, freedom, peace, and national independence. "Our party," declares the platform, "looks to institutional and structural reforms based on democratic ideals and the establishment of a thoroughgoing democratic state." It continues, "Our party, subscribing to universal principles of peace and freedom, looks to improvement and readjustment of international relations and the achievement of full independence."

In economic affairs, the Liberal Democratic Party subscribes to a liberal philosophy which emphasizes individual initiative and free enterprise. But at the same time it speaks in favor of a "welfare state" and the stabilization of the people's livelihood through governmental measures. For example, the party has come out publicly in favor of such social welfare measures as public health insurance, low-cost housing for workers, and expansion of care for the aged.

The Liberal Democratic Party implies that Occupation-sponsored reforms broke too sharply with Japanese traditions, a point of view shared widely by conservatives, and the party sets forth in its platform the desirability of amending the constitution and of revamping the educational system, the civil service, and the system of local government. The aim of the Liberal Democratic Party is to revive some of the prewar practices that were abolished under the Allied Occupation.

In foreign affairs, the Liberal Democratic Party pledges continued co-operation with the free world. On defense matters, however, it pledges the establishment of a small self-defense force appropriate to Japanese national strength. At the same time the platform states that the party will seek reduction of the number of U.S. bases in Japan and revision of the administrative agreement between Japan and the United States. On the Communist issue, the party declares itself to be opposed to communism and other antidemocratic activities.

The ideology of the Japanese Social Democratic Party as expressed in its platform differs substantially from that of its conservative rival. The Socialists contend that Japan is only nominally independent because foreign troops are stationed and foreign bases are maintained in Japan. They contend that monopoly capital, the capitalist class, and its instrument, the Japanese government, are under the control of the United States.

The Social Democratic Party looks upon itself as a class party led by the working class and supported by peasants, fishermen, medium and small merchants, and the intellectuals. However, it pledges to seek political power through democratic means.

The Socialists are opposed to the administrative agreement between Japan and the United States and are in favor of trying to negotiate security pacts with Soviet Russia and Communist China on a bilateral basis. At the same time they also favor attempts to seek collective-security arrangements involving Japan, Russia, and the United States. The Social Democratic Party has declared its opposition to present attempts to rearm Japan.

The Socialists affirm that they stand for democracy, peace, and the preservation of the present constitution. Their aim is to improve the people's livelihood, eliminate unemployment, and bring other economic reforms. They advocate the repeal of certain laws, such as the antisubversives law, and statutes regulating strikes which they regard as inimical to the best interests of the working class.

As is evident from the foregoing brief summary of the platforms and policy statements of the two parties, a wide gulf separates the Liberal Democrats and the Social Democrats. The existence of this gulf has made it difficult for the two parties to work together in the Diet and has led to heated tempers and prolonged wrangling and on occasion to the outbreak of violence. When the party in power and the opposition party differ markedly on numerous basic issues, as do the two

Japanese parties, the ability of the parliamentary mechanism to achieve some sort of accommodation between contending forces is usually severely tested.

PARTY ORGANIZATION

In terms of structure, Japanese parties are highly centralized. The headquarters of all parties are located in Tokyo, and although there are a number of prefectural and local party offices, the important work of the party is handled by the national headquarters organization.

The Liberal Democratic Party is led by its president, who in recent practice has been elected by a secret ballot at a meeting of prominent party members. At present there are, under the president, at least four important party officials, namely, the secretary-general and chairmen of the Political Research Committee, of the Executive Committee, and of the National Organization Committee.

The secretary-general's job is to keep the party machinery functioning, to help raise funds, to act as the party's spokesman, to plan election strategy, to advise the president, and to negotiate with other parties. The secretary-general has a number of deputies to assist him in carrying out his duties.

The chairman of the Political Research Committee takes the lead in formulating party policy. The committee reviews and even drafts bills to be presented to the National Diet. The committee is organized into subcommittees which parallel the ministries, and it has a staff of research specialists.

The chairman of the Executive Committee nominally oversees the work of the secretary-general and the Policy Research Committee and other committees. The Executive Committee shares with the party convention and the party caucus of Diet members the power to make high-level party decisions. In recent years the Executive Committee has grown in size in order to provide better representation for various factions and groups within the party, and as a result it appears that the influence wielded by the committee has declined.

The National Organization Committee has been elevated in importance, and its changing status represents an attempt to secure "grassroots" strength for the party. The committee has established permanent prefectural branches in order to facilitate the recruitment of new party members, especially among the youth. How successful this attempt to broaden the party's base will prove remains to be seen.

The headquarters staff which works under the general supervision of the secretary-general is divided into a number of sections and divisions, such as youth, women, industry, labor, agriculture, publications, education, and so on. At the present time the headquarters staff of the Liberal Democratic Party is rather large, numbering around 120 persons, because many staff members of the two parties were retained after the amalagamation of the Democratic and Liberal parties.

The local organization of the Liberal Democratic Party is still weak. The party has hundreds of branches in cities, towns, and villages, but they are not particularly active except at election time. An official of the party has been quoted to the effect that he hopes the party will be able to recruit 1 million members who would be willing to pay dues amounting to 200 yen annually (about 55 cents).[2]

The Socialist Party does not have a president, and the official who is usually considered the leader of the party is the chairman of the Central Executive Committee. The secretary-general is in charge of the headquarters staff and wields considerable power. In 1957, Asanuma Inejiro, who held this post, had more than a hundred staff members under him.

The Socialist Party's Policy Deliberation Committee corresponds roughly to the Political Research Committee of the Liberal Democratic Party. The committee, which is divided into a number of sub-committees, not only deliberates on pending policy questions, but also deals with the party platform and other problems such as the relation of the party to labor unions.

Like the conservative party, the Socialist Party has many local branches. Although the true situation cannot be certainly known, their local organizations appear to keep in closer touch with the Tokyo headquarters than do the branches of the Liberal Democratic Party. It is said that there are about 50,000 members formally registered on the roster of the Socialist Party and that of this group perhaps 30,000 pay their dues regularly. The party reputedly hopes to increase its dues-paying membership to about 100,000 persons.

Both parties hold conventions periodically (usually once a year) for the purpose of electing officers and passing on party policy. In general conservative party conventions are cut-and-dried affairs, and beyond providing publicity for the party and an occasion for party members to get together, they do not seem to serve as a device for

[2] Masamichi Inoki, *Nihon no Ni Dai Seito* [Japan's Two Parties] (Tokyo, 1956), p. 90.

determining policy. The Socialist Party conventions, on the other hand, are often characterized by stormy sessions, with much argument and debate.

THE SOCIAL BASIS OF PARTIES

As already noted, there is at least from the ideological point of view a substantial difference between the conservative and the socialist parties. The former is committed to the perpetuation of an economic and social order based on capitalistic principles, and the latter seeks to reduce drastically the role of private capital. One would surmise, therefore, that these two parties would appeal to and obtain support from different social and economic groups. Because the element of personal loyalty often exerts a powerful influence, the picture can sometimes be distorted, but it may be said in a very general way that there exists a relationship between parties and social and economic groups.

The conservative party considers itself a national party and seeks support from all strata of the population. The conservatives are backed most heavily in rural communities where traditional values persist and where the type of politician frequently found in the conservative camp has an appeal. Data taken from public opinion polls, from interviews, and from first-hand observation by journalists and others suggest that at least one-third to one-half of those engaged in agriculture and fishing prefer the conservatives. Since just under one-half of Japan's population still lives in rural communities, agrarian support is an important asset. It is also true, however, that in recent years the socialists have gained strength in certain rural areas. The change in sentiment may come in some instances from the movement of industry into the countryside and in other instances from the influence exerted on their kin by younger sons of farm families who have migrated to the cities.

Another important source of conservative strength is provided by the owners of commercial and industrial establishments in the towns and cities. The historical development of capitalism in Japan was such that small individually owned and operated enterprises survived in the face of industrialization and the growth of large industrial combines. Support from this segment of the population is important because in the smaller business enterprises, where a high degree of paternalism characterizes employer-employee relationships, employers are often able to influence the political attitudes of those who work for them.

Finally, conservative forces enjoy the support of high-level administrative personnel in government agencies and of corporation executives. Some corporations contribute funds to both parties, but there is no question that large corporate enterprise is on the side of conservatism and that it helps fill the coffers of the party, especially when an election is about to take place.

On the other hand, the Socialists, in keeping with their commitment to Marxist principles, explicitly seek to base their power on the working class. The Socialist Party enjoys the open support of many labor unions, including the General Council of Trade Unions of Japan (Sohyo), which boasts more than 3 million members. Labor unions, moreover, represent an important source of financial aid for the Socialist Party.

The fact that most labor union leaders identify themselves with the socialist cause, however, does not automatically determine the political attitudes of the rank and file. Available data indicate that somewhere between 40 and 45 per cent of the industrial workers favor the Socialist Party. By and large it is those workers employed in large plants who are most class conscious and inclined toward socialism.

Additional socialist support comes from intellectuals—professors, writers, students. In recent decades the Japanese intellectual world has felt the strong impress of Marxist thought, with the result that it is a little unfashionable to be an intellectual and not cast one's lot with the socialists.

Finally, the Socialist Party has made inroads into the urban white-collar class. The complexity of Japanese industrial organization has fostered the need for numerous salesmen, clerks, office workers, and other specialists who are forced to live on low incomes and with relatively little job security. To many of these people the socialist program and promises have strong appeal.

In view of the foregoing relationship between political parties and social groupings, a sudden shift in the present balance between conservative and socialist forces appears unlikely, barring, of course, a cataclysmic change, such as a serious economic depression. Thus continued conservative strength seems assured. But it is also worth remembering that time seems to be on the side of the socialists. Further industrialization will undoubtedly enlarge the working class and gradually reduce the number of those engaged in agriculture. There is, moreover, a rough correlation between socialist support and the amount of formal education, and as the educational level of the nation rises the number of those who will turn to socialism should also rise.

Finally, historical experience seems to show that in Japan those who have just reached voting age tend to vote for radical candidates, whereas the older age groups tend to vote for the conservatives. The present age composition of the Japanese population is such that about 1,700,000 individuals reach voting age every year, while the annual death rate is about 700,000 persons. Mathematically, therefore, the left-wing forces are acquiring new supporters while the conservatives tend to loose supporters through death. The net socialist increase is of course reduced by the shift of voters from the socialists to the conservatives as they grow older. A rough calculation of the relative annual change in party support has been made as follows:

	Decrease	*Increase*	*Net increase*
Conservatives	600,000 (death)	900,000 (shift)	300,000
Radicals	900,000 (shift)	1,700,000 (new)	800,000

These are very crude calculations, but they do suggest that if the present trend continues the left wing will gain about 500,000 votes per year. In 1955 the conservatives obtained some 11 million more votes than the socialists, so it would appear that the day when the socialists will win a majority of seats in the House of Representatives is some years distant.

· VII ·

The Power Structure

WHENEVER a group of men seek to work together to achieve some common objectives, there is a need for leadership. A few individuals must give directions for the majority to follow; otherwise various individuals are likely to work at cross-purposes to the detriment of common ends. Social action, therefore, calls for leaders, but at the same time a man cannot be a leader without having followers. Thus power always involves human relationships. The relationship cannot be equal, however, for by definition the leader is the one who exercises a stronger voice in group decisions, partly by consent and partly by constraint.

In surveying the power structure of the Japanese state the situation at the local level will first be considered, then the national level, and finally the relationship between the local and national levels.

Political Power at the Local Level

In Chapter IV the relation of the individual to the group was considered, and it was pointed out how, as a rule, the individual is subordinated first to his family and then to informal local groups. Under these circumstances, an individualist who insists on following the dictates of his own conscience will often find himself ostracized and excluded from community affairs. Conversely, a willingness to cooperate and conform to accepted norms of behavior will lead to social approval. Thus it may be said that social behavior, particularly in rural areas, is highly circumscribed by tradition, custom, and community sentiments concerning what is proper and improper.

Among these sentiments are notions about the kind of persons who should hold leadership positions. Robert Ward notes that there "exist in almost all *buraku* [hamlets] one or more elders who are generally regarded as outstandingly wise and experienced in all lines and particularly in respect to matters such as village or prefectural politics which transcend the normal daily experience of most members of the community." [1]

Traditionally, in rural Japan, landed property and long residence in the community were determinants of social prestige and political influence, and important local government posts were rotated among a few families which possessed these qualifications. This is still true to some extent today. For example, a tenant farmer has been quoted as saying, "It is a commonplace that all official positions should be circulated among those who, having inherited wealth from their ancestors, are regarded as 'gentlemen' [*danna*], even though they may be stupid." [2]

The fact that members of long-established landed families generally enjoy power is in part because the people in the community expect them to take the responsibility of leadership and in part because those who belong to such families have at their disposal certain economic levers. Landed families often rent a portion of their holdings to tenant farmers, and this gives them a certain economic power, for the tenant's livelihood comes to depend on the willingness of his landlord to continue to rent land to him. Moreover, since credit is difficult to obtain, wealthy families can use their loan-making ability in order to enhance their influence in the community. The exercise of power is, however, seldom brutal and naked, but is tempered by a sense of paternalism, and there is always a degree of give-and-take between the influential and the influenced.

Not all local leaders come from long-established landed families. Both the postwar land reform program, which reduced large landholdings, and social changes, which have invaded the countryside as well as the cities, have contributed to modifications in leadership. In

[1] Robert E. Ward, "Patterns of Stability and Change in Rural Japanese Politics," in University of Michigan, Center for Japanese Studies, *Occasional Papers,* no. 1 (1951), p. 4.

[2] Masamichi Royama, *Noson Jichi no Henbo* [Changes in Local Government in Rural Areas] (Tokyo, 1948), p. 16.

some areas local shopkeepers, schoolteachers, Buddhist priests, and others not typically landowners can now be found among the local political elite. In any case, whatever their occupational background, there are everywhere in rural areas local leaders who are able, by the use of material wealth or the manipulation of political symbols, to affect the electoral behavior of the people in their area and influence decisions made by political bodies with which they are affiliated.

A somewhat similar situation with regard to the structure of power may be found in sectors of society other than rural communities. An interesting study of the Japanese labor-boss system among construction workers shows how a building contractor in paying low wages makes his workers dependent upon his "benevolence" and how the contractor acts as a kind of "father" to his workers by mediating their quarrels, finding wives for unmarried workers, personally taking care of them when ill, and in general looking after their welfare.[3] Hence in this case a highly personalized reciprocal relationship has been established between the boss and his workers, and the power relationship thus established can be utilized for political ends if and when it is to the advantage of the boss to do so. Similar social situations may be frequently found in fishing villages, in mining towns, and among gangs of hoodlums and racketeers.

The subordination of the individual to the group is buttressed by an ideology which places value on social harmony. Individuals who insist on their "rights" and bring dissension into the open are not welcome. For this reason, appeals to law and the courts to settle quarrels or to seek redress of wrongful acts are much less frequent than might be supposed. The socially approved way to seek solutions to these problems is through mediation and compromise with the help of local elders and other leaders. Thus there often exists what might be called "informal government" at the local level. Many problems, such as the bringing of sanctions against those who violate the mores, the adjudication of disputes, and to some extent the provision of social welfare measures, are handled by "informal government" without their being brought within the purview of the formal institutions of government.

Another consequence of the preference for social harmony is the avoidance of majority rule in arriving at group decisions. As one observer notes: "In Japan it is considered brash for an individual to

[3] Iwao Ishino and John W. Bennett, *The Japanese Labor Boss System* (Columbus: Ohio State University Research Foundation, 1952).

make a definite, clearcut decision regarding himself or others. He must maintain a reserve (enryo) and must restrain his own opinions."[4] Consequently, a group does not come to a decision through open debate of the issues involved, followed by voting. Rather a group decision is arrived at by consensus, with the chairman more or less "divining" the unexpressed will of the group.

In this connection, the following quotation taken from a news account of Hatoyama Ichiro's election as president of the Liberal Democratic Party is illuminating: "His election, however, did not come about as many of his supporters might have wished. Contrary to traditional unanimous installation of a new president in keeping with a prearranged understanding the choice this time took the form of balloting, which also publicly exposed intra-party strife."[5]

One result of this system of decision making is that unity is often very superficial and that not all those who participate in the decision are prepared to abide by it. Apparently many people believe that it is not inconsistent to agree to a course of action in a meeting and then ignore it as soon as the meeting has disbanded.

Political Power at the National Level

The tone and character of national politics depends to some extent on the men who are at the helm. As has been noted, in the Meiji period power came to be concentrated in the hands of an oligarchy which stemmed in the main from the lower ranks of the samurai class in several fiefs of western Japan. Although the establishment of a parliament in 1890 provided an institutional structure for a wider sharing of power, in practice the oligarchy managed to keep a tight hold on the government, at first by monopolizing the most important executive posts and later by manipulating their protégés from behind the scenes. For example, of those leaders who held cabinet posts between 1885 and 1918, about 55 per cent came from four geographical areas—the former feudal fiefs of Satsuma, Choshu, Tosa, and Hizen. It was not until about the end of the First World War that the influence of the oligarchy disappeared from the political area.

Among those who fell heir to the control of the government with the passing of the oligarchs were the higher bureaucrats, an overwhelming proportion of whom were graduates of Tokyo Imperial

[4] Fred Kerlinger, "Decision-Making in Japan," *Social Forces*, XXX, no. 1 (Oct. 1951), 38.

[5] *Japan News Letter*, no. 14 (April 6, 1956).

University; senior army and navy officers; and party politicians, some of whom had previous experience in or connections with business. Very clearly, men with different backgrounds joined the ranks of the elite; yet it is doubtful that they represented an essentially new type of leadership. Robert Scalapino has succinctly characterized the political leaders of this era as follows:

Japanese leaders have never been accepted on the basis of their ability to sway the minds and hearts of the masses; rather, public speech-making and oratory have been classified as vulgar by a large proportion of the political elite. Neither has independent thought and action achieved acclaim. The leader prototype has been a man distinguished by age, culture, and character—an individual with many "connections" and a capacity for intricate behind-the-scenes negotiations.[6]

As the foregoing passage suggests, Japanese leaders did not base their power on a mass following, but rather on establishing and maintaining connections with other elite individuals and groups. It was as if there was a silent conspiracy to keep the masses out of the picture and prevent them from having a voice in important political decisions.

The Allied Occupation, on the other hand, with a different political philosophy, purposefully sought to widen the base of the power structure. Woman suffrage was granted for the first time; institutional changes described in Chapter V were undertaken in an attempt to make the government more responsive to the public will; and, finally, many prewar leaders were removed, at least temporarily, by the purge. Moreover, the hold which the military had on the government was destroyed, paving the way for resumption of full civilian control of the government. Thus, defeat and occupation provided an almost unprecedented opportunity for new leadership to come to the fore.

Since institutionally the National Diet occupies a strategic place in the power structure, it would be instructive to see what changes have occurred in its personnel. As a result of the purge in 1945, a little over 90 per cent of the prewar Diet members affiliated with the Progressive Party, and some 44 per cent of those in the Liberal Party were denied the right to hold public office. It is not surprising, therefore, that in the first postwar election held in 1947 many "new faces" were elected. Of the 141 successful Liberal Party candidates, 102 or

---

[6] Robert Scalapino in *Modern Political Parties*, ed. by Sigmund Neumann (Chicago: University of Chicago Press, 1956), p. 328.

72 per cent were newcomers. The percentages for the Progressive
Party and the Social Democratic Party were even a little higher,
running about 76 per cent in both cases.

Various types of people were represented among the newcomers,
but an important group were men connected with business, either as
owners of enterprises or as corporation executives. In fact, there has
been a long-term trend in the direction of larger representation of
businessmen in the Diet. It is difficult to get accurate statistical data
on the occupational background of Diet members, for many of them
are engaged in several occupations. Table 5, however, gives a rough

Table 5. Occupational background of the members of the House of
Representatives, 1937–1949

Occupation	1937	1942	1946	1947	1949
Government officials	9	23	17	39	15
Members of armed forces	3	—	—	—	—
Doctors, pharmacists	10	7	14	7	4
Authors, publishers, journalists	51	61	30	35	34
Lawyers	87	70	51	46	43
Bank and corporation employees	72	87	109	116	153
Employees in commerce and industry	17	27	—	25	54
Agriculturalists	80	74	62	50	37
Mining employees	2	—	—	—	2
Educators	8	12	35	12	14
Other occupations	54	46	88	102	92
No occupation	73	59	38	34	92
Total	466	466	466	466	466

Source: *Jiji Nenkan,* 1952, p. 720.

outline of general trends. As might be expected, the conservative party
roster has more businessmen and corporation executives, whereas the
socialist party has proportionately more lawyers and, recently in
particular, officials of labor unions.

Between 1950 and 1951 the purge was rescinded for many individuals, enabling them to return to political life. In the 1952 national
elections a little over 30 per cent of those elected from the two conservative parties, the Liberal Party and the Progressive Party, were
so-called depurgees. In the 1955 national elections about 65 per cent
of the successful candidates of the Democratic Party had prewar
political experience, and a little less than 40 per cent of the Liberal

Party representatives had been active in the prewar period. That so many could make a successful comeback after some seven years of absence from public activity perhaps testifies to the essential continuity of political life in Japan.

When the uppermost levels of the elite structure are examined, evidence of continuity is even more apparent. Among prominent leaders of postwar parties have been such men as Ashida Hitoshi, Yoshida Shigeru, Shidehara Kijuro, and Shigemitsu Mamoru, all former foreign office officials; Hatoyama Ichiro, a prominent prewar politician; and Kishi Nobusuke, an ex-bureaucrat, who was purged by the Occupation authorities. Scalapino notes that "conservative party leaders thus far have been older men whose political experience was first established in the prewar period. Age, experience (though not necessarily political party experience), and access to funds continue to be primary qualifications for conservative leadership in Japan." [7]

The situation with respect to top leadership in the Social Democratic Party is essentially no different. In his study of Japanese socialist leadership, George Totten concludes:

When one considers, for example, the dozen or so top leaders in each wing [of the socialist party], the proportion of prewar leaders is striking: only one of the Right Wing was not a party functionary before the war, while only one-fourth of the Left were not. The observation that even today's Japanese Socialist leadership stems largely from the prewar generation is borne out by the fact that 70 per cent of the Right and 45 per cent of the Left are over fifty years old, and of the dozen top-rank Right Wing leaders, all except Sone are close to or over sixty. [8]

With the possible exception of the left wing of the Socialist Party, the top levels of political parties in Japan have not been strengthened by the infusion of new blood. As already indicated, institutional change has occurred. Yet it is a fact that many people who hold key positions within the institutional structure are those who by prior experience and training are more likely to feel at home in the old structure. If the parties are to develop effective programs and win the confidence and support of the electorate, they will, of necessity, need to recruit new and energetic leaders. Furthermore, if and when new types of leaders are recruited, they will probably reach the top through par-

[7] *Ibid.*, p. 341.
[8] George Totten, "Problems of Japanese Socialist Leadership," *Pacific Affairs*, XXVIII (June 1955), 160–161.

ticular channels. The conservative parties have four major sources of leadership recruitment.

(1) *The bureaucracy.* Since under the new constitution the majority of cabinet members must also be members of the National Diet, cabinet status, which carries with it high honor and great prestige, is denied to career civil servants. Those who have ambitions of becoming cabinet ministers must therefore at some point run for a seat in the National Diet. Ex-bureaucrats were particularly well represented in the old Liberal Party; in 1949 about 20 per cent of its members in the lower house were in this category. If one party succeeds in staying in office for an extended period and if the public continues to place high value on those who hold or have held official positions, the bureaucracy will probably continue to be an important source of party leaders.

(2) *Business.* Over the long term, an increasing number of business-men have been getting seats in the House of Representatives. With the high cost of election campaigns, as well as expenses such as entertainment, which burden those in office, men who have outside sources of income enjoy an advantage. In the postwar period repre-sentatives with a business background have been drawn from among owners of small- or medium-sized business establishments and from the middle ranks of big business.

(3) *The professions.* Of those with professional backgrounds, lawyers and journalists tend to predominate. Lawyers have a natural affinity for a job which primarily involves lawmaking. Lawyers are also able, as a rule, to maintain their practice even while holding a seat in the Diet, and this is helpful from the point of view of income. Journalists, on the other hand, can become well known through their writings and thus are in a position to capitalize on their fame for political purposes.

(4) *Local politics.* Local politics holds the promise of becoming one of the important channels of leadership recruitment. Here again, changes in the institutional structure have had their effect. In the postwar period many local government posts, such as governorships of prefectures, which were formerly appointive, have become elective. In addition, there has been a trend recently in which candidates for local office run under a party ticket rather than as independents. "The importance of the locally elected official," says Kenneth Colton, "is seen in the number of ex-governors elected in the July 1956 House

of Councilors elections, and in the frequency with which press analyses speculated on a candidate's chances by reference to the degree he was supported by prefectural assemblymen." [9]

These same channels are, of course, available to socialist leaders, but as might be expected there are fewer such leaders drawn from the bureaucracy or business. For the left wing of the Socialist Party, trade unions have been an important stepping stone. Many young socialist leaders have risen in the union hierarchy and then have run for office with the support of organized labor. In general, however, the socialist cause has been hampered by its inability to attract in large numbers men who have distinguished themselves and have won the admiration and respect of leading members of the community.

In the final analysis, it must be admitted that the choice of men who are put into positions of responsibility is partly related to popular attitudes regarding political leadership. It is therefore instructive to consider the matter of electoral behavior.

Electoral Behavior

Japanese writers often describe electoral behavior by reference to the three "ban," namely, *kamban* or signboard, *jiban* or foundation, and *kaban* or satchel.

Kamban, or signboard, poster, or billboard, signifies the candidate's reputation and his standing in the community. A man who has had a distinguished career as a government official, or is a prominent businessman, or is the head of an important local organization can get votes because of his name. For instance, a "big name" has an advantage particularly in the election to the House of Councilors from the nation at large. In this kind of election, *kamban* is often more important than party label, political ideology, or issues.

It used to be that candidates who were unsure of their standing could add to their drawing power by getting prominent individuals to speak on their behalf in their district. However, a legislator, who presumably knows from experience, has stated that nowadays voters are not so easily fooled.[10] One would suppose that voters are getting more sophisticated, for prior to the war a man who had been a

[9] Kenneth Colton, "The Conservative Political Movement," *Annals of the American Academy of Political and Social Science,* Nov. 1956, pp. 52–53.

[10] Kan'ichi Tsuji, *Jingasa* [Rank and File] (Tokyo, 1953), pp. 37–42.

cabinet minister was almost certain to be elected, but recently there have been instances where ex-ministers have not made the grade at election time.

The "attraction" exerted on voters by a candidate as an individual may be crudely measured in several ways. For instance, there are the results of a survey made on the eve of the 1949 national elections in an industrialized section of Tokyo. Voters were asked whether they cast their ballots for a candidate or for a party, and the answers have been tabulated in Table 6. As is shown, somewhere between one-fifth and one-half of those questioned said that they voted for candidates.

Table 6. Basis for voting: candidate vs. party

Age of voter	For candidate	For party	For both candidate and party	Don't know	Other
20–24	22% (33%) *	30% (41%)	25% (21%)	23% (5%)	(0%)
25–29	25 (33)	31 (47)	2 (20)	11 (0)	(0)
30–39	33 (39)	39 (40)	21 (19)	7 (1)	(1)
40–49	52 (34)	17 (42)	20 (21)	11 (3)	(0)
50–	48 (37)	15 (33)	20 (9)	17 (12)	(10)

* The figure in parentheses shows percentage of workers as distinguished from the population at large. Percentages apparently were rounded off, as the last age group totals more than 100.

Source: Ukai Nobushige, "Koba rodosha no tohyo kodo," *Sekai*, no. 84 (Dec. 1952), p. 93.

There seems to be a tendency—less obvious in the case of workers—for older voters to prefer to vote for candidates rather than for party affiliation.

Another way to get an idea of the personal influence which affects electoral behavior is to take the case of a candidate who has switched parties. Hirano Rikizo, a well-known socialist who had been active in the prewar period, ran for the House of Representatives in 1947 as a socialist and received 58,916 votes, to head the list. But he was purged by the Occupation for his wartime activities and so was unable to continue political life until 1952, when he ran on the Co-operative Party ticket. Even though the Co-operative Party was a minor party, obtaining only 1.2 per cent of the national vote, Hirano was able to win his seat with 47,183 votes. In the next election in 1953 he returned to the socialist fold and campaigned under the right-wing Socialist banner, polling 40,727 votes. In 1955, however, he changed his affiliation to a minor party and failed to be re-elected since he received only 20,794 votes. The case of Hirano demonstrates the ability of a candidate with a name to get votes regardless of changes in party affiliation, but it also shows that strength based on a personal following can decline suddenly.

A third example of the personal factor in voting is the strong support a candidate often gets from his "friends and neighbors." Localism is still a strong factor in Japanese politics, and many people tend to vote for the candidate who lives in their immediate vicinity, presumably on the theory that such a candidate is most likely to best represent local interests.

A run-down of election statistics indicates in numerous instances a close relationship between vote-getting ability and the place of residence of the candidate. Table 7 showing the distribution of votes

Table 7. Relationship between place of residence of candidates and votes cast, 1955

| City or town | Successful candidates | | | |
	J. Koizumi (Democrat)	S. Shimura (Left Socialist)	T. Noda (Democrat)	S. Yamamoto (Democrat)
Yokosuka-shi	38,234 *	17,149 *	5,245	17,370
Kawasaki-shi	8,592	27,116	31,948 *	15,192
Kamakura-shi	2,453	4,678	10,808	9,925 *
Zushi-shi	3,287	2,781	3,127	3,014
Miura-shi	3,130	2,603	793	3,314
Hayama-machi	1,863	835	869	1,222

* Total vote cast at place of residence of the candidate.

in the second electoral district in Kanagawa prefecture illustrates this relationship. In this district two out of the four successful candidates polled very heavy votes in their home areas.

Thus it can be said in a very general way that personal qualifications are often important; but it is also true that the personal element is not equally important for all voters. The tendency to vote for candidates rather than for party is more pronounced among older voters and among peasants, fishermen, and owners of small business enterprises. On the other hand, government officials, urban white-collar workers, teachers, students, and industrial workers are more apt to vote along party lines.

The second "ban" is *jiban,* or foundation or footing, and it refers to the political organization that a successful politician needs if he is to be returned to office time and time again. In order to be sure of securing the necessary number of votes on election day, a politician must make himself popular with the electorate and especially with influential community leaders. One legislator has written that he carries a notebook containing 400 names of prominent individuals to whom he writes frequently. In order to learn the names of people in his district, the same legislator studied photographs he had taken whenever he attended important social gatherings.[11] A frequently used tactic is to send picture postcards to voters, particularly when a potential candidate goes abroad. There are stories to the effect that conscientious politicians going on foreign trips have their aides at home cable lists of names of persons who were inadvertently overlooked when postcards were sent out.

There are other techniques of winning voter approval. A politician who wants to be successful must make it a point to attend public functions, speak to organized groups, such as women's groups, send flowers to funerals of prominent local leaders, contribute generously to worthy causes, distribute gifts, make social calls on such occasions as New Year's Day, entertain local dignitaries who come to visit the Diet when it is in session, find jobs for worthy young men, and do chores for constituents, such as interceding on their behalf with government agencies. The following account describes how a former representative from Tokyo, Takagi Masutaro, built his political organization:

This man [Takagi] was very thorough in what he did for elections. During festivals he was the first to present an offering with his name inscribed on it. At school graduations, he distributed cake, decorated with his name, among students. Naturally he went around making calls during the New Year holiday season; and he always assisted at weddings and funerals. During the Diet sessions he always mounted the rostrum several times. Whenever the interests of the townspeople were involved, he would attend the committee sessions, even if he was not a member of that particular committee; and he would have a transcript of the meetings distributed among the voters.[12]

As present electoral districts (for the House of Representatives) are fairly large, embracing in some instances a whole prefecture, a politician cannot hope to establish close personal ties with every voter.

[11] Kan'ichi Tsuji, *Jingasa*, p. 36.
[12] Yoshinao Washio, ed., *Seikai Gojunen: Kojima Kazuo Kaikoroku* [Fifty Years in the Political World: The Memoirs of Kojima Kazuo] (Tokyo, 1951), p. 248.

He must therefore rely on others to get out the vote for him on election day. A member of the lower house, for example, will have several followers, whom he more or less controls either through personal ties or through financial aid. Such followers may be active in prefectural politics, perhaps holding a seat in the prefectural assembly, and they in turn will have followers operating at a lower level, in city and town politics, for example, and so on down the line until there will be at the base of the pyramid informal neighborhood groups, tradesmen's organizations, women's groups, and the like.

No doubt it takes diligent effort to build a *jiban*, but once built it often lasts. There have been instances in which a political organization has been inherited by a politician's widow or son and even by a favored disciple.

The third "ban" is *kaban*, or satchel, which symbolically holds money used for election purposes. In Japan, as in the United States, large sums are needed to carry on a successful election campaign. Every candidate must open campaign headquarters, print and distribute thousands of posters and leaflets, entertain friends and supporters, and rent sound trucks to go up and down the streets calling out the candidate's name and urging voters to cast their ballots for him. There is also, in some instances, vote buying, either directly or through so-called "election brokers." A big item of expense is money needed to lubricate the political machine. Those at the top levels of the organization must provide funds for their immediate followers, who in turn pass on a portion of what they receive to their followers, down to the lowest levels of the organization.

Because money almost always lies at the root of political corruption, attempts have been made to regulate by law the amount candidates are permitted to spend on a campaign. The total amount legally allowed is determined by dividing the number of registered voters by the number of representatives elected from that district and multiplying by 4 yen. Everyone assumes that no candidate takes such legal limits seriously, and one legislator says that five to six times the amount permissible by law is generally enough.[13]

Attempts are also made to control election expenditure by requiring political parties and organizations to report to the government contributions received. These reports show that the conservatives collect funds from individual wealthy businessmen, from corporations, both large and small, and from trade associations. The socialists, on the

[13] Tsuji, *op. cit.*, p. 42.

other hand, are supported in the main by labor unions, which often assess each member for this purpose. In order to be certain that they will always have friends no matter who gets into office, some corporations contribute to both the conservatives and the socialists. In addition, individual candidates raise money from sundry sources. Since about a thousand candidates compete for seats in the House of Representatives, a large amount of money goes into circulation every time an election is held.

The Determinants of Voting

The individual voter must now be considered, to determine if possible what makes him vote the way he does. As in the United States, tradition is one of the elements, although in Japan loyalty seems to be focused more on individuals than on party labels. For instance, some voters who have been consistently supporting a political leader will transfer their support to his son who succeeds him.

An element which is probably growing in importance is economic interest. The conservatives generally favor the interests of business and of property holders, and thus it is not surprising that businessmen, landowners, corporation executives, and higher bureaucrats tend to vote for conservative candidates. The socialists, because of their Marxian orientation, think of themselves as basically a class party built around the proletariat. Surveys show that socialists tend to be favored by organized workers in large plants, but that those employed in small establishments where a paternalistic relationship exists between owner and employee are more likely to prefer conservative candidates. As might be expected, the conservative strength is centered in the rural areas, whereas the industrialized cities form the strongholds of the Socialist Party.

A third element which may determine the way one votes is manipulation by others. There are always some individuals—found most often in small rural communities—who will vote according to instructions from other people, either out of indifference or of fear. For some voters, politics, especially at the national level, is difficult to understand and remote from problems of everyday life. Accordingly, they are easily persuaded by a local leader to vote for a particular candidate, as can be seen from the following account by Paul Dull:

As elections approached, the *senkyoya* [local political boss] made known the candidate he supported. However, the statement of advocacy was couched in the proper symbols, symbols to which his followers would respond. There was nothing so crude as the *senkyoya's* telling his followers to vote for a candidate. The *buraku senkyoya* [political boss of the hamlet] might be politically sophisticated (although not necessarily so); the *buraku* [hamlet] inhabitants were, for the most part, unaware of the dynamics of politics and merely responded to their leader's words conveyed through proper symbols such as a candidate's idealism, sincerity, past reputation, and his willingness to work for the tangible benefit of the *buraku*.[14]

In some instances actual coercion takes place. Let us assume that a local bigwig has promised to deliver a certain number of votes to a candidate. This local leader will then ask voters in his area over whom he can exercise persuasion to vote for his candidate, using as leverage such things as power to control credit. In rural communities it is not too difficult for a local political boss to find out whether or not a voter has actually followed his instructions. A local leader, for example, has been quoted to the effect that when a voter has cast his ballot as he has been told he will usually drop in on the way home from the polls to report the fact, whereas someone who has not will avoid him.[15]

Finally, the way in which institutional arrangements affect voting behavior must be examined. At present Japan is divided into 118 electoral districts which send between three and five representatives to the lower house. Each voter, however, writes in the name of only one candidate. This means that a candidate needs the support of merely a minority of voters in his district to be among the top three to five. The percentage of votes necessary to win will depend, of course, on the number of candidates running and the spread of votes among them.

Many Japanese voters do not like to "waste" votes, that is, they are reluctant to support a man who seems to have no chance of winning or a man who is likely to win by a wide margin. There have been instances in which a candidate who secured the largest number of votes in one election dropped very low in the following election. Campaigning, therefore, becomes a tricky art, and candidates try to avoid giving the impression that they are sure to win.

The Legislative Process

One of the functions of elected officials is lawmaking, and it is pertinent to know something of the way in which these men make

[14] Paul S. Dull, "The *Senkyoya* System in Rural Japanese Communities," in University of Michigan, Center for Japanese Studies, *Occasional Papers,* no. 4 (1953), p. 30.

[15] "Aru Mura De Kiku" [We Heard in a Certain Village], *Asahi Shimbun,* Jan. 6, 1955.

the laws. In present-day Japan, bills which are put into the legislative
hopper may originate in several places. An individual member may
present a bill if it has the approval of 20 or more members in the
lower house and of 10 or more members in the upper house. Bills
necessitating an appropriation of funds call for 50 and 20 signatures
respectively. Proportionately the number of bills actually submitted
by individual Diet members is small. Other sources of bills are
the various committees of the Diet, policy research committees of
the political parties, and the cabinet.

The great majority of bills are sponsored by government agencies
and come to the Diet via the cabinet. In the course of their operations,
bureaus and agencies may find that they must carry out some administrative action or that existing legislation is inadequate or unworkable. In such an instance, a section or a bureau in a ministry
will draft a bill, very often with the assistance of the Bureau of
Legislation. This bureau is under the cabinet, and its job is, among
other things, to see that the proposed measure is in line with existing
legislation, that it has no loopholes, and that it is technically and
legally correct. After the bill has been discussed at various levels
within the ministry concerned and has secured the backing of that
ministry, it is sent to the cabinet.

In the case of important bills, steps are taken to get the views
of outsiders through the medium of advisory committees. These committees—consisting of scholars, government officials, and representatives of various groups—can make known their views or, if they
are so asked, can even draw up detailed provisions of the proposed
law.

At the beginning of each Diet session, the cabinet gets a list of
bills presented by the ministries and agencies. Those bills that are
carefully drawn up and meet no opposition from other agencies
usually stay on the list, are approved by the cabinet, and eventually
are introduced in the Diet.

When a bill reaches the lower house, it is referred to an appropriate
committee on the recommendation of the Ways and Means Committee. If the Ways and Means Committee believes the bill to be
of such importance that it should be brought to the attention of all
legislators as well as the public, it may be explained in a plenary session
before it is referred to a committee.

As a part of its deliberations, the committee will often hold public
hearings to give interested parties an opportunity to present their
views, and it may summon cabinet members and other officials to

provide information and answer questions. After the committee has approved a bill by a majority vote, it is put on the calendar and in due time comes before a plenary session of the Diet.

The chairman of the committee will report to the plenary session the decision of the committee, together with a summary of the deliberations. If there is a minority report, this will also be placed before the plenary session. A motion to amend the bill must have the support of at least 20 members in the lower house (10 in the House of Councilors); a bill calling for appropriations or an increase in appropriations must have 50 supporters in the lower house and 20 supporters in the upper house. Members who wish to speak on the bill must, as a rule, ask the secretariat of the House of Representatives to put their names on the list which the Speaker will use in recognizing members. The Speaker can limit the time allotted to those speaking, and an effort is made to give equal time to both proponents and opponents of the bill. When the debate comes to an end, members will vote on the bill; usually those in favor will be asked to stand. When the vote is close, however, or when more than one-fifth of those present take issue with the Speaker's decision, voting is by ballot. As soon as a bill is passed by one house, it is sent to the other.

Voting in the Diet is strictly controlled by political parties. Chitoshi Yanaga writes:

In the Diet the party caucus, which is the center of practical party politics, is used constantly. For the Japanese who have a strong predilection for consultation in making decisions in any sphere or any level, the party caucus is a natural procedure. Without it, it would be impossible to manage political affairs. Members of the Diet are rigidly bound by the decisions of the caucus and few dare to disregard them.[16]

Bureaucratic Behavior

Although the Diet makes laws, often it is the bureaucracy which draws up proposed legislation; and it is certainly the bureaucracy which administers laws put on the statute books by the legislature. As Carl Friedrich says, "All realistic study of government has to start with an understanding of bureaucracy (or whatever else one prefers to call it), because no government can function without it." [17]

[16] Chitoshi Yanaga, *Japanese People and Politics* (New York: Wiley, 1956), p. 267.

[17] Carl J. Friedrich, *Constitutional Government and Democracy* (Boston: Little, Brown, 1941), p. 57.

The Japanese bureaucracy has certain characteristics which affect its role in the political system. Before the war the bureaucracy was a closely knit organization, staffed largely by graduates of Tokyo Imperial University with training in law. As a result, civil servants took a highly legalistic approach to administrative problems, and in cases in which there was no statute or precedent to provide guidance, decisions were delayed. Although in the postwar period graduates from other universities have entered the civil service in somewhat greater numbers, many of the top posts are still held by Tokyo University graduates, and the bureaucracy remains to a large degree parochial and legalistic in its outlook.

Traditionally officials held an exalted place in society, and, accordingly, they were arrogant when dealing with the public. Under the 1947 constitution, "all public servants are servants of the whole community and not any group thereof," but in practice the notion that a bureaucrat is a "public servant" remains somewhat alien to Japanese mentality. Japanese government agencies still have much to learn about public relations and the art of becoming more responsive to public wishes and needs.

A third characteristic of the Japanese bureaucracy is its fragmentation. The various sections, bureaus, and ministries which make up the administrative structure are highly jealous of their status and prerogatives. One branch of the government will often refuse to share information and reports with other branches, so that sections within the government will be working at cross-purposes or will be duplicating work. In many instances there is little or no co-ordination of governmental activities.

In Japan, as elsewhere, what government does or fails to do affects the interests of many people. For example, the government regulates, directly or indirectly, all kinds of economic activities through its power to grant licenses, its control of foreign exchange, its allocation of subsidies, its purchases of goods and services for defense and other needs, and so on. Given the nature of the bureaucracy, it is to the advantage of those who have frequent dealings with government agencies to establish close personal ties with important government officials.

There are several ways by which this may be achieved. In the past, companies hired bureaucrats, who by custom retired from government service in their forties and fifties, for the purpose of maintaining personal connections with agencies. One account states that "enterprising businessmen offer comfortable posts—virtual sine-cures—to pensioned officials in exchange for public favors arranged through their junior colleagues who remain in service." [18] The National Public Service Law enacted in the postwar period attempts to discourage this practice by prohibiting an official for a period of two years from taking a post with a firm which had dealings with his agency.

Another method is to become well acquainted with important officials by entertaining them lavishly. Businessmen have been known to send their private cars to government offices to pick up officials and take them to golf courses and geisha parties. The newspaper *Asahi* once quoted a businessman as saying that if anyone wants to have an application acted upon "you have to become so friendly with officials that you can pick up the telephone and get section chiefs and bureau chiefs to act." [19]

Finally, a more permanent and institutionalized relationship between a government agency and interest groups is established through organizations known as *gaikaku dantai* or auxiliary organizations. The Ministry of Agriculture, which distributes large sums as subsidies, is said to have some 300 such organizations attached to it. These organizations, which get financial aid from the government agencies, help to provide liaison between a particular agency and the public concerned with its work and also furnish certain services such as publishing reports—some of them written by government officials—and specialized journals and magazines. Another link between government agencies and these auxiliary organizations is supplied by civil servants who retire from government service and take jobs as officers of such organizations. Finally, these organizations serve as convenient steppingstones to elective office. For example, an administrator in the Ministry of Agriculture may first become an officer of one of the auxiliary organizations connected with the ministry and then use his contacts with the farm population to get support for his candidacy.

[18] Hugh H. MacDonald and Milton J. Esman, "The Japanese Civil Service," *Public Personnel Review*, Oct. 1946, p. 223.

[19] In the Dec. 31, 1954, issue.

· VIII ·

Problems of

Contemporary Japan

ANY government, if it is to survive, must be able to provide reasonably workable solutions to problems that confront the nation. In the case of Japan the tasks of statesmanship are formidable, for the problems to which solutions must be found are deep-seated and difficult. Because it is beyond the scope of the present work to treat these matters in detail, three topics—in the field of the economy, defense, and foreign relations—which appear to be particularly significant will be discussed briefly in this chapter.

Economic Problems

Japan's economic goals are no different from those of many other nations, namely, to provide stable employment, economic and social security, and a rising standard of living for its population. To attain these goals, Japan must have a viable economy; but this is not so easily achieved.

As it well known, Japan is poor in resources. Despite the fact that a little less than one-half the population is engaged in agriculture, Japan cannot produce enough food to meet requirements and must now import at least 20 per cent of the food consumed annually. Japan, moreover, is deficient in most of the raw materials required by the industrial machine and is completely dependent upon foreign sources for raw cotton, raw wool, rubber, bauxite, and phosphate rock. Japan must also import much of the iron ore, salt, zinc and petroleum needed and about one-third of the coking coal. Thus it is evident that Japan must import if the population is to be fed and the important industries kept running.

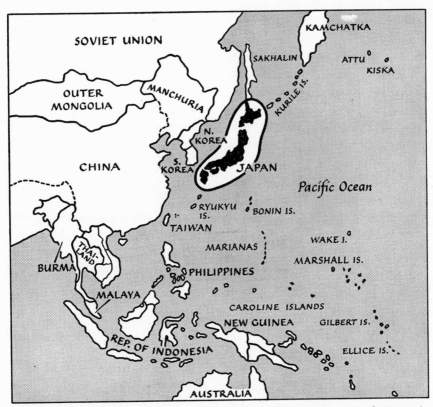

Map 6. Present area of Japan. (As redrawn from the *New York Times.*)

In order to pay for these essential imports Japan must convert raw materials into manufactured goods and sell them to foreign customers. Another way to pay for imports is to furnish services, such as carrying ocean freight in Japanese-owned merchant ships. Since the surrender in 1945, Japanese economy has made a remarkable recovery, particularly when the circumstances are considered. During the war the cities of Japan were severely damaged as a result of air raids, and following the defeat investments and colonies abroad as well as traditional markets were lost. Despite these handicaps, by 1954 Japan's level of manufacturing, when compared to the period between 1934 and 1936, had risen 74 per cent, and real income per capita was 5 per cent higher.

Even these gains were not sufficient, however, to enable Japan to balance imports against exports. Before the war Japan's share of the total world trade was about 5 per cent, but in 1955 it was only about one-half of that. In terms of volume, Japan's exports in 1955 were about one-half the 1937 level, and imports were about three-fourths the prewar level. In the decade following the end of the war, Japan has been able to stay in the black, so to speak, only because the United States has provided some $5 billion, in the form either of direct aid or of military procurement and spending by U.S. armed forces in Japan.

Clearly in order to improve the economy Japan must expand foreign trade considerably. This, however, is not easily accomplished, with the obstacles that now exist. In many instances the flow of Japanese goods to foreign consumers is impeded, in varying degrees, by tariff barriers, import quotas, boycots, competition from other nations, and restrictions on the conversion of foreign exchange. For example, in recent years American producers have lodged protests against the continued importation of plywood, textiles, and tuna from Japan. At present Japan purchases large amounts of cotton, iron ore, coal, and other raw materials from the United States and then sells goods made from these raw materials in nondollar areas, resulting in the depletion of Japanese dollar reserves.

Another matter which further complicates the picture is the establishment of a Communist regime on the Chinese mainland. Before the war, China—parts of which were under the direct or indirect control of Japan—was an excellent market for consumer goods and a source of raw materials, including coal, iron ore, and soybeans. Understandably many Japanese businessmen look back with nostalgia on the prewar China trade and argue that many of Japan's economic ills could be solved by increased trade with Communist China.

During the last decade, Japan's trade with the Chinese mainland has remained at a low level, partly because of political reasons. The United States has been particularly anxious to prevent the Chinese Communist regime from acquiring strategic materials from the free world, with the result that Japan has refrained from selling many items. But even if American policy with regard to this matter should be relaxed—and it seems certain that Japan will be allowed to trade more and more with the mainland—there is still the question of what

China would use to pay for imports. The Chinese Communists have embarked on an ambitious industrialization program and will need their iron ore and coal, which otherwise they might sell to Japan in exchange for capital goods. An American economist has come to the conclusion that "in terms of present ability to supply Japan's import needs, the Communist bloc has little to offer Japan." [1]

There is, finally, the element of Japanese production costs which serves to act as a brake on further growth of foreign trade. Over the years there has been a gradual shift in the Japanese economy from textiles to metals and chemicals. Textiles, to be sure, are still important, but their relative position is fairly certain to decline even more. Production costs of metals and machinery, however, are higher in Japan than elsewhere. It is said that the man-hours needed to produce a ton of pig iron or steel in Japan is twice the amount needed in Great Britain. [2] To maintain Japan's competitive position industrial efficiency must be raised, and this means in part that Japanese industrial output must be increased without adding substantially to the labor force engaged in manufacturing.

But, as a Japanese economist notes, "the Japanese economy is beset with the perennial problem of oversupply of people who seek work; and the energetic introduction of labor-saving machinery, while improving the competitive position abroad of Japan's manufactured products, creates at the same time internal strains on the employment front." [3] Japan's population now numbers about 90 million, and whereas the net increase of births over deaths is declining, the population is still increasing about 1 million per year. Moreover, the age composition of the population is such that about a million people are being added to the labor force annually. Unless Japan's economy can expand to absorb increases in the labor supply, chronic unemployment will be the result, and it requires no great imagination to see that large-scale unemployment will contribute to social and political instability. For this reason, various Japanese government agencies are constantly engaged in economic planning, regulation, and aid in an effort to solve economic problems. How successful these efforts will be in the long run remains to be seen.

[1] Jerome B. Cohen, "Problems in Foreign Trade and Investment," *Annals of the American Academy of Political and Social Science,* Nov. 1956, p. 100.

[2] *Ibid.,* p. 97.

[3] Shigeto Tsuru, "Internal Industrial and Business Trends," *Annals of the American Academy of Political and Social Science,* Nov. 1956, p. 94.

Defense Problems

Because of its large population (fifth largest in the world), its industrial capacity, and its strategic position off the continent of Asia, Japan cannot remain aloof from international developments, particularly as they relate to the Great Powers. Japan must necessarily consider the problem of national defense in a world marked by tension. Yet it must be noted that the Japanese, despite their long record of militarism, have shown in the postwar decade a preference for international co-operation and even for pacifism. They have begun to rearm only with reluctance.

The recent history of Japan's defense problems has been characterized by curious and ironical twists and turns. After the end of the war the aim of the United States and other nations was to destroy Japan's ability to wage war, and toward that end steps were taken to demobilize completely the Japanese armed forces. A provision was even written into the 1947 constitution forever renouncing "war as a sovereign right of the nation and the threat or use of force as a means of settling international disputes."

Within a few years, however, American policy was reversed because of increased tension between the United States and the Soviet Union and the Chinese Communist victory on the mainland. In June 1950, two weeks after the outbreak of war in Korea, General MacArthur authorized the creation of a National Police Reserve of 75,000 men. This marked the beginning of Japan's rearmament.

Since then there has been a gradual strengthening of Japan's armed forces. In the security treaty signed between the United States and Japan in 1951, it was anticipated that American forces and troops maintained in Japan to provide for its defense would be gradually withdrawn as Japan increased its armed forces.

In 1952 the National Police Reserve force was changed to a National Safety Force of 110,000 men, equipped and organized with American help. Seven frigates were also leased to Japan by the United States in order to provide the beginnings of a Japanese navy. Two years later, in 1954, the National Safety Force was changed into the National Defense Force, and provisions were made for an air force. By 1956 more than 180,000 men were in uniform within the three branches of the armed forces.

To achieve even this modest build-up required extensive political maneuvering on the part of Japanese leaders. From the beginning the socialists have been opposed to rearmament and have advocated instead a policy of "neutralism." In this the socialists have had the support of numerous intellectuals, women, and young men. Resistance to rearmament rests on both psychological and financial grounds.

Many people share the underlying fear that rearmament will ultimately lead to the revival of militarism and that the government will again be dominated by professional soldiers. There is also the fear that rearmament will invite attack and invasion rather than prevent it. Those who think along these lines argue that it would be easier to avoid involvement in case of another world war if Japan had no army, navy, or air force. Finally, some resist rearmament in the belief that Japanese forces might be used less to defend Japan's national interest than to further the policies of other nations such as the United States.

The realities of the situation, however, pose a dilemma for those who oppose rearmament. Japan has by treaty granted the United States the right to maintain bases and station troops in Japan. The presence of foreign troops has offended the Japanese sense of nationalism, has led to problems of jurisdiction over American troops, and has created conflict between military needs, such as bigger airfields, and the interests of those Japanese residing in the vicinity of bases. Many people would like to see American troops withdrawn, and they realize that probably the best way to bring this about would be to build up Japanese military strength. These considerations led to a meeting in Washington in 1957 between President Eisenhower and Prime Minister Kishi Nobusuke, which resulted in an agreement calling for the gradual withdrawal of American forces from Japan beginning in 1957 and continuing thereafter.

It has been mentioned that financial considerations also affect thinking on the problem of rearmament. The high cost of modern weapons of war such as radar, jet planes, guided missiles, and so on impose a heavy burden on small nations like Japan. Because the United States has been contributing to the total cost of rearmament, Japan's outlay, though it has been increasing over the years, is still not very large. In the fiscal year 1956 total appropriations for defense purposes came to 13.6 per cent of the budget and about 2.2 per cent of the national income. Undoubtedly as American aid decreases in the future, Japan's share will increase substantially; and there is a question whether Japan will be able to afford the most up-to-date weapons in sufficient quantity to be really effective in case of hostilities.

So far Japan has managed to rearm through very broad interpretation of the constitutional clause prohibiting rearmament. The time will come, however, when it will be necessary to amend the constitution in order to push forward the rearmament program. For example, without an amendment conscription would probably be impossible.

At present the socialists control more than one-third of the seats in the National Diet, and so long as they maintain their present stand of opposition to rearmament, constitutional amendment is not feasible. Any Japanese action on full-scale rearmament is therefore likely to remain stalemated for some time.

Foreign Relations

Historically Japan has gone through extended periods of relative isolation from its neighbors. Even today many Japanese might find it preferable, given the world situation, to adopt an attitude of Swisslike neutrality and avoid involvement in the power struggles among nations. However desirable such a policy might be in solving some of Japan's problems, it would be difficult to carry out. Many factors compel Japan to have continuing contacts with foreign countries—strategic position, the fact of being the most industrialized nation in Asia, dependence on foreign trade for very existence. More than many other countries, Japan is confronted with the problem of maintaining friendly relations with neighboring nations.

It is therefore unfortunate that several external and internal factors tend to impede the development of amicable relations between Japan and other countries. For instance, continued tension between the United States and her allies and the Soviet bloc has posed diplomatic problems. The policy of the conservative government in Japan is to maintain an alliance with the United States and at the same time come to some kind of working arrangement with Soviet Russia and Communist China, particularly with reference to trade matters. If Japan leans too far in the direction of friendship with these Communist countries, friendly relations with the United States will be jeopardized. Yet the Japanese government cannot maintain a completely hostile attitude toward Communist China and Soviet Russia, first, because Japan lies in the shadow of Communist military power and, second, because there are domestic pressures from socialists and others who want a more "independent" policy.

Relations with the countries of Southeast Asia will have a vital bearing on the economic future of the Japanese nation. Potentially

Southeast Asia could provide some of Japan's raw materials, which are now procured elsewhere, and would absorb more Japanese manufactured goods as well as services. In countries such as the Philippines and Indonesia, the legacy of hatred toward Japan inherited from wartime occupation and the fear of possible revival of Japanese militarism have been greatly diminished in recent years. Agreements reached between Japan and some of the Southeast Asian countries for the payment of reparations by Japan has also helped to bring about more cordial relations.

Japan's relations with its nearest neighbor, South Korea, have been most unhappy. The so-called Rhee Line has proved to be an important point of dispute. This boundary line, established by President Syngman Rhee, lies from 60 to 170 miles off the Korean coast, and Japanese fishermen are forbidden to enter the waters thus set off. Fishermen who have crossed this boundary have been seized and imprisoned. Conflicting claims over property and the treatment of Koreans residing in Japan have also engendered hostile feelings between the two countries. The United States is allied with both countries and because of the antagonism between Japan and Korea has sometimes been placed in a difficult position.

Without doubt, the maintenance of friendly relations with the United States is of utmost importance from the Japanese point of view. Fortunately, when all things are considered, the two nations have succeeded to a remarkable degree in achieving harmony. This does not mean, however, that there have been no areas of dispute. The maintenance of military bases and the stationing of United States troops in Japan may well lead to continued friction over the requisitioning of farm lands, problems of jurisdiction over American personnel, and incidents between Japanese civilians and American soldiers.

Another issue of some duration has involved the testing of atomic weapons in the south Pacific. For understandable reasons, the people of Japan are particularly sensitive to atomic weapons, and public opinion is easily aroused on the subject. On numerous occasions Japan has protested the testing of these weapons because of the fear of fallout and the contamination of fishing grounds. Left-wing political groups in Japan have used this issue to create an image of the United States as a callous and warlike nation.

A third source of friction is the American occupation of Okinawa. Under the terms of the San Francisco Treaty, "residual sovereignty" of Japan over Okinawa was recognized, with the implication that eventually the territory would be restored to Japan. But, in the meantime, the United States controls the area and has established numerous military installations. Additional land now in cultivation is being taken over for military use, and heated discussions have resulted between the American military authorities and the local residents who are forced to give up their farm land. The Okinawans have appealed to Japan for help in their dispute with the United States, and they have received support from the Socialist Party and many important Japanese newspapers.

The Okinawa case, along with other problems relating to foreign policy, has helped to accentuate the gulf between the conservatives who control the government and the socialists who form the opposition. Thus, even if it is only indirectly, the United States and other nations are exerting an influence in the matter of political stability and the creation of a political consensus within Japan.

As to the betterment of international understanding between Japan and other nations, there are domestic obstacles which must be considered. During the past century, foreign relations have preoccupied many of Japan's leaders. The drive, for example, to modernize the country in order to become strong was sustained by the determination to make Japan a leading member of the community of nations. The Meiji leaders, with their samurai background, were habituated to thinking of nations, as well as individuals, not as equals but rather as units arranged in a hierarchical structure, and they set as their goal the attainment for Japan of a position in the upper levels of the world hierarchy. As modernization was begun, the notion of Japan as the leader of Asia took root, and with the advent of the twentieth century the Japanese looked upon themselves in that light.

Japan's defeat in the Second World War with the subsequent decline in status from a world power to that of a small nation has produced profound psychological effects among the Japanese population. Seemingly nations cannot undergo a marked change in status without some violent repercussions in the attitude of their citizens.

Certainly the initial response after the end of the Second World War was withdrawal from active consideration of foreign relations problems and shifting of responsibility for such matters to the Occupation authorities. With the end of the Occupation in 1952 came a renewed sense of nationalism and a desire to pursue a more independent foreign policy. Nevertheless, there were indications that many people remained unsure as to Japan's position in the world.

A public opinion poll carried out in 1954 in Tokyo and in one of the prefectures produced the following results in answer to the question "Do you think Japan can become a first-rate power again?" [4]

	Tokoyo	Prefecture
Cannot	35.8%	42.6%
Can	35.8	27.6
No need to become first-rate power	7.3	3.7
Other replies	3.4	4.2
Don't know; no answer	17.7	21.9

Thus, according to this survey, somewhere between one-fourth and one-third of those polled believe that Japan can regain its status as a first-rate power; the others either believe that the status cannot be regained or are uncertain about it.

In the same poll, another question was asked: "What aspects of Japan can we boast about to other people?" [5] The response was as follows:

	Tokoyo	Prefecture
Culture, spiritual power	18.4%	9.8%
Natural beauty of country	1.9	4.6
Fine arts	14.0	16.7
Emperor system, family system	4.1	5.1
Other	12.9	7.0
None	16.8	21.4
Don't know	31.9	35.3

This shows that much uncertainty exists concerning those elements of Japanese culture in which the citizen may take pride. For about one-half of those questioned there is apparently nothing in the Japanese culture which stands out as distinctive and worthy.

It might therefore be concluded that nations, like the individuals who comprise it, need the satisfaction of important and worth-while achievements. Perhaps in the long run the most difficult problem to solve will be that of the psychological adjustment to Japan's altered position in the world.

[4] Naikaku Soridaijin Kanbo Chosashitsu, *Kokumin Seiji Ishiki ni kansuru Chosa* [Research on the Political Consciousness of the People] (Tokyo, 1954), p. 15.
[5] *Ibid.*

SUGGESTED READING

III: The Historical Background

Bellah, Robert. *Tokugawa Religion: The Values of Pre-industrial Japan.* Glencoe, Ill.: Free Press, 1957. An interesting attempt to evaluate religious factors involved in the development of an industrial society in Japan.

Borton, Hugh. *Japan's Modern Century.* New York: Ronald Press, 1955. A narrative account with some interpretation of major trends in recent Japanese history.

Maxon, Yale Candee. *Control of Japanese Foreign Policy: A Study of Civil-Military Rivalry, 1930–1945.* Berkeley: University of California Press, 1957. The story of the failure to achieve co-ordination between the civil and military branches of the government.

Norman, E. Herbert. *Japan's Emergence as a Modern State.* New York: Institute of Pacific Relations, 1940. Somewhat outdated, but still the best introduction in English to the Meiji political and economic scene.

Reischauer, Edwin. *Japan, Past and Present.* Rev. and enl. ed. New York: Knopf, 1953. An excellent introduction to Japanese history.

Sansom, George B. *Japan: A Short Cultural History.* Rev. ed. New York: Appleton-Century, 1943. A classic work covering Japan's historical development to the early 19th century.

——. *The Western World and Japan.* New York: Knopf, 1950. Covers the 19th century with particular reference to the Western impact.

Schwantes, Robert S. *Japanese and Americans: A Century of Cultural Relations.* New York: Harper, 1955. A thoughtful study of the cultural relations between the United States and Japan.

Smith, Thomas C. *Political Change and Industrial Development in Japan: Government Enterprise, 1868–1880.* Stanford: Stanford University Press, 1955. Describes the role of government in Japanese industrialization.

Yanaga, Chitoshi. *Japan since Perry.* New York: McGraw-Hill, 1950. An encyclopedic account useful mostly as a reference work.

IV: The Social and Economic Structure

Benedict, Ruth. *The Chrysanthemum and the Sword.* Boston: Houghton Mifflin, 1946. An anthropologist's interpretation of Japan; interesting and provocative but must be used with care.

Cole, Allan B. *Japanese Society and Politics: The Impact of Social Stratification and Mobility on Politics.* Boston: Department of Government, Boston University, 1956. A brief but excellent exposition of changes in the elite structure.

Embree, John. *Suye Mura: A Japanese Village.* Chicago: University of Chicago Press, 1939. A pioneering study of a village in southern Japan.

Haring, Douglas G. *Personal Character and Cultural Milieu.* 3d rev. ed. Syracuse: Syracuse University Press, 1956. Contains chapters on Japanese personal character.

Lockwood, William L. *The Economic Development of Japan: Growth and Structural Change, 1868–1938.* Princeton: Princeton University Press, 1954. An outstanding treatment of Japanese economic development.

Maruyama, Masao. "The Ideology and Movement of Japanese Fascism," *Japan Annual of Law and Politics,* no. 1 (1952). An abstract of an important work by a leading Japanese political scientist.

Nagai, Michio. *Dozoku: A Preliminary Study of the Japanese "Extended Family" Group and Its Social and Economic Functions.* Columbus: Ohio State University Research Foundation, 1953. A report on the extended-family system in Japan.

Norbeck, Edward. *Takashima: A Japanese Fishing Village.* Salt Lake City: University of Utah Press, 1954. An anthropological survey of a fishing village.

Reischauer, Edwin. *The United States and Japan.* Rev. ed. Cambridge, Mass.: Harvard University Press, 1957. An excellent general account of modern Japan.

Stoetzel, Jean. *Without the Chrysanthemum and the Sword.* New York: Columbia University Press, 1955. An analysis of political and social attitudes among Japanese youth by a French sociologist.

V: Governmental Organization

Japan, Ministry of Education. *Kokutai no Hongi.* Trans. by John Owen Gauntlett. Cambridge, Mass.: Harvard University Press, 1949. A translation of an official statement of *kokutai.*

Maki, John M. "The Prime Minister's Office and Executive Power," *Far Eastern Survey,* vol. XXIV (May 1955). Discusses the functions of the Prime Minister's Office to which are attached numerous specialized agencies.

Quigley, Harold S. *Japanese Government and Politics: An Introductory Study.* New York: Century, 1932. A standard work on the prewar Japanese government.

——, and John E. Turner. *The New Japan: Government and Politics.* Minneapolis: University of Minnesota Press, 1956. Particularly good on the background of the postwar constitution.

Smythe, Hugh, and Masaharu Watanabe. "Japanese Popular Attitudes toward the Emperor," *Pacific Affairs,* vol. XXVI (Dec. 1953). Quotes public opinion polls on the Emperor system.

Steiner, Kurt. "The Japanese Village and Its Government," *Far Eastern Quarterly,* vol. XV (Feb. 1956). An evaluation of reforms in local government structure.

Supreme Commander for the Allied Powers. *Political Reorientation of Japan, Sept. 1945 to Sept. 1948.* 2 vols. Washington, D.C.: U.S. Government Printing Office, 1949. An official account of the role of the Occupation in modifying Japanese political institutions.

Ward, Robert E. "The Origins of the Present Japanese Constitution," *American Political Science Review,* vol. L (Dec. 1956). Reveals the part played by the Occupation in the drafting of the new constitution.

Wildes, Harry Emerson. *Typhoon in Tokyo.* New York: Macmillan, 1954. A critique of the Occupation by a participant.

Yanaga, Chitoshi. *Japanese People and Politics.* New York: Wiley, 1956. Contains a detailed description of the organization of the postwar government.

VI: *Major Political Forces*

Colbert, Evelyn S. *The Left Wing in Japanese Politics.* New York: Institute of Pacific Relations, 1952. A description of the left wing with particular reference to the socialists.

Farley, Miriam S. *Aspects of Japan's Labor Problems.* New York: John Day, 1950. Discusses changes in Japanese labor under the Occupation.

Ike, Nobutaka. *The Beginnings of Political Democracy in Japan.* Baltimore: Johns Hopkins Press, 1950. Treats the origins and early growth of Japanese political parties.

Levine, Solomon B. "Management and Industrial Relations in Postwar Japan," *Far Eastern Quarterly,* vol. XV (Nov. 1955). Discusses changes in employee-employer relationships and their implications for industrial relations.

Neumann, Sigmund, ed. *Modern Political Parties,* Chicago: University of Chicago Press, 1956. Contains a concise account of Japanese political parties by Robert A. Scalapino.

Saffell, John. "Japan's Post-War Socialist Party," *American Political Science Review,* vol. XLII (Oct. 1948).

Scalapino, Robert A. *Democracy and the Party Movement in Prewar Japan: The Failure of the First Attempt.* Berkeley, University of California Press, 1953. The best work in English on Japanese political parties.

Swearingen, Rodger, and Paul Langer. *Red Flag in Japan: International Communism in Action, 1919–1951.* Cambridge, Mass.: Harvard University Press, 1952. A detailed study of the Japanese Communist movement.

Totten, George. "Problems of Japanese Socialist Leadership," *Pacific Affairs,* vol. XXVIII (June 1955).

Uyehara, C., S. Royama, and S. Ogata. *Comparative Platforms of Japan's Major Parties.* Medford, Mass.: Tufts University, Fletcher School of Law and Diplomacy, 1955.

VII: The Power Structure

Colton, Hattie Kawahara. "The Workings of the Japanese Diet," *Pacific Affairs,* vol. XXVIII (Dec. 1955).

Colton, Kenneth. "Conservative Leadership in Japan," *Far Eastern Survey,* vol. XXIV (June 1955). An analysis of leadership recruitment among conservative groups.

Dull, Paul S. "The Senkyoya System in Rural Japanese Communities," in University of Michigan, Center for Japanese Studies, *Occasional Papers,* no. 4 (1953). Describes techniques used by a political boss.

Esman, Milton J. "Japanese Administration—A Comparative View," *Public Administration Review,* vol. VII (Spring 1947). A first-hand account of attempted reforms in the Japanese bureaucracy.

Ike, Nobutaka. *Japanese Politics: An Introductory Survey.* New York: Knopf, 1957. A study of Japanese political behavior.

Ishino, Iwao, and John W. Bennett. *The Japanese Labor Boss System.* Columbus: Ohio University Research Foundation, 1952. A preliminary study of the behavior of labor bosses.

Roser, Foster. "Establishing a Modern Merit System in Japan," *Public Personnel Review,* vol. XI (Oct. 1950).

Ward, Robert E. "The Socio-political Role of the Buraku (Hamlet) in Japan," *American Political Science Review,* vol. XLV (Dec. 1951). Provides insight into the nature of rural politics.

Williams, Justin. "Party Politics in the New Japanese Diet," *American Political Science Review,* vol. XLII (Dec. 1948). A description of the legislature by an Occupation official who served the Japanese government in an advisory capacity.

VIII: Problems of Contemporary Japan

Borton, Hugh, and others. *Japan between East and West.* New York: Harper, 1957. Contains six essays covering domestic politics, communism, economic position, diplomacy, relations with Communist China, and so on.

Japan since Recovery of Independence. In *Annals of the American Academy of Political and Social Science,* Nov. 1956. An up-to-date appraisal of the state of affairs in Japan by 17 specialists.

Mendel, Douglas H. "Revisionist Opinion in Post-Treaty Japan," *American Political Science Review,* vol. XLVIII (Sept. 1954). An analysis of popular attitudes toward rearmament and other issues.

United States and the Far East, The. New York: Columbia University, American Assembly, 1956. A symposium on the current American position in the Far East.

PERIODICALS

Those interested in following current developments should consult the publications listed below.

Contemporary Japan, a quarterly journal which carries articles on current
and historical topics, is particularly useful for documents and extracts of
Japanese periodicals.

Japan Quarterly, published by the Asahi Newspaper Company, often contains good articles by leading Japanese writers.

Japan Times, an English-language daily published in Tokyo, carries, in
addition to news, abstracts of editorials appearing in leading Japanese
newspapers.

Oriental Economist, a monthly journal, is well informed on economic developments.

This Is Japan, published at irregular intervals since 1954 by the Asahi Newspaper Company, is a handsome volume, profusely illustrated and a joy
to read.

PART THREE : INDIA

By Norman D. Palmer

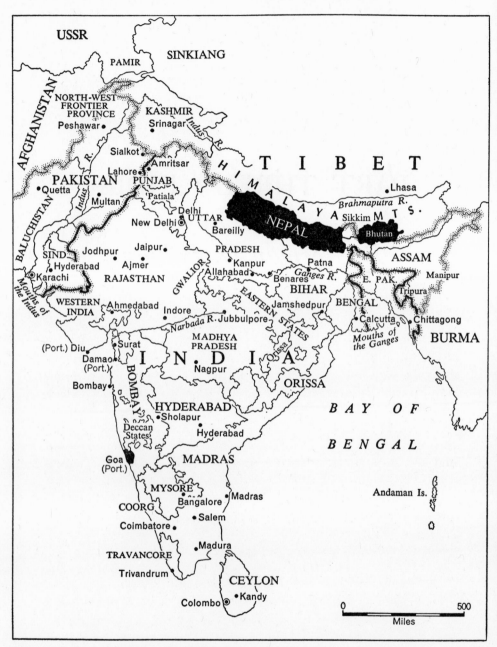

Map 7. India and Pakistan in 1947. (From *The Far East*, by Fred Greene, copyright 1957, Rinehart & Co., Inc.)

· IX ·

The Political Heritage

of Modern India

BECAUSE historical records are few and scanty, not much is known about the early inhabitants of the Indian subcontinent; but it seems likely that the pattern of conquest, infiltration, and absorption, which is so familiar in modern India, reaches far back into the darkness of prehistory. First traces of the earliest-known Indian civilization were discovered hardly more than a generation ago. At Mohenjo-Daro in Sind and at Harappa in the western Punjab the remnants of an ancient Indus Valley civilization came to light which dates back at least to the third millennium B.C. It was an urban civilization, of considerable complexity, with highly developed arts and crafts. After a period of substantial prosperity and for reasons about which we can only speculate, this early civilization declined and died away.

Patterns of Government in Hindu India

Some centuries later, Aryan invaders entered India from the north and began to mingle with the primitive stocks, the so-called Dravidians. These Aryan peoples brought with them ideas and institutions which, under the generic name of Hinduism, have taken deep root in the Indian soil. The essence of the Hindu religious philosophy is its extraordinary fluidity, eclecticism, and adaptability. There are hundreds, even thousands, of Hindu gods and goddesses; indeed almost every ethnic strain in Indian life has contributed to the Hindu pantheon, and all mix together, with remarkably little jealousy or jostling. The sacred books of Hinduism, the *Vedas* and *Upanishads,* are eclectic and tolerant collections, which have been read as justifying a mixture of all creeds, cults, and philosophies. At the same time, there is a remarkably strict aspect to Hinduism. From earliest times the Hindu has considered the cow a sacred animal; he will go far out of his way to avoid harming it, to avoid tasting its flesh, to avoid using a by-product of its skin, flesh, or horns.

More striking still is the typically Hindu concept of caste. Originally the Aryans were organized into tribes, with specific social functions (priests, warriors, and the like). These tribes very gradually over a period of many centuries became exclusive marriage groups. Divided and subdivided, sometimes territorially, sometimes according to occupation, sometimes by the sheer accidents and circumstances of history, they developed into full-fledged castes, with highly elaborate regulations regarding not only those whom they can marry, but also those with whom they can eat (commensality), those to whom they can talk, and those whom they can touch. The caste system is still one of the deepest influences on Indian social life.

In the fourth century B.C., Alexander the Great made a brief incursion into western India. Shortly after his fleeting visit the Mauryan dynasty established a powerful empire in north India, with a capital at Pataliputra. An important figure at the court of the first of the Mauryan emperors was Kautilya (also known as Chanakya or Vishnugupta), "the greatest Indian exponent of the art of government, the duties of kings, ministers, and officials, and the methods of diplomacy." [1] Kautilya's *Arthasastra* is one of the world's earliest classics in political science and public administration, although the text was discovered and translated only in the present century. The greatest of the Mauryan rulers was Asoka (273–232 B.C.), one of the great names in history. Asoka gave a powerful impetus to Buddhism, which is a particularly tolerant and contemplative offshoot of Hinduism. A convert to the arts of peace, he ruled benevolently over a vast empire including much of north India, the Deccan, and Afghanistan. It is wholly appropriate that the capital of one of his huge pillars, with its four lions (now in the Buddhist museum at Saranath), is often

[1] J. F. Fleet, Introductory Note to Kautilya's *Arthasastra,* trans. by Dr. R. Shamasastry (4th ed.; Mysore, 1951), p. v.

reproduced today as a symbol of independent India and that the wheel on this capital was adopted for the national flag of India.

The Mauryan empire collapsed soon after the death of Asoka, and political fragmentation and disunity prevailed for six centuries, until the rise of the Gupta empire in the fourth century A.D. Under Chandragupta II (380–413), nearly all of India was united under one rule, with the center of power in north India. Indian culture reached a high point during the Gupta period. It was the golden age of Sanskrit studies, and the great university of Nalanda attracted students from all parts of Asia. The Gupta rulers also increased the prestige of India as a maritime power and sponsored the establishment of Hindu kingdoms, particularly in Southeast Asia. More than a century after the collapse of the Gupta dynasty, in the seventh century A.D., there was a momentary revival of Hindu power under Harsha, the ruler of a state north of the present site of Delhi. Harsha extended his control over most of the territory once embraced in the Gupta empire and ruled firmly and well for more than forty years; but he was the last of the great Hindu rulers of north India.

By A.D. 1000 Hindu civilization, which had reached great heights in literature and philosophy and had enjoyed occasional periods of political eminence, showed signs of fatal decay. There was, as Nehru has written, a "decline all along the line—intellectual, philosophical, political, in techniques and methods of warfare, in knowledge of and contacts with the outside world." [2]

Clearly the great achievements of what might be called the Hindu period of Indian history were not in the arts of politics. The prevailing political pattern was fragmentation. The prevailing form of government, in the larger political units which rose and fell with bewildering rapidity, was absolutism. Occasionally that absolutism was benevolent, but if it was controlled at all it was limited by inefficiency or weakness in administration. There was little that could be called democratic in ancient India, any more than in other parts of the world; but some examples of representative institutions, usually local and embryonic, can be found, and these have very understandably been glorified by modern Indian nationalists.[3] If republican forms of

[2] Jawaharlal Nehru, *The Discovery of India* (New York: John Day, 1946), p. 221.

[3] A report on the first general elections in India contained the following analysis by the Election Commission (*Report on the First General Elections in India, 1951–52* [Delhi, 1955], I, 7–8):

"It is perhaps not commonly known that republican forms of government existed in many parts of ancient India. There are numerous references to such government in fact existed, they were certainly the exception, even on local levels. The village panchayats (councils of five), in particular, merit careful study,[4] especially since the present government of India is trying to revive and extend these ancient village institutions in an organized and somewhat more democratic form.

Mughal Government and Administration

Islam was brought into India not long after it became firmly established in the Arabian peninsula in the seventh century; but the story of Islam in India really begins with Mahmud of Ghazni, who made many raids into India between 998 and 1030. In the late twelfth and early thirteenth centuries Mohammed Ghori, from what is now Af-

---

Governments in the Buddhist literature. Even in the 4th century B.C., there was a republican federation known as the Kshudrak-Malla Sangha, which offered strong resistance to Alexander the Great. The Greeks have left descriptions of many other republican states in India, some of which were described by them as pure democracies while others were said to be 'aristocratic republics' . . . . in some of these republics every adult male member had the right to vote and to be present in the general assembly which decided all public affairs. . . .

"Apart from the evolution of the democratic form of government in sovereign states in ancient India . . . the genius of India also evolved, as a natural growth, the system of autonomous and almost self-sufficient village communities, under every system of government. These communities, which lasted through the ages, were run on truly democratic lines. . . . In later days, they went by the name of village panchayats and were a vital force in the social life of the countryside.

"Even after the republican states were absorbed within empires, the system of regulating the local corporate life through popular assemblies survived for a very long time. . . . During the Muslim period, the affairs of the trade corporations and the villages continued to be carried on by popular assemblies. A fundamental change came with the British administration when revenue, judicial and legal affairs were centralised and conducted away from the villages. This factor, coupled with the consequent decay of the agricultural and industrial economy of the countryside, resulted in the deterioration of the corporate life of the rural communities and gradually the organisations based on the popular will faded out.

"In the context of history, therefore, the establishment by the Constitution of the democratic and Parliamentary form of Government in the country on the basis of adult franchise was like the rejoining of a historic thread that had been snapped by alien rule."

For varying views and interpretations see A. S. Altekar, *State and Government in Ancient India* (Benares, 1949); U. N. Ghoshal, *A History of Hindu Political Theories* (2d ed.; London, 1927); K. P. Jayaswal, *Hindu Polity* (Calcutta, 1924); Beni Prasad, *The State in Ancient India* (Allahabad, 1928); Beni Prasad, "Political Theory and Administrative System," in R. C. Majumdar and A. D. Pusalker, eds., *The Age of Imperial Unity* (2d ed.; Bombay, 1953); Benoy Kumar Sarkar, *The Political Institutions and Theories of the Hindus* (Leipzig, 1922).

[4] See J. G. Drummond, *Panchayats in India* (Bombay, 1937); Rattan Lal Khanna, *Panchayat Raj in India* (Chandigarh, 1956).

ghanistan, extended his sway over a good part of northern and north-western India. After his death in 1206, one of his generals established the Delhi Sultanate. For a century and a half the Sultans of Delhi ruled over much of north India and also conquered kingdoms in the Deccan and farther south. In the late fourteenth century the Delhi Sultanate virtually collapsed, and in 1398 Timur—or Tamerlane—swept out of Central Asia into India and sacked Delhi. By the mid-fifteenth century, the Delhi Sultanate had revived, but it never regained its former power; and in 1526 Babur, a descendant of Timur and Genghis Khan, defeated the armies of the Delhi Sultanate and established the great Mughal dynasty in India.

The greatest of the Mughal rulers of India was Akbar (a grandson of Babur), who ruled from 1556 to 1605. Akbar established a control over most of India, except in the extreme south, which was firmer and more efficient than anything that India had experienced for many centuries. "The Mogul Empire at the beginning of the seventeenth century was probably the best organized and most prosperous then existing in the world."[5] The empire was organized into provinces. It was highly centralized and had an efficient civil service and tax system. Able administrators, Hindu as well as Muslim, served the Great Mughal. Akbar followed a policy of religious as well as political toleration and sought to unite Hindus and Muslims. He tried to formulate a new religion which would combine the best features of Islam, Hinduism, and other religions.

For a century following his death Akbar's successors maintained the splendor of the Mughal court and even expanded the boundaries of the empire; but they were far less able and far less tolerant than the Great Mughal. Jehangir was ineffective, and his son, Shah Jahan, builder of the Taj Mahal, not only imposed staggering burdens on the people, but reversed his grandfather's policy of religious toleration. The last of the great Mughal rulers, Aurangzeb (1659–1707), continued these oppressive policies. Obsessed with the aim of uniting India under his rule, he spent years in arduous campaigns against other Muslim kingdoms and against the Sikhs, the Rajputs, and especially the Mahrattas. For a time he ruled over more of India than any other man in the long history of the subcontinent, but he was never able to give real unity and stability to his unwieldy kingdom. Upon his death the Mughal empire fell apart. After a century and a half of

[5] T. Walter Wallbank, *India in the New Era* (Chicago: Scott, Foresman, 1951), pp. 37–38.

dazzling magnificence and despotic power the great period of Muslim
rule in India was at an end.

Obviously the Muslim contribution to Indian civilization has been
a great and lasting one in many fields. Politically the Mughals determined the patterns of control on the provincial level and above,
but they always had to rely upon large numbers of non-Muslim administrators, and they had to enter into agreements with many Hindu
rulers. Large parts of India never experienced direct Muslim rule,
and the Muslims had little effect, even during the period of imperial
splendor, upon the villages of India, where the great majority of the
people lived. Relatively few of the many millions of Muslims in India
and Pakistan today are descendants of the Mughals or other Muslim
invaders of India; the great majority are descended from Hindus
who (usually because of dissatisfaction with their caste position)
adopted the Muslim faith and way of life. The introduction of Islam
into India never produced anything like a real Hindu-Muslim synthesis. In the words of K. M. Panikkar:

The main social result of the introduction of Islam as a religion into India
was the division of society on a vertical basis. Before the thirteenth century,
Hindu society was divided horizontally by castes. Islam split Indian society
into two sections from top to bottom. . . . It was two parallel societies
vertically established on the same soil. At all stages they were different
and hardly any social communication or intercourse of life existed between
them.[6]

Thus the relationship between Hindus and Muslims, and the success
or failure of their experiments in "peaceful coexistence," became a
main theme of modern Indian history.

British Rule to 1857

The century following the death of Aurangzeb was a period of confusion in the political history of India. Mughal rule was reduced
almost to impotence; Hindu power revived, especially among the
Mahrattas and Sikhs; Afghan and Persian invasions were beaten back;
the British and French came into conflict; and the power of the
British East India Company grew steadily in importance. The governmental influence of this originally private corporation was extended
by a curious combination of force and persuasion.

After an ineffectual revolt against Aurangzeb, the Mahratta people

[6] *A Survey of Indian History* (London, 1948), p. 162.

had slowly built up a confederation extending from the present state of Bombay into northern India and the frontiers of Bengal. But in 1761 their army was destroyed by invading Afghans in the Punjab, and toward the end of the century the Mahratta leader was forced to seek refuge with the British in Bombay. In 1802 he agreed, in return for a promise of protection, to receive British troops at his court and to pay an annual tribute. "The treaty," in the opinion of A. B. Keith, "unquestionably must be accepted as giving the British the Empire of India, for it reduced the head of the Mahratta confederation to a position of complete inferiority, and in matters external of absolute subordination, to the British." [7] Most of the lesser Mahratta chiefs refused to be bound by the treaty, and war followed in 1803–1805. As a result of the fighting, Mahratta power was checked, and it soon faded into insignificance in comparison with the growing British influence.

The French had become active in India only in the latter part of the seventeenth century, when the French East India Company was organized by Louis XIV's great finance minister, Colbert. During the confusion which followed the death of Aurangzeb, the French increased their influence and reached a peak of power during the twelve years (1742–1754) when Dupleix was Governor-General of the French East India Company's holdings, centered at Pondicherry. By force and diplomacy Dupleix more than held his own until his plans were checkmated by the activities of a young clerk of the British East India Company named Robert Clive. In 1754 Dupleix was recalled in disgrace. Shortly afterwards Dupleix' chief ally, the Nawab of Bengal, was defeated by forces of the British East India Company under Clive, and the main French power in India was broken. Until very recently the French maintained a foothold in Pondicherry; but after Indian independence, they ceded their holdings. Portugal, on the other hand, which has maintained a small enclave at Goa since the early seventeenth century, has steadfastly refused to give it up. For India today the question of Portuguese "imperialism" at Goa is a sensitive one. Since 1754, however, neither the French nor the Portuguese have had any influence in India remotely comparable to that of the British.

Robert Clive did much to lay the foundations of effective British power in India and was rewarded by appointment as Governor-General of the East India Company. During succeeding decades other able Governors-General, notably Warren Hastings (1772–1785), Lord

[7] *A Constitutional History of India, 1600–1935* (2d ed.; London, 1937), p. 114.

Cornwallis (1786–1795), Lord Wellesley (1798–1804), Lord William Bentinck (1828–1835), and Lord Dalhousie (1848–1856), consolidated and extended the holdings of the company. By the 1840s, most of the subcontinent was under British control, either directly or indirectly through treaties with Native States.

The period of British rule in India can be divided into two main subperiods, with the "Sepoy Mutiny" (1857) as the watershed. The first period was one of rule by the British East India Company; the second of rule by the British government itself, which continued to combine direct with indirect rule, as during the days of "John Company."

When it began to be a governing as well as a trading corporation, the British East India Company itself became subject to government regulations. The first bills were passed as early as 1773. Three years of investigation into Indian affairs (1781–1784) preceded the passage by Parliament of Pitt's India Act of 1784, which further limited the powers of the company. The act established a Board of Control, the President of which was virtually "a Secretary of State for India." It also provided for the appointment of the Governor-General by the British government. The parliamentary investigations of the early 1780s led to the famous trial of Warren Hastings, which started in 1788 and ended only in 1795 with Hastings' acquittal. Lord Cornwallis, the first Governor-General after the Act of 1784, laid the basis for a more honest and efficient system of administration. The governor-generalship of Lord William Bentinck (1828–1835), "the first of the modern rulers of India," was marked by significant steps in administrative and social reform. Parliament, after an intensive review, renewed the charter of the East India Company for twenty years in the Charter Act of 1833, but it closed down the company's commercial activities and gave more power to the Governor-General in Council. By this time the interests and welfare of the people of India had become matters of genuine concern to the British government, and Bentinck undertook a number of social reforms. Among these were the abolition of suttee (the suicide of widows after the death of their husbands), the suppression of lawlessness by fanatical devotees, known as Thugs, of the goddess Kali, and efforts to eliminate female infanticide.

The Charter Act of 1833 added a law member to the Governor General's Council, who was to prove an important addition. The first law member, the famous Lord Macaulay, inaugurated a systematic codification of criminal law. In time an impressive legal structure was developed. Lord Macaulay's name is also associated with perhaps the most lasting of all Lord William Bentinck's reforms, the selection of English as the medium of education in India and the decision to follow Western methods in teaching promising young Indians. In his famous Minute on Education in 1835 Lord Macaulay recommended this step; as a result, he predicted, there would develop "a class of persons, Indian in blood and colour, but English in taste, in opinion, in morals and in intellect," and these Western-trained Indians would set the pattern for the entire country. Thus for over a century higher education in India was based on Western models, and English was the accepted medium in the schools and courts and in all government business. Even today, in independent India, this pattern still prevails, although Hindi and other languages are gradually being used for purposes of instruction and although the role of English is now a hotly debated subject. Today the government of India must decide what parts of the British-imposed system of education should be preserved and what should be replaced by methods more in keeping with India's traditions and needs.

Macaulay and other English Liberals held Indian culture and customs in low esteem, and they directly challenged deep-rooted Indian practices and institutions. At the same time, unlike most of the Englishmen who helped to shape India's destiny in the half century or more following the "Mutiny," they looked forward with anticipation to the remote day when Indians would be granted self-government. "When it comes," said Macaulay, "it will be the proudest day in English history." [8]

British Rule from 1857 to 1900

In 1957 both India and Pakistan commemorated the centenary of "the War of Independence," which British historians have referred to as the "Sepoy Mutiny." In *The Discovery of India* Nehru himself wrote: "It was much more than a military mutiny, and it spread rapidly and assumed the character of a popular rebellion and a war of Indian independence." [9] In a symbolic sense Nehru may be right; but the "Mutiny" was in historical fact far from "a popular rebellion and a war of Indian independence." It was confined to a limited area

[8] Quoted in Guy Wint and Sir George Schuster, *India and Democracy* (London, 1941), p. 78.
[9] Nehru, *The Discovery of India*, p. 324.

(starting in Meerut, spreading to Delhi, Cawnpore, Lucknow, and a few other places in north central India) and to a limited number of Indians, mostly Sepoys (Indian soldiers) of the British Indian army. The cause of the uprising was primarily a "revulsion against western influence." "The repeated annexation of territories by a foreign power, the spread of Western mode of education and new ideas of life—all combined revealed to the Hindu mind a consistent effort to substitute a western for a Hindu civilisation." [10] The exact occasion which set off the uprising was relatively trivial, but it "ignited the mass of combustibles which the more serious crime had collected." [11]

Although the "Mutiny" of 1857 never developed into a national resistance movement and never endangered British rule, it did have momentous consequences. It marked the end both of the East India Company as a ruling power in India and of the Mughal dynasty in even its feeblest form. It ushered in the great epoch of British rule in India, yet at the same time it unleashed forces which less than a century later were to force the British out of India entirely. After 1857 British rule was firmer and more efficient, perhaps more benevolent and farseeing as well, than it had been in the days when the British government and the East India Company were sharing the responsibilities of governing India. But the gulf between British rulers and Indian people became wider, and much of the warm intimacy of previous days gave way to aloofness and distrust. The Muslims, in particular, were at an increasing disadvantage after the "Mutiny," and they were carefully excluded from positions of trust and responsibility.[12]

In the period following the "Mutiny" the British developed an impressive structure of government and administration for India. The great parliamentary landmarks are the Indian Councils Acts of 1861 and 1892, the Morley-Minto reforms of 1909, the Government of India Act of 1919 (following the Montagu-Chelmsford report of 1918), and the Government of India Act of 1935. During these years Indians gained an increasing but never dominant voice in provincial government, in the legislative assemblies, and even in the Executive Council (after 1909). But the governors were always the key figures in the provinces, and the Governors-General (called Viceroys when acting

[10] S. N. Ray, "The Sepoy Mutiny of 1857," *Radical Humanist*, XXI (May 12, 1957), 237.
[11] *Ibid.*
[12] See Chapter XIV, the "British Rule" section.

as the representatives of the Crown) were supreme in British India as a whole, though increasingly subject to control from London. There the key figure was the Secretary of State for India, assisted by a council and by officials of the India Office. The provinces were subdivided for administrative purposes into divisions and districts. Districts were under the supervision of district officers (sometimes known as collectors), whose role in the entire system of British administration was a particularly vital one. A district officer had numerous functions and responsibilities, both official and unofficial; his chief formal duties were to administer justice, to collect revenue, and to preserve law and order. In the eyes of ordinary Indians the district officer was the British Raj.

Some efforts were made to establish advisory boards for the district officers, composed of both nominated and elected members. The results were fairly impressive in the municipalities, but disappointing in the villages and rural areas. A famous Resolution on Local Self-Government of 1882, associated with the name of the Viceroy at the time, Lord Ripon, declared: "It is not primarily with a view to improvement in administration that this measure is put forward and supported. It is chiefly designed as an instrument of political and popular education." [13] Actually, the British had little success in developing any satisfactory system of local government below the district level.

Whereas in the development of district administration there was a fusion of Indian and English traditions and usage, in the building up of local bodies almost no concession was made to native prejudices or ways of thinking. There was the great difficulty that no separate indigenous local government tradition existed (except for the village organization) distinct from the centralized administration of the state, upon which nineteenth-century officials could build.[14]

The main task of administration in British India devolved upon the members of the Indian Civil Service, who set standards of efficiency and incorruptibility which have seldom been equaled in any other civil service. Even today former ICS officers are the backbone of the administrative system in both India and Pakistan, although the withdrawal of the British members and depletions due to resignations, retirements, and deaths foreshadow the passing of this great service. One of the oldest of civil services, the ICS came into being as early

[13] Quoted in Hugh Tinker, *The Foundations of Local Self-Government in India, Pakistan, and Burma* (London: Athlone Press, 1954), p. 44.

[14] *Ibid.*, p. 334.

as the eighteenth century. After 1853 appointments were made by the British government in place of the East India Company, on the basis of open competition. As late as 1892 the ICS numbered only 992 officers, and only 21 of these were Indians. But after 1900, increasing numbers of Indians were taken into the service, through rigid examination, and on the eve of independence a major part of the service was Indian.

Just prior to the 1857 "Mutiny" the British Indian army consisted of approximately 233,000 Sepoys and 45,000 British troops, a ratio of more than five to one. After the "Mutiny" the army was completely reorganized, and the ratio of Indian to British troops was never more than two to one. Henceforth the Indian contingents were drawn more heavily than before from the "martial" races, the Sikhs, the Pathans, the Punjabi Muslims, and the Gurkas of Nepal. More than ever before the Indian army became a professional force.

After the "Mutiny," too, an earlier policy of seeking the annexation of Native States was abandoned. Most of the Indian princes had remained loyal to the British during the "Mutiny," and as a reward the British government entered into agreements giving them assurance of British aid in retaining their holdings. Thus the Princely States were brought within the British orbit. British residents were stationed in most of the more than 500 states, large and small, and often these agents had more real power than the native princes.

Toward Self-Government

Indian nationalism as an organized movement had its beginnings about 1885, the date of the founding of the Indian National Congress; but in effect its history is much longer and is the history of two movements, perhaps more properly of several. For there is a long background of Hindu nationalism as well as a more recent one of Muslim nationalism; and the two currents, though they have often flowed alongside one another, have never really mingled.

Raja Ram Mohan Roy (1770–1833) is sometimes referred to as the father of the nationalist movement among the Hindus. Although he lived several decades before the great age of Indian nationalism, his influence was manifest long after his death. In 1828 he founded the Brahmo Samaj as a Hindu reform movement. His faith was securely rooted in the *Upanishads*, but he found in this orthodox Hindu classic a note of universal acceptance which led to a tolerant attitude toward other religions and societies. Within India, Ram Mohan Roy advocated

Chart 4. The development of self-government in British India *

	VICEROY & EXECUTIVE COUNCIL	LEGISLATURE	PROVINCIAL GOVERNMENTS
1861 Indian Councils Act	5 MEMBERS — ALL BRITISH	Indian Civil Service 12 BRITISH / Non-Officials (appointed) SOME INDIANS	In the majority of the provinces, there was one-man rule by the Governor
1909 Morley-Minto Reforms	1 INDIAN 6 BRITISH	LEGISLATIVE COUNCIL — Indian Civil Service 36 BRITISH / Elected 27 INDIANS / Non-Officials (appointed) 5 INDIANS	COUNCIL, including one Indian, appointed by the Governor
1919 Montagu-Chelmsford Reforms	3 INDIANS 4 BRITISH	COUNCIL OF STATE — Indian Civil Service 3 INDIANS 17 BRITISH / Elected 22 INDIANS 2 BRITISH / Non-Officials (appointed) 5 INDIANS 1 BRITISH (Upper House) — LEGISLATIVE ASSEMBLY — Indian Civil Service 5 INDIANS 21 BRITISH / Elected 97 INDIANS 8 BRITISH / Non-Officials (appointed) 14 INDIANS (Lower House)	Provincial Legislatures not shown — DYARCHY Some portfolios transferred to Indians
1935 Government of India Act	NO CHANGE FROM 1919	COUNCIL OF STATE — Indian Civil Service 3 INDIANS 17 BRITISH / Elected 22 INDIANS 2 BRITISH / Non-Officials (appointed) ALL INDIANS — LEGISLATIVE ASSEMBLY — Indian Civil Service 10 INDIANS 16 BRITISH / Elected 97 INDIANS 8 BRITISH / Non-Officials (appointed) 14 INDIANS	PROVINCIAL SELF-GOVERNMENT All portfolios transferred to Indians
1946 First All-Indian Council	14 INDIANS	COUNCIL OF STATE — Indian Civil Service 7 INDIANS 6 BRITISH / Elected 20 INDIANS 2 BRITISH / Non-Officials (appointed) ALL INDIANS — LEGISLATIVE ASSEMBLY — Officials (appointed) 17 INDIANS 3 BRITISH / Elected 94 INDIANS 8 BRITISH / Non-Officials (appointed) 20 INDIANS	1935 RIGHTS CONTINUE

The provisions of the 1935 Constitution, which would have federated British India with the Indian States ruled by the Princes, never came into force

* From British Information Services.

social reform, through the adoption of Western science, religion, and educational methods. His teachings flowered in 1885 with the formation of the Indian National Congress, a party which, though it has always claimed to be nonsectarian and open to members of any religious faith, has never failed to be predominantly Hindu in its composition and sometimes in its policies.

Muslim nationalism, though slower to develop, also had its founding father. After the "Sepoy Mutiny," Sir Sayyid Ahmad Khan (1817–1898) "launched a Muslim modernism which sought to reconcile traditional Islam with modern needs." [15] He contributed to a synthesis of Eastern and Western ideas and also to the development of a Muslim political consciousness, by founding, in 1875, a Muslim College at Aligarh (now Aligarh Muslim University). Sir Sayyid believed that the Muslims should preserve their own culture and institutions, but he favored co-operation with the British. He was also "clear that there was a Muslim national consciousness quite distinct from the Hindu, and for that reason discouraged Muslims from any participation in the Indian National Congress. . . . In his whole attitude was implicit the concept of Pakistan [as a separate Muslim nation]. It only needed the prospect of British withdrawal, something which in his day still seemed remote, to bring it to the surface." [16] Sir Sayyid's influence culminated after his death in the founding of the Muslim League (1906).

After the "Mutiny," Hindu nationalism became increasingly manifest. In 1875 Swami Dayananda Saraswati, a Hindu ascetic, founded the Arya Samaj, under the slogan "Back to the Vedas." Thus Dayananda preached "a militant assertion of primitive Hinduism." [17] His movement attracted a considerable following, especially in the Punjab and the United Provinces. In this same period the Bengali ascetic Ramakrishna found in the philosophy of Vedanta proof that all roads lead to truth and that all religions are one. His influence was and is greater on the religious than on the political side; but his devout follower, Vivekananda, founded the Ramakrishna Order and preached the importance of India's ancient religious and philosophic heritage for the modern world. He was a leading figure of the Indian Renaissance, which did so much to give Hindus confidence in themselves and their traditions and which profoundly affected the developing nationalist movement.

In the 1880s the nationalist movement entered a new and more

[15] Sir Percival Spear, *India, Pakistan, and the West* (London, 1952), p. 190.
[16] *Ibid.*, pp. 190–191.   [17] *Ibid.*, p. 184.

concerted stage with the founding of the Indian National Congress. Among the active promoters of the Congress were Surendranath Banerjea, Dadabhai Naoroji, and an Englishman, Octavian Hume. Its first meeting was held in Poona in December, 1885. Thereafter it met regularly in annual sessions. At first the British authorities looked with some favor upon the Congress. It seemed to be a moderate movement, and it proclaimed its loyalty to the British connection while it worked for a larger measure of representative government. Octavian Hume, known as the "father of Congress," was in charge of the Congress Secretariat until 1907, and several Englishmen were elected as presidents of the Congress. As time went on, however, the Congress increased its demands and began to include in its ranks some Indians who were *persona non grata* to the British rulers of India.

Until well into the twentieth century the British authorities refused to take the Congress seriously, and they were constantly predicting its decline. "The Congress," wrote the great Viceroy, Lord Curzon, about 1900, "is tottering to its fall, and one of my great ambitions while in India is to assist it to a peaceful demise."[18] Lord Curzon not only greatly underestimated the growing strength of the nationalist movement, but he contributed unwittingly to its support by some of his own acts. Two of his "reforms," in particular, gave impetus to Indian nationalism. One was the Universities Act of 1904, which was interpreted in India as a means of making government control over education more effective and which "convulsed educated India from one end of the country to another."[19] The other was his decision to partition the province of Bengal, an act which infuriated the Hindus of Bengal.

Until the First World War the National Congress was generally controlled by moderate nationalists—men like Surendranath Banerjea and Dadabhai Naoroji and later Pherozeshah Mehta and G. K. Gokhale. "Gokhale was the outstanding Indian political leader up to the First World War,"[20] and Gandhi later regarded Gokhale as his political *guru*. After 1905 the Congress adopted a stronger line and demanded a real degree of self-government (*swaraj*). For some time a struggle had been going on in the ranks of the Congress between the moderates, led by Gokhale, and the extremists, led by Tilak. Tilak was a great champion of Hindu orthodoxy. Rightly or wrongly, he be-

[18] Lord Ronaldshay, *The Life of Lord Curzon* (London, 1928), II, 151.
[19] Surendranath Banerjea, *A Nation in the Making* (London, 1925), p. 175.
[20] Wallbank, *India in the New Era*, p. 80.

came associated with a militant brand of nationalism which sometimes found expression in acts of violence. In the pages of the two newspapers which he published in Poona, one in English, the other in Marathi, Tilak justified the use of force in furtherance of national aims. Nationalist extremists were particularly active in Bengal during the decade following the partition of the province, as well as in Bombay and the Punjab. They received support from Congress organizations outside of India, notably in London, Paris, and San Francisco. Besides Tilak their best-known leaders were Bepin Chandra Pal in Bengal and Lala Lajpat Rai in the Punjab.

At the annual meetings of the Congress in 1906 and 1907 a showdown took place between the moderates and extremists, amid scenes of wild disorder. The moderates won the day, and in 1907 the extremists withdrew from the Congress. The triumphant moderates drew up a new constitution for the Congress and remained in control of Congress machinery until the death of Gokhale in 1915. Many of the extremists, including Tilak and Lala Lajpat Rai, were either imprisoned or deported. The moderates continued to advocate peaceful and constitutional methods to achieve their goals. By the end of the First World War, however, their day was over. Most of them were essentially nineteenth-century liberals who admired British ways and institutions; and in their last years increasing dissatisfaction was felt with the slow progress of the movement.

While the Congress Party was torn by factional strife, various short steps in the direction of representative government were taken, in consequence of the Morley-Minto reforms of 1909. The underlying idea of these political changes was to "associate the people [of India] to a greater extent with Government in the decision on public questions"; and to this end, they granted to the Indians a few carefully hedged privileges. Through direct or indirect elections, Indians were given places in provincial councils and the central Legislative Council. For the first time, Indian members were appointed to the Viceroy's Executive Council and to the executive councils of the governors of Bombay and Madras. For the first time, also, separate electorates were provided for the Muslims. Separation of the electorates along communal lines was in one sense a forward step, as the very existence of electorates was a novelty in India. On the other hand, it implied the abrogation of all responsibility by the Hindu politician for the Muslim voter and by the Muslim politician for the Hindu voter—even though they inhabited the same village. Thus the seeds of partition were in one sense planted by the first British "liberal" reforms.

"Democratic" as they looked on the surface, the Morley-Minto reforms insisted at bottom on the "fundamental principle that the executive government should retain the final decision on all questions." [21]
In a famous statement in the House of Lords in December 1908, Lord
Morley emphatically repudiated the idea that the proposed reforms
"were in any sense a step towards parliamentary government." And he
added: "If it could be said that this chapter of reforms led directly
or necessarily up to the establishment of a Parliamentary system in
India, I for one would have nothing at all to do with it. . . . a Parliamentary system in India is not the goal to which I for one moment
would aspire." [22]

Conceived in this spirit, the Morley-Minto reforms were received
with little enthusiasm in India, and they were soon overtaken by
the march of events. During the First World War most Indians loy-
ally supported the British cause, but Indian spokesmen became increasingly dissatisfied with the failure of the British to make any substantial concessions to political unrest and nationalist sentiment. The
radical Tilak returned from exile in 1914, re-entered the Congress
Party, and regained a large, even a dominant, following within the
party in the remaining three years of his life.

But even at the height of the war, there were evidences that the
British were aware of the need of putting their relations with India
on a new footing. In 1917 the Viceroy, Lord Chelmsford, specifically
recommended a greater measure of self-government. On August 20,
1917, the new Secretary of State for India, Samuel Montagu, made this
historic statement in the House of Commons:

The policy of His Majesty's Government, with which the Government of
India are in complete accord, is that of the increasing association of Indians
in every branch of the administration and the gradual development of
self-governing institutions with a view to the progressive realisation of
responsible government as an integral part of the British Empire.[23]

Shortly afterwards Mr. Montagu went to India where, in company with
the Viceroy, he visited the major centers and heard a variety of points
of view. The result of his visit was the Montagu-Chelmsford report
of 1918, which led to the Government of India Act of 1919.

This famous act charted the lines of government in Indian until

[21] *Report on Indian Constitutional Reforms, 1918* (London, 1918), Cd. 9109,
p. 7.
[22] *Indian Speeches, 1907–1909* (London, 1909), p. 91.
[23] Quoted in *Report of the Indian Statutory Commission, 1930* (London, 1930),
Cd. 3568 (Report of the Simon Commission), I, 2.

1935. It established a kind of quasi-federal system for British India, with a bicameral legislature at the Centre, consisting of the Council of State and the Assembly. In the latter body the majority of the members were elected representatives, with some official members who were nominated. In the provinces the act inaugurated the ingenious but cumbersome system of dyarchy, one of the unique features of India's constitutional system before independence.[24] In each province the government was to be of a dual nature, with the various legislative subjects classified as "reserved" or "transferred." Reserved subjects were to be handled by the governor, assisted by an executive council, but without the participation of the provincial legislature. On the other hand, transferred subjects, such as education, agriculture, and health, were entrusted to Indian ministers who were to be responsible to the provincial legislature. Generally speaking, the governor was expected to accept the advice of his ministers on these matters. The system was not as radical as it might seem, for the act included carefully worded provisions whereby the provincial governors and the Viceroy could block or override the wishes of the elected majority in the assemblies. The act also contained elaborate provisions for communal electorates. After it was passed, the franchise was given to 5,179,000 male voters (only 33,000 had been eligible to vote prior to 1919).

Liberal and forward-looking as the Act of 1919 seemed to be, it was out of date before it was even promulgated. In its very first year the central legislature, composed largely of liberals and moderates, resolved to press for further concessions. Moreover, any good effects which the act might have had were more than offset by resentment over certain unfortunate events of 1919, notably the repressive Rowlatt Acts and the Jalianwalla Bagh tragedy in Amritsar, where some 400 persons were killed and 1,200 were wounded when British troops fired upon an unarmed crowd.

After the First World War the nationalist movement entered a new phase, under the leadership of Mahatma Gandhi, who had just returned to India after many years in England and South Africa. It was doubtless a fortunate thing both for India and for England that Gandhi appeared in a leading role at this time, when the stage seemed to be set for an orgy of violence and bloodshed.

It is impossible to assess the manifold contributions of Mohandas K.

[24] See A. Appadorai, *Dyarchy in Practice* (Madras, 1937), and "Kerala Putra," *The Working of Dyarchy in India* (Bombay, 1928).

Gandhi to the nationalist cause. In a critical period he diverted the movement into constructive channels—although at times it got out of control—and he identified it with the mass of the people. He related it directly to India's past and to modern needs. He preached and himself practiced the doctrines of nonviolent nonco-operation (*ahimsa*) by techniques which he called *satyagraha* (soul force). He did all he could to promote good relations among all the people of India, especially between Hindus and Muslims. He gave depth and substance to India's cause, and he won for it world-wide attention and sympathy. He sought to win independence for India, not only in a political but in a spiritual sense. He gave "a moral and a spiritual standing to India's revolution." [25]

At first his efforts seemed to be unsuccessful. The Calcutta session of the Indian National Congress in 1920 accepted his policy of "progressive non-violent non-cooperation" as a weapon in support of the Khilafat movement (a Muslim protest movement in support of Turkey against threatened Allied reprisals). His methods were also viewed as a step toward greater self-government, "within the British Empire if possible, without if necessary." In December 1916 both the Congress and the Muslim League met in Lucknow, and there they agreed to co-operate in the cause of Indian unity and self-government. This "Lucknow Pact" was in effect for several years and was cemented by Gandhi's support of the Khilafat movement, in which the Muslims were intensely interested. To Gandhi this was "such an opportunity of uniting Hindus and Mohammedans as would not arise in a hundred years." But the differences between the Congress and the Muslim League were deep-seated, and the basis of their co-operation was a flimsy one. In 1922, as a result of the revolution in Turkey, the Sultan was deposed and in 1924 the caliphate was abolished. At about the same time the association between the Congress and the League came to an end. The nonco-operation campaign reached a climax in 1921, but was shortly called off by Gandhi himself because of repeated acts of violence. Obviously the people of India were not yet ready to make effective use of the methods of *satyagraha*.

In 1922 Gandhi was arrested and imprisoned. In the following year, while he was still in confinement, two leaders of the Congress, C. R. Das and Pandit Motilal Nehru, were able to reverse the decision of the Congress not to co-operate in British legislative councils. The Con-

[25] Gertrude Emerson, "Non-Violent Non-Cooperation in India," *Asia*, XXII (Aug. 1922), 674.

gress thereupon contested elections; its members entered both provincial and central legislatures and turned them into effective sounding
boards for the nationalist movement.

For four years after his release from jail in 1924 Gandhi remained
aloof from politics. Meanwhile the nationalist movement became increasingly radical. This trend was furthered by the rise of able,
young, and militant nationalists, including Jawaharlal Nehru and
Subhas Chandra Bose. Again a rift was developing between moderates
and extremists, but this time there was a leader of sufficient stature
and detachment to mend the rift.

In December 1928 Gandhi returned to active political work and
soon was able to effect a compromise between the various groups in
the Congress. At its annual meeting in 1929 in Lahore the Congress,
under Gandhi's urging, adopted a pledge of complete independence
and decreed that all members should take the pledge on January 26,
to be observed as Independence Day. By decision of the government
of a free India, January 26 twenty-one years later was chosen as the
day on which the constitution would enter into effect and on which
India would become a republic.

In March 1930 Gandhi led his famous salt march to the sea, symbolizing the national boycott of British goods, and this act was a signal
for a nation-wide campaign of civil disobedience. Gandhi was arrested
in May, and by mid-summer some 60,000 members and supporters of
the Congress were also in prison.

Widespread disorders and moral pressures directed at England, due
to the all-British composition of the Simon Commission on Indian
constitutional reforms, led the Labour Government in 1930 to hold
a Round Table Conference in London, to discuss the whole "India
problem," with the co-operation of leading Indians. Fifty-seven eminent Indians attended the first Round Table Conference, which was
held in London from November 1930 to January 1931, but the Congress
refused to send any representatives.

Immediately after the conference adjourned, hundreds of political
prisoners, including Gandhi, were released, and in March 1931 Gandhi
reached an agreement with Lord Irwin in the so-called Delhi Pact.
Under this agreement the campaign of civil disobedience was to be
halted and the Congress was to be represented at the second Round
Table Conference. When the second conference was held, from September to December 1931, Gandhi alone spoke for the Congress. In
fact, he gave the impression that he spoke for India. Unfortunately,

little was accomplished either at the second Round Table Conference or at the third, where neither the Indian Congress nor the British Labour Party was represented.

Yet the pressure continued to mount for a settlement of the India problem. Finally, in the spring of 1933, Parliament appointed a Joint Committee on Indian Constitutional Reform. Its report, issued in November 1934, became the basis for the famous Government of India Act of 1935. The act was a long and complex measure, running to 451 clauses and 323 printed pages. The London *Times* of August 3, 1935, called it a "great constructive measure, the greatest indeed that a British Government has taken in hand in this century."

The Act of 1935 provided for the separation of Burma and India, and it gave a new constitution to India. Dyarchy in the provinces was abolished. The eleven provinces of British India were given a greater degree of independence from the Centre; and responsible government, limited by certain safeguards and emergency powers in the hands of the governors, was introduced in a really meaningful sense. After the act was passed, the franchise was extended to some 30,000,000 persons. A complex system of separate communal electorates was established. The Act of 1935 further provided the framework for a federal India, comprising both British India and the Native States. This significant step, however, was to be taken only when half the rulers of Princely States agreed to it. The powers of the central government and of the provincial governments were spelled out in three long lists of areas subject to federal, provincial, and concurrent jurisdiction. A kind of dyarchy appeared in the Centre through provisions giving the Governor-General full authority in defense and foreign affairs and providing for responsible government in other matters—subject, however, to special authority of the Governor-General in finance and economics and to wide emergency powers.

The Government of India Act of 1935 was ill-fated from the beginning. As V. P. Menon remarked, "the Act had more enemies than friends."[26] One wonders whether the outcome would have been happier if the Indians had been able and willing to implement the federal provisions of the Act of 1935. In spite of lengthy negotiations with the princes, the Viceroy was unable to put the federal provisions of the act into effect; and opposition to this promising experiment in central government came from many other sources. With the out-

[26] *The Transfer of Power in India* (Princeton: Princeton University Press, 1957), p. 54.

break of the Second World War the efforts to establish a federal India along the lines charted by the Act of 1935 were shelved, never to be revived in the same form. Thus, as Menon sadly observes, "in the clash of politics, the struggle for power, the wrangle for ascendancy, and the scramble for gains on the part of the political organizations, politicians and the Princes, the scheme of federation, became a tragic casualty." [27]

After considerable delay a large measure of responsible government was actually granted to the provinces of British India for a limited period of time. The enlarged franchise was put into effect, and elections for the provincial assemblies were held early in 1937. In five of the eleven provinces the Congress obtained a clear majority. In Bombay it won nearly half the seats and soon gathered enough support to dominate the Assembly; in Assam and the North-West Frontier Province it was the largest single party. At first the Congress representatives refused to accept office because the governors would not pledge not to use their "powers of interference or set aside the advice of ministers in regard to their constitutional activities." Thus interim governments had to be organized in the five provinces where the Congress had been especially successful. Within a few months the impasse had been resolved by a statement from the Governor-General which the Congress interpreted as meeting its demands, and in July 1937 Congress ministries were formed in Bihar, Bombay, the Central Provinces, Madras, Orissa, and the United Provinces. Shortly thereafter a coalition ministry in which the Congress was the dominant group was set up in the North-West Frontier Province, and in October 1938 a similar coalition was formed in Assam. On the whole, these Congress ministries made an impressive record, and their relations with the governors were generally good; but they resigned en masse in November 1939 as a part of the Congress opposition to the circumstances under which the British brought India into the Second World War.

Various developments in 1937–1939 widened the gulf between the Congress and the Muslim League. When Congress ministries were in office in most of the provinces, no Muslims were included unless they abandoned the League and joined the Congress. It was Dr. Ambedkar, spokesman of the untouchables and not a Muslim, who said that this decision "means the political death of the Muslims as a free people." [28] Faced with the prospect that in the foreseeable future they would be a permanent minority in a Hindu-dominated state, large numbers of Muslims began to support the League actively, and the League leaders began to think seriously in terms of a separate state. Their demands were formulated more specifically in the famous Lahore Resolution of 1940, which called for the creation of independent Muslim states in areas "in which the Muslims are numerically in the majority, as in the north-western zones of India." Thereafter the League championed partition and eventually the creation of a single Muslim state of Pakistan. These steps were naturally anathema to the Congress leaders, but by the early 1940s they were in no position to check the separatist trends.

In the spring of 1939 a crisis developed within the Congress; Subhas Chandra Bose, president in 1938 and re-elected in 1939, opposed the views of Gandhi, whose retirement from politics had been no more than nominal. Gandhi won the day, and Bose was forced to resign. He immediately formed a more radical group known as the Forward Bloc. During the war he managed to escape to Germany, where he developed a great admiration for nazism, and then went to Malaya to form the Indian National Army, under the aegis of the Japanese. He apparently expected to enter India as a conqueror, but toward the end of the war he was killed in an airplane crash on Formosa. Thousands of Indians believe he is still alive, and his is still a name to conjure with in many parts of the country; but in 1939 his work with the Congress was over.

Meanwhile the advent of the Second World War complicated and intensified the struggle for independence. As soon as the British declared war on Germany, in September 1939, the Viceroy, Lord Linlithgow, announced that India too was at war with Germany. Promptly the Congress leaders called upon the Congress ministries in eight provinces to resign in protest as of early November 1939. The Muslim League welcomed this move by celebrating on December 22 a Deliverance Day. Forthwith, in early 1940, the Congress accepted a recommendation of Gandhi to launch a campaign of nonviolent protest against the war. Thousands of Congressmen were arrested as they tried to launch this program. When Winston Churchill replaced Neville Chamberlain as British Prime Minister, a new round of negotiations on the subjects of independence and co-operation began. But, although the Muslim League drifted ever closer to a position of all-out support for the British war effort, the Congress steadfastly refused its co-operation unless it received guarantees of immediate independence.

In 1942 Sir Stafford Cripps was sent to India on a special mission to win the co-operation of the Indians against the Japanese, who were already moving into Burma. Sir Stafford arrived in India on March 22, and a week later, at a press conference, he released the British government's draft proposals for the immediate and long-range future. Britain would not abandon its basic responsibility for the defense of India during the war, but after the fighting was over it would work with Indian representatives for "the creation of a new Indian Union." Negotiations, primarily with Congress leaders, failed to produce an agreement. On April 11 Sir Stafford admitted that "past distrust has proved too strong to allow of present agreement." The next day he left for England. As V. P. Menon observed:

The result of the Cripps negotiations, instead of bridging the gulf between the Government and the political parties in India, only served to widen it. The manner in which the negotiations had broken down tended to strengthen the doubts and suspicions in the minds of political leaders that there was no genuine desire on the part of His Majesty's Government to part with power.[29]

In August 1942 the Indian National Congress issued a sensational resolution calling on the British directly to "Quit India," and the party leaders set about preparing for another campaign of civil disobedience, at the very moment when the Japanese were approaching the borders of India. The British did not hesitate. They promptly arrested all the leaders of the Congress Party, and although Gandhi was released, because of ill-health, in May 1944, the majority of the Congress leadership spent the remainder of the war years in British jails.

Thus India went through the war as a divided camp, with the major nationalist movement opposed to the war effort and with the population becoming increasingly dissatisfied and disillusioned. Thousands of Indian troops who served on faraway battlefields also "recognized and felt the new trends sweeping across India."[30] Subhas Chandra Bose and his Indian National Army had many sympathizers in India, even though they were co-operating with the Japanese; and the trial of officers of Bose's army in the Red Fort in Delhi in the latter part of 1945 aroused widespread resentment against the British and support for the accused. To the public mind of India, Bose and

[29] *The Transfer of Power in India*, p. 138.
[30] Phillips Talbot, "The Independence of India," *Foreign Policy Reports*, XXIII (June 15, 1947), 77.

his followers seemed to have been trying to drive the British out of India. They were therefore national heroes, however misguided.

Relations between the Congress and the Muslim League were particularly strained by the war. Postwar elections to the central Legislative Assembly and to the provincial legislatures left no doubt that the League had won the support of the great majority of Muslims, just as the Congress had become the recognized spokesman for the great majority of non-Muslim Indians.

The growing strength of the nationalist movement in India was undoubtedly one major factor in the winning of independence; another was the impact of the war itself, for the basic discontents which brought new power to the Congress Party were precisely those which weakened the British hold on the subcontinent. But at the end of the war India was a house dangerously divided against itself. The British themselves were the first to feel that the situation was getting beyond their control. Their first action after victory in Europe was to release most political prisoners and to hold extensive conferences, in both India and England, on the subject of India's future. As a result of these conferences, Lord Wavell, who had succeeded Lord Linlithgow as Viceroy in October 1943, broadcast new proposals, designed, so he said, "to ease the present political situation and to advance India towards her goal of full self-government." He called a political conference of representative Indian leaders at Simla to form a new executive council, which was to be composed almost entirely of Indians.

The conference was held at Simla from June 25 to July 14.[31] The twenty-one Indians invited represented the major parties and groups in the country. They included Jinnah, president of the Muslim League, and Maulana Azad, then president of the Congress. Gandhi did not attend, by his own choice, but he was in Simla during the conference and available for consultation. Nehru took no part in the deliberations. It was hoped that a meeting between spokesmen of the Congress and the Muslim League, under the sponsorship of the Viceroy, would produce agreement regarding the creation of a new central government. "Very soon, however," Menon wrote many years later, "it became transformed into the familiar pattern of futile discussions between the Congress and the Muslim League, and between party leaders and the Viceroy."[32] Thus the Simla Conference ended in the usual impasse.

[31] See Menon, *The Transfer of Power in India*, ch. viii (pp. 182–215), "The Simla Conference." Menon served as one of the secretaries of the conference.
[32] *Ibid.*, p. 214.

This time the failure was a particularly ominous one. As Menon regretfully noted, "The Simla Conference afforded a last opportunity for the forces of nationalism to fight a rear-guard action to preserve the integrity of the country, and when the battle was lost the waves of communalism quickly engulfed it. Only the Hobson's Choice of partition was left." [33]

The Transfer of Power

The electoral victory of the British Labour Party in July 1945 aroused great expectations in India, and the end of the war in August raised urgently the question of India's future political status. The Viceroy went to London for instructions and announced on his return in mid-September that "His Majesty's Government are determined to do their utmost to promote in conjunction with the leaders of Indian opinion the early realisation of full self-government in India." Elections for the central Legislative Assembly, held in late 1945, resulted in overwhelming victories for the Congress in non-Muslim constituencies and for the Muslim League in the Muslim constituencies, giving the Congress 57 and the League 30 of the 102 elected seats. As a result of the elections to the provincial legislatures the Congress formed ministries in six provinces, and the League in two, namely, Bengal and Sind.

In January 1946 a British parliamentary delegation of ten members toured India and talked with most of the important leaders. From March 24 to June 29 a special mission composed of three members of the cabinet—Lord Pethwick-Lawrence, Secretary of State for India; Sir Stafford Cripps, President of the Board of Trade; and A. V. Alexander, First Lord of the Admiralty—visited India to seek a reconciliation of the Congress and the Muslim League, but its efforts were in vain. In the absence of agreement among the Indians themselves the mission put forward its own proposals. Rejecting the idea of two sovereign states in the subcontinent, the mission proposed the establishment of "a Union of India, embracing both British India and the States," with residuary powers vested in the provinces or in the Princely States. Special provisions were to be included for the protection of minorities, especially Muslims and Sikhs. A Constituent Assembly would be created to draw up the constitution for the new Union. In the meantime an interim government, composed of representatives of the major political parties in India, would carry on the work of administration.

Both the Congress and the Muslim League had reservations regard-

[33] *Ibid.*, p. 215.

ing the rather complicated scheme proposed by the Cabinet Mission, but both agreed to participate in elections for the 296 seats in the Constituent Assembly which were assigned to the provinces of British India (the 93 seats allotted to the Indian States were to be filled after negotiations with the rulers of the states concerned). The Congress won all the general seats except nine, and the League won all but five of the seats allotted to Muslims. Now, however, the Muslim League rejected the long-term plan of the Cabinet Mission, which, it charged, had "played into the hands of the Congress." In late July the League went so far as to adopt a plan of "direct action." "This day," declared Jinnah, "we bid goodbye to constitutional methods."

With some misgivings the Viceroy decided to go ahead without the co-operation of the Muslim League. On August 6 he asked Nehru to form an interim government. With the approval of the Congress Working Committee Nehru informed the Viceroy that the Congress would welcome the co-operation of the Muslim League but was prepared to form a government without it. The new interim government, headed by Nehru, was sworn in on September 2. In the beginning it did not include any nominees of the Muslim League, but in mid-October, after long negotiations on the part of the Viceroy with Jinnah, Gandhi, and Nehru, the League decided to participate. The five members it nominated included one member of the scheduled castes, but not Jinnah himself. As Menon notes, "The Muslim League had decided to enter the interim Government with but one purpose—and that was not to allow the Congress to consolidate its position to the detriment of the League's interests." [34] It also refused to participate in the deliberations of the Constituent Assembly until it had specific guarantees that the Muslims of India would not be dominated by the Congress and the Hindu majority. Nehru, Jinnah, Liaquat Ali Khan, and the Sikh leader Baldev Singh went to London in early December 1946 to discuss the forthcoming Constituent Assembly with leaders of the British government, but again no agreement could be reached.

In spite of the refusal of the Muslim League to participate, the Constituent Assembly met as scheduled on December 9. The highlight of the first session was the introduction by Nehru of a resolution stating that the Union of India should be "an independent Sovereign Republic," with residuary powers vested in the autonomous units and with adequate safeguards for minorities and for backward communities and areas.

Early in 1947 the situation in India remained tense because of the

[34] *Ibid.*, p. 318.

inability of the British representatives to secure agreement on basic matters between the Congress and the Muslim League. The League continued to refuse to join the Constituent Assembly, and the Congress demanded that in the light of this refusal the representatives of the League should be dismissed from the interim government. Underlying the jockeying on immediate issues was a basic distrust which had constantly bedeviled all efforts at unified self-government. The League was insisting on a separate Pakistan, whereas the Congress wanted a single Union of India, a house of many rooms but not two separate establishments.[35]

Under these circumstances, with tension mounting in India and with increasing pressure upon it to resolve the deadlock, the British government decided to set a definite date for British withdrawal from India. On February 20 Prime Minister Attlee announced in the House of Commons that it was the "definite intention" of his government "to take the necessary steps to effect the transference of power to responsible Indian hands by a date not later than June 1948," and that if unhappily by that date a constitution for an independent India had not been worked out

by a fully representative Constituent Assembly . . . His Majesty's Government will have to consider to whom the powers of the central Government in British India should be handed over, on the due date, whether as a whole to some form of central Government for British India, or in some areas to the existing provincial Governments, or in such other way as may seem most reasonable and in the best interests of the Indian people.

On the same day the British government announced that Lord Wavell would shortly be succeeded as Viceroy by Lord Mountbatten, who would supervise the work of "transferring to Indian hands responsibility for the government of British India in a manner that will best ensure the future happiness and prosperity of India."

The announcement of the Labour government was widely hailed in both England and India. Nehru publicly described it as a "wise and courageous" declaration which "not only removes all misconcep-

[35] In an interview with Eve Curie in the early 1940s Jinnah said: "How can you even dream of Hindu-Moslem unity? Everything pulls us apart: We have no intermarriages. We have not the same calendar. The Moslems believe in a single God, and the Hindus are idolatrous. Like the Christians, the Moslems believe in an equalitarian society, whereas the Hindus maintain the iniquitous system of castes and leave heartlessly fifty million Untouchables to their tragic fate, at the bottom of the social ladder" (Eve Curie, Journey among Warriors [Garden City, N.Y.: Doubleday, Doran, 1943], p. 463).

tion and suspicion, but also brings reality and a certain dynamic quality to the present situation in India." Jinnah refused to endorse the declaration and reiterated his demand for a separate state of Pakistan. The debates in the British Parliament revealed the grave apprehensions which many members held as to the consequence of this step. Spokesmen of the Labour government admitted that the decision was fraught with grave risks, but they believed the risks were necessary.

Lord Mountbatten arrived in India on March 22, 1947. It was soon apparent to him that India was going from bad to worse, and he determined to effect the transfer of power as rapidly as possible. A new plan was drawn up after extended conferences and communications with Indian leaders and with the British cabinet in London. On June 2 and 3, after his return from London, Mountbatten met with seven Indian leaders, including Nehru and Jinnah. He also saw Gandhi, who had been preaching at his prayer meetings against partition, to explain the steps which had led to the new plan. Gandhi was observing a day of silence, but in a friendly note he indicated that he sympathized with the Viceroy's position. On June 3 Prime Minister Attlee announced the new plan in the House of Commons and in a radio broadcast. The essence of the proposal was that the British government intended to hand over its responsibilities in India before the end of the year to one or two governments, as determined by the Indians themselves. That same night, in broadcasts over All-India Radio, Lord Mountbatten explained the plan to the Indian people, and Nehru, Jinnah, and Baldev Singh followed with pleas to their people to give the plan a fair test.

By this time Lord Mountbatten and most of the Indian leaders were convinced that partition, however undesirable, was the only solution to the existing situation. Even today it is difficult to determine objectively at what point in India's history partition became "inevitable" and how the responsibility for this "solution" should be shared. Perhaps the best answer was given by Gandhi, to whom the very idea of partition was repugnant, at a prayer meeting shortly after the June 3 plan was announced: "The British Government is not responsible for partition. The Viceroy has no hand in it. In fact he is as opposed to division as Congress itself. But if both of us, Hindus and Muslims, cannot agree on anything else, then the Viceroy is left with no choice."

In June and July the decision for partition was taken by votes in the legislative assemblies of Bengal, the Punjab, and Sind, by a meeting of certain representatives of tribal groups and of the Quetta Municipality in Baluchistan, and by referenda in Sylhet and the North-West Frontier Province. Thereupon the British government began to prepare the draft of an Indian Independence Bill. Introduced in the House of Commons on July 4, it was passed by the Commons on July 15, by the Lords on the following day, and received the Royal Assent on July 18. Seldom in the history of the British Parliament had a measure of such epochal significance been put through so speedily and with so little debate. "This is a bill," declared the Secretary of State for India, "unique in the history of legislation in this country. Never before has such a large portion of the world population achieved complete independence through legislation alone." Significant though it undoubtedly was, the act simply confirmed decisions that had already been made. It provided that "as from the fifteenth day of August, nineteen hundred and forty-seven, two independent Dominions shall be set up in India, to be known respectively as India and Pakistan."

At the close of his meeting with Indian leaders on June 3 Lord Mountbatten produced a thirty-three page document entitled "The Administrative Consequences of Partition." "The effect it made on those present," reported V. P. Menon, "was indicated by the complete silence which followed. For the first time the party leaders had been made to realize the magnitude of the task that confronted them." [36] The task was indeed formidable, and the time was short. As Lord Birdwood observed (like Menon he was intimately involved in the mechanics of partition): "There was thus left just under two and a half months in which to complete the greatest political and administrative operation in history." [37] Of particular importance were the decisions regarding the division of the armed forces and the civil service and the drawing of boundaries in the two great provinces of Bengal and the Punjab, which were to be partitioned also. For each province the decisions were made by boundary commissions consisting of two High Court judges nominated by the Congress and two nominated by the Muslim League, with Sir Cyril Radcliffe as chairman of both commissions. Quite wisely, the Radcliffe awards were not announced until August 16, the day following independence for the two Dominions. They were widely criticized at the time of their announcement and at later periods, but they were nevertheless accepted as the basis

[36] *The Transfer of Power in India*, p. 397.
[37] *India and Pakistan: A Continent Decides* (New York: Praeger, 1954), p. 34.

for the redrawing of boundary lines in the Punjab and Bengal, subject to such modification as might be made by later negotiations.

Another major problem that had to be dealt with in the few weeks between early June and mid-August 1947 was that of the Indian States. There were 562 of these states in early 1947, ranging in size from Jammu and Kashmir and Hyderabad, which were larger than many independent countries in the world, to states of only a few hundred acres. Together they covered 45 per cent of the area and had 28 per cent of the population of the entire subcontinent. Some of these states, such as Mysore and Cochin, were truly progressive, and 60 of them had representative assemblies; but in general the Indian States were far behind British India in a political, economic, and social sense, and most of the states were regarded as backward and autocratic, relics of the past and allies of the imperial power, Britain. Their independence guaranteed by the British, the states were a major obstacle to any federal program; they had, for example, prevented the federal provisions of the Act of 1935 from being implemented. In a declaration of May 12, 1946, the British stated clearly that although they could not and would not force the hand of the princes, they nonetheless hoped and expected that the Princely States would voluntarily accede to either India or Pakistan.

In the spring of 1947 representatives of the states took their seats in the Constituent Assembly. Immediately following the historic announcement by the British government on June 3, 1947, the interim government in India created the States Ministry headed by Sardar Vallabhbhai Patel, with V. P. Menon as Secretary, to deal with the problem of the Indian States. For his success in persuading—or in some cases forcing—the Princely States into the Union of India, Sardar Patel was widely hailed as the main architect of Indian unity. "The work accomplished by him at the States' Ministry amounts to a silent revolution." [38] Before August 15, 1947, the rulers of all the states contiguous to the territories of the new Union of India, with the exception of Hyderabad, Kashmir, and Junagadh, had signed an Instrument of Accession and a Standstill Agreement. Within two years after independence, the territorial unity of the Union was assured by the merger, consolidation, or integration of virtually all the states which fell within the confines of the new nation. Whether the later integra-

[38] N. Srinivasan, *Democratic Government in India* (Calcutta, 1954), p. 108. See also V. P. Menon, *The Story of the Integration of the Indian States* (New York: Macmillan, 1956).

tion was a violation of the original understandings under which the princes agreed to enter the Union of India and whether the government of India has abided by the pledges which Patel made to them in good faith are still delicate and moot questions in India today.

Thus, after long years of foreign rule and in a country divided against itself, India achieved independence in August 1947. The cost of partition, with all its attendant evils and tragic aftermath, still lay in the future. On the night of August 14 the Constituent Assembly met to usher in the nation's independence. In a moving speech Nehru declared:

Long years ago we made a tryst with destiny, and now the time comes when we shall redeem our pledge, not wholly or in full measure, but very substantially. At the stroke of the midnight hour, when the world sleeps, India will awake to life and freedom. A moment comes, which comes but rarely in history, when we step out from the old to the new, when an age ends, and when the soul of a nation, long suppressed, finds utterance. It is fitting that at this solemn moment we take the pledge of dedication to the service of India and her people and to the still larger cause of humanity.

· X ·

India since Independence:

The Political Record

IN the face of unfavorable conditions at home and abroad India's achievements since independence have been impressive indeed. The new nation has survived many crises, and Indians have a developing sense of national unity and a growing confidence that their country can face with equanimity whatever vital issues may be encountered. Step by step major obstacles have been overcome and the democratic structure has been strengthened.

At the outset two great problems involved dealing with the tragic circumstances that followed partition and ensuring the political unity of the country. The government managed very effectively the critical situation of the refugees and then turned its attention to their rehabilitation and to preparations for their entry into the normal activities of the country. Within two years after independence most of the Indian States in or contiguous to those portions of British India which were to be a part of the Union of India were integrated in various ways into the Union, thus averting what might have been a serious or even a fatal handicap to the unity of the emerging nation.

Work was begun promptly on the drafting of a constitution. After extensive discussion of the proposed draft in the Constituent Assembly and throughout the country, the constitution went into effect on January 26, 1950, and India thereupon became a republic. As soon as preparations could be made following the adoption of the constitution, India held its first nation-wide general elections in 1951–1952, and thereafter the parliamentary institutions began to function on a more normal basis. In the spring of 1957 the second general elections were held. The constitutional system that emerged was patterned heavily after Western and especially British models, but it has been adapted very successfully to India's needs and environment, and the precedents that have been established in the first years of democratic government augur well for the future.

In 1951 India launched her First Five Year Plan (finalized in late 1952), a gigantic experiment in democratic planning. At the expiration of this plan in the spring of 1956, most of the goals had been achieved, and the country immediately entered upon the even more ambitious Second Five Year Plan.

Agitation for a redrawing of the boundaries of the states of India along essentially linguistic lines was at first opposed by the government of India; but in 1953 Andhra was set up as a separate state, and on November 1, 1956, after the report of the States Reorganization Commission had been submitted and debated and after the inner circles of the Congress Party and the government had agreed upon basic matters, the map of India was redrawn internally with the creation of fourteen states and six centrally administered territories. Linguistic and regional problems are still troublesome, and they will doubtless stand in the way of effective national unity for many years to come. So will the traditions of communalism and caste, in spite of the efforts to do away with the worst features of these ancient practices.

In economic, social, and political objectives there is a remarkable degree of agreement in India. The Five Year Plans and the broad outlines of foreign policy have attracted an impressive measure of support. The tremendous popularity and prestige of Jawaharlal Nehru have won country-wide support for the dominant Congress Party and for the government which Nehru heads and have helped to consolidate the foundations of national unity and to win acceptance of the concept of the secular state. There is still a vast gap between objectives and performance, between professions and deeds, between the old and the new, between social conservatism and resistance to change.

The Cost of Partition

India arrived at independence only at the cost of partition, with all its difficulties and bitterness. Rejoicing over the winning of freedom was muted by the unhappy events which marred the birth of the two nations. India awoke to independence, to use Nehru's figure of speech, to discover that a first-class crisis threatened to plunge the entire subcontinent into a bloodbath and to place an impossible burden on the already-harassed political authorities of the new states. Even before the announcement by the British government of its forthcoming abdication, communal rioting had broken out in Calcutta and other parts of the subcontinent. When it became known that two of the great provinces, the Punjab and Bengal, would likewise be cut in two, rioting and killings became more frequent. In spite of the strained relations between India and Pakistan, their leaders co-operated as best they could to avert the impending tragedy; nevertheless, during a few weeks in the fall of 1947, the subcontinent witnessed one of the greatest orgies of violence and uncontrolled fanaticism in modern times.

The worst scenes occurred in the Punjab. No one can tell how the trouble started or who should bear the major responsibility. In the western Punjab the Muslims attacked the homes and the persons of the Hindu and Sikh minority, and in the eastern Punjab the Hindus and Sikhs vented their wrath on the Muslim minority. Thousands of people were killed, often in the most brutal ways. Trains were derailed and their passengers massacred, refugee columns ambushed, homes set on fire and their inhabitants butchered in the streets. The Punjab Boundary Force had to be disbanded because its members too became infected with the communal fury.

As hundreds of Muslims began to move out of Delhi and as refugees from West Punjab streamed in, bringing harrowing tales of atrocities with them, Delhi also, in the very political center of India, witnessed terrible scenes. V. P. Menon, an eyewitness of these scenes, has given an eloquent description of the state of the refugees who came to Delhi in these trying days:

The uprooted millions were in a terrible mental state. They had been driven from their homes under conditions of indescribable horror and misery. Not many had the time to plan their evacuation; most had to move out at the shortest possible notice. They had been subjected to terrible indignities. They had witnessed their near and dear ones hacked to pieces before their eyes and their houses ransacked, looted and set on fire by their own neighbors. They had no choice but to seek safety in flight, filled with wrath at what they had seen, and full of anguish for numberless missing kinsmen who were still stranded in Pakistan and for their women-folk who had been abducted.[1]

Fortunately, the rest of the country remained relatively unaffected by the communal frenzy, although there were threats of trouble in West Bengal. Serious rioting was averted in Calcutta only by the influence of Mahatma Gandhi, who went to India's largest city and started a fast in protest against communal disturbances. Lord Mountbatten did not exaggerate when he referred to Gandhi as "the one-man boundary force who kept the peace while a force 50,000 strong was swamped by riots."

The governments of India and Pakistan, encouraged by Lord Mountbatten, co-operated in helping to move thousands of people to and from each other's territories and in preserving some semblance of law, order, and sanity. In India an emergency committee was set up; Lord Mountbatten served as chairman, and Nehru and Patel were among its members. A special committee was created to deal with the situation in Delhi and New Delhi. In October the worst of the troubles was over, although the flow of refugees continued. By the middle of 1948 over 12,000,000 people had crossed the Indo-Pakistan borders, creating one of the greatest refugee problems of modern times. About 5,500,000 Hindus and Sikhs had moved from West Pakistan into India, about the same number of Muslims had left East Punjab and other parts of India for West Pakistan, and approximately 1,500,000 non-Muslims had crossed the borders of East Pakistan into West Bengal. Nearly half a million Hindus later left Sind for India, and the influx of Hindus from East Pakistan into West Bengal still goes on.

India has made heroic efforts to cope with the tremendous refugee problem. The first task was to care for immediate needs. At one time the government of India was running some 160 camps, accommodating a million and a quarter people. There were 150,000 in two camps outside New Delhi alone. The next step was to provide centers for the rehabilitation of the refugees and to find means for integrating them into the life of the country. All over India, refugees began their new lives, with substantial government assistance. On the whole the

[1] V. P. Menon, *The Transfer of Power in India* (Princeton: Princeton University Press, 1957), p. 418.

refugee problem has been brought under control, but even today, more than a decade after independence, thousands of refugees huddle in improvised shelters in Delhi, Calcutta, and other large cities of India.

Thus at the outset of independence India was faced with a human tragedy of formidable dimensions. The terrible weeks of August and September 1947 left a lasting impression on Indian minds. Trouble had been anticipated along the new frontiers of India and Pakistan, especially in divided Bengal and the Punjab, but few people foresaw mass destruction. Many Indians still find it hard to understand why such a catastrophe occurred. It was a heavy burden for the new state to bear. As V. P. Menon has observed: "The communal holocaust, the two-way exodus of refugees, their protection and the rehabilitation of those who had come to India—all these provided the Government of India, at a time when the administrative machinery was already out of joint as a result of partition, with a task as stupendous as any nation ever had to face." [2]

The Integration of the States

As soon as the communal disturbances accompanying partition had been brought under control, the government of India turned its attention to problems of consolidation and internal development. A matter of pressing importance was the necessity of integrating into the Union of India the Native (Princely) States which had acceded to India prior to independence. Within two years this important task was accomplished. Again the chief credit belongs to Vallabhbhai Patel and to the States Ministry which he headed. The policy of the government of India was to subordinate the Native States to the central government by moving well beyond the Standstill Agreements that had been made prior to independence, to associate the more than 500 Native States into viable units, chiefly by consolidating them with former governor's provinces or chief commissioner's provinces or by forming unions of states, and to modernize and democratize the Native States to the fullest extent possible. Briefly put, the aim, as the first White Paper on Indian States declared, "was the integration of all elements in the country in a free, united and democratic India." [3] Integration

[2] *Ibid.*, p. 434.
[3] See Government of India, Ministry of States, *White Paper on Indian States* (New Delhi: Government of India Press, 1st ed., 1948, rev. ed., 1950).

meant that the princely rulers had to give up their effective power. Some continued to have appointive posts in the territories where they had once held almost absolute sway, and some took active political roles, but most were simply pensioned off.

The process of integrating the Indian States assumed three main forms. In the first place, many of the smaller states were merged and then joined to the former provinces of British India (governor's provinces). Secondly, some Native States were consolidated into States Unions and placed under the direct administration of the central government, and the administration of a few individual states, for special reasons, was at least temporarily of the same nature. Thirdly, many other Native States were joined into Unions of States. Eventually, five States Unions were thus created, and together with the only three Princely States to retain their original form until the reorganization of 1956—Mysore, Hyderabad, and Jammu and Kashmir—they became Part "B" states under the constitution of 1950. Altogether, 216 Native States were merged into former governor's provinces; 61 were placed under the administration of the central government, mostly merged into States Unions; and 275 were merged into five States Unions which became separate units of the Union.

A mere recital of the steps by which the more than 500 Princely States were made integral parts of the Indian Union cannot even suggest the drama of the story. That drama has recently been described by V. P. Menon, who was Patel's right-hand man in the States Ministry.[4] Menon describes the negotiations which Patel and others in the States Ministry carried on with the princely rulers, trying to persuade them to relinquish their power voluntarily and thus to help in the integration of the new India. Some rulers, like the fabulously wealthy Nizam of Hyderabad, were reluctant to surrender their power at all. Others took a dim view of having their territories merged with other states. Occasionally these mergers involved states whose rulers had been bitter rivals or even enemies for many decades. To persuade the Maharajah of Gwalior and the Maharajah of Indore to join in the new state of Madhya Bharat was a feat of no small dimensions, in view of the long-standing rivalry between these two states. No fewer than 222 states, estates, and talukas were merged to form the United State of Kathiawar, later known as Saurashtra. Menon's lively account of the process by which Saurashtra was brought into being may be com-

[4] V. P. Menon, *The Story of the Integration of the Indian States* (New York: Macmillan, 1956).

mended as a fascinating study of a most difficult operation. The accession, integration, and democratization of the Native States of India constituted a major achievement of the leaders of India and especially of Vallabhbhai Patel, who called the operation a "bloodless revolution which has affected the destinies of millions of our people."

Special problems arose with regard to Jammu and Kashmir, Hyderabad, and a small state in the Kathiawar area, Junagadh. The case of Junagadh was rather easily settled, although it caused friction between India and Pakistan and raised problems of considerable import. Located only a short distance from the southeast borders of West Pakistan, Junagadh had a Muslim ruler and an overwhelmingly Hindu population. In September 1947 the ruler of Junagadh formally acceded to Pakistan, and Pakistan accepted the accession. When this action became known, disturbances broke out in the state. India disapproved of the arrangement and presumably encouraged the Hindus of the state to voice their protests. The ruler was forced to flee, and the Muslim Diwan, under great pressure, invited the Indian government to send in troops to restore order. On India's insistence a plebiscite was held in Junagadh in February 1948 and resulted in an almost unanimous vote for accession to India. The merger was accomplished in the following January.[5]

The case of Hyderabad posed far more serious problems for the government of India. One of the largest of the Native States and one of the most feudal, Hyderabad occupied a huge area in the center of the Deccan. From the point of view of the Indian government the integration of Hyderabad into the Union of India was a necessity. The Nizam, however, was a Muslim and had other ideas; he was strongly backed in his desire to preserve an independent existence by militant Muslim leaders and organizations inside his state and perhaps also by the government of Pakistan. He rejected the invitation to accede to India before the transfer of power. In November 1947 he did agree to sign a Standstill Agreement with India. For several months Lord Mountbatten and Sir Walter Moncton, who was the Nizam's constitutional adviser, worked with Patel and other Indian officials to persuade the Nizam to change his mind. In June 1948 the negotiations broke down, and India imposed a complete economic blockade on the state. Within Hyderabad a campaign of violence, spurred on by Muslim fanatics and Communists, kept the Hindu majority in a state of terror. The Nizam appealed to the Security Council

[5] See *ibid.*, ch. vi.

of the United Nations for aid in settling his dispute with India. While the Security Council was considering the advisability of placing the dispute on its agenda, in the face of India's strong insistence that Hyderabad was not a sovereign state and therefore could not bring a dispute before the UN, the government of India, on September 13, 1948, sent troops into Hyderabad. After no more than token resistance the Nizam capitulated, and the state was placed under a military administration. The Indian government allowed the Nizam to continue as head of the state. In November he acceded to India, and in January 1950 he became Rajpramukh (i.e., governor) of his state, which became a Part "B" state in the Union.[6] When all the states were reorganized along linguistic lines, in November 1956, the state of Hyderabad passed out of existence, and the Nizam announced his retirement. Most of what had been Hyderabad was shared by the enlarged states of Bombay and Andhra Pradesh, and the city of Hyderabad became the capital of the latter state.

The government of India now regards the state of Jammu and Kashmir as fully integrated into the Indian republic, even though the "final" steps in this process were not completed until January 1957, when the constitution which had been adopted by the Constituent Assembly in Kashmir went into effect. The Pakistan government takes an entirely different view. It maintains that the status of Kashmir is still to be determined by a plebiscite, promised by Governor-General Mountbatten in October 1947 and reaffirmed by Nehru and other Indian leaders on many subsequent occasions. It holds that the principle of popular consent which motivated Indian actions in the cases of Junagadh and Hyderabad was violated by India in the case of Kashmir. A brochure issued by Pakistan Publications in 1957 stated:

According to its logic in the cases of Junagadh and Hyderabad, India should have turned down the offer of a Hindu Ruler to accede to India, in spite of the fact that 77 per cent of State's population was Muslim. . . . But in the case of Kashmir, the arguments which India had advanced in the cases of Hyderabad and Junagadh were ignored.[7]

The details of the dispute between India and Pakistan over Kashmir are discussed in the later section on foreign policy.[8] Here brief refer-

---

[6] *Ibid.,* chs. xvii–xix.

[7] *Kashmir: The Powder Keg of Asia* (Karachi: Pakistan Publications, 1957), p. 5.

[8] See also Lord Birdwood, *Two Nations and Kashmir* (London, 1956); Josef Korbel, *Danger in Kashmir* (Princeton: Princeton University Press, 1954); Menon, *Integration of the Indian States,* ch. xx.

ence will be made to the evolving status of Kashmir within the Union of India.

Like the Nizam of Hyderabad, the Hindu Maharajah of Kashmir did not accept an invitation to accede to the Union of India prior to August 15, 1947. He entered into a Standstill Agreement with Pakistan, but apparently he thought in terms of preserving his independence from either of the emerging Dominions. He was subject to strong pressure from Pakistan to accede to that state. Pakistan even imposed an economic blockade on Kashmir. But tribal invasions of the Maharajah's state in October 1947 forced him to appeal to India for help. Acting on the advice of Lord Mountbatten, the government of India agreed to send military aid only if the Maharajah would accede to the Indian Union. This he did on October 26, 1947. A few hours later Indian troops landed by air in Srinagar and within a few days had pushed back the invaders. A letter from Governor-General Mountbatten to the Maharajah of Kashmir, dated October 27, 1947, made it clear that India's acceptance of the accession was provisional and that "as soon as law and order have been restored in Kashmir and her soil cleared of the invader, the question of the accession should be settled by a reference to the people." The plebiscite has never been held. In spite of the efforts of Dr. Frank Graham and other representatives of the United Nations, which has been concerned with the Kashmir dispute ever since India brought it before the Security Council on January 1, 1948, demilitarization and other essential preliminary steps could not be agreed upon by the two parties directly concerned. As time went on, new factors entered the picture, so that India's present position seems to be that the pledge of the plebiscite is no longer binding. As early as 1947 the Kashmir National Conference approved the Maharajah's decision to accede to India. Sheikh Abdullah, who was the Muslim leader of the National Conference until his dismissal and arrest in August 1953, favored close association with India until a few weeks before his fall from power. The state of Jammu and Kashmir was listed as one of the Part "B" states of the Indian Union in the constitution of 1950, but retained a special limited relation to Union authority. The Delhi Agreement of July 1952 spelled out the details of Kashmir's special relationship with India. This agreement was ratified by both the Indian Parliament and the Constituent Assembly of Kashmir. In 1952, upon the recommendation of Sheikh Abdullah, then Prime Minister of the state, the Constituent Assembly declared that the Maharajah's rule was at an end and elected his son,

Yuvraj Karen Singh, as the first Sadar-i-Riyasat or elected head of the state.

The government of Bakshi Ghulam Mohammed, which replaced Sheikh Abdullah's regime in August 1953, was strongly pro-Indian and took the position that Kashmir had irrevocably cast its lot with that of India. With the obvious approval of the Indian government, a newly elected Assembly, composed chiefly of followers of the Bakshi government, drafted and adopted a constitution for the state. Article 3, which became operative immediately on the adoption of the constitution in November 1956, stated categorically that the "State of Jammu and Kashmir is and shall be an integral part of the Union of India." When this constitution entered fully into effect on January 26, 1957, both the Bakshi regime and the government of India announced that the integration of Kashmir into the Indian republic was now complete.

Constitution Making

These three states were the last to be integrated into Indian territory; but long before this process of integration was complete, India had set about creating a constitution. Indeed, the essential character of the Indian state after the achievement of freedom was largely determined before the British government decided to withdraw from India. The new nation, it was clear, would be a democratic state, modeled mainly along British lines. The new constitution would be patterned after the Government of India Act of 1935, with such changes as seemed necessary to safeguard fundamental freedoms and to serve the needs of an independent democracy. Free India would be a federal state, and it would have a written constitution. Although the British system of cabinet responsibility would prevail, an effort would be made to adapt features of other constitutional systems as well. The new constitution would be framed by a Constituent Assembly.

Under the plan advanced by the British Cabinet Mission a Constituent Assembly was elected by the provincial assemblies in July 1946 and began to function immediately, even though its representative character was weakened when the Muslim League refused to allow its elected members to attend. The first session was held in New Delhi on December 9, 1946. Dr. Rajendra Prasad, later President of the Indian republic, was elected permanent president. An important Resolution on Aims and Objectives, moved by Nehru on December 11, and adopted on January 22, 1947, expressed the Assembly's "firm and solemn resolve to proclaim India as an Independent Sovereign Republic and to draw up for her future governance a Constitution." At its third session (April 22–May 2, 1947) the Constituent Assembly set up committees on the Union constitution and provincial constitutions, under the chairmanship of Nehru and Patel, respectively. When the fourth session met on July 14, the decision to partition the subcontinent had been announced, and only a short time remained to prepare for the assumption of full independence. The Constituent Assembly was broadened by the addition of representatives from the Native States and of members of the Muslim League from parts of the country which would be included in the Union of India. The Assembly began to discuss the principles of the new constitution, starting with the reports of the Nehru Committee. After midnight of August 14 the Assembly began to function in two capacities: as the Provisional Parliament of India, with a Speaker (G. V. Mavalankar) in the chair, and as the Constituent Assembly with sovereign powers, presided over by a president (Dr. Rajendra Prasad). The Assembly continued to function in this dual role until the work of constitution making was accomplished.

On August 29, 1947, two weeks after India became independent, the Constituent Assembly set up a drafting committee of seven distinguished members, including N. Gopalaswami Ayyangar, K. M. Munshi, Alladi Krishnaswami Iyer, and T. T. Krishnamachari, with India's most distinguished "untouchable," Dr. B. R. Ambedkar, as chairman. B. N. Rau, later a judge of the International Court of Justice, acted as constitutional adviser, and S. N. Mukerji was principal draftsman. Both because of their positions as Prime Minister and Deputy Prime Minister and because of their enormous personal influence, Nehru and Patel also played a major role in the work of constitution making. Perhaps the chief credit should go to Dr. Ambedkar, the able chairman of the drafting committee, for his vast legal knowledge, his ability as a presiding officer of the committee, and his effectiveness in defending the constitutional proposals in the Constituent Assembly.

Relying heavily upon British models and upon the Government of India Act of 1935, the members of the drafting committee made a careful study of the constitutions of all the democratic countries of the world and adopted features from several. Thus the provisions regarding the Supreme Court of India owed much to the American constitution. In the framing of the vital sections dealing with fundamental rights and with the "directive principles of state policy," the commit-

tee borrowed certain provisions and ideas from the constitutions of
Ireland, Australia, Canada, and the United States.

The first draft of the constitution was ready in the incredibly short
time of under six months. It was the subject of extensive discussion
in the country, which resulted in some changes, before it was taken
up by the Constituent Assembly eight months later. The Assembly
spent an entire year considering the constitutional proposals in great
detail. "During this period as many as 7,635 amendments were tabled
and 2,473 of these were actually discussed by the Assembly." [9] The
debates in the Constituent Assembly during these months were generally on a very high level. Although they did not probe to the fundamentals of government as did the debates in the American Constitutional Convention, they are of fundamental importance for all students
of comparative government. Unfortunately India produced nothing
comparable to the Federalist Papers to enlighten the people of the
country on the nature and significance of the new constitution.

The third reading of the Constitution Bill began on November 14,
1949, and was concluded on November 26 by its adoption. The final
session of the Constituent Assembly was held on January 24, 1950.
It elected Dr. Rajendra Prasad as President of the republic of India
under the new constitution. Two days later, India was proclaimed a
republic and Dr. Prasad assumed office as its President. This date is
commemorated every year as Republic Day. The Constituent Assembly
carried on as India's Provisional Parliament until the summer of 1952,
when the first regular Parliament elected under the constitution took
over.

The Constitutional System

India's constitution is the longest document of its kind in the world.
It consists of 395 articles and 9 schedules. The text of the document in
an official version runs to 254 pages, and the table of contents and
the index to 64 pages more. For its unusual length there was both
reason and precedent. "The Indian Constitution, unlike some others,
is not merely a declaration of principles. It is a detailed and intricate
body of organic law containing many elements that in some other countries are to be found in the statutory rather than the constitutional
law." [10] Because of regional and social variations, the great variety
of legal practices and customs, the relative lack of experience in self-

[9] N. Srinivasan, *Democratic Government in India* (Calcutta, 1954), p. 138.
[10] Editorial, "A Constitution for India," *New York Times,* Nov. 28, 1949.

government, and the need to provide for emergencies, the framers of the constitution took pains to be explicit. They felt that many points which might otherwise have been left to regular legislation, and even many objectives which could not be legally enforceable, should be spelled out in the basic constitution document.

Undoubtedly the example of the Government of India Act of 1935 did not make for brevity. This act was one of the longest and most intricate acts ever passed by the British Parliament. As has been noted, the constitution of India borrowed heavily from this act; in fact, many sections were incorporated almost without change. Professor N. Srinivasen has called the constitution "a palimpsest" of the Act of 1935. "The new Constitution may indeed be described as the working Constitution of the country under the old Act adapted to its new political status." [11]

Briefly stated, the constitution of India makes India a democratic secular state with what is essentially a parliamentary system and a federal structure. In practice, no doubt, this generalization must be qualified in many ways. Perhaps it would be more accurate to say that in India democracy is the goal rather than the reality—in other words, that India is a democracy-in-being and that the prospects for the successful evolution of democratic institutions are still unknown. The leaders of India, and most of all Nehru himself, are dedicated to the concept of the secular state, but there are strong communal forces in the country pulling in a different direction. Although India has essentially a parliamentary system, patterned, as Nehru himself stated, "largely after the British model, with necessary variations," some of the "variations," such as the emergency powers of the President and the role of the Supreme Court, suggest a strange blending of parliamentary and nonparliamentary forms.

Although India is "a Union of States," according to Article 1 of the constitution, experts in government are still arguing whether there is in fact a federal system. If so, it is a peculiar kind of federalism, with many unfederal features. Here again an influence is noted from the Government of India Act of 1935, which provided for a federation of British India and the Native States, though these provisions were never implemented. In free India the federation was peculiar in that it was created by the transfer of power from both foreign and native rulers. Thus from the outset the Indian federation had strong centralizing characteristics. These are perpetuated in the constitution, which

[11] Srinivasan, *Democratic Government in India*, p. 143.

vests residuary powers in the Centre and gives the central government an authority over the constituent units of the federation—the states— which in times of emergency may amount to a virtual suspension of the federal structure. Professor Kenneth Wheare, a distinguished British authority on constitutional systems, has expressed the view that the constitution of India "establishes, indeed a system of government which is at most quasi-federal, almost devolutionary in character; a unitary State with subsidiary federal features rather than a federal State with subsidiary unitary features." [12] Most authorities would challenge the latter part of Professor Wheare's interpretation. They would agree that India is "at most quasi-federal," but they would insist that it is "a federal State with subsidiary unitary features." Most federations have felt the need to give ample authority to the central government; hence few existing federations are more than quasi-federal in character. The framers of the Indian constitution were determined to give the Centre enough power to hold the Union together against the many disruptive forces which they knew to be at work in the Indian environment. Thus, as Professor Srinivasan has pointed out, "the new Constitution of India has effected an adjustment of federal-state relations suited to the conditions of India that is *sui generis*." [13] It is a pattern which deserves the careful attention of students of comparative government.

A people which has known only authoritarian rule, either foreign or domestic, now has a constitution which proclaims boldly in the first words of the Preamble: "WE, THE PEOPLE OF INDIA, having solemnly resolved to constitute India into a SOVEREIGN, DEMOCRATIC REPUBLIC . . . do HEREBY ADOPT, ENACT AND GIVE TO OURSELVES THIS CONSTITUTION." A lengthy section (Articles 12 through 35) spells out the fundamental rights which are guaranteed to every person. These rights are grouped under the following subheadings: Right to Equality, Right to Freedom, Right against Exploitation, Right to Freedom of Religion, Cultural and Educational Rights, Right to Property, Right to Constitutional Remedies. Article 17 states unequivocally: " 'Untouchability' is abolished and its practice in any form is forbidden." The widespread prevalence of "untouchability" in India today does not lessen the importance of this provision in India's fundamental law; rather it points to

[12] "India's New Constitution Analysed," *A.L.J.*, XLVIII, 21, quoted in Alan Gledhill, *The Republic of India* (London, 1951), p. 92.
[13] Srinivasan, *Democratic Government in India*, p. 147.

the difficulty of trying to correct long-standing social abuses by legal means and offers a positive hope for the future.

Article 21 of the constitution reads as follows: "No person shall be deprived of his life or personal liberty except according to procedure established by law." And Article 31 (1) states: "No person shall be deprived of his property save by authority of law." These provisions call attention to the fact that there is no due process clause in the Indian constitution, such as is found in the Fifth and Fourteenth Amendments to the American constitution. American experts on constitutional law have often pointed to this omission, which was a deliberate one, as an indication that the constitution of India lacks a vital reserve power to protect the citizen against arbitrary acts of the government. In the important case of *A. K. Gopalan v. The State of Madras* the Supreme Court of India held that the term "procedure established by law" in Article 21 of the Indian constitution "cannot be interpreted to lay down a vague standard such as the principles of natural law" and thus was not equivalent to the American due process clause. Justice William O. Douglas of the United States Supreme Court, however, in his careful comparative study of American and Indian constitutional law, professed to "discern in Indian judicial decisions a flavor of due process when it comes to questions of *substantive* law." "Suffice it to say," he concluded, "that the concepts embodied in due process are also embodied in Indian constitutional law, where other clauses do service for a due process clause." [14]

Article 22 provides protection against arrest and detention in certain cases, but it also contains clauses which have allowed the Indian Parliament to pass the Preventive Detention Bill, one of the toughest bills on the statute books of any democratic state.

The section on fundamental rights in the constitution is followed by a brief and interesting section (Articles 36 through 50), borrowed apparently from the Irish constitution, entitled "Directive Principles of State Policy." The nature of these principles is suggested by the wording of Article 37: "The provisions contained in this Part shall not be enforceable by any court, but the principles therein laid down are nevertheless fundamental in the governance of the country and it shall be the duty of the State to apply these principles in making laws." Dr.

[14] William O. Douglas, *We the Judges: Studies in American and Indian Constitutional Law from Marshall to Mukherjea* (New York: Doubleday, 1956), pp. 28, 29.

B. R. Ambedkar stated in the Constituent Assembly that the object of the directive principles was "to prescribe that every government . . . shall strive to bring about economic democracy." Most of the principles are in fact concerned with economic and social policy. The broad goals are stated in Article 38: "The State shall strive to promote the welfare of the people by securing and protecting as effectively as it may a social order in which justice, social, economic and political, shall inform all the institutions of the national life."

Article 40 expresses an intention to revive an ancient institution of village democracy, the panchayat, and to make it the basis of the system of local self-government. Article 45 lays down the ambitious objective of "free and compulsory education for all children" up to the age of 14 within a period of ten years following the adoption of the constitution.

Most of the constitutional provisions, as would be expected, relate to the organization and functions of the governments in the Union and in the states. India, according to Article 1, is "a Union of States." Originally the states were divided into three classes: Part "A," Part "B," and Part "C." Part "A" states were the former governor's provinces of British India, into which many Native States had been merged. Part "B" states were the five newly created Unions of Native States plus the Native States of Jammu and Kashmir, Hyderabad, and Mysore. Part "C" states were created out of the former chief commissioner's provinces, to which, after independence, some Native States had been joined. Thus in its origin the federal Union of India was composed of three main types of states, with the first two having roughly equal status, but with the Part "C" states being definitely on a lower level. Altogether there were 27 states (which became 28 in 1953 with the creation of Andhra as a Part "A" state). This division was abolished when the states reorganization went into effect in November 1956. Today there are 14 states in the republic of India, all having equal status, plus 6 centrally administered Union territories.

In theory all executive power of the Union of India is vested in the President. He is chosen by the elected members of both houses of the Indian Parliament and of the legislative assemblies of the states for a term of five years and is eligible for re-election. There has been much controversy and disagreement over the constitutional position and powers of the President. If the framers of the constitution had been trying to follow the British model, with such variations and adaptations as they felt to be desirable, one would assume that the President was, to use Bagehot's term, the head of the "dignified" parts of the constitution, whereas effective power would rest in the Prime Minister and the cabinet and the Parliament. That is the position which the President does in fact occupy, and it is certainly the role which the respected first President of India, Dr. Rajendra Prasad, has chosen to play. The constitution states that "the Ministers shall hold office during the pleasure of the President," but the very next article reads: "The Council of Ministers shall be collectively responsible to the House of the People." Moreover, as M. Ramaswamy has pointed out, "the President of India has no constitutional means at his disposal to implement any decision he might wish to take in the public interests when the decision depends for its execution upon legislative or fiscal action, so long as the cabinet and Parliament are hostile to the course he wishes to adopt." [15]

But the constitution of India does give the President a special position and special powers which would seem to make him a far stronger head of state than the British sovereign. He has many powers to promulgate ordinances when Parliament is not in session and wide emergency powers, which in effect would enable him to take over the government of any state or states if he should find that the security of India is threatened "whether by war or external aggression or internal disturbances" or that "a situation has arisen in which the government" of a state "cannot be carried on in accordance with the provisions of the Constitution" or that "a situation has arisen whereby the financial stability or credit of India or any part of the territory thereof is threatened." These special powers are so sweeping that Professor B. M. Sharma has concluded:

The Constitution of India contains a vast reservoir of powers for the President, and in what manner these shall be exercised is the moot question on the answer to which shall largely depend the exact nature of the executive of India, whether it will be purely parliamentary, like the British king, or he will effectively exercise some of his powers independently of the Council of Ministers. For even if he adopts the latter course he will not be guilty of violating the Constitution. [16]

Article 77 of the constitution provides that "all executive action of the Government of India shall be expressed to be taken in the name of the President." He appoints the Prime Minister and other Minis-

[15] M. Ramaswamy, "The Constitutional Position of the President of the Indian Republic," *Canadian Bar Review*, XXVIII (June–July 1950), 651–652.
[16] B. M. Sharma, *Federalism in Theory and Practice* (Lucknow, 1951), II, 564.

ters, and the Prime Minister has the duty of keeping him informed of "all decisions of the Council of Ministers relating to the administration of the affairs of the Union and proposals for legislation." The President may not be a member of either house of the Parliament, but Article 79 states that the Parliament of the Union "shall consist of the President and two houses."

The Vice-President of India is elected for a term of five years by members of both houses of Parliament in joint session. He is ex-officio chairman of the Council of States, but he may not be a member of that body or of the House of the People or of any state Legislature.

Considerable speculation has been aroused by the brevity of the provisions in the constitution regarding the Council of Ministers, and particularly regarding the failure to make clear the precise relation between the President, the Prime Minister, and the Council of Ministers. The Prime Minister and the Council of Ministers are "to aid and advise the President in the exercise of his functions"; but they are also "collectively responsible to the House of the People."

Parliament in India is composed of two houses, the Council of States (Rajya Sabha) and the House of the People (Lok Sabha). The Council of States has a membership of no more than 250; 12 members are nominated by the President of India, and the rest are representatives of the states, chosen for the most part by the elected members of the state assemblies. Approximately one-third of the members retire every second year, but the Council itself is not subject to dissolution. India has a weak upper chamber, without even the special dignities and privileges of, say, the House of Lords.

The House of the People has a membership of approximately 500, practically all of whom are directly elected. The maximum life of the House is five years, but it may be dissolved at any time by the President, acting upon the advice of the Prime Minister. In its organization, its procedure, the power and privileges of its members, and the relations between the two houses, the Parliament of India is very similar to the British Parliament. In its actual operation and its place within the constitutional system the similarities are less marked.

The Supreme Court of India, consisting of a Chief Justice and seven other judges, appointed by the President and holding office until they reach the age of 65, is "placed at the apex of a single, unified judiciary which administers both federal and state laws alike throughout the country." [17] It has extensive original jurisdiction in cases which

[17] Srinivasan, *Democratic Government in India,* p. 282.

involve the government of India and any of the states, conflict between states, or enforcement of fundamental rights. In certain cases it also has appellate jurisdiction over appeals from high courts. The President may consult the Supreme Court on "a question of law or fact," on a matter of public importance, or on constitutional questions. To some extent the Supreme Court of India has the power of judicial review and is therefore the guardian of the constitution, but it does not have the place in the Indian system of government which the Supreme Court has in the American system. Parliament may extend the court's jurisdiction, but may also limit it. "The court's authority is intended to be more a barrier to executive arbitrariness and violations of the Constitution than to legislative acts. Any assumption of power by the court to frustrate the social policies decided upon by the Legislature can be prevented in the last resort by an amendment of the Constitution," [18] and this process is considerably easier than in the United States.

For Part "A" and Part "B" states the constitution originally provided responsible government very much along the lines of that established in the Centre, subject of course to the residuary powers of the central government. The executive power in Part "A" states was vested in a governor and in Part "B" states in a Rajpramukh, each appointed by the President of India. The chief minister and other ministers were to be appointed by the governor or Rajpramukh, but the council of ministers was collectively responsible to the Legislative Assembly of the state. The state legislature was to consist either of one house, known as the Legislative Assembly, or of two houses, known as the Legislative Council and the Legislative Assembly. Each state was also to have a high court, district courts, and such subordinate courts as might be deemed necessary. Part "C" states were to be administered by the President acting through a chief commissioner or a lieutenant governor. Parliament could create a legislature, either nominated or elected, for any Part "C" state and also a council of advisers or ministers. The reorganization of the Indian States in November 1956 eliminated the three classes of states and placed all fourteen new states on the same basis. Hence their government is conducted mainly along the lines charted in the constitution for Part "A" states.

In any federal union the relations between the Centre and the component units are of crucial importance. This was particularly true in India, where federalism was a novel experiment and where an effort

[18] *Ibid.*, p. 291.

was made to give sufficient powers to the Centre while at the same time granting as much autonomy as possible to the states. The Seventh Schedule of the constitution enumerates the powers of the Centre and the states in a Union List, a State List, and a Concurrent List. Ninety-seven items are included in the Union List, 66 in the State List, and 47 in the Concurrent List. During a period of national emergency, Parliament has "power to make laws for the whole or any part of the territory of India with respect to any of the matters enumerated in the State List."

Part XIV of the Indian constitution contains provisions for recruiting and employing members of the public services, with major responsibility being vested in the Union Public Service Commission and the State Public Service Commissions. Part XV deals with elections and election procedures. An Election Commission was charged with preparation of the electoral rolls and with the conduct of all elections for the central Parliament, for legislatures of every state, and for President and Vice-President. In a country where very few people in the past had been eligible to vote, where most of the population were illiterate and backward, and where women in particular had played little part in political life, the framers of the constitution took a bold step, indeed a "calculated risk": they decreed universal adult suffrage for all the citizens of India, except those obviously disqualified, over the age of 21. Special provisions were necessary for the most backward of India's underprivileged millions, those who belonged to the so-called scheduled castes and scheduled tribes. Seats were reserved for these groups, roughly in proportion to their numbers, in the House of the People and in state legislative assemblies. The Fifth Schedule contained elaborate provisions for the administration and control of scheduled tribes, with special attention to the administration of backward tribal areas in Assam.

In a multilingual country, with strong attachments to various regional and local languages, the constitution makers took another bold step by decreeing that "the official language of the Union shall be Hindi in Devanagari script" and that "for a period of fifteen years. . . . the English language shall continue to be used for all the official purposes of the Union for which it was being used." At stated periods after the adoption of the constitution, the President was to appoint a commission to make recommendations for "the progressive use of the Hindi language" and for the use of other languages for official purposes. All proceedings in the Supreme Court and in the high courts were to be in English, as before independence. The legislature of each state could adopt "one or more of the languages in use in the State" for official purposes. In addition to Hindi, thirteen languages of India were recognized in the constitution. These were Assamese, Bengali, Gujarati, Kannada, Kashmiri, Malayalam, Marathi, Oriya, Punjabi, Sanskrit, Tamil, Telegu, and Urdu.

A bill to amend the constitution may be introduced in either house, and in most cases the proposed amendment will become effective if it is passed in each house "by a majority of the total membership of that House and by a majority of not less than two-thirds of the members of that House present and voting" and if it receives the assent of the President. In certain cases the proposed amendent must also be ratified by the legislatures of half the states. On the whole it is relatively easy to amend the Indian constitution.

The Constitution in Operation

The work of constitution making in India was a truly impressive performance. Few persons in the Assembly or in the country at large challenged the basic character of the document. Some wondered whether the constitution gave the government sufficient authority to deal with the many fissiparous tendencies in Indian society; others, though granting the need for authority to cope with these tendencies, expressed concern lest the extensive powers given to the Centre, especially the emergency powers, provide opportunity for a would-be dictator to overthrow the democracy. In other words, two questions basic to the success of constitutional government were raised: (1) Were the guardians of the constitution given adequate powers to discharge their responsibilities? (2) Who would guard the guardians? Neither of these potential dangers has so far developed into a direct peril to the state.

When the constitution went into effect on January 26, 1950, India became a republic and began to take steps to establish the regular institutions of democratic government. More than two years later, after the first nation-wide elections were held, the Constituent Assembly acting as the Provisional Parliament gave way to India's first regular Parliament. It had made the basic decisions and had functioned well during the first years of India's great experiment as a "sovereign, democratic republic." It had also made an important extraconstitutional decision that India, though about to become a republic, wished to remain within the Commonwealth of Nations. The formula whereby a republic could remain a part of this unique association headed by a monarch was worked out in April 1949 at a conference of Commonwealth Prime Ministers convened for the express purpose of considering this problem. It was solved by a simple declaration of the governments of the Commonwealth countries. India expressed her willingness and desire "to continue her full membership in the Commonwealth of Nations and her acceptance of the King as the symbol of the free association of its independent member nations and as such the Head of the Commonwealth." The governments of the other Commonwealth countries declared that they "accept and recognize India's continuing membership in accordance with the terms of this Declaration."

However excellent the work of the draftsmen, the real test of any constitution is its actual operation. How has the constitution of India worked in the Indian environment? Obviously this question cannot be definitively answered, for less than a decade has passed since the constitution went into effect. But on the whole the Indian experiment in democracy seems to be succeeding. The political leaders have been scrupulous in observing the constitution, and they have established certain conventions which augur well for the future. The successful conduct of two national elections and several elections in the states, the economic progress of the country under the two Five Year Plans, tangible evidence that the government is trying to deal with ancient wrongs and to institute programs of economic and social reform—these achievements have given the people of India a growing confidence that they will be able to cope with the many grievous problems that still confront them.

The machinery of government seems to be operating well, on the formal level, although very often it is operating in ways not envisioned by those who created it. Again we are reminded that whereas the structure of the government of India is very familiar to any student of Western democratic government, in actuality the government does not operate along familiar lines. The levels of decision making differ fundamentally, and the main decisions are made to a large degree outside normal channels. This fact calls attention to the great influence of "nonpolitical" forces in India, to the role of personalities and charismatic leadership. Most of the major policies are in fact determined within the Congress Party and not by the agencies of government; and within the Congress Party they are made by Jawaharlal Nehru and a handful of associates. The Working Committee of the party is actually the most important policy-making body in India.

Thus the institutions of government are to some extent agencies to carry out decisions made elsewhere; but there is a close identification between the Congress Party and the government, and the leaders of the Congress are careful to work within the constitutional system. Nevertheless, there is a kind of unreality about the operation of the governmental agencies in India, and any examination of their functioning soon leads to other sources of influence and power.

Among the conventions that seem to be established is one that the President of the republic shall indeed be the head of the "dignified" parts of the constitution and that he shall use his extraordinary powers only upon the advice of the Prime Minister and the cabinet. In actual fact his position has been far closer to that of the English sovereign than to that of the American President or even of the President of the French republic. Thus a very important precedent has been established with regard to the role and responsibilities of the head of the state.

Dr. Rajendra Prasad, India's first—and thus far only—President, has played this role in an admirable way. Dr. Prasad is a kindly gentleman, greatly beloved by the people and highly respected by all. Before his election as President of India he served with inconspicuous distinction as a president of the Indian National Congress and as president of the Constituent Assembly. He has deliberately chosen to remain aloof from party politics, and to be a harmonizing and a unifying influence. His relations with Prime Minister Nehru have apparently been close and cordial. He has invariably accepted the advice of the Prime Minister on political matters, and Nehru has been careful to consult him on major questions and to keep him informed at all times. At the expiration of his first term as President Dr. Prasad was unanimously re-elected. It was a fitting tribute to the way he had conducted himself as India's first head of state, giving dignity and prestige to the office without taking advantage of his prerogatives.

Although Dr. Prasad has elected to play a limited and useful role in the Indian political system, the emergency powers bestowed upon him under the constitution have been invoked several times, because of governmental instability and factional bickering in the Punjab in 1950, in PEPSU (Patiala and East Punjab States Union) in 1953, in Andhra in 1954, and in Travancore-Cochin in 1956. In each instance the President's rule was continued for several months until, after new elections, more stable governments could be formed in the states concerned. In 1954 it seemed possible that the new state of Andhra might have a Communist government, and in 1957 India's first Communist government did in fact come to power in Kerala (formerly Travancore-Cochin). These events raised the question of using the emergency powers of the constitution in case a Communist regime in one of the states proved to be disruptive of the democratic state. Thus far the Communist regime in Kerala has carefully operated in a constitutional manner; but it is comforting to realize that the government of India does have the constitutional authority to deal with a threat to the political stability of the Union or of its component units. Experience thus far is that the emergency provisions of the constitution are useful, indeed necessary, and have not been abused.

India has also been fortunate in its Vice-President. Dr. Sarvepalli Radhakrishnan, a distinguished Indian educator and one of the world's great philosophers, has been a valuable member of the government, even though his official responsibilities have been nominal. He has great prestige in India and an international reputation; a former professor at Oxford, he has been President of UNESCO, and his books are read widely in many countries. He is frequently consulted by both the President and the Prime Minister, and he has presided over the Council of States with grace and charm; a wave of his finger or one of his famous epigrams, delivered at the right moment, has invariably been more effective than any rules of order.

In India, as in other parliamentary systems, the Prime Minister is the most important official of the state; but the present Prime Minister is particularly important because he is Jawaharlal Nehru. In the last stages of the struggle for independence Nehru was overshadowed only by Gandhi in the top leadership of the Congress Party. He was Chief Minister in the interim government that was set up in India in 1946, and he has been Prime Minister of India since independence. From the time of Gandhi's assassination in January 1948 he has occupied a position of unquestioned pre-eminence in Indian life. His great power and influence are derived less from his position as Prime Minister than from his dominance over the Congress Party and from his tremendous personal popularity in the country. In a land where personal leadership is often more important than office or issues, Nehru is a charismatic leader par excellence; in fact, there is a real danger that as long as he lives too much reliance will be placed on his individual popularity and that when he dies or retires (and he is nearly seventy years old) he will leave a dangerous void. Fortunately Nehru himself is aware of his own shortcomings and the pitfalls of great power. Fortunately too he is steeped in the tradition of liberal democracy and is thoroughly devoted to the democratic way. But he is also an impatient and an impulsive man, who is eager to achieve great things quickly and who sometimes rides roughshod over lesser people. On the whole he has played his part well. That part, as he envisions it, is much greater than to be the Prime Minister of India. It is to lead the movement for the achievement of a social revolution in India.[19]

The Council of Ministers—the cabinet—in India has been very much dominated by Nehru and the Congress Party, from which its members have almost invariably been drawn, although it has contained several respected elder statesmen, such as Maulana Azad, Gopalaswami Ayyangar, Kidwai, and Rajagopalachari, and able administrators such as John Mathai, C. D. Deshmukh, and T. T. Krishnamachari. Since the death of Sardar Patel in 1950 there has been no Deputy Prime Minister, no one who could hold his own with Nehru, no one who could complement Nehru as Patel did. The collective responsibility of the Council of Ministers to the Parliament has meant very little to date, since the Congress Party has had such an overwhelming majority in the Parliament.

The Indian Parliament is playing an increasingly significant part in Indian political life, but it still does not make central decisions as one would expect in a parliamentary system. Although in its organization and procedure it closely resembles the Parliament of Britain, its actual place in Indian political life is hardly comparable to that occupied by the Mother of Parliaments. The great decisions in India are not made in or by the Parliament, or even by the dominant party in the country, but by a small group within that party.[20] Almost every leading Congress M.P. holds some important post or posts in the party hierarchy. There is close liaison between the leaders of the Congress Party and the Congress Party in Parliament.[21] The parliamentary party has an elected leader and a chief whip nominated by the leader. Eleven officeholders plus twenty-one elected members form the Executive Committee. "The constitution of the Party in Parliament lays down that, so far as possible, all important Government motions, Bills and resolutions should be placed before the Executive Committee in ad-

[19] See Ajoy Kumar Gupta, "The Indian Parliament and States Reorganization," *Parliamentary Affairs*, X (Winter, 1956–1957), 105, 107, 111.

[20] See Lanka Sunderam, "The Role of an Independent Member," in A. B. Lal, ed., *The Indian Parliament* (Allahabad, 1956), p. 68.

[21] See Norman D. Palmer and Irene Tinker, "Decision-Making in the Indian Parliament," a paper prepared for the conference on "Leadership and Political Institutions in India," held at the University of California, Berkeley, in August 1956.

vance of their consideration by Parliament." [22] The party standing
committee provides a useful way for the Congress M.P.'s to keep informed on issues, and the state groups give them an opportunity, often
after consultation with opposition members from the same state, to
make representations on particular issues to their party leaders or to
the government.

No effective opposition to the Congress has yet developed within
the Parliament. Rarely has the vote against a measure sponsored by
the Congress ministry—that is, the government—exceeded 100, and
no one opposition party has ever had enough members in the House
of the People (50) to qualify as a recognized opposition party. "It is
. . . unfortunate that the main opposition group in the parliamentary
life of India should be the essentially non-parliamentary Communist
Party." [23]

In a sense the committees of the Parliament serve as a partial check
on the government. Standing committees were abolished in 1952. At
present the two financial committees, the Public Accounts Committee
and the Estimates Committee, are particularly influential. Regarding
the latter committee Professor Morris-Jones wrote:

The indirect influence of the Committee . . . is probably even more important than its direct influence on the Government. . . . To a very real
extent, this type of committee, inspired as it is by the idea not simply of
economy nor even of efficiency alone but also of acting as a check against
an oppressive or arbitrary executive, achieves a special political significance
as a substitute for a real Opposition.[24]

Ad hoc select committees or joint select committees are created for
every bill that is sent to committee; relatively few bills pass through
committee consideration, but these bills are usually of particular importance. In the opinion of Professor Morris-Jones:

The whole structure of Parliamentary Committees reflects and at the same
time reinforces this mood of watchfulness over the Government. It provides
the student of politics with an interesting if slight modification of parliamentary government of the British type. More important . . . it saves the
Indian Government with its large majority from the worst temptations of
autocracy.[25]

[22] W. H. Morris-Jones, *Parliament in India* (Philadelphia: University of Pennsylvania Press, 1957), p. 187.
    [23] *Ibid.*, p. 330.   [24] *Ibid.*, pp. 307–308.   [25] *Ibid.*, p. 315.

Within its limited sphere the Parliament of India is playing an increasingly useful role. The future of the Council of States seems rather uncertain; it is not yet operating well in the traditional role of an upper chamber, and its membership is not very different from that of the lower house. But the House of the People is rapidly winning for itself an established place in Indian political life. It is still a relatively new and inexperienced body, and its members are even more inexperienced. The party leaders, however, are men of long political experience, and the first Speaker of the House, G. V. Mavalankar, was a veteran parliamentarian. The language problem has been another complication and may be even more of a handicap as more members use regional languages in the debates and as the use of English diminishes.

As would be expected, the Supreme Court of India is somewhat more limited than the United States Supreme Court in its authority to act as guardian of the constitution. With respect to land reform and other social measures its jurisdiction has been further limited by the First and Fourth Amendments to the Indian constitution (in 1951 and 1955). Nevertheless it has proved to be a major bulwark of constitutional government. Although it has scrupulously refrained from passing upon political questions, it has freely exercised its extensive powers of judicial review. It has "laid down the basic principles governing the problem of delegation of legislative power," [26] and it has done much to reconcile the fundamental rights guaranteed in the constitution with the limitations which have occasionally been placed upon these rights.

Any observer of the Indian scene is poignantly aware of the vast gap between the fundamental rights guaranteed in the Indian constitution and the limited reality of these rights in India today. Moreover, the limitations upon some of these rights are serious. For example, Article 22, guaranteeing protection against arbitrary arrest and detention, contains provisions which have been invoked to provide the basis for the Preventive Detention Act, a tough measure which authorizes the arrest and detention for many weeks without trial of persons who are even suspected of contemplating acts which would be inimical to public safety and order; and the amendment to Article 31, which removes from the judicial sphere the question of what is reasonable compensation for expropriated property, may seriously impair the guarantee

[26] Douglas, *We the Judges,* p. 166.

contained in the first paragraph of Article 31 that "no person shall be deprived of his property save by authority of law." The continued prevalence of untouchability in many parts of the country seems incampatible with its constitutional prohibition in Article 17.

Despite all the reservations which must be entered, genuine efforts are being made to give meaning to the constitutional provisions regarding fundamental human rights. Obviously in the area of social reform constitutional provisions backed by court decisions cannot immediately correct age-old injustices; but they can certainly be of great value, and they can mark the road along which the nation desires to move. The record of the Indian government and Parliament in the field of social legislation is impressive; it contrasts with the British reluctance to interfere in any way, if this could possibly be avoided, with popular customs and ways of life.[27] The Indian authorities have not hesitated to tackle head on some of the most deep-seated customs which are regarded as undesirable and undemocratic, such as the practice of untouchability, Hindu customs concerning marriage and property matters, and other oppressive codes of behavior. A study of the legislative history of the Hindu Code Bill and of the efforts first to obtain consent to a comprehensive measure and then to push through the major features in separate pieces of legislation would be most revealing. Resistance to changes in customs was strong, but pressure for modification of certain practices was stronger. The Hindu Marriages Act of 1955, a major piece of the Hindu Code Bill, heralded a revolution in the marriage law among most of the Indian population.

Among the many paradoxes of Indian political life since independence has been the simultaneous development of strong centralizing and decentralizing tendencies. These conflicting tendencies appear in the evolving relations between the Centre and the states in India. The constitution provided for a federal system having an unusual degree of central control, with residuary powers vested in the central government. The government has endorsed "the socialistic pattern of society,"

[27] See K. Lipstein, "The Reception of Western Law in India," *International Social Science Bulletin,* IX (1957), 90: "The startling contrast between the pace of progressive legislation in India after independence and before appears, therefore, to justify the criticism that the policy of the British administration to interfere as little as possible with the customs of the population in matters of personal status, family law and succession, however well intentioned, acted as a brake on progress and retarded a possible natural line of advancement and development of Hindu society." This article is a report of the discussions on the subject indicated at the meetings of the International Association of Legal Science, held in Barcelona in September 1956.

and Indians traditionally look to the strong authority of the Centre for guidance and aid on a wide variety of matters. Hence it is hardly surprising that India presents one of the most extreme manifestations of centralization in democratic state. In a country dedicated to democratic planning on a vast scale, the central government has given direction and leadership to this co-ordinated effort, and its role has been all the greater because the states, as well as private business, have failed to make their expected contributions in finances and effort.

On the other hand, Paul Appleby, an American specialist, has pointed out that the central government has relied on the states "for a large part of its administration." [28] In fields like development planning and education the Centre has had to rely on the states to carry out policy, and often it has encountered stubborn resistance or reluctance to act. The states have also been the strongholds of linguistic feelings. Reorganizing the political map of India along essentially linguistic lines has probably weakened a major threat to national unity. But the second general election in the bilingual state of Bombay dramatically demonstrated that the stresses resulting from frustrated linguistic aspirations are still great. The price of nation-wide concessions to these aspirations has been high. In one of his reports on public administration in India Dr. Appleby asks: "Will India be able to maintain and develop its national unity and strength in the face of its linguistic divisions and its extraordinary dependence upon the States for a large part of its administration?" [29]

One powerful force for harmony between the Centre and the states has been the fact that the governments in New Delhi and in almost all of the states have been formed by the same party. After the general elections of 1951–1952 the Congress Party formed governments in all the states and maintained these governments until the second general elections in 1957, with the exception of the short-lived government formed by the minority Praja Socialist Party in Travancore-Cochin and the periods when the Punjab, PEPSU, Andhra, and Travancore-Cochin were under President's rule. Following the second general elections, the Congress maintained its control in all the reorganized states except Kerala. The Congress has always been careful to keep some of its leading members in the state governments. Thus some years ago

[28] Paul H. Appleby, *Re-examination of India's Administrative System with Special Reference to Administration of Government's Industrial and Commercial Enterprises* (New Delhi: Government of India Press, 1956), p. 47.
[29] *Ibid.*

five chief ministers in states—B. C. Roy in West Bengal, Pant in Uttar Pradesh, Shukla in Madhya Pradesh, Rajagopalachari in Madras, and Moraji Desai in Bombay—were sometimes referred to as Nehru's "five warlords." It is, however, perhaps a commentary on present political trends that two of these men—Pant and Desai—are now members of the central cabinet, while Rajagopalachari is in retirement and Shukla is dead. Only Roy remains in active service in a state, and he will probably retire in the near future. Factional squabbles within the Congress Party have harried the administration in a number of the states, such as Rajasthan, although in some cases strong action by the national leaders has helped to restore the party's prestige in these states and to improve the quality of the administration.

Although Congress ministries still control all but one of the states, in several of the state legislative assemblies there are sufficient opposition members to act as a real check upon the majority party. This gives a flavor to political life in some key states, such as West Bengal, Bombay, Uttar Pradesh, Bihar, and Orissa, which is lacking at the Centre. Possibly the composition of the state assemblies is a better barometer of trends in Indian politics than the make-up of the House of the People. Certainly there seems to be a greater popular interest in what goes on in the capitals of the states than in New Delhi, which is a long distance, psychologically as well as geographically, from most of the Indian people.

In local government and administration the district officer is still the key figure, as he was in the days of British rule. "As agents of State government, but with national status and all-India outlooks, District Officers have the job of translating the vast bulk of governmental decisions into effective action." [30] In addition to their traditional duties as chief officers for enforcing law, administering justice, and collecting taxes, they are now usually the chief development officers as well. As efforts to develop local self-government increase, elected agencies such as district boards and village panchayats may take over many of the functions of the district officers; but "for the foreseeable future" the latter promise "to remain the key leadership figures throughout District-level India, local self-government to the contrary notwithstanding." [31]

[30] Richard L. Park, "District Administration and Local Self-Government," a paper prepared for the conference on "Leadership and Political Institutions in India," held at the University of California, Berkeley, in August 1956.

[31] *Ibid.*

In the 1880s Lord Ripon made heroic efforts to reform local self-government in India. He sought "to revive and extend the indigenous system of the country" and "to make full use of what remains of the village system."[32] His primary objective was political education, not administrative efficiency; to prevent the new middle class from becoming "a source of serious political danger," he wished to give them "a training in the working of political institutions."[33] The leaders of independent India have tried to follow the same policies, though often for different reasons. One of their main objectives has been to improve the living conditions of village India, where some 80 per cent of the population live. Through the Community Development Program and the National Extension Service, both integral parts of the Five Year Plans, a major effort is being made in this direction. The government of India is also trying to revive the ancient agency of village democracy, the panchayat, in accordance with Article 40 of the Indian constitution, and to fit the panchayat into the normal machinery of government. Most of the states have passed panchayat legislation, and the number of panchayats has increased greatly in recent years. It is still too early to assess the results of this experiment in the revival of an institution which once played a major role in Indian life.

Although the great majority of the Indian people live in villages, there are 5 cities with a population of over a million, and some 70 more with a population of over 100,000. There is considerable variation in the pattern of municipal government in India and in the degree of self-government which the inhabitants enjoy. In the days of the British East India Company, Bombay, Madras, and Calcutta were organized as "Presidency towns"; this implied relatively great autonomy. By 1870 there were about 200 municipalities in the subcontinent.[34] Thus Indian towns have often had a long record of experience in municipal government. Today urban areas are generally governed as townships or as corporations. Officials appointed by the state governments have the largest measure of effective authority, but there are also elected officers, and usually there is some kind of elected council. Most of the larger cities are governed as corporations, each with a commissioner appointed by the state government, an official head us-

[32] L. Wolf, *Life of Ripon* (London, 1921), II, 100.
[33] See L. S. S. O'Malley, ed., *Modern India and the West* (London, 1941), pp. 745–746.
[34] See table showing "Dates of Establishment of Some Early Indian Municipalities," in Hugh Tinker, *The Foundations of Local Self-Government in India, Pakistan, and Burma* (London, 1954), pp. 30–31.

ually known as the mayor, and a legislative council. The municipal government is divided into departments, dealing with such matters as revenue, water, education, health and welfare, sanitation, slum clearance, and relief.

Much attention is being given in India today to problems of public administration. The administrative problems of running a huge underdeveloped country such as India are obviously enormous, and there is a real danger that India may not be able to develop the necessary machinery. Even more serious is the problem of orientation to administration. In the opinion of Dr. Paul Appleby:

Perhaps nowhere else have so many systematic barriers been erected to prevent the accomplishment of that which it has been determined shall be done. . . . Indian leadership has had the tremendous problem of shifting from the negative, antigovernmental attitude that was necessary to the drive for independence to a positive, operating, institutional responsibility appropriate and necessary to program achievements planned by independent and revolutionary India.[35]

Fortunately a good many Indians had practical experience in administration under the British, and the Indian members of the Indian Civil Service whose services were available after independence have stiffened the administrative structure of the country. Those who are still active are today in key positions in the central government or in the states. An Indian Administrative Service has been established to recruit qualified young Indians for permanent civil service positions. Additional personnel are recruited in many other ways. The Public Service Commissions in the Centre and in the states are doing excellent work, but their efforts are limited in scope and in imagination. The recently organized Indian Institute of Public Administration may become a center for more serious study of administrative problems and for the advanced training of top administrative personnel. In general, aside from the top administrators, the work of administration in India is being carried on by relatively untrained and often unqualified persons, and no really effective measures are being taken to remedy the situation.

There is much criticism of the quality of administration in the country. According to Dr. Appleby, the four most prevalent criticisms on the popular level "are that government has too many employees, that it is permeated with dishonesty, that it is inefficient and that its work

[35] Appleby, *Re-examination of India's Administrative System*, pp. 17, 46.

is unnecessarily hampered by 'red tape.'" He believes that many of these criticisms are overdone or miss the point. He is more concerned with administrative structures; with "personnel recruitment, development and arrangement; financial provision, fiscal policy, financial administration, and procedures, on paper and otherwise, maximizing expedition, responsibility, good judgment, effective delegation, etc." [36] Perhaps the basic question facing India's civil service is whether the people and the Parliament will pay enough to attract proper personnel and will grant those personnel scope enough to operate efficiently.

[36] Paul H. Appleby, *Public Administration in India: Report of a Survey* (New Delhi: Government of India Press, 1953), p. 9.

· XI ·

Political Parties in India

WHEN the political process in India is analyzed, not only the formal functioning of institutions should be kept in mind, but also political parties, leaders and leadership patterns, pressure groups, and public opinion. Here again much is found that is familiar and much that is unfamiliar, sometimes to a striking degree. In this chapter the Indian party system will be analyzed; in the next the focus will be upon political dynamics.

Attitudes toward Political Parties

In the newly formed democracy of India, the party system is not yet a healthy one. Some influential leaders, in fact, have advocated the development of a "new political system" in which parties in the usual meaning of the term will not exist at all. Gandhi himself often espoused this new approach, without making clear how his ideals of a *sarvodaya* society could replace the institutions of representative government. The two outstanding "nonpolitical" leaders of India today, Vinoba Bhave and Jayaprakash Narayan, whose influence in politics is greater than that of any conventional political leader except Nehru himself, would like to do away with political parties. The Radical Humanists repeatedly point to the absence of a well-developed party system and argue that parties are both unnecessary and undesirable.

In the political atmosphere of India, where the party system is not functioning well, where parties prior to independence had little opportunity to develop or to perform their customary roles, and where the masses of the people are illiterate, it is hardly surprising that parties are viewed with a rather jaundiced eye. Under the circumstances it could be argued that there are advantages in the absence of a balanced party structure. Richard L. Park has expressed this view in words which apply to India in particular and to other Asian countries as well:

An independence movement is not the best breeding ground for political parties in the Western sense. In the search for unity in opposition to the ruling imperial power, the Asian nationalist movements exerted every effort to bring all factions together into one independence-bound organization. . . . After independence, as was natural, these movements tended to break down, with groups of minority views leaving the parent body to form new political groupings.

. . . a well-organized political party system might have hindered the relative stability. Much of the success of the legislative and planning programs in these countries can be traced to the large, disciplined majorities held by the party in power in the respective parliaments. The hard test of parliamentary government, of course, will come when this situation no longer prevails.[1]

On the national level Indian political parties may be divided into four main groups: (1) the Congress Party; (2) the communalist parties, notably the three groups known as Jan Sangh, the Hindu Mahasabha, and the Ram Rajya Parishad (the Rashtriya Swayamsevak Sangh, though ostensibly nonpolitical, actually has considerable political influence); (3) the socialist parties, notably the Praja Socialist Party and the Socialist Party of India; and (4) the Indian Communist Party. Besides these major groupings there are numerous parties which are of some importance on the state or regional level and innumerable so-called parties which center around individual leaders. Another prominent characteristic of Indian political life is the existence of a number of groups which are both political parties and pressure groups or which are at once parties and organizations for the promotion of economic, social, or religious objectives. At the Centre, because of the dominance of the Congress, India seems to have virtually a one-party system, but in many regions and states of India opposition to the Congress is strong and is apparently growing. Moreover, there are trends

[1] "Problem of Political Development," in Philip W. Thayer, ed., *Nationalism and Progress in Free Asia* (Baltimore: Johns Hopkins Press, 1956), pp. 103–104.

within the Congress Party which may portend a lessening of its influence and power, especially after Nehru passes from the scene.

The Indian National Congress

The Indian National Congress was the directing organization of the struggle for independence in India, and since that goal was achieved it has been the dominant political party. It is the party of Gandhi and of Nehru. "It utilizes the aura of a successful nationalist movement, to which it has added the prestige of government authority and high international importance." [2] It has both the advantages and the disadvantages of its past record and inheritance. As the spearhead of the independence movement, it attracted the support of people of very diverse viewpoints and interests who were willing to overlook their differences in the interests of the freedom struggle. When it became the ruling party of a new nation, it preserved much of the atmosphere and prestige of its past, but in the new setting it had to change many of its objectives and techniques. Under the responsibilities of authority it naturally "ceased to enjoy that overwhelming mass appeal which made it a truly national organization in the heyday of its struggle for freedom." [3] Thus the membership of the Congress has been subject to considerable variation. Indeed, almost all the political parties of modern India represent groups which split off from the main Congress party or which have at various times been merged in the Congress.

During the Second World War the Congress took a firm stand of nonco-operation and nonparticipation, as a result of which most party leaders were jailed. At this time the British naturally favored other groups, including the Muslim League and even the Communists, who supported the war effort. But the leaders of the Congress took a prominent part in the negotiations leading to independence in August 1947 and were active in the interim government and Constituent Assembly which were inaugurated in 1946. After the attainment of independence the Congress did not cease to function, as many people expected it would, but continued in the triple role of party, government, and social welfare organization. Gandhi, its great mentor, argued that it had outlived its usefulness "in its present shape and form, i.e., as a propa-

[2] Gene D. Overstreet and Irene Tinker, "Political Dynamics in India" (Berkeley: Modern India Project, University of California, March 1957; from material prepared for the India volume, Country Survey Series, Human Relations Area Files), p. 27.

[3] P. D. Gupta, "Political Parties and Elections in India," a lecture delivered at Subhas National College, Unnao, February 23, 1953.

ganda vehicle and parliamentary machine"; [4] he recommended that it be disbanded as a political organization and converted into a Lok Sevak Sangh, a social service organization. But, as N. V. Rajkumar explains, "Unable to contemplate the idea of dissolving an institution which was the only organizational body which could run the administration of the country and tackle the manifold problems that political freedom brought in its wake, the Working Committee with great regret dissented from Gandhiji's basic approach." [5]

Since 1947 the Congress has passed through many crises and has experienced several changes in orientation; but it has retained its unquestioned predominance at the Centre and, except for rare and not too successful experiments in a few states, has controlled the machinery of government throughout the country. It has profited greatly from its prestige as the party of national independence, although critics point out that there is a vast difference between the organization which spearheaded the independence struggle and the party which is now in power in India. It has also profited from the great popularity and prestige of Jawaharlal Nehru and from the weakness and division of the opposition. By death, retirement, or resignation it has lost some of its most important leaders. Many groups have left its ranks, including the Socialists in 1948; but it has gained new recruits, and aside from the Communist Party it is the only organized and disciplined national party of any importance in India.

Nevertheless, its organization and discipline leave much to be desired. As Nehru himself pointed out quite forcefully to his associates after the general elections of 1957, it needs to recapture some of the dynamism which it once possessed and to regain popular confidence by high standards of austerity and integrity. At the local level it seems to be losing support, and its representatives at this level are often people of inferior quality and questionable character. Its top leadership is still good, and its central organization seems to be functioning well. The major organizational problems relate to the proper relations between the agencies of the party and of the government, between the Congress parliamentary party and the Working Committee and other top organs of the national party, and between the central agencies of the party and state and local committees. Its policy seems to involve a

---

[4] From a suggested draft for an All-India Congress Committee (AICC) resolution which Gandhi gave to the Constitution Subcommittee of the Congress on January 30, 1948, a few hours before his assassination.

[5] *Development of the Congress Constitution* (Delhi: AICC, 1948), p. 98.

left-of-center orientation which, it hopes, will retain its identification
with the people, enable it to resist the divisive tendencies of communalism, casteism, and linguistic differences, cut the ground from
under the Socialists by embracing most of their approaches and policies, and provide a satisfactory democratic alternative to communism,
whose followers now seem to be concentrating on achieving unparlia-
mentary ends through parliamentary means.

After surviving the first crises of independence, the party found
itself faced with internal conflicts in 1950. For the first three years
Nehru had concentrated his personal energies on the vast tasks of
national unity and survival, and he had left the internal affairs of the
party largely up to others, notably to the strong hand of the Deputy
Prime Minister, Vallabhbhai Patel. But Patel favored the conservative
elements in the party, whereas Nehru appealed to the younger and
more liberal groups. Both wanted the party to follow a moderate and
middle-of-the-road policy, but Patel had little sympathy with the
mounting demand for major economic and social reforms, whereas
Nehru felt that the Congress must espouse a left-of-center orientation
lest it cut itself off from the people and go the way of the Kuomintang
in China.

Hence a crisis developed within the party in 1950 when Purshottam-
das Tandon, a white-bearded orthodox Hindu "of the old school,"
who enjoyed the support of Patel, was elected as president of the
Congress over Acharya Kripalani, a candidate much more acceptable
to Nehru. Nehru regarded this development as a challenge to his
leadership and as a trend in the wrong direction. Above everything
else he aspired to convert India into a modern secular state with a
socialist orientation, and he was alarmed at the victory of the Patel-
backed Hindu conservative. In the fall of 1951 the Prime Minister
forced a showdown by resigning from the Congress Working Committee and other party posts. Tandon thereupon offered his resignation as president. A special meeting of the All-India Congress Committee accepted Tandon's resignation and elected Nehru as president
of the Congress.[6] Although he was on record against combining the
posts of Prime Minister and president of the Congress, Nehru announced that he would accept the party office because he felt that

[6] See Susanne Hoeber Rudolph, "The Working Committee of the Indian Congress Party" (a paper prepared for the Center for International Studies, Massachusetts Institute of Technology, Jan. 14, 1955), pp. 35–37; Robert Trumbull,
"Nehru Keeps His Prestige despite a Party Setback," *New York Times*, Sept. 10,
1950.

the party was moving away from the masses and because "something must be done to arrest its disintegration." He held the post as president for more than four years, until he gave way to a candidate of his choice, U. N. Dhebar, in January 1955.

During this period both the government and the party consolidated their strength and moved in a generally socialist direction. In the spring of 1953 Nehru held talks with Jayaprakash Narayan and other leaders of the Praja Socialist Party, apparently to explore the possibilities of closer co-operation, perhaps even of coalition, with his only "loyal opposition." Although these talks were suspended by mutual agreement without leading to any specific understanding, they were indicative of the direction of Nehru's thinking. His letters to Narayan revealed impatience with the pace of economic and social change and a wish to unite all like-minded persons and groups in speeding up the "social revolution." At the annual sessions of the Congress and at regular meetings of the All-India Congress Committee and of the Working Committee, resolutions were passed which culminated in the historic Avadi resolution of January 1955 laying down the objective as "a socialistic pattern of society":

In order to realize the object of the Congress as laid down in Article I of the Congress Constitution and to further the objectives stated in the Preamble and Directive Principles of State Policy of the Constitution of India, planning should take place with a view to the establishment of a socialistic pattern of society, where the principal means of production are under social ownership or control, production is progressively speeded up and there is equitable distribution of the national wealth.

This orientation greatly strengthened the standing of the Congress in the country and weakened the power of the leftist parties and groups which supported similar aims.

The issue of linguistic states threatened to create serious divisions within the party and actually resulted in serious electoral setbacks for the party in Bombay state. Aside from this still-unresolved situation, however, the Congress emerged from its many gyrations over the linguistic states issue with generally increased strength.[7] "The initial turmoil apart, States Reorganization has fulfilled the political aspirations of the people in various parts of the country and thus eliminated

[7] For a full account of the initial proposals for states reorganization see *Report of the States Reorganization Commission* (New Delhi: Government of India Press, 1955).

a factor which might have affected the party's popularity in the country." [8] The Congress has also shown a "tremendous flexibility and capacity to adapt to public opinion on specific issues." [9]

The central organs of the Congress Party are the annual Congress session, the All-India Congress Committee (AICC), and the Working Committee. On the state level the key organ is the Pradesh (State) Congress Committee, which sets up such subordinate committees, down to the level of the taluka (subdistrict), as it deems appropriate. Above the lowest levels all members of Congress committees must be "active" members. An active member must "wear khadi, be a teetotaller, oppose untouchability, favor equality of opportunity, believe in intercommunal unity, perform 'constructive activity,' pay Rs. 1 annually and collect another Rs. 10 for Congress." There are fewer than 80,000 "active" Congress members, but some 6,000,000 "primary" members, who accept the objectives of the party but who are not subject to the obligations and responsibilities of the "active" members.

The AICC is composed of one-eighth of the delegates of each Pradesh Congress Committee and is elected by the PCC.[10] It meets at irregular intervals, usually on the call of the Working Committee. The Working Committee is a small and active body consisting of the president of the Congress and twenty members chosen by the president from the membership of the AICC. Two of its important subsidiary bodies are the Parliamentary Board, which exercises supervision over the Congress ministries in the states, and the Central Election Committee, which screens Congress candidates for the central Parliament and to some extent also for state assemblies. Thus, "in addition to . . . power over the state parliamentary parties, the Working Committee retains a crucial hand in the all-important business of personnel selection, both for the central parliament (through the Central Election Committee) and for the state ministries (through the Parliamentary Board)." [11] It also has a "crucial hand" in the shaping of governmental policy on the national level. Of particular interest is the relationship between the Working Committee and the Congress Party in Parliament, with its separate offices and secretariat. Although

[8] S. L. Poplai, ed., *National Politics and 1957 Elections in India* (Delhi, 1957), pp. 11–12.

[9] *Ibid.*, p. 10.

[10] See Susanne Hoeber Rudolph, "The All India Congress Committee and the Annual Congress Session" (a paper prepared for the Center for International Studies, Massachusetts Institute of Technology, Jan. 14, 1955).

[11] Rudolph, "The Working Committee of the Indian Congress Party," p. 23.

at times there has been some working at cross-purposes, there can be little doubt that the Working Committee is the more important body; indeed, it is possibly the most important decision-making body in India. According to Nehru, "the basic policy of the Party is laid down by the Annual Session, and it is interpreted and implemented by the AICC. The Working Committee, as the executive of the Congress, is charged with carrying out this policy." Actually, as Susanne Rudolph has pointed out, "the real power relationship of the three national organs of the Congress Party . . . is the reverse of the stated power relationship . . . the Working Committee makes both basic and *ad hoc* policy, and submits it to the other two organs for their approval." [12]

In the nearly seventy-five years of its existence the Congress has played a major role in the political life of the country. It has passed through many stages and survived many crises. Some of the greatest figures of modern India have been among its leaders. After independence it ceased to be the umbrellalike organization within which all groups took shelter and became the dominant political party in free India as well as the government of the country on both national and state levels. It is still the chief political organization in India. As long as Nehru is actively in control of the affairs of the party and of the country, the position of the Congress can hardly be effectively challenged on the national scene, and it seems likely to retain its strength in most of the states. Whether it can retain its influence after Nehru goes, whether it can find new momentum and dynamism under other leaders—these are great unanswered questions in India's political future.

Paradoxically, the disintegration of the Congress could be either a blessing or a tragedy. It might be a blessing if it gave way to a healthy party system, with at least two democratic parties strong enough to compete for political power; but it would be a tragedy if the removal of its strong hand impeded the progress of India's great experiment in democracy and economic development and particularly if its passing strengthened the forces of communalism or of communism. The best-organized political opposition to the Congress today is the Communist Party; its victory would present a threat to the survival of India as a democratic state. One of the ironies of the Indian political scene is that an effective democratic opposition seems to be

[12] Rudolph, "The All India Congress Committee and the Annual Congress Session," p. 22.

out of the question as long as the Congress exists in its present form, while at the same time the disintegration of the Congress might have adverse effects on the entire prospects for democracy in India.

Communal Parties

Communalism is one of the most powerful and most divisive forces in Indian life, but thus far no "communal" party has had any success in national politics and very few have made much of an impact even on the state or local level, where forces of religious traditionalism and orthodoxy are stronger. Most of the communal parties represent varieties of orthodox Hinduism; among these the Hindu Mahasabha, the Jan Sangh, and the Ram Rajya Parishad are the most significant, with the Rashtriya Swayamsevak Sangh, allegedly nonpolitical, as "the Hindu communal organization of greatest potential strength." Leading non-Hindu communal parties are the Akali Dal, representing certain groups in the Sikh community, the Scheduled Castes Federation, devoted to the interest of the untouchables, and the Jharkhand Party, the principal party espousing the cause of the scheduled tribes.

The Akhil Bharat Hindu Mahasabha was formed in the early 1900s by persons who wanted to ensure the dominance of Hinduism in Indian society. It gained momentum and became active politically in opposition to the Muslim League and to the "modern" leaders of India who wanted to make independent India a secular state. In response to the Muslim League's demand for a separate Pakistan, the Mahasabha raised the slogan of "Akhand Bharat," an undivided India true to Hindu traditions. It has consistently advocated tougher policies toward Pakistan.

When Gandhi was assassinated in January 1948 by a Maharashtrian Brahman who had been a member of the Hindu Mahasabha, the Mahasabha announced that it was retiring from the political arena; but it rode out the storm of criticism after Gandhi's death and resumed political activity in time to contest the first general elections in 1951–1952. It fared badly in these elections, winning only 4 seats in the House of the People and only scattered seats in some of the state assemblies. In the second general elections in 1957 it fared even worse. Only 2 members of the party were returned to the House of the People, and the president, N. C. Chatterjee, the vice-president, Dr. N. B. Khare, and the general secretary, V. G. Deshpande, all lost their parliamentary seats.

The most successful politically of the Hindu communal parties is the Bharatiya Jan Sangh. Founded in 1951 by Dr. Shyama Prasad Mookerjee, the Jan Sangh gained the largest vote of any of the communal parties in both general elections, returning 3 members to the House of the People in the first general elections and 4 members in the second. As long as Dr. Mookerjee was its leader, the Jan Sangh gave promise of bringing various conservative and communal groups together in a united front. Dr. Mookerjee was a former vice-chancellor of Calcutta University and the son of a distinguished Bengali jurist and educator. At one time he was president of the Hindu Mahasabha. Shortly before he formed the Jan Sangh, he was a member of the central cabinet, but he resigned over the issue of India's policy toward Pakistan. A particularly powerful speaker and an effective parliamentarian, he became a kind of unofficial leader of the opposition in the House of the People. He organized and headed a loose coalition of communal and conservative groups in the House known as the National Democratic Party. Dr. Mookerjee died in June 1953, however, while in "protective custody" in Srinagar, where he had been confined after he had made a dramatic but unauthorized entry into the state of Jammu and Kashmir in protest against the treatment of the Hindus in Jammu. After his death the communal parties had no commonly accepted spokesman, and the Jan Sangh had difficulty in holding itself together. Dr. Mookerjee's successor as president resigned to rejoin the Congress party. In spite of its lack of leadership and internal difficulties, the Jan Sangh polled nearly twice as many votes in the second general elections as it did in the first, and in addition to 4 members in the House of the People it elected 17 members to the State Assembly in Uttar Pradesh, 10 to the Assembly in Madhya Pradesh, and scattered members in other state assemblies.

The Ram Rajya Parishad, the most orthodox of the leading Hindu communal parties, polled nearly 3 per cent of the votes and elected 3 members to the House of the People in the general elections of 1951–1952, but in 1957 it was unable to return even one member and it had little success in elections to the state legislative assemblies. It has almost disappeared as a political force.

As has been noted, the most important of the Hindu communal organizations, the Rashtriya Swayamsevak Sangh (RSS), is not a political party but a tightly organized, highly disciplined, paramilitary, hierarchical body of dedicated persons whose "primary aim is to establish within its own group a model of a revitalized Hindu society and eventually to secure the adoption of this cultural form in the whole country." [13] The head of the RSS is the *Sar Sanghcalak,* an office which is passed down from one incumbent to his chosen successor. Both the men who have served to date in this role, Dr. Keshav Hedgewar and Guru Madhav Rao Golwalkar, have been strong personalities. Also influential in the organization are the Organizers, an appointed executive hierarchy taking a vow to devote their lives to the work of the Sangh. Every member of the RSS is carefully screened and tested. He joins a cell of about fifty persons and participates in exercises, ceremonies, group discussions, and other forms of training.

The Rashtriya Swayamsevak Sangh, then, is today the one important Hindu communal organization in India. When communalism is at a low ebb, the devotion of its members and ancillary appeals of its organizational style have kept it strong as the communal parties have faded. If communalism once again eclipses language as the primary divisive force in India, the Sangh may reemerge in a bid for general public support.[14]

For some years a militant Sikh party, the Shiromani Akali Dal, has been active in the Punjab and PEPSU. Its leader has been a colorful and dramatic firebrand named Master Tara Singh, an elderly and heavily bearded gentleman who looks like Michelangelo's Moses. Several of its members have held important positions in the assemblies and governments of the Punjab and PEPSU. It led the demand for a separate Sikh state—Sikhistan—but the majority of its members finally accepted the compromise which was proposed by the Congress Party and the central government. The agreement was so complete, in fact, that in October 1956 the majority of the ruling body of the Akali Dal voted to join the Congress Party for political activity and to continue only as a religious organization. This agreement was repudiated by Master Tara Singh himself shortly before the general elections in 1957, on grounds of bad faith on the part of the Congress, and some Akali Dal members, with their leader's blessings, ran against Congress candidates in the elections. They had very little success, however, for the majority of the members of the organization remained loyal to their new association with the Congress. Faced with this virtual repudiation by his own followers, Master Tara Singh announced that

---

[13] Richard D. Lambert, "Hindu Communal Groups in Indian Politics" (a paper prepared for the conference on "Leadership and Political Institutions in India," held at the University of California, Berkeley, in August 1956), p. 15. See also J. A. Curran, Jr., *Militant Hinduism in Indian Politics: A Study of the R.S.S.* (New York: Institute of Pacific Relations, 1951).

[14] Lambert, "Hindu Communal Groups in Indian Politics," p. 19.

he would retire for a time to consider the proper strategy for the future.

Another type of communalism in politics is represented by the Scheduled Castes Federation (SCF) and the Jharkhand Party. The Federation was formed by India's most famous untouchable, the late Dr. B. R. Ambedkar, an English-educated lawyer, in opposition to the policies of the British government and the Indian National Congress regarding the untouchables. It is a well-known fact that Dr. Ambedkar and Gandhi did not agree on the proper treatment of the untouchables. The Federation had some influence in the negotiations in 1945–1947 leading to the transfer of power, but it faded into obscurity in 1947–1950 while its founder was Law Minister in the first cabinet of free India and chairman of the committee which drafted the Indian constitution. The constitution abolished untouchability and contained some special provisions for the scheduled castes, but Dr. Ambedkar was dissatisfied with the failure of the government and the Congress Party to institute prompt measures to implement the constitutional guarantees, and he resigned from the cabinet a few weeks before the start of the first general elections. The Scheduled Caste Federation was revived in time to contest the general elections in some areas, and it polled nearly 2.5 per cent of the votes for the House of the People. Dr. Ambedkar became increasingly embittered against the Congress Party, and he publicly expressed his regrets that he had served as a member of a Congress ministry and had been used as "a political hack" in drafting a constitution which in retrospect he repudiated. In 1956 he and several thousand of his followers staged a mass public acceptance of Buddhism. The SCF is still in existence, though Dr. Ambedkar died in 1957, but some of its members have left the party, apparently in the belief that they can best promote their interests through the Congress or some other of the stronger parties.

Political organization among the scheduled tribes of India is still largely lacking, and the problem of the assimilation of the tribesmen into the life of the country is a vexing one. The chief tribal party, which has considerable support in Bihar, Assam, and Manipur, is the Jharkhand Party, whose leader is Jaipal Singh, an able, English-educated member of one of the tribes. The party demands a separate Jharkhand state, and it champions the interests of the tribal people generally, including those along the Indo-Burmese borders, the Nagas, who are virtually without political representation and some of whom insist upon an independent state of their own.

Socialist Parties

In view of its present dedication to the objective of "a socialistic pattern of society" the Congress itself should perhaps be discussed under the heading "Socialist Parties." Indeed, all the prevailing trends in India seem to be socialistic. "Socialism is no longer the great divide: all are socialists now and everyone's socialism is diluted in varying degrees." [15] Nehru does not now regard himself as a Marxist, although he is frank to confess that there is much about Marxism, and also about communism, that appealed to him; but he has considered himself to be a socialist for many years, and he has been looked to as a spokesman by various leftist members and groups within the Congress.

As organized political movements socialist parties have passed through three main periods since they became a political force of some significance a quarter of a century ago. Leadership in the first period was provided by the Congress Socialist Party (CSP), which remained a party within a party until 1948. During the second period, from 1948 to 1952, the Socialist Party led a rather confused independent existence and received a rude shock in the first general elections. In 1952 the Socialist Party and the Kisan Mazdoor Praja Party merged to form the Praja Socialist Party, which has been the leading independent socialist party since that time, although it is now in another period of crisis.

In 1934 the first important socialist party in India was formed as a group within the Indian National Congress. It aspired to unite the non-Communist left wing of the nationalist movement and eventually, with the support and perhaps even under the leadership of Jawaharlal Nehru, to gain control and form the government of a free India. These hopes, of course, were never realized, although the Congress Socialist Party undoubtedly exerted some influence on Nehru and other leaders who have tried to keep the Congress Party to the left of center.

From the outset, however, the new party was characterized by internal ideological disharmonies since it embraced views ranging from the orthodox Marxist through the Fabian Socialist to a type of Gandhian socialism. This original disunity has led to a preoccupation with ideological abstractions which, along with personal disputes, have proved to be a constant source of instability and disruption.[16]

[15] Asoka Mehta, "The Political Mind of India," *Foreign Affairs*, XXXV (July 1957), 686.
[16] Overstreet and Tinker, "Political Dynamics in India," p. 35.

These observations hold equally true for the independent socialist parties which emerged after the Congress Socialist Party left the Congress fold. They describe difficulties and dilemmas which socialist parties in India have always faced and which are still unresolved.

In trying to unite the leftist elements in the country the CSP early admitted Communists as members. This proved to be a serious mistake. Communists gained positions on the CSP's National Executive and took a large section of the CSP membership with them in urging the Congress to support the war effort after 1941. During the war the CSP advocated more forceful methods of resistance to the British than the Congress leaders, under Gandhi's influence, adopted. They remained within the Congress, but they became increasingly alienated from its inner circles and from Nehru. They had little use for Patel and his stanchly conservative views. They drew closer to Gandhi, however, and he did his best to help them to improve their position within the party. They were not given any important posts in the interim government in 1946–1947 or in the Congress ministry which led India during the first years of freedom. In 1947 a new constitution for the Congress Party contained a provision which required all internal organized parties to dissolve or to leave the Congress. Reluctantly and with grave misgivings the CSP decided to leave the Congress and emerge as an independent party, appealing for support to members of the Congress and nonmembers alike.

It was . . . *not* primarily differences over ideology, program, or policies that forced the Socialists out of the Congress (although these existed) . . . but the *organizational impossibility of Socialist leadership achieving control of the Congress.* The main obstacle was Sardar Patel and the provincial leaders who worked under his control. Had this not existed, it is quite probable that the Party leadership would have been absorbed as a leading section of the Congress leadership and no opposition Socialist Party would have emerged.[17]

Thus the Socialist Party emerged from the Congress "as a *reluctant opposition,* and an *over optimistic one.*"[18] It had a number of able leaders, but they were divided on ideological and other grounds, and in the rank and file there was little co-operation and enthusiasm. The

[17] Thomas A. Rusch, "Evolution and Devolution of Socialist Leadership: Disinheritance and Disintegration" (a paper prepared for the conference on "Leadership and Political Institutions in India," held at the University of California, Berkeley, in August 1956), p. 25. Italics in original.

[18] *Ibid.* Italics in original.

party was badly organized and even more badly financed. Nevertheless, it entered the first general elections with high hopes. It polled over 10 per cent of the votes for the House of the People, but it won only 12 seats, whereas the Communist Party and its allies, which received only about half as many votes, elected 27 members to the House. A partial reason for this paradoxical result was the unwise Socialist policy of running candidates in many constituencies, instead of concentrating in constituencies where the chances for victory were bright, as did the Communists. All the nationally prominent members of the Socialist Party who ran for the House of the People were defeated.

In 1952 the Socialist Party joined with the Kisan Mazdoor Praja Party, which had been formed in 1951 by an orthodox Gandhian, Acharya Kripalani. The product of this fusion was the Praja Socialist Party (PSP). The new party gave a Gandhian trend to the Socialist movement. Kripalani was elected president and Asoka Mehta general secretary. For a time the merger seemed to give promise of developing into an effective opposition to both the Congress and the Communists, but soon the new party was seriously weakened by the resignation, retirement, or death of some of the key leaders and by factional disputes among those who remained.

"Six major events are responsible for bringing to fruition the basic discords inherent in the Party previously: the J. P.–Nehru talks (1953), the Bhoodan movement of Vinoba Bhave, the experience of Socialist government in the state of Travancore-Cochin (1954–55), the Avadi session of the Congress (1954), the Gaya Party Thesis adopted in 1955, and the linguistic agitations of 1956." [19] Reference has already been made to the talks between Nehru and Jayaprakash Narayan over the possibility of some kind of co-operation between the Congress and the PSP in the task of national development. The fourteen-point program which Narayan submitted to Nehru had been approved by the high command of the PSP, but some of the top leaders were not in favor of the discussions in the first place and the whole episode, which received great publicity in India and which aroused speculations that Nehru was thinking of Jayaprakash as a possible successor, provoked considerable controversy in Socialist ranks. The PSP has given its strong support to Bhave's Bhoodan Yagna Movement (land gift movement), and its outstanding leader, or former leader, Jayaprakash Narayan, has presumably turned his back on politics to

[19] *Ibid.*, p. 29. Narayan is often referred to familiarly as "J.P."

devote himself to Bhoodan work. When a Socialist government was formed in Travancore-Cochin in 1954, with the support of the Congress Party, which had a plurality but not a majority in the State Assembly, the national leaders of the PSP approved of the experiment; but the behavior of the Socialist-led ministry in Travancore-Cochin caused a group in the top leadership of the PSP, consisting of Ram Manohar Lohia and some of his followers, to demand the resignation of the Socialist government. Refusal of this demand led to internal friction within the central leadership of the PSP and to the election of Acharya Narendra Deva as a kind of "neutral" chairman.

The resolution adopted at the Avadi session of the Congress Party for "a socialistic pattern of society" was publicly welcomed by PSP leaders like Asoka Mehta who desired co-operation with the Congress and was publicly condemned by those, like Dr. Lohia, who wished to remain wholly aloof from the dominant party. At the PSP general conference at Gaya in 1955 a statement prepared by the national chairman of the party, Acharya Narendra Deva (who died a year later), and intended "as a compromise between various adherents of Gandhian, democratic, and Marxian socialism" [20] was adopted by the membership in the face of the opposition of such key leaders as Kripalani, Asoka Mehta, and Purshottam Tricumdas.

The socialist orientation of the Congress Party accentuated differences of viewpoint within the top leadership of the PSP over the proper policy to follow regarding the Congress. One group, of which Asoka Mehta was a leading spokesman, favored a policy of collaboration with the Congress on common objectives and warned against the dangers of playing into the hands of the Communists by ignoring "political compulsions" and realities. Another group, led by Ram Manohar Lohia, rejected the policy of collaboration with the Congress as fatal to the party and insisted that instead of being "a tail of the Congress" the PSP should become a truly revolutionary party. The divergence in viewpoint reached a climax in 1955, when the National Executive of the PSP first reprimanded and then expelled Lohia and some of his followers from the party for issuing public statements against other party leaders and party policies. Lohia promptly formed a new party, which he called the Socialist Party of India. He took with him "at least 30% of the former party's strength . . . the active leadership of six state organizations, the entire Socialist youth movement, and one-seventh of its legislative representation. His primary support

[20] *Ibid.*, p. 37.

lies in South and Central India and among the youthful elements in the P.S.P. who had little or no attachments to the Congress." [21] In spite of its afflictions, however, the party made a fine showing in the 1957 elections. By concentrating its energies (it contested only about half as many seats as it had in the previous election), the party minimized its losses; and though its popular vote for the House of the People fell from over 16 per cent to about 10 per cent, its representation in the House dropped only from 20 to 18. In the state assemblies it increased its representation from 125 to 195, returning 20 or more members to the assemblies in Bihar, Bombay, Uttar Pradesh, and West Bengal.

"No party," wrote Asoka Mehta in 1957, "has gone through such hard times as the P.S.P." However, contemplating the results of the general elections and the surprisingly good showing of the PSP, especially in the states, he wrote of his party: "That in spite of this it has come through unscathed suggests that it has a place among the people." [22]

The Communist Party of India

In the Indian House of the People the largest single group in opposition to the dominant Congress Party is composed of the 29 M.P.'s (about 6 per cent of the total) who represent the Communist Party of India. The CPI has one or more members in each of the state legislative assemblies, and in the assemblies of three states, Kerala, West Bengal, and Andhra, it has a formidable representation—60 (48.5 per cent), 46 (18 per cent), and 35 (11.6 per cent) respectively. In Kerala, as a result of the second general elections, it became the majority party in the Assembly (thanks to the adherence of five independent members), and it formed in this South Indian state the first Communist government in democratic India.

It is very difficult to estimate the real strength of the Communist movement in India. As in all countries, especially non-Communist countries, it operates largely beneath the surface. There is much in the Indian environment which provides fertile soil for the spread of communism. Much of the appeal of communism in India is

due to the extremely slow economic improvements in India, and to the inability of the masses to examine political slogans and promises critically and

[21] *Ibid.*, p. 36.

[22] Asoka Mehta, "The Political Mind of India," *Foreign Affairs*, XXXV (July 1957), 687.

intelligently and to appreciate the price they would have to pay if the Communists were given a chance to fulfill their promises. . . . But the greatest asset of the Communists has always been the romantic appeal and the reflected glory of the revolutionary power of Russia and now of China. . . . If in spite of their defeat the Communists have received more votes at the polls in recent elections than is good for India, it only shows that they still benefit from their assets of poverty, popular ignorance and international tension.[23]

In spite of their efforts to exploit all kinds of popular grievances and discontent, the CPI draws its main support from the disaffected intellectuals, especially from the "educated unemployed."

Communism came to India shortly after the Bolshevik Revolution in Russia. During the 1920s Communist groups were established in a few Indian cities, and they attempted to infiltrate the trade union movement. They received guidance from M. N. Roy and other Indians who were then active in the international Communist movement, and at an early period they apparently had close contacts with the British Communist Party, which seems to have been the main channel for policy guidance and direction until at least the years after the Second World War. In the late 1940s and early 1950s it seemed that international direction was coming chiefly through the Cominform. Recently the guidance has appeared to come directly from the head centers of international communism, chiefly from Moscow and perhaps increasingly also from Peking.[24]

In spite of Lenin's advice to Asian Communist movements to work with the national bourgeoisie, the Indian Communists—perhaps under the influence of M. N. Roy, who publicly disagreed with Leninists regarding the proper strategy to follow in Asian countries—were extremely critical of "bourgeois nationalism" until the mid-1930s, when they conformed to the shift in the international party line and adopted the strategy of the "united front." In 1934 the Communist Party of

---

[23] Ellen Roy, "Indian Party Politics" (a lecture delivered in Chicago, June 27, 1955, under the auspices of the Chicago Council on Foreign Relations), *Radical Humanist*, XIX (July 24, 1955), 356. Mrs. Roy is the widow of M. N. Roy, who for some years was the leading Indian Communist and an agent of the Comintern and who later abjured communism and founded the Radical Humanist movement in India.

[24] For details on the relations of the Communist Party of India with the international Communist movement, see M. R. Masani, *The Communist Party of India* (New York: Macmillan, 1954), and John H. Kautsky, *Moscow and the Communist Party of India: A Study in the Postwar Evolution of International Communist Strategy* (New York: Wiley, 1956).

India was formed as an organized section within the Indian National Congress. Its members were able to gain representation in the higher councils of the Congress Socialist Party and of the Congress itself. But when Russia entered the Second World War the CPI, like Communist parties in all countries, called for full participation in the struggle against the Axis, whereas the policy of the Congress was one of strict nonco-operation in the war effort. For this deviation from Congress policy and for its determined stand against partition, the CPI was expelled from the Congress in 1945.

Shortly after India became independent, the party, again in conformity with "the new cold war line of the international Communist movement," launched a program of direct action against the government. Although it was unable to stir up much trouble in most parts of the country, for a time in 1948 it had spectacular success in a remote Telegu-speaking section of Hyderabad state known as Telengana. There it was able to arouse the discontented peasants against the landlords and local authorities. For several months Telengana was virtually in Communist hands, in armed revolt against the government, and the Communist leaders associated with this coup gained great prestige within the inner ranks of the CPI. But the victory in Telengana was brief. Within a few months, as a result of firm and intelligent government action and Vinoba Bhave's first great crusade in his Bhoodan Yagna campaign, Communist influence in Telengana was reduced.

The Telengana affair was a warning to the rest of the country, and it did much to expose the soothing appeals of the Communists as hypocritical. The failure of the direct-action movement created confusion and division within the ranks of the Indian Communists. With some guidance from the British Communist Party, however, they veered around in time to contest the first general elections, with surprising success. The CPI and its allies received 5.4 per cent of the vote for the House of the People, and although they contested only a few constituencies, they gained 27 seats in the House, scoring notable successes in West Bengal, Madras, and Travancore-Cochin.

In 1953, reflecting the impact of the "new look" in international communism following the death of Stalin, the CPI began to take a more charitable view of the Congress Party and of Nehru. This softer line was expressed at the party's Third Congress, held at Madurai, where an effort was made to work out a compromise between various factions within the party and between the desire to oppose the Congress and yet to support the policy of "peaceful coexistence." [25] The Avadi resolution of the Congress Party and the trend of India's foreign policy raised further problems of strategy and tactics for the CPI. Although belatedly welcoming these developments, the party continued to look for opportunities to checkmate the Congress in the country. In early 1955 it undertook a major test of strength in elections in the newly created state of Andhra, where it had scored sensational victories in the general elections of 1951–1952; but its strategy backfired, and it suffered such severe losses that from being a potential threat to the Congress control of the new state it was reduced to a minority group of little influence in the State Assembly.

By the time the CPI held its Fourth Congress, at Palghat in April 1956, the effects of the Andhra debacle, the Bandung Conference, Nehru's visit to Russia, the visit of Bulganin and Krushchev to India, and the resolutions and revelations at the Twentieth Congress of the Russian Communist Party forced the Indian Communists to reassess their position. The party declared that though it "must act as a Party of Opposition in relation to the present Government" the "democratic front" which it hoped to establish "will not be an anti-Congress front."

The CPI contested the second general elections under considerable difficulties; but the results were generally gratifying to them. They nearly doubled their vote for the House of the People and increased their representation in that body from 27 to 29. They retained their strength in West Bengal, regained some of their losses in Andhra (where elections to the State Assembly were held only in the Telengana area), won 18 seats in the Bombay State Assembly (where they had held one before), and won more seats in Kerala than the Congress. In Bombay their victories were due largely to the support of anti-Congress electoral alliances. In a constituency in Bombay city S. A. Dange, a leading Indian Communist, won the seat to the House of the People by the greatest plurality accorded any candidate in India. In Kerala, as previously noted, the Communists have formed a government, with the support of five Independents they backed in the elections. The chief minister is E. M. S. Namboodiripad, a member of the Politburo of the CPI. The unique experiment of a Com-

[25] A. K. Ghosh, *On the Work of the Third Party Congress* (New Delhi: Communist Party of India, 1954), p. 5.

munist government in an Indian state is being closely watched, not only in India but throughout the world.

The organization of the CPI follows the standard pattern of Communist parties generally. The basic unit on the local level is the town or local conference, in which all the cells in the area participate. Each conference, from the town or local conference through the district and provincial conferences, has an executive committee and a secretary. The party congress, at the top of the hierarchy, elects the Central Committee, which chooses the Politburo and the general secretary. As in other Communist parties, the CPI has been controlled from the top, by a relatively limited number of people. There have been five general secretaries since 1934: Dr. G. Adhikari, P. C. Joshi, B. T. Randadive, Rajeshwar Rao, and A. K. Ghosh.[26] These men have been identified with different policies and approaches, but it is hard to decide how much these differences have been due to the shifts in the international party line and how much to differences in convictions and personalities. The parliamentary group has apparently not had a decisive influence in the inner circles of the party; with Dange now in the Parliament this situation may change.

The Indian Communists, says Ellen Roy, "are no different from other Communists, except that they have to their credit probably more mistakes, more turn-abouts and somersaults than Communists elsewhere." [27] Indeed, "the Communist Party of India appears to be characterized by a higher degree of indiscipline . . . than any other Communist Party of which we have detailed knowledge." [28] Divisions within the party have existed ever since its founding, and at times the confusion of the Communists has been almost ludicrous. But they have survived their inner differences and the gyrations of the international party line. As the strongest opposition group in the Indian Parliament, as a major political factor in several key states, and as the dominant party in Kerala, they have tangible political strength; more important, however, they are operating effectively, beneath the surface of Indian life, in trade unions, student groups, peasant organizations, among the most influential and discontented segments of Indian society. They remain a disturbing element and a basic threat to democracy in India.

[26] See Gene D. Overstreet, "Indian Communist Approaches to Leadership" (a paper prepared for the conference on "Leadership and Political Institutions in India," held at the University of California, Berkeley, in August 1956).

[27] "Indian Party Politics," p. 356.

[28] Overstreet, "Indian Communist Approaches to Leadership," p. 9.

Other Parties and Groups

The Indian political scene is characterized by a bewildering number of political parties, most of which are hardly more than groups in local areas supporting individual personalities. Nearly 200 so-called parties announced their intention to contest the first general elections, and so many of these actually put up candidates that straight contests were the exception rather than the rule. Fourteen parties were recognized by the Election Commission as national parties in the first general elections, and fifty as state parties. Only five of the recognized national parties received more than 3 per cent of the vote, the minimum requirement to be recognized as a national party as stipulated by the electoral laws—the Congress, the Socialists, the Kisan Mazdoor Praja Party, the Jan Sangh, and the CPI. As a result of the showing in the first general elections, only four parties—the Congress, the Jan Sangh, the PSP, and the CPI—were recognized as national parties in the second elections. Seven others which had been recognized as national parties were recognized only as state parties for the allotment of election symbols. These were the Forward Bloc (Marxist) in West Bengal, the Hindu Mahasabha in four states, the Ram Rajya Parishad in six states, the Scheduled Castes Federation in seven states, the Revolutionary Socialist Party in Kerala, the Revolutionary Communist Party in Manipur, and the Krishikar Lok Party in Madras and Rajasthan. Other parties recognized as state parties included the Peasant and Workers Party in Bombay, the Tamil Nad Toilers Party in Madras, the Akali Dal Party in the Punjab.

One of the most significant aspects of the second general elections was the generally good showing made by regional or state electoral coalitions. These alliances and the Independents were generally more successful than opposition parties. Indeed, Asoka Mehta is convinced that this is an important development in Indian politics:

Opposition to the Congress is emerging not in terms of rival national parties but mostly through various regional groupings: Ganatantra Parishad in Orissa, Jharkhand Party and the Janata Party in Bihar, the Dravida Munnetra Kazhagam in Madras, Samyukta Maharashtra Samiti in Maharashtra (Bombay State), Maha Gujerat Parishad in Gujarat (Bombay State), and the various tribal organizations in the tribal areas of Assam. Collectively, these parties have won more seats in the State Assemblies and the Lok Sabha than any national party in opposition to the Congress. As a matter of fact, it is not easy for a national party to satisfy and articulate the emotional discontent of a region. When a region wants to express its discontent it prefers a party whose allegiance is to the region alone and whose horizons are limited. This is perhaps the biggest danger that Indian democracy faces during the next 20 years when it will be under the severe strains of economic development. [29]

[29] "The Political Mind of India," pp. 682–683. Material from "The Political Mind of India," by Asoka Mehta, appearing in the July 1957 issue of *Foreign Affairs*, is quoted by special permission. Copyright by Council on Foreign Relations, New York.

· XII ·

Political Dynamics

POLITICAL parties have not yet found their place in Indian political life. They have received their major tests in the two general elections which have been held since independence, and they are influenced to an indeterminate degree and in ill-defined ways by public opinion and by interest and pressure groups. In this chapter elections and electoral procedures will be discussed, and some analysis of the nebulous subjects of public opinion and pressure groups, conventional and unconventional, will be attempted.

Elections and Electoral Procedures

On every count India's two general elections were major achievements. The people of India had had little experience in voting—elections in British days were confined to a few people with special qualifications—and none at all in the complex processes of a nation-wide general election. Simply to prepare election rolls and conduct elections was a tremendous task. Over 173 million persons were eligible to vote in the first general elections, and at least 20 million more in the second. About half the eligible voters actually voted in each election. Because most voters were illiterate, special arrangements had to be made to enable them to vote intelligently. Symbols were used for the parties, and the multiple-ballot-box technique allowed the voter to drop the ballot paper—a sheet bearing only a serial number stamped on it—into the ballot box bearing the symbol of the party of his choice. Special provision was also made for choosing representatives of the scheduled castes and scheduled tribes. The result was a fairly large number of double-member constituencies and even one triple-member constituency. Because of the shortage of trained election officials and certain problems of geography and climate, the elections were held over a period of some four months in 1951–1952 and three weeks in 1957 (although the voting in a few remote places did not take place until some weeks later). The first general elections required the preparation of 600,000,000 ballot papers, 2,600,000 ballot boxes, 132,500 polling stations, and 196,000 booths. The services of 900,000 personnel were required to supervise the voting.

Preparations for the first general elections were started soon after India became an independent state. The remarkable boldness and unanimity with which the constitution makers decreed universal adult suffrage for India have been noted. The constitution provided for an Election Commission and "one general electoral roll"; it also authorized the Indian Parliament to make appropriate laws regarding elections, electoral rolls, and the delimitation of constituencies. In January 1950, at about the time the constitution went into effect, the Parliament set up an Election Commission with wide powers, and in April Mr. Sukumar Sen was appointed chief election commissioner. Eventually Election Commissions were set up in each state as well. Much of the credit for successfully preparing the general election, conducting these elections, hearing election petitions, and carrying out basic arrangements must go to the Election Commissions and to Mr. Sen, who has held the post of chief election commissioner since 1950. In April 1950 Parliament passed the first electoral law dealing with the qualifications of voters and the preparation of the electoral rolls. The Representation of the People Act of 1951 dealt with procedures of elections, election expenses, election offenses, and similar matters.

The main work in preparing the electoral rolls was completed by the end of 1949, since the first general elections were originally scheduled for the spring of 1950. The rolls had to be revised almost up to the beginning of the voting in the fall of 1951. Complete accuracy in the rolls was out of the question, but the Election Commissions directed that great care should be taken to register every qualified voter. Much of the work was done by house-to-house canvass. Even then several million people were not registered; these included some 2,800,-000 women, who would give only the names of their husbands or fathers, and an even larger number of refugees. The delimitation of the constituencies proved to be another arduous task. Most of this work was done by Delimitation Commissions, with advisory committees consisting of members of Parliament. Eventually 3,772 constituencies were set up, 489 for the House of the People and the remainder for the state assemblies. This meant that every elected M.P. would represent approximately 720,000 persons. The decision to include in each parliamentary constituency an equal number of State Assembly constituencies helped to simplify the procedure.

Election Commissions and government agencies generally made herculean efforts to instruct the voters in their rights and duties. The work of the parties in this respect left much to be desired. Undoubtedly the elections were a great educational experience for millions of Indians, and they were conducted without major disturbances. During the campaign the candidates and party workers concentrated on local issues and interests; they also tried to make the voters identify the symbol with the party. Candidates who ran for the 489 seats to be filled in the House of the People numbered 1,874, and there were 15,361 for the seats in 22 state assemblies. Nearly 85 parties were represented, and there were also independent candidates. Over 9,000 candidates forfeited their deposits because they got less than one-sixth of the total vote in their constituencies; included in this number were nearly 5,000 Independents. Only the Congress Party put up candidates for most of the seats in the House of the People. It was therefore the only party which operated on a truly national scale.

The results of the elections were about as anticipated.[1] The Congress Party polled only about 45 per cent of the total votes cast for seats in the House of the People, but it elected 362 members, or 74 per cent of the total. The Communist Party returned 27 members, the Socialist Party 12, the Kisan Mazdoor Praja Party 9. No other party had any significant representation. Of the elected members 37 ran as

[1] For details see Election Commission, *Report on the First General Elections in India, 1951–52* (New Delhi: Government of India Press, 1955), I, 10; S. V. Kogekar and Richard L. Park, eds., *Reports on the Indian General Elections, 1951–52* (Bombay, 1956); *India Press Digests* (University of California), vol. I, no. 4, and Monograph Series no. 3 (Dec. 1956); Richard L. Park, "Indian Election Results," *Far Eastern Survey*, XXI (May 7, 1952), 61–70; Irene Tinker and Mil Walker, "The First General Elections in India and Indonesia," *Far Eastern Survey*, XXV (July 1956), 97–110; Gene D. Overstreet and Irene Tinker, "Political Dynamics in India" (Berkeley: Modern India Project, University of California, March 1957; from material prepared for the India volume, Country Survey Series, Human Relations Area Files), pp. 44–65.

Independents. In the state assemblies the Congress won a majority of the seats in all but 4 states. In Travancore-Cochin, Madras, Hyderabad, and West Bengal the main opposition to the Congress came from the Communists; in Orissa and Rajasthan it was from a right-wing coalition in which the princes figured prominently; in the Punjab it came from the Sikh party, the Akali Dal. Most of the nationally prominent leaders of the opposition parties were either defeated or did not run at all.

On the whole, the voters demonstrated great interest, if sometimes a bit of confusion, in the process of voting. It is of course impossible to tell what considerations influenced their decisions. Doubtless many voted for the Congress because it was the party of Gandhi and of Nehru; some may have voted for Congress candidates because their symbol was a pair of bullocks. Many villagers undoubtedly cast their ballots as directed by their headman or other leader. Women turned out in large numbers, and possibly many of them voted as their husbands had instructed. There were a number of voters who worshiped the ballot box or stuffed something besides the ballot paper into the box; there were several hundred cases of attempted impersonation and some reports of intimidation. The practice of stamping each voter's hand with a round mark in indelible ink seemed to be effective in preventing voting more than once. Since the ballot was cast in secret, it could be placed outside a box; and a voter might not deposit it at all, but retain it and perhaps sell or give it to some unscrupulous candidate who wished to rig the election. The fact that the ballot bore a serial number which was recorded opposite the name of the voter led to apprehension and to charges that the voting was not really secret at all. This practice was followed, however, only to allow an election tribunal to check the voting in case of a challenge or to check the balloting in double-member constituencies to make sure that the same voter had not cast two ballots for the same candidate.

After the general elections, the first regularly constituted Parliament of independent India met in the summer of 1952. Since its maximum life was five years, the second general elections had to be held sometime before the summer of 1957. In the interim the election lists were kept up to date by periodic revisions, the last changes being made only a few weeks before the voting began in late February 1957. For a time it seemed that the agitation and uncertainty created by reorganization of the states might force a postponement of the second general elections or even jeopardize the entire electoral process. After vigorous debate, the political map of India was redrawn, effective November 1, 1956. The changes in state boundaries and the reduction of the number of states to fourteen, each of equal status, greatly complicated the process of preparing the electoral rolls and delimiting constituencies; it also created emotional tension where the government's decisions on state boundaries gave rise to strong feelings of frustrated regionalism. But the elections were held as scheduled.

India's second general election was held in a much shorter period of time than the first, but for the most part it was conducted along similar lines and the results were not markedly different, with a few exceptions.[2] On the national level it was practically an election without issues. Naturally, the opposition parties leveled a variety of charges against the Congress, but there was almost unanimous support for the broad policies of the Indian government, at home and abroad. The elections were fought largely in terms of personalities and local issues.

Peaceful as they were in most ways, in some parts of the country the second general elections gave rise to violent disagreements over the government's action in reorganizing the states just three months before the elections. Most criticisms concerned the government's failure to satisfy the demands of certain linguistic groups, particularly in Bombay and the Punjab.

Redrawing the state boundaries to conform to linguistic groupings had long been a popular issue in India. The Congress Party itself first gave strong support to linguistic demands at its Nagpur session in 1920; and in the following year regional units of the Congress were reorganized along linguistic lines. Thus the Congress early committed itself to the linguistic principle and over the years repeatedly

[2] For background of the second general elections see S. L. Poplai, ed., *National Politics and 1957 Elections in India* (Delhi, 1957); J. R. Chandran and M. M. Thomas, eds., *Political Outlook in India Today: A Pre-election Study* (Bangalore, 1956); *Thought,* Feb. 23, 1957 (special election issue); fifteen "Election Preview" articles published in *Times of India,* Feb. 1957. For election results see Asoka Mehta, "The Political Mind of India," *Foreign Affairs,* XXXV (July 1957), 679–688; *India News,* II (April 15, 1957), 3; "India: Big Events, Few Changes," *Round Table,* June 1957, no. 187, pp. 285–288; "India's Second General Election," *World Today,* XIII (June 1957), 232–241; James R. Roach, "India's 1957 Elections," *Far Eastern Survey,* XXVI (May 1957), 65–78. Many of the comments in this chapter on both general elections are based on the observations, interviews, and investigations of the author, who was in India shortly after the conclusion of the first general elections and during the entire period of the voting in the second general elections.

reaffirmed its adherence to this principle. In 1946, however, a Congress election manifesto stated that linguistic considerations would control political divisions "not in every case, but as far as it was possible in the circumstances of each case." In 1947 Nehru remarked: "First things must come first, and the first thing is the security and stability of India." The major shift in Congress policy came in 1948, with the report of the Constituent Assembly's Commission on Linguistic Provinces (known as the Dar Commission). This report not only stressed the financial, economic, and administrative considerations in states reorganization; it also held that formation of provinces exclusively or even mainly along linguistic lines would be inadvisable. Soon after this, a committee of the Congress Party headed by Nehru, Patel, and Pattabhi Sitaramayya endorsed the findings of the Dar Commission, but opened the door to widespread agitation by adding that overwhelming public opinion must be satisfied and agreeing to the possible creation of an Andhra state. The Congress as a whole held to this position in the elections of 1951. But after the elections the government found ways to delay the creation of Andhra and yielded in 1953 only after Potti Sriramulu, by fasting unto death, had roused the Telegu-speaking peoples of Madras state to violent agitation.

Finally, in December 1953, the government appointed a commission to examine "objectively and dispassionately" the question of states reorganization. The "guidance" provided by Parliament for this commission pointed clearly along the lines laid down by the Dar Commission. When its report was delivered in 1955, however, the States Reorganization Commission seemed to have followed, with but two major exceptions, the linguistic principle. Of the 16 states and 3 Union territories it proposed to create, only 2 states were to remain bilingual, Bombay and the Punjab. The Marathi-speaking people of Bombay had long been demanding a unilingual Maharashtra state with Bombay city as its capital; the Sikhs in the Punjab wanted a Punjabi-speaking state. Both demands were rejected, though all other major linguistic demands were satisfied; as a result, strong political agitation marked by occasional violence broke out in these two states, and dissatisfaction with the government's reorganization proposals was felt in virtually every state of the Union. Numerous compromises were broached by various groups and Congress policy vacillated, but the solution embodied in the States Reorganization Bill of 1956 retained a bilingual status for Bombay and the Punjab, postponing final action on the position of Bombay city for several years. Continuing agitation by the Sikhs led to a unique "regional formula" for dividing governmental functions within the Punjab along linguistic lines. The political vitality of the linguistic issue is evidenced by the resounding defeat which the Congress Party suffered in parts of Bombay state in the second general elections. Two strange electoral coalitions, the Maha Gujerat Parishad in Gujerat and the Samyukta Maharashtra Samiti in Maharashtra, united to bring down the Congress candidates. The parties adhering to these coalitions were united on so few other issues that the importance of the linguistic issue was strikingly demonstrated.

In the voting for state assemblies, the Congress suffered greater reverses than were anticipated in Bihar, Uttar Pradesh, and Bombay, but it still won a majority in these states and in all the other state assemblies except those of Kerala and Orissa. In all states except Kerala it was able to continue its Congress governments. Even in this problem state the gains of the Communists were not substantial, and they can be accounted for in part by the incorporation in the new Kerala state of the Malabar section of former Bombay state, where Communist strength was already great. In Orissa, where the Congress won only a few seats more than a coalition party dominated by land-lords and princes, the main opposition came not from the left but from the right. The Congress actually improved its position in a few states, including the Punjab, Rajasthan, Mysore, and Madras.

The outcome of the voting for the House of the People was re-markably similar to that in the elections of 1951–1952. The Congress gained a few more seats, the Communists gained two and the Jan Sangh one, and the Praja Socialists lost two seats. Again, as in 1951–1952, the Congress gained approximately three-fourths of the repre-sentation in the House of the People and remained in power in all but one of the states, though polling less than half the total votes (see Table 8). Again about 50 per cent of the eligible voters actually cast their ballots.

The techniques of campaigning and of voting were like those em-ployed in 1951–1952. In the campaign there was more house-to-house canvassing, and fewer mass meetings were held. As in the first general elections, national leaders, including Nehru himself, campaigned vigorously. Again the All-India Radio was barred to candidates and party representatives, although the election manifestoes of the major parties were read over the air and voting instructions were broadcast frequently. On the whole, the voters cast their ballots with greater confidence and possibly with greater independence, although many voters were still unfamiliar with voting procedures, and many election irregularities were repeated. Again the campaigning and balloting passed off without serious incident.

Table 8. Relative percentage of votes obtained by Congress party in first and second general elections *

State	1951–1952	1957
Assam	43.9	56.6
Bihar	42.1	43.1
Bombay	52.8	48.2
Kerala	42.3	38.2
Madhya Pradesh	45.2	47.9
Madras	35.5	42.0
Mysore	49.0	50.9
Orissa	38.0	38.5
Punjab	38.4	46.0
Rajasthan	39.8	44.0
Uttar Pradesh	47.9	42.7
West Bengal	38.4	46.3
Andhra (Telengana area) †	37.5	46.5

* Adjusted to take into account changes caused by the reorganization of the states in 1956.

† Only the Telengana area of Andhra Pradesh went to the polls in 1957 because the rest of the members of the state's Legislative Assembly had been elected in 1956. Of the 196 seats filled in 1956, the Congress won 146.

Shortly after the second general elections, the government announced that it had accepted a recommendation of the Election Commission to replace the multiple-ballot-box system by a system of marked ballots, such as is used in most democratic countries. Under the new system the ballot paper will contain the names of all the candidates along with party symbols. The ballot will be marked in secret, but will be placed in a ballot box in the presence of polling officials, and the presiding officer will check the official mark on the back. The new method will be less expensive and complicated, and it will also eliminate the difficulties and abuses of the multiple-ballot-box system. On the other hand, it will be more difficult and confusing for the illiterate voter.

India's two general elections were great lessons in democracy which came home to almost every Indian. For the first time the humblest citizen could feel that he was participating in the processes of democracy and that his opinion counted. Even if many Indians were bewildered by the whole process, the exercise of the franchise had a continuing impact and educational value. The way the elections were conducted demonstrated that democracy, though foreign to the experience and outlook of most Indians, could be practiced in an underdeveloped Asian country among mostly illiterate people. Few of the achievements of independent India have been more impressive than this "act of faith," the adoption of universal suffrage and the successful conduct of "the world's largest elections."

Public Opinion

Indian public opinion is a will-o'-the-wisp which almost defies analysis by the standard techniques of public opinion measurement that have been developed in the West. An Indian Institute of Public Opinion exists, but its observations have not yet attained anything like reliability.[3] Indians are too radically divided, on too many different levels and in too many different directions, to have distinct, formal opinions on very many topics. Such public opinions as exist concerning topics which do not touch daily life have usually been the opinions of a very small group of "intellectuals." There is hardly anything in India analogous in scope and effectiveness to the newspaper editorials, radio and television commentators, trade unions, voluntary associations, and letter-writing public in America. The vast majority of the people in India are illiterate and isolated in a more than geographical sense; they live, literally, in a world of their own. Except in a dim and negative way, they have little impact on those who make the political decisions. On the other hand, a certain tendency is evident to "Indianize" Indian politics, particularly on the regional and state levels, and here the Indian masses are slowly becoming involved and articulate. Here too, political horizons are narrower, and traditional attitudes more apparent. Here one notes the continued strength of religious orthodoxy and social conservatism, a widespread suspicion of government, a heavy burden of inertia.

Yet, overall, there can be no question that public opinion is becoming influential in India. It expresses itself in vague popular demands,

[3] For the results of various polls conducted by the Institute see its journal, *Monthly Public Opinion Surveys.* Vol. II, nos. 16, 17, 18, and 19 (Jan., Feb., March, and April 1957), comprise a quadruple special issue containing the results of the first national public opinion poll conducted in India. It was specially designed to test public opinion research methods in India.

unformulated, intangible, but irresistible. The issue of linguistic states was decided by a surge of public opinion that proved, ultimately, impossible to deny. Particularly in South India, resistance to the introduction of Hindi in the schools appears to be very powerful. A mass *satyagraha* movement against Portugal arose over the issue of Goa; it continued despite the appeal of the Prime Minister and the government to call it off. Even in world politics, where a remarkable consensus seems to exist among Indians of all parties, criticism is sometimes heard to good effect. This was illustrated by the protests within India over Nehru's delay in condemning roundly the Russian brutalities in Hungary in 1956.

Thus, one senses considerable unevenness in the texture of public opinion in India. Certain issues are tender ones, and the least tremor will touch off violent waves of protest; on others, seemingly no less important, the apathy is profound. Much of Nehru's tremendous popularity is apparently due to his sensitivity to public moods, his efforts to keep the Congress Party in touch with the people, his innumerable public appearances. He realizes, probably far better than his idolators, that there are definite limits to his power, that it is based on a delicate mixture of consent and persuasion, which he must be continually on the alert to preserve.

In shaping Indian public opinion, nonpolitical organizations, individuals, and considerations are particularly important.

There is a strong tendency on the part of political forces in India to operate outside the framework of responsible political institutions, an inclination which presents a serious challenge to those institutions. Furthest removed from the framework of conventional politics are movements expressing the tradition of non-responsible leadership, exercising moral influence on formal political authority. Originating in the Brahmanic code, this tradition was strengthened by Gandhi who attempted political and social reform outside government and frequently outside party.[4]

Thus movements such as Bhoodan Yagna, extraparliamentary techniques such as fasts and *satyagraha,* "unconventional" leaders such as Gandhi and Bhave have a tremendous influence on Indian political life. It may even be said, as Professor Morris-Jones has suggested, that these "nonpolitical" and "unconventional" aspects of Indian life are at the very heart of Indian politics.[5]

[4] Overstreet and Tinker, "Political Dynamics in India," p. 7.

[5] W. H. Morris-Jones, *Parliament in India* (Philadelphia: University of Pennsylvania Press, 1957), pp. 2, 37–40.

Because of the widespread illiteracy, geographical distances, and local patterns of Indian life, communication of all sorts is difficult, and the effective channels are often very different from those which are available in highly developed industrial states. There are no television stations, and the only radio network, All-India Radio, is controlled by the government and has only a limited impact.

Although All-India Radio broadcasts in regional languages as well as English, the audience which hears any of these broadcasts is limited both by the small number of radio sets in villages and by the variety of local dialects used throughout the nation. Motion pictures have a wider audience than does the radio, but they are widely used for escapist melodramas which tend, if anything, to reinforce traditional values of society.[6]

Foreign motion pictures, even poor ones, are popular. Indians like to boast of the fact that they have the third largest motion-picture industry in the world, surpassed only by the United States and Japan.

There are scores of newspapers, mostly weeklies and dailies, in all the regional languages and in English. Because "the press appears to be aimed primarily at national and regional elites, and its circulation is mainly urban," [7] most of the really influential newspapers are published in English. Among these are such excellent papers, with far more than a local circulation, as the *Hindu* (Madras), the *Times of India* (Bombay and Delhi), the *Statesman* (Calcutta and New Delhi), the *Amrita Bazar Patrika* (Calcutta and Allahabad), and the *Hindustan Times* (New Delhi). No Indian newspaper has a circulation of much over 100,000 copies, and most of them have far less than this. They reach a larger audience, however, than the circulation figures would suggest, for many nonpurchasers read them, and they are read to many who are illiterate. Most of the Indian newspapers are strongly political in their views, and the better ones provide, within space limitations, extensive coverage of national and international events. Lengthy and numerous editorials are common, but there are relatively few political columnists, and some of the best of these, such as A. D. Gorwala, are under heavy pressure to curb their pens in writing of government policies and leaders.

Periodicals abound in India, but very few, except some film magazines, have a sizable circulation. Most are fly-by-night organs of opinion with a circulation of a few thousand at most. The *Eastern*

[6] Overstreet and Tinker, "Political Dynamics in India," pp. 9–10.
[7] *Ibid.*, p. 10.

Economist, published in New Delhi, is an excellent journal along the lines of the London *Economist.* Several of the scholarly or professional journals are of high quality; among these, in the field of politics and foreign affairs, are the *India Quarterly,* organ of the Indian Council of World Affairs, and the *Indian Journal of Public Administration,* published by the Indian Institute of Public Administration.

India has one of the most effective "undergrounds" in the world. That is to say, information gets around rapidly, by word of mouth and by devious means beyond the comprehension of outsiders. Personal contacts are of the utmost importance. "In personal contact the visual impression plays a weighted role; the belief in *darshan* (the beneficial effect of being in the presence of a great man) is still strong, and to receive *darshan* one needs only to see, not listen." [8] The importance of *darshan* is generally recognized by India's leaders. Gandhi traveled ceaselessly about the countryside, often on foot, and thousands were content just to see him and to be in his presence. He used the spinning wheel and prayer meetings as effective instruments of popular education. Nehru, burdened as he is by heavy official responsibilities, devotes a considerable amount of time and energy to public appearances in all parts of India; he professes to derive strength and refreshment from his contacts with the people, and they turn out in great numbers to see and hear him. Vinoba Bhave moves about on foot from one village to another in his crusade for spiritual regeneration and sacrificial giving of land; and Jayaprakash Narayan, vowing to abjure politics, devotes most of his time to this work. These men are truly charismatic leaders. The role of charisma in Indian life cannot be overestimated, in a land where "the belief in *darshan* . . . is still strong." It is quite apparent that "the personality of leaders and their ability to have a direct impact on their audience will doubtless continue to play an outsized role in Indian politics for some time." [9]

Pressure Groups, Conventional and Unconventional

Like public opinion generally, the nature of pressure groups in India and their influence on Indian politics are just beginning to be topics for serious study. There are many such groups, and their influence is

[8] *Ibid.*

[9] *Ibid.,* p. 11. See also Myron Weiner, "Some Hypotheses on the Politics of Westernization in India" (a paper prepared for the conference on "Leadership and Political Institutions in India," held at the University of California, Berkeley, in August 1956), pp. 2–4.

obviously great. One of the clearest general analyses of these groups was presented in a paper prepared for the Human Relations Area Files by Gene D. Overstreet and Irene Tinker:

Three main types of pressure groups may be distinguished in the Indian setting: 1) special-interest organizations of fairly recent origin representing modern bases of social and economic association familiar to the Western observer, such as trade unions and business groups, social welfare agencies, or youth and women's organizations; 2) organizations representing traditional social relationships, such as caste and religious groups; and 3) organizations representing the Gandhian ideological heritage.[10]

The "modern interest groups" are multiplying rapidly. They are still mostly influenced and controlled by a small group of intellectuals, and they usually have a strong political flavor. Some, in fact, are closely associated with political parties or movements. This is illustrated by trade unions, peasants' organizations, student groups, and cultural associations.

The number of industrial workers in India is still very small in comparison with the number of agricultural laborers, and they are not strongly organized; but an organized labor movement has been of some importance for a generation, and today four major unions claim a membership of approximately 3,500,000. The leadership is still concentrated markedly in the intelligentsia. "Trade Unions in India exert little influence on the policies and character of political organizations. They are rather ancillaries of the leading parties, for which they seek to extend power and further political aims." [11] The first major union was the All-India Trade Union Congress (AITUC), formed in 1920. After stormy years of intense conflict within the organization, it came strongly under Communist influence, and other political parties turned to the formation of competing unions. At present it is clearly allied with the CPI. Its general secretary, S. A. Dange, is one of India's leading Communists; he was elected to the Indian House of the People from Bombay city in the general elections of 1957. To counter the AITUC the Congress Party took the initiative in forming the Indian National Trade Union Congress, which now has nearly half the members of trade unions in India. The two smaller trade unions also have political affiliations or inclinations—the Hindu

[10] Overstreet and Tinker, "Political Dynamics in India," p. 11.

[11] Laxmi M. Singhvi and Bidyut K. Sarkar, *India: Government and Politics* (New Haven: Human Relations Area Files, 1955), p. 114.

Mazdoor Sabha with the Socialists and the United Trade Union Congress with some of the smaller leftist parties, leaning strongly toward the Communists.

Peasant organizations (*kisan sabhas*) have existed for some time, and a number have been politically active. Among these are the All-India Kisan Sabha, which is dominated by the Communists; the Hind Kisan Panchayat, led by the Socialists; and the United Kisan Sabha, associated with smaller leftist parties. Both the Socialists and the Congress have tended in recent years to support the Bhoodan Yagna Movement rather than any more politically inclined peasant associations.

Indian students are politically conscious, perhaps to an unfortunate degree, and student associations have been hotbeds of competing political activities. When the All-India Students' Federation came under Communist influence, a new association, the National Union of Students, was formed, with the blessing of the Congress party. Many other student groups, of a national or local character, including welfare groups, philosophical societies, and debating societies, were drawn into political activity.

Cultural associations have been a fertile field for the Communists. Cultural delegations have visited Communist China and the Soviet Union, and delegations have come to India from China and Russia. The All-India Peace Council, which is associated with the Communist-dominated World Peace Movement, and the Indo-Chinese Friendship Association often parrot the international Communist line, in spite of the fact that the great majority of their members are sincere non-Communists.

Women's organizations are becoming increasingly active. At times the most important of these associations, the All-India Women's Conference, has been strongly influenced by the Communists, but it is now affiliated with the Congress Party. It is primarily concerned with welfare activities and with improving the legal and social status of women. It was particularly active as a "pressure group" while the Hindu Code Bill, in its various parts, was being considered by the Indian Parliament.

The second main type of pressure groups—caste and religious groups—includes organizations which have functioned or which still function both as political parties and as associations to promote the interests of a particular group or community. These include such important "parties" as the Scheduled Castes Federation, the Akali

Dal, and even, to some degree, the Hindu Mahasabha. Organizations devoted to the interests of special religious groups include the All-India Conference of Indian Christians, the Parsi Central Association and Political League, and the Anglo-Indian Association. Caste groups are particularly numerous. The Marwari Association, for example, is dedicated to the interests of a community which has achieved a conspicuous place in the business life of India. The Harijan Sewak Sangh is one of the many associations which "work to ameliorate the social and economic status of the lower castes through legislation and social work . . . —a part of the complex of Gandhian constructive institutions." [12]

For the most part the political leaders of modern India have not been businessmen, and the policies of the Indian government since independence have placed increasing restrictions on the operations of the Indian business community. In a welfare state, dedicated to the achievement of "a socialistic pattern of society," the role of "private enterprise" is limited by the over-all objectives of national planning and development. The Indian government considers that the main function of private enterprise is to help in fulfilling the goals laid down in the Five Year Plans. Indian business leaders often complain of the restrictions which are placed upon them by nationalization and social control of economic life. Partly because of the economic exploitation of the country by foreign interests, but also because of the practices of indigenous business concerns, there is widespread aversion to "predatory capitalism" in India. Thus Indian businessmen have less scope for activity and less influence on politics than the business leaders of most democratic states. On the other hand, some businessmen have had considerable influence in Indian politics, even during the days when Gandhi controlled the independence movement. It is well known that the Mahatma, who reacted against modern industrialization and was dedicated to the *sarvodaya* society, was a close friend of a great Indian industrialist, Birla, and received substantial support from the Indian business community. In India today the concentration on economic development requires the intimate association of businessmen in all phases of planning and development.

Practically all the major industries in India have associations, and most of these are aligned with the most influential of the business organizations of India, the Federation of Indian Chambers of Commerce

[12] Overstreet and Tinker, "Political Dynamics in India," p. 18.

and Industry. "This body maintains a research office in New Delhi which approaches the status of a lobbying agency." [13]

The third variety of pressure group is in many respects unique to the Indian setting, performing functions and filling needs which affect all levels of Indian life. Their work appeals to the humblest villager and to the most sophisticated Westernized political leader.

These agencies formally disavow the normal pressure group function of influencing political institutions, seeking instead the fundamentally different goal of effecting change outside the institutional framework through creating the essential moral impetus. However, they possess great prestige and exercise significant influence through the power of example and through close personal contact with government.[14]

Most of these groups have their roots in Indian traditions and attitudes. Many of them were founded by Mahatma Gandhi or came into being under the stimulus of his teachings and example. They are designed to promote the great goal of the Mahatma of a *sarvodaya* society, classless and casteless, emphasizing the regeneration of the individual and the welfare of all, a society almost without government and formal institutions, in which voluntary constructive work would provide for most needs. In this way Gandhi hoped to bring out the best in the human spirit and to avoid the abuses and complications of modern technological life. The political leaders of independent India are departing from the spirit and practice of Gandhi's teachings, but they are conscious of the profound significance of these teachings and of the great influence that they have in the country as a whole; and they are encouraging the co-operation of Gandhian associations and movements in such aspects of the national effort as welfare work and the community development projects.

The all-encompassing association of the Gandhian constructive workers is called the Sarvodaya Samaj. The Samaj is a body of members only, however, and has no formal organization except an annual conference. The primary organized agency of the Sarvodaya movement is the Sarva Seva Sangh. . . . Affiliated with the Sarva Seva Sangh are a number of specialized groups including the All-India Village Industries' Association, the Go-Seva Sangh (a society for cow protection), the All-India Spinners Association, the Hindustani Prachar Sabha (a society for the promotion of Hindustani), and the Talimi Sangh (a society for the promotion of basic education).[15]

[13] *Ibid.*, p. 15.   [14] *Ibid.*, p. 19.   [15] *Ibid.*, p. 20.

By far the most dramatic effort to make Gandhi's ideals a living reality in Indian life is the Bhoodan Yagna Movement of Acharya Vinoba Bhave. Its purpose is to achieve a nonviolent revolution of the kind that Gandhi envisioned. Acharya Kripalani has called it "the greatest revolution since Gandhiji."

Called the Bhoodan Yagna (land gift movement) because voluntary redistribution of land was its first goal, it has since added the aims of *sampattidan* (donation of wealth), *koopdan* (donation of wells), *baildan* (donation of bullocks), and *jivandan* (donation of personal service to the cause)—all culminating in the goal of *gramdan* representing communal ownership of village land and the establishment of village democracy as envisaged by Gandhi.[16]

In the fall of 1951 Vinoba Bhave set out on foot from Sevagram on the first stage of a movement which was to attract world-wide attention and to create a tremendous stir in the Indian countryside. One of Gandhi's closest followers, he looked like a bearded Gandhi, and he wore the same scanty dress. After going to Delhi and New Delhi to explain the purpose of his movement and to dramatize it, he began a walking tour of Indian villages which won for him the sobriquet "India's Walking Saint." [17] After his initial successes in the Telengana area of Hyderabad, where Communist propaganda had produced a state of revolt, he moved to Bihar and intensified his efforts. Within a few years he had been given several million acres of land and many other gifts, including several hundred entire villages—the *gramdan* villages. Yet the economic results of the movement have been disappointing. Very little of the land has been redistributed, and much of it is of little value anyway. Bhave was not interested in developing an organization, and he expressed a desire to eschew politics; but he has been quite willing to receive the assistance and support of government authorities in his work. Several states have enacted legislation to facilitate the redistribution of the land donated to the Bhoodan Movement, and the top leaders of India, including the President, Dr. Rajendra Prasad, himself an old Gandhian from Bihar, Prime Minister Nehru, and the Vice-President, Dr. Radhakrishnan, have gone out of their way to visit Bhave and to express their approval of the movement. As has been noted, the Praja Socialist Party has been particularly interested in Bhoodan, and its outstanding leader,

[16] *Ibid.*
[17] See Hallam Tennyson, *India's Walking Saint: The Story of Vinoba Bhave* (Garden City, N.Y.: Doubleday, 1955).

Jayaprakash Narayan, is devoting himself to this work and has presumably retired from political life. Because of its great popular appeal and potentiality, the Communists are taking a special interest in the movement, although Bhave himself, like Gandhi, is a strong critic of communism and of Communist methods.

Vinoba Bhave is generally regarded as the nearest approximation to a Gandhi in India today, and his Bhoodan Movement is in the true Gandhian tradition. "Only in India, one feels, could there be such a movement. . . . It shows how powerful still is the moral force of the Gandhian outlook." [18] Although professing to be wholly non-political, it undoubtedly has a powerful influence on Indian politics. Its main significance is perhaps more spiritual than economic or political. "But whatever may be the fate of its specific program—much of which in the long run is incompatible with the prevailing modernist goals of industrialization and secularization—the Sarvodaya movement in general," and the Bhoodan Movement in particular, "represents an important predisposition to non-responsible forms of organization and action which may influence the future development of political institutions in India." [19]

[18] Lady Hartog, *India: New Pattern* (London, 1955), p. 34.
[19] Overstreet and Tinker, "Political Dynamics in India," p. 21.

· XIII ·

Economic Development

and Foreign Relations

INTERNALLY a major objective of the government of India is to increase the productive capacity and to raise the standards of living of the large and growing population. This is a task which will tax to the utmost the economic and human resources of the country. At the present time the major effort is being made through the Second Five Year Plan, which represents one of the most significant experiments in economic planning on a nation-wide scale in the world.

Externally India is interested in cultivating friendly relations with all nations, in avoiding too close commitments to any group, and in working for international peace and co-operation. In spite of the policy of "nonalignment," the leaders of India are poignantly aware of the stake which their country has in the course of world affairs and of the disastrous consequences to their country and people of another global war. It is understandable, however, that at the moment their attention is focused more on their pressing internal problems than on the world scene.

Economic Development

"The central objective of public policy and of national endeavour in India since Independence has been promotion of rapid and bal-

347

anced economic development." [1] To achieve this end, large-scale economic planning, directed and controlled by the government, has been undertaken. Even before independence the Congress Party, at Nehru's urging, established in 1938 a Planning Committee which drew upon the help not only of the Congress Party but also of numerous industrialists, labor representatives, and economists. As Frank Moraes has noted, however, "it was soon obvious to [Nehru] . . . that national planning on a comprehensive scale could only take place under a free national government prepared to introduce fundamental changes in the country's social and economic structure." [2] The resolutions passed at the annual sessions of the Congress Party, both before and after the creation of the Planning Committee in 1938, supported state intervention in the economic life of the nation. The adoption of the "socialistic pattern of society" resolution at the sixtieth annual session of the Congress Party at Avadi, Madras, in January 1955 was supported by its proponents as a logical development of Congress policy rather than as an innovation.

The constitutional basis for government action in the sphere of economic planning is found in Article 39 of Part IV, "Directive Principles of State Policy," which pledges that the state shall direct its policy toward securing:

(a) that the citizens, men and women equally, have the right to adequate means of livelihood;

(b) that the ownership and control of the material resources of the community are so distributed as best to subserve the common good; and

(c) that the operation of the economic system does not result in the concentration of wealth and means of production to the common detriment.

To translate these goals into reality, the government of India, in March 1950, established a Planning Commission, whose principal tasks were to "formulate a Plan for the most effective and balanced utilisation of the country's resources," to "appraise from time to time the progress achieved in the execution of each stage of the Plan and recommend the adjustments of policy and measures that such appraisal may show to be necessary," and to examine "the principal

---

[1] *Second Five Year Plan* (New Delhi: Government of India, Planning Commission, 1956), p. 1.

[2] Frank Moraes, *Jawaharlal Nehru* (New York: Macmillan, 1956), p. 421.

problems affecting the social and economic development of the country."

The Planning Commission has worked under the direct supervision of the government of India and especially of the National Development Council, which was set up to provide a high-level agency to consider the place of planning in the political life of the country. The importance of this co-ordinated effort in national planning is suggested by the fact that Prime Minister Nehru is chairman of both the Planning Commission and the National Development Council and has been very active in these roles. Economic planning on a national scale has also involved the closest possible co-operation between the central government and the states and between the government and the "private sector" in the country, as well as the maximum public participation and support.

In July 1951 the Planning Commission prepared a draft outline of a plan of development for the period of five years from April 1951 to March 1956. After widespread review and comment by both government and private groups and individuals, the First Five Year Plan was submitted and approved by the Parliament. It called for a total outlay of Rs. 2,069 crores (a crore is 10,000,000), or approximately $4.3 billion.[3] A major target of the planners was to increase agricultural production, particularly food grains, and irrigation facilities. A concerted effort to expand industrial production was deliberately postponed until the Second Plan in the hope that concentration on agriculture and related areas would yield a direct rise in the living standards of the people. The government had exceeding good fortune, for the monsoons during the First Plan period were good, yielding sufficient rain to ensure abundant harvests.

The over-all results of the First Five Year Plan were also encouraging. National income over the five-year period increased by some 18 per cent. Food-grain production went up by 20 per cent. The output of cotton and major oilseeds increased by 45 per cent and 8 per cent respectively. Over 6 million acres of land were brought under irrigation through major works, and another 10 million through minor works. Industrial production increased steadily. The interim index (1946 = 100) of industrial production was at 161 for 1955 as compared to 105 for 1950 and 117 for 1951. (The revised index with 1951

[3] See below, p. 351, for the final allocation of funds in the First Five Year Plan period.

as a base shows a 22 per cent increase as of 1955.) Electric power output increased from 6,575 million KWH in 1950–1951 to 11,000 million KWH in 1955–1956. The output of cement for the same period increased from 2.7 to 4.3 million tons.

One phase of the plan which attracted widespread attention was the program for community development and national extension services. According to Prime Minister Nehru, this represents one of the most exciting and important developments in India today and in time may produce a revolution in the countryside. In October 1952 55 community development projects were launched. By the end of the First Five Year Plan development schemes had been initiated in areas comprising 123,000 villages and a population of 80 million people. Community development projects were under way in 300 development blocks (each representing about 100 villages with a population of between 60,000 and 70,000 people covering an area of approximately 150 to 170 square miles), and 900 more blocks were under the National Extension Service scheme.[4] The Community Development Program and National Extension Service involved very sizable problems of financing, administration, personnel recruitment, and popular education and co-operation. In the annual evaluation report on the progress of these programs covering the final year of the First Plan period, it was noted that distinct advances had been made "in terms of provision of basic amenities needed by the people —education, health and sanitation, water supplies, communications."[5]

Although the First Five Year Plan achieved most of its objectives, its implementation revealed a number of areas where even greater effort and concentration of material resources were required. These factors came to the fore in the early stages of the drafting and implementation of the Second Five Year Plan.

The Second Plan called for an expenditure of Rs. 4,800 crores ($10 billion), an expenditure more than twice that of the First Plan. The principal objectives of the Second Plan are:

(a) a sizeable increase in national income so as to raise the level of living in the country;

---

[4] "Welfare of the Villages," *India News*, II (Jan. 26, 1957), 8; *Second Five Year Plan: A Draft Outline* (New Delhi: Government of India, Planning Commission, 1956).

[5] *Evaluation Report on Working of Community Projects and N.E.S. Blocks* (New Delhi: Government of India, Programme Evaluation Organisation, Planning Commission, 1956), p. 1.

(b) rapid industrialization with particular emphasis on the development of basic and heavy industries;

(c) a large expansion of employment opportunities;

(d) reduction of inequalities in income and wealth and a more even distribution of economic power.[6]

Table 9 sets forth comparative figures for the First and Second Five

Table 9. India's two Five Year Plans

	First Five Year Plan		Second Five Year Plan	
	Total provision	Per cent	Total provision	Per cent
	$ million		$ million	
I. Agriculture and community development	749.70	15.1	1,192.80	11.8
II. Irrigation and power	1,388.10	28.1	1,917.30	19.0
III. Industry and mining	375.90	7.6	1,869.00	18.5
IV. Transport and communications	1,169.70	23.6	2,908.50	28.9
V. Social services	1,219.30	22.6	1,984.50	19.7
VI. Miscellaneous	144.90	3.0	207.90	2.1
Total	4,947.60	100.0	10,080.00	100.0

Source: *India News,* vol. II, no. 2, Jan. 26, 1957.

Year Plans by major heads of development. The figures for the First Plan are sums already expended, those for the Second are planned. It should be noted that the total investment in the First Plan exceeded the original goal by about 15 per cent.

As implementation of the Second Plan has proceeded, the problem of resources for financing it has become critical. The total deficit envisaged by the planners over the five-year period was Rs. 1,100 crores, of which it was believed that Rs. 200 crores could be raised by withdrawal of foreign exchange reserves, leaving a net deficit of Rs. 900 crores (approximately $1.9 billion). This, it was hoped, would be met by foreign aid and loans from institutions such as the World Bank.

The heavier emphasis on industrialization, especially on heavy industry, caused India to increase sharply withdrawals from the foreign credit balance. The closing of the Suez Canal in 1956, which resulted

[6] *Second Five Year Plan: A Draft Outline,* p. 7.

in higher costs on commodities imported from the West, inflation throughout the world, and the inability of the government to raise the required amount of foreign exchange through foreign loans and aid have forced the Indian government to embark on a series of rather drastic financial measures. In October 1957 the Indian government authorized the withdrawal of all $630,000,000 of its sterling assets, held in Britain, in an attempt to solve its balance of payments problems. This, however, is at best a temporary solution since, as Finance Ministry officials noted, the sterling reserve held in Britain was the equivalent of only eight months' imports into India. The need for increased foreign aid has been delayed, but not solved. Since the required amount of foreign aid is not likely to be forthcoming, rather large cuts have already been made in the planned outlays in the Second Five Year Plan.

Other factors also have forced a scaling down of the targets of the Second Five Year Plan. Among these are a serious drought in 1957 which compelled India to import far more food than planned and "added costs of the Plan of about 20 per cent because of the rise in prices both at home and abroad." [7] The *Eastern Economist,* the leading economic journal of India, concluded that what was required was "a substantial slowing down of the rate of the development to near the 1956–57 level," and it offered the following consolation for "this hard advice": "We need not give up our higher or more exacting aspirations. One can surely pause for breath in order to run a longer race." [8] India is certainly embarked on a very long race. In spite of present difficulties, India's planners and government leaders insist that the plan must and will be pressed and that in any event "the hard core" can be saved.

Foreign Relations

In spite of pressing internal problems and the policy of nonalignment India has, since 1947, played an active and generally consistent role in foreign affairs, based on a remarkable consensus at home. Whatever outside criticisms may be made of India's foreign policy, it makes sense to most Indians who have any views at all on such matters. It has given India an influence in the world which is far

---

[7] "The State of the Plan," *Eastern Economist,* XXVIII (March 22, 1957), 422. This is a special budget number, with a Blue Supplement on "The State of the Plan."

[8] *Ibid.*

greater than India's actual power would seem to warrant, and it is almost the only policy which could win such widespread support within the country.[9]

In power-political terms India is a weak country, with few of the advantages which a nation must possess to be influential in world affairs. To be sure, it is the most populous of the democratic states, but in view of the extremely low standards of living, widespread illiteracy, and social fissures, the people are perhaps more a weakness than a source of strength at the present time. India occupies a vast territory in a strategically important part of the world, but resources are limited and there are distressing problems of internal unity. Nevertheless, India is the largest non-Communist state in Asia, the largest and most important of the "underdeveloped" countries, the leading nation in the "uncommitted" world, and a leading spokesman of the newly emergent nations, especially of the Asian-African group of states in the United Nations. India regards itself as a major bridge between East and West, whether these two terms be taken to refer to the Communist and non-Communist worlds or to Asia and the West. However irritating or shortsighted India's position of non-alignment may seem to a partisan eye, it has resulted in greater influence in the councils of the nations than association with the West would give.

UNDERLYING FACTORS

The foreign policy of India, like that of any other country, is conditioned by certain basic factors such as geographic, strategic, and historical considerations, domestic pressures and influences, and basic characteristics of national life. It is also profoundly affected by the policies and attitudes of other states and by the general course of international developments.[10]

In geographic and strategic terms India occupies a vital part of the earth's surface.[11] Since relations with Pakistan are most unsatisfactory, there is a strategic problem within the natural frontiers of the Indian subcontinent; India is also interested in removing the last vestiges of

[9] See N. D. Palmer, "India's Outlook on Foreign Affairs," *Current History*, XXX (Feb. 1956), 69.

[10] For summaries of basic factors in India's foreign policy see J. C. Kundra, *Indian Foreign Policy, 1947–1954: A Study of Relations with the Western Bloc* (Groningen, 1955); K. P. Karunakaran, *India in World Affairs, August 1947–January 1950* (Calcutta, 1952).

[11] See K. M. Panikkar, *Geographic Factors in Indian History* (Bombay, 1955).

colonial possessions within the subcontinent, as represented by the territories, notably Goa, which Portugal refuses to give up. The nation is directly concerned with the security of the Indian Ocean area, but has no immediate problem in this respect, so long as the defense of the region depends essentially upon British and American sea power, with such collateral support as the Indian navy can provide. Flanked on the north by the world's highest mountains, India would seem to be almost immune from attack from this quarter; but there is an awareness of the strategic importance of these frontiers and of the possible threat from the great powers beyond the mountain ranges, Russia and China. If Nepal and Bhutan are included within its strategic frontiers, India has the longest border which any non-Communist state shares with a Communist state, and the greatest of the Communist powers is not far to the northwest. There are "floating frontiers" both in the Ladakh section of Jammu and Kashmir and in the North-East Frontier area.

In countless ways India's long historical experience has shaped its policies as an independent state. Its leaders have been made particularly sensitive to foreign domination in a cultural and psychological as well as a political sense, and they are especially concerned with remaining aloof from great-power politics in order to concentrate on serious internal problems. India is struggling to behave externally as well as internally in keeping with its traditions and beliefs. The present policy of nonalignment may be explained almost solely in terms of present weaknesses and opportunities as related to the existing international situation; but the careful student of Indian society and history is likely to conclude that the policy has even deeper roots in the Indian past and that somehow it is linked with the great traditions of Indian philosophy and experience, such as the Buddhist teachings of the middle way, the ancient faith in *ahimsa*—meaning nonviolence in more than a physical sense—and many other Gandhian teachings based on Indian values. Many of the leaders of modern India, including Nehru himself, are inclined to shape their policies in the light of immediate considerations, such as influence the policies and actions of national leaders elsewhere, but they know that India's historical experience and traditions must shape its foreign relations, and they realize the importance of domestic considerations and pressures in shaping foreign policy.

Prior to 1947 the foreign policy of India was largely determined in

Westminster, and it did not necessarily reflect the views of India's leaders or of Indians generally. During the First World War, for example, many Indians rallied around the British war effort, and thousands of them fought in Europe and elsewhere overseas. During the Second World War, Indians again fought in Europe, North Africa, and other parts of the world, and India was officially at war with the Axis powers; but the Indian National Congress was opposed to India's involvement in the struggle, so long at least as India was not free, and throughout most of the war years it advocated a policy of noncooperation. Even though India was not independent, it was a member of the League of Nations, and many Indians gained international experience in the League councils and at various international conferences. Nevertheless, India entered the family of nations in 1947 with relatively little experience and with relatively few commitments. This proved to be both an advantage and a handicap.

FOREIGN POLICY OF THE INDIAN NATIONAL CONGRESS

Well before 1947, however, a kind of Indian foreign policy did emerge in the Indian National Congress, the spearhead of the freedom movement. One of the first resolutions passed by the Congress at its first annual session in 1885 was a protest against the annexation of Upper Burma. In 1904 the Congress protested against a recent expedition to Tibet, on the ground that it was "but part of a general forward policy, which . . . threatens to involve India in foreign entanglements." [12] Until the end of the First World War, the Congress took relatively little interest in questions of foreign policy and generally supported the British position on such issues. Immediately after the war the Congress began to take a more active and independent line, in foreign as well as in domestic policies. Resolution after resolution expressed opposition to imperialism and especially to European rule, sympathy with peoples struggling to be free, hatred of war, desire for peace, and antipathy toward foreign entanglements.

In 1925 the Congress authorized the All-India Congress Committee to establish a foreign department. Jawaharlal Nehru became head of this department and the chief spokesman of the Congress in the field of foreign affairs. Thus for a generation he has been the voice of

[12] N. V. Rajkumar, ed., *The Background of India's Foreign Policy* (Delhi, 1957), p. 37. All subsequent quotations from Congress resolutions are taken from this very useful collection.

India in foreign policy; in fact, he has established a record in this field which is unequaled by any other democratic statesman. This fact should be remembered, for it helps to explain India's remarkable consistency in foreign policy and it is a reminder that, as Nehru himself stated in 1955, "our foreign policy is not a sudden growth, but a natural outcome of our thinking for many years past." [13]

Before the outbreak of the Second World War the Congress strongly dissociated itself from British policy. A resolution of the Working Committee in August 1939 declared:

The past policy of the British Government, as well as the recent developments, demonstrate abundantly that this Government does not stand for freedom and democracy and may at any time betray these ideals. India cannot associate herself with such a Government or be asked to give her resources for democratic freedom which is denied to her and which is likely to be betrayed.

This policy was carried to the point of almost complete noncooperation during the war.

After the war, Congress resolutions welcomed the emergence of the United Nations, deplored the position allotted to the smaller nations, lent moral support to freedom movements everywhere, particularly in Asia, and deprecated the politics of the atom bomb which "has brought to a crisis the immoral and self-destructive elements of the present-day political, economic and spiritual structure of the world." Indian spokesmen, including Gandhi, Nehru, and Mrs. Sarojini Naidu, took a prominent part in the First Asian Relations Conference, held in New Delhi in April 1947.[14] In a sense this was a precursor to the conference on Indonesia which was held in New Delhi in January 1949, on the invitation of the government of India, and to the important Asian-African Conference at Bandung in April 1955, which was sponsored by the "Colombo Powers," including India. These meetings marked the growing role of Asian countries in world affairs. The idea is one which Nehru has often expressed. "In this crisis in world history," he declared at the Asian Relations Conference, "Asia will necessarily play a vital role. The countries of Asia can no longer be used as pawns by others; they are bound to have their own policies in world affairs."

[13] Address at the annual session of the Congress Party in Madras in January 1955.
[14] See *Asian Relations: A Report of the Proceedings and Documentation of the First Asian Relations Conference, New Delhi, March–April 1947* (New Delhi, 1948).

PANCH SHILA

Thus even before they assumed the responsibilities of independence, India's spokesmen had charted the broad outlines of the foreign policies which India has followed with little deviation since 1947. "The main objectives" of India's foreign policy, stated Nehru in an address at Columbia University in October 1949, are

the pursuit of peace, not through alignment with any major power or group of powers but through an independent approach to each controversial or disputed issue, the liberation of subject peoples, the maintenance of freedom, both national and individual, the elimination of racial discrimination and elimination of want, disease, and ignorance, which afflict the greater part of the world's population.

The belief that nonalignment or independence is the path to peace furnishes a partial explanation for India's aversion to the power politics and military pacts of the major powers. In a letter to the presidents of the Pradesh Congress committees in July 1954 Nehru wrote: "Peace can only be preserved by the methods of peace. A warlike approach to peace is a contradiction in terms." And military pacts represent to him "a war-like approach to peace," "a wrong approach," "a dangerous approach," which "sets in motion all the wrong tendencies and prevents the right tendencies from developing." He is particularly opposed to SEATO and the Baghdad Pact, which "apart from their being, I think, basically in the wrong direction, affect us intimately and in a sense tend to encircle us from two or three directions." [15]

Instead of relying on military pacts, Nehru recommends acceptance of the *Panch Shila*, the five principles of peace. These principles were first spelled out in the treaty between India and Communist China regarding Tibet in the spring of 1954; they were repeated in the Nehru–Chou En-lai declaration of June 1954 and in many other pronouncements which Nehru has made. They recur in the communiqué issued at the close of the Bandung Conference. The five principles are mutual respect for territorial integrity and sovereignty, nonaggression, noninterference in internal affairs, equality and mutual benefit, and peaceful coexistence. "These principles," said Nehru in December 1955 at the time of the visit of Bulganin and Khrushchev, "form the basis of our relations with other nations. If *Panch Shila* were fully

[15] Speech in the Lok Sabha on February 17, 1953.

and sincerely accepted by all countries, then peace would be assured to everyone and cooperation would follow."

A policy based upon such nebulous principles, upon "deciding each issue on its own merits," upon "independence" or nonalignment may at times be no policy at all. India's spokesmen have often been taxed with unwillingness or incapacity to recognize present dangers and real issues, with a tendency to take refuge in moral abstractions, and with naïveté or worse regarding the Soviet-Communist threat. Their policy is often characterized as one of neutralism. This is a word which they generally reject. They insist that India's policy of non-alignment is a sound policy, well suited to promote India's national interests and the cause of world peace. They indignantly deny that it is a negative or escapist policy. "I should like to make it clear," asserted Nehru in 1949, "that the policy India has sought to pursue is not a negative and neutral policy. It is a positive and vital policy that flows from our struggle for freedom and from the teachings of Mahatma Gandhi." [16]

RELATIONS WITH PAKISTAN

India's relations with Pakistan are of central importance in the total picture of India's foreign relations. Unhappily the two nations that emerged in the Indian subcontinent began their separate existences in a state of mutual tension and recrimination, and they are still at odds on several major issues and a multitude of minor ones. Josef Korbel believes that "the real cause of all the bitterness . . . is the uncompromising and perhaps uncompromisable struggle of two ways of life, two concepts of political organization, two scales of values, two spiritual attitudes that find themselves locked in deadly conflict." [17] Other observers believe that though the Indian concept of the secular state differs widely from the Pakistan concept of an Islamic state, the two nations can settle their differences amicably and co-exist peaceably in the subcontinent.

For some years before partition, relations between Hindus and Muslims, and between the Indian National Congress and the Muslim League, steadily deteriorated. Chiefly responsible were Muslim apprehensions of their future in a predominantly Hindu state and the Muslim League's urgent demand for a separate state of Pakistan.

[16] Address at Columbia University on October 17, 1949.
[17] *Danger in Kashmir* (Princeton: Princeton University Press, 1954), p. 16. See also Lord Birdwood, *Two Nations and Kashmir* (London, 1956).

The tragic circumstances of partition widened the gulf between the two new nations; "they were divided by a pool of Punjabi blood." [18] Many other issues arising from partition—notably the treatment of minorities in the two countries, problems of the settlement of claims of evacuee property, and economic difficulties—have bedeviled Indo-Pakistan relations ever since 1947. Perhaps most important of all the causes of friction, aside from underlying distrust, have been the problems of the canal waters and, above all, Kashmir.

East Pakistan usually suffers from too much water; great loss of life and property is caused by the frequent floods. Most of West Pakistan, on the other hand, suffers from too little water. At least three important rivers of the Indus River system, on which life depends in West Pakistan, flow in part through Indian territory. In 1948 an agreement was signed between India and Pakistan whereby over a period of years India would divert a good share of the water from the rivers running through Indian territory. Pakistan, with considerable financial assistance from India, would make alternate arrangements for needed water by more efficient use of the waters which run through West Pakistan and by a series of link canals. Shortly after this agreement was reached, efforts to implement it and to settle other problems arising from the canal-waters question became bogged down in endless negotiations between the two countries, in Washington and elsewhere. The International Bank for Reconstruction and Development made some specific suggestions, some of which were accepted by both parties; but the whole question is still a major issue in dispute between the two neighbors. It is likely to become even more serious as relations between the two countries harden generally and as India diverts some of the waters in question for its large multipurpose river-valley-development and irrigation schemes before Pakistan has worked out effective plans to make up the loss of the water which will result.[19]

The Kashmir question is one of the thorniest issues in contemporary international relations, even though it is not a Communist–non-Communist dispute and even though the chief disputants are fellow

[18] Taya Zinkin, "Indian Foreign Policy: An Interpretation of Attitudes," *World Politics,* VII (Jan. 1955), 188.

[19] Speaking in the Rajya Sabha on August 21, 1957, Mr. S. K. Patil, Minister for Irrigation and Power, announced that India had informed the World Bank that it would be willing to extend the transitional period with respect to the canal waters to 1962. "We cannot go any further," he added, "without jeopardizing the vital interests of millions of our people."

members of the Commonwealth who want to find a way out of the dilemma. But under present circumstances no solution seems possible. India continues to insist that all Kashmir is legitimately a part of the Union of India and that Pakistan is illegally occupying a part of Indian territory. Pakistan insists that the future of the disputed area should be determined by a plebiscite, in accordance with India's pledge in late 1947 and repeated United Nations recommendations. India apparently has withdrawn its commitment to hold a plebiscite in Kashmir, allegedly on the grounds that Pakistan would not accept the necessary preconditions for a plebiscite or withdraw its troops from "Azad Kashmir." India holds that American arms aid to Pakistan and certain other developments have changed the whole complexion of affairs. India justifies its position in Kashmir largely through the accession of the Maharajah of Kashmir to India in late October 1947 and the alleged aggression of Pakistan in Kashmir. The Indian position on this issue is, as clearly stated by President Rajendra Prasad in his address to the Parliament on March 19, 1957, that the "Jammu and Kashmir State is and has been a constituent State of the Union of India since October 1947, like other States which acceded to the Union." To Indians the inauguration of a constitution for Kashmir on January 26, 1957, was simply a formal recognition of a status which had in fact existed for nearly a decade.

Pakistan, of course, completely rejects these claims, and the Security Council of the United Nations, which has had the Kashmir question on its agenda ever since India brought it before the Council in January 1948, seems to agree with Pakistan that the future of Kashmir is still to be determined. India has been increasingly critical of the UN's position on this question and especially of the position taken by Britain and the United States in debates and votes in the Security Council. Thus India's attitude on this issue has hardened at a time when Pakistan's spokesmen and many of its people are becoming increasingly vehement on Kashmir.

Until some agreement is reached regarding the status of Kashmir, relations between India and Pakistan will continue to be jeopardized by tension and suspicion, with even some danger of an explosion in the subcontinent. If an amicable agreement could be reached on this issue, Indo-Pakistan relations generally might be very much improved; and in a more relaxed atmosphere the two countries could reduce their defense expenditures, deal more hopefully with the other issues in dispute between them, and concentrate more effectively on basic problems of economic development, social welfare, and political survival.

OTHER ASPECTS OF FOREIGN RELATIONS

India is also greatly concerned about relations with other near neighbors, notably Nepal, Burma, Ceylon, Afghanistan, and the two great Communist powers whose vast territories extend to, or close to, the frontiers of India. The Indian attitude toward the Soviet Union and communism has often been characterized as ambivalent, although to most Indians it seems consistent. The example of Soviet Russia has exercised an almost hypnotic fascination for many Indians, few of whom are Communists. They are particularly impressed with the success of the Soviet efforts to change Russia within a remarkably short space of time from an underdeveloped country to one of the two most powerful states of the world. They also admire Soviet policies toward nationalities within the borders of the USSR and toward Asians generally. They tend to exaggerate the successes of the Soviet experiment and to minimize or ignore the costs in human terms. India has posed as the leading champion of Communist China's claims to membership in the United Nations and to a major role in world affairs. Indian spokesmen have been assiduous in cultivating the leaders of the People's Republic of China, in playing upon the theme of the long friendship between the two great Asian countries, and in emphasizing the doctrine of peaceful coexistence as embodied in the *Panch Shila.* They are undoubtedly aware of the fact that India and China are trying to deal with essentially the same problems in fundamentally different ways and that the future of communism and democracy in Asia may be determined in large part by the relative success or failure of these two great experiments; but they are inclined to emphasize areas of agreement rather than zones of competition. The low point in relations between India and Communist China came in 1950, when Chinese Communist troops occupied Tibet. India protested vigorously then and subsequently has showed a special concern for the security of its Himalayan frontiers and for its relations with Nepal.

India has sought to cultivate close relations with the Arab states of the Middle East and especially with Egypt. In part this may be due to a desire to thwart any ambitions which Pakistan might entertain of leadership in the Muslim world. As would be expected, the Indian leaders sharply denounced the British and French intervention in Egypt in the fall of 1956. They were slower and less vehement in criticizing the Soviet Union for its brutal repression of the uprising in Hungary, which preceded the Suez crisis by a few days.

Many people of Indian origin live outside India, mainly in Ceylon, Burma, Malaya, and East and South Africa. Relations between India and these countries have often been colored by the treatment of these people. India has shown a special solicitude for their welfare, even though the Indian government has never claimed them as Indian citizens. This question has been a source of particular tension between India and Ceylon and South Africa. In South Africa, Gandhi first experimented with the techniques of *satyagraha* which he later applied with such effect in India. The position of persons of Indian origin in South Africa has become a matter of world concern as a result of recent policies in the Union of South Africa, policies known as apartheid. Frequent discussions of the problem have occurred in the United Nations, with India in a leading role, and India has given continuous attention to the problem.[20]

Outside of South Africa, Indian interest in African developments has been expressed in many ways. Indians have maintained concern for persons of Indian origin in Kenya, Uganda, and elsewhere in East Africa; in the United Nations they have taken a special interest in the status of peoples of trust territories and nonself-governing areas; they have strongly supported the nationalist movements in the continent, especially the recent movements in Tunisia, Morocco, and Algeria; and they have welcomed the new states that have emerged in Africa. India seems to regard itself as a special champion and protector of the newly independent and still-dependent peoples of Africa, and African nationalist leaders look to India for guidance and support.

With independence, relations between India and Britain naturally took on an entirely different complexion, but the two countries are still bound by many ties, both tangible and intangible. Notwithstanding all the differences in culture and outlook and the bitter feeling that inevitably developed between a subject people and a paramount power, the British impact upon India was a profound one, and its influence is manifest today in countless ways. India's political, administrative, legal, and educational systems are based on British models. Even attitudes of mind and patterns of political behavior reflect the impact of the British connection. Free India chose to remain within

[20] See Karunakaran, *India in World Affairs,* ch. vii.

the Commonwealth, even after becoming a republic in January 1950. It has many economic ties with Britain. It is a member of the sterling area, and its currency is tied to the British pound. After the war India had large sterling balances, steadily drawn upon in recent years, chiefly for purposes of economic development.

Relations with the United States have assumed a growing importance since the Second World War and particularly since India became independent. Indians have been quite outspoken in their criticisms of certain aspects of United States foreign policy. They have accused the United States of concentrating too heavily on the "so-called" Soviet-Communist threat and of giving insufficient attention to other problems, including the struggles of undeveloped areas to achieve political freedom and economic security. They have charged that the United States relies too heavily on "wrong approaches" to peace, such as military pacts and "collective security." They have been critical of American policy in Asia, particularly of American support of reactionary regimes and of colonial policies; they suspect American protestations of sympathy with independence movements and dislike American policy toward both Communist and Nationalist China. They have argued that the United States has harmed them in areas of their most immediate concern; and they point to policies such as arms aid to Pakistan, American criticism of the Indian position on the Kashmir question, and American encouragement of the formation of SEATO and the Baghdad Pact, which in their eyes bring the cold war to the very frontiers of India. (This presumably implies that it was far away before!) In spite of all these disagreements, however, relations between India and the United States have been generally good; there is a vast reservoir of mutual good will, interest, and respect between the leading democratic states of the East and the West.[21]

Despite India's policy of nonalignment, its spokesmen have not been reluctant to express their views on many international issues or to participate in a wide variety of co-operative international endeavors. Apparently they see their major role as mediatory, helping to bridge the gulf between the Communist and non-Communist worlds, between Asia and the West, between the developed and underdeveloped countries. India assumed important mediatory or

[21] See Phillips Talbot and S. L. Poplai, *India and America* (New York: Harper, for the Council on Foreign Relations, 1958). This volume is based to a large extent on the data papers and discussions of two study groups, one set up by the Council on Foreign Relations in New York, the other by the Indian Council of World Affairs in New Delhi.

supervisory roles in Korea and Indo-China and at many international conferences. It has not hesitated to join international associations of a nonmilitary nature. It is a member of the Commonwealth, perhaps the most successful of all international associations, even though the central member is the former ruling power and even though it is bound in this association with two "unfriendly" countries, Pakistan and the Union of South Africa. India is one of the "Colombo Powers" and is a leading participant in and beneficiary of the Colombo Plan. It belongs to the sterling area, a unique international economic grouping, and in many respects is the leader of the Asian-African group in the United Nations. Its role in the UN has been a conspicuous and busy one. India attaches great importance to the world organization, which it regards as primarily an agency for the peaceful settlement of disputes and for international co-operation on the broadest possible front. Indian spokesmen tend to minimize the responsibilities of the UN with regard to maintaining peace and resisting aggression and to emphasize the UN's potential in the advancement of human rights and fundamental freedoms.[22]

Thus India is both a committed and an uncommitted nation. It believes that there is no conflict between the brand of nationalism for which it stands and the cause of international co-operation. India is allergic to military arrangements but not to international commitments of other sorts. This position was reaffirmed by Jawaharlal Nehru in July 1957. Speaking in the Lok Sabha, he said: "Broadly speaking, I am against breaking of any kind of associations of nations. I want more associations and not less."

SUGGESTED READING

IX: The Political Heritage of Modern India

GOVERNMENT AND POLITICS IN THE PRE-BRITISH PERIOD

Altekar, A. S. *State and Government in Ancient India.* Benares, 1949. Demonstrates that monarchy was not the only form of government known to ancient India.

Basham, A. L. *The Wonder That Was India: A Survey of the Culture of the Sub-Continent before the Coming of the Muslims.* London, 1954. Especially ch. iv, "The State: Political Life and Thought." One of the most comprehensive one-volume treatments of Indian history, culture, and institutions.

[22] See *ibid.*, chs. viii–xi, and *India and the United Nations* (New York: Manhattan Publishing Co., 1957), a report of a study group set up by the Indian Council of World Affairs in New Delhi.

Brown, D. MacKenzie, *The White Umbrella: Indian Political Thought from Manu to Gandhi.* Berkeley: University of California Press, 1953. Part One, "Ancient Political Thought," contains a brief commentary on "The Nature of Indian Thought" and excerpts from four classics of the Hindu period: the *Manu Samhita*, the *Santiparvan* of the *Mahabharata*, Kautilya's *Arthasastra*, and the *Sukraniti*.

Ghoshal, U. N. *A History of Hindu Political Theories—From the Earliest Times to the End of the First Quarter of the Seventeenth Century A.D.* 2d ed. London, 1927. A widely known work, first published in 1923.

Jayaswal, K. P. *Hindu Policy—A Constitutional History of India in Hindu Times.* Calcutta, 1924. Jayaswal is a leading exponent of the thesis that "republican institutions" existed in ancient India.

Kautilya. *Arthasastra.* Trans. by R. Shamasastry. 4th ed. Mysore, 1951. An Indian political classic, the work of "the greatest exponent of the art of government, the duties of kings, ministers, and officials, and the methods of diplomacy."

Majumdar, R. C., and A. D. Pusalker, eds. *The Age of Imperial Unity.* (*The History and Culture of the Indian People,* vol. II.) 2d ed. Bombay, 1953. Ch. xvii, "Political Theory and Administrative System," by Beni Prasad, is particularly recommended.

Majumdar, R. C., H. C. Raychaudhuri, and Kalikinkar Datta. *An Advanced History of India.* London, 1950. A standard work.

Moreland, W. H., and A. C. Chatterjee. *A Short History of India.* 3d ed. London, 1953. A well-known brief history, chiefly political.

Prasad, Beni. *The State in Ancient India—A Study in the Structure and Practical Working of Political Institutions in North India in Ancient Times.* Allahabad, 1928.

Sarkar, Sir J. *Mughal Administration.* 3d ed. Calcutta, 1935. An excellent brief survey.

Sherwani, H. K. *Studies in Muslim Political Thought and Administration.* 2d ed. Lahore, 1945. Especially ch. ix, "Syed Ahmad Khan."

Srivastava, A. L. *The Mughal Empire, 1526–1803.* 2d ed. Agra, 1957. Emphasizes administrative and social aspects of Mughal rule.

GOVERNMENT AND POLITICS IN THE BRITISH PERIOD

Birdwood, Christopher Bromhead, Baron. *A Continent Experiments.* London, 1946. The last years of British rule in India, described by a man who held high rank in the British Indian army.

Campbell-Johnson, Alan. *Mission with Mountbatten.* London, 1951. A valuable account by Lord Mountbatten's private secretary.

Coupland, Sir Reginald. *India: A Re-statement.* London, 1945. A brief commentary by a recognized authority.

——. *The Indian Problem: Report on the Constitutional Problem in India.* London, 1944. 3 vols. in 1. Vol. I, "The Indian Problem, 1833–1935";

vol. II, "Indian Politics, 1936–1942"; vol. III, "The Future of India." A constitutional history of India during an eventful century.

Dodwell, H. H. F., ed. *The Indian Empire, 1858–1919, with Chapters on the Development of Administration, 1818–58. (The Cambridge History of India,* vol. VI.) Cambridge, Eng., 1932.

Griffiths, Sir Percival J. *The British Impact on India.* London, 1952. A remarkably objective treatment by a Britisher who had long experience in India.

——. *The British in India.* London, 1946. A brief history.

Keith, A. B. *A Constitutional History of India, 1600–1935.* 2d ed. London, 1926. A standard work.

Lumby, E. W. R. *The Transfer of Power in India, 1945–47.* London, 1954. An excellent brief survey.

Menon, V. P. *The Transfer of Power in India.* Princeton: Princeton University Press, 1957. A detailed study by a prominent Indian civil servant who participated in many of the events which he describes.

Moreland, W. H., and A. C. Chatterjee. *A Short History of India.* 3d ed. London, 1953. Especially good on constitutional questions.

O'Malley, L. S. S., ed. *Modern India and the West: A Study of the Interaction of Their Civilizations.* London, 1941. An astute interpretation.

Proceedings of the Round Table Conference. 3 sessions, 1931–1932. Cmd. 3778; Cmd. 3997; Cmd. 4238.

Report of the Indian Statutory Commission, 1930. Cmd. 3568–3569. Report of the Simon Commission.

Report on Indian Constitutional Reforms, 1918. Cmd. 9109. Montagu-Chelmsford report.

Singh, Gurmukh Nihal. *Landmarks in Indian Constitutional and National Development,* vol. I, 1600–1919. 3d ed. Delhi, 1952. By a respected Indian political scientist and government official. Widely used in India.

Tinker, Hugh R. *The Foundations of Local Self-Government in India, Pakistan, and Burma.* London, 1954. Especially good for the period 1882–1937.

Woodruff, Philip (pseud. for Philip Mason). *The Men Who Ruled India.* Vol. I, *The Founders of Modern India.* London, 1953. Vol. II, *The Guardians.* London, 1954. Delightful studies, emphasizing the role of leading personalities.

THE NATIONALIST MOVEMENT

Banerjea, Sir Surendranath. *A Nation in the Making: Being the Reminiscences of Fifty Years of Public Life.* London, 1925. The memoirs of one of the founders and early leaders of the Indian National Congress.

Buch, M. A. *Rise and Growth of Indian Militant Nationalism.* Baroda, 1940. Throws light on less-publicized aspects of the Indian nationalist movement.

Desai, A. R. *Social Background of Indian Nationalism.* Bombay, 1948. An excellent historical and sociological analysis.

Lajpat Rai, Lala. *Young India: An Interpretation and a History of the Nationalist Movement from Within.* New York: H. B. W. Huebsch, 1916. By a prominent nationalist leader.

Lovett, Sir Harrington Verney. *A History of the Indian Nationalist Movement.* London, 1920. A stanch defense of the thesis that "Britain cannot abdicate her responsibilities" in India. The author spent nearly 35 years in India as an ICS officer.

Moraes, Frank. *Jawaharlal Nehru: A Biography.* New York: Macmillan, 1956. A "life and times" biography, and hence in effect a history of modern India.

Nehru, Jawaharlal. *The Discovery of India.* New York: John Day, 1946. Written in prison in 1944; reflections on Indian history, society, and national character.

——. *Toward Freedom: The Autobiography of Jawaharlal Nehru.* New York: John Day, 1942. Provides revealing insights into the personality of the most important of living Indian statesmen.

Sitaramayya, P. B. *The History of the Indian National Congress (1885–1935).* Allahabad, 1935. The standard official history, by a prominent member of the Congress.

——. *The Nationalist Movement in India.* Bombay, 1950. The author was a leading figure in the nationalist movement in its last phases.

Tendulkar, D. G. *Mahatma: Life of Mohandas Karamchand Gandhi.* 8 vols. Bombay, 1951–1954. A detailed record of the life and teachings of the greatest of modern Indians, the "Father of the Nation."

X: India since Independence

GENERAL WORKS

Birdwood, Christopher Bromhead, Baron. *India and Pakistan: A Continent Decides.* New York: Praeger, 1954. Extensive discussions of internal and external problems; eight chapters on Kashmir.

Griffiths, Sir Percival. *Modern India.* (Nations of the World series.) New York: Praeger, 1957. One of the best volumes on India since independence.

Hartog, Mabel Helene, Lady. *India: New Pattern.* London, 1955. Impressions of the "New India" by one who knew the "Old India" well.

Lyon, Jean. *Just Half a World Away: My Search for the New India.* New York: Crowell, 1954. Penetrating and well-written observations, on major political and social changes now under way in India.

Mellor, Andrew. *India since Partition.* New York: Praeger, 1951. A brief popular report.

Menon, V. P. *The Story of the Integration of the Indian States.* New York: Macmillan, 1956. The definitive work, by Vallabhbhai Patel's right-hand man in the States Ministry.

Trumbull, Robert. *As I See India.* New York: Sloane Associates, 1956. The author was *New York Times* correspondent in India for seven years.

Vivek (pseud. for A. D. Gorwala). *India without Illusions.* Bombay, 1953. Articles by a well-known Indian columnist, reprinted from *The Times of India,* Dec. 1950–June 1953.

Wallbank, T. Walter. *India in the New Era: A Study of the Origin and Development of the Indian Union and Pakistan.* Chicago: Scott, Foresman, 1951. An excellent historical survey.

White Paper on Indian States. Rev. ed. Government of India, Ministry of States, March 1950. First edition was revised in July 1948. An official report on a major achievement.

Wofford, Clare, and Harris Wofford. *India Afire.* New York: John Day, 1951. Personal impressions of the Indian "revolution" by two Americans.

THE CONSTITUTIONAL SYSTEM

Appleby, Paul H. *Public Administration in India: Report of a Survey.* Delhi: Manager of Publications, 1953. A widely discussed report by an American expert.

Basu, D. D. *Commentary on the Constitution of India.* 3d ed. 2 vols. Calcutta, 1955. A detailed commentary.

Gledhill, Alan. *Fundamental Rights in India,* London, 1955. A legal analysis by a well-known British authority on Indian jurisprudence.

——. *The Republic of India: The Development of Its Laws and Constitution.* London, 1951.

Gorwala, A. D. *Report on Public Administration.* Government of India, Planning Commission, 1951. A famous public document.

Jennings, Sir W. Ivor. *Some Characteristics of the Indian Constitution.* Madras, 1953. Lectures at the University of Madras in 1952.

Joshi, G. N. *The Constitution of India.* 3d ed. London, 1954. One of the best and most substantial commentaries.

Lal, A. B., ed. *The Indian Parliament.* Allahabad, 1956. Among the many contributors are Indian M.P.'s and others with first-hand experience in the workings of parliamentary institutions in India.

Majumdar, B., ed. *Problems of Public Administration in India.* (Indian Political Science Association, publ. no. 1.) Patna, 1954. Contains papers by many authors.

Morris-Jones, W. H. *Parliament in India.* Philadelphia: University of Pennsylvania Press, 1957. The best treatment of the Indian Parliament.

Report of the States Reorganization Commission, 1955. Detailed recommendations for the political reorganization of India, with valuable background material.

Sharma, M. P. *Local Self-Government in India.* 2d ed. Bombay, 1951. A brief text.

Singh, Trilochan. *Indian Parliament* (*1952–57*). New Delhi, 1954.

Srinivasan, N. *Democratic Government in India.* Calcutta, 1954. Traces the development of parliamentary government in India and presents a concise summary of the salient features of the constitution of 1950.

Subramania Ayyar, C. S. *Planning the Indian Welfare State: A Study of the Constitutional Aspects of India's First Five-Year Plan.* Madras, 1954. A legal analysis, with frequent quotations from leading cases.

XI: Political Parties in India

Bhargava, G. S. *Leaders of the Left.* Bombay, 1951. Personal portraits.

Chatterjee, N. C. *Awakening of India: Problems of Today.* New Delhi, 1952. By a leader of the Hindu Mahasabha.

Curran, J. A., Jr. *Militant Hinduism in Indian Politics: A Study of the R.S.S.* New York: Institute of Pacific Relations, 1951. Mimeograph. A concise study of the Rashtriya Swayamsevak Sangh.

Kautsky, John. H. *Moscow and the Communist Party of India: A Study in the Postwar Evolution of Communist Strategy.* Cambridge, Mass.: Technology Press, and New York: Wiley, 1956. An analysis of the gyrations in the party line of the CPI against the background of international Communist strategy and tactics.

Lakhanpal, P. S. *History of the Congress Socialist Party.* Lahore, 1946.

Lal Bahadur. *The Muslim League: Its History, Activities, and Achievements.* Agra, 1954.

Madhok, Balraj. *Dr. Syama Prasad Mookerjee: A Biography.* New Delhi, 1954. A biography of a prominent Bengali educator and politician, who occupied high positions in the Indian National Congress and who was the founder and president of the Bharatiya Jan Sangh.

Masani, M. R. *The Communist Party of India: A Short History.* London, 1954. A brief but comprehensive study, with effective use of Communist documents.

Mehta, Asoka. *Democratic Socialism: Mid-Twentieth Century Synthesis.* 2d ed. Hyderabad, 1954. By one of the chief spokesmen and a leading theoretician of the Praja Socialist Party.

Nehru-Jayaprakash Talks. Bombay, 1953. Issued by the Praja Socialist Party. An important exchange of views in 1953, which attracted nation-wide attention and comment.

Overstreet, Gene D., and Irene Tinker. "Political Dynamics in India." Berkeley, Calif.: Modern India Project, Univ. of Calif., March 1957. Mimeograph based on a chapter prepared for the India volume of the Country Survey Series published by the Human Relations Area Files.

Prakash, Indra. *A Review of the History and Work of the Hindu Mahasabha and the Hindu Sanghatan Movement.* New Delhi, 1952.

Rajkumar, N. V. *Indian Political Parties.* New Delhi, 1948. Published by the All-India Congress Committee.

Rudolph, Susanne H. *The Action Arm of the Indian National Congress: The Pradesh Congress Committee. The All-India Congress Committee and the Annual Congress Session. The Working Committee of the Indian Congress Party: Its Forms, Organization, and Personnel.* Cambridge: Massachusetts Institute of Technology, Center for International Studies, 1955. Mimeograph. Three detailed studies.

Sitaramayya, P. B. *The History of the Indian National Congress (1885–1935).* Allahabad, 1935. A detailed official history, by a leading Congressman.

Weiner, Myron. *Party Politics in India: The Development of a Multi-Party System.* Princeton: Princeton University Press, 1957. Emphasizes Socialist and communalist parties; also contains considerable material on general trends in the party system in India.

XII: Political Dynamics

ELECTIONS AND ELECTORAL PROCEDURES

All India Election Guide. Madras, 1956. A reference book published on the eve of India's second general elections.

India, Election Commission. *Report on the First General Elections in India, 1951–52.* New Delhi, 1955. 2 vols. Vol. I, General; vol. II, Statistical.

"The Indian Experience with Democratic Elections," *Indian Press Digests,* Monograph Series no. 3, Dec. 1956. Summaries of first general elections and by-elections between 1952 and 1957.

Kogekar, S. V., and Richard L. Park, eds. *Reports on the Indian General Elections, 1951–52.* Bombay, 1956. Published under the auspices of the Indian Political Science Association. Reports on the first general elections in each of the Indian States.

Mehta, Asoka. *The Political Mind of India.* Bombay, 1952. Analysis of first general elections by a prominent Indian Socialist.

——. "The Political Mind of India," *Foreign Affairs,* XXXV (July 1957), 679–688. Comments on results of the second general elections in 1957.

Monthly Public Opinion Surveys. Issued by the Indian Institute of Public Opinion, New Delhi. "The Indian General Elections: An Analysis of Political Opinion Based on India's First Gallup Poll," vol. II, nos. 16, 17, 18, and 19 (Jan., Feb., March, and April 1957).

Park, Richard L. "Indian Election Results," *Far Eastern Survey,* XXI (May 1952), 61–70.

Poplai, S. L., ed. *National Politics and 1957 Elections in India.* Delhi, 1957. Published on eve of second general elections; contains policy statements and election manifestoes of the four major parties and an informative commentary on "Parties between the Elections" by Sisir Gupta.

Rajkumar, N. V., ed. *The Pilgrimage and After: The Story of How the Congress Fought and Won the General Elections.* New Delhi, 1952. Issued by All-India Congress Committee.

Roach, James R. "India's 1957 Elections," *Far Eastern Survey,* XXVI (May 1957), 65–78.

Sharma, Bodh Raj. *Report on Elections in the Punjab.* Jullundur, 1952.

Singh Sud, S. P., and Ajit Singh Sud. *Indian Elections and Legislators.* Ludhiana, 1953.

Tinker, Irene, and Mil Walker. "The First General Elections in India and Indonesia," *Far Eastern Survey,* XXV (July 1956), 97–110.

Venkatarangaiya, M. *The General Election in the City of Bombay, 1952.* Bombay, 1953.

PUBLIC OPINION AND PRESSURE GROUPS

Misra, B. R. *V for Vinoba.* Calcutta, 1956. Examines "the significance of the Bhoodan movement in the context of the agrarian problems of Indian economy." The author is a great admirer of Vinoba Bhave.

Monthly Public Opinion Surveys. Issued by the Indian Institute of Public Opinion, New Delhi. The following surveys are particularly valuable and pertinent:

  Vol. I, no. 1. "The Structure of Indian Political Opinion."

  Vol. I, no. 3. "Attitudes towards Caste, Class, and Social Rights."

  Vol. I, no. 4. "The Understanding of the Plans and Community Development."

  Vol. I, no. 5. "The Character of the Indian Middle-Classes."

  Vol. I, no. 6. "Attitudes to Unemployment."

  Vol. I, nos. 7, 8, and 9. "Cold War Controversies."

  Vol. I, nos. 10, 11, and 12. "The Measurement of Attitudes to the Private and Public Sectors and the Socialist Pattern of Society."

  Vol. II, nos. 16, 17, 18, and 19. "The Indian General Elections: An Analysis of Political Opinion Based on India's First Gallup Poll."

Overstreet, Gene D., and Irene Tinker. "Political Dynamics in India." Berkeley, Calif.: Modern India Project, Univ. of Calif., March 1957. Especially the sections on "Political Awareness and Activity in India" and "Pressure Groups."

Singvi, Laxmi M., and Bidyut K. Sarkar. *India: Government and Politics.* New Haven: Human Relations Area Files, 1955. Especially ch. iii, "Political Dynamics."

Tennyson, Hallam. *India's Walking Saint: The Story of Vinoba Bhave.* Garden City, N.Y.: Doubleday, 1955. An intimate picture of Vinoba Bhave and his Bhoodan Yagna Movement, by a sympathetic Englishman.

XIII: *Economic Development and Foreign Relations*

ECONOMIC DEVELOPMENT

Chandra, J. G. *India's Socialistic Pattern of Society.* Delhi, 1956. With a foreword by U. N. Dhebar, president of the Congress Party. A valuable exposition of the official viewpoint.

Eastern Economist, XXVIII (March 22, 1957). Special budget number, with a Blue Supplement on "The State of the Plan." Almost every issue of the *Eastern Economist,* published in New Delhi, contains valuable information and comments on economic development and planning in India.

Economic Development with Stability: A Report to the Government of India by a Mission of the International Monetary Fund. Washington, D.C.: International Monetary Fund, 1953. A survey of development problems and fiscal policies.

Evaluation Report on Working of Community Projects and N.E.S. Blocks. New Delhi: Government of India, Programme Evaluation Organization, Planning Commission, 1956.

First Five Year Plan. People's ed. New Delhi: Government of India, Planning Commission, Jan. 1953.

Fisher, Margaret W., and Joan V. Bondurant. "Indian Approaches to a Socialist Society," *Indian Press Digests,* Monograph Series no. 2, 1956. A useful compilation and analysis of Indian viewpoints.

Gadgil, D. R. *Economic Policy and Development.* New York: Institute of Pacific Relations, 1955. Includes several essays on problems of economic development in India, by a leading Indian economist.

Monthly Public Opinion Surveys. Issued by the Indian Institute of Public Opinion, New Delhi. "The Understanding of the Plans and Community Development," vol. I, no. 4; "The Measurement of Attitudes to the Private and Public Sectors and the Socialistic Pattern of Society," vol. I, nos. 10, 11, and 12.

Planning Commission, Government of India. *The New India: Progress through Democracy.* New York: Macmillan, 1958. An attempt "to set out for readers abroad the underlying approach and main features of India's economic and social programs." Prepared at request of the Planning Commission by a special study group, including two representatives of the Ford Foundation.

Second Five Year Plan: A Draft Outline. Government of India, Planning Commission, Feb. 1956.

Sovani, N. V. *Planning of Post-War Economic Development in India.* Poona, 1951. A study of government planning of economic development during the period 1947–1950, with suggestions for future planning.

Vakil, C. N., and P. R. Brahmananda. *Planning for an Expanding Economy: Accumulation, Employment, and Technical Progress in Underdeveloped*

Countries. Bombay, 1956. Contains a critical evaluation of the Second Five Year Plan.

——. *Planning for a Shortage Economy: The Indian Experiment*. Bombay, 1952. An analysis of the First Five Year Plan, by two prominent Indian economists.

FOREIGN RELATIONS

Gupta, Karunakar. *India's Foreign Policy in Defence of National Interest*. Calcutta, 1956.

India and the Commonwealth. 2 vols. Prepared for the Commonwealth Relations Conference, 1954, Lahore. New Delhi, 1954. Vol. I, Political and Strategic, by K. P. Karunakaran; vol. II, Economic, by B. N. Ganguli.

India and the United Nations. (National Studies on International Organization series, sponsored by the Carnegie Endowment for International Peace.) New York: Manhattan Publishing Co., 1957. Report of a study group set up by the Indian Council of World Affairs.

Karunakaran, K. P. *India in World Affairs, August 1947–January 1950*. Calcutta, 1952. The first of a series of volumes on "India in World Affairs," sponsored by the Indian Council of World Affairs.

Kundra, J. C. *Indian Foreign Policy, 1947–1954: A Study of Relations with the Western Bloc*. Groningen, 1955. An objective and informative study.

Levi, Werner. *Free India in Asia*. Minneapolis: University of Minnesota Press, 1952.

Palmer, N. D. "India's Outlook on Foreign Affairs," *Current History*, XXX (Feb. 1956), 65–72.

Rajkumar, N. V., ed. *The Background of India's Foreign Policy*. New Delhi, 1952. Issued by All-India Congress Committee. A useful compilation of the resolutions of the Indian National Congress on foreign policy and international affairs, from 1885 to 1952.

Rosinger, L. K. *India and the United States: Political and Economic Relations*. New York: Macmillan, 1950.

Singri, Laxmi M., and Bidyut K. Sarkar. *India: Government and Politics*. New Haven: Human Relations Area Files, 1955. Contains ten chapters on foreign relations, prepared by Bidyut Sarkar.

Sundaram, Lanka. *India in World Politics: A Historical Analysis and Appraisal*. Delhi, 1944.

Talbot, Phillips, and S. L. Poplai. *India and America*. New York: Harper, for the Council on Foreign Relations, 1958. Based on discussions and conclusions of two study groups, one set up by the Indian Council of World Affairs, the other by the Council on Foreign Relations.

Zinkin, Taya. "Indian Foreign Policy: An Interpretation of Attitudes," *World Politics*, VII (Jan. 1955), 179–208.

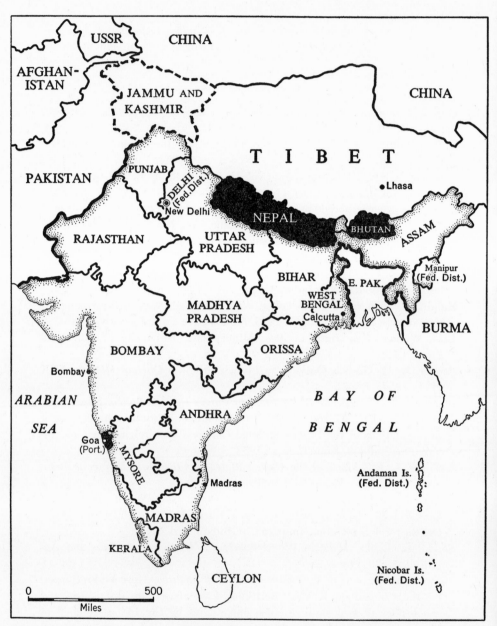

Map 8. India and Pakistan in 1956. (From *The Far East,* by Fred Greene, copyright 1957, Rinehart & Co., Inc.)

PART FOUR : PAKISTAN

By Keith Callard

· XIV ·

Pakistan and Its Origin

IN AUGUST 1947 the name Pakistan appeared for the first time on the map of the world. Pakistan is not merely a new state, claiming a status of sovereign equality among nations, but a new people and a new territory. At no time in previous history had the two wings of modern Pakistan shared a common identity, whether ethnic, political, linguistic, or economic. East and West Pakistan comprise two large pieces of former Indian territory which have one feature in common— a population that is predominantly Muslim.

The process of dividing India into two new states was bitter, bloody, and costly beyond measure. The majority of India's inhabitants had no wish to see their country partitioned. They believed that, given independence and good will, a free, democratic, and progressive state could be built in which every Indian would find a place. The Muslims, one-quarter of the total, refused to co-operate. They claimed to be a separate nation, having nothing in common with the Hindu majority except the accident of living in the same country. Even though they lived together in one village and might see each other every day of their lives, Muslim and Hindu were never part of the same community. They differed in religion, in morals, in diet, in dress, in education, in family laws. They did not eat in one another's houses, and their children did not intermarry. Under such circumstances, physical nearness bred suspicion, not comradeship.

377

The prospect of the end of British rule brought apprehension to many Muslims. On the one hand it meant freedom and independence; but on the other it might mean the permanent status of a minority under the domination of an alien and unsympathetic majority. Mohammed Ali Jinnah, who is rightly called the founder of Pakistan, said: "We are opposed to a united India constitution with Central Government, Federal or otherwise. We are opposed to this because it will mean our transfer from the British *raj* to the Hindu *raj*. A united India means a Hindu racial and cultural majority dominating over Muslims whose civilisation, culture and social structure of life is totally different." [1]

The Mughal Empire

The earliest Muslim influence reached the shores of India in the seventh and eighth centuries, and Sindh was under the rule of an Arab commander by 712. Apart from this enclave in the extreme northwest, establishment of Muslim power in India really began with the conquests of Mahmud of Ghazni. In the early part of the eleventh century Mahmud annexed the Punjab and carried out raids to the west and south. A hundred and fifty years later the Ghaznavid power was overthrown by another Turkish dynasty—the Ghuris—who captured Delhi in 1193 and established control of most of northern India. The latter part of the fourteenth and the early fifteenth century witnessed the breakup of Turkish rule and the division of power among a series of small kingdoms. A wide area of dominion was established by the Lodi kings (1451–1526).

Substantial areas of India had been ruled by Muslims for five hundred years before the beginning of the Mughal empire. Babur, the first Emperor, captured Delhi and Agra in 1526, and his grandson Akbar (reign 1556–1605) extended the rule of the Mughals over the greater part of northern and central India. The Mughals were Central Asians who came to India by way of Afghanistan. They came as conquerors over the Khyber Pass, seeking to possess the riches of the Indian peninsula. They were sustained by a strong martial faith which made the subjugation of the infidel appear an act of piety. The India that was their prey was a land of an ancient and varied civilization, superior in material wealth and intellectual subtlety to the Central Asian homeland of the Mughals. As the invaders settled, they learned

[1] Jamil-ud-Din Ahmad, ed., *Some Recent Speeches and Writings of Mr. Jinnah*, II (Lahore: Shaikh Muhammad Ashraf, 1947), 380.

much from their new subjects. Akbar was a man of tolerance, which he demonstrated by attempting to found a new, composite religion.

The reign of Aurangzeb (1658–1707) was marked by a new adherence to strict Islamic orthodoxy. Under his successors, the Mughal court was remarkable for magnificence and debauchery rather than tolerance and sound administration. From this same time the power of the empire began to decay. The peacock throne remained the symbol of authority, but its effective strength was limited by overambitious viceroys, the increasing claims of the European foreigner, and the rebellion of Maratha and Sikh princes. The Mughals and their subordinates remained a ruling class, but they were surrounded by corruption, treason, and decay. Following the battle of Plassey (1757) the preponderance of power passed to the East India Company. In 1858, after the turmoil of the Mutiny,[2] the trappings of the Mughal court were swept away, and the ninety years of direct British rule began.[3]

British Rule

The next half century held depression and uncertainty for Muslim interests. Before 1858 the vestiges of the Mughal empire, anachronistic though it had become, had allowed Muslims to feel that they were still a ruling group. The conduct of official business in Persian (the court language) and the persistence of Islamic law in personal matters had given employment to Muslims educated in the old style and having a knowledge of Arabic, Persian, and Urdu. Direct British administration, which had been extending itself for eighty years, meant that the government carried on more of its functions in the English language and through legal and administrative devices established by Englishmen. Indians who desired a career in government service therefore had to know English and possess some of the elements of a Western-style education.

In these matters the Hindu proved himself much more adaptable than the Muslim. The Hindu had learned Persian as a language foreign to his culture and background: he was quite prepared to abandon

[2] The uprising of 1857 has traditionally been called by British historians the Indian (or Sepoy) Mutiny. In India and Pakistan it is now fashionable to describe it as the War of Independence. In truth it was more than the first and less than the second. It is certainly a mistake to view it as the product of nationalism as that term is now understood.

[3] For a more complete discussion of the establishment of British control and for the events leading to independence see Chapter IX.

it and turn to English. The Muslim, on the other hand, regarded Persian or Persianized Urdu as his own language and looked on the old form of education as an important aspect of his religion. British officials now filled the senior posts; Hindus were recruited for clerical positions, and Muslims, if employed at all, were used in inferior, manual occupations. For the Indian middle classes there were almost no careers outside the army, government service, or law. In 1871 Sir William Hunter wrote of the Muslims of Bengal:

A hundred years ago, the Musalmans monopolized all the important offices of state. The Hindu accepted with thanks such crumbs as their former conquerors dropped from their table, and the English were represented by a few factors and clerks. The proportion of Muhammadans to Hindus . . . is now less than one-seventh. . . . in fact, there is now scarcely a Government office in Calcutta in which a Muhammadan can hope for any post above the rank of porter, messenger, filler of inkpots and mender of pens.[4]

The Muslim upper and middle classes thus found that they were badly equipped to prosper in the nineteenth century. The Indian peasant has always lived a hard life, beset by famine, disease, and oppression, and the Muslims, in some regions of India, were among the lower levels of village existence. Most of them were converts from Hinduism; many had accepted the new faith in part because of the hardship imposed on the lower castes in the Hindu social system. Islam gave them pride of spiritual equality though not of material prosperity. There was one means by which a Muslim villager, especially from the Punjab and the North-West Frontier,[5] could improve his position—that of service in the Indian army. But the vast majority of villagers depended on the soil and the weather. If crops were good, they prospered: if crops failed, the peasants starved.

In the years after 1858 the Muslim community stood apart from other Indians. It had lost its special function as a governing elite and had found no alternative. The Muslims were distrusted by the British for having played a predominant part in the Mutiny. They were ignored or brushed aside by the Hindus, who saw them as fallen tyrants. And they lacked self-confidence, for they could perceive the weak-

[4] W. W. Hunter, *The Indian Musalmans* (reprinted from 3d ed.; Calcutta: Comrade Publishers, 1945), pp. 161–162.

[5] The area known as the North-West Frontier is made up of the North-West Frontier Province, the princely states along the frontier, and tribal areas. This area has dominated the military scene for thousands of years as an invasion route. (The North-West Frontier Province was merged into West Pakistan in 1956.)

nesses of the old order and the technological superiority of the British structure, with its railways and telegraphs and its regular, disciplined armies. There was no leadership to be found in the wreckage of the old order, and there were almost no Muslims equipped to master the new sciences that the West had brought to India.

Political Awakening

Slowly and against considerable opposition there began to emerge new leaders who took much that the West had to offer without abandoning their basic faith in Islam. In the year of the Mutiny the three Presidency universities were founded at Bombay, Calcutta, and Madras. With the development of the steamship and the opening of the Suez Canal it became easier and more normal for young Indian students to go to the universities of Britain and continental Europe. In 1875 Sir Sayyid Ahmad Khan, who had been deeply impressed by his visit to England, established the nucleus of the Aligarh Muslim University.

Toward the end of the nineteenth century the British rulers of India began to take steps to associate more Indians with the upper levels of government. A few were taken into the higher civil service; municipal councils, chosen mainly by election, were given substantial powers of local administration; and the number of Indian representatives on the provincial legislative councils was substantially increased.

British policy toward India from 1830 to 1947 was always the reflection of three separate points of view. First, there was a minority who believed that Britain's finest day in India would be when power was transferred in peace to a free Indian government. Second, there was another minority who believed in a permanent Indian empire, the brightest jewel in the British crown, which must be ruled firmly, justly, and without concessions to nationalist sentiments. And third, there was the majority who at all times felt that the Indian empire was a good thing while it lasted and that, though changes would be necessary, they should be introduced with caution. This was the normal opinion of the senior administrators who spent their lives in India.

To the minds of perceptive Indians, British policy posed the issue of who was to receive the increasing share of power. If, even in the remote future, India were to become independent, there would be a struggle to determine who would rule. Half a century before the Muslim League raised its demand for Pakistan, Sir Sayyid Ahmad Khan used these words:

Now suppose that all the English . . . were to leave India . . . then who would be the rulers of India? Is it possible that under these circumstances two nations—the Mohammedan and Hindu—could sit on the same throne and remain equal in power? Most certainly not. It is necessary that one of them should conquer the other and thrust it down. To hope that both could remain equal is to desire the impossible and the inconceivable.[6]

The Muslims were a minority in India, outnumbered three to one by the Hindus. Their share of the middle class, commercial, professional, and official, was far smaller. Therefore they asked for protection against being overwhelmed by the larger community. In particular, they wanted a reserved quota in the public services and special provisions to ensure Muslim representation in the legislatures. In 1906, reform was in the air, and the Muslim community made its first organized political moves. A deputation under the Agha Khan asked the Viceroy for special safeguards in the event of an extension of representative government. Later in the same year, under equally aristocratic sponsorship, the Muslim League was formed at Dacca in East Bengal.

The Indian National Congress [7] had been in existence for more than twenty years. It had begun as a respectable, upper-middle-class organization with some British membership and guidance. It was now becoming more vigorous and more radical and falling under the influence of Hindu revivalism that was both anti-Western and uncongenial to the Muslims. Two issues at this period served to divide the interests of the two communities. The Muslim request for safeguards was conceded in the Morley-Minto reforms of 1909. The Muslim community was given reserved seats in the legislatures, to be filled by Muslims voting in separate constituencies; the number of Muslim seats was somewhat higher than their proportion of the population would have indicated. This provision led Muslim candidates to campaign along communal lines since they were appealing for Muslim votes only. Many Indians have seen in this law the true progenitor of Pakistan.

The second divisive issue arose over the partition of Bengal. This enormous province was divided in 1905, in part with the intent of allowing the mainly Muslim East Bengal to govern itself apart from the predominant influence of the Hindu middle class of Calcutta. The Hindus protested bitterly and with violence, and the partition was

---

[6] Quoted in Richard Symonds, *The Making of Pakistan* (3d ed.; London: Faber and Faber, 1951), p. 31.

[7] See Chapters IX and XI.

annulled in 1912. This was seen by the Muslims as a betrayal by the British and as an indication that they would have to fight more vigorously to preserve their status.

It would be wrong to suppose that from the establishment of the Muslim League there was nothing but antagonism between this party and the Congress. It was possible for individuals to be sincere members of both organizations. In 1916 they agreed upon the Lucknow Pact, which outlined a constitution for an autonomous India.

In the First World War the British government promised India a major advance toward full self-government. At the war's end, the leaders of Indian nationalism were determined to force the pace and were profoundly disappointed at the meagerness of the concessions offered. The Muslims also found themselves with a grievance. The Muslim world had always paid at least nominal deference to the position of the Caliph, as the successor to the Prophet Muhammad. The Caliph was then the Sultan of Turkey, which was the only surviving independent Muslim power of any magnitude. The Turks lost in the war, and as a consequence it seemed that Turkey was to be dismembered. Indian Muslims, even though they had backed the Allied war effort, protested against such harshness. They were therefore in a mood to join Gandhi's civil disobedience movement in order to further the somewhat incongruous twin objectives of self-government and the preservation of the caliphate. Ultimately the Turks preserved their territory but abandoned their Caliph, and his Indian supporters were left without a cause.

The agreement with the Indian National Congress and the caliphate agitation caused the Muslim League to recede into the background, and the reforms of 1919 enlarged the degree of representative government in the provinces and maintained the provisions for separate electorates for Muslims. The question of a final transfer of power was too remote to cause intense rivalry. The Muslim demands for continued and increased safeguards were presented to the Simon Commission and to the Round Table Conferences that followed.[8] Muslim leaders were unwilling to discuss possible powers of a future central government until they were assured of enhanced representation in the provincial legislatures.

Political Ideas

At this stage few Muslims had contemplated the erection of a separate state, although certain social and political ideas had begun to

[8] See p. 260.

produce a tendency towards Muslim separatism. Western countries
have become accustomed to the concept that loyalty is owed primarily
to the state and that the state is the nation, organized for purposes of
government. These propositions, however, were by no means obvious
to the educated Indian in the early years of the present century.

The Indian's loyalty, his sense of solidarity, began at home. First
came his family with all its ramifications. Then there were the ties
within the village, especially to those of the same caste or religious
community. Beyond this were wider religious bonds and regional
patriotism, based on language or history and connected perhaps with
loyalty to a big landowner or an Indian prince. And beyond these lay
the idea of India, remote and somewhat alien, as a British-erected and
British-controlled conglomeration. Most Indians, Muslim or Hindu,
were therefore pluralists, unable to accept one object of loyalty placed
ahead of all others. "Where God commands, I am a Muslim first, a
Muslim second and a Muslim last and nothing but a Muslim. But
where India is concerned, I am an Indian first, an Indian second and
an Indian last and nothing but an Indian." [9] These words were used
by Muhammad Ali (1878–1930), who was to find that the two loyalties would tear him apart.

It was the idea of nationalism in any form that was new in the Indian subcontinent, not the older sectional loyalties. Muslim separatism
was one response to the new doctrine. Indian nationalism, the doctrine
that there was one nation in India, had the advantage that it promised
the quickest route to the transfer of power from British to Indian
hands. But concentration upon national unity was bound to cause conflict with the other loyalties. The best that could be offered the Muslims was the status of a religious minority in a secular state. And in a
cultural sense that state was likely to evolve a unified social outlook
that would be predominantly Hindu in tradition and content.

Muslim social and political thought in this period was primarily
directed to insisting that the bonds of Muslim solidarity should not be
overlooked. The Muslim felt the call of Indian nationalism, but he
wished to preserve a high place also for Islam. Almost every Muslim
thinker, whichever side of the fence of nationalism he chose, tried to
preserve some degree of special status for Islam and its followers. Many
attempted to stay astride that fence until the events of 1940–1947
forced them to make a choice.

The first concern of Muslim middle-class thinkers was that the
Muslim community should not be left hopelessly behind in the ac-

[9] Quoted in Symonds, *The Making of Pakistan*, p. 43.

quisition of the new ideas and techniques offered by the West. Sir Sayyid Ahmad Khan (1817–1898) was the first major writer to urge his coreligionists to learn from the European. He concerned himself with proving to the British that the Muslim community was loyal and should be trusted. He then urged Muslims to educate themselves and play a part in public life. He was not an anti-Hindu although he felt that the Muslim community would have to display much more vigor if it were to avoid submergence.[10]

Sayyid Ahmad had sought to show that Islam was no barrier to scientific inquiry and social progress. Amir Ali (1849–1928) told the Muslims that, compared with Christianity, they possessed a religion and a culture for which no apology was needed. His message was that Muslims should be proud of and true to their own heritage, which was ample enough to permit incorporation of new ideas. "Sir Sayyid had maintained that Islam was not inimical to liberal progress. Amir Ali presented an Islam that is that progress." [11] The effect of this line of argument was to encourage Indian Muslims to look upon Islam as their proper object of identification rather than India. They felt themselves brothers of Muslims everywhere as well as residents of the Punjab or of the United Provinces.

This strain of pan-Islamic sentiment was in the forefront of the case presented by the exponents of the Khilafat movement (to preserve the caliphate). Muhammad Ali, the leader of the movement, was able for several years to combine his ardent desire for the end of British rule with his devotion to Islam. Even Abul Kalam Azad, who was to become president of the Congress and a minister in Nehru's cabinet, proclaimed the identity of Islamic and nationalist causes in the defense of the caliphate.[12]

The Khilafat movement was doomed to frustration, and it was barren of ideas except for the emphasis on the unity of all Muslims. The movement demonstrated, however, the readiness of large masses of Muslims to respond to a call based upon Islam. It was a mass movement which had many of the features of a holy war. As it declined, the line between Muslim separatism and Indian nationalism became more marked—some leaders turned primarily to the defense of Muslim communal interests and others to the cause of a united India.

Thus far the aim of Muslim thinkers had been to preserve the iden-

[10] See Wilfred Cantwell Smith, *Modern Islam in India* (London: Gollancz, 1946), pp. 24–26.

[11] *Ibid.*, p. 49.

[12] *Ibid.*, pp. 201–202.

tity of the community. The next stage in the development of the ideas of Muslim separatism was the injection of a spirit of dynamism, and the leading figure in this regard was Sir Muhammad Iqbal (1876–1938). Iqbal was a poet, philosopher, lawyer, and politician. His primary concern was to combine the progressive driving force of the Western countries and the tradition of Islam. He condemned the tendency to accept passively the situation brought about by others. The Muslims everywhere must act, individually and collectively. He was less certain and less consistent about the nature of those actions, but he was sure that their inspiration could be found only in Islam. In 1930, when he was president of the Muslim League, he suggested the creation of a separate Muslim state in northeast India. At the time the idea seemed fantastic, but it made an impression on the minds of others, even though, for some years, it was to remain an inspiration rather than a practical objective.

The Pakistan Movement

The discussions of 1928–1932 led ultimately to the Government of India Act of 1935 which granted near autonomy in the provinces and promised a major advance toward self-government at the center. Provincial elections were held in 1937, and the result was a general victory for the Congress. The Muslim League, led by Mohammed Ali Jinnah, had contested the elections on the basis that it would co-operate fully with the Congress if its status was recognized as the true spokesman of the Muslim community. Congress ministries were formed in seven of the eleven provinces, but no gesture of co-operation as between equals was made in the direction of the League. On the contrary, in one province the Congress agreed to nominate Muslim League members to the cabinet only on the condition that they accept party discipline and cease to function as a separate entity.

For the first time Muslims found themselves in the position that they had begun to fear—that of being subject to a mainly Hindu government able to claim the sanction of an electoral victory. This fear acted as a spur to the Muslim League, which had fought the election without carrying the argument to the level of the peasants and the urban laborer.[13] In the by-elections that took place after 1937 the League showed signs of new strength and determination. Many mem-

[13] The franchise was limited by property and education qualifications, and the Muslim League had effectively represented only its more-educated portions.

bers of minor parties (including two provincial chief ministers) also joined the League in the name of Muslim solidarity.

Soon after the outbreak of the Second World War the Congress ordered its provincial ministries to resign as a protest against the declaration of war on behalf of India without the consent of Indian leaders. This was an opportunity for the League, and Mr. Jinnah proclaimed a Day of Deliverance. The stage was then set for the League to demand an independent state. The formal adoption of this proposal came in 1940 at Lahore. The resolution demanded "that the areas in which the Muslims are numerically in a majority, as in the northwestern and eastern zones of India, should be grouped to constitute 'Independent States' in which the constituent units shall be autonomous and sovereign." This was the Pakistan Resolution. It took by surprise the rest of the world, which was busy watching the battles of France and Britain. The very name Pakistan was unfamiliar. It had been coined six or seven years previously by a student at Cambridge; the idea had been advocated in general terms by the poet and philosopher Iqbal. But practical men had dismissed the scheme as unworkable, a vision incapable of fulfillment. It had scarcely been mentioned in the general elections of 1937. Now it was the official policy of a party that claimed the sole right to speak for one-fourth of India's population. There were many who called it a bluff, a propaganda device to be used in subsequent bargaining.

The later war years saw the Congress leaders in jail or in flight. The League gave conditional approval to the war effort and clung to its position of power. Moreover, it converted itself into an agency with mass influence. The campaign for Pakistan provided its spokesmen with a rallying cry that could transcend all lesser claims to loyalty and obedience. The cause could appeal to the backward-looking and the orthodox who longed to live under the rule of believers in the true faith; it could also cast its spell upon the young and the innovators who, as Muslims, would otherwise be left as a minority in a united India.

Immediately after the war the government of India took steps to hold new elections for both the central and provincial assemblies. Although the Congress emerged clearly as the strongest party, the League carried almost all the provincial Muslim seats except in the North-West Frontier Province and took every Muslim seat in the central Assembly. Its claim to represent the large majority of Muslims could no longer be denied.

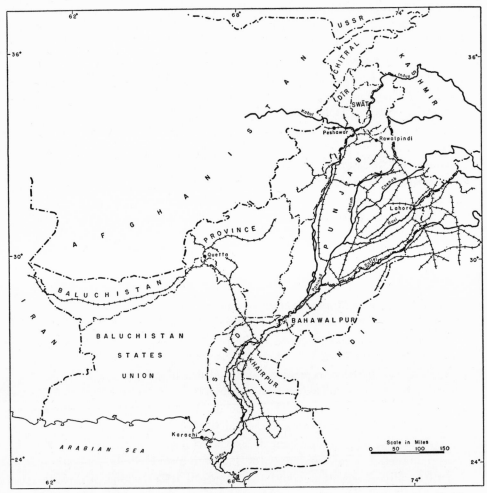

Map 9. West Pakistan. Note substantial difference of scale in Maps 9 and 10.

The Congress could, and did, deny the right of the League to be the sole spokesman for all the Muslims of India. The president of the Congress at this period was Abul Kalam Azad, whose presence served to vindicate the Congress's claim of being a nation-wide organization and also infuriated the League.

After the elections the British Cabinet Mission visited India [14] and produced its proposals for a loose federal system of government with the provinces ranged into "groups," two of which would have been predominantly Muslim. A Constituent Assembly was to be chosen by the elected members of the provincial assemblies, and the Viceroy's

[14] See p. 267.

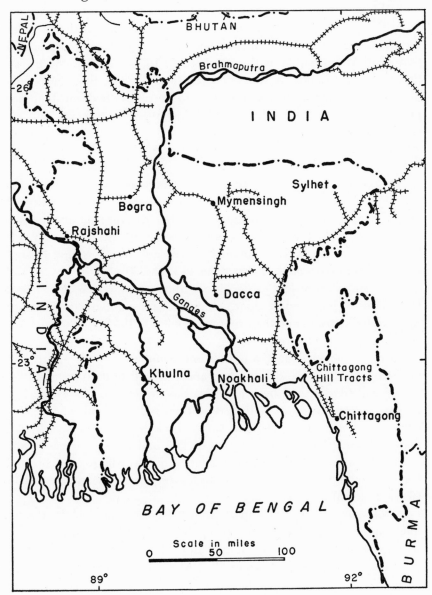

Map 10. East Pakistan.

Executive Council was to be reorganized as an interim cabinet and include members drawn from both the Congress and the League.

Neither of the major parties could agree entirely to this scheme. The interim cabinet was established, however, and the Constituent

Assembly constituted. After some delay League representatives entered the cabinet but stayed away from the Assembly. At this point the British government set a time limit for the transfer of power and sent Lord Mountbatten as the last Viceroy to superintend the transition to independence. It was not until June 3, 1947, that the people of India learned that the country was to be partitioned and that two new independent states—India and Pakistan—were to come into existence at midnight on August 14.

The New State

Pakistan was made up of two sizable fragments severed from the structure of the old India. The legislatures of the Punjab and Bengal met and decided upon partition, with the Muslim-majority areas—West Punjab and East Bengal—forming Pakistan. A referendum was held in the North-West Frontier Province and in the Sylhet district of Assam, and each chose Pakistan, as did Sindh and Baluchistan. The princely states were left to decide for themselves which of the new Dominions to join. Bahawalpur, Khairpur, and eight relatively minor states in Baluchistan and the Frontier acceded to Pakistan. So much for the enumeration of territories.

What happened in fact was that one country, even though it had been inhabited by two nations, was abruptly and brutally torn in two. Communal tension had been rising as the struggle for the succession to power intensified. Appalling riots occurred in Bombay and Calcutta, and the province of Bihar suffered widespread violence. Immediately before partition the system of law and order had effectively ceased in large sections of the Punjab. The British troops who had been available in the last resort were leaving, and so were many British civil officials.

In that summer of 1947, apart from brief rejoicings on the day of independence, fear and hatred were the principal emotions. Rumors of rape, murder, and arson augmented the horror of the immense atrocities that had in fact occurred. A Muslim surrounded by Hindus, or vice versa, never knew if he would live through the night. In some instances, especially in the princely states, the authorities participated in massacre and mass expulsion of those who belonged to the alien community. No one will ever know the full death toll. Estimates range up to 1 million, with a figure for refugees of more than 12 million.[15]

---

[15] See Symonds, *The Making of Pakistan*, pp. 83–84; E. W. R. Lumby, *The Transfer of Power in India* (London: Allen and Unwin, 1954), ch. v.

This human disruption was the harder to deal with because of the accompanying dislocation of government and commercial services. From the point of view of administration and economics, India had been a single unit before 1947. Substantial powers were centralized in New Delhi, and the main commercial centers for the whole country were Bombay, Madras, and Calcutta. The new Dominion of India inherited all these centers of government and trade. In addition there were many large provinces which had not been divided and which had been relatively unaffected by violence or the movement of population. India suffered at partition; Pakistan was devastated. East Bengal, Pakistan's largest province, had been severed from its main urban focus in Calcutta and was separated from its new federal capital by a thousand miles of unfriendly Indian territory. The Punjab was also partitioned and had been the scene of the worst of the violence and arson. Lahore, its capital, less than twenty miles from the border, was left in flames, and its large population of Hindu and Sikh shopkeepers, clerks, and mechanics had fled. The province of Sindh had to act as host to the new central government which was established at Karachi and to refugees who poured in by the hundred thousand.

Out of this chaos the government of the new state had to bring order. It had to begin by creating itself. There had been few senior Muslim civil servants, and one or two of these had elected to stay on the Indian side of the border. Hindu and some British officials had withdrawn from their posts in Pakistan to serve India or to retire. There was no organized nucleus around which a government could be built, no offices, no telephones, no typewriters, no files. Some officials and implements had arrived from Delhi, but others were delayed en route or failed to arrive. There was no reserve in provincial service to be drawn upon.

Mohammed Ali Jinnah

Above all the confusion, one figure stood forth resolute and confident. He was Mohammed Ali Jinnah (1876–1948), the first Governor-General of Pakistan and the Quaid-i-Azam (Great Leader) of the nation. No one could differ more markedly from the stereotype of the Asian nationalist politician than Mr. Jinnah. For most of his life he dressed in well-tailored European clothes, and he wore an eyeglass. Even when he adopted local costume, he chose a form of dress (*sherwani*) somewhat resembling a black frock coat with a high buttoned collar. He had an ascetic appearance, and the first impression he made was of cold but brilliant intensity. He never suffered fools gladly and disdained the tricks of the politician that win easy popularity.

In his youth Jinnah went to England for a legal education and returned to establish a highly successful practice at the Bombay bar. Politics soon claimed him, and election to the central Legislative Council followed in 1909. He was a member of both the Congress and the League and was the principal promoter of the Lucknow Pact when he first became president of the League. He was rightly regarded as a leading exponent of Hindu-Muslim unity. By temperament and reason he was unattracted by either Gandhi's civil disobedience or the movement to preserve the caliphate. He returned to active political leadership at the time of the preparation of the Muslim case for the Simon Commission and the Round Table Conferences. After the failure to reach agreement Jinnah remained in London and contemplated spending the balance of his career at the English bar. But in 1934 he was persuaded to return to his native land and to assume that command of the Muslim League which he never afterward relinquished. In no sense did he become a popular leader until after the 1937 elections and the subsequent adoption of the Pakistan Resolution.

Although he had great respect for the tradition of Islam, he was not an orthodox Muslim and could never have been described as a religious fanatic. His loyalty was primarily to the Muslim people of India and their common cultural heritage. He was far too much a master and a student of the common law to consider a return to the simplicity of the Islamic state patterned after that of the Holy Prophet and of those who immediately followed. At no stage did Jinnah want a state inhabited solely by Muslims. But he believed that a Muslim-majority state would be the best guarantee of the survival of the Muslim community throughout the subcontinent and of harmony between the two major communities. After 1937 he became convinced that no safeguards within a single state could ensure the effective preservation of the Muslim group identity.

In his capacity as president of the Muslim League, Jinnah felt himself to be almost the incarnation of the Indian Muslim nation. He towered above his subordinates and sought lieutenants who would serve him rather than colleagues who might argue with him. His will was inflexible, and his continued insistence on Pakistan was so obdurate that the Viceroy and the Congress abandoned hope of any change on his part or that of his followers.

The First Year (1947–1948)

The immediate task facing the new government was to establish its control and ensure minimum services throughout its territory. The exact boundaries were not known until immediately after partition, and it was months before the normal lines of responsibility could be established. The army had to be partitioned, and the attempt to maintain a joint command throughout the disturbed areas was never completely effective. The Hindu and Sikh civil servants, railwaymen, clerks, bankers, and shopkeepers had to be replaced with Muslims, whether qualified or not. Provision had to be made for the hundreds of thousands of refugees, to provide them with food, shelter, and some medical attention.

The government was organized according to the provisions of the 1935 Government of India Act, with some modifications introduced for Pakistan in the few weeks preceding and following the date of independence. The principal figure was the Governor-General, Mr. Jinnah. Other Dominions of the Commonwealth had reduced the office of Governor-General to that of a figurehead. In Pakistan it was the office that corresponded most closely to that of the Viceroy who had been the real head of the government of British India. The Prime Minister, Liaquat Ali Khan, was quite content to serve as the first lieutenant of the Quaid-i-Azam, a role that he had played during the struggle to secure the new state.

The immediate task of combating the emergency fell upon the executive branch of government. The legislature, known as the Constituent Assembly, met in the week before independence, but it then adjourned for six months. It was composed, for the territories of Pakistan, on the same basis as the Constituent Assembly established in 1946 for the subcontinent as a whole. That is, its original 69 members were chosen by the provincial assemblies. Additional members were added to represent the tribal areas and the princely states, and readjustments were made to reflect the movements of population that had taken place. Its job was twofold: to write a constitution and to act as an interim parliament. Each of the four provinces (East Bengal, Punjab, Sindh, North-West Frontier Province) had a similar constitution, with a governor appointed by the central government and a cabinet responsible to a single-chamber legislature.

The first six months of the new state were occupied in attending to the most urgent problems and hoping that some of the others would solve themselves if left alone. Gradually the government became aware of the resources available to it and the magnitude of the various claims upon them. By the spring of 1948 the first crisis was over, and it was clear that Pakistan was going to survive.

The struggle to achieve independence and the fight to maintain it had taken all the strength that Mr. Jinnah possessed. After a prolonged period of increasing weakness he died in September 1948. The nation had lost its Great Leader, the one man whose order was obeyed unquestioningly by all.

1948–1951

There was no dispute over the succession. Effective power passed to the Prime Minister, Liaquat Ali Khan, though his authority was never to equal that of Mr. Jinnah. The new Governor-General was the former chief minister of East Bengal, Khwaja Nazimuddin.

The government had to deal with a series of difficult issues—the framing of a constitution, Kashmir,[16] canal waters,[17] food production, industrialization, the balance of payments. It was unable to achieve any spectacular successes. A preliminary draft of the constitution was issued in 1950, but severe criticism was encountered from those who regretted the absence of distinctive Islamic provisions and those who wanted more autonomy for East Bengal. The draft was referred back to a committee of the Assembly.[18]

The progress made in other directions was real but not dramatic. Various economic development projects were begun, especially in the field of textile manufacture. A State Bank was established and monetary control extended over the economic system. There were no major changes in law or in administration. There was nothing that a man could point to at the end of a year and say, "This marks a distinct step forward."

There were some items to be counted as discredit. Political factions, especially in the provinces, began a process of intrigue that was to place in continued doubt the life of every government. A series of provincial ministers in Sindh was dismissed on grounds of corruption and political irregularities. Self-government had to be suspended in the Punjab in 1949 because of the impossibility of finding a stable and reliable ministry.[19] Official corruption, black-marketing, and general

---

[16] See below pp. 457–459.   [17] See below p. 460.
[18] A more detailed account of these developments may be found in Keith Callard, *Pakistan: A Political Study* (London: Allen and Unwin, 1957; New York: Macmillan, 1958), pp. 89–101.
[19] *Ibid.*, pp. 26–29.

inefficiency were part of the price that had to be paid for the dislocation of government and economy caused by partition. The high hopes
and firm faith that had sustained the people in the early months were
being dissipated by petty frustrations and the absence of clear signs
of substantial improvement. At this point, in October 1951, Liaquat
Ali Khan was assassinated.

The murderer was an Afghan living as a political refugee in Pakistan, and his motive has never been clearly established. The consequences of his act were all too plain. In four years Pakistan had lost
both of its pre-eminent leaders, and there was no one of equivalent
stature to take their place.

1951–1954

Nazimuddin, whose piety and integrity have never been questioned, stepped down from the dignity of the governor-generalship
and became Prime Minister. Ghulam Mohammed, the former Finance
Minister, was elevated to the office of Governor-General. Most of the
other members of the cabinet retained their offices, and a former civil
servant, Chaudhri Mohamad Ali, was promoted to the finance portfolio.

The problems facing the administration were not changed, and the
government's ability to cope with them was lessened by the loss of
its leader. Differences over the future constitution became aggravated. The advocates of an Islamic state demanded and received concessions. The East Bengalis also sought to advance the interests of
their half of the country. The political situation in the provinces offered little chance of stable and vigorous administration.

In the early months of 1953 there were widespread riots in West
Pakistan in support of demands which combined religious and political elements. And there was a food shortage that threatened large
areas of the country with starvation. The Governor-General, whose
position since Jinnah's death had been regarded as mainly formal,
now intervened. He dismissed the Prime Minister and reconstituted
the cabinet with Mohammed Ali, the former ambassador to the
United States, at its head.

The Constituent Assembly, though dubious about the constitutional
propriety of this action, did not openly challenge the new government.
Technically it was still a government of the Muslim League, which
filled almost every Muslim seat in the central and provincial legislatures. The League was split in many directions. There were those who
wanted a constitution based on Islamic principles, and there were

those who favored secularism in political life. Many of the Bengalis and some representatives from other provinces fought for provincial rights which they believed were being denied. There were supporters and opponents of the Governor-General and his nominee for Prime Minister. The political instability that plagued the provinces was now reproduced in Karachi.

The situation was made more complex by the result of the provincial election of 1954 in East Bengal. The eastern province, which contains more than half the total population of the country, voted overwhelmingly against the Muslim League and in favor of a coalition of parties that demanded greater provincial autonomy. This election did not affect the seats of the Bengal members of the Constituent Assembly, but it served to indicate that they had lost the confidence of their electorate.

A new provincial government, under the party label of the United Front, was installed. It found the province on the verge of major riots, and within a few weeks the central government suspended it from office. A strong governor, Major General Iskandar Mirza, was sent from Karachi to rule until it seemed possible to restore popular government without risking public tranquillity.

The Governor-General hoped to have a constitution approved without further delay. The Assembly was determined to limit the present and future powers of the Governor-General. The result was delay, intrigue, and maneuver. In September 1954 the Assembly passed bills aimed at reducing the power of Ghulam Mohammed. A month later he announced:

The Governor-General having considered the political crisis with which the country is faced has, with deep regret, come to the conclusion that the constitutional machinery has broken down. He, therefore, has decided to declare a State of Emergency throughout Pakistan. The Constituent Assembly as at present constituted has lost the confidence of the people and can no longer function.[20]

1954–1957

A new cabinet was formed with the same Prime Minister and several other ministers, but also included were the commander in chief of the army, a top civil servant with a military background, a businessman, and representatives of groups that had opposed the Muslim League. Democracy seemed to be at a low ebb. Self-government was

[20] *Gazette of Pakistan, Extraordinary,* Oct. 24, 1954.

suspended in the eastern half of the country, and the national legislature had been dismissed. Further, the provincial ministers and legislators of West Pakistan were not outstanding for democratic practice.

The government proposed to frame a constitution by administrative order and to merge the western provinces into a single unit. However, the fundamental constitutional deadlock had already been referred to the courts.[21] A series of Federal Court decisions required a return to something resembling the pattern laid down by the Indian Independence Act. The government was forbidden to go ahead with making a constitution by administrative decree. A new Constituent Assembly was to be set up, elected by the provincial assemblies.

The court's ruling was accepted, and the second Constituent Assembly held its first meeting in July 1955. Shortly afterward the government was once more reconstructed. Chaudhri Mohamad Ali replaced Mohammed Ali as Prime Minister, and Ghulam Mohammed was succeeded as Governor-General by Iskandar Mirza. The commander in chief left the cabinet, which became once more a group of political party leaders. The Muslim League was still the major component, but it had to share power with the United Front, since the League could not claim the support of the new members from Bengal.

The initial party composition of the second Constituent Assembly was as follows:

Muslim League	26
United Front	16
Awami League	13
Congress	4
Scheduled Castes Federation	3
United Progressive Party	2
Others	16
	80

In early 1956 many of the Muslim Leaguers and "others" joined the Republican Party.

The new Constituent Assembly immediately began to work on three major pieces of legislation. First, it had to clear away the legal and constitutional tangle left by the dismissal of its predecessor and by the interim of emergency rule. Second, it acted to amalgamate the three provinces and the princely states of West Pakistan into a single province. Finally, it adopted the new constitution. The draft, prepared

[21] See Sir Ivor Jennings, *Constitutional Issues in Pakistan* (Cambridge, Eng.: Cambridge University Press, 1957).

by the government, was introduced in January 1956, debated and passed in February, and proclaimed on March 23.

The adoption of the constitution was not to be a prelude to a period of political calm. The United Front, which filled most of the seats in the East Pakistan [22] Assembly, had split into two major segments. It had been formed as an electoral alliance and began to dissolve as soon as victory was won. In West Pakistan the Muslim League was about to disintegrate. One section adopted the name Republican Party [23] and chose a leader, Dr. Khan Sahib, who had never been in the League though he had joined the emergency cabinet in 1954. The Republicans formed a provincial ministry and held a narrow majority in the West Pakistan Assembly. Although the League was in opposition to the Republicans at Lahore, both parties continued to support the central cabinet of Chaudhri Mohamad Ali. This unstable equilibrium lasted until September 1956, when the Muslim League moved into opposition at the center as well as in the provinces. Simultaneously one segment of the United Front—the Awami League—ousted the other from the government of East Pakistan. The national leader of the Awami League, H. S. Suhrawardy, who had been leader of the Opposition, was called on to form a government. This he was able to do, with the support of the Republicans who were at that time the largest party in the National Assembly. In October 1957 the Republicans broke away from the coalition. Mr. Suhrawardy resigned, and a new government was formed under the Muslim League leader, I. I. Chundrigar. This cabinet collapsed, in its turn, in December 1957, and Firoz Khan Noon (Republican) became Prime Minister.

[22] The constitution changed the name of East Bengal to East Pakistan, and the other province was West Pakistan.

[23] A more detailed account of the political parties is given below in Chapter XVII. See also Callard, *Pakistan*, ch. ii.

· XV ·

Economic and Social Structure

ACCORDING to the census of 1951, Pakistan had a population of about 76 million. Of these, 42 million lived in East Pakistan. The vast majority was composed of poor and illiterate villagers. Those who could read and write in any language totaled 19 per cent. Those who lived in cities and towns comprised 10.4 per cent of the total (only 4.4 per cent in East Pakistan).

There are immense contrasts between various sections of the country. One thousand miles of Indian territory separate East and West Pakistan. But this is not the only factor that keeps them apart. There are six main languages spoken in Pakistan. A small minority dispersed throughout the country possesses a knowledge of English, which is still the main vehicle of official and commercial transactions. In East Pakistan the language is Bengali, which uses a script derived from Sanskrit and serves to form a link with the Hindu Bengalis living in West Bengal on the Indian side of the border. The languages of West Pakistan are Urdu, Punjabi, Sindhi, and Pushtu. They have some elements in common, though they are far from being merely dialects of a central tongue. They are mostly written in the Urdu (or Persian) script and use a vocabulary that borrows heavily from Arabic and Persian. The cultural traditions of the two wings of Pakistan are, in consequence, substantially different. Persian is still the classical language for many West Pakistanis, and Persian verse is widely quoted.

There are those who do not hesitate to say that Urdu is a more truly "Islamic" language than Bengali, which has been affected by its Hindu heritage. This, of course, is denied heatedly by Bengali Muslims.

The Economy

There are further grounds for difference beyond language. East Pakistan occupies the delta of the Ganges and Brahmaputra rivers, where these combine to form a massive flow of water. This water marks the main difference between the physical character of East and of West. The problem in the East is to drain it away to the sea. Each rainy season the delta is flooded and the distributaries change their courses; for many months water is the only feasible means of transport in areas not served by the few railways. In the West, on the other hand, water has to be hoarded and shared out by an immense network of canals over the parched land or raised from wells by primitive means. The crops which give men their livelihood are also different. In the East rice is the staple food and jute the principal cash crop; in the West wheat and cotton are important.

Most of the cities and industry are in the West, and the average standard of living is lower in the East. Much of the land in the West is owned by a limited number of large landholders, whereas in East Pakistan there are few very large estates and the program of land reform is further reducing their number.

Within West Pakistan there is a great variety of conditions. The North-West Frontier contains regions in which the life of the people must be much the same as when Alexander marched through. The basis of life is tribal, with the elders of each clan maintaining law and making the major decisions. Each man still carries a rifle on his shoulder and lives in a hut with thick mud walls, behind which his family and possessions are withdrawn at night. Thousands of Baluchis are nomads, pasturing their sheep and goats in the hills in summer and coming down to the plains in winter. The peasants of Sindh till irrigated fields in a state of near serfdom for the benefit of their hereditary landlords.

The women of Pakistan are mostly excluded from participation in the general life of the community. Where poverty requires, the women work, either alongside the men in the fields or in groups in the cities. But they keep themselves apart from strange men. And those families that can afford it, especially the middle classes, confine their women at home; but if they venture abroad, they do so under a veil that covers them from head to toe, and they are escorted by a male relative or servant. This custom of the seclusion of women does not exist without protest or attempts at reform. Some women are now obtaining higher education—though at one university that permits "mixed" classes a curtain is hung down the center of the classroom to ensure segregation. The wives of some political and business leaders have abandoned the veil and appear in public freely and even take part in political life. Such women are almost entirely limited to the three or four large cities in which foreign cultural influences are strong.

Religion

The reason for the seclusion of women is the Islamic precept that a woman is to observe the strictest modesty. Islam is a factor that permeates every aspect of individual and social life in Pakistan. This is not surprising since the very reason for the creation of Pakistan was the feeling by Muslims that their faith and its associated tradition and culture placed them so far apart from their fellow Indians as to make them a separate nation. The central feature of the struggle for Pakistan was this sense of a separate identity as Muslims, as believers in Islam.

For a Muslim, his religion means obedience to the clear and definite commands of God as revealed by the Prophet Muhammad. These commands can be read directly in the Quran and understood almost equally well from the sayings and traditions of the Prophet. Such divine laws are not mere general principles, capable of being interpreted in widely differing senses. Many of them are precise and practical and regulate such matters as the manner of saying prayers, the proper laws of inheritance, the prohibition of alcohol and the flesh of swine, and the status of nonbelievers. The Muslim has tended to see the source of all law in his religion. If a matter is not explicitly provided for, it can be discerned by analogy from the nearest precedent or by deduction from an established principle.

This represents the traditionalist's view of the role of Islam. It was certainly not completely acceptable to Mr. Jinnah or to many other political leaders in Pakistan. In many instances the minds of these leaders operate on two levels. One is the realm of tradition and faith; the other, the area of their Western secular education. At one particular time and in one company they think in an Oriental language and organize their thoughts in Islamic terms; at another they think in English and use the vocabulary of John Stuart Mill or Woodrow Wilson. Such Pakistanis want all the advantages that can be learned from the experience of others, but, at the same time, they wish to feel the assurance that they are obedient to the word of Allah. Without Islam, Pakistan has no meaning. The nation's first Prime Minister said: "Pakistan was founded because the Muslims of this Sub-Continent wanted to build up their lives in accordance with the teaching and traditions of Islam, because they wanted to demonstrate to the world that Islam provides a panacea to the many diseases which have crept into the life of humanity today." [1]

The Islamic State

Throughout the long discussions of the new constitution there was a continuing demand that Pakistan should be an "Islamic state," and the name of the country finally adopted is the Islamic Republic of Pakistan. The opening words of the constitution run as follows: "In the name of Allah, the Beneficent, the Merciful. Whereas sovereignty over the entire Universe belongs to Allah Almighty alone, and the authority to be exercised by the people of Pakistan within the limits prescribed by Him is a sacred trust . . ."

The constitution contains several comparable allusions to Islam, but most of them take the form of declarations of principle rather than enforceable matters of administration or law. Thus it is provided that the state shall endeavor to prevent the consumption of alcohol [2] and to make the teaching of the Quran compulsory for Muslims. Two clauses have more definite significance. The first requires the President of Pakistan to be a Muslim. Since 86 per cent of the people are Muslim, it is unlikely that any other would have been chosen. The second clause lays down that "no law shall be enacted which is repugnant to the Injunctions of Islam" and that "existing law shall be brought into conformity with such Injunctions." The Constituent Assembly debated at length whether a special religious court or the Supreme Court should be able to declare invalid any law that contravened Islamic requirements. In the end the issue was left to the conscience of the Muslim members of the legislatures. These are to be advised by a Presidential Commission on Islamic laws which will suggest modifications of existing law and suitable forms for enacting Islamic provi-

[1] Constituent Assembly of Pakistan, *Debates,* V, 2, March 7, 1949.

[2] It is to be noted that, ten years after independence, prohibition is by no means total in Pakistan.

sions. The commission is to report within five years from March 1957, when it was appointed.

The Minorities

When Pakistan was formed, about one-quarter of its population consisted of non-Muslims. The upheaval of 1947 saw the transfer of millions of Muslims into Pakistan and the departure of millions of non-Muslims. The 1951 census indicated the non-Muslim population as 14.1 per cent of the total (see Table 10).

Table 10. Non-Muslim population (1951 Census)

	East Pakistan	West Pakistan	Total
Caste Hindu	4,187,000	162,000	4,349,000
Scheduled caste	5,052,000	369,000	5,421,000
Christian	107,000	434,000	541,000
Buddhist	319,000	—	319,000
Parsi	—	5,000	5,000
Other	40,000	2,000	42,000
Totals	9,705,000	972,000	10,677,000
Percentage of minorities in total population	23.2%	2.9%	14.1%

Most of the Hindus in Muslim-majority areas either had a positive dislike for the prospect of Pakistan as a separate nation or were indifferent. There was no reason why they should feel the same emotional drive toward an Islamic state as their Muslim neighbors. On the contrary, the two-nation theory that lay behind the Pakistan movement seemed to imply that they would be reduced to the status of a permanent minority, excluded by their religion from full participation in citizenship of a Muslim state. The arguments for a separate Pakistan had always been twofold: first, that there was a bond which made all Muslims brothers; second, that Muslims were different from Hindus and did not wish to live under Hindu rule. The negative argument of fear of Hindu domination seemed at times to be stronger than the positive argument of the creation of a pure Muslim society.

The doctrine of Indian nationalism declared that men born in India were Indians first before the consideration of any claims of religious or local loyalties. The two-nation theory declared that a man was primarily a Muslim. Mr. Jinnah, however, always emphasized that this implied no threat to non-Muslims once the state of Pakistan was conceded. "Now I think we should keep that in front of us as our ideal and you will find in course of time Hindus would cease to be Hindus and Muslims would cease to be Muslims, not in the religious sense, because that is the personal faith of each individual, but in the political sense as citizens of the State." [3]

As can be seen from the figures in Table 10, the largest group of non-Muslims which remained in Pakistan consisted of the Hindus (caste and scheduled caste [4]) of East Pakistan. They raised objections to the proclamation of an Islamic state, and some Hindus have continued to leave the country for India. Their main complaint has been that the Hindu community is regarded with suspicion in Pakistan. They have been accused of too much sympathy with India and lukewarm loyalty to Pakistan. Many Hindus feel that their sons will have opportunity for a better career if they transfer to the Indian side of the border where their coreligionists are in control.

The largest single grievance was the Muslim insistence on maintaining the system of separate electorates. This was introduced in 1909 to ensure adequate representation for the Muslim minority in the legislatures. It served to concentrate political divisions along communal lines and was always criticized by Indian nationalist leaders. It was continued in Pakistan because the Muslims had come to regard it as a proper safeguard of minority interests and because it prevented the Hindu electorate in East Bengal from being mingled with the Muslim voters. The system was carried farther in Pakistan, and a separate electorate was provided for the scheduled castes.[5] This split the Hindu community in two and reduced its political influence even more. The question of separate versus joint electorate was a major political issue, with the Muslim League on the side of segregation and the Awami League and the Hindus for joint electorates. The matter was left open by the constitution, but the Electorate Act of 1957 ruled in favor of a joint electorate.[6]

One of the earliest committees established by the Constituent Assembly was that on fundamental rights and on minorities. Its report

[3] Constituent Assembly of Pakistan, *Debates*, I, 20, Aug. 11, 1947.

[4] The scheduled castes are the low castes or outcastes.

[5] Under the 1935 Government of India Act the scheduled castes were given reserved seats, but all Hindus voted for the various candidates.

[6] Keith Callard, *Pakistan: A Political Study* (London: Allen and Unwin, 1957; New York: Macmillan, 1958), pp. 240–254.

was substantially incorporated in the constitution which guarantees freedom of religion, religious education, equal opportunity for public employment, and the preservation of linguistic and cultural characteristics. These community rights are in addition to those respecting the fundamental rights of the individual.

· XVI ·

The Structure of Government

THE constitution of Pakistan was not adopted for almost nine years after independence. For twenty years those interested in public affairs had discussed the merits of the 1935 Government of India Act, even though its provisions were never fully implemented in their original form. The practical experience of the politicians, journalists, and students of government had been in relation to that constitutional act. The objections raised against it were seldom that it provided an unsuitable form of government but rather that effective power was confined to the wrong persons.

The Constituent Assembly cast a few glances at the United States and other democratic countries but finally decided to proceed along the lines that were already familiar, making some changes to meet the altered circumstances. Thus the constitution of 1956 bears a strong resemblance to its parent, the Act of 1935, and hence to its brother the constitution of India.

The Central Government

Pakistan adopted a system of cabinet government, in the tradition of all other countries of the Commonwealth. Until 1956 Pakistan owed formal allegiance to the Queen, though she herself had no function to perform. Her representative in Pakistan was the Governor-General, and it was by virtue of his status as the agent of the Crown that he was able to make the full use of his ill-defined powers in dismissing a Prime Minister and dissolving the Constituent Assembly. The Crown as a symbol was not appropriate for Pakistan, and it was not to be expected that the new nation would continue to regard a person of strange race and religion as its focus of allegiance. Pakistan has therefore proclaimed itself to be a republic, and the head of the state is called the President.

The transition from dominion to republic caused no disruption, and the last Governor-General became the first President, being elected by the Constituent Assembly. Future Presidents are to be chosen by the combined vote of the National Assembly and the two provincial assemblies. The President must be at least forty years old and a Muslim (Article 32). He holds office for a term of five years and may be elected not more than twice. He may be removed by impeachment on a charge of violation of the constitution or gross misconduct, if this is voted by three-quarters of the total membership of the National Assembly. In the event of a vacancy a new election for a full term is to be held as soon as possible. There is no Vice-President, and in the event of the absence of the President or a vacancy, the Speaker of the Assembly acts as President until the official President returns or a new election is held.

In the United Kingdom the acts of the government of the day are taken in the name of the monarch, even though the cabinet of the day has made the real decision. This is a matter of convention and is not laid down in any statute or written constitution. Pakistan, having a written constitution and wishing to adopt a similar device, has defined the relationship of the President to the government of the day. The constitution says: "The executive authority of the Federation shall vest in the President and shall be exercised by him, either directly or through officers subordinate to him" (Article 39). He is also granted supreme command of the armed forces. It thus appears as though the President is to have real power. This impression is quickly corrected by another clause of the constitution which runs: "In the exercise of his functions, the President shall act in accordance with the advice of the Cabinet or the appropriate Minister or Minister of State, as the case may be, except in cases where he is empowered by the constitution to act in his discretion" (Article 7, sec. 7).

The first act that the constitution expects the President to perform in his discretion is choosing a Prime Minister. His choice is limited both by express wording and by the facts of political life.

The Prime Minister is to be a member of the Assembly who "in his opinion, is most likely to command the confidence of the majority of the members of the National Assembly." If there is a two-party system and each party is loyal to its leader, then the element of presidential choice disappears. But if something like the French confusion of parties prevails, then the President is faced with a real and influential range of choice. There can be little doubt that Mr. Mohammed Ali was chosen by the Governor-General, and only after his appointment did the two men set about creating a parliamentary majority. Equally clearly Mr. Suhrawardy in 1956 was the leader of the Opposition and had a strong claim to the summons of the President.

The Prime Minister has to inform the President of all cabinet decisions and give any further information that the President may seek. Further, the President may question the action of an individual minister, in which case the Prime Minister is obliged to submit the matter for the consideration of the entire cabinet.

The President has also a conditional power to dismiss the Prime Minister. He is to exercise his authority only if "he is satisfied that the Prime Minister does not command the confidence of the majority of the members of the National Assembly" (Article 37, sec. 6). Clearly there should be some safeguard against an authoritarian Prime Minister who refuses to vacate office after being defeated. If the party situation is unclear, the very act of dismissal might induce the loss of confidence that otherwise would not have occurred. The proof could only be the ability of a new cabinet to achieve a vote of confidence. For this purpose it is required that the National Assembly must be summoned not later than two months after the appointment of a new Prime Minister.

Other ministers, ministers of state, and deputy ministers are appointed on the advice of the Prime Minister. They must be members of the Assembly when appointed, although if a minister loses his seat at a subsequent election he is allowed six months to find another before being put out of office. The cabinet has normally consisted of 10 to 14 ministers assisted by 3 or 4 ministers of state or deputy ministers. The cabinet is collectively responsible to the National Assembly.

The other functions which the constitution assigns to the President in his discretion are significant and are designed to take certain acts "out of politics." In this category are the appointments to three commissions: the Election Commission, which conducts all federal and provincial elections; the Delimitation Commission, which establishes the boundaries of electoral constituencies; and the Public Service Commission, which controls recruitment for government employment.

Few written constitutions work in practice in exactly the manner that the wording would seem to require. In Pakistan the constitution has been in force for only a brief period, but it has to be viewed in the light of the preceding experience. The relative position of the President and the Prime Minister has not led to the clear recognition of the latter as the primary initiator and controller of government policy. The office of President is directly descended from that of Governor-General which in turn succeeded that of Viceroy. The first Governor-General was Jinnah. No one could expect that he would confine himself to ceremonial functions and the passive acceptance of the advice of his ministers. In fact, he issued orders which his lieutenants obeyed. This was his custom as Quaid-i-Azam of the Muslim League, and as head of state his position was even further beyond argument. Under the second Governor-General the leadership of the Prime Minister was equally clearly acknowledged, and it seemed that the normal tradition of cabinet government in other countries might become accepted in Pakistan. The third Governor-General, however, was Ghulam Mohammed, who dismissed one Prime Minister and dominated his successor. Iskandar Mirza, the last Governor-General and the first President, is a man of authoritative temperament and a believer in seizing the initiative. He had been an army officer, a political officer on the Frontier, a strong governor of East Bengal, and Minister of the Interior. He has not dominated his four successive Prime Ministers (Chaudhri Mohamad Ali, H. S. Suhrawardy, I. I. Chundrigar, and F. K. Noon), but neither has he retreated into dignified impotence.

Parliament

Parliament consists of the President and one house called the National Assembly.[1] The constitution provides for 300 seats although, for a period of 10 years, 10 additional seats are to be reserved for women. The seats are divided equally between East and West Pakistan.

---

[1] The constitution was proclaimed on March 23, 1956, but elections for the first parliament under the constitution were not due to be held until 1958. In the interim the Constituent Assembly transformed itself into the provisional National Assembly. The description of parliamentary practice given below is therefore based largely on the experience of the two constituent assemblies.

A candidate for election must be a citizen of Pakistan and at least 25 years old. A member forfeits his seat if absent without leave from the Assembly for 60 consecutive sitting days.

Elections are conducted by the Electoral Commission though the provisions governing eligibility to vote are laid down in the constitution and supplemented by act of parliament. Voting takes place in single-member constituencies, and every adult citizen is entitled to one vote provided that he is qualified by residence in a given constituency. Women for a ten-year period may have a general vote and an additional vote for a woman member.

The National Assembly is summoned, prorogued,[2] and dissolved by the President. Its full term is five years, but it may be dissolved at any earlier date. The Assembly is required to meet at least twice a year, and one session must take place in East Pakistan. The President may address the Assembly and may send messages.

The general organization and procedure of the house follow the main lines of British development. The house elects a Speaker and a Deputy Speaker to preside and enforce the rules. The business of the house can be divided into four main categories. Proposals for legislation are discussed and adopted; resolutions may be moved on matters of public policy; the government's plans for raising and spending revenue are to be sanctioned; and further devices are used to enable the house to be informed about and to supervise the conduct of the administration.

In the Constituent Assembly most business was dealt with by the house as a whole though from time to time an item was referred to a committee. The total membership never exceeded 80, however, and most of these supported the government of the day. With 300 members under the constitution, greater use of committees is to be expected.

A bill, when presented to the house, may be debated on three occasions. First, there is a general discussion on the general principles of a measure. If approved and not referred to a committee, the bill is discussed clause by clause, and detailed amendments may be moved. Finally, in amended form the measure is discussed once more and submitted for final approval.

When approved by the house a bill is presented to the President for his assent. Within ninety days he has to approve, to announce his refusal of assent, or to return the bill with a request for amendment.

---

[2] Prorogation is the term used in Commonwealth parliaments for the adjournment at the end of a session.

Should assent be refused, it may still become law if passed again by the house with a majority of two-thirds of the members present and voting. When a bill is returned by the President for reconsideration, a simple majority of the house is sufficient to secure the acceptance of the measure. The purpose of this veto power is somewhat obscure. The government of the day is expected to have a majority in the house. It is therefore to be presumed that no measure will be passed against the will of the administration. The ninety-day period might, however, be useful as a device for delay.

Parliamentary control over the government has always centered upon the control of the purse. As is normal under cabinet government, any proposal involving the expenditure of public money must have the approval of the government. The constitution goes further than the practice elsewhere when it provides that no bill or amendment concerning "the imposition, abolition, remission, alteration or regulation of any tax" may be moved without the President's recommendation (Articles 58, 59). This would appear to prevent the Opposition from moving a tax cut.

The procedure for the approval of the government's financial program provides the occasion for two general discussions of official policy as well as some probing into detail. There is a wide-ranging discussion immediately after the presentation of the budget. This is followed by individual demands for grants (appropriations) though parliamentary time never permits every item to be debated. Finally, when approval is being granted to the tax measures, another debate takes place on general or particular issues.

The public accounts of both the national and provincial governments are inspected by the Comptroller and Auditor-General who is appointed by the central government. Once appointed, he has the same security of tenure as a high-court judge. The federal audit reports are submitted to the National Assembly and examined by the Public Accounts Committee. Examination at this stage is concerned more with financial regularity than with the wisdom of the policy that led to the expenditure.

A further method open to members of parliament to criticize the actions of the government occurs at Question time. As at Westminster, a member may ask a particular minister for information on matters for which he is responsible. Notice must be given of such questions, but if the answer is not considered satisfactory, a "supplementary" question may be asked. The minister cannot, of course, be compelled to reply but naturally wishes to appear competent and well informed. Under certain circumstances defined in the rules, a single member or a group may move various motions seeking a statement of policy or censuring the action, or lack of action, of the government. The first Constituent Assembly contained almost no opposition, and the second had a relatively brief existence. There have been few major parliamentary clashes between the government and a vigorous opposition, although the debates of 1955–1957 have shown that the parliament in Pakistan has been able to force a government to submit to strong criticism and to defend its own proposals at every stage.[3] As long as a government is sure of a majority in the house, it feels certain of accomplishing its will, subject only to constitutional restrictions. The place of parliament becomes more vital when the government has to seek to hold together a dubious majority that threatens to disappear on crucial issues. Many of the recent tense debates have gained their significance because of the possibility of a revolt among the ranks of the government's supporters and the chance of a parliamentary defeat.

Emergency Provisions

Any government in Pakistan must bear in mind the fact that it is much closer to the threshold of disorder than is the case in longer-established democracies. The need to contemplate quick action in an emergency has therefore been recognized by the constitution.

When the Assembly is not in session, the government has a general power to promulgate ordinances which have the same force as an act of parliament. An ordinance must be laid before the Assembly when it reconvenes, and its provisions lapse six weeks from the day of the Assembly's meeting or sooner if the Assembly adopts a resolution of disapproval (Article 69).

There are further provisions to deal with a more serious emergency. "If the President is satified that a grave emergency exists in which the security or economic life of Pakistan, or any part thereof, is threatened by war or external aggression, or by internal disturbance beyond the power of a Provincial Government to control, he may issue a Proclamation of Emergency." Under the authority of a proclamation the government may suspend the guarantee of constitutional

---

[3] Thus there were heated and prolonged debates on the unification of West Pakistan, the validation of laws, the constitution, and the two acts relating to electorates.

fundamental rights and may take over the functions of a provincial government.[4] The national parliament may make laws during the emergency on matters within provincial jurisdiction. There is no time limit to the operation of a proclamation of emergency. Such a proclamation, however, is to be laid before the Assembly "as soon as conditions make it practicable for the President to summon that Assembly" and ceases to operate if disapproved. In effect, Article 191 is a form of constitutional dictatorship under which all forms of political activity may be brought under the control of the central government and the liberty of the citizens restricted without means of redress. The courts would continue to function, and they and public opinion would provide the only chance of exercising restraint upon a government that was prepared to abuse the emergency provisions.

The Provinces and the Federal System

In 1947–1948 Pakistan contained eighteen "units" of government, each with some degree of local autonomy. There were the four governor's provinces (East Bengal, West Punjab, Sindh, and the North-West Frontier Province); each had a legislature and a full range of powers and responsibilities. British Baluchistan was administered by a chief commissioner, and the four Baluchistan states were under the rule of local princes, though they were soon to be merged into the Baluchistan States Union. There were four more small states under princely rule on the North-West Frontier. There were also the larger and more developed states of Bahawalpur and Khairpur. In 1948 the Karachi district was separated from Sindh to become the federal capital. In addition, there remained a section of Kashmir and extensive tribal areas. The system of government ranged from complete autocracy to full representative government.

East Pakistan has remained a single province. It was obvious, however, that changes would have to come about in West Pakistan. The prospect of losing a separate identity was unpopular with those who were in power in the smaller units and with those who feared that local interests and traditions might be overwhelmed by the predominance of the Punjab in any merger or federation. Little progress was made in the first Constituent Assembly, and after its dissolution the government proposed to amalgamate West Pakistan by administra-

---

[4] This power under Article 191 is in addition to that under Article 193 which relates to a crisis within a province. The provisions of Article 193 are outlined below at p. 415.

tive order. This move was blocked by the courts, but was forced through the second Assembly before the main proposals of the constitution were introduced. West Pakistan became a single province late in 1955.

The argument was by no means over, and many groups, especially those representing the Frontier and Sindh, have pressed for a re-division of the province. This proposal has been adopted by the National Awami Party and in September 1957, for tactical reasons, was endorsed in the West Pakistan Assembly by the ruling Republican Party.[5] Its implementation, however, would require action by parliament.

Provisions for the government of the provinces are contained in the single constitution for the entire country. Each province has a governor, appointed by Karachi, a provincial assembly of 300 members (plus 10 temporary seats for women), and a cabinet under a chief minister that is collectively responsible to the provincial assembly.

When Pakistan first came into existence, it was faced with an emergency that could be met only by strong centralized action. The provinces had to act as agents of the national government in the restoration of order and the establishment of administrative machinery. But in a country so diverse in territory and people there are strong reasons why a large measure of local authority should be permitted. This applies with special force to East Pakistan, which is removed from the national capital by distance and difference of living conditions and outlook.

A constant theme in the ten years since partition has been the demand of the provinces for greater autonomy. This has normally been countered by the central government urging that limited resources and the risk of friction and instability make central control inevitable. It is hard to maintain that provincial self-government has been an example of successful democracy and efficient administration. There has been no year since independence when at least one provincial government was not in danger of being overturned by intrigue within the ranks of its own supporters.

To combat this political factionalism the central government made repeated use of its emergency powers. In the original form these had been designed to enable the Viceroy to suspend self-government

[5] *Dawn*, Sept. 18, 1957. (*Dawn* is the leading English-language newspaper of Karachi and was founded by Mr. Jinnah.)

in a province in the interest of preserving law and order and the maintenance of the British connection. The centrally appointed governor then ruled as an agent of the central administration, exercising the power of the legislature as well as the cabinet. In Pakistan, before the new constitution, "governor's rule" was imposed on three of the four provinces for periods exceeding a year in each case. The primary reason in two instances was that no stable cabinet of politicians could be found. In the third instance the province of East Bengal, having just completed its elections, was loudly demanding concessions that the center was not prepared to grant.

The provincial politicians have resented this power of the center to depose a cabinet and suspend a legislature (though some of them have sought to invoke it when their enemies are in power). It was therefore a subject of heated debate in the Assembly when the new constitution was under discussion. The emergency clause adopted (Article 193) is slightly more limited in scope than its predecessors. It provides that the central government may issue a proclamation which transfers the powers of the provincial government to the governor and the authority of the provincial legislature to the national parliament. Parliament may then in turn confer this lawmaking power on the President. Such a proclamation ceases to be effective unless approved by the National Assembly within two months; if the Assembly approves, the total life of a proclamation may extend up to six months. There seems to be nothing in the constitution that would prevent a new proclamation of emergency being issued immediately after an old one had expired. This, however, is a point on which the courts would have to rule.

Within a year and a half of the adoption of the constitution Article 193 had been invoked on three occasions. Two of these, in East Pakistan, were to bridge a relatively minor constitutional hiatus. The third was a three-and-a-half-month suspension in 1957 in West Pakistan where the provincial government had encountered the normal evaporation of its voting support in the Assembly.

The emergency power is clearly the most formidable weapon available in the event of a clash between a province and the center. There are many other constitutional provisions which lead in the same direction. In the first place the governor is appointed by Karachi, and although in normal times he is expected to take the advice of his cabinet, he cannot be removed except by the central authorities. There is no provincial counterpart to the power of the National Assembly to impeach the President. If a provincial ministry is unable to persuade the governor to accept its views, the only recourse is an appeal to the central cabinet. It was under these circumstances that M. A. Gurmani, the governor of West Pakistan, was asked to resign in August 1957.[6]

The power to make laws is divided in the constitution into three lists of subjects—federal, concurrent, and provincial. As the titles imply, the provinces have exclusive jurisdiction over the third list, share the second, and are forbidden to touch the first. Where an otherwise valid provincial law conflicts with federal law, it must give way. The items on the federal list comprise mainly foreign affairs, defense, interprovincial trade, and federal taxes. The exclusive jurisdiction of the provinces extends to public order and the administration of justice, land and agriculture and forests, water, local government, education, health, industries, and trade and commerce within a province. This is a considerable extension of the area of provincial jurisdiction exercised before 1956. Its effect, however, is substantially diminished by the wide scope of the concurrent list, where federal law takes priority. This list includes such items as civil and criminal law, economic and social planning, banking, insurance and corporations, trade unions, and social security. No doubt the courts will have to determine the exact boundaries where one set of powers ends and the others begin, but the general intention seems to be that of giving the center power, in its discretion, to regulate all matters except land, agriculture, and local government.

This impression is strengthened by the direction to the provinces that their governments must act to ensure compliance with acts of parliament and in such a manner "as not to impede or prejudice the exercise of the executive authority of the Federation" (Article 126). For similar purposes the central government has the right to issue instructions to the provinces. In the other direction, central functions may, with provincial consent, be delegated to a province.

The heart of an effective system of federation is finance. The distribution of the powers of taxation remain much as they were before 1956. The principal independent sources of provincial revenue are taxes on land and agricultural income, succession duties on agricultural land, and a variety of stamp and excise duties. In 1954–1955

---

[6] *Ibid.*, Aug. 28, 1957. This removal of a governor brought about the resignation of a central cabinet minister on the grounds that it was not in accordance with the spirit of the constitution (*ibid.*, Aug. 31, 1957).

East Pakistan received less than one-half its total revenue from these sources, and the units of West Pakistan an even smaller proportion.[7]

Substantial provincial income is derived from rent and the profit on irrigation schemes and commercial activities. The remainder of provincial revenue comes from central grants and shared taxes. One-half the proceeds of the income tax is divided between the provinces in the ratio of 45 to 55, with the larger share going to West Pakistan. East Pakistan receives 62.5 per cent of the export duty on jute, and this amounts to about one-fifth of its total revenue. The proceeds of the sales tax are also divided between the center and the provinces.

When all these taxes are added together, they yield a pitifully small income to the provincial governments. The per capita annual revenue of East Pakistan in 1955–1956 was only 5.6 rupees ($1.12), and that of the Punjab 12 rupees ($2.40). The central government received about 17 rupees per head for the same period, a small share of which was transferred to the provinces as grants-in-aid.

The decision on the financial relations between the center and the provinces is reached on the advice of the National Finance Commission, which represents all three governments. It is improbable that the center could be compelled to yield a larger share of revenue than it is willing to concede. It will have to argue its case before the commission, however, and public and political pressure will find a convenient focus.

In the light of the foregoing, it must be concluded that Pakistan is not in reality a federal state. Although the provinces cannot be swept out of existence by the central power, they can be reduced to virtual impotence and may find that at intervals all power has been removed from local hands. There are, however, ten "entrenched" clauses of the constitution which may not be amended without provincial approval. These protect the territories of the provinces, their legislatures, the legislative lists, and the Finance Commission. Other articles may be amended by act of parliament if approved by two-thirds of the members present and voting (Article 216).

Local Government

In some parts of the world local self-government has been credited with providing the foundation of democratic ideals and practices. The Indian subcontinent has always been a land of villages, and many local matters have always been decided by custom or group decision. In

[7] The North-West Frontier Province obtained only 15 per cent.

some parts of India and at certain periods the village *panchayat* or council of elders was a recognized institution of the local administration of justice. In the period preceding British rule the *panchayat* could not be regarded as a democratic system of local government. Appointed or hereditary local officeholders provided the link between the village and higher authority. The local sense of community has always been blurred by communal, caste, and other sectional loyalties.

During the period of direct British rule it was felt safest to begin experiments with representative government at the local level. Some kind of municipal body came into being quite early in the Presidency cities and most of the larger towns. The Resolution of 1882 laid down the general principles of a system of local institutions in rural as well as urban areas. The details were left to each province to implement, but the main outline was similar in most areas and has persisted to the present day. Municipal boards governed the towns, and district and subdistrict boards were established for rural areas.

Municipalities in Pakistan have found it hard to concentrate on questions of sewers and streets and markets and public health. The political life of the last twenty years has proved too exciting, and municipal business is often pushed to one side to make way for a resolution on Kashmir or French rule in Algeria. Lord Ripon, who sponsored the reform of 1882, was clear that his purpose was to provide opportunity for training in public affairs rather than to promote local efficiency. In some senses he has succeeded better than he could have imagined.

Many district and municipal boards in West Pakistan have been suspended for many years. Others, such as the Karachi Municipal Corporation, have carried on a running battle with higher authorities in order to continue in existence. Elections have been conducted in an atmosphere of confusion, and no general tradition of responsibility to the electorate has emerged. The state of affairs is much more hopeful in East Pakistan. There has been lively public interest in municipal affairs, though this has involved the same readiness to stray from local matters. The electoral process has been much better used, however, and the power of the voter has been recognized. It must be admitted that, neither before nor after 1947, have provincial governments and district officials acted to promote effective and strong local self-government. As recently as 1957 the chief minister of East Pakistan announced the beginning of "an era of educational reforms" with the transfer of primary education from the district boards to the provincial government.[8]

The Public Services

Contemporary Pakistan cannot be understood without giving due regard to the role of the bureaucracy. A special part of the constitution is devoted to this subject. It would be true to say that Pakistan could have survived since 1947 without politicians but that it would have collapsed without the civil service.

The Indian Civil Service, before 1947, was a remarkable organization. It was designed to keep the control of the essential parts of the machinery in the hands of those who would take orders from their duly constituted superiors and execute those orders without fear or favor. The ICS was the central service around which gravitated all other elements of the administration. Its membership never exceeded some 1,300 men. From 1870 some Indians had been included in its ranks, and by 1939 more than 40 per cent were Indians. By a process of education, selection, training, and tradition these men had become assimilated to the pattern of the service as established by its British founders.

Not many members of the ICS were Muslims, and a small number of these chose to serve in India rather than Pakistan. Less than a hundred officials, with some British staff who agreed to remain, were thus the central core of the new administration. Recruitment has been proceeding year by year, but the total strength of the Civil Service of Pakistan (CSP) is still only about 400.

The CSP is fully conscious of the fact that it is an elite. Its recruiting announcement states: "The Civil Service of Pakistan is the successor in Pakistan of the Indian Civil Service, which was the most distinguished Civil Service in the world." [9] Its candidates are drawn from among the best university graduates. Those who are successful in meeting requirements go to the Civil Service Academy at Lahore for nine months' training. This is followed by field training in East Pakistan and by an assignment for about six months to the United Kingdom or another country of the Commonwealth. The CSP officer is then ready for a posting to a district.

[8] *Dawn*, Aug. 20, 1957.
[9] Government of Pakistan, *Careers in the Pakistan Central Superior Services* (Karachi, 1954), p. 3.

CSP officers fill almost all senior administrative jobs at all levels of government, central, provincial, and in the districts. A limited number of senior posts in the provinces may be filled by promoted members of the provincial services, but most are reserved for the CSP provided that sufficient officers are available. Before independence the governorship of most provinces had been reserved for the Indian Civil Service. In 1947 Pakistan appointed British ICS officials to three of the four provinces. Although the job of governor is not specifically reserved for CSP members, it is still possible for them to achieve that position. A senior civil servant was appointed governor of West Pakistan in August 1957.

In a district the CSP officer is the personification of the government. All government activities come under his command or supervision. The district officer is in charge of the maintenance of law and order, revenue collection, and social services, and he is also a magistrate with substantial powers. According to the custom of the area, a man in charge of a district may be known as the district magistrate or collector or deputy commissioner. There are 67 districts in Pakistan, the largest of which contains about 4 million people. The district officer is responsible for all aspects of their well-being and acts as the agent of both central and provincial governments and as the supervisor of local authorities.

The districts are grouped into divisions, each under the control of a commissioner who reports in turn to the provincial government. The provincial and federal governments are organized in much the same manner. They are divided into ministries (in Karachi) and departments (in the provinces). Each is in charge of a minister, though one minister may at times hold more than one portfolio. Immediately under the minister, who is a politician, comes the secretary, who is a permanent official and a member of the CSP. Almost without exception these men are general administrators and have no technical or specialist background. A member of the CSP is liable to transfer to any assignment suitable to his rank in any department or any part of the country. Indeed, there are tenure rules designed to prevent overlong assignments to provincial or national headquarters. The administrator is thus kept consistently in touch with the districts, where the effects of government action will ultimately be felt.

If the government needs specialist advice, it may call upon advisers or upon the "attached" departments, which are staffed by specialists. The government of West Pakistan has laid down the distinction between the two types of agency. "It should be the responsibility of the Secretariat to formulate policy, while it should be the responsibility of the Attached Departments to implement that policy." [10] In practice it has not been easy to draw the line.

This highly centralized structure of administrative services enables a few men in key positions to control the whole apparatus of government. The CSP, with the aid of the higher police officials who are also organized on a national basis, are able to govern the country by themselves. They had this experience under British rule and again during the periods when self-government was suspended in the provinces. They form a small homogeneous group of high education, considerable administrative ability, and wide experience. In each capacity they tend to excel the elected politician, who is often tempted to resort to intrigue to lessen the dominant influence of the bureaucrat.

The government machine acts also as an instrument of central authority over provincial and local agencies. This control was necessary during the years when British Indian authorities were threatened by political movements (such as the Congress) which shared power at some levels of government. Many local politicians have urged that the situation should be reversed now that the nation has secured its independence. But the bureaucracy has not allowed its influence to be seriously challenged. When Iskandar Mirza, the first President of Pakistan, was commenting on his role in East Bengal under emergency law, he said: "You cannot have the old British system of administration [and] at the same time allow politicians to meddle with the civil service. In the British system the District Magistrate was the king-pin of administration. His authority was unquestioned. We have to restore that." [11]

In the central government it has been the civil servants who have tended to invade the offices of politicians rather than the reverse. Ghulam Mohammed (Finance Minister and Governor-General), Chaudhri Mohamad Ali (Finance Minister and Prime Minister), and Iskandar Mirza (Minister of the Interior, Governor-General, and President)—all joined branches of the public service in British days and achieved high positions before independence.

Finally, there are the constitutional safeguards for the public serv-

[10] Keith Callard, *Pakistan: A Political Study* (London: Allen and Unwin, 1957; New York: Macmillan, 1958), p. 293.

[11] *Dawn*, Oct. 31, 1954.

ices. These were included in the Act of 1935 to protect civil servants from possible adverse interference by elected politicians. Under the constitution no disciplinary action may be taken against a public servant "by an authority subordinate to that by which he was appointed" (Article 181). In other words, a member of a central service, though serving in a province, cannot be punished by the provincial authorities. In any disciplinary case the civil servant must be given a chance to defend himself and is entitled to at least one appeal against an adverse finding. The constitution also guaranteed the status of the federal and provincial Public Service Commissions, which conduct recruitment and act as advisers on personnel policy and disciplinary cases. These commissions are appointed by the President or the governors acting in their discretion, that is, without cabinet advice.

The Courts

The judiciary is part of the public services of Pakistan. More than fifty senior judicial appointments, including those as judges of the high courts and as district and sessions judges, are included in the total cadre of the CSP. The judicial branch of this service is recruited in equal proportions from CSP officers, who have already acquired administrative experience, and the bar. The CSP man will previously have tried cases as a magistrate, though this will have been only a small element of his former duties.[12] Before being eligible for a high-court judgeship a person must have practiced law for ten years or served as a district judge for three years. Appointment to a high court is made by the President after consultation with the Chief Justice, the provincial governor, and the provincial chief justice. To qualify for the Supreme Court, five years on a high court or fifteen years at the bar is required. The Chief Justice is appointed by the President (i.e., the government), and other members by the President after consultation with the Chief Justice. All judges have security of tenure. A high-court judge can be removed only with the concurrence of the Supreme Court, and a Supreme Court judge by a two-thirds vote of the National Assembly.

[12] The constitution contains a provision that "the State shall separate the Judiciary from the Executive as soon as practicable." This is not aimed primarily at ending the recruitment of judges from the ranks of the CSP. It is intended to take away the magisterial functions of the district officer. A start in this direction was made in the Punjab in 1954.

The judiciary, especially in the higher branches, has been regarded with pride and respect in Pakistan. Both Islamic and British traditions lay stress on the rule of law. The system of jurisprudence owes more to the common law than to the Sharia (the compilation of Islamic law). The legal system of British India consisted of the imposition of English procedures and prejudices on top of the complex mass of local rules and customs. The highest court of appeal until 1950 continued to be the Judicial Committee of the (British) Privy Council. Since the courts of Pakistan regard themselves as bound by precedents, the broad principles of British legal interpretation continue to apply. Some British judges continued to serve on Pakistani courts for a decade after independence, and many of the autochthonous judges and lawyers were trained at the English bar.

The Supreme Court (formerly the Federal Court) has shown itself prepared to take issue with the powers of government at the height of an emergency. When the Governor-General dismissed the first Constituent Assembly, the president of the Assembly sought redress from the courts. The chief court of Sindh granted an injunction against the government that would have restored the Assembly and invalidated the title to office of half the cabinet. The government appealed, and the Federal Court handed down a series of historic judgments defining the relationship between the Crown and the elected legislature. Some of the citations went back as far as Bracton, and the sound of sonorous Latin seemed slightly incongruous in the courtroom at Lahore. The judgments, however, were contemporary in their application, and although the dissolution of the Assembly was permitted to stand, the Governor-General was told in strict terms that he had no title to proceed without a lawmaking assembly.[13]

The Armed Forces

Pakistan received a share of the weapons and supplies of the former Indian forces. A large proportion of the fighting troops of the Indian army had been composed of Muslims from the Punjab and the Frontier. Muslims were less well represented in the technical branches and in the navy and air force. A number of British officers remained both in active commands and for training purposes—the commander in chief of the air force was until 1957 a British officer.

British influence is noticeable still in the character of the senior

[13] Sir Ivor Jennings, *Constitutional Issues in Pakistan* (Cambridge, Eng.: Cambridge University Press, 1957), pp. 4–6.

Pakistani commanders. They are nearly all men who received their training and early experience under British auspices. They were true professional soldiers in appearance and attitude of mind and have been little tempted to meddle in matters of politics. As a group they would favor any government that could make its will effective. If necessary they would employ their troops to back such a government and to maintain law and order. The period of martial law in the Punjab in 1953 [14] was just such an example of the use of the military to reimpose order. The entry of the commander in chief into the cabinet in 1954 was for a comparable reason. The politicians having made a mess of things, the army indicated that it was prepared to back a strong administration. General Ayub Khan took no known part in political matters and withdrew from the cabinet as soon as the new Assembly began to function.

[14] Widespread rioting occurred in Lahore and elsewhere and was due to a campaign that combined religious and political features. The civil government lost control, and the army stepped in. See Government of the Punjab, *Report of The Court of Inquiry to Inquire into the Punjab Disturbances of 1953* (Lahore, 1954).

· XVII ·

The Political Process

IN the final stage before partition, Indian politics narrowed into a struggle between the Indian National Congress and the Muslim League, with the British government acting as referee and scapegoat. Other Indian parties and groups were forced aside or were compelled to merge with one of the main combatants. By 1946 the question "Should India be independent?" had been answered. The only issue remaining was whether there should be one or two successor governments.

The Muslim League was the party of Pakistan. Pakistan was the entire program of the Muslim League. Before 1947 an Indian living in the Punjab or East Bengal might be opposed to partition and the idea of a separate Muslim state. After 1947 such opposition amounted almost to treason. Those who believed that the Pakistan movement was mistaken had either to move to Indian soil or to hide their convictions as carefully as possible. Many of the leaders of anti-Pakistan parties went to India; such was the case of Kiran Sankar Roy, who had been chosen as the first leader of the Opposition in the Pakistan Constituent Assembly. Others—Abdul Ghaffar Khan, for example—were imprisoned or placed under official surveillance.

The months of rioting and bloodshed gave no time for the development of political opposition. The choice for the Hindu and Sikh groups in West Pakistan was migration or death. When the turmoil subsided, the need for political representation of the non-Muslim was almost at an end in West Pakistan, and many of the leaders were missing from East Pakistan.

The Decline and Fall of the Muslim League

When Pakistan was created, Mr. Jinnah was the leader of the Muslim League. He became Governor-General and issued invitations to various individuals to join the cabinet. It was not a question of asking a party leader to form a cabinet of his own choosing. Liaquat Ali Khan had been Jinnah's principal lieutenant, and he and several other cabinet ministers were Muslim Leaguers of long standing. Others, such as Ghulam Mohammed, were included because of personal experience in administration rather than political leadership. The Muslim League was the progenitor of the state, and its function was to secure the stability of the new structure. There was little thought in 1947 of a struggle for political power within Pakistan.

The League had an overwhelming majority in the Constituent Assembly and all four provincial assemblies. The only organized party in opposition was the Pakistan National Congress, which was the successor in Pakistan to the Indian National Congress. Since it was composed almost entirely of Hindus from East Bengal, it could not hope to present itself as an alternative government in a predominantly Muslim country.

The Muslim League was the party of Pakistan—and of Jinnah. Political parties in India normally started at the top and later, if at all, achieved a broad popular base. This was especially true of the League. From its origin in 1906 until after the elections of 1937 it was composed mainly of the wealthy and the educated. It claimed to speak on behalf of the Muslim masses, but its composition was in no sense representative. When Mr. Jinnah returned from England in 1934, the League was little more than a name. He took charge of it, and within the party his authority was never seriously challenged. After the relatively poor showing in the 1937 election, Jinnah set to work to carry the League to the people. It was the case of a leader organizing a mass following, not that of a mass movement producing its own leaders.

The struggle for Pakistan required the submission of individual wills and ambitions to the overriding cause. There were many local leaders who faltered in this and either accepted office when Mr. Jinnah had decided to the contrary or co-operated with the Congress when Mr. Jinnah wished to oppose. They were expelled from the party and were supplanted by others more ready to obey the orders of their commander in chief.

In 1947 Pakistan was won, and within its boundaries the foes of the League were put to flight. The All-India Muslim League held its last meeting in December 1947 with Mr. Jinnah presiding. The Pakistan Muslim League then became its successor and proceeded to draw up a constitution.[1] The League consists of the convention, the council, the Working Committee, and provincial, district, and city leagues. Membership in a primary league is open to a Muslim Pakistani, over 18 years of age, who is in agreement with the aims of the League and pays a triennial subscription of two annas ($.03).

The convention is an assembly of the members of the central and provincial League councils and is the ultimate authority within the party. No convention, however, was held during the first ten years of Pakistan's existence. Arrangements were made for a meeting in October 1954, but the political crisis of the dissolution of the Assembly forced a cancellation.

The League council is the principal controlling and policy-forming organ. It consists of some 400 members—180 elected by each provincial council, League members of the National Assembly, party office-holders, and some nominated persons. The council is expected to meet at least twice a year, but in practice its sessions have been less frequent. Meetings are summoned by the president, though any 75 members are entitled to demand a special session. The council elects the officers of the League and may amend the constitution. It has power "to affiliate, suspend, dissolve or disaffiliate a Provincial Muslim League." The council may delegate any of its functions to the Working Committee or to the president.

The office-bearers elected for three-year terms by the council are the president, the vice-president, the general secretary, the treasurer, and two joint secretaries. All these officers are members of the Working Committee, which also comprises not more than 22 members of the council nominated by the president. This committee has power "to control, direct and regulate all the activities of the various Provincial Leagues in consonance with the aims, objects, rules and declared policy of the Pakistan Muslim League." It may take disciplinary ac-

---

[1] The original constitution of the Pakistan Muslim League was approved in 1948 but was substantially amended in 1952 and 1956. The references that follow refer to the constitution as amended.

tion against any individual member or constituent organization, subject to a right of appeal to the council.

An additional central organ of the League is the Parliamentary Board elected by the council every three years. It consists of 12 elected members (6 apiece from East and West Pakistan) and the League president as chairman. Its job is to select candidates for the central legislature and to supervise the provincial parliamentary boards when selecting provincial candidates. This process is known locally as allocating the party ticket and at times bears a marked resemblance to a competitive examination. The following announcement appeared in the press in 1951:

The Central Parliamentary Board of the Pakistan Muslim League invites applications from persons wishing to seek election on the Muslim League ticket to the NWFP [North-West Frontier Province] Legislative Assembly in the forthcoming general elections.

Applications should reach the Honorary Secretary of the NWFP Provincial Muslim League, Peshawar, by October 15 at the latest.

Each application should be accomplished by a sum of Rs.500 as application fee.

In the case of applicants who fail to obtain the Muslim League ticket, three-fourths of the application fee will be returned, provided they fulfil the terms of the pledge [to be loyal to the successful candidate].[2]

In most democracies, politicians would agree—at least in theory—that party interests should never come before those of the state and its parliamentary institutions. Those countries that have recently attained independence have found it necessary to readjust their scale of loyalties. Before 1947 the state, for Indian Muslims, was British India, but the nation was the concept of Pakistan, as represented by the Muslim League. Support for the League was not a question of favoring the "ins" or the "outs" in the effort to install a new government for a term of office. The larger loyalty was to the League, the lesser, if any remained, was to the existing state. Some Pakistanis carried over this outlook into the age of independence. "I say to you," wrote Mr. Jinnah's sister, "support the Muslim League, because the League alone won Pakistan and can serve and consolidate Pakistan. . . . Don't oppose the League but come into it and remove its defects. If you destroy the League you destroy Pakistan."[3] The first Prime Minister, Liaquat Ali Khan, was making a similar point when he said: "So far as I am concerned, I had decided in the very begin-

[2] *Dawn*, Oct. 3, 1951.   [3] *Pakistan Standard*, Aug. 14, 1954.

ning, and I reaffirm it today, that I have always considered myself as the Prime Minister of the League. I never regarded myself as the Prime Minister chosen by the members of the Constituent Assembly." [4]

When Pakistan came into being, most of the senior leaders of the League became members of the various governments, and the role of the party receded into the background. Mr. Jinnah, while he lived, was the Great Leader in party matters as in all aspects of state policy. The party after its reorganization in 1948, however, chose Choudhry Khaliquzzaman as its organizer and, later, president. The party constitution of 1948 maintained the principle that the party should act as a watchdog over the central and provincial governments. Holders of party office were forbidden to hold cabinet posts, and members of the parliamentary boards were debarred from standing for election to the legislatures. The idea behind this arrangement was that the party could better represent the common people if its leaders were insulated against the temptations of power. Such a relationship was bound to lead to friction.

At the center Liaquat Ali Khan was strong enough to overcome any difficulties placed in his way, but there is no doubt that his position as a member but not the leader of his party's national organization was the cause of embarrassment. In the provinces the party machinery became the continuing source of opposition to the government. This led to prolonged instability in Sindh and the suspension of self-government in the Punjab in 1949.

The party constitution was amended in 1950, and the Prime Minister and the provincial chief ministers were chosen as party presidents. In the center, the change in the office of Prime Minister resulted in change of the party head. But the official appointment preceded the party election when Nazimuddin and then Mohammed Ali became Prime Minister—in this case there was a considerable interval when Nazimuddin, the dismissed minister, continued to be the titular head of the party which formed the government. The change when Chaudhri Mohamad Ali succeeded Mohammed Ali followed a different pattern. The Muslim League parliamentary party (members of the Assembly) elected Chaudhri Mohamad Ali, who then became Prime Minister. He was not a party politician by nature or experience, and he made no attempt to assume the presidency of the League. By this

---

[4] *Dawn*, Oct. 9, 1950. Still less, apparently, did Liaquat Ali regard himself as the Prime Minister chosen, according to the constitution, by the Governor-General.

time the cabinet was a coalition, and he was able to balance its sectional interests by maintaining a distance between himself and the League organization. In January 1956 the Prime Minister moved the nomination of Sardar Abdur Rab Nishtar as president, and at the same time the constitution was changed once more to separate the party leadership from the cabinet.

This change resulted in a return to the earlier friction between the party leaders inside and outside the government. The Prime Minister was accused of disloyalty to his party. His reaction was sharp: "Let me make it clear that in any action that I have to take as Prime Minister I cannot be bound by a resolution of any political party. I have to do what I consider to be right under the constitution, and for that I am responsible to the Cabinet and to the Parliament." [5] Four months later Chaudhri Mohamad Ali resigned as Prime Minister and as a member of the League. He complained with some bitterness that the party had rendered his position untenable.[6] The League was not included in the following government, and the question of the relations between this party and the administration did not arise again until I. I. Chundrigar became Prime Minister in October 1957.

In the provincial Muslim Leagues the conflict between government and party was repeated, but the level of rivalry and intrigue was more intense. Between 1947 and 1955 there were seven ministries in Sindh and four in the Punjab, and each province suffered a prolonged suspension of self-government. Each of these ministries was, in name, a government of the Muslim League, and the party had at all times an immense majority in the legislatures. The size of the majority had much to do with the dissension within the party. When there is no fear that a strong opposition may overthrow the government, political loyalty gives way to individual maneuver. It would be true to say that no legislative session passed in these two provinces without some serious attempt to undermine the administration. Each government protected itself after its own fashion with carefully distributed favors for present or potential supporters and tangible signs of disapproval toward those who contemplated mutiny.

To judge by the wording of the League constitutions, the presidents, both central and provincial, should have had little trouble in dominating the party. Each appointed the majority of the members

<hr>

[5] *Pakistan Observer*, May 15, 1956. This statement is in marked contrast with that of Liaquat Ali, six years previously.

[6] *Dawn*, Sept. 9, 1956.

of his Working Committee, and the unwieldy councils were seldom in session. But this is to ignore the real nature of political parties in Pakistan. Political activity usually begins with a few men of position and influence in a community. These may be landlords, businessmen, hereditary religious leaders, or simply young lawyers with a talent for oratory. The next stage is to find a small nucleus of supporters and, if the would-be politician lacks money, a patron. Local politics becomes a struggle for predominance among groups of such men; provincial politics merely increases the scale of operations. Thus a few score prominent men, each with a retinue of political liverymen, form changing patterns of alliances to obtain and hold power. The ordinary member of the party—the two-anna man—is enrolled largely to give voting support to a particular local leader. It is often hard to join such a party since the officeholders make sure that prospective members are "sound" before allowing them to obtain an enrollment form.

There is nothing novel or improper in the idea that a party should be a tactical alliance for achieving power. What has distinguished the parties of Pakistan, especially the Muslim League, is the speed with which the alliances are made and dissolved. This is partly caused by the absence of a genuine opposition, though the tendency to dissolve into fragments persisted even after the emergence of large opposition groups. It is also due to the absence of any clear division of political forces by long tradition or by differences on major policies.

Before 1947 the policy of the Muslim League could be summed up in one word—Pakistan. The new state could be portrayed as all things to all men. And the struggle for Pakistan was a valid reason for postponing or eliminating all personal or sectional differences. Once the state was accomplished, the first tasks of the government were so clear and urgent that there could be little room for dispute except as to the appointments to office. All were agreed that Mr. Jinnah's leadership was beyond question, and some part of his political mantle fell on the shoulders of Liaquat Ali Khan.

The Muslim League was in power at all levels of government from 1947 to 1954. Nationally there was no call to face the prospect of a general election until 1958.[7] Each of the four provinces, however, conducted one general election on the basis of an adult franchise, before the proclamation of the new constitution. These elections were held in the Punjab and the North-West Frontier Province in 1951

[7] The second Constituent Assembly was elected by the provincial assemblies.

and in Sindh in 1953. In each case members of the League won an overwhelming proportion of the seats, though a large number of independent candidates served to divide the popular vote. The League secured not less than 80 per cent of the seats in each province.

The façade of party unity was thus preserved, and the impression of public support was not seriously challenged. The real opposition was to be found within the ranks of the League, although in a few instances prominent individuals had taken their followers into opposition. Thus the main opposition party in the Punjab elections was led by the deposed chief minister, the Khan of Mamdot. In Sindh one deposed chief minister led an opposition group while another continued to lay claim to be the true head of the provincial Muslim League. The situation was confused, and the choice open to the voter was not very wide.

The electorate in Pakistan had no previous experience of an adult suffrage election. Unfortunately the examples of 1951–1953 could not be looked upon as a lesson in democratic procedures. An official inquiry reported: "It was widely and persistently complained that these elections were a farce, a mockery and a fraud upon the electorate." [8] Mr. Suhrawardy, then in opposition, used even stronger language: "The elections [in the Punjab] were a farce, intimidation and coercion, fraud and manipulation of ballot papers and ballot boxes were practised on an unprecedented scale." [9]

The Politics of East Pakistan

What has been said in the preceding paragraphs applies primarily to West Pakistan. Until 1954 East Bengal was politically quiescent. There were two chief ministers, Nazimuddin, who departed to take high office in Karachi, and his successor, Nurul Amin. There seemed to be no plots and counterplots, and the outward unity of the provincial Muslim League was unbroken. But the provincial government was strangely reluctant to contest by-elections or to dissolve the provincial assembly. The members of the legislature had been chosen before partition to sit in the Assembly of undivided Bengal. Their term of office, however, was deemed to begin from the date of the

[8] Electoral Reforms Commission, Report, in *Gazette of Pakistan, Extraordinary,* April 24, 1956, p. 922. It should be noted that these elections were held before the establishment of the Election Commission.

[9] H. S. Suhrawardy, *Address to the Nation* (Lahore, n.d.), delivered at Dacca, May 8, 1953, pp. 6–7.

first meeting after independence, in March 1948. Five years later the government hoped shortly to have a new constitution, and the life of the provincial house was extended until March 1954. The constitution was not adopted, and the election was finally held under the provisions of the Government of India Act.

Although the provincial government seemed secure, it had become clear that major differences had arisen between East Bengal and the central government. The basic grievance felt by the Bengalis has been a feeling that they were regarded as inferior by the rulers of West Pakistan.

Sir, I actually started yesterday and said that the attitude of the Muslim League coterie here was of contempt towards East Bengal, towards its culture, its language, its literature and everything concerning East Bengal. . . . In fact, Sir, I tell you that far from considering East Bengal as an equal partner, the leaders of the Muslim League thought that we were a subject race and they belonged to the race of conquerors.[10]

East Pakistan contains more than half the population of the whole country, but it is poorer and almost totally lacking in industry. Many Bengalis feel that a primary charge upon the national government should be the accelerated development of the east wing to the point where it possesses standards equivalent to the west. The central authorities, on the other hand, have often insisted that the utmost use of existing resources must be made and that the west is better suited for industrial development. This divergence of view has led to a series of requests by East Pakistan, many of which have not been met by the national government. The Bengalis have then proceeded to ask for greater decentralization to provide them with the authority and the resources to do for themselves what Karachi is unwilling to perform. This is not feasible when the major powers and tax sources are allotted to the central government.[11]

During the discussion of the new constitution the members from Bengal pressed hard, with partial success, for increased authority for their province. They also fought vigorously for a distribution of seats in the national legislature that would not deprive them of the benefits of their numerical majority. A number of complex formulas were

[10] Constituent Assembly of Pakistan, *Debates*, I, 530, Sept. 7, 1955. The speaker was Ataur Rahman Khan, who was to become chief minister of East Pakistan.

[11] For a discussion of the distribution of power and revenue see above, pp. 414–417.

considered when it was expected that there would be four provinces and two houses of the legislature. Finally, with two provinces and one house, the equal division of seats was accepted.

The issue which caused the greatest anger and resentment in East Bengal was that of the national language. Nearly 55 per cent of the total population speaks Bengali, whereas 28 per cent speak Punjabi and 7 per cent Urdu. Bengali employs a script that is derived from Sanskrit, and Urdu and Punjabi use the Persian script. The principal language of the Indian Muslims before 1947 was Urdu, which can be understood over the greater part of the subcontinent. The West Pakistanis suspected Bengali because it forms a link with West Bengal (in India) and because much Bengali culture bears strong influences of Hinduism. Some of the advocates of Urdu as the main national language managed to convey the impression that the defense of Bengali was both un-Islamic and opposed to the interests of national unity.

It was made clear from the start that the national leaders intended to insist on Urdu as the state language. Mr. Jinnah made a speech in the capital of East Bengal which could leave no doubt concerning his own view. "But let me make it very clear to you that the State Language of Pakistan is going to be URDU and no other language. Anyone who tries to mislead you is really the enemy of Pakistan. Without one State Language, no nation can remain tied up solidly together and function." [12] When the first constitutional proposals were published, they contained the flat recommendation, "Urdu should be the national language of the State."

The subordination of Bengali was never acceptable to the people of East Pakistan. They suffered from many other disadvantages, and if this proposal were adopted, they would be separated further from influence and power by the barrier of language. The students of Dacca University protested violently against the imposition of Urdu, and in the resulting riot some of the demonstrators were killed. The issue had now become a sacred cause. After four years of growing bitterness the central leaders gave way and admitted equal status for Urdu and Bengali. The constitution recognizes this concession and provides further that English may be used for official purposes for twenty years.

Karachi is more than a thousand miles from East Pakistan. The national government is therefore remote from the problems and feelings of Bengal. It has recruited its civil servants and armed forces

[12] *Quaid-e-Azam Speaks* (Karachi, n.d.), p. 133.

mainly from the west, although genuine attempts have been made to increase the proportion of Bengalis. Those Bengalis who go to Karachi as politicians or government employees tend to find either that they remain outsiders with no real influence or that they have been absorbed into the cultural pattern of West Pakistan and cease to act and feel as Bengalis.

Throughout this period of mounting Bengali irritation the position of the government of East Bengal was not easy. As a Muslim League administration it could not afford to quarrel openly with the national leadership at Karachi. Yet its own sympathies were largely on the side of those who wanted increased autonomy and more consideration from West Pakistan and the central government.

In spite of known resentment against Karachi, informed observers still expected the Muslim League to win a majority in the new Assembly, although it was conceded that a much stronger opposition was to be expected. The results of the election left no doubt as to the feelings of the electorate. Out of 309 seats the Muslim League secured 10, and the main coalition of opposing parties—the United Front—obtained more than 230. The monopoly of the Muslim League had been broken, and within three years that party was to find itself excluded from office in both provinces and at the center.

The Awami League

The largest single component of the United Front was the Awami (People's) League. This party had its origins in the period from 1949 to 1950 and was formed by grouping together a number of political leaders who had quarreled with the leaders of the Muslim League. In the North-West Frontier Province the Pir of Manki Sharif was forced out of the League and moved into opposition. In East Bengal, Maulana Bhashani, a former president of the Assam Muslim League, felt that a new party was needed to speak for the common people. In the Punjab the Khan of Mamdot was deposed as chief minister in 1949 owing to rivalry within the Muslim League. He organized his followers as the Jinnah Muslim League. Shortly afterward, he consolidated his group with the Awami League under the title Jinnah Awami Muslim League, and the new party gained 29 seats at the provincial elections.[13]

The task of organizing these small opposition groups into a na-

[13] In 1953 Mamdot and his adherents rejoined the Muslim League. In 1956 he transferred to the Republican Party.

tional party fell to H. S. Suhrawardy. He too had been a Muslim
Leaguer and had been chief minister of undivided Bengal in the days
immediately before partition, when he made an unsuccessful attempt
to secure a united independent Bengal based on Hindu-Muslim co-
operation. In 1947 he decided to remain in Calcutta working for
communal peace between the Muslims and the Hindu majority in
West Bengal. He had been elected to the first Constituent Assembly
and even while living in India traveled to Karachi to participate in
its sessions. In 1948, however, he was deprived of his seat on the
ground of nonresidence in Pakistan. About a year later he moved to
Pakistan and began to rebuild his political influence.

Mr. Suhrawardy is a professional politician with long experience
as a legislator and cabinet officer during the period of British rule. He
completed his education at Oxford and was trained for the bar. He is
a fluent and persuasive speaker though not a great orator. Like many
politicians he is noticeably more radical in his ideas and attitudes
when in opposition. In office he has demonstrated a remarkable ability to maintain support and to outmaneuver his opponents.

The Awami League held a convention in Lahore in 1952. Its constitution is similar to that of the Muslim League, with a convention,
council, and Working Committee, and Mr. Suhrawardy was convener.
The manifesto of the party, adopted at that time, is filled with high-
sounding phrases, but few of them have any concrete significance.
The following proposal was advanced in the field of economic policy:
"The State should be self-sufficient and even surplus in food and national requirements; it must be in a position to export finished
products; the agriculturists must be assured a reasonable price for
their produce, and the labourers a reasonable wage. The cost of
living must be proportionate to the income."

During the period of its consolidation and growth the Awami
League bore no responsibility for administration. Since it was also
virtually excluded from the legislatures, it could hardly be called
upon to bear the duties of a responsible opposition. It was able,
therefore, to take advantage of almost all the feelings of discontent
in any part of the country. In East Pakistan its supporters were
mainly young men who had been no more than students during the
struggle for Pakistan. Their general outlook was radical in economic
and social matters, and they were ardent supporters of the demand for
autonomy for East Bengal. The principal leader of this group was
Ataur Rahman Khan.

A somewhat different style of politics, though with the same ends, was provided by Maulana Bhashani. The Maulana [14] was a born malcontent and a fanatic with millennial visions of what might be accomplished if only the rule of the saints could be established. He lived an austere personal life and attacked wealth and privilege. When the Awami League formed a government, he preferred to remain outside, acting as spokesman for the ordinary people. He had little knowledge of the problems of administration, finance, or international affairs. His appeal was less to the students of the colleges, who played such a prominent part in Bengali politics, than to the peasants in the villages.

Mr. Suhrawardy as national leader operated mainly from West Pakistan and established himself as a potential alternative Prime Minister. He stressed the need for a strong opposition.

Next, we believe that an opposition party is necessary for the proper functioning of democracy, this is the only influence that can keep the rulers in check and at work, and can create public opinion. The Muslim League, on the other hand, labels opposition as disruption, demands that there shall be no parties other than itself, and all other parties must be crushed out of existence.[15]

The first major chance to move toward power came with the East Bengal election of 1954. Late in the previous year the Awami League entered an alliance (the United Front) with the Krishak Sramik Party and some lesser groups. They agreed to sponsor a combined list of candidates against the Muslim League. Local committees chose the individual candidates, and it was often uncertain which section of the United Front claimed their primary allegiance. This prepared the way for prolonged confusion at a later stage over claims to predominance.

The United Front proclaimed a manifesto known as the Twenty-one Points. It contrived to promise something for everyone. It announced a firm adherence to Islam and urged that no laws should be passed contrary to the requirements of the faith. *Zamindari* (landlord system) was to be abolished without compensation, and the land was to be distributed to the peasants. The crucial item was point 19, the demand for provincial autonomy:

Secure all subjects, including residuary powers, except Defence, Foreign Affairs and Currency, for East Bengal, which shall be fully autonomous and

---

[14] Maulana is a religious title, the nearest Western equivalent of which might be doctor of theology.

[15] Suhrawardy, *Address to the Nation*, pp. 6–7.

sovereign as envisaged in the historic Lahore Resolution, and establish Naval Headquarters and ordinance factory in East Bengal so as to make it militarily self-sufficient.

When the elections were held, the United Front carried almost every seat it contested and emerged with a majority as great as that previously enjoyed by the Muslim League. A new ministry was appointed under the leader of the Krishak Sramik Party. The elections and their results had caused some commotion throughout the province. This erupted in two major riots in which hundreds of lives were lost. The central government had been alarmed by the program of the Front and by the character of some of its leaders. The riots provided the pretext for the proclamation of a state of emergency, and self-government was suspended before the new Assembly had a chance to meet.

When the central cabinet was reorganized after the dissolution of the Constituent Assembly, Mr. Suhrawardy became Minister of Law. He was the only representative of the Awami League in a ministry still dominated by the Muslim League, and he found himself somewhat isolated. In the middle of 1955 he left the cabinet and became leader of the Opposition in the second Constituent Assembly. At the same time self-government was restored in East Bengal, but the Awami League was excluded from the new United Front ministry and formed the Opposition there also.

The next shift in the balance of political forces occurred a year later, after the new constitution had come into operation. The East Bengal ministry appeared unable to obtain a majority in the legislature and was replaced by the Awami League, with some minority support, under Ataur Rahman. Chaudhri Mohamad Ali resigned as national Prime Minister, and Mr. Suhrawardy formed a coalition government in co-operation with the Republican Party.

The Krishak Sramik Party

The Krishak Sramik (Peasants and Workers) Party consists of the personal following of A. K. Fazlul Huq. Fazlul Huq has been a leading and highly controversial figure in the politics of Bengal for more than half a century. He participated in the founding of the Muslim League, and his subsequent career carried him in and out of that organization on several occasions. He was the mover of the Lahore Resolution in 1940. In 1937 he led his own Krishak Proja Party and secured a large number of seats in the Bengal Assembly. He became chief minister and held office for six years. After partition he accepted the office of advocate-general for East Bengal. In 1953 he broke with the Muslim League government and began to form a party to contest the forth-coming provincial election.

Fazlul Huq is a magnificent orator in Bengali, and though his technique does not appeal to the sophisticated, he has a mass follow-ing throughout his province. His main argument during the cam-paign was the demand for a greater measure of autonomy for East Bengal. He was the leading figure in the United Front, and there can be no doubt that his name and personal influence did much to swell the total vote against the Muslim League. After the March 1954 victory he became the chief minister during the six weeks before governor's rule was proclaimed. His visit to Calcutta, while in office, was the occasion for a series of press reports indicating that he wanted complete independence for East Bengal and closer ties with West Bengal. The central government, after his dismissal, described him as a "self-confessed traitor to Pakistan." When the second Constituent Assembly was formed in 1955, however, the national government needed his assistance, and he entered the cabinet. At the same time his principal lieutenant became chief minister of East Bengal with a ministry composed mainly of the Krishak Sramik Party but with support from the non-Muslims and others. A few months later Fazlul Huq became governor of East Pakistan, a post that he continued to hold even after his party was replaced as the provincial government by the Awami League. He was dismissed by the central government early in 1958.

Non-Muslim Parties

In the various elections held before 1956 the non-Muslims voted in separate constituencies for candidates drawn from their own com-munity. Although the Christians, Parsis, and Buddhists were repre-sented at the center or in the provinces, the two major groups of non-Muslims were the Hindus and the scheduled-caste Hindus. The Pakistan National Congress was the principal representative of the upper-caste Hindus and had a substantial following among the scheduled (low) castes. The Congress was the official opposition in the first Constituent Assembly and in the Assembly of East Bengal until 1954. Being confined to the Hindu community,[16] it could never

---

[16] The Congress was open to members of all communities, but for obvious reasons very few Muslims in Pakistan wished to be connected with it.

hope to become a government with a majority. Its main role was therefore that of defender of minority rights and interests. It lay continually under the suspicion of disloyalty. Many of its members had opposed the creation of Pakistan and maintained friendly contacts with members of the Indian Congress across the border. Naturally the Congressmen could not be expected to have precisely the same feelings toward Pakistan as those of the Muslim nationalists.

The Congress Party fought on two main issues. First, it opposed the proclamation of an Islamic state and all features in the constitution that conferred a special status on one faith. Second, it argued vehemently against the continuation of the system of separate electorates, whereby the minorities were penned politically into little boxes and prevented from exercising effective influence on matters of wider concern. The Muslim League was pledged to the concept of two separate nations, the Muslim and the Hindu. It had fought for separate electorates to enhance its own position as a minority community. Both by tradition and by its line of reasoning the League wished to continue separate electorates to preserve the purity of Muslim politics and to ensure proportional representation of Hindus in the legislatures. The Awami League came round to the support of joint electorates, and in 1956–1957 the law was altered to provide simple territorial constituencies for the country as a whole.

The Scheduled Castes Federation also was the successor of an All-India organization. The scheduled castes had always had some doubts about their position under a predominantly caste Hindu administration. The Federation therefore pressed for special seats in the legislatures and for special quotas of jobs in the public services. The Muslim League had used members of the scheduled castes to substantiate their claim that the old Indian National Congress was primarily a body of upper-caste Hindus. Thus a scheduled-caste Hindu was named by the League to the interim government of 1946–1947 and was continued in cabinet office in Pakistan after partition. The community has often been divided in its political view, and members in the legislatures have at times followed the lead of the Muslim League, the Awami League, the Krishak Sramik Party, and the Congress. The result has been that as a group the scheduled castes have had little political weight. The Federation, the largest political body representing the scheduled castes, obtained 27 seats (out of 309) in East Bengal and 3 (out of 80) in the second Constituent Assembly.

The Republican Party

The Muslim League won large majorities in all three provinces of West Pakistan, but these gave no stability since they were divided into a dozen major factions which struggled ceaselessly for power. One of the reasons for amalgamating the provinces in 1955 was the hope that, on a larger stage, the scope for petty conflicts would be lessened. The government of West Pakistan was appointed before the legislature came into being. M. A. Gurmani became governor, and Dr. Khan Sahib chief minister. Dr. Khan had been chief minister of the North-West Frontier Province immediately before partition. He was then a member of the Congress Party and had opposed the creation of Pakistan; the governor dismissed him a week after the new state came into existence. He was invited to join the emergency central cabinet of October 1954 as a sign that old quarrels had been forgotten and as an indication that in a moment of crisis all patriotic citizens should be prepared to serve the state.

The West Pakistan Assembly was chosen in January 1956 by election by the members of the old provincial assemblies. As was to be expected, a majority of its members belonged to the Muslim League. This made Dr. Khan Sahib's position somewhat equivocal. He had no party of his own and was unwilling to join the League. A large section of the League elected a party leader and demanded that he be summoned to form a government as the head of the largest party in the Assembly. The chief minister responded by dismissing those members of his cabinet who were not prepared to be loyal to him. In April 1956 Dr. Khan Sahib announced the formation of the Republican Party. He was able to hold a narrow majority in the Assembly, and most of the Muslim League members of the National Assembly joined the Republicans. In September the Muslim League members were dropped from the central cabinet, which was reconstituted under Mr. Suhrawardy with support from the Awami League, the Republicans, and some non-Muslims. The Republican majority in West Pakistan held through two short sessions of the Assembly, but the party was divided on the issue of separate or joint electorates. In March 1957, when the situation in the Assembly was highly confused, self-government was suspended and the governor assumed power under Article 193. In July, Dr. Khan Sahib resigned as leader and was replaced by Sardar Abdur Rashid,[17] who was then called on to form a cabinet. He was succeeded in 1958 by M. A. Qizilbash.

The Republican Party came into being solely because of the splits within the Muslim League. It was formed largely to prevent certain Muslim Leaguers, notably M. A. Khuhro and M. M. Daultana,[18] from taking power. Apart from personal loyalties and enmities and a desire to remain in office, there was little in common among the Republicans. In order to adopt a constitution and to work out a policy, the party held a convention in Lahore in September 1956. The constitution is basically similar to that of the Muslim League with a leader, national council, national convention, and provincial and local units. The only item of its program which is specific is related to the two-nation theory and its consequences:

To assert that there is more than one nation in Pakistan is to assert that some citizens of Pakistan are Pakistani nationals and some are not, that Pakistan is the national homeland only of some of her citizens and not of all. To assert this is to free some of our nationals from the demands of allegiance to the State and loyalty to the country; it is to invite disloyalty and disruption.

Apart from this item, the other aims of the party are pious aspirations rather than proposals that could be implemented by an administration. Section headings include "the expedition of progress," "realisation of goodness," "disbursement of happiness," and "the consolidation of peace."

The National Awami Party

The parties described above have been based on personal and local factors rather than ideology. The Awami League has, to a certain extent, developed a degree of responsiveness to the views of its ordinary members, but its policy is made mainly by a handful of leaders. In all cases it would be true to say that the leaders built the party rather than that the party produced its leaders. Fixed principles have normally been subordinated to personal maneuvers to obtain power.

The National Awami Party (NAP) is, in this sense, also an association of leading figures, backed by their personal followings. But it also possesses a number of ill-assorted ideologies. This party is a

[17] Rashid had been chief minister of the Frontier Province in 1953–1955 and had served in Dr. Khan's cabinet.

[18] M. A. Khuhro had been chief minister of Sindh, and Daultana chief minister of the Punjab. Both were in Dr. Khan's cabinet until April 1956.

union of malcontents, men who, by temperament, find themselves in opposition under any government. The party was formed in July 1957 as the result of an agreement between the leaders of eight minor groups.

In West Pakistan, for example, the Azad (Free) Pakistan Party had achieved a considerable measure of publicity largely owing to the character and position of its leader, Mian Iftikharuddin.[19] He was a minister in the Muslim League government of the Punjab immediately following partition, but resigned because that government was unwilling to adopt more radical solutions to social problems. His politics are of the extreme left, and he has often been called a fellow traveler. In foreign affairs he has been a principal critic of Pakistan's ties with the Commonwealth and the United States.

Other segments of the NAP are led by G. M. Syed and Abdul Ghaffar Khan. Syed was a major political figure in Sindh before partition and had been a member of both the Congress and the Muslim League. He was a strong advocate of Sindhi interests and opposed the amalgamation of the provinces. Abdul Ghaffar Khan, the brother of Dr. Khan Sahib, used to be called the Frontier Gandhi. He was a member of the first Constituent Assembly, but for most of its duration he was in prison on security grounds. He wanted autonomy for the Pathan people of the frontier and also opposed the creation of West Pakistan.

Such minor parties in West Pakistan were mostly local organizations, but they were agreed in demanding the redivision of the province into linguistic units and radical social reforms. In 1956 they combined to form the Pakistan National Party. At first they supported Dr. Khan Sahib in the provincial assembly. Failing to obtain any reconsideration of the unification scheme, they withdrew their assistance. This led to the suspension of self-government in 1957.

In East Pakistan the National Awami Party has two main components. The Ganatantri Dal (People's Party) was formed in 1953. Its leadership was mainly Muslim, but it admitted others on equal terms and contested some non-Muslim seats. Its outlook is secular and socialist. There is also Maulana Bhashani, one of the founders of the Awami League. He was opposed to his party on issues of internal social reforms and on the question of Pakistan's alliances with the Western powers.

Bhashani attempted to bring the Awami League back to the path

[19] Iftikharuddin is a wealthy man and the proprietor of a leading newspaper.

of virtue. Responsibility for the conduct of government in both
Karachi and Dacca had induced a cautious outlook in the main leaders of the party. The Maulana was therefore outvoted in the Awami
League council in his attempt to alter official policy. His response
was to summon a convention to inaugurate the National Awami Party.
The constituent resolution declared that the new party would "aim
at freeing the country from imperialism, ameliorating the condition
of the people and establish, through constitutional means, democracy
in the country and autonomy in both the Wings of Pakistan." [20]

Religious Parties

Although Pakistan is a proclaimed Islamic state, political activity
has not passed, to any substantial degree, into the hands of religious
leaders. The Muslim League, which established Pakistan, continues
to be led by professional politicians, many of them lawyers by training. Men of rigid Islamic orthodoxy are to be found in most of the
parties that have been described, but they control none of them.

This is not to say that religion plays no part in political life. Almost
every Muslim, politician or layman, would agree that the clear injunctions of Islam ought to be followed in public as well as in private
life. The attempt to give constitutional expression to Islamic ideals
was much more than window dressing. Pakistan would indeed be
without meaning if it failed to give Muslims a sense of being able
to accomplish their own Islamic destiny.

Some politicians have attempted to ride into public favor by taking
up a religious issue. Thus in West Pakistan the campaign against a
particular Muslim religious sect was led by men who were both
religious leaders and politicians. The result was explosive, involving
widespread rioting and the imposition of martial law. On most issues
public opinion has looked to the politician rather than to the man of
religious learning. The cry of "Islam in danger" is, however, still
powerful and might serve to produce a violent reaction if the interests
of the faith seemed to be in danger.

There are two parties which are religious in their leadership
and policy. The more important is the Jamaat-i-Islami (Union of
Believers). It is led by an able politico-religious theorist, Maulana
Maududi. The Jamaat attempts to be more than a political party. It is
a militant religious order owing obedience to its commander. It un-
dertakes social service activities as well as political teaching and agi-

[20] *Dawn*, July 26, 1957.

tation. Its members are subject to rigorous discipline and are expected to lead lives of austerity. Many individuals have admired this spirit of devotion even if they have not agreed with the political program of the group. Others have hoped that some teacher would provide an authoritative exposition of the relevance of Islamic doctrine to current problems. Maududi has attempted to play this role and has attracted attention though not a mass following.

The lesser religious group has confined its operations to East Pakistan. The Nizam-i-Islam (Rule of Islam) Party is conservative and orthodox, whereas that of Maududi is radical and experimental. It joined with the United Front in opposing the Muslim League in 1954 and secured 19 seats in the provincial assembly.

Other Parties

If the Communist Party deserves mention in a discussion of politics in Pakistan, it is because of its international rather than its internal importance. No Communist leader of any importance has appeared in Pakistan, and the main activities of the party have been concentrated in an effort to place individuals within labor, student, and political groups. The party was allowed to operate openly until 1954 but achieved no success at the polls in the four provincial elections. In East Bengal some alleged Communists secured United Front nominations and were successful, but only four were elected as party members. Later in 1954 the party was suppressed by law, but one reputed Communist was elected to the second Constituent Assembly.

One further party deserves mention. Its formation illustrates the tendency of the older parties to split and the extent to which parties are formed by one or two prominent individuals. The former Prime Minister Chaudhri Mohamad Ali, having broken with the Muslim League, formed his own party, the Tehrik-i-Istehkam-i-Pakistan (TIP or Pakistan Solidarity Movement). He had at least one supporter in the National Assembly but no visible popular following.

The Art of Politics

If a Western observer should enter the National Assembly in Pakistan, the nature of the proceedings would be immediately apparent. Most of the speeches, especially by ministers, are given in English. The Speaker presides, with the government benches on his right and the Opposition on his left. The atmosphere is parliamentary, with its Question period, points of order and privilege, and motions of adjournment. This is politics as practiced by men of Western education many of whom have had twenty years or more of parliamentary experience.

The politics of the streets and fields is a different matter. The ordinary man is illiterate but not stupid. He quickly forms an opinion about his rulers, that they are honest men or corrupt, that they are strong or weak. It is a judgment of character rather than policy. Gossip about political leaders, often well informed and usually malicious, can be heard in the bazaar of any small town or the coffeehouses of the cities.

Public opinion, in the sense of a well-informed critical appraisal of policies and events, is limited to a small group of the educated living in the few large centers. For popular appeal, in Pakistan as elsewhere, an issue has to be reduced to a simple contrast between right and wrong. Thus "Home rule for Bengal" and "Kashmir is ours" are slogans that can be readily understood and have an emotional appeal.

In the towns mass political activity takes the form of mass meetings which last for hours and are harangued by a series of orators. Leaders among the crowd begin chanting slogans which are taken up in unison by thousands of voices. The effect, from a distance, resembles a college football crowd; at close quarters it is rather more alarming. A meeting is often followed by processions through the streets with the crowds still chanting and waving banners and placards. If the issue is controversial, violence often results, and processions and meetings are frequently banned by the magistrates.

In the rural areas mass activity of this kind is not possible, but missionary speakers tour the country to impart their message. Political consciousness is much more highly developed in East Pakistan, where mass participation in major issues has been evident for half a century. In West Pakistan the power of the landlords in the Punjab and Sindh has been diminished only slightly since independence.

Political life in Pakistan has reached the stage at which the people have begun to realize that they have power. But this has to be set against the long tradition by which "government" had power and the people could do no more than petition for redress of grievances. Government, both cabinets and the civil service, still behave in an authoritarian manner, but this no longer passes without challenge. Responsible government, however, is a more subtle matter than this, and it is too early to suggest that it is fully understood or accepted in Pakistan.

· XVIII ·

Pakistan and Its Problems

IN the days before 1947 there were many who doubted whether Pakistan could ever be established as a working state. There is no existing parallel of a country which functions divided into two portions, almost equal in population but separated by a thousand miles of alien territory. True federalism is never an easy form of government to work since its very nature causes some degree of friction between the interests and attitude of the component units. Federalism with only two components runs the risk of becoming a perpetual struggle for supremacy, and yet a central administration in a divided country is difficult of achievement.

Experience in Pakistan before 1956 and provisions made in the constitution indicate that the central government is to retain the major share of power. If there is a conflict between one province and the center, the latter is always in a position to have the last word. Federalism can, however, take another form—the central government should itself be composed and function as a representative body. Thus the cabinet should be evenly divided between East and West. The civil service and the army should give equal attention to both wings of the country in their policies of recruitment and promotion. In the allocation of federal expenditure the claims of each province should be considered. (The standing grievance of Bengal is that this has not

447

happened or has not been carried to the point that would be fair to its interests.)

National Unity

The first task of any government in Pakistan is that of holding the country together and maintaining the consent of the people-at-large to the continuance of the state if not to that of the government of the day. The Muslim League had the virtue that it was equally strong in both provinces; but its policy alienated East Pakistan to the extent that the party was all but effaced in that province. The Awami League exists in West Pakistan but draws its strength from the east; the reverse is true of the Republican Party. A coalition is usually an uneasy alliance unless there is real agreement on a clear policy. In Pakistan no distinction between right and left has emerged. Individuals in every party want radical changes, but the assumption of office has usually resulted in a more conservative outlook.

The principal problem in maintaining national unity is that of relations between East and West Pakistan. A second issue is the status of non-Muslims. Pakistan, by definition, is a state with a preponderance of Muslims, in which the principles of Islam shall guide social action. There is nothing in the constitution, however, that imposes serious discrimination upon the non-Muslims. Nevertheless there can be no doubt that the Hindu, in particular, does not feel himself to be a full citizen with standing equal to that of his Muslim compatriots. There has been a slow but steady drift of Hindus from East Pakistan to India. The middle classes, who might provide leaders, have been the first to go. A young educated Hindu feels that he will have a better chance of a career in Calcutta than in Dacca. The government of Pakistan has tried to reduce the efflux though it does not prevent the departure of those who wish to leave.

A Free Society

It is highly misleading to suppose that national independence and a free society are equivalent terms. Before 1947 Indians lived in a society that was free within limits defined by an alien power. Since independence those limits have changed—though not very much—but they are now set by a government that belongs to the country. There is a psychological difference, but to the man who finds himself in jail it is more apparent than real.

Any government must maintain order. In settled countries where the basic social purposes are a matter of general agreement, civil disorder is a minor concern. Pakistan is newly self-governing and emerged into separate existence during a period of turmoil and repression. The main laws and regulations limiting political activity which might endanger peace have been continued from the period of British rule. The constitution, however, has balanced them with a series of fundamental rights, enforceable in the courts.

Some of the limits on political activity are to be found in the ordinary criminal law. Thus section 144 of the Code of Criminal Procedure permits a magistrate to forbid a public meeting or to order a specified individual not to make a speech. Section 144 has been proclaimed with great frequency and is often in force for periods of several months. Other sections of the criminal law restrict what may be said or written in the course of political debate. A person who "brings or attempts to bring into hatred or contempt, or excites or attempts to excite, disaffection towards the Government established by law in the provinces" commits an offense punishable by a maximum sentence of transportation for life. (Before 1947 this meant exile to the penal colony of the Andaman Islands.) This clause has been used very rarely, but its presence alone can serve as a restraint.

The press in Pakistan is subject to control. Many newspapers, especially those printed in local languages, have been wildly irresponsible and malicious. In an illiterate society rumors can easily be started, and the truth is hard put to hold its own. The law therefore requires that publishers may be required to give deposits that are liable to forfeiture without a judicial trial. There is also provision for the suppression of a paper or for precensorship. In 1948 in Karachi the central government took action against seven newspapers, barring four and imposing censorship on three.

The most serious limitation of civil liberty in Pakistan consists of the laws authorizing preventive detention. Such laws have a long history in the subcontinent. The Bengal State Prisoners Regulation of 1818 is still in force throughout Pakistan. Detention may be ordered by the central government for reasons of state connected with foreign affairs or as a precaution against internal commotion. More widely used have been the Security of Pakistan Act and its provincial counterparts.[1] Under the constitution, parliament may make laws concerning "preventive detention for reasons connected with defence, foreign

[1] The Awami League government of East Pakistan secured the repeal of the provincial Security Act in 1956.

affairs, or the security of Pakistan," and the provinces may make similar laws "for reasons connected with the maintenance of public order." The power to detain without trial is limited by the fundamental rights under the constitution. Each case of detention has to be referred to an advisory board appointed by the chief justice of the federation or province. Unless the advisory board confirms the detaining order, no person may be held for more than three months.

Article 5 of the constitution declares that "all citizens are equal before law and are entitled to equal protection of law" and, further, that "no person shall be deprived of life or liberty save in accordance with law." This wording leaves no redress against an unjust law unless the courts develop some equivalent of the American doctrine of substantive due process of law. In similar fashion the constitution guarantees freedom of speech and expression subject to "any reasonable restrictions imposed by law in the interest of the security of Pakistan, friendly relations with foreign states, public order, decency or morality, or in relation to contempt of court, defamation or incitement to an offence." The draftsmen of these clauses were attempting to foresee all possible consequences of a literal interpretation of the guarantee of the fundamental rights. The result seems to leave the individual only one word of defense against legislative tyranny. The word is that restrictions must be "reasonable."

The safeguards of life and liberty are limited by extensive powers of the state. The right to property is subject to similar conditions: "No person shall be deprived of his property save in accordance with law." Property may be taken for public purposes by a law which provides for compensation and fixes the amount and specifies the principles on which the compensation is to be paid. There is no guarantee that the compensation shall be equivalent in value to the property acquired. Further, nothing in Article 15 affects the validity of any existing law or the acquisition of any property which is classed as evacuee property.[2]

Many free societies have laws upon their statute books which might severely limit the freedom of the citizen. Such laws are available for emergency use only, and it is clearly understood by the government as well as public opinion that under ordinary circumstances they will not be employed. Pakistan has lived through ten years of crisis. Yet it would be wrong to suggest that lawful political opposition has been prevented or that there has been a reign of terror. Ministers and gov-

[2] Evacuee property is property belonging to persons who have migrated to India.

ernments have been violently criticized, and their overthrow has been secured by political activity. There has been upon occasion a real danger of internal disturbance, and any government would have had to be armed to meet it. The exact steps taken may be open to criticism, but it is clear that after ten years Pakistan remains a country where free political discussion and agitation are the rule rather than the exception.

Economic Development

One of the chief aims of all nationalist movements struggling to achieve independence has been to accelerate the pace of economic development. The majority of the inhabitants of Pakistan live not far above the starvation line. They remember vividly the disastrous famine of 1943–1944 when the dead in Bengal were numbered by the hundred thousand. They hear of the prosperity and security of the workers in the economically advanced countries, and they insist that something must be done to raise local standards.

It was clear from the beginning that independence for Pakistan would harm the economy of the new state which consisted of two separated sections carved out of the economic unity of prepartition India. Pakistan was deprived of the commercial and industrial facilities formerly provided for those areas by the major economic centers of Bombay and Calcutta. Further, many of the businessmen and skilled workers of non-Muslim communities fled to India, and their place was only partially filled by refugees coming from the reverse direction. Those owners and operators of businesses who remained in Pakistan found an immense demand for their products and were able to make large profits. The conclusions of a leading economist in 1955 are not, therefore, surprising.

It is . . . probable that the per capita income after 1954–55 would be less than what it was about seven years ago. Inequalities in income have increased. A smaller national income, relatively to the size of the population, more unequally distributed than before, implies that the living standards of the masses of the people which were already very low, have deteriorated still further.[3]

Nearly ninety people out of every hundred live in villages. Although this figure includes rural craftsmen and others, most of these live

[3] M. L. Qureshi (chief economist, Planning Board, Government of Pakistan), *Address Delivered at the Conference of the Pakistan Economic Association* (Peshawar, 1955), p. 11.

directly or indirectly from the produce of the land. The majority are poor peasants, holding their land either as tenants of a landlord or directly from the state. In West Pakistan a very small group of land-lords disposes of a vast amount of land. In Sindh shortly before the war it was reported that 70 per cent of the total farm land was in the hands of 7 per cent of the owner group. Ten years later another inquiry indicated that more than one-fifth of the cultivable area of the Punjab was in the hands of about .5 per cent of the owner group.[4]

The attention of most of Pakistan's politicians has been given to constitutional issues and the struggle for power. The landlords have been sufficiently strong and skillful in West Pakistan to divert attention from land reform to other matters, and no major party has adopted a systematic left-wing program. Some minor improvements have been made, however, giving greater security to the tenant and freeing him from some of the feudal obligations to his landlord. No general redistribution of landholdings has been attempted. East Pakistan, by contrast, has begun a complete revision of the pattern of land rights. The State Acquisition and Tenancy Act of 1950 provides for the abolition of rent-receiving interests. A normal limit of about 33 acres is to be placed on individual holdings and subletting is forbidden, though a form of sharecropping is to be allowed. The former rent receivers are to be compensated on a scale that varies with the size of their holdings. The Muslim League government proceeded slowly with the program of acquisition, taking over a few large estates each year. The United Front made use of a procedure for summary large-scale acquisition and promised to complete the job by 1956. Court action subsequently slowed but did not halt this undertaking.

No country is now willing to remain a producer of primary products and rely upon others for its supplies of manufactured articles. Possession of large industries is a source of national pride even though the goods produced may be more expensive and of poorer quality than the imported article. Pakistan has undertaken a program of industrial development that is very large when measured against the available material resources. At the time of partition there were almost no industries in Pakistan. In ten years large numbers of jute, cotton, and woolen mills have come into operation, and the country is now practically self-sufficient in these products.

The program of industrialization has involved direct public invest-

[4] Government of Pakistan, *The First Five Year Plan 1955–60 (Draft)* (Karachi, 1956), II, 117.

ment, private initiative, and varying combinations of the two. The major government agency in this field is the Pakistan Industrial Development Corporation, which has provided financial backing for a large proportion of new industrial undertakings. Besides the textile industries, the PIDC has also launched enterprises in paper, sugar, chemicals, fertilizers, and cement and in shipbuilding and engineering. The index of industrial production, which covers seventeen major industries, rose from 100 in 1950 to 350 in 1955.

Pakistan is not well endowed with natural resources. Iron ore has recently been discovered, and plans for its processing have been drawn up. There are small coal deposits in West Pakistan, but substantial imports are required. A major field of natural gas has been brought into production at Sui in Baluchistan and is distributed by pipeline to Karachi and industrial centers in the Punjab. In 1947 Pakistan had only 5 per cent of the installed capacity for electricity in the subcontinent. Several large hydroelectric plants have now come into production and are supplemented by coal-burning stations.

The foreign trade of Pakistan is made up of exports of raw materials and imports of machinery and manufactured goods. Four-fifths of export revenue is provided by raw jute and raw cotton, with tea and wool, hides, and skins making up most of the remainder. The balance of payments has fluctuated widely with the movement of world prices of these primary products. Some years have seen a surplus as high as $170 million, but these have been more than offset by even larger deficits. In 1949 when the pound sterling was devalued, the Pakistan rupee did not follow and maintained its higher value until 1955 in order to take advantage of continuing demand for Pakistan's exports. Both imports and exports are subject to government control, and both are taxed, mainly for revenue purposes.

Pakistan had almost no class of capitalists and no developed investment market. Savings from the rural sector of the economy are traditionally hoarded or put back into the land. The industrial and commercial sector was small and composed largely of family enterprises. Major industrial expansion has therefore needed state assistance or foreign investment. Pakistan, like most newly independent countries, has been reluctant to see vital industries controlled entirely by foreigners. The government has therefore laid down varying proportions of voting control for different industries that must be retained in Pakistani hands. There is also strong encouragement for foreign firms to employ as many Pakistanis as possible in senior positions.

Apart from this, official policy has welcomed foreign private investment. The main source of capital has been the United Kingdom.

The census of 1951 reported a total labor force of 22 million, of
which 17 million were engaged in agriculture. Even in the industrial
sector the growth of trade unions has been slow. In 1954 there were
nearly 400 registered unions with a total membership of 420,000.
Three-quarters of these are grouped into the All-Pakistan Confederation of Labour, with a subordinate federation in each province. Government policy has been favorably disposed toward the growth of
unions but has given little active encouragement. The leadership of
many unions rests in the hands of educated men who have no experience in the type of work performed by the members. This has advantages in dealing with management but may lead to the advancement
of the leader's political career rather than the advantage of the
workers.

There is general agreement that Pakistan must have a planned,
though not necessarily socialist economy. Resources were too scarce
and the managerial class too small to consider uncontrolled investment, production, and distribution. In the early years the machinery
for economic planning was designed mainly to co-ordinate the activities of the State Bank and the various government agencies controlling imports, tariffs, and investment. In 1950–1951 all existing
development schemes were listed together and described as a Six
Year Plan. The plan was, however, more a compilation of desirable
projects than a workable scheme for practical achievement. In 1954
a Planning Board was established to review the progress of development, survey available resources, and prepare future plans. The draft
of a Five Year Plan was produced in 1956.

Social Policy

Pakistan is pledged by its constitution to the creation of a welfare
state. The Directive Principles of State Policy are not enforceable in
the courts, but they stand as a declaration of intention for the guidance
of legislators and officials. The state is to "endeavour to secure the
well-being of the people, irrespective of caste, creed or race, by
raising the standard of living of the common man, by preventing the
concentration of wealth and means of production and distribution
in the hands of the few to the detriment of the interest of the common
man." Further, the state is to establish a system of social security and
to provide for the sick and infirm. It is also to aim at the provision of

"free and compulsory primary education within the minimum possible period."

These are noble ideals. Unfortunately they are so far from the existing state of affairs as to sound unreal to the ears of the "common man." In 1954 Pakistan had one doctor for every 13,000 people and one nurse for 51,000.[5] Comparable figures for the United Kingdom were one doctor for 1,000 and one nurse for 300. Underground drainage for sewage disposal was available to about 2 per cent of the population. Hundreds of thousands, even in the federal capital, lived in miserable shacks built of tin cans and sackcloth. The government is taking some action, but progress is slow. Refugee colonies have been built on the outskirts of several of the large towns to house a part of the homeless. The village AID (Agricultural and Industrial Development) scheme has improved the sanitation of the villages besides encouraging the development of cottage industry. All such plans are limited by the paucity of government revenues and the need to spend large sums on defense and major industries which are slow to benefit the general standard of living.

Foreign Policy

It is characteristic of all intense nationalist movements that the rest of the world appears merely as a background to the successive acts of the national drama. Thus the struggle for Pakistan was set amid the events of the Second World War and the early years of the Cold War. It would be untrue to suggest that Pakistanis felt themselves unaffected by world politics, but their interest was focused primarily upon the achievement of national independence. Firoz Khan Noon, who was to become Prime Minister of Pakistan, said in 1946: "If the Hindus give us Pakistan and freedom, then the Hindus are our best friends. If the British give it to us then the British are our best friends. But if neither will give it to us, then Russia is our best friend." [6]

Once Pakistan had been established, the immediate concern of its foreign policy was to secure recognition of its sovereign statehood. Pakistan felt that the two new Dominions were equal successors to the international status of British India. The Indian government, on the other hand, considered that India was the principal heir and that Pakistan was a new state based on the decision of certain parts of the

[5] Government of Pakistan, *The First Five Year Plan 1955–60 (Draft)*, II, 482.
[6] Quoted in A. B. Rajput, *The Muslim League Yesterday and Today* (Lahore: Shaikh Muhammad Ashraf, 1948), p. 109.

subcontinent to secede. The Secretariat of the United Nations seems to have taken the Indian view since the membership of India continued without re-election whereas Pakistan was admitted with no delay but only as the result of an application and election to membership.

The major problems of Pakistan's foreign policy arose from the partition of India. By all the factors of history, geography, and economics the interests of India and Pakistan were intermingled. The very boundaries of the two states were not defined until the day of partition had arrived. The definition of their respective territories was left to a Boundary Commission with members from each Dominion and Sir Cyril Radcliffe as chairman. Neither government was satisfied with the commission's award, which had to be decided by the vote of the chairman. An important area of the Punjab, in the district of Gurdaspur and with a Muslim majority, was allotted to India, and the Chittagong Hill Tracts, with a non-Muslim majority, went to Pakistan. There were many lesser causes of uncertainty and irritation.

The Boundary Commission had not decided the distribution of the princely states between the two Dominions. The British relationship with the Indian princes had been described as "paramountcy." This meant that the states retained internal self-government subject to the acceptance of guidance from British resident advisers. When independence came to British India, paramountcy lapsed, and it became the right of each prince (there were more than 600 of them) to decide for himself, with or without consulting his people, whether to join India or Pakistan or to try to achieve independent existence. The Viceroy urged the princes to make their choice between the two Dominions before independence day and to bear in mind the influence of geography, economics, and the composition of the population. The large majority had no alternative but to join India. Three states, however, were the cause of serious dispute between Indian and Pakistan. They were Junagadh, Hyderabad, and Jammu and Kashmir.[7]

Junagadh was a small state on the west coast of India about 200 miles south of the nearest territory of Pakistan. Its ruler was Muslim whereas the majority of the people were Hindus. The prince signed a formal accession to Pakistan but found himself opposed by a large section of his people. India massed troops on the border, and the ruler fled. His minister then invited India to enter the state to preserve order. A plebiscite was held later which decided in favor of union

[7] Jammu and Kashmir had been one state for a century, but there were historical and cultural differences between the two regions.

with India. The official view of the government of Pakistan is that the state legally forms part of her territory and that India's forcible occupation cannot be recognized.

Hyderabad constituted a much more significant example of a similar problem. It was the most important Indian state, and its ruler, the Nizam, was a man of immense wealth and great prestige. He was a Muslim, and his state had become a major center of Islamic culture. Osmania University had acted as an important stimulus to the growth of the Urdu language and literature. The majority of the state's population was Hindu, with the Muslims acting as a ruling class. Hyderabad had no coast line and was entirely surrounded by India. The Nizam's government tried to proceed toward complete independence and signed a "Standstill Agreement" with India in November 1947. The situation inside the state deteriorated rapidly, with Muslim and Hindu extremists resorting to violence and the Communist Party provoking a peasants' revolt. In September 1948 Indian troops marched into Hyderabad, and the issue was settled by force. Pakistan was not an immediate party to the dispute, but developments appeared to confirm Pakistani suspicions of India's aggressive intentions against areas under Muslim rule. Pakistani sympathies were, of course, on the side of the Muslim minority.

It is the quarrel over Kashmir that has proved the insuperable obstacle to friendly relations between the two countries. Kashmir was in a position shared by no other princely state, in that it could contemplate a real threefold choice—accession to India or to Pakistan or independence. Kashmir had frontiers with both new Dominions as well as with China, Tibet, and Afghanistan. Natural communications in 1947 were almost entirely with Pakistan. The Indian contact with the state was through the Gurdaspur District, which as a Muslim majority area Pakistan felt should never have been assigned to India. There was one poor road from India that was impassable in winter. The population of Jammu and Kashmir totaled more than 4 million of whom three-fourths were Muslim. There was a concentration of Hindus and Sikhs in Jammu, and a scattered population of Buddhists in the region adjoining Tibet.

The Maharajah of Kashmir was a Hindu. He was on unfriendly terms with the Indian National Congress, which was opposed to autocracy, and with the Muslim League, which had no sympathy for Hindu princes. India and Pakistan have argued for ten years about the facts and the legal rights of the Kashmir dispute. The outline of events is clear. The Maharajah acceded to neither Dominion but entered into a Standstill Agreement with Pakistan. Rioting took place within the state and was soon converted into war by the invasion of Muslim tribesmen from the North-West Frontier of Pakistan. These tribesmen were armed and provided with transport to the border of the state, but it is not certain that the invasion was planned by the Pakistan government. The Maharajah, in danger of being driven out of the state, appealed to India for armed assistance. The Indians insisted that he first sign an instrument of accession to India, but at the same time they declared that the people of the state must be free to make the final decision once law and order had been restored. Indian troops were flown to the state's capital and routed the tribesmen who had lingered on the way to indulge in looting and arson. Soon Indian forces were approaching the Pakistan frontier. The government in Karachi then ordered the army to intervene to prevent the whole of Kashmir from falling into Indian hands. The fighting continued through 1948 until a cease-fire was arranged in January of the following year.

In the meanwhile the issue had been taken to the United Nations. The Indian case was simple. Kashmir had acceded to India, and the presence of Pakistani troops was consequently an invasion of Indian soil. The Security Council should therefore condemn Pakistan as an aggressor, and India would then assume control of the state. After this had been done, a plebicsite could be held in peaceful conditions so that the will of the people might be ascertained.

Pakistan had not accepted the validity of the accession of Kashmir to India. Prime Minister Mohamad Ali made this clear in a speech in the National Assembly. "If anything, here was an act of naked Indian aggression against a defenceless people, committed under cover of a fraudulent and invalid instrument of accession, surreptitiously obtained from a Hindu ruler who had lost the confidence and support of his people and whose writ had no longer any force within the state." [8] Pakistani indignation was made much greater because it seemed that India had been able to use force against Junagadh and Hyderabad to "rescue" Hindu people from Muslim princes but professed to be morally outraged when Pakistan wished to apply similar tactics in Kashmir.[9]

[8] National Assembly of Pakistan, *Parliamentary Debates*, I, 306, March 31, 1956.
[9] An account of the Kashmir dispute from the point of view of its effect on Indian foreign policy may be found in Chapter XIII, which also deals with the internal situation in that part of Kashmir held by India.

Essentially for both disputants the issue at stake is one of pride and prestige. Pakistan is utterly convinced that Kashmir must be a part of that country since it is a Muslim-majority area. Any other solution is unthinkable since it would deny the essence of Pakistan—the claim of the Muslims of India to be one separate nation with a right to a state of their own in areas where they constitute a majority. For India the converse is true. The reality of a secular democratic India will best be demonstrated if a Muslim-majority area becomes freely reconciled to its place within the Indian Union. To surrender Kashmir would act as an irritant to extreme Hindu sentiment and might provoke increased communal tension within India. This is a continuation, after partition, of the old argument between Muslim separatism and a united India. By its nature there can never be a compromise except that produced by sheer weariness of continuing the quarrel.

In the meanwhile Kashmir is divided, with the richer and more populous area under Indian control. Elections were held in 1957, but no party was permitted to campaign for accession to Pakistan. In January of that year India announced the "irrevocable" accession of Kashmir in spite of a Security Council resolution urging no change in status until a plebiscite had been held. Opinion in Pakistan has begun to despair of a satisfactory solution but is in no sense resigned to the ultimate absorption of Kashmir in India.

The fighting in Kashmir produced a direct clash between the armies of India and of Pakistan. On other occasions, notably in 1951, both countries have massed their armies behind their main frontiers, and general war has seemed perilously close. A small power directly confronting a larger neighbor always has reason for anxiety when relations between the two enter a period of friction. Pakistan is especially vulnerable in the event of war. Its territory is divided into two sections with a thousand miles of India in between. Communication between the two would be impossible by land or air, and the sea involves a prolonged voyage around India in the face of an Indian navy which is far superior to the ships of Pakistan. Pakistan's resources for the production of munitions are slight; the country has only two major ports, both of which would be vulnerable to blockade. The Pakistani air force is relatively small, and most of its bases are within reach of Indian attack. The army of Pakistan is sizable and well trained, but with restricted supplies and air support its effect would be limited. War would be disastrous for both sides, even if some sort of victory could be won. Responsible leaders of the armed forces and the governments know this very well. Unfortunately the state of tension that has existed at times in the ten years since independence means that the possibility of war, however suicidal, cannot be ignored.

A further cause of dispute between Pakistan and India has arisen over the distribution of the waters of the Indus basin. The Punjab contained one of the largest and most complex systems of irrigation to be found anywhere. Most of the irrigated land in 1947 lay in the West (Pakistani) Punjab. On the other hand, the upper reaches of five of the six main rivers lie in India or Indian Kashmir. The Indians wished to use some of this water for schemes of irrigation on their own side of the border, and they began to undertake projects that would reduce the flow of water in Pakistan. The World Bank was called upon to act as mediator, and negotiations have proceeded for seven years without an agreement being reached. The Indians are proceeding with some of their plans for diversion of water, and the authorities in Pakistan have become increasingly alarmed.

Other points of conflict between Pakistan and India have arisen from the attitude of each country toward its minorities. Stories of Hindu mistreatment of Muslims find a wide audience in Pakistan, and the converse is true in India. There have been lengthy arguments between the two governments on the subject of the disposition of property left behind by refugees, and no agreed scheme of compensation has been found. Between 1948 and 1951 there was a virtual stoppage of trade between the two countries since India refused to recognize the continued high value of the Pakistani rupee after its Indian counterpart had been devalued.

In all these issues Pakistanis have felt that India has never accepted their nation as an equal. The struggle for Pakistan before 1947 was in large measure the attempt to force the Indian National Congress to deal with the Muslim League as the representative of a separate but equal nation. The validity of this claim was never accepted by the Congress. Equality with (Hindu) India was therefore a dominant idea in the minds of Pakistanis even before their state came into being. This idea has continued to be the primary motive of Pakistan's foreign policy since 1947, and relations with all other countries are seen as they affect this basic objective.

Pakistan was created to be the homeland of the Muslims of the Indian subcontinent. As such the Pakistani nation can be expected to take an interest in the progress of Muslims everywhere. An article of the constitution declares that "the State shall endeavour to strengthen the bonds of unity among Muslim countries." Classical Islamic doctrine treats of Muslims as forming one people, and the institution of the caliphate preserved in theory the ideal of allegiance to a single ruler. In this sense the requirements of Islam cut across the concept of nationhood for Pakistan. Indeed there were some religious leaders who opposed Pakistan because it tended to deify the nation and detract from the unity of all believers.

Many pious Muslims in Pakistan believe that their government should work steadily toward a pan-Islamic state or at least toward a Muslim bloc that would act as a unit when the interests of Muslims were in conflict with those of others. The government encouraged the activities of a number of unofficial organizations which aimed at closer understanding between Muslim peoples. It also originated a series of Muslim International Economic Conferences, the first and third sessions being held in Karachi in 1950 and 1954. In 1952 the prime ministers of twelve Muslim states were invited to Karachi, but the conference was abandoned because of the reluctance of some of the governments concerned. Heads of state or of government of Turkey, Iran, Iraq, Saudi Arabia, Jordan, Egypt, Syria, Indonesia, and Afghanistan have exchanged state visits with their Pakistani counterparts.

In the United Nations and elsewhere, Pakistan has given vigorous support to independence for Muslim peoples in Libya, the Sudan, Morocco, Tunisia, Algeria, and Malaya. There was also support for Iran during the oil dispute and for Egypt in the early stages of the Suez crisis. The Arab countries have been able to count on Pakistani influence in their conflict with Israel. "I would like to make it clear," said Prime Minister Suhrawardy in 1956, "that Pakistan has never recognized Israel, and my policy definitely is that we shall not recognize Israel under any circumstances." [10]

In these actions Pakistan has a genuine feeling of the duty of all Muslims to stand together. This is based on a simple code of friendship—that your friends are my friends and your enemies my enemies. Unfortunately the rest of the Muslim world has not been anxious to reciprocate, especially since the evidence of friendship demanded by Pakistan is support of its case against India. The Arab states, besides internal quarrels, have ambitions of their own which have little to do with the advancement of the realm of Islam. When Israel, Britain, and France attacked Egypt, the initial reaction in Pakistan was to offer support to the victim. Nasser, who hated the Baghdad Pact, was

[10] *Pakistan News* (London), Nov. 24, 1956, quoting a press statement of Nov. 14, 1956.

not impressed and refused to permit Pakistani forces in the United
Nations Emergency Force or to receive a visit from Mr. Suhrawardy.
Opinion in Pakistan felt betrayed. "It is nevertheless a matter of deep
regret that in the veins of this turbulent egotist not the blood of Islam
should seem to flow but the turbid waters of the Nile. Nasser will
never be our friend; he will never think in terms of Islam except when
it suits his own interest." [11]

It is unfortunate that Pakistan has not enjoyed good relations with
neighboring Afghanistan. There had been a long record of friction
between India and Afghanistan along the North-West Frontier.
Afghan influence with the Pushtu-speaking tribes was considerable
since they inhabit areas on both sides of the border. After partition,
the Afghans reopened old claims either for frontier adjustments or for
an independent state of Pakhtunistan. On the other hand, Afghanistan
has since had good relations with India, and Pakistan has placed a
sinister interpretation on this cordiality.

Apart from India, the people of Pakistan feel more closely connected with Britain than with any other country. In the history of
India before 1947 Britain appeared as the predominant world power.
India became involved in Britain's wars, and Britain defended India
against external aggression. Indians were naturally aware of the
activities of the British government and the stand of British political
parties, since India's prospects depended on British decisions. For
Pakistan some measure of British sympathy was an essential condition
for the creation of an independent state. Hence, immediately after
independence, Pakistan hoped to rely on British and Commonwealth
influence to strengthen its position. Many British civil servants and
officers of the armed forces remained in the service of Pakistan, and
Britain was the major supplier of private capital for industry. But the
British government, like those of the other countries of the Commonwealth, declined to take sides in the differences between India and
Pakistan.

This attitude has led to a feeling in Pakistan that membership in
the Commonwealth is of no great advantage in the overriding issue
of foreign affairs—relations with India. British policy in the Middle
East has also drawn criticism, both from the left and from pious
Muslims. The Working Commitee of the Muslim League passed the
following resolution in November 1956:

[11] *Dawn*, Dec. 1, 1956, editorial, "So This Is Nasser!"

The behaviour of the British government in their dealings with Muslim countries, particularly towards Iran when that country nationalized its oil industry, towards Saudi Arabia over the Buraimi Oasis dispute, and towards Egypt over the nationalization of the Suez Canal; their attack on Yemen, and last but not the least, their brutal aggression against Egypt in company with France and Israel has convinced the people of Pakistan that its continuance as a member of the Commonwealth is positively harmful and, therefore, there is a universal demand for withdrawal of Pakistan from the Commonwealth.

A few months earlier, however, the Foreign Minister (Hamidul Huq Chowdhury) had stated the position of the government: "As regards the Commonwealth countries, we have the friendliest and most cordial relations with the United Kingdom." [12] And when, in March 1956, the Constituent Assembly was asked to take a vote on the matter, the support for continued membership of the Commonwealth was almost unanimous (42 to 2).

The Cold War has always seemed remote from Pakistan. Internal communism has not posed a serious threat, and Russia and China, although a stone's throw from Pakistani frontiers, have not appeared a menace. If there has been any threat to security, it has come from India. But Pakistan has been actively in search of friends. Neither the Muslim world nor the Commonwealth was willing to help strengthen Pakistan in relation to India. Under the Truman regime the United States seemed even more anxious to make friends with India and to overlook Pakistan. The stand taken by Chester Bowles (U.S. ambassador in New Delhi) seemed to indicate the possibility that the United States might lend major assistance to India in order to provide Asia with leadership as an alternative to China. When the Republicans took office in 1953, the situation changed. Mr. Dulles was anxious to show that there were free countries in Asia which were neither Communist nor neutralist. In April 1953 the Governor-General dismissed Nazimuddin and replaced him as Prime Minister by Mohammed Ali, who had been ambassador in Washington. Mohammed Ali had a genuine admiration and affection for the United States, and his relations with officials of the American government were excellent. A month later Mr. Dulles came to Karachi. In November the Governor-General, the Foreign Minister, and the army commander in chief

[12] National Assembly of Pakistan, *Parliamentary Debates*, I, 83–84, March 26, 1956.

arrived in Washington. It was therefore no great surprise when, in 1954, Pakistan signed a Mutual Defense Agreement with the United States and entered SEATO and the Baghdad Pact.

Indian leaders were highly vexed at this turn of events which appeared to them to bring the Cold War to their doorstep. But the vehemence of the Indian protest did much to make the Western alliance palatable in Pakistan, where otherwise neutrality would have been much more attractive. The Awami League initially condemned the link with the United States; but as soon as the League assumed power, the advantages of an alignment with a great power became apparent, and Mr. Suhrawardy became a staunch defender of the alliance and a major source of strength for the Baghdad Pact. The alignment with the West has been aided, inside Pakistan, by a natural dislike of communism, and this is combined with hostility produced by Russian signs of favor toward both Indian and Afghan claims against Pakistan. Nonetheless, many Pakistanis feel that the Western alliance is valuable only if it strengthens Pakistan against India. Prime Minister F. K. Noon made this quite clear in March 1958: "I can tell the world this much that our people, if they find that their own freedom is in jeopardy and threatened by India, they will break all Pacts in the world in order to save their own freedom and that they will go and shake hands with the people whom we have made enemies for the sake of others." [13]

SUGGESTED READING

Ahmad, Jamil-ud-Din, ed. *Some Recent Speeches and Writings of Mr. Jinnah.* Lahore: Shaikh Muhammad Ashraf. Vol. I, 5th ed., 1952; vol. II, 1947.

Ahmad, Mushtaq. *The United Nations and Pakistan.* Karachi: Pakistan Institute of International Affairs, 1955. Written mainly for a Pakistani audience, it shows their view of world affairs.

Akhtar, S. M. *The Economics of Pakistan.* 3d ed. Lahore: Publishers United. Vol. I, 1954; vol. II, 1955.

Albiruni, A. H., pseud. *Makers of Pakistan and Modern Muslim India.* Lahore: Shaikh Muhammad Ashraf, 1950. A useful account of the lives of such men as Sayyid Ahmad, Iqbal, and Jinnah.

Ambedkar, B. R. *Pakistan; or, The Partition of India.* 3d ed. Bombay: Thacker & Co., 1946.

[13] *Dawn, March* 10, 1958. The statement was made in the National Assembly on March 8.

Arnold, F. B., ed. *Pakistan: Economic and Commercial Conditions,* May 1954. (Overseas Economic Survey.) London: H.M.S.O., 1955.

Birdwood, Christopher Bromhead, Baron. *A Continent Decides.* London: Robert Hale, 1954. Also published as *India and Pakistan.* New York: Praeger, 1954. An interpretation of the causes and process of partition, with much sympathy for the cause of Pakistan.

———. *Two Nations and Kashmir.* London: Robert Hale, 1956.

Bolitho, Hector. *Jinnah.* London: John Murray, 1954. A readable biography without profound insight into Indian history.

Brecher, Michael. *The Struggle for Kashmir.* Toronto: Ryerson Press, 1953. Based mainly on the proceedings of the United Nations.

Brown, W. N. *The United States and India and Pakistan.* Cambridge, Mass.: Harvard University Press, 1953.

Calder, Grace J. "Constitutional Debates in Pakistan," *Muslim World,* Jan., April and July 1956, pp. 40–60, 144–156, 253–271.

Callard, Keith. *Pakistan: A Political Study.* London: Allen and Unwin, 1957; New York: Macmillan, 1958.

———. "The Political Stability of Pakistan," *Pacific Affairs,* XXIX (March 1956), 5–20.

Campbell-Johnson, Alan. *Mission with Mountbatten.* London: Robert Hale, 1951. A day-by-day record by Mountbatten's press attaché, who was critical of the part played by the Muslim League.

Coupland, Sir Reginald. *India: A Re-statement.* London: Oxford University Press, 1945. This and the following are works of major importance surveying Indian history from 1833 to 1945 and analyzing its constitutional and political implications.

———. *Reports on India.* London: Oxford University Press. Part I, 1942; parts II and III, 1943.

Davis, Kingsley. *The Population of India and Pakistan.* Princeton: Princeton University Press, 1951. A demographic study.

Faruki, Kemal A. *Islamic Constitution.* Karachi: Khokhropar Gateway Publications, 1952. The outline for a constitution on an Islamic basis, representing a line of thought far removed from Western political ideas.

Feldman, Herbert. *A Constitution for Pakistan.* Karachi: Oxford University Press, 1956. An account of the political crises of 1953–1955.

Gledhill, Alan. *Pakistan: The Development of Its Laws and Constitution.* London: Stevens, 1957.

Griffiths, Sir Percival. *The British Impact on India.* London: Macdonald, 1952. A valuable assessment, written by a former senior official in British India.

Human Relations Area Files, Inc. *The Economy of Pakistan.* Vols. I and II. New Haven, 1956. This work and the two following are useful compilations of fact.

——. *Jammu and Kashmir State*. New Haven, 1955.

——. *Pakistan: Government and Politics*. New Haven, 1956.

Hunter, Sir William. *The Indian Musalmans*. Reprinted from 3d ed., 1876. Calcutta: Comrade Publishers, 1945. A classic work, invaluable to the understanding of the growth of Muslim separatist sentiment.

Jennings, Sir Ivor. *Constitutional Problems in Pakistan*. Cambridge, Eng.: Cambridge University Press, 1957.

Jinnah, Mohammed Ali. *Quaid-e-Azam Speaks*. Karachi, n.d. Mr. Jinnah's speeches, 1947–1948.

Keith, Sir Arthur Berriedale. *A Constitutional History of India, 1600–1935*. 2d ed. London: Methuen, 1937.

Korbel, J. *Danger in Kashmir*. Princeton: Princeton University Press, 1954. An account by a member of a United Nations commission.

Lambert, R. D. "Religion, Economics, and Violence in Bengal," *Middle East Journal*, IV (July 1950), 307–328.

Liaquat Ali Khan. *Pakistan: Heart of Asia*. Cambridge, Mass.: Harvard University Press, 1951. The North American speeches of Pakistan's first Prime Minister.

Lumby, E. W. R. *The Transfer of Power in India*. London: Allen and Unwin, 1954.

Maron, S. "The Problems of East Pakistan," *Pacific Affairs*, XXVIII (June 1955), 132–144.

——, ed. *Pakistan: Society and Culture*. New Haven: Human Relations Area Files, 1957.

Maudoodi, Syed Abul Ala. *Islamic Law and Constitution*. Karachi: Jamaat-e-Islami Publications, 1955.

Menon, V. P. *The Transfer of Power in India*. Princeton: Princeton University Press, 1957. A detailed record from 1939 to 1947 by a senior Indian civil servant who was close to the center of power.

Narasimham, Sarat C. V. *The Other Side*. Karachi: Sorodo Publications, 1955. Speeches by Hindu leaders in Pakistan.

Pakistan, Government of. *The Constitution of the Islamic Republic of Pakistan*. Karachi, 1950.

——. *The First Five Year Plan 1955–60 (Draft)*. Vols. I and II. Karachi, 1956.

Punjab, Government of the. *Report of the Court of Inquiry to Inquire into the Punjab Disturbances of 1953*. Lahore, 1954. The Munir report provides invaluable material on the problems of governing a country such as Pakistan.

Qureshi, Ishtiaq H. *The Pakistani Way of Life*. New York: Praeger, 1956. An introduction to the history and culture of Pakistan.

Rajput, Allah Bakhsh. *Muslim League Yesterday and Today*. Lahore: Shaikh Muhammad Ashraf, 1948.

Saiyid, Matlubul Hasan. *Mohammad Ali Jinnah.* 2d ed. Lahore: Shaikh Muhammad Ashraf, 1953.

Sayeed, Khalid Bin. "The Jama'at-i-Islami Movement in Pakistan," *Pacific Affairs,* XXX (March 1957), 59–68. An account of a significant political-religious group.

Smith, Wilfred C. *Islam in Modern History.* Princeton: Princeton University Press, 1957. See especially ch. v, "Pakistan: Islamic State."

——. *Modern Islam in India.* London: Gollancz, 1946. An excellent analysis of Muslim social and political thought.

Spear, Sir Percival. *India, Pakistan, and the West.* London: Oxford University Press, 1949.

Stephens, Ian. *Horned Moon.* London: Chatto & Windus, 1953; Bloomington: Indiana University Press, 1955. A mixture of political reflections and travel diary by the former editor of an Indian newspaper who prefers Pakistan to modern India.

Symonds, Richard. *The Making of Pakistan.* 3d ed. London: Faber and Faber, 1951.

PART FIVE : INDONESIA

By George McT. Kahin

· XIX ·

The Precolonial and

Colonial Background

GEOGRAPHY has had a strong influence upon the course of Indonesia's history and has always conditioned severely the course of its political development. It is the only major state based upon a widely flung archipelago; and whereas the four islands of Japan with their less than 150,000 square miles of area constitute in a practical sense one fairly integrated geographical unit, Indonesia's 576,000 square miles of territory (over 730,000 square miles if Western New Guinea is included) are spread out over several thousand islands covering an area wider from east to west than the United States and from north to south roughly the distance between Seattle and Los Angeles. Its population of approximately 85 million—making it the world's sixth most populous country—is distributed over islands varying tremendously in size and density of population. Sumatra, whose area is slightly larger than Japan or California, supports a population of about 13 million. Bali with an area slightly less than half that of Connecticut almost equals it in population—just over 2 million. The 213,000 square miles of Indonesian Borneo are inhabited by less than 4 million people, but Java, with an area of only 48,500 square miles (slightly less than New York state) supports a population of about 55 million.

Constituting a bridge between Asia and Australia and lying athwart the principal channels of trade between the Indian and Pacific oceans, the Indonesian archipelago has for some two thousand years been a crossroads of both international commerce and outside ideas and culture. Whereas nearly two millennia of commercial contact with China appear to have had no important cultural consequences for Indonesia, equally old trading contacts with India provided the channel for the introduction of Buddhist, Hindu, and later Mohammedan ideas.

Indonesia's fragmentation into a widely strewn archipelago tended to stimulate a degree of cultural, particularly linguistic, diversity among its islands' scattered groups of inhabitants. This was only partially off-set by culturally integrating factors, such as the generally intensive commerce among the major islands and between them and the world outside—trade which served to spread the culture of the relatively powerful maritime political centers of Java and Sumatra, and later of Celebes and Borneo, along their coasts and often across the narrow seas to the smaller islands. Intra-Indonesian commerce diffused an Indonesian lingua franca, based chiefly upon east coast Sumatran Malay, into the most distant of the port areas of the archipelago. And it was via these channels of commerce that Islam, an even more important element of cultural integration, was spread. By early in the twentieth century nearly 90 per cent of Indonesia's population was at least nominally Mohammedan, and today Indonesia is the world's largest Islamic nation. The extension of Netherlands colonial rule introduced another important element of cohesion. The Dutch established their first bridgehead in Java as early as 1619, but the expansion of their control was initially slow. Not until the middle of the eighteenth century were they firmly in control of all Java, and not until the eve of the First World War had they secured their position in areas of such intransigent resistance as Bali and northern Sumatra. Thus although it is true that Netherlands rule carved out Indonesia's present political boundaries and provided it with its longest period of sustained political integration, it is important to note that Dutch authority was not consolidated in many important areas of Indonesia until very recent times. The extent of political integration resulting from Dutch colonial rule should not, therefore, be overly emphasized.

Precolonial History and Government

Prior to the arrival of the Dutch, Indonesia was no mere geographical designation, and its present boundaries bear to some extent the stamp of its earlier history. Indeed, the domain ultimately administered by the Netherlands was roughly congruent with that incorporated into the two great Indonesian empires of the ninth and fourteenth centuries, Shrivijaya and Majapahit. Shrivijaya, whose capital lay near the present site of Palembang in southern Sumatra, was a maritime state which for several centuries dominated Indonesian commerce and the international trade passing through the Indonesian archipelago. At the height of its power it appears to have exerted varying degrees of control over most of the politically important parts of Indonesia, over some of the Philippines, and over the Malay peninsula. Astride the currents of international commerce that eddied back and forth through the Straits of Malacca, Shrivijaya, and presumably the smaller kingdoms that preceded it, was at an early date in contact with religious ideas emanating from India—Buddhism in particular—and by the middle of the seventh century it had become a center of Buddhist learning of international renown. Buddhist ideas had also entered Java at an early date; however, toward the end of the thirteenth century, with the rise of the power of the state of Majapahit, Hinduism had clearly superseded it as the dominant religion. But Javanese Hinduism always incorporated important residues of Buddhism, indigenous mysticism, and animism. It was thus a religion whose Hindu elements had been severely conditioned by the Javanese cultural environment and adapted so as to harmonize with pre-Hindu religious ideas. At the zenith of its power, in the latter part of the fourteenth century, Majapahit's sea power and commerce dominated the Indonesian archipelago, the Philippines, and the Malay peninsula. But if one can speak of Majapahit as an Indonesian empire, it must be pointed out that, as had been the case with Shrivijaya, it was at best a very loosely knit political entity wherein the power center's leverage on many parts of Indonesia was fitful and unsustained. By the middle of the fifteenth century its strength had begun to wane, and concurrently so did the position of Hinduism. Indeed, roughly coincident with Majapahit's decline was Islam's spread among the major port cities of the north Java coast, and with its final demise at the end of the sixteenth century Islam superseded Hinduism as the major religion of Java.

Islam penetrated Indonesia peacefully, not by the sword, but via commerce and missionaries. Although as early as 1292 Marco Polo had found a Mohammedan community near the northern tip of Sumatra, Islam's spread through Indonesia did not become rapid until the middle of the fifteenth century, its most spectacular period of expansion coming during the sixteenth and seventeenth centuries coinci-

dent with the impact of the power of the Christian Portuguese and
Dutch. It is highly probable that this acceleration was related to the
impingement of European Christian power, first Portuguese and later
Dutch. The Portuguese aimed at eliminating the position of Indian
Muslim merchants both in the Indian Ocean and farther east, and they
were no less bent upon supplanting the substantial position in Indonesian commerce held by Javanese merchants and merchant princes
—a policy later pursued by the Dutch with greater vigor and more success. Since Portuguese trade objectives were linked with a crusading
missionary zeal in behalf of Christianity, it is understandable how the
affinity of commercial interests between Muslim Indian traders and
Indonesian harbor princes and merchants should help dispose these
Indonesians to be receptive to Islam. When in 1511 the Portuguese
finally captured the Malayan emporium of Malacca, key entrepôt of
Indonesian trade, they found that the dominant political element in
this great Islamic city was Javanese, its army largely Javanese, most of
its shipbuilders and other craftsmen Javanese, and the major components of its extensive merchant class Javanese and Indian. Although
strong enough to appropriate a considerable share of Indonesian trade,
the Portuguese were not able to marshal sufficient power to subjugate
the relatively small Javanese and Sumatran states that arose after the
fall of Majapahit.

The Dutch arrived early in the seventeenth century in greater
strength and, with their seizure of Malacca from the Portuguese in
1640, became the paramount European power in the Indies. Initially
because of internal dissension among the Javanese states and skill in
playing off one of them against the other, they were able with relatively
small forces to maintain their tiny bridgehead in west Java at the port
which they had occupied in 1619 and rechristened Batavia. Within the
course of the century, however, they increased their strength and became the major power on Java, their expansion slowed only by the declining kingdom of Mataram. This state, founded in 1582 in what had
been the heartland of the old empire of Majapahit, for a while controlled as much as two-thirds of Java and small parts of southern Sumatra and Borneo, but never approached Majapahit or Shrivijaya in
power. In the middle of the seventeenth century it was obliged to
come to terms with the Dutch. With a steadily diminishing power and
a shrinking area, it maintained a tenuous semi-independence until 1755,
when the Dutch divided its residual area into two small states, Surakarta

and Jogjakarta. Following a spirited but unsuccessful Jogjakarta-based rising from 1825 to 1830, the Dutch severely reduced the size of even these remnants of old Mataram, leaving them as they existed until the end of Netherlands rule—two tiny enclaves in south central Java, each granted a partial autonomy, with its *sunan* or Sultan maintaining his palace and court entourage, but reigning rather than ruling.

Little is known concerning the political organization of precolonial Indonesia. Very early two rather different kinds of states began to emerge. The most numerous, and usually the smaller, were the harbor principalities which dotted much of the coast of Sumatra and Java. A few of these were also to be found along some of the coasts of Borneo and parts of Celebes, where they constituted enclaves flanked by vast territories inhabited by tribal political groups. These states were based primarily upon inter-Indonesian and overseas trade, and only secondarily upon control over adjacent hinterlands with rice-producing peasants. Their rulers were either themselves directly involved in this commerce or else received considerable indirect benefit from it. The second type were the inland, predominantly agricultural, semibureaucratic states of central and eastern Java. Several of them, Majapahit in particular, developed substantial interests in inter-Indonesian and overseas commerce and in the process absorbed many of the harbor principalities; but their initial, and usually their major, basis of power rested on inland rice-growing areas, generally river plains where irrigation played an important part and where high concentrations of agrarian population were possible. All these precolonial states appear to have been characterized by a considerable degree of decentralization. Only their heartland areas seem to have been politically and administratively integrated, their lesser, but often important, outlying districts usually enjoying considerable independence. Moreover, within the confines of both Mataram and its semivassal states, as well as within the contemporary independent west Java sultanate of Bantam, numerous villages lying some distance from the capitals apparently enjoyed substantial autonomy, a quality verging on virtual independence among those most distant. Even before the consolidation of Dutch rule there appears to have been among the villagers of Java a tradition of autonomy and of striving to keep the power of the capital at a distance. Although in the villages, particularly among those in the outlying districts, there may have been elements of democratic government, the capital and central areas of these states were organized along authoritarian lines with power concentrated in the hands of an autocratic ruler and his court entourage.

These precolonial states, especially those on Java, appear to have shared a roughly similar political ethos, what Heine-Geldern has termed "the cosmological basis of state and kingship," [1] belief in the parallelism between the natural universe and the world of men. The political community was regarded as being constantly and critically influenced by natural forces, both terrestrial and extraterrestrial, the principal purpose of the state being to harmonize itself and the human activity which it encompassed with these forces. Man, and thereby political activity, was to conform and to work in harmony with this cosmological environment. The ruler was believed to be the incarnation of a god and to have magical or mystical properties enabling him to contact the natural forces and their divine representations. Thus he was in a pivotal position to mediate between these forces and his subjects and to secure harmony between them. Being *au courant* with the posture of these forces, sometimes symbolized as the two great world snakes—the Nagas—he could tell when their shifting patterns of order reflected a harmony propitious for important decisions.

This idea of individual and state activity harmonizing with the cosmos, so vital to the political order of pre-European and particularly pre-Islamic Indonesia, is not dead today. Although certainly much less influential now than in the past, it is of greater importance in the individual and political lives of present-day Javanese than most Westerners are aware. The important contemporary residue of this sort of thinking is the still widely revered idea of harmony—harmony with the forces of nature, harmony within the political community, and conversely the conviction that inharmonious conduct is a disruptive force which society should rightly frown upon. It is this outlook which undergirds the still prominent belief in Java and many other parts of Indonesia that basically important political decisions should be an expression of full harmony and should not be based upon a 51 per cent, or even a 90 per cent, majority. And there are not a few Western-educated Indonesians in important government posts today inclined to avoid or defer certain important decisions unless they feel through mystical insight, or they are informed by a wise man better endowed with this quality, that the Nagas are in harmony.

[1] Robert Heine-Geldern, *Conceptions of State and Kingship in Southeast Asia* (Southeast Asia Program, Cornell University, Data Paper no. 18; Ithaca, N.Y., 1956).

Netherlands Control through Indirect Rule

The authoritarian political organization which characterized the central area of Mataram during its period of vigor was taken over by the Dutch as they absorbed its districts and in its essentials was extended by them throughout almost all of Java. Thus a political system, which in the pre-Dutch period had in actual practice been highly authoritarian largely in areas near to the capital and lesser administrative centers, was so strengthened with Dutch power that the outlying districts as well were forced into the same political mold. Commanding limited resources and being expected to show a high annual profit on its small capital, the Dutch East India Company was not in a position to pay the high costs that a system of direct administration would have entailed. The inexpensive system of indirect rule that it pursued was sufficient to secure the sort of political control necessary for the attainment of its economic objectives. In essence this provided for the utilization of the indigenous power structure, or more precisely its amenable elements. The Dutch maintained the aristocratic character of the societies of Java, taking over for themselves the apex of the pyramid of power and retaining at the second and third echelons of authority that considerable portion of the indigenous aristocracy willing to work with and under them.

Because the company's economic objectives demanded that new and additional burdens be placed on the peasants, it enlarged and strengthened the power of the co-operating elements of the aristocracies of Java vis-à-vis the peasantry. Since these aristocrats could if threatened call upon Dutch military force to back them up, they were able to disregard the interests and sentiments of the peasantry in a way which previously had rarely been possible outside the heartland areas of the old states. Vis-à-vis Dutch authority the position of the indigenous aristocracy of Java became weaker, but in its relationship to the Javanese peasantry it became strengthened. This increased power could be exercised all the more effectively because concurrently the peasantry in the outlying areas was progressively losing its traditional bargaining power—namely, the ability to abandon the area of a harsh king or local aristocrat and move on to the district of one whose rule was less onerous or to virgin areas distant from the center of any aristocrat's power. For the *pax Nederlandica,* however oppressive, eventually put an end to the frequent warfare and raids that had previously been so common among the Javanese states, thus promoting condi-

tions favoring the rapid growth of Java's population and the consequent decrease of virgin arable lands.

The central role of the aristocratic Javanese agents of the Dutch
was to ensure that the indigenous population of their areas delivered
them a large proportion of their crops, a fixed proportion of which they
passed on to the company. In return they were granted important
benefits, being permitted to impose exactions of *corvée* labor as well
as crop deliveries over and above what the company demanded. Indeed, they were generally free to add as much more as could be
squeezed out of the villages in the areas under their control.

Well before the demise of the Dutch East India Company in 1798
the Chinese had come to occupy a key position in its system of economic exploitation in Java, one equal in importance to that of the indigenous aristocracy. Each of these elements was indispensable both
to the successful functioning of the company and to the roughly similar system pursued by the government of the Netherlands soon after
the end of company rule. Neither of these systems, nor for that matter the social legacy of Dutch rule as a whole, can be understood without some mention of the tremendous expansion of the economic role
of the Chinese in Indonesia under the aegis of Netherlands rule. Although prior to the establishment of Dutch power Chinese merchants
had been active throughout the Indies, the Indonesian princes severely
limited and controlled the area of their settlement, and their principal
function was limited to that of intermediaries in the exchange of goods
between the Indies and China. But with the spread of the Dutch East
India Company's power in Java, the scope and intensity of Chinese
activity expanded tremendously. The company consciously promoted
this, initially regarding the Chinese as its special protégés, protecting
and favoring them because of the conviction that its exploitation of
the Indies could be most efficiently achieved through them.[2] Although
at first the company's territorial administrative agents were nearly all
recruited from the indigenous aristocracy, increasingly it came to
lease areas of Java to Chinese entrepreneurs, a practice often taken
over by its Javanese aristocratic agents who themselves frequently

[2] These Chinese were in Indonesia on sufferance of the Indonesian rulers, with
the government of China at this time giving them no support; on the other hand,
the Javanese merchants were generally closely tied in with indigenous power.
Thus it was understandable why the Dutch preferred working through the alien
Chinese who were the more tractable because they could not look for support to
any Javanese prince.

subleased their authority to Chinese.[3] In addition, the company farmed out various monopolies to them—exclusive rights to collect road tolls, levy bazaar fees, collect customs, and sell salt. Because of this and their hold on the rice trade stemming from their control of the economies of leased villages, the Chinese came to dominate the internal commerce of Java. In the process Java's indigenous merchant class was largely eliminated, never again recovering its strength. This fact has had an important influence upon the character of present-day Indonesian society, on its ideological orientation, and on the economic policies its leaders have pursued.

Rampant and widespread corruption in its administration in Indonesia combined with a reckless financial policy under which stockholders were paid dividends averaging 18 per cent per year led to the collapse of the Dutch East India Company in 1798. The area it controlled was then placed under the direct authority of the Netherlands government. There was no real break with the company's policies, however; its key economic and political institutions were retained. During the brief interlude of British rule (1811–1816) attendant upon the Napoleonic wars, efforts were made by Stamford Raffles to reduce powers of the Javanese aristocracy; but very little of his program was realized, and much of what was accomplished was abandoned following the return of Netherlands authority.

After the withdrawal of the British in 1816 the policy of the Netherlands government until 1830 was indecisive and wavered between opening the Indies to individual enterprise and reverting to a system of government monopoly very much along lines the company had followed. Finally, primarily as a result of financial considerations stemming from the large-scale rebellion in central Java of 1825–1830 and the costs of the unsuccessful war with Belgium, the Netherlands government adopted a system providing for government monopoly. The new system, known variously as the Cultivation System and the Net Profit Policy, lasted as a whole until 1877, after which it was pro-

[3] Such Chinese actually stood on a contractual basis with the company or the Indonesian regents and other aristocrats from whom, for a stipulated payment in gold or produce, they leased political and economic authority over one or more villages, or in some cases whole districts, for a certain number of years. By the end of the eighteenth century 1,134 of Java's villages had been leased to them. They were in a position to maintain a substantial economic hold within a district long after their lease of political authority had expired, for frequently they utilized their short periods of control to effect lasting credit relationships with the peasantry.

gressively restricted until it was completely abolished in 1919. From the standpoint of the Netherlands its success can be measured by the fact that as of 1877 it had paid off the East India Company's and subsequent government debts of 178 million guilders and in addition brought to the Netherlands home treasury a net profit of 664.5 million guilders.[4] In theory the Cultivation System called for one-fifth of the peasant's rice fields being planted with a commercial export crop designated by the government, with the peasant exempted from paying a land tax; in practice not only was he forced to continue payment of this tax, but rarely was he able to limit to one-fifth of his total the area of his land planted with the government crop. "One-third, one-half, and even the whole of these irrigated fields were used for growing designated crops for the Government, and instead of 66 days per year, which originally was the normal period, the interest of certain Government cultures necessitated those liable to service working 240 days and even more." [5]

Under the Cultivation System the fundamental elements of the partially eroded system of political relationships developed by the company were re-established. Indeed, it could hardly have succeeded without the support of the Javanese aristocratic hierarchy. The supervisory staff of European civil servants was increased, but local authority was no longer leased to Chinese, and throughout practically all of Java this aristocracy was the only real point of contact between Dutch power and the indigenous population. To secure the aristocracy's effective support the government actually enhanced the position of its upper ranks, the regents, to a point beyond that which they had enjoyed under the company. Their office was made hereditary; they were frequently given a modest grant of land; their powers were strengthened as against lesser officials including the village headman; and, of key importance, they were given a direct financial interest in the system's operation—a percentage of the crops collected from the peasantry. As a prominent Dutch jurist on the Indies was later to write concerning this system:

[4] Indonesian nationalist leaders were later to remark that of this sum 236 million guilders was applied to the reduction of the Netherlands public debt, 115 million for the reduction of Dutch taxes, 153 million for the construction of the Dutch state railways, and 146 million for the improvement of fortifications in the Netherlands (J. S. Furnivall, *Netherlands India* [New York: Macmillan, 1944], p. 210).

[5] G. H. van der Kolff, "European Influences on Native Agriculture," in B. Schrieke, *The Effects of Western Influence on Native Civilizations in the Malay Archipelago* (Batavia, 1932), pp. 108, 111.

Over against his subordinate civil servants and the population the regent was elevated to become a feudal prince, who in turn however, had to carry out the will of the resident [the top territorial Dutch administrative official]. From the population servile submission was demanded and even the village leadership, by nature identical with the interest of the people, was made a tool in the hands of the regents and their subordinate district heads.[6]

The Cultivation System, its basic elements roughly the same as under the Dutch East India Company, thus tended to solidify the pattern of Java's social structure which had begun to emerge under company rule. The authoritarian content of Javanese society was increased, in particular the relationship between the village and the political structure above it. Throughout Java the village headman came to be dependent for his position on the Dutch and the Dutch-backed aristocratic hierarchy above him to an extent approximating what had existed earlier between headman and Sultan in the limited heartland of Mataram. The collectivist aspect of peasant society, probably already reinforced during the period of company rule, became much stronger during the forty years of the Cultivation System. As Furnivall has pointed out, "So great were the demands on landholders, that landholding was no longer a privilege but a burden which occupants tried to share with others."[7]

In 1877 with the beginning of what was termed the Liberal Policy, the Cultivation System gradually gave way, in many areas very slowly indeed, to a laissez-faire system which for the first time allowed private capital considerable freedom. In Sumatra, Borneo, and Celebes Dutch authority penetrated into areas where its writ had previously been absent or only nominal, generally instituting a system of indirect administration through the local aristocracies and opening the way for large-scale private investment by Western (largely Dutch) capital in plantation agriculture and mining. Whereas this was important in Sumatra and to a lesser extent in Borneo and Celebes, it had relatively little impact on Java. Not only was the Cultivation System maintained in parts of Java until very late, in some areas until 1919, but elsewhere on the island the pattern of the economy changed slowly. In those areas of Java not affected by Western plantation agriculture the ending of forced cultivation, individual liability for taxation, and an increasing pressure of the population on the available arable land gradu-

[6] P. H. Fromberg, "De Inlandsche Beweging," *Verspreide Geschriften* (Leiden: Leidsche Uitgeversmaatschappij, 1926), p. 558.

[7] *Netherlands India,* p. 141.

ally broke down the collective land ownership that the company and
the Cultivation System had fostered. The increased supplanting of
collective by individual land ownership did not, however, entail a
commensurate disintegration of the collectivist (communal) pattern
of social relationships. Although the chief objective characteristic of
agrarian collectivism—common ownership and/or disposition of land
—has for the most part disappeared,[8] much of the collectivist psy-
chology induced by this previously long period of collectivist organization remains.

Among the most important measures introduced by the government
following the switch to a laissez-faire policy were its land laws of the
1870s. While allowing the European entrepreneur to rent, for a limited
period, land cultivated by an Indonesian, they forbade its purchase by
any non-Indonesian. This enlightened policy had long-term consequences beneficial to Indonesian society. It was spared the large-scale
alienation of peasant landholdings to Western, Chinese, or Indian
creditors such as occurred in many other parts of Southeast Asia. Consequently the pattern of agrarian society during the last few decades
of Dutch rule in Java, and indeed throughout most of Indonesia, was
relatively balanced and free of the socioeconomic extremes which
characterized most other Asian agrarian communities. In Java, the
rapidly mounting population was, however, already beginning to undermine this balance. And because of the diminishing reserves of non-
cultivated arable land and the growing disparity between the agricultural base of the village and the population dependent upon it, the
number of landless peasants increased significantly during the 1930s.
This in combination with the decrease in communal lands was beginning to induce a greater degree of economic differentiation at the village
level than had previously obtained. Nevertheless, the long period of
collectivist agrarian organization had left most Javanese villages with
a set of values which has helped preserve social equality in the face
of diminishing economic equality.

The colonial society which we have been describing was, then, one
wherein the indigenous elite's surviving elements had come to terms
with the colonial power, serving as its key agents in an inexpensive but

[8] As late as 1882, 53 per cent of landholdings in Java were collectively owned
(either as general village lands or for the support of village officials), 35 per cent
of landholdings being in this category as late as 1907, with 17 per cent (the last
year for which statistics are available) in 1932.

effective system of indirect rule and as a political buffer between Dutch authority and a peasantry which still looked to this elite for guidance. On Java this was matched by a roughly similar buffer in economic relationships, one originally provided by the Javanese aristocracy and Chinese jointly, at the end of the nineteenth century by the Chinese alone. Although commencing about 1910, coincident with a set of more enlightened policies designed to improve village conditions, the number of Dutch officials having some direct contact with the peasantry became for the first time significant, until the end of Netherlands rule a probable majority of Indonesians still viewed the political order as one where power which affected them issued primarily from the hands of their own traditional aristocratic ruling class. And for the most part these traditional leaders continued to serve more as the agents of the Dutch colonial regime than as representatives of their people's interests.

Emergence of a New Indonesian Elite and the Rise of Nationalism

Beginning in the second decade of the twentieth century a new, Western-educated elite finally began to emerge. But its numbers remained so few and the Dutch so circumscribed its role that throughout the course of Netherlands rule it was unable to effect a sufficiently widespread and sustained relationship with either the peasantry or urban and plantation labor to educate them to the realities of their political environment. For a brief period this new elite, led by a small group of influential Islamic leaders strongly influenced by recently generated Modernist Islamic currents emanating from Cairo and elsewhere in the Near East, was able to establish enough contact with the peasantry of Java to create the first and only peasant-based nationalist organization during the entire period of colonial rule. This movement, Sarekat Islam (United Islam), grew so fast, by 1919 enrolling the support of more than 2 million members, that the Dutch became thoroughly alarmed and saw to it that henceforward contact between Indonesian nationalist leaders and the peasantry was made extremely difficult. Thereafter, the repression of the colonial authorities so limited the political activities of these leaders that never again during the period of Netherlands rule were they able to develop the contacts with the peasantry that had been basic to the burgeoning of Sarekat Islam. One consequence of this was that most of the men who emerged at the end of the Second World War as leaders of an independent Indonesia had little understanding of the basic character and outstanding problems of their country's peasantry.

Soon after the spectacular rise of Sarekat Islam an intense competition ensued for control over its membership between its original Islamic leadership and that of the newly founded Indonesian Communist Party, during the course of which Sarekat Islam lost most of its mass backing. And when at the end of 1926 the Communists attempted a revolt, they so lacked supporters and their effort was so weak and unco-ordinated that the Netherlands East Indies government suppressed them with ease and dispatch. Thereafter, until the Japanese occupation, the Communists, few and divided among themselves, operated underground and quite ineffectively, and the Sarekat Islam was unable to recapture its previous commanding position. During this period the dominant role in the nationalist movement was played by secular, non-Communist Indonesians, among whom Soekarno was the outstanding leader. The repressive apparatus now at the disposal of the Dutch was so powerful, however, that he and other prominent nationalists, such as Mohammad Hatta and Soetan Sjahrir, were unable to build up the organizations necessary to provide the movement with sufficient power to challenge the Dutch. After a few years of moderately successful organizational work in the late 1920s and early 1930s these three leaders along with a number of others were summarily arrested and not released from their places of detention until the Japanese invasion.

Neither in its prewar phase nor in its postwar revolutionary period was the Indonesian nationalist movement headed by either a landed aristocracy or a substantial middle class. The modern Indonesian political elite—the men who led their country's nationalist movement and struggle for independence and who are the political leaders of Indonesia today—has been the product of an only recently available Western education and to a lesser extent of the impact of Modernist Islamic thought. Although in Indonesia education has traditionally been highly esteemed, the Islamic educational facilities existing there in the first decades of the twentieth century, and those available to the considerable number of Indonesians who went to Mecca for study, were not well suited to equip Indonesians to meet their country's modern needs. For this, as an increasing number of them were aware, modern Western education was necessary. Not until very late, however, was such education, particularly secondary education, made available to Indonesians, the Dutch trailing the British in India in this respect by approximately half a century. Moreover, for some time even the limited facilities open to Indonesians were reserved for the sons of aristocrats, and even for them opportunities were exceedingly limited. Those who held the dominant positions in the formation of Dutch colonial policy had no interest in preparing Indonesians for independence and little interest in training them for responsible positions in government or business. The meager amount of educational facilities opened to Indonesians was enough to spark the nationalist movement, but far too little to prepare Indonesians for the efficient administration of their own country.

Opportunities for Indonesians to acquire a secondary education were so few that during the period 1910–1914 in all of Indonesia an average of only 4 Indonesians graduated from high school per year. The yearly average had increased to 11 for the period 1920–1921, to 157 during the years 1929–1930, and by 1940 had reached only 240 (out of an Indonesian population of around 70 million).[9] This stands in sharp contrast to the situation obtaining in British India. Although the quality of its high schools and colleges was probably on the average less than that of those in Indonesia, opportunities for Indians to attend were vastly greater than for Indonesians in colonial Indonesia.[10] With its population approximately only four times as large as that of Indonesia, British India by 1917 was providing a high school education to 216,160 students, as against 7,474 receiving such education in Indonesia twenty-three years later, in 1940. Moreover, while the preponderant majority of those receiving this education in India were Indians, only 1,786 of the 7,474 were Indonesians—most of the facilities in Indonesia being reserved for Europeans. For Indonesians the situation with regard to college-level education was even worse. The first technical college in Indonesia was opened only in 1919, the first law school in 1924, and the first medical college in 1926. In British India as early as 1891 there were 15,589 students enrolled in college, and by 1920 more than 50,000 were enrolled as against just 2 Indonesians attending college that year in Indonesia. As late as 1940 there were only 630 Indonesians attending colleges in Indonesia with only 37 being graduated in that year. (A much smaller number were

[9] In 1940 junior high schools (grades 7–9) in Indonesia graduated 1,130 Indonesians.

[10] Although categories are not strictly comparable, they certainly admit of rough comparison.

enrolled in colleges abroad.) In the same year there were 12,179 students attending public colleges in the Philippines, a country with a quarter the population of Indonesia.[11]

This situation was not in any sense indicative of a lack of desire among Indonesians for Western education. Rather it reflected a dearth of opportunities resulting from limited facilities and a heavy discrimination against Indonesians with regard to their use. Even before the great depression of 1929–1930, the Netherlands Indies government had shown a reluctance to expand opportunities in Western education for Indonesians, the nature of the Dutch colonial regime not being attuned to this. Thus an extensive survey made by a government commission just prior to the depression determined that 25 per cent of all Indonesians who had graduated from Western schools were unable to find jobs in which their education could be utilized and concluded that Western education for Indonesians was on too large a scale and that the "tempo of expansion exceeds the scope of social development." [12] There were two major reasons why this commission was obliged to come to these conclusions. First, again in contrast to India, the Indonesian commercial class capable of taking advantage of Western education was pathetically diminutive, and additionally European business firms were generally averse to hiring Indonesians.[13] Second, and again in contrast to the situation in British India, the Dutch administration in the Indies was reluctant to take Indonesians into the upper levels of its bureaucracy.

[11] The statistics cited above are drawn from the following sources: *Indisch Verslag*, 1941, II (Batavia, 1941), 102–107; I. J. Brugmans and Mr. Soenario, "Enkele Gegevens van Socialen Aard," *Verslag van de Commissie tot Bestudeering van Staatsrechtelijke Hervormingen* [Report of the Commission for Study of Constitutional Reform] (Batavia, 1941), I, 63; *Hollandsch-Inlandsch Onderwijs-Commissie* [Dutch-Native Education Commission], vol. XII, Résumé (Batavia, 1931), pp. 24–25; *Census of India, 1901*, vol. I, pt. i, Report by H. H. Risley and E. A. Gait (Calcutta, 1903), p. 183; Indian Statutory Commission, *Review of Growth of Education in British India*, Interim Report, Cd. 3407 (London: H.M. Stationery Office, 1929), p. 22; *The Philippines*, vol. II, Subcontractor's Monograph, Human Relations Area Files, Inc. (New Haven, 1955), p. 802 (figure includes enrollment at the University of the Philippines; a considerable number of other Filipinos attended private colleges).

[12] *Hollandsch-Inlandsch Onderwijs-Commissie*, vol. VIa, *De Werkgelegenheid in Nederlandsch-Indie voor Nederlandsch Sprekenden* [Opportunities for Employment in the Netherlands Indies for Speakers of Dutch] (Weltevreden, 1931), pp. 73–78.

[13] Even during the year just previous to the depression of 1929–1930 Western business firms in Indonesia employed only 126 Indonesians in positions paying $100 per month or more (computed from figures appearing in *ibid.*, pp. 28–29).

Indonesia at the conclusion of Dutch colonial rule was a country with practically no indigenous middle class. If one can speak of an Indonesian middle class on Java, its commercial element had been almost eliminated. The tiny remnant still surviving at the end of the Cultivation System may have received some minor benefit from the introduction of a laissez-faire economy, but there appears to have been little or no increase in its numbers. The conditions of the company and the Cultivation System had so blunted the sensitivity of the native population on Java to the urges of capitalist economics that in Java there was little response among them to any opportunities for entrepreneurial activities which the new system may have opened up.[14] Into the resulting vacuum crowded the aggressive, already-established resident Chinese merchant class supplemented by thousands of immigrants from southeast China. Armed with industriousness and commercial ability acquired in the fiercely competitive society of their own country, they eagerly exploited opportunities which the Indonesian population was rarely equipped to dispute with them and which did not tempt most Netherlanders. Nearly all of that part of the middle class in Indonesia which was not European was Chinese. There existed only a handful of Indonesian entrepreneurs, a most meager handful in Java, and what hard data are available suggests that the numbers of even this tiny residual element were declining rather than growing during the last years of Dutch rule. Some indication of the economic position of Indonesians as compared with the Chinese and Europeans in the nonagrarian sector of colonial society at the close of Dutch rule is given in Table 11.

The figures suggest that during the period 1925–1940 the tiny sliver of the Indonesian population that might be classified as middle class shrank in proportion to the total Indonesian population. Moreover, it appears that during the period 1925–1940, despite a substantial population increase, the entrepreneurial component of the Indonesian middle class declined both relative to the bureaucratic component and in absolute numbers.[15] Of those Indonesians who at the end of Dutch rule

[14] In Sumatra, Borneo, and Celebes—by contrast—opportunities in copra and small-holder's rubber production and trade probably somewhat strengthened the position of Indonesian entrepreneurs. Any increase in the number and/or wealth of Indonesian entrepreneurs outside of Java would appear, however, to have been more than offset by a decline in their numbers on Java, with a resultant over-all decrease for Indonesia as a whole.

[15] The very slight increase of Indonesians with incomes of 5,000 guilders or more in 1930 and 1940 over 1925 appears to have been significantly less than the number of new openings at that salary level made available for Indonesians in the government service. A government report indicated that, as early as 1925, of the

Table 11. Number of assessments (for purposes of income tax) on earnings in guilders * for the years 1925, 1930, and 1940. (Total population for each group is given in the column heads.)

Income in guilders	1925 †			1930 ‡			1940 §		
	Indonesians 53,724,197	Europeans 206,040	Chinese and other foreign Asians 1,210,692	Indonesians 59,143,775	Europeans 242,372	Chinese and other foreign Asians 1,344,878	Indonesians 69,700,000	Europeans 1,700,000‖	Chinese and other foreign Asians 1,700,000‖
1,000–1,500	24,338	5,529	17,322	29,896	6,590	22,298	14,426	9,257	15,699
1,500–3,000	17,184	18,080	17,551	20,766	17,812	22,496	12,085	20,435	18,204
3,000–5,000	2,928	17,016	6,553	4,731	18,993	8,573	3,595	18,246	6,161
5,000–10,000	920	18,905	3,353	1,558	23,752	4,752	1,034	17,226	2,842
10,000–25,000	192	8,157	1,162	307	11,161	1,616	195	5,050	815
25,000–50,000	16	1,046	182	20	1,275	270	7	403	94
50,000–100,000	1	356	76	2	367	78	1	116	25
100,000 and over	—	160	19	1	124	20	2	19	3

* The guilder was equal to approximately one-half US dollar. The figures in this table relate exclusively to nonagrarian income. Indonesian peasants paid a land tax but were not required to pay an income tax.

† *Indisch Verslag*, 1931, vol. II, Table 109, p. 172. Population figures for 1925 are estimates based on figures for the 1920 and 1930 census reports. See *ibid.*, Tables 11, 12, 13, pp. 16, 17, 18.

‡ *Ibid.*, Table 108, pp. 168–169.

§ *Indisch Verslag*, 1941, vol. II, Table 110A, pp. 184–185. Population figures for 1940 are estimates of N. Keyfitz, based on an estimated population increase for Indonesians of 1.5 per cent per year for Java and Madura and 2 per cent for the other islands. (Keyfitz estimated that the population of Europeans plus Chinese and other Asians together totaled 1,700,000.) See N. Keyfitz, "The Population of Indonesia," in *Ekonomi dan Keuangan*, vol. VI, no. 10 (Oct. 1953), pp. 641–655, table on p. 652.

‖ Separate population figures for these last two groups are not available.

in 1941 had received a Western primary education or above and who had found employment in which this education was utilized, probably about two-thirds worked as civil servants in the Netherlands East Indies government.[16] Thus insofar as there did exist an Indonesian middle class at the close of Dutch rule, it was preponderantly a bureaucratic middle class. This majority element, as well as the sizable minority of Western-educated Indonesians unable to secure jobs which made any effective use of their education, had no direct stake in capitalism, regarding it as something largely outside of their own sphere of life, the province of alien Europeans and Chinese. They were not opposed to government's having a major role in economic affairs and tended to be warmly receptive to the socialist ideas to which Western education had given them access. These Indonesians, and in particular those who assumed positions of leadership in the nationalist movement and the revolution, usually tended to regard capitalism as an aspect of colonialism, many actually equating the two. By and large they looked on capitalism as the way of the European overlord and his Chinese associates, a system whose benefits by-passed Indonesians.

It is thus understandable why Marxism, in particular Marxist ideas concerning the relationship between capitalism and colonialism, has had such a wide appeal for Indonesians. Although an undoubted majority of the modern Indonesian political elite have been affected by these

---

4,016 Indonesians assessed as having incomes between 3,000 and 20,000 guilders about 53 per cent were civil servants. Figures are computed from *Mededeelingen van het Centraal Kantoor voor de Statistiek, 69: Eenige Bijzonderheiden Betreffende het Aantal Aangeslagenen in de Inkomstbelasting en hun Belastbaar Inkomen over het Jaar 1925* ["Bulletin of the Central Bureau of Statistics, 69: Some Particulars concerning the Number of Persons Assessed in the Income Tax and Their Assessable Incomes for the Year 1925"] (Weltevreden, 1929), p. 23. Had a similar investigation been made in 1940, it would have undoubtedly shown an even higher percentage.

[16] Of the 33,044 employment-seeking Indonesians who by 1928 had received at least a primary education along Western lines, 45 per cent were employed as civil servants. Since only 75 per cent of all such graduates had managed to obtain jobs where a knowledge of Dutch was needed, this meant that in 1928 of those Indonesians able to find employment in which their Western education was used approximately 60 per cent then found it with the colonial government (*Hollandsch-Inlandsch Onderwijs-Commissie*, vol. VIa, pp. 46, 28–29, 15–16, 73). This percentage must have increased during the next decade. Even in the year before the depression of 1929, less than 2 per cent of all of those Indonesians having a Western education through the sixth grade or above who lived in urban areas were self-employed and only slightly over 2 per cent had Indonesian employers. More than 83 per cent worked for wages, and the remainder were unemployed (*ibid.*, p. 46).

ideas, most of them have been highly eclectic in their approach to Western political thought and often mix their Marxism with the ideas of non-Marxist political theories. Whereas most of them have been attracted to and influenced by Lenin's analysis of colonialism, often profoundly,

Chart 5. Economic differentiation in the nonagrarian sector of colonial Indonesian society in 1940, indicating percentage of each population group in the several income categories: Income in guilders (the guilder equaling approximately one-half US dollar) * as shown by income tax assessments †

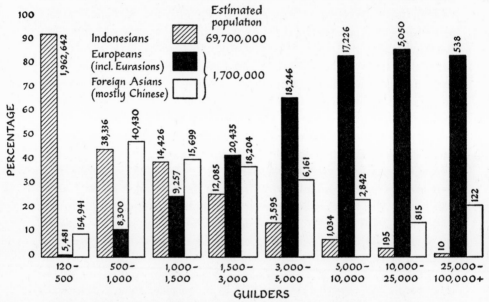

* It should be observed that many living costs, particularly that of food, were considerably less in Indonesia than in the United States at that time.

† This chart is based upon statistics appearing in the Netherlands East Indies official government statistical yearbook, *Indisch Verslag,* 1941, vol. II, Table 110, p. 181, and Table 110A, pp. 184–185.

the large majority have been drawn to revisionist strands of Marxism leading in the direction of democratic socialism rather than communism. There has, however, always been a significant minority who have espoused communism. Another by no means insignificant minority, though eschewing communism, has undertaken (sometimes more unconsciously than consciously) to wed Marxian economic concepts with largely indigenously rooted ideas of paternalistic authoritarianism. Finally, it should be noted that most of the strongly Islamic political leaders, especially those most receptive to Modernist Islamic ideas, are socialistically oriented, some of the most influential calling themselves "religious socialists." They have argued that Muhammad preached so-

cialist economic doctrines twelve centuries before Marx, but their socialism, though probably fully harmonious with any enlightened interpretation of Muhammad's teachings, also bears the print of the social
democratic strand of Marxism.

The fact that so large a proportion of the Indonesian middle class
found jobs with the civil service should not induce the conclusion that
the Netherlands provided the Indonesians with any significant preparation for self-government. The facts were quite different. Although
during the last decade of their rule the Dutch were giving their own
colonial officials a training which was probably superior to that provided by any other colonial power, in Indonesia they built up no equivalent of the Indian Civil Service. Whereas the British during the last
decades of their rule in India turned over a very substantial amount
of the country's administration to highly trained Indians, this was decidedly not the case with the Dutch in Indonesia. A breakdown of the
component elements of the Netherlands Indies Civil Service at the end
of Dutch rule makes this abundantly clear. As late as October 1940,
out of the 3,039 higher-ranking civil service positions only 221 were
held by Indonesians. The other Indonesian civil servants held posts
largely devoid of any real decision-making function wherein the chief
requirement was to carry out decisions arrived at by the generally
paternalistic-minded Dutch officials who stood above them. Even in the
upper-middle ranks Indonesians filled no more than 40 per cent of the
positions. "Function must be equivalent to education" was the official
Dutch rationale for this system; and so long as they were denied this
education, Indonesians could thereby be barred from the positions
where they might have had the training in governmental administration
which their counterparts in India and the Philippines enjoyed and
which contributed so much to the political viability of those countries
following their independence.

Not only was the record a somber one with regard to preparation of
Indonesians in governmental administration. In addition, again in contrast to the record of the British in India and Burma and of the United
States in the Philippines, Indonesians were allowed no real experience
with the institutions of national self-government, parliamentary or
other. The most that the Netherlands was willing to countenance was a
largely advisory People's Council on which elected Indonesians as late
as 1940 held only 19 out of 60 seats and which had no significant function other than providing a sounding board heeded or disregarded at
will by Dutch colonial officials.

Thus during the colonial period Indonesians were denied access to constructive political roles. Those who were forthright in pressing demands for independence were arrested, jailed, and deported to remote islands. Those who tried to co-operate with the colonial authorities in the expectation that this would lead to significant grants of administrative responsibility to Indonesians within an increasingly autonomous, though Dutch-controlled, Indonesia were bitterly disappointed. Being thus denied any really constructive role or responsible position in colonial society, educated Indonesians assumed the only posture consistent with their nationalist convictions—one of opposition, an opposition without responsibility. For the independent Indonesia that emerged after the Second World War, this was to have unfortunate consequences not confined to lack of administrative training and experience in self-government. Because of this condition, many Indonesians could not entirely rid themselves of their negative attitude toward government in general. Their long participation in a politics of opposition had endowed them with an opposition orientation which, though useful during the period of revolution and the long struggle against the Dutch, militated against a constructive role in government once Indonesia had attained its independence. This residuum in conjunction with another derived from the same set of colonial circumstances, namely, a reluctance to assume responsibility for decisions, particularly when confronting new problems demanding new answers, constituted in their combination a colonial legacy hardly suited to the political and administrative exigencies confronting the Indonesian elite upon the attainment of independence.

· XX ·

The Revolution and the

Revolutionary Government

THE Indonesian elite's dissatisfaction with Dutch rule was such that many welcomed the Japanese invasion of early 1942, believing that under Japan their situation could not be worse and might well be better. The harshness of Japanese rule soon disabused them of any such expectations. The sufferings of Indonesians at the hands of the Japanese reinforced their nationalism and did not dispose them to welcome the return of the Dutch. The weak, half-hearted defense put up by the Dutch army dealt a heavy blow to Netherlands prestige, and Indonesians tended to hold the Dutch responsible for their sufferings inasmuch as the Netherlands was regarded as having neither effectively protected Indonesia nor permitted Indonesians to bear arms to protect themselves. This and the persistent anti-Dutch propaganda of the Japanese spread anti-Dutch sentiment more widely among the mass of the population than ever before.

The Japanese Occupation

Nationalism grew apace during the three and a half years of Japanese occupation, but in the various parts of the archipelago its growth as an organized movement was rather uneven, there being three separate Japanese military occupation zones in Indonesia.[1] Each was administratively distinct, with little intercourse between them. One Japanese army occupied Java and, although responsible to the Japanese Southeast Asia command headquarters in Saigon, enjoyed considerable autonomy. Under it the Indonesian nationalist movement was given the greatest latitude for development. Sumatra was administered by a separate Japanese army, likewise directly responsible to Saigon but inclined to give nationalists less scope. Celebes, Borneo, the Moluccas, and the Lesser Sundas were under a division of the Japanese navy, with headquarters at Macassar which followed a severely repressive policy that in general allowed Indonesian nationalists no more latitude than had the Dutch.

On Java long-exiled influential nationalist leaders were allowed substantial freedom of movement; some were permitted a contact with the Indonesian masses which, although limited and controlled, was much greater than had been countenanced by the Dutch. The Japanese were willing to grant them such opportunities in order to secure their help in harnessing Indonesia more effectively to Japan's wartime economic requirements—in particular assistance in mobilizing forced labor and in organizing peasant deliveries of rice. Those nationalist leaders willing to lend themselves to this work, Soekarno in particular, were given opportunities for touring the countryside, making speeches to the peasantry, and utilizing the radio network. In the process they were able to engage in a considerable amount of nationalist propaganda.

The Japanese occupation greatly furthered the spread of an all-Indonesian language. This language, based primarily upon Sumatran Malay (and closely related to the old commercial lingua franca of the Indonesian port cities), had earlier been promoted by Indonesian nationalists with only modest success. After the outlawing of Dutch and an abortive attempt to get the Indonesians to use Japanese in schools and in administration, the occupation command authorized the use of Indonesian for these key functions. As a consequence a national language, a basic vehicle of any nationalistic movement, took real root in Indonesia.

One of the most important results of the occupation was the virtual

---

[1] For accounts in English of the Japanese occupation see H. J. Benda, *The Crescent and the Rising Sun* (New York: Institute of Pacific Relations; The Hague: van Hoeve, 1958); Willard H. Elsbree, *Japan's Role in Southeast Asian Nationalist Movements, 1940–45* (Cambridge, Mass.: Harvard University Press, Institute of Pacific Relations, 1953); G. McT. Kahin, *Nationalism and Revolution in Indonesia* (Ithaca, N.Y.: Cornell University Press, 1952), pp. 101–133.

social revolution which expediency obliged the Japanese to put through, a measure which gave a sharp fillip to the growth of nationalist sentiment. Arriving with almost no military government personnel and believing it necessary to intern practically all Netherlanders, they were obliged to turn to Indonesians to help them staff many administrative and technical positions previously held by the Dutch. Until the last months of the war the Japanese filled the top posts themselves, but Indonesians who had formerly occupied the lower ranks of the services frequently were suddenly pushed up into positions two or three levels above what they had held in the Dutch colonial administration. Generally they were able to fill these positions with a degree of competence which quite surprised them. It became apparent to many that the skills of the Dutch colonial official, whom for so long they had been taught to regard as their superior, were well within the compass of their own abilities. This realization engendered a powerful self-confidence which increased their belief in their ability to govern themselves. Moreover, those who had personally benefited from this revolutionary upward social mobility naturally had a vested interest in maintaining these changes. To them, this meant resistance to any return of Dutch rule; for they felt that its re-establishment would mean loss of their new posts.

Toward the end of the war expectation of an Allied attack on Java persuaded the Japanese that to have any hope of the Indonesians' support they would have to promise them independence and yield them some upper-level administrative posts. Beginning in early October 1944, just after an announcement by the Japanese Prime Minister that Indonesia would be given independence "in the very near future," occupation authorities on Java began to relax controls over the activities of nationalist leaders, giving them greater opportunities for contact with the people. By early 1945 the Japanese began to take some short and halting steps in the direction of limited Indonesian self-government. A significant number of top-level administrative positions were gradually opened to Indonesians. (Again it was only on Java, and to a much lesser extent on Sumatra, that the Japanese made these concessions to Indonesian nationalism; in the areas administered by the navy the lid was clamped tight until almost the very end.) Although these positions remained usually under close Japanese supervision and always under ultimate Japanese control, they were important in generating a feeling of self-confidence among the Indonesian elite, a belief in their ability to handle the key positions previously held by Dutch officials.

Expectation of an Allied attack also brought the Japanese to establish an auxiliary army, a lightly armed militia known as the Peta, numbering some 120,000 men by mid-1945. It was this Japanese-trained, but Indonesian officered, militia which was to provide the principal military force behind the revolution, both in its early stages, when ironically it turned on the Japanese troops and fought them, and later when it fought British and subsequently Dutch forces. In addition, the Japanese gave a very limited military training—but no arms—and the function of security guards to a considerable number of village and urban youth; when the Peta later as a revolutionary army expanded its ranks, it was able to draw on this source.

In March 1945 the Japanese appointed a committee of some 60 Indonesians, most of them prominent, representing the principal social and ethnic groups of Java and Madura, and 7 Japanese to work out plans for the political and economic organization of an independent Indonesia. At meetings in May and July its members reached agreement on a set of broad national political principles. The Indonesians appear to have dominated these discussions, the Japanese members, for whatever reasons, taking relatively modest parts. The major role was played by Soekarno; much of the discussion was between him and certain Islamic leaders who wished the principles to have a more strongly Islamic cast than he believed was consistent with that religion's relatively undogmatic character in most of Indonesia and with the fact that the country had important non-Islamic minorities. Soekarno prevailed, and the set of five principles, *Pantjasila*, finally adopted —through a compromise between differing views held by the committee members—was a synthesis wherein his own thinking was dominant. In fact the *Pantjasila* was Soekarno's own statement made in an off-the-cuff speech (and recorded stenographically) toward the end of the meeting wherein he presented his own ideological synthesis in an effort to bridge his position and that of the more doctrinaire Islamic leaders while changing his own views as little as possible in the process.

The *Pantjasila*, although vague and not fully acceptable to some nominally Islamic Western-educated Indonesians as well as some prominent Islamic leaders, was to become the nearest approach to an official Indonesian national philosophy. The Five Principles in the order then presented by Soekarno were nationalism, internationalism (or humanitarianism), representative government, social justice, and belief in God in a context of religious freedom. His nationalism had a geopolitical element and defined the Indonesian nation as covering "the entire archipelago of Indonesia from the northern tip of Sumatra

to Papua." It was not, however, to be chauvinistic, but was to harmonize with other nationalisms to form an international community,
"one family of all nations," wherein each member would maintain his
national identity. Representative government would incorporate the
Islamic principle of consultation, and the envisaged house of representatives would provide Muslims with ample opportunity for working toward an Islamic political order while at the same time giving
adherents of other religions an equal chance to advance their own
ideas. But representative government would mean little if not under-
girded by social justice. In America and the countries of Western Europe, Soekarno argued, "the capitalists are in control," and in them
political democracy is unaccompanied by economic democracy. "Political democracy," he stated, citing the French revisionist socialist
Jean Jaures, does not ensure "economic democracy." If social justice
was to be secured for the Indonesian people, both kinds of democracy
would be necessary; "if we are seeking democracy, the need is not for
the democracy of the West, but for . . . politico-economic democracy."

Late in July 1945 the Japanese command on Sumatra provided for
the establishment of a roughly similar committee to make preparations
for independence, but in the areas under its control the Japanese
navy made no such concession. Not until August 7, 1945, when Japan's
Southeast Asia headquarters ordered the establishment of an all-
Indonesian Independence Preparatory Committee, was it possible for
Indonesian nationalists from the navy-administered areas to come to
Java to consult with Javanese and Sumatran leaders. This committee,
with Soekarno as chairman and Mohammad Hatta as vice-chairman,
was composed of 11 members from Java, 4 from Sumatra, 2 from
Celebes, and 1 each representing the Lesser Sundas, the Moluccas, and
the Indonesian Chinese community. Its announced function was to
make preparations for transfer of governmental authority to it by the
Japanese.

The Revolutionary Struggle

Japan's surrender resulted in the sudden removal of the repressive
apparatus that had for so long held the Indonesian nationalist movement in check. It found the Indonesian members of the Peta anti-
Japanese as well as anti-Dutch and equipped with the arms necessary
to contest any reimposition of outside control. When the Japanese commander in Java made clear that rather than promote Indonesian in-

dependence he would obey the Allied orders to maintain the status quo pending the take-over by Allied troops, Soekarno and Hatta, urged on by the anti-Japanese underground organizations and student groups, on August 17, 1945, proclaimed Indonesia's independence.

Some Japanese officers, stupefied by their country's sudden surrender, acquiesced to the Indonesians' seizure of stocks of arms in their custody; but others ordered their troops to resist the Peta and students. The scope and tempo of this fighting quickly increased, with the Peta, reinforced by newly armed student organizations, engaging in heavy fighting against Japanese forces for control of key cities. The first phase of the Indonesian revolution had begun. Sumatra followed Java's example, and in parts of that island, too, fighting broke out between Indonesians and Japanese. This was not the pattern, however, in Borneo, Celebes, the Lesser Sundas, or the Moluccas. There the Japanese had not allowed Indonesian nationalists to organize or to form militias, and consequently they had little trouble in maintaining control until Allied troops, generally Australian, took over. The Australians, not confronted by any strong and active Indonesian nationalist organization with which they felt obliged to come to terms, did not hesitate to reinstall Dutch civil administrators promptly.

In Java and Sumatra the situation was very different. When the British, the Allied troops assigned there, first landed in Java some six weeks after the declaration of independence, they were amazed to find the newly born Indonesian Republic a going organization, possessing an effective militia and a functioning, if somewhat rudimentary, administration. Moreover, they soon discovered that the Republican regimes on Java and Sumatra were solidly linked to and backed by the Indonesian masses. Although the Indonesians were glad to have the British accept the surrender of Japanese troops and send them home, they naturally could not agree with that part of the Allied mandate which called for the British to turn over authority to the Dutch before pulling out. Heavy fighting resulted. The British ultimately had to send Japanese troops into battle to shore up an Indian division which except for its Ghurka component had proved unreliable, several hundred Indians deserting to the Indonesian side.

It rapidly became clear to the British that unless they were willing to bring to Indonesia a greatly increased strength of soldiers and equipment they would have to alter their policies and find some measure of common ground with the leaders of the Indonesian revolution. Continuation of a military policy found no backing at home, and the

British soon began to deal with the Republic of Indonesia as a *de facto* government. In addition they urged the Dutch, whose troops they had meanwhile begun to shoehorn into some of the port areas they held, to negotiate with the Republic so that a peaceful compromise might be effected. Following the disarming and removal of the Japanese, Britain put great pressure on the Netherlands to come to such an agreement, making it clear that all British troops would leave Indonesia by November 1946.

Late in November, Netherlands and Republican authorities finally signed an ambiguously worded document, the Linggadjati Agreement, which it was hoped would avert the outbreak of war and meet the basic demands of both parties. This provided for the protection of Dutch economic interests in Indonesia and for Dutch recognition of the Republic's *de facto* authority over Java and Sumatra. Ultimately the Republic was to be merged in an Indonesian federation containing at least two other units—Borneo and "the Great East" (Celebes, the Lesser Sundas, the Moluccas, and Western New Guinea). This federal state would then co-operate with the Netherlands in establishing a vaguely defined Netherlands-Indonesian Union to emerge at the beginning of January 1949.[2] During the ensuing eight months of relative peace the Dutch consolidated their control over the islands outside of Java and Sumatra and reinforced their troop strength in the Javan and Sumatran port cities turned over to them by the retiring British. Dutch efforts to reassert political control over Indonesia followed two courses: first, an attempt to destroy the Republic and its armed forces by military means and, second, a politics of divide-and-rule calculated to isolate the Republic from other areas of Indonesia and create a political system—a so-called federal order—wherein pro-Republican elements would be smothered, or at least decisively outvoted, by representatives from a congeries of some fifteen Dutch-sponsored and Dutch-controlled component states.[3] But successful prosecution of their tactics of indirect rule, however refined and skillful, was ultimately dependent upon the other prong of their strategy, a decisive and crushing military victory over the forces of the Republic —an objective they were to find unobtainable.

In July 1947 the Dutch charged the Republic with violating the

[2] For a full account of the Linggadjati negotiations and an analysis of the agreement see Charles Wolf, Jr., *The Indonesian Story* (New York: John Day, 1948).

[3] For an account of the strategy and tactics employed by the Dutch see Kahin, *Nationalism and Revolution*, pp. 351–390.

Linggadjati Agreement, refused to abide by its arbitration clause, and launched an all-out attack. After their forces had overrun the Republic's richest districts in Java and Sumatra, they were induced by the United Nations to halt further advance and to sign in January 1947 another military truce and political agreement with the Republic, the Renville Agreement. In essence this gave the Dutch temporary control of the areas they had penetrated in return for their pledge to hold a UN-sponsored plebescite in them to determine whether or not their populations wished to be governed by the Republic. It was very clear that in any such plebescite an overwhelming majority would declare for the Republic, and the Dutch never held one. Instead, and likewise in contravention of the Renville Agreement, in these disputed areas they energetically set about to sponsor and build up amenable puppet or semipuppet states such as they had already begun establishing in Borneo and Celebes.

Into the truncated territory left the Republic on Java, a deficit food area, fled approximately a million refugees from those parts Dutch forces had entered. A tight Dutch blockade, extending even to medical supplies and quite in violation of the Renville Agreement, made living conditions extremely harsh. Because of this and because Indonesian leaders saw the United States and the European democracies unwilling to take effective measures to bring the Netherlands to live up to its commitments under the agreement (while they for the time being regarded Soviet Russia as supporting the Republic), the pro-Communist minority inside the Republic grew in numbers and influence. The Stalinist Communists were emboldened and, apparently responding to the new international line, laid plans for taking over the government and ousting Soekarno and the cabinet headed by Hatta. Their preparations were only partially completed when their effort was prematurely triggered by second-echelon Communist leaders operating from the central Java city of Madiun. After bitter fighting extending from mid-September through mid-November 1948, the Republic's army (the large majority of its units remaining loyal) suppressed the rebellion.[4]

Just six weeks later, in defiance of the UN-sponsored Renville Agreement, the Netherlands launched an all-out military campaign against the Republic's weakened forces. But Indonesian resistance was determined and sustained, and by the late spring of 1949 it was clear

[4] An account of the Madiun rebellion and its background can be found in Kahin, *Nationalism and Revolution*, pp. 256–303.

that the Dutch could not marshal sufficient military strength in Indonesia to enforce a political decision through military power. It was likewise clear that any prolongation of their costly military effort would result in an even more widespread destruction of the Netherlands' 2-billion-dollar investment in Indonesia and be a continuing heavy drain on its manpower and wealth at home. As Dutch holdings were increasingly exposed to the Republic's scorched-earth policy, more and more Dutch businessmen joined liberal elements in the Netherlands long committed to the idea of Indonesian independence. This in conjunction with powerful adverse world opinion, including substantial pressure from the United States, finally brought the Netherlands government to come to terms with the realities of Indonesian nationalism. At the Round Table Conference held at The Hague during the late summer of 1949 a settlement was reached which ended the hostilities and provided for Indonesia's full independence. In essence the Dutch exchanged their claim to sovereignty over all Indonesia except Western New Guinea (with the proviso that its status be decided during the coming year on the basis of negotiations between Indonesia and the Netherlands) for the preservation of their economic stake in Indonesia and a shipping agreement and a debt settlement distinctly favorable to the Netherlands, Indonesia being saddled with nearly $1,130,000,000 of the colonial regime's obligations, much of which had been incurred since 1945 in financing the effort to suppress the Republic.

Effect of the Revolution on Indonesian Government

The circumstances attending Indonesia's long and difficult struggle for independence decisively shaped the nature of its government. The political institutions forged during the heat of nearly five years of revolution were developed under unique conditions, quite different from those obtaining after independence. By its very nature the revolutionary struggle exerted powerful centripetal pressures which greatly eased the tasks of government. The necessity for Indonesians to stand shoulder to shoulder against a common enemy induced a consciousness of common political purpose and a political integration, at the same time enhancing the individual's willingness to sacrifice for the common good. The Republic was able to wage a war against tremendous odds for more than four years on a printing-press currency backed by nothing more than the symbols of nationalism and independence. Thus during the long period of struggle there was no great pressure to provide formulas of political organization calculated to satisfy regional sentiments.

The character of the revolutionary Republic's political institutions, institutions which were to have a profound influence upon postrevolutionary Indonesian government, was also strongly affected by the struggle for power within the ranks of revolutionists.[5] And to some extent it was influenced by a belief (which reinforced the position of certain leaders) that Indonesia's bargaining position against the Dutch in the forum of world opinion would be stronger if it had a government which was rid of any important residue of the Japanese occupation and any suggestion of fascist orientation.

The course of the revolution also influenced ideological outlook. The attraction of Indonesians to socialist ideas was reinforced by the leveling process which the revolution visited upon a society that even before had few valleys and peaks. For many, disappointment with both the United States and Soviet Russia—from whom they had hoped for greater support against the Dutch—and the conviction that their four-year struggle for independence was won primarily by their own efforts and the heavy sacrifices of their own people lessened the attraction of either the American or the Soviet system and reinforced their inclination to work out uniquely Indonesian governmental institutions. In addition this disillusionment with the two great powers tended to induce an even stronger determination than is found among most ex-colonials to follow an international course aligned with neither.

At its first meeting on August 18, 1945, the 21-member Independence Preparatory Committee added 6 people to its membership, including the commander of the Jakarta Peta garrison and 3 members of one of the anti-Japanese underground organizations. It then elected Soekarno and Hatta respectively President and Vice-President of the newly proclaimed Republic of Indonesia and appointed a commission of 7, including these two leaders, to make a final draft of a national constitution, a document already largely written during the last month prior to the Japanese capitulation. Within a week this work was completed and the constitution promulgated. Though considered definitely provisional, it was not replaced until the end of 1949.

The 1945 constitution described a political order somewhat like the American. The center of power was to be lodged with a President

---

[5] An account of the internal politics of the revolution in this early, formative period can be found in Kahin, *Nationalism and Revolution*, pp. 147–212.

assisted by an appointed cabinet directly responsible to him. In addition to holding executive powers the President would share legislative power with an elected Congress. The major departure from the American system was the provision for a sort of periodical constitutional convention to be known as the Consultative Assembly, a large elected body to meet every five years which would elect the President and Vice-President and initially formulate the definitive constitution, in later meetings amending it if necessary and determining the broad lines of general governmental policy. There was also provision for a High Advisory Council, whose composition was to be defined by law and which was to advise and provide information requested by the President and have the right to submit proposals to the government.

Although the 1945 constitution envisaged three major lodgments of power—an elected Consultative Assembly, the presidency, and an elected Chamber of Representatives—the circumstances of the revolution never allowed sufficient opportunity to hold the national elections which were the necessary antecedents for creation of the Consultative Assembly and the Chamber of Representatives. Only the Transitional Provisions of the 1945 constitution were in an operational sense of importance. These stipulated that until the formation of the two elected bodies all state powers would be exercised by the President assisted by a central national committee which would have a purely advisory function. Thus on August 29 Soekarno dissolved the Independence Preparatory Committee and in its place established the Komite Nasional Indonesia Pusat (Central Indonesian National Committee), or KNIP as it came to be known. Assisted in his selections by Hatta, he appointed 135 members to the new body, including those of the dissolved Independence Preparatory Committee. Those selected were considered to be outstanding Indonesian nationalists and the most important leaders of the principal ethnic, religious, social, and economic groups in Indonesia; few could be classified as amenable political stooges. A cabinet directly responsible to the President was appointed, for the most part made up of those Indonesians who had served as department heads under the Japanese during the last months of their rule. Thus the government established at the outset of the Indonesian revolution was one in which power was largely concentrated in the presidency.

This system lasted for only two and a half months, until November 15, 1945. Widespread opposition to its concentration of power soon emerged, a large part of the criticism being equally concerned with the survivals of Japanese rule evidenced by the cabinet's membership. Much of the pushing power behind the revolution came from the armed youth organizations, whose members were deeply affected by the ideas of the leaders of the major anti-Japanese undergrounds, in particular by Soetan Sjahrir and Amir Sjarifuddin. These youth groups along with a large minority of the KNIP accused several key members of Soekarno's cabinet of being close to the Japanese in their thinking and of possessing what they termed "fascist mentalities." They were disturbed that these men were in control of key sectors of government and in positions to exert substantial influence on the course of policy. And, although the majority were reconciled to Soekarno's assumption of the principal post of leadership in the revolution, they opposed his exercising the overwhelming and unrestrained power called for in the transitional regulations of the constitution.

In response to this powerful sentiment, on October 7, 1945, 50 members of the KNIP presented a petition to Soekarno urging that legislative authority be shared by the President with the thus far advisory KNIP. Cognizant of the strong backing of this element and fearful of the challenge from a third group headed by the nationalist-Communist leader Tan Malaka, Soekarno gave in to this demand (undoubtedly with Hatta urging him to do so). Thereby he strengthened his ties with the Sjahrir and Sjarifuddin groups and those who shared their dislike of some of the high officials left in office by the Japanese. On October 16, 1945, a presidential decree, signed by Vice-President Hatta, provided that pending the establishment of the Consultative Assembly and Chamber of Representatives called for in the constitution the KNIP would be vested with their legislative authority, thereby sharing legislative power with the President. All legislation now had to be approved by the KNIP as well as by the President, with the KNIP having the same right as he to introduce legislation. The decree also stipulated, as had been requested in the petition, that the KNIP delegate its powers to a small permanently sitting representative body known as the Working Committee (Badan Pekerdja) which was to be composed of members of the infrequently convoked parent body (the KNIP) and responsible to it.[6] Although the KNIP was required to convene a minimum of only once a year, the Working Committee was to meet at least every ten days. The KNIP elected the two men who had been the principal leaders of the anti-Japanese underground—

[6] The term Working Committee was one derived from the Indian National Congress, whose history most Indonesian nationalists knew.

Sjahrir and Sjarifuddin—respectively as chairman and vice-chairman of the newly established Working Committee. They accepted their posts on condition that they be empowered to select its other 13 members, a demand which the KNIP granted. Thereupon the Working Committee became a key factor in the Republic's government, exercising to the full its colegislative powers and under Sjahrir overshadowing both President and cabinet.

At the end of October 1945, Sjahrir published a small booklet, *Our Struggle (Perdjuangan Kita)*, which had great impact upon the thinking of politically active Indonesians, especially those who remained dissatisfied with the still substantial power in the hands of the cabinet and regarded its members as too close to the Japanese in their thinking. Sjahrir strongly castigated what he described as the fascist and opportunistic mentality of many members of the government, both in the cabinet and in the upper level of the bureaucracy. He warned that these men might lead the government in the direction of fascist totalitarianism and jingoist nationalism and called for their prompt removal from office. There was a heavy rallying behind him; those who had earlier called for the President's sharing power with the KNIP now demanded that the cabinet be responsible to the KNIP rather than to the President. The positions of those in the cabinet and in the bureaucracy who owed their posts to the Japanese were seriously weakened, and although Soekarno had not been included in the attack, there is no doubt that it temporarily decreased his political stature. Sjahrir's position was further strengthened because of the feeling among a number of influential Indonesians that a government required to deal with the victorious Allies ought to show as little residual Japanese influence as possible.

Thus on November 11 the Working Committee called for the introduction of cabinet responsibility to parliament, that is, to the KNIP. Soekarno and Hatta promptly accepted this proposal, dismissing the old cabinet and opening the way for establishment on November 14, 1945, of a new cabinet headed by Sjahrir, one no longer under the authority of the President and responsible only to the representative body of the government. With the Working Committee (now under a new chairman and vice-chairman) still serving as deputy of the KNIP during the long periods between its meetings, the cabinet in effect became responsible to the Working Committee. Although not specifically spelled out at this time, it was expected that should a difference arise between cabinet and Working Committee the matter would be referred for resolution to the KNIP. In practice all disagreements which arose were resolved between them without either making an appeal to the KNIP.[7] The Working Committee never challenged the cabinet's assumption of the major executive role, but it reserved the right to scrutinize closely its discharge of that power through a frequently employed right of interpolation. In the legislative field the Working Committee came close to being the cabinet's peer. By mid-1948 out of the 98 legislative acts passed during its existence, it had itself initiated 15. During the year's span between the KNIP meetings of March 4, 1946, and February 17, 1947, it rejected 10 and passed 20 of the bills which had been approved by cabinet and President, adding its own amendments to many. One reason for the positive and efficient role played by the Working Committee was its small size. Until March 1947 its membership did not exceed 24, and thereafter it was increased to only 45. This made possible discussion along traditional Indonesian lines, that is, discussion resulting in a conclusion based upon the broad consensus of the group as a whole rather than one based upon majority vote. Whereas the KNIP, had it been disposed to be an active legislative body, was much too large for discussion and decision making along traditional Indonesian lines, the Working Committee was of optimal size and usually followed this process in arriving at its most important decisions. Another reason for the Working Committee's efficiency was its members' freedom from close connection with political parties and their usual tendency to view issues apart from party considerations, showing themselves in most cases to be above party in their conduct.[8]

[7] No clear agreement ever emerged as to what would happen if the cabinet in the face of a disagreement with the Working Committee refused to accept a KNIP judgment backing up the Working Committee. It was the position of Mr. Assaat, chairman of both the KNIP and the Working Committee, that should "a serious conflict arise between the KNIP and the cabinet where the President is convinced that the KNIP no longer represents the people, he may dissolve the KNIP and establish a new one which is more representative"; he argued, however, that should there be a continuation of the disagreement between the cabinet and the new KNIP, the President would be required to dissolve the cabinet rather than the new KNIP (*Hukum Tata Negara* [Constitutional Law; Jogjakarta, 1947], p. 33).

[8] Not only was the original nucleus of the Working Committee appointed before the formation of most of the political parties, but in addition its membership was originally selected as being representative of "political trends, communal groups, or the provinces" rather than of parties. Thus during 1946–1947 out of a membership of 25, 8 members had been elected as representing the 8 provinces of Indonesia, 1 the Chinese community, 1 the Christian element, 4 "the national democratic trend," 2 the Muhammedan trend, with the remaining 9 regarded as representing the "workers, peasants, socialists, the youth movement, and the women's

During its month's operation under Sjahrir's chairmanship (October 16, 1945—November 12, 1945) prior to the establishment of cabinet responsibility to parliament, the Working Committee had called for the creation of a diversity of political parties. It took this important measure largely to obviate the possible growth of a totalitarian political order —one of the reasons which had prompted it to demand that the KNIP be transformed into a body with legislative authority and which later brought it to demand that the cabinet be responsible to the KNIP rather than the President. The Working Committee was particularly concerned lest a monolithic party organization be created wherein those who had worked with the Japanese would exercise control because of their still dominant position throughout most of the bureaucracy.[9] It was to preclude this and ensure that these elements would be politically undercut that the Working Committee on October 30, 1945, called for the formation of several political parties reflecting various trends of opinion. This position was promptly endorsed by the cabinet and President in a government regulation of November 3 which noted that "if democratic principles are to be observed it is not permissible that only one party should be allowed to function." There followed a rapid establishment of parties, and those who had hoped to form a single national party were never again to have a favorable opportunity. While parties proliferated, they did not develop real roots in the population; for national elections, although repeatedly scheduled, were not held during the revolutionary period. The impact of the parties on the political scene was not immediate. But whereas in the formation of his first cabinet (November 14, 1945—March 12, 1946) Sjahrir was able to disregard them completely, in forming his third and last cabinet (October 2, 1946—July 3, 1947) he was obliged to meet them half way in their demand for cabinet representation.

Although it is true that during the four-year revolutionary period the principal legislative and executive roles were played by the Working Committee and the cabinet, one should not minimize the importance of the presidency. Soekarno and Hatta appear to have participated in

movement." Although at a later date most members of the Working Committee established party affiliations, even then their work on the committee usually gave little evidence of party considerations.

[9] An abortive move to establish such a party had been made on August 22, 1945, when the Independence Preparatory Committee had decided on the formation of a single national party. Ten days later this decision was withdrawn and the proposal shelved, but there was considerable expectation that it might be reactivated.

all major governmental decisions, and as far as can be ascertained, none was ever taken to which they were strongly opposed. Promulgation of any law or decree was regarded as requiring the signature of either the President or the Vice-President, and it was Soekarno's position that signing was no mere formality but an indication of presidential approval which he had the right to withhold when he was in disagreement. Thus to the writer he stated: "Theoretically I can veto any law of parliament. However, I have never done so, because my system was to keep in very close contact with Assaat [chairman of both the Working Committee and the KNIP] and to influence the Working Committee. Agreements were worked out ahead of time, and thus collisions between presidency and Working Committee were avoided." [10] The fact that both President and Vice-President generally acted in close concert during this period helped ensure that their views would usually diverge little from those held by the cabinet and the Working Committee. For in the process of finding common ground between themselves the two leaders were likely to be that much closer to the views of these other two organs of government. On only one occasion did differences come to a head. This occurred at the end of 1946, with the President's assuming in rather dramatic fashion his prerogative for appointing members to the KNIP. It was primarily in order to get that body to ratify the Linggadjati Agreement and provide for peaceful negotiations with the Netherlands that Soekarno, backed by both Hatta and Sjahrir's cabinet, decreed that the KNIP be expanded in membership from 200 to 514 members. The Working Committee challenged this measure, and the issue was therefore referred to the Working Committee's parent body, the KNIP, for resolution. Meeting in full session in February of 1947 the KNIP was initially inclined to support the Working Committee and finally was only dissuaded from doing so by a vigorous speech of Vice-President Hatta wherein he made clear that he and Soekarno would resign if defeated on this issue.[11]

[10] Muntok, Bangka, May 4, 1949.

[11] It was the position of Mr. Assaat, chairman of the KNIP, that this event tended to fix the general principle (never again tested) that whenever on a matter of presidential prerogative the President was opposed by the KNIP he and the Vice-President would be obliged to resign, the KNIP then electing a new President and Vice-President. Although there was no clear agreement as to what powers were included in the sphere of presidential prerogative, there was a considerable and influential body of opinion which held that in addition to the power of appointing the membership of the KNIP it also included—though probably most would have argued subject to subsequent KNIP ratification—declaration of a state of emergency, initiation and promulgation of ordinances during such a period, decla-

Soekarno, in addressing this session of the KNIP, stated that in his opinion, pending elections which would determine the composition of the representative bodies of the state, "it is the task of the President himself to nominate and appoint members because of the fact that the President himself is regarded as the representative of the whole people." Even then his views concerning the proper qualities of a representative body foreshadowed the controversial position which he was to take in 1957: he held that the KNIP should incorporate members of occupational groups, the regions, the principal non-Indonesian minorities, the armed organizations, as well as of the political parties. In the enlarged KNIP the parties actually held only 222 out of 514 seats as against a previous 129 out of 200, and the appointments reflected Soekarno's view that a party's representation should be determined not merely by the number of its members, but also by its degree of organization and integration. Thus while acknowledging that the major Islamic party, the Masjumi, enrolled several times as many members as either the Socialist, Labor, or Communist parties, he held that nevertheless because of greater integration and superior organization these last three were entitled to 35 seats each in the KNIP as against 60 for the Masjumi.[12] This same philosophy was reflected in the composition of the Republic's High Advisory Council, one of the few organs of government provided for in the 1945 constitution which functioned as described. Its membership of 10 to 19 members, selected by Soekarno in consultation with Hatta, related only incidentally to party and embraced distinguished regional leaders as well as individuals representing important religious and ethnic groups.[13] Its importance as an advisory body to the President was assured by the KNIP's early relinquishment of this function. Although the Working

---

ration of war, the making of peace, and conclusion of treaties. Assaat believed, however, that there was a general consensus that unless the point of difference between President and KNIP was vital to the country and the President irrevocably committed to his action (e.g., signing of a treaty with the Netherlands which the KNIP rejected) he would, once the difference was apparent, generally be prepared to yield to the KNIP and consequently remain in office (discussion with the writer, Jogjakarta, September 17, 1948).

[12] Conversation of the writer with President Soekarno, Jogjakarta, December 12, 1948. Soekarno stated that in determining party strength he consulted with Hatta after having received reports from local officials giving estimates of party strength within their areas.

[13] An original membership of 10 (1 a woman) was expanded to 19 in April 1948, when it included 8 representatives from outside Java (3 being Sumatrans), 1 Chinese, and 1 Eurasian. At the end of 1949 its membership stood at 13.

Committee repeatedly sought to have the Council abolished, regarding it as undemocratic, Soekarno found it useful and successfully contested such efforts.

In times of acute crisis when for one reason or another the cabinet could not function effectively, plenary emergency powers were exercised by the President. It was, however, never clear to what extent the decision to vest the President with them was a prerogative of the President or lay within the competence of cabinet and/or Working Committee.[14] During the revolutionary period there were three such occasions, each brief. The first was from June 29 to October 2, 1946, being precipitated by the kidnaping of Prime Minister Sjahrir during an unsuccessful *coup d'état* led by Tan Malaka. Soekarno assumed full powers on the basis of his own decree, surrendering them following the coup's suppression and Sjahrir's formation of a new and broader cabinet. (In this case the rump cabinet had urged Soekarno to issue the decree, and following its promulgation the Working Committee concurred.) The second instance was from June 27 to July 3, 1947, in connection with the critical situation arising from the deadlock in negotiations with the Dutch, Sjahrir having urged concessions which went further than the rest of the government were initially prepared to go. By presidential decree, ratified by the Working Committee the following day, full powers were again assumed by Soekarno pending the formation of a new cabinet a week later with Sjarifuddin as Prime Minister. The third instance occurred as a consequence of the Communists' Madiun rebellion and lasted from September 15, 1948, to December 15, 1948. In this case the cabinet with the concurrence of the Working Committee passed an act vesting President Soekarno with full emergency powers.

The relative efficiency and quality of Indonesia's government during the revolutionary period may be explained in part at least by three important factors. One was the previously noted solidarity induced by the common struggle against the Dutch. A second was the generally smooth working relationship between the government's representative body and the cabinet, a situation which was not to obtain during most

[14] See A. K. Pringgodigdo, *The Office of President in Indonesia as Defined in the Three Constitutions in Theory and Practice* (Cornell Modern Indonesia Project, Translation Series; Ithaca, N.Y., 1957), pp. 15–16. Soekarno's own position was clear. To the present writer he stated: "I have the right to declare a state of emergency, during which I can govern by decree, and to do so I do not need consent of parliament, though of course I would always talk it over with the ministers beforehand" (Muntok, Bangka, May 4, 1949).

of the postrevolutionary period. In practice the cabinet had to deal only with the Working Committee of the representative body (KNIP) and for all practical purposes was responsible only to it. With the Working Committee composed of a small group of competent men, it was reasonably easy for them to reach agreement in a short time. Thus the cabinet could generally count upon the Working Committee's knowing its own mind and reaching a decision fairly quickly, qualities which were much more difficult to develop in the large, heterogeneous, and loosely organized KNIP and which were to prove equally difficult to achieve in the postrevolutionary parliament. Moreover, the size and quality of the Working Committee's membership meant that discussion, informal as well as formal, between it and cabinet members could yield mutual understanding, common ground, and finally agreement relatively quickly. Such rapport would not have been possible had the cabinet been obliged to deal directly with the KNIP, and it was not to prove possible between cabinet and parliament in the postrevolutionary period when the intermediary Working Committee had been abolished.

A third reason for the relative effectiveness of government in the revolutionary period lay in the generally harmonious relationship between President and Vice-President. The policies emanating from the presidency were moderated by the fact that such co-operation implied a degree of compromise between the views of these two men. In addition, when during the last two years of the revolutionary period the hardening of party lines made it increasingly difficult in times of crisis to form cabinets based upon a parliamentary majority, this harmony ensured that emergency, transitional "presidential cabinets" could be formed with Vice-President Hatta acting as Prime Minister. The composition of such cabinets did not become a question of bargaining between the various political parties, the key post being held by a man of great prestige who stood above party, and it was generally believed that a cabinet so established could not be forced to resign by a vote of nonconfidence in the KNIP. During periods of crisis two such cabinets were formed. The first was established following the Renville Agreement on January 29, 1948, in order to ensure that the Republic undertake the unpopular task of implementing it and endured until August 4, 1949. It was not based upon a party coalition commanding a majority in parliament, although the major parties were represented in it, and Hatta conducted his government in a way which in fact ensured consistent majority support. The second, essentially a reshuffle of the first, lasted from August 4, 1949, to December 20, 1949, and was created under Hatta's leadership to set the stage for the final negotiations with the Dutch at The Hague. It should be reiterated that the possibility of establishing such presidential cabinets was dependent upon a reasonably harmonious relationship between Hatta and Soekarno, a harmony which was to decrease rapidly after 1950 and give place to a complete rupture by 1956.

Government in Sumatra and in the Dutch-controlled Areas

During the first two years of the Republic's existence, that is, until the first Dutch military campaign of July 1947, its authority extended to all of Java and Sumatra except for a few enclaves embracing those major ports held first by the British and later by the Dutch. In the remainder of Indonesia, it will be recalled, the Dutch were enabled to take over with very little trouble. Although most politically conscious Indonesians in Borneo, Celebes, the Lesser Sundas, and the Moluccas were strongly pro-Republican, the Dutch were able to put down their few efforts at armed resistance with relative ease. The central government of the Republic, with its capital during most of this period at Jogjakarta in central Java, certainly spoke for that large majority of Indonesians on Java and Sumatra (well over four-fifths of Indonesia's population), but its relationship with Java was much closer than with Sumatra. The Netherlands navy and air force so effectively controlled communications between the two islands that only rarely were the Republic's officials able to run their blockade. Following the military campaigns of the summer of 1947, wherein approximately one-half of Java and about a quarter of Sumatra (including almost every important port) were overrun by Dutch troops, the problem of communication became even more difficult. Thus, although during the revolutionary period the top administrative posts in Sumatra were held by officials appointed or endorsed by the central government of the Republic and though many of its major policies were followed insofar as possible by the Sumatran Republican administrations, of necessity these administrations were highly autonomous.[15] Financially they

---

[15] This autonomy had been recognized by a central government decree of 1945, providing that the province be administered by a governor appointed by the central Republican government and assisted by a locally selected Sumatran national committee (KNI). Actually this legislation merely formalized the existing situation. Until the beginning of April 1946 the only contact between Sumatra and the Republican government on Java was by radio, and not until then were cabinet ministers of the Republic's government able to reach the island. This mission,

were completely independent of the central government, printing their own currencies, usually tying them to the Straits dollar. The Republic's armed forces in Sumatra were obliged to finance themselves, often quite independently of the local civil administrations, and to rely primarily upon the local Indonesian population for food and supplies.[16] Thus during the course of the revolution the several regions of Sumatra by and large governed themselves through their own highly autonomous Republican administrations, operating only under broad directives from the central government and doing so only to the extent that they regarded this as feasible. They fended for themselves militarily against the Dutch, financed themselves, and undertook directly the local measures which they deemed necessary for their economic and social well-being.

Meanwhile in the substantial areas controlled by the Netherlands outside of Java and Sumatra, and after mid-1947 in those parts of these two islands which its army had overrun, the Dutch endeavored to establish a new political order of their own. By early 1949 they had created in these areas fifteen so-called "states" which were represented to the outside world as being run by local Indonesians and possessing a high degree of self-government. Although elaborate governmental façades were set up, in every case the outwardly Indonesian regime was controlled tightly and effectively by the Dutch colonial adminis-

---

headed by two Sumatra-born leaders—Amir Sjarifuddin, Minister of Defense, and Mohammad Natsir, Minister of Information—succeeded in partially reorganizing Sumatra's administration, establishing a network of local national committees and a Sumatran central national committee. It was, however, able to reinforce only slightly the meager authority of the Republic's governor on Sumatra, Tengku Hasan. Upon the initiative of Mohammad Hatta a second reorganization was effected under central government legislation of July 10, 1948. This divided Sumatra into three separate provinces—North, Central, and South Sumatra—and dissolved the existing all-Sumatra KNI, establishing in its place three such bodies, one for each province. Heading each of the provinces was a state commissioner (a local leader of considerable political stature) appointed by the central government. Each was charged with representing Jogjakarta (the central government) in his province and ensuring as much co-ordination as was feasible between his administration and the major directives of the central government. Another mission sent to Sumatra in 1948 and headed by the Republic's Minister of Economic Affairs, Sjafruddin Prawiranegara, was able to establish some rather slender financial ties between Jogjakarta and the Sumatran areas which resulted in the central government's receiving some benefit from the blockade-running barter trade between certain Sumatran areas, particularly Atjeh, and Singapore. All these efforts, however, bore limited results, and throughout the revolution the autonomy of the Sumatran administrations remained very great.

[16] They derived some additional income from "contributions" of Chinese merchants in return for protection and assistance in their lucrative smuggling trade with Singapore.

tration. In those states created in former Republican territory following the military campaign of mid-1947, Republican guerrilla units sometimes controlled as much of the area as the Dutch; but in those set up outside of Java and Sumatra, Netherlands military and police control was effective, and pro-Republican elements were either jailed or induced to keep quiet because of the overwhelming force which they confronted. In some of these areas the Dutch were able to win the support of a small minority which foresaw that under the Republic its aristocratic status and semifeudal privileges would be lost. And in almost every case there were a few political opportunists from other walks of life willing to collaborate in a positive sense in order to benefit from the financial remuneration, the automobiles, and the other things that the Dutch made available to them. Other Indonesians grudgingly co-operated in order to secure a living for their families, but remained pro-Republican at heart. The overwhelming majority of the Indonesian populations of these Netherlands-sponsored states were, however, opposed to the regimes with which they were saddled and looked wistfully to those areas of Java and Sumatra still able to hold out against the Dutch, regarding them as champions of their own cause.

It should be noted, then, that throughout the long period of the revolution only on Sumatra and Java, and after the middle of 1947 only in parts of these islands, were the Indonesian people administratively linked to the Republic. And only on Java itself (only half of Java after mid-1947) were they effectively incorporated into its government. Thus the major part of the Indonesian archipelago went through the more than four years of the revolution either as highly autonomous units with ties more psychological than substantive connecting them with the Republic's central government (as on Sumatra), or as units completely separated from it and under Netherlands control. The desire for independence and common opposition to the Dutch rallied all these areas and ensured a psychological unity throughout the revolution, one demanding a united and fully independent Indonesia. But this psychological bond was a mixture of positive and negative elements. True, it was to an important extent based upon an increasing sense of national identity and the belief that independence would open the way to a better life. At the same time, however, it was activated by the powerful negative dynamic of opposition to colonial rule—a component of Indonesian nationalism which was to lose much of its strength as a force for national cohesion once independence had been won.

· XXI ·

The Postrevolutionary Setting

FOUR years of revolution with a common objective and the attendant spread of a national language brought to Indonesians a great increase in political consciousness and national awareness. Particularly marked among urban elements, this was often discernible at the village level as well, the turmoil of Japanese occupation and revolution having done much to break down the introverted parochialism previously characteristic of most Indonesian villages. The rapid spread of a national educational system, down to and including the village, significant even during the revolution but tremendous in scale (if not always in quality) thereafter, considerably reinforced this tendency.

Heightened Expectations

Another important psychological residue of the revolution was the heightened expectations which the achievement of independence induced. They characterized in particular the outlook of educated and semieducated elements, especially those who had played the most active roles in the revolution, but were also to be found in varying degrees among a large part of urban and plantation labor and in some areas among the peasantry. Economic benefits as well as social and political status formerly seen as having been preserves of the Dutch were now regarded as the legitimate right of Indonesians. This feeling was understandably strongest among those who had won new self-confidence during the revolution and Japanese occupation by demonstrating ability to handle a wide range of positions previously regarded as outside the scope of their competence. But the idea was widespread that careers should be open to talent and that positions should be based upon ability and upon achievement demonstrated during the revolution. Education was seen as the postrevolutionary generation's principal channel of advancement, an avenue of social mobility extending down to the village. Although within a few years party connection increasingly became a criterion for career advancement, usually it did not supersede education in importance.

This emphasis upon education as a basis for advancement, though undoubtedly salutary in general, frequently penalized the middle generation—the young men and women in their twenties and early thirties who had provided so much of the vanguard of the revolution, often shouldering aside their more timorous colonial-conditioned elders and at decisive moments assuming the leadership and taking the decisive actions without which the revolution would have failed. Having in so many cases dropped out of school or college during the Japanese occupation and/or shelving their schooling to throw all their energies into the four-year revolutionary struggle, they were in educational terms a "lost generation." Beginning in 1950 some were able to return to their studies, but most had been out for so long, often having a wife and children to support, that this was quite impossible. Thus they were in an awkward position, for although their revolutionary record and practical experience gave them a claim to the positions of responsibility they had assumed or aspired to, on educational grounds they were in a weak position to compete. And now many of the older-generation revolutionary nationalists who had been happy to give them their head during the revolution felt that the time had come to reassert a position of superiority based on education as well as age and, since a reasonable degree of security was now attached to the upper governmental and political positions, ensure that these should rest largely in their own hands.[1]

---

[1] When those older nationalists who could point to a good revolutionary record took this position of emphasizing age, education, and length of bureaucratic service (often stretching many years back into the Japanese and Dutch colonial periods) as being criteria for governmental or party rank of equal or greater importance than revolutionary record, they were able to push aside and supersede many of those young, imaginative, and dynamic leaders who had won their spurs during the revolution at the cost of disrupting their schooling and of falling far behind in educational qualifications. But in addition, this opened the way for hundreds of

Although many of the younger ex-revolutionaries did not actually lose their government or party posts, often they were smothered by new positions opened up above and beside them and filled by their elders.[2] Those so by-passed became understandably bitter and discouraged, their expectations frustrated. Thereby their country was deprived of much of the imaginative thinking and willingness to take resolute action which had made this group's service so valuable during the revolution. In failing to provide its young revolutionary vanguard with opportunities for social service commensurate with the positions it filled during the revolution, the leaders of postrevolutionary Indonesia dissipated one of their country's most valuable assets, contributing to its problems as well as weakening its political viability.

Economic Conditions

Postrevolutionary expectations operated in an unpromising economic milieu. For after the revolution Indonesia was immensely poorer in developed economic resources than during the prewar colonial period —the wartime bombing raids, long and bitter fighting in the revolution, and frequent recourse to scorched-earth policies, both preceding the Japanese occupation and during the revolution, had resulted in the devastation of wide areas. The extent of damage or total destruction to transportation and communication facilities, oil installations, plantation equipment, sugar centrals, and the few industrial enterprises which the prewar economy had supported was tremendous; their restoration would require great effort, large financial outlay, and a substantial period of time. With respect to the government's financial substance, it should be recalled that as a consequence of the Round Table Agreement Indonesia had been saddled with a heavy indebtedness to the Netherlands, one which from the outset was a significant drain upon its economy. Moreover, because of the destruction of some of the few prewar industrial and processing enterprises, Indonesia's postwar economy was even more lopsided, even more preponderantly dependent upon the export of a few generally unprocessed raw materials (rubber, tin, oil, and copra) than before the war. And, as then, the prices of

---

fair-weather nationalists, timorous Republicans as well as former Federalists, to argue that their age, education, and bureaucratic experience outweighed their lack of revolutionary record and entitled them to positions which many ex-revolutionaries held or felt a right to.

[2] In the army this situation did not arise; for among its officers there was only a meager handful of the older generation, and only a few of them could point to experience that extended back before the revolution and Japanse occupation.

most of these exports on the world market fluctuated widely, making it difficult for the government to undertake long-term economic planning. With the government dependent primarily upon export and import taxes for its revenue, this problem was to become especially crucial.

Although the revolution and the Japanese occupation had seriously eroded the economic base of the country, its population had increased considerably, at least 15 per cent over the prewar figure, with most of this increase in already-overcrowded Java. During the revolution the Javanese peasantry did temporarily improve its position by repudiating its indebtedness to Chinese moneylenders, but the ratio between peasants and the available supply of arable land had become more unbalanced. Concentration of land ownership and absentee landlordism remained slight, but the average peasant's plot on Java had become smaller and his level of living had probably dropped, with the substantial degree of economic equality which persisted being maintained "through a division of the economic pie into smaller and smaller pieces," a sort of "shared poverty." [3]

Most of Indonesia's economy above the village level remained capitalistic in character and still preponderantly in the hands of non-Indonesians, primarily Netherlanders and Chinese. Although the amount of Western capital invested in postwar Indonesia remained large (Dutch investments despite destruction suffered during the revolution still standing in the neighborhood of a billion dollars), its political leverage was now infinitely less than had been the case during the colonial period. Western economic enterprise now had to deal with a government whose leaders were nearly all strongly socialist, many of them unsympathetic to any increase in the role of foreign capital and most of them dedicated to the idea of its eventual displacement by socialization or transfer to the hands of Indonesian capitalists. In addition Western and Chinese business were now confronted by large and militant trade unions, something the colonial government had never countenanced. Formation of these labor unions had been encouraged by the revolutionary government, and the postrevolutionary government remained sympathetically inclined toward them, framing legislation advantageous to their growth and to their bargaining position vis-à-vis capital. Membership in these unions soon reached be-

[3] Clifford Geertz, "Religious Belief and Economic Behaviour in a Javanese Town: Some Preliminary Considerations," *Economic and Cultural Change*, IV, no. 2 (Jan. 1956), 141.

tween 1.5 and 2 million, and it was precisely in the plantations, oil fields, and industrial enterprises where Western capital was most active that they enrolled most of their members. Increasingly the trade unions took on a political orientation, the majority of them becoming adjuncts of political parties, in particular the Indonesian Communist Party.

Just as during the colonial period, Indonesia's 2.5 to 3 million Chinese continued to dominate the lower and middle levels of the capitalist sector of the economy. As a consequence of the revolution they had to a large extent lost their previously strong position as dispensers of agrarian credit, most of them leaving the countryside for the cities and thereby swelling the proportion of Chinese domiciled there; but they were quick to move into those sectors of economic enterprise from which European capital was withdrawing. As government policy sought to promote the economic interests of Indonesians, primarily through granting highly preferential treatment in distributing import licenses, some traditional Indonesian trading elements, largely in Sumatra and Borneo, were able to take direct advantage of these opportunities. In many areas, however, particularly in Java, these measures indirectly benefited Chinese more than they helped Indonesians. Most Indonesians lacked the requisite entrepreneurial experience and subleased their privileges to Chinese so endowed with this quality as to make substantial profit even though required to give the Indonesian license holder a sizable cut. An undoubted affinity of economic interests developed between such Indonesian "fronts" and their Chinese associates, but this was to result in no discernible social integration. The Chinese community continued to stand apart from the Indonesian, the distance between them having if anything been increased during the course of the revolution when most Chinese took what they termed a "neutral" position, one hardly likely to elicit sympathy from the hardpressed Indonesians. Even that majority of the Chinese population willing to accept Indonesian citizenship was not regarded as Indonesian by most ethnic Indonesians and found itself discriminated against by governmental economic policy.[4] Thus the role of Indonesians in the capitalist sector of their country's economy remained almost as small after the revolution as before, the slight increase of their importance between 1950 and 1958 stemming primarily from preferential governmental policies.

[4] See Donald E. Willmott, *The National Status of the Chinese in Indonesia* (Cornell Modern Indonesia Project, Interim Reports Series; Ithaca, N.Y., 1956).

The Bureaucracy

A great and striking difference between postrevolutionary and colonial Indonesian society was in the bureaucracy. Whereas before the revolution Western-educated Indonesians had been given only very slight access to its middle and upper ranks, these had now become their exclusive preserve. In the bureaucracy heightened expectations could to a degree at least be rewarded; for, as traditionally, it was still regarded by Indonesians as a profession of great prestige. The economic rewards were, however, disappointing, salaries (in terms of purchasing power) being much smaller than during the colonial period. This resulted not only from the poverty of the postrevolutionary government and an increasingly serious monetary inflation, but from inflation of the bureaucracy itself. By the early 1950s the national civil service had become four times as great as before the war, nearly 600,000 as against approximately 150,000.

The necessity of incorporating the Dutch-sponsored Federalist civil service into that built up during the revolution in the Republic induced from the outset a loss in morale among both elements. Those from the Republic felt that revolutionary service and sacrifice should be rewarded; they were often disillusioned in finding themselves placed under someone who had greater experience or educational qualifications but who had served in one of the Dutch-controlled states and whom, as a consequence, they frequently regarded as opportunistic and lacking in patriotism. On the other hand former Federalists working under a civil servant whose only training had been acquired under the revolutionary Republic frequently felt aggrieved because the Republican lacked their experience or education.

Unfortunately it proved virtually impossible to stiffen the administrative backbone of the new state by utilizing experienced Dutch and Eurasian civil service personnel. From the standpoint of cold logic the government's dismissal of so many of the undoubtedly competent Dutch and Eurasian administrative officers and technicians who had served the colonial government may seem unreasonable. But the nature of Indonesian nationalism ran counter to such logic. Distrust of the Dutch was increased as a result of an attempted coup against the new Indonesian government (the Westerling Affair) by demobilized officers and men of the Dutch colonial army less than two months after the Netherlands had formally relinquished sovereignty. As a consequence many actually loyal and capable Dutch civil servants were regarded with suspicion and kept from positions in which they could have been very useful. Moreover, Indonesia is perhaps unique among the newly emancipated Asian nations in that its Eurasian population, which had competently filled many of the upper-middle administrative positions in the colonial bureaucracy, with few exceptions declared unequivocally for the colonial power, during the revolution aligning themselves solidly with the Dutch against the Republic. Thus, although many Eurasians remained in Indonesia after the Netherlands' withdrawal, they were rarely welcome in the higher administrative and technical positions, even though often better trained than Indonesians.

The Indonesian bureaucracy was not a harmonious and unified group. The postrevolutionary loss of morale was soon increased as the competition of political parties resulted in its growing politicization, appointments frequently being made more in terms of political patronage than merit. As they maneuvered for control of parliament, and especially as they prepared for the national elections, the parties often utilized their power to influence appointments to the bureaucracy as a means of filling strategic positions in the territorial administrations as well as in certain key ministries with men who could be relied upon to advance party interests. Consequently, although the bureaucracy can be regarded as a force of some consequence in the Indonesian political scene, its impact has not been as great as might be expected on the basis of the high proportion of the Western-educated Indonesian elite it has incorporated. Where the influence of its members has been felt, it has frequently been in terms of party advantage rather than calculated to promote views or interests of the bureaucracy as a whole.

This, then, was the bureaucracy called upon to be the instrument of a government covering the world's geographically least integrated major state, a bureaucracy charged not merely with routine administration, but also with carrying out a wide range of social services far surpassing those previously undertaken by the highly trained officials of the colonial government. It was a bureaucracy notable primarily for its size, too large for the government to pay its members adequately, lacking in efficient organization, and bereft of the high morale and *élan* that had previously existed among that part of its membership which had served the revolutionary government. Most crucial of all, there were few possibilities for improving its quality, the overwhelming majority of its members being woefully lacking in experience and only a very small proportion equipped with even a secondary education. Thus postrevolutionary Indonesia emerged without the governmental capital so vital to the political viability of a new state—a well-trained civil service such as India fell heir to or at least the well-trained nucleus for one such as Pakistan inherited. Nor had the Netherlands' colonial legacy provided any substantial pool of educated men which might have been drawn upon to compensate for this lack. Indonesia began its postrevolutionary existence with what was undoubtedly the weakest civil service by far of any contemporary major state.

The Army

With respect to its armed forces, too, Indonesia did not enjoy as substantial a colonial inheritance as India or Pakistan. Instead of an integrated monolithic army with members having a common background of training and led by highly trained professional officers with substantial careers behind them, Indonesia's postrevolutionary army is highly heterogeneous and only a handful of its officers has had prewar experience. It incorporates two broad components—the semi-guerrilla revolutionary army and sizable elements of the disbanded Dutch colonial army (KNIL). Not only are they poorly suited to work harmoniously with one another, but even within the larger of them, the revolutionary army, there are ideologically diverse elements, frequently with different backgrounds of training.

According to the Round Table Agreement, troops of the Royal Netherlands Army, numbering about 80,000, were to be withdrawn from Indonesia as rapidly as possible, and the Netherlands Colonial Army (KNIL)—a predominantly Christian Indonesian and Eurasian force of some 65,000 men—was to be dissolved by July 26, 1950. Actually the demobilization of the KNIL took considerably longer and was not completed until June 1951. This was a delicate process, inasmuch as only a very small number of these troops elected to settle in the Netherlands, most of them wishing to stay in Indonesia. Indonesian leaders were understandably reluctant to incorporate these former adversaries into the new Indonesian army. But it was believed even more dangerous to return all of them to civilian life, thereby setting free of military discipline a formidable group of professional fighting men whose loyalty to the new government was at best dubious and many of whom would be further antagonized if denied the opportunity to continue in their chosen career. Consequently it was regarded as necessary to absorb approximately half of this ex-colonial force into the new army. Very soon the government experienced serious trouble from some of those demobilized elements not incorporated into the new army; it was from this group that Captain "Turk" Westerling recruited the soldiers for his abortive *coup d'état*. Westerling, a recently retired Dutch officer, already notorious because of his responsibility for atrocities during 1946 in southern Celebes, on January 23, 1950, led a force of recently demobilized Netherlands colonial troops into battle against a small Indonesian army unit quartered in Bandung, drove them out, and briefly occupied the city. Three days later his men infiltrated Jakarta for the purpose of launching a coup against the government, but were discovered and ejected by former Republican forces before they could act. Shortly thereafter Westerling fled to Singapore in a Dutch military plane.

An equally grave question centered about the future of some 100,000 Republican guerrilla soldiers in Java, Sumatra, Celebes, and Borneo who had not been part of the regular forces of the revolutionary army. Clearly, unless they were incorporated into the new army, provision had to be made for absorbing them into civilian life—a task which was hard enough as a psychological problem, but was particularly difficult because of the economic and administrative weakness of the government.

Even within the major component of the new Indonesian army, the regular detachments of the revolutionary forces, there were many serious factors impeding unity. Only the revolution itself, common battle against the colonial enemy, had kept its diverse elements together during 1945–1949. But with this integrating factor removed, their differences tended to be accentuated. Except for a tiny handful who had received training as noncommissioned officers, and even more rarely as commissioned officers, during the last years of the colonial regime, its officers were divided into two major groups—those who had been trained by the Japanese in the Peta and subsequently fought for the Republic in the revolution and those who had not had any previous military training but received all their experience during the course of the revolution itself. A large proportion of this second group were men of some education, mostly former teachers or high school students. A significant proportion of the Japanese-trained and indoctrinated group tended to feel that the army should quite properly have a voice in politics, often taking a sympathetic view of authoritarian political organization and holding democratic government in low regard. A majority of those officers trained exclusively during the revolution were inclined, however, in part because of their educational background, to view politics as something that an army officer should

eschew and were at the same time proponents of democratic government. Both of these major groups could be broken down further according to ideological inclination, there being several political currents
discernible.[5]

A further important division within the officer corps—one already
discernible during the last two years of the revolution—became extremely important during the postrevolutionary period, its growth being stimulated by the dispatch of a sizable minority of the younger
and generally better-educated officers abroad for advanced training,
especially to the United States, Western Europe, and the Philippines.
Such experience often increased the generally existing propensity
among the better-educated officers to urge a reorganization and rationalization of the army in order to make it smaller, more efficient, and
technically better trained—more like the professional armies of the
West. Their point of view understandably generated strong opposition
among that large component of officers trained under the Japanese—a
group which possessed less education and fewer technical qualifications
and which consequently feared, with some justification, that under
such a program they would be regarded as the most expendable element. For their part they argued that what was needed was a large
army, trained and organized as during the revolution, with emphasis
upon guerrilla tactics and revolutionary spirit.

Probably more important than these differences were the divisions
which emerged in the army on the basis of regional indentification. The
course of the Indonesian revolution, with its long period of grueling
guerrilla warfare, enforced a pattern of military operations which made
for a divided and regionally rooted military establishment, one effective in fighting the Dutch but not well suited to maintaining a unified
military organization once independence had been achieved. There was

---

[5] One of the most important was strongly Islamic and receptive to the idea that
the state should be organized in at least general conformity with Islamic tenets.
There was also a considerable Marxist (more often pseudo-Marxist) current
which could be roughly subdivided into democratic socialist and national Communist sectors. There was an important relatively moderate current, nominally
or passively Islamic, but not inclined to press for an Islamic basis to politics or
government, and, though generally socialist, not militantly so. Within the group
of Japanese-trained officers there was a small but influential element, particularly
heavily indoctrinated by the Japanese, who were strongly attracted to the political
and social code of the Japanese officer caste, especially to the ideas of Toyama,
leader of the Black Dragon Society, and to the sort of thinking evidenced among
the Japanese army's Young Officers group. These were advocates of a highly
authoritarian political order wherein the army would be regarded as "the soul
of the nation" and entitled to play a central role.

a natural tendency for army personnel to be recruited in the regions where they fought, and to conduct successful guerrilla warfare the revolutionary army had to develop close and sympathetic rapport with the local populations. There resulted an identification of local army units with the inhabitants of the regions in which they operated and a tendency for soldiers and officers to regard themselves as representatives of the local population, a conviction which did not die with the attainment of independence. Thus in the postrevolutionary period a large part of the troops stationed in the various regions (particularly in Sumatra) were those which had fought there during the revolution and developed roots among the population. These roots were strong and in many cases were maintained afterwards. During the revolution, moreover, many officers had become accustomed to playing roles which were in part political as well as military. It was not merely a matter of regarding themselves as the vanguard of the revolution, often seeing themselves in this respect as peers of the political leaders in Jogjakarta. In addition the nature of the military struggle against the Dutch frequently required commanders to exercise a wide range of political and administrative functions in the areas where they operated. So accustomed did many of them become to playing these extramilitary roles that following the revolution they were often reluctant to relinquish them.[6]

It should be therefore apparent why from the outset postrevolutionary Indonesia was beset by security problems of great magnitude, problems that were to tax seriously its limited financial and administrative resources. For a country as vast and geographically unintegrated as Indonesia the problem was made more acute because of the lack of adequate air and naval forces (one destroyer and a few corvettes) and the absence of trained personnel to man larger forces. During the first year of its existence the new government was, after great difficulties, able to cope with and largely eliminate the problem posed by adven-

[6] Moreover, during the postrevolutionary period because of the promulgation from time to time of a state of martial law ("war and siege") in a number of districts where security conditions have been poor, Jakarta has delegated to military commanders extensive civil powers. In some areas the range of administrative and economic problems which territorial commanders have been obliged to shoulder has been so extensive and burdensome that they have had insufficient time to devote to the military training of the units under them. Although commanders of military districts have frequently complained of this and have sometimes sought to avoid such responsibilities, among the officers under them there has often been a reluctance to relinquish such civil powers once they have been assumed. (With the emergence of acute political crisis in late February 1957 the whole of Indonesia was placed under a state of martial law, thereby endowing all the territorial commanders with extensive civil powers and functions.)

turers and recalcitrants among demobilized (though sometimes still intact) units of the Dutch colonial army. But the problem of rehabilitating some 100,000 ex-guerrillas, training them and finding them places in civilian life, was to prove more difficult, and the close of 1957 found it still only partially solved. In the mountains of western Java and the interior of southern Celebes militantly Islamic ex-guerrillas dedicated, ostensibly at least, to the proposition of establishing a theocratic Islamic state (Darul Islam) have maintained themselves up to the present (though in western Java with a dwindling base and reduced strength), directing a violent and destructive hit-and-run guerrilla warfare against the government. The even more formidable problem of unifying, rationalizing, and reducing the size of the new army has remained largely unsolved and has exerted, directly or indirectly, a profound influence on the course of political events.

The Political Elite

Government and politics in postrevolutionary Indonesia have been dominated by a handful of people, probably not many more than a thousand. Most of this tiny political elite are in the upper ranks of the bureaucracy, in the cabinet, in the leadership of the political parties (both in and outside parliament), in the army, in journalism, and in the universities. Although incorporating a number of influential people whose education has been leavened by a considerable Modernist or orthodox Islamic ingredient and in a few instances by heavy doses of Japanese indoctrination (especially in the case of some army officers), the outstanding characteristic of nearly all members of this elite is Western education, secondary school or above.[7] This similarity in educational background and a common colonial and revolutionary conditioning have tended to promote considerable homogeneity in their approach to socioeconomic problems, nearly all of them espousing some variant of socialism. A very minor portion have been attracted to communism, and a few, including a small but active number of army officers, have inclined toward other types of totalitarianism. The preponderant majority, however, have been in varying degrees proponents of democratic ideas. Nevertheless during the period 1950–1958 increasing disunity developed, even among those who had been united during the

[7] See Soelaeman Soemardi, "Some Aspects of the Social Origin of Indonesian Political Decision-Makers," *Transactions of the Third World Congress of Sociology*, III (1956), 338–348.

revolution. There were differences over whether and to what extent the state should be organized along Islamic lines and whether or not the Communists should be permitted a part in the government; and there were differences over Soekarno's proper role in government and the extent of his authority in the army, the urgency of the West Irian (New Guinea) issue and the right way of solving it, the kind of decentralization best suited to Indonesia's interests, the proper way to reorganize the army, the manner in which national elections should be carried out, and the necessity for and proper nature of a drive against corruption. But purely personal differences were frequently of greater importance. Given the tremendous possibilities in postrevolutionary society for rapid upward advance, the very minuteness of this elite may well have been detrimental to its inner harmony. With the floodgates of social mobility opened, it was perhaps natural that the sudden availability of many new and heretofore unobtainable positions should generate a competitive scramble, one rendered particularly sharp because the competitors knew one another (and one another's limitations and virtues) so well. The situation might not have been characterized by such bitterness had the competition been more impersonal—as could presumably have been the case if the elite had been larger, less intermarried, and less knowledgeable of one another's character. The numerous political parties, moreover, based as much (or more) on personalities as on issues and platforms, tended to aggravate the situation, the multiparty system working frequently against solidarity and providing channels for promoting intra-elite conflict.

Since the revolution Indonesia's political elite has generally exercised its leadership without the necessity of any great amount of consultation with the mass of the population. (The major exceptions have been the national elections of 1955–1956, the provincial elections of 1957, and apparently the regional anti-Jakarta political movements of 1957–1958.) The village level of society presents a more democratic character than before the revolution, and the village leaders—most of them now elected—must often come to terms with a more politically conscious village populace and new and sometimes aggressive unofficial local leaders. Nevertheless, by and large the villagers—leaders and led—still look to governmental levels above them for initiative in a number of traditional as well as new spheres of activity. They are used to and still expect the exercise of authority from above, and in general the relationship between the national or regional capital and the village remains strongly authoritarian in character, with little or no feeling on the part of its inhabitants that the government in Jakarta or the regional capital is "their" government or in any way their agent.

There are occasionally, however, some relatively important decisions taken by the elite where an area of consensus broader than its own membership is required and where the area is expanded to incorporate what might be termed the literate subelite. This sector of the population roughly corresponds with the more politically conscious elements among Indonesia's two to three million newspaper readers, generally individuals possessing an education which has stopped at or gone no more than a couple of years beyond the primary level. The Indonesian press has for the most part been vigorous, forthright, and often politically sophisticated; consequently where the decision on a political issue needs to be based in a relatively broad consensus, it has been effective in arousing the political concern of the literate subelite. Moreover, several of the political parties are able to mobilize significant sectors of public opinion on such occasions through rallies and oral agitation as well as through their newspapers.

On those very rare occasions when governmental decisions have required an even broader base (there probably have been less than a half dozen since 1950), this subelite—working primarily, though not exclusively, within the political parties and the labor and peasant organizations or through such components of the bureacracy as the Ministries of Information, Interior, or Religion—has served as the link between the elite and the masses. The literate subelite can as yet only to a limited extent be characterized as mediator between the two, since the relationship is still largely one-sided, that is, from the top down. But its mediating role is increasing, and as the masses become more politically conscious this function of the subelite, and thus its political power, will expand. In the last two years it has been at the provincial level—between provincial elite and mass—that its importance appears to have grown most rapidly.

Some Traditional Factors Affecting Decision Making

Despite the revolution, the hierarchical cast of government inherited from the colonial and precolonial periods has remained strong. Persistence of traditional attitudes toward authority has discouraged the growth of self-reliance among subordinate officials, the majority of whom feel uneasy about exercising initiative and continue to look upward in the hierarchy for instruction concerning many matters which they should be capable of resolving themselves. With few exceptions initiative is still expected to come from the top, and it is usually deemed improper for a subordinate to introduce something new. Many even of those qualified individuals in the highest levels of government continue to show the imprint of a colonial experience wherein they were conditioned to eschew important decisions and leave them to paternalistic Dutch officials, a conditioning which today frequently results in deferring or avoiding decisions of pressing importance. Where there is no way of evading a decision, they frequently strive to escape full responsibility by sharing it with others, particularly with those relatively few colleagues who are not averse to shouldering responsibility. The resultant number of meetings concerned with relatively trivial problems is staggering. These cut deeply into the time and energy of the few key men in the government, whose preoccupation with minor matters has become a major factor in hindering the formation of governmental policy as well in delaying administrative decisions.

The problem is exacerbated because of the limited number of Indonesians who received administrative training or higher education under the Dutch, with most of those who did now being absorbed into the very top levels of the bureaucracy and into the ministries. In other words nearly all of the tiny pools of experts are lodged at the very top of the governmental decision-making pyramid. Because of both traditional factors and the limited supply of *expertise* the system forces a host of routine as well as important decisions—political, administrative, and technical—to the top levels of the hierarchy. Thus many more decisions are passed to the top in Indonesia than is true in probably any other major nontotalitarian country.

A traditionally rooted element in the decision-making process which continues to have importance is the emphasis upon social solidarity and harmony—a cultural value particularly strong among the Javanese which begets the widely shared conviction that openly stated conflict is to be avoided as disruptive. It is this precolonial legacy which underlies and helps explain the distinctively Indonesian approach to democracy, the coming to agreement through extensive discussion aimed at yielding a synthesis of views, an often implicit consensus known as *mufakat*. Such generally sensed agreement is reached not through majority vote, but in a way somewhat reminiscent of the Quaker "sense of the meeting." This is a consensus which is felt rather than physically measured. It eschews voting, for voting produces an opposition minority as well as the majority. Hence a number of influential Indonesian political leaders are averse to decision-making procedures that involve voting. They are convinced that these stimulate disharmony and make differences explicit, crystallizing points of view to an extent where they are too hard to be mellowed or melted down into a common synthesis through further discussion.

Mufakat procedure has worked particularly well at the village level, where the sphere of decision making is well charted and largely concerned with matters of traditional concern, most of them easily relatable to past precedent. But while *mufakat* is possible on a small scale (we have noted that this was one reason for the success of the Working Committee in the revolutionary government), it is not easily adapted to decision making by large bodies of individuals with considerably different backgrounds such as have made up Indonesian parliaments both before and after the elections of 1955. Parliamentary decisions are reached on the basis of a simple majority vote and have come to be regarded by many Indonesians as contributing to and reinforcing national differences of opinion.

Despite undoubted virtues, the *mufakat* system does slow the process of decision making. In the cabinet the usual practice has apparently been for decisions of major importance—especially where there is reason to believe significant differences of opinion exist—to be made on this basis rather than by simple voting (the method followed in reaching most minor and middle-range decisions). This also appears to be the general pattern in a number of the top-level bureaucratic councils. With such a paucity of people qualified to take decisions in behalf of the government, the few key men must attend an unending number of deliberative sessions to arrive at decisions generally made by a single responsible individual in most governmental systems; in addition those sessions which involve major decisions are often very long, sometimes a whole series of meetings over a considerable span of time being required to arrive at the consensus necessary before action can be taken. For in order to maintain harmony in the cabinet and within ministerial councils and other bodies, it is frequently necessary to discuss and debate a question for a long time if a common denominator sufficiently precise for laying the basis of a new policy is to be discovered. Sometimes the inability to attain *mufakat* will result in the shelving of a major issue, since it is regarded as more important to maintain harmony —even though the problem remains—than to arrive at a decision based upon a simple majority and a consequent open disruption of solidarity.

· XXII ·

Government and Politics in

Postrevolutionary Indonesia

THE Round Table Conference agreement signed at The Hague in November 1949 stipulated: "The Netherlands unconditionally and irrevocably transfers complete sovereignty over Indonesia to the Republic of the United States of Indonesia and thereby recognizes said Republic of the United States of Indonesia as an independent and sovereign state." The latter accepted this sovereignty "on the basis of the provisions of its Constitution which as a draft has been brought to the knowledge of the kingdom of the Netherlands." The transfer of sovereignty was therefore explicitly unconditional, and there is no justification for interpreting acceptance as binding Indonesia to the constitution operative at the time or as limiting its right to amend or basically change that constitution at will. But part of the price of the Netherlands' relinquishment of its claim to sovereignty had been the stipulation that transfer of authority be made not to the Republic alone, but to a federal Indonesia of which the Republic would be merely one of sixteen component units. Although the federal system of government bequeathed by the Hague Agreement remained intact for only a scant six weeks and thereafter progressively disintegrated until replaced by a unitarian form of government in mid-August 1950, less than eight months after its inception, this legacy was to have long-term consequences significant in

shaping the character of the subsequent government and the problems confronting it, some of which still persist.

Formation of a Federal Government

Much of the groundwork for the Hague Conference had been laid in
Java during the middle of 1949 in the course of preliminary negotiations, the Inter-Indonesian Conferences, held between delegations
from the Republic and from the "Federalists"—the representatives of the
fifteen Dutch-created states. Foremost among the accomplishments of
these conferences were the outline draft of a constitution for the envisaged federal order and the agreement that its constituent states
should have no military forces of their own. This last provision, reaffirmed later at the Hague Conference where it was also stipulated that
the Dutch colonial army was to be dissolved, meant that the supporting
bayonets upon which these Dutch-created states rested would soon be
withdrawn, leaving nothing but the federal constitution itself to protect
them from the popular demand that they be liquidated.

After some reworking by the Republican and Federalist delegations
to the Hague Conference the draft constitution agreed upon earlier at
the Inter-Indonesian Conferences emerged as the constitution of the
projected federal Republic of the United States of Indonesia (RUSI),
being signed by both delegations on October 29, 1949. This federal state
to which the Republic's representatives were obliged to agree was a
weirdly unbalanced and distorted organism. Its very composition testi-
fied to the artificial nature of the federal order which the Dutch had
been sponsoring and made clear that in constructing it they had been
more concerned with promoting a strategy of divide and rule, calculated
to eventuate in a political order which they could indirectly control,
than in establishing a federal order honestly dedicated to Indonesia's
very real need for a political decentralization consistent with basic geographic, economic, and cultural factors. The constitution provided for a
federation composed of sixteen states. Whereas the largest component,
the Republic of Indonesia (the residual area left to the revolutionary
Republic following the Renville Agreement, comprising approximately
half of Java and three-quarters of Sumatra), had a population of more
than 31 million, the coequal state of Riau, comprising the tiny Riau
archipelago just off Singapore, had a population of only about 100,000.
The small islands Bangka and Billiton each constituted a state, and the
meager population of Indonesian Borneo was divided into no less than
five. Each of these sixteen states, regardless of its population, was rep-

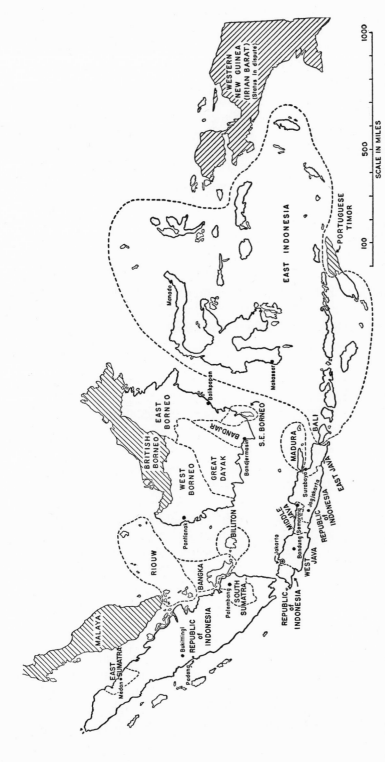

Map 11. Federal Indonesia. Boundaries shown are of the Republic of the United States of Indonesia on December 27, 1949. (Pasundan is designated here as West Java.) With the exception of Middle Java, whose boundaries date from early March 1949, all approximate the boundaries of fourteen or more months previously. The major exception is West Borneo, whose southwest corner had for a brief period been detached to form the short-lived autonomous area of Kota Waringen. (From *Nationalism and Revolution in Indonesia,* by George McTurnan Kahin, copyright 1952, Cornell University Press.)

resented by two senators. The Senate was granted colegislative authority with the House of Representatives on matters "referring particularly to one, several or all participant territories or parts thereof, or concerning the relation between the Republic of the United States of Indonesia" and these constituent states. Only a two-thirds majority of the members of the House at a session where at least two-thirds of its total membership was present could override the Senate in such matters. Further protection was provided the Dutch-created federal components by a provision that 100 of the 150 members of the House should come from the 15 Dutch-created states (apportioned according to their respective populations), whereas the Republic of Indonesia, the federation's major component, would have only 50 representatives (approximately 10 less than it was entitled to on a basis of population). Since each of the states was free to decide on the matter of selecting its representatives to both houses of the parliament, whether by election or appointment, it appeared that the elements installed in power by the Dutch would be able to maintain their positions by seeing to it that those representing their states were "reliable."

The position of the Dutch-sponsored states in the new political order was not, however, as strong as these provisions might suggest. Quite apart from the fact that the overwhelming majority of their populations were in opposition to the regimes with which the Dutch had saddled them, the constitution incorporated provisions which in the long run were to make possible their legal dissolution. Although the "Government" (cabinet plus the President) was obliged to share legislative power with the House of Representatives on all matters and with the Senate as well on those matters in the compass of its authority, it was expressly stipulated that the cabinet would not be responsible to either of the existing representative bodies (Article 122). It was held that since most of their members had not been elected (and those few who were had been chosen under conditions which fell far short of any democratic norm) cabinet responsibility was not appropriate. Elections were scheduled to be held within a year (Article 111), after which (so the constitution implied but did not expressly stipulate) cabinet responsibility to the two representative bodies would commence. In addition Article 139, one that was to assume great importance in the liquidation of the Dutch-sponsored constituent states, stated that "the Government on its own authority and responsibility has the right to enact emergency laws for the regulation of such matters of federal governing power as demand immediate provisions on account of urgent circumstances," these regulations requiring, however, the subsequent endorsement of the House. Moreover, the prospects for the survival of this federal system were weakened because of the unsympathetic attitudes of the federal government's President and Prime Minister—Soekarno and Hatta.[1]

The Unitarian Movement and Creation of a Unitary Government

Immediately upon its assumption of office the Hatta cabinet was confronted by growing local demands, given encouragement by Soekarno and a number of other high government leaders, that the federal legacy of the Netherlands be scrapped in favor of a unitarian political order. Indeed, the dominant and overshadowing political development during the eight-month Hatta cabinet (December 1949–July 1950) was the unitarian movement, a widely based and increasingly powerful popular demand for replacing the federal order, regarded as a tainted vestige of colonial control, by a unitary system of government which would restore the revolutionary Republic to a position of dominance. Thus a major part of the time and energies of Hatta and his cabinet were absorbed

---

[1] The Inter-Indonesian Conferences had established a National Preparatory Committee, composed of Federalist delegates from the Dutch-sponsored states and delegates from the Republic, and had charged it with, among other things, selection of the President of the projected United States of Indonesia and of the *formateurs* of its first cabinet. Although this committee contained 60 Federalists as against only 20 Republican members, the prestige of Soekarno was so great and the relative stature of the leading Federalists so puny by comparison that even the most intransigent of the Federalists realized that it would be a travesty to elect anyone other than this man who had become the principal popular symbol of the revolution. On December 16, 1949, a sixteen-man *ad hoc* committee, which was selected by the larger National Preparatory Committee and in which each member state had one vote, unanimously elected Soekarno President of the United States of Indonesia. (The federal constitution, it may be noted, did not provide for a Vice-President.)

An agreement reached at the Inter-Indonesian Conferences, and later incorporated into the federal constitution, provided that the President "in agreement with the delegates" of the component states select a group of three men charged with the formation of a cabinet (actually four were appointed—two Republicans and two Federalists). Just as Soekarno had dwarfed every Federalist who might have had the temerity to present himself as a candidate for the presidency, so did Hatta overshadow every possible Federalist candidate for the post of Prime Minister. In the cabinet which was formed on December 20, 1949, the Republican element held a dominant position, eleven posts as against five for the Federalists, Hatta serving concurrently as Prime Minister and Minister of Foreign Affairs and the Federalists holding only one key portfolio, Internal Affairs, which went to Anak Agung.

in the effort to keep this transition orderly and confined to constitutional channels.

The active phase of the movement was precipitated by the attempted coup of demobilized Netherlands colonial soldiers led by Captain Westerling. Not only did this do serious harm to Indonesian-Dutch relations, sowing serious distrust and suspicion among Indonesians with regard to Netherlanders still in Indonesia. In addition the incident caused grievous damage to the position of the Federalists, since it was discovered that Sultan Hamid, one of their chief leaders and a member of the cabinet, had played a major part in planning the affair. Evidence that some officials of the Dutch-sponsored Pasundan (West Java) government had ties with Westerling further discredited the Federalists. Popular indignation was so strong and widespread that Federalist representatives in parliament had no recourse but to support the cabinet's emergency law of February 8 calling for Pasundan's relinquishing its powers to a state commissioner appointed by the cabinet. This set in train a whole series of similar moves, wherein under strong local pressure the governments of most of the federal states undertook to end their existence, symbolizing the change by amalgamating themselves with the old Republic. The process was held up in East Indonesia where troops of the recently demobilized Netherlands Indies Army temporarily resisted the landing of former Republican troops. By early May, however, following a conference between Hatta and the heads of the states of East Indonesia and East Sumatra, these last two of the fifteen Dutch-created states agreed to give up their identities and join the old Republic in the establishment of a new unitary Republic of Indonesia.

On May 19, 1950, leaders of the federal government (acting in behalf of the governments of the states of East Indonesia and East Sumatra) reached an agreement with those of the Republic of Indonesia on the basic character of the new unitary state.[2] During the next two months

[2] Its provisional constitution was to be framed "through revision of the RUSI [federal] Provisional Constitution in such a manner that it . . . contain the essentials of the Constitution of the Republic of Indonesia . . . and additionally appropriate sections of the Provisional Constitution of the RUSI." It was to be drawn up by an "Assembly for Changing the Constitution" made up of the House of Representatives of the outgoing federal government and the Working Committee of the Republic's KNIP, and it was understood that as soon as possible elections would be held for a constituent assembly which would frame a final constitution. Until superseded by new legislation, existing acts and regulations were to remain in force, "with the understanding that, wherever possible, the laws of the member-state, the Republic of Indonesia . . . be adhered to." It was agreed that the Senate would be abolished, that the cabinet would be made re-

representatives of the federal government's House of Representatives and of the Republican KNIP met together to work out a draft unitary constitution based upon this agreement. By July 20, 1950, they had completed their work and presented their draft to the federal House and Senate and to the Working Committee of the KNIP for approval, with the understanding that these bodies could not amend it, but only approve or disapprove. After some three weeks of discussion they reached general agreement and by large majorities approved the draft, which on August 15 was signed by President Soekarno and Soepomo, Minister of Justice in the federal (RUSI) government, and promulgated as the "Provisional Constitution of the Republic of Indonesia." It is this unitary constitution which, despite its provisional and expected short-term history, is still operative.

Although pro-Republican sentiment and the demand for the liquidation of the remnants of the old Dutch-created federal system had triumphed, an important residue survived. In order to ensure the smooth transition from a federal to a unitary government Republican leaders believed it necessary to placate the largely Dutch-selected representatives from the Dutch-sponsored states who held seats in the outgoing RUSI Senate and House. Thus, in conformance with the Charter of Agreement of May 19, Article 77 of the unitary constitution made a major concession to this group by providing that the new state's unicameral legislature incorporate the memberships of the federal government's Senate and House of Representatives together with those from the Republic's High Advisory Council and KNIP Working Committee.[3] As a consequence, more than 40 per cent of the membership of the

_____

sponsible to a unicameral parliament, that Soekarno would be President and (implicitly at least) that Mohammad Hatta would be Vice-President. The new state's provisional unicameral legislature was to be created out of the combined memberships of the federal House of Representatives and the Working Committee of the Republic's KNIP with a provision that other members could be added.

[3] In the new House of Representatives 130 members could be classified as Republicans and 106 as Federalists (it should be recalled, however, that some Federalists had actually been strongly pro-Republican in outlook). Of those classified as Republicans, 46 had been members of the KNIP's Working Committee (as of 1950), 13 had been members of the Republic's High Advisory Council, 50 had constituted that one-third of the federal government's House of Representatives drawn from the Republic's KNIP, another 19 had been appointed by the Republic, while it was a constituent unit of the federal government, to represent the former territory of Pasundan after that state's amalgamation with the Republic in February 1950 following the Westerling affair, and 2 had been drawn from the Senate. Of those classified as Federalists, 27 came from the Senate and 79 from the federal government's House of Representatives.

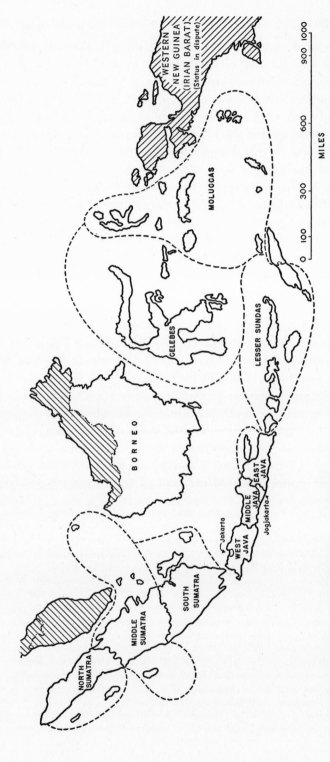

Map 12. Unitary Indonesia, 1950–1956. Boundaries of the provinces of the Republic of Indonesia are as established in late August 1950. Jogjakarta is a special territory with the status of province; Jakarta, the national capital and its immediate en- virons (Greater Jakarta), is a municipality with provincial status. (From *Nationalism and Revolution in Indonesia*, by George McTurnan Kahin, copyright 1952, Cornell University Press.)

parliament which was to govern Indonesia from mid-1950 until the spring of 1956 was made up of individuals who had worked with the Dutch in the states established by them and who for the most part owed their current parliamentary positions to this earlier collaboration. Some were men of political probity and ability, but there were many whose careers had been marked by political opportunism and frequently by widely known involvement in governmental corruption. Not only did this make the unitary state's largely nonelected parliament less representative than had been the Republic's nonelected parliament, it also introduced at the outset an unhealthy political atmosphere, weakening both the moral authority and the ability of the representative body that was charged with governing Indonesia during the critical six-year period prior to the national elections; and there is no doubt that the long delay in holding these elections stemmed, to an important extent, from the fact that many of these men realized that elections would spell the end of their parliamentary careers.

Soekarno and the Presidency

A central factor in the government and politics of postrevolutionary Indonesia has been the country's President, Soekarno. He has been a major political force in his own right; one might even say that he is the strongest organized political force in Indonesia. He has consistently maintained that in filling the office of President he is not obliged to diminish his role as his country's revolutionary nationalist leader. Although the extent to which he has continued to play this politically charged extraconstitutional role is not agreeable to a considerable proportion of the political elite, it undoubtedly is to millions of the Indonesian rank and file, particularly in Java. For almost thirty years he has been regarded by Indonesians as their most prominent nationalist leader. He has been a charismatic personality without peer in Indonesia, and, indeed, in few other countries in the world. His powers of oratory and his personal charm and dynamism have provided him with the means for enlisting mass backing that no Indonesian leader has thus far been able to rival. Had he constituted himself a political party and run for office in the elections of 1955, he would probably have emerged with more votes than any other party. And undoubtedly the fact that he did indirectly back the Indonesian Nationalist Party (PNI) in those elections was a major reason for its emerging as the party with the largest number of votes.

Although he has shown great talent as a nationalist and revolutionary leader and continues to display shrewdness in politics, Soekarno has not demonstrated comparable aptitude in providing Indonesia with the leadership it has needed to meet some of the most important of its post-revolutionary problems. From the outset he realized that the problem of national unity would be a formidable one, estimating in 1949 that its achievement would require another ten years; [4] but his approach to this problem has not been marked by sympathetic understanding of regional sentiments, and he has not shown leadership in working out a formula calculated to provide for the governmental decentralization that development of such unity requires. Soekarno has brought together Islamic, Javanese mystical, and Western political thought—including a considerable component of the revisionist Marxism of the 1920s—in a synthesis which has had widespread appeal as a nationalist ideology. But some of those who have been his close supporters observe that in general he has given little attention to relating this synthesis in any effective sense to economic realities and that the revisionist Marxism which he has drawn upon has manifested itself in a rather rigid cast with little adaption to changing conditions.

In recent years an increasing number of Indonesian leaders have entertained doubts as to Soekarno's political wisdom. Their major cause for alarm has been his conviction that the Indonesian Communists constitute a lesser danger than the proponents of an Islamic state and his consequent willingness to go along with the Communist Party in combating the major Islamic party, the Masjumi. These critics believe that the Communists pose the greatest and most immediate danger, and many of them are convinced that the Masjumi cannot be subdued without greatly strengthening the Communists in the process. They feel that Soekarno has underrated the ability of the Masjumi's moderates to maintain control and that by joining the Communists in opposing them he, in fact, undermines their ability to contain the influence of Isa Anshary and other dogmatic advocates of an extreme form of Islamic state.[5] Soekarno himself, it should be observed, probably regards the

[4] Discussions with the writer, Muntok, Bangka, May 2–4, 1949.

[5] Soekarno's concern with the dangers posed by such dogmatists as Isa Anshary has been by no means groundless. Thus following Soekarno's speech of January 27, 1953, wherein he stated that the Indonesian state could not be based upon Islam and that such a policy would drive areas with non-Islamic majorities to secede, Isa Anshary on April 12 made a public statement generally regarded as an oblique reference to Soekarno that there was "a cold war in Indonesia between Islam on the one hand and those who call themselves Islamic and aren't. The central question is whether Islam is to be based upon God's laws or not."

Communists' switch to supporting him and his policies during the last four years as nothing more than a temporary marriage of convenience. But in terms of his own objectives and priorities he has found it useful to co-operate with them. To understand his position, one must realize that up until fairly recently at least he does not seem to have greatly feared the Communists, apparently confident that when it should suit him he could turn on them and crush them.[6]

Furthermore, many leaders basically sympathetic with Soekarno's adamant resolve to bring West Irian (Western New Guinea) into the Indonesian fold are disturbed that he has made this so much a personal issue involving his own prestige. They believe that his preoccupation with this problem has diverted him from giving attention to more pressing matters and that he tends too much to regard the attitude of Indonesians and foreign countries toward the Irian issue as a touchstone for evaluating their loyalty to him or their friendship for Indonesia. They were pleased to see him make extensive trips abroad during 1956, believing that this would be politically healthful, would make his approach to international affairs less parochial, and would allow him to see Indonesia's problems in wider perspective. On his travels he seemed to find as much that was good in the United States as in Soviet Russia, but he was particularly impressed with Communist China. As a consequence many Indonesian leaders, including a number who remain well disposed toward him, are concerned over his profound admiration of Mao's success in organizing and harnessing the energies of the Chinese people. They are not afraid that Soekarno will become a Communist, but they do fear that this increases his disposition to lead Indonesia away from Western democratic practices and toward a more monolithic and autocratic political order. Some fear that his extreme nationalism and his impatience with the policies of the Western powers, especially their unsympathetic attitudes toward Indonesia's claim to West Irian, will impel him to lead Indonesia into dependence upon Soviet Russia or Communist China or both.

Because of these attitudes and his decreasing willingness to heed the counsel of qualified leaders to whom he formerly listened, Soekarno has become more and more estranged during the past years from a growing number of other former revolutionary leaders and from a majority of Indonesian intellectuals. But although there has been among many of those so disaffected a consistent tendency to indulge in a

[6] This was the general impression received by the writer in talks with President Soekarno in Jakarta in October 1954 and February 1955.

wishful thinking that downgrades his political importance, there is no doubt that he still remains by far the most influential political leader in Indonesia.

It has earlier been noted that a major weakness of Indonesia's government was the nonelected, conglomerate parliament which functioned from 1950 until 1956—a body which because of the nature of its membership lacked moral authority from the outset. A second important weakness stemmed from the 1950 constitution's vagueness in defining the position and role of the President. The powers it clearly grants the President are themselves hardly impressive. He has the explicit right of designating those who are to form a new cabinet (the *formateurs*), selecting one or several individuals to fulfill this function. In accordance with the recommendation of the formateur or formateurs, he appoints the Prime Minister, who may or may not be one of the formateurs.[7] In addition to various ceremonial functions the only other clear-cut constitutional power of the President is his right to appoint the unitary state's first Vice-President, though even this is "upon the recommendations submitted by the House of Representatives" (Article 45). Under the still-existing 1950 constitution it is, then, only with regard to these two matters that the President has been given the prerogative to act without reference to the cabinet.

There are, however, several attributes of the constitution which have greatly facilitated Soekarno's assumption of a major governmental role. First is the provision that "the President and the Vice-President are inviolable" (Article 83), a term apparently borrowed from the phraseology relating to the monarch in the Dutch constitution. This means that there is no method of impeaching or removing in any way the President (or Vice-President) from office or of calling him to account for his actions. Moreover, it is stipulated that the President (and the Vice-President) cannot be replaced prior to an elected constituent assembly's drafting of a new constitution which would designate the provisions for election to these offices,[8] and it has been clear that it would be a considerable period before an elected constituent assembly would draft a new constitution. (The Constituent Assembly elected in 1956 is still deliberating, no new constitution having yet emerged.) In addition the President is granted the right to dissolve the House of

[7] A. K. Pringgodigdo, *The Office of President in Indonesia as Defined in the Three Constitutions in Theory and Practice* (Cornell Modern Indonesia Project, Translation Series; Ithaca, N.Y., 1957), p. 23.

[8] See Pringgodigdo, *The Office of President in Indonesia*, p. 30, and Article 141 and the official Elucidation to the provisional constitution.

Representatives (Article 84), being required to order the election of a new House within thirty days. Although it has been argued that such an action would need cabinet support, this is not made explicit in the constitution, and the President might well be able to assert such a prerogative successfully. He has never yet attempted to do so, but it is clear that the possibility that he could gives him at least indirect influence with parliament over and above that of his own personality as the great revolutionary leader and ceremonial head of state.

Sitting in his constitutionally unassailable position and responsible constitutionally to no one, Soekarno has been free to interpret a number of ambiguous provisions in the constitution in ways which have allowed him to play a role far in excess of what is usually regarded as its spirit and intent, but not necessarily in excess of its letter. Much of this ambiguity centers about the term "the Government," a term which was defined in the 1949 constitution as comprising President plus one or more cabinet ministers, but which was not defined at all in the 1950 constitution. Article 83 of the 1950 constitution, seemingly one of explicit clarity, stipulates that "the Ministers shall be responsible for the entire policy of the government; jointly for the entire policy, and each Minister individually for his share in the government." The intent of the article itself would therefore seem to give to a cabinet and the parliament to which it is responsible sole authority for all legislation and other governmental regulations, sharing this authority with the President only with respect to the relatively few cases where the constitution explicitly confers authority on him, namely, dissolution of parliament, award of decorations, granting of pardons, conclusion and ratification of treaties and other agreements with foreign powers, appointment of diplomatic representatives, declaration of war (to be concurred in by parliament), and declaration of a state of emergency. According to this interpretation, except in these functions the President does not share with the cabinet in the exercise of power, but acts within the Government only as agent of the cabinet, promulgating and countersigning its legislation—fulfilling this function automatically and in full conformance with its wishes.

In view, however, of the historic definition of the term "Government" in Indonesia and the present constitution's explicitly absolving the President of governmental responsibility, there is also basis for arguing that although the cabinet is indeed "responsible" for all legislation it must share *authority* for it with the President, he and the cabinet together constituting "the Government." Quite apart from whichever interpretation is right, there is certainly nothing in the constitution to restrain a President should he wish to assert his own judgment and refuse to endorse his name to and promulgate a particular piece of legislation put forward by the cabinet. And, as has been noted, during the revolution Soekarno was convinced that he did have this right of veto, even though then too he never employed it openly. Thus, although until 1957 Soekarno did not publicly challenge the cabinet's right to play the paramount role in initiating legislation, on a number of important occasions between 1950 and 1957 he quietly, but effectively, delayed or vetoed legislation of which he did not approve. Whatever the wisdom of his stand on these occasions, such actions tended to undermine the principle of cabinet responsibility to parliament. When confronted by such presidential interference, a cabinet has had no alternative but to acquiesce or resign—except in those situations where it has been in close enough rapport with dominant elements in the army to secure their support in offsetting the power exerted by the President.

Another unhappy ambiguity in the constitution is that concerning the President's relationship to the armed forces. Article 85 of the constitution can only be read as indicating that authority over the armed forces must be shared by President and cabinet, stating as it does that "all decrees of the President, including those concerning his authority over the armed forces of the Republic of Indonesia, shall be countersigned by the Minister(s) concerned." On the other hand, Article 127, with equal explicitness, states that "the President is in supreme command of the armed forces." Although these statements can be interpreted as being fully compatible and providing for presidential subordination to the cabinet in such matters, it is also possible to argue (and frequently has been argued) that authority over the armed forces is shared by President and cabinet and even that in this sharing the initiative for appointment of officers lies with the President.

In addition Soekarno has on a number of important occasions exerted substantial political influence by appealing over the heads of cabinet and parliament to the people in public addresses which have sometimes deviated considerably from policies of the cabinet in question, on occasion making statements in clear defiance of the Prime Minister's request not to. Important also has been his close connection with what has always been one of the largest political parties, the Indonesian Nationalist Party. Standing in particularly close relationship to its older-generation leaders he has sometimes induced them to reverse a position already taken in parliament or in cabinet meeting.

Soekarno's great political stature, his continuing insistence upon playing the part of revolutionary nationalist leader over and above that of President, and the constitution's vagueness in defining his position have meant that he has been able to pull decisive levers of power without having to assume constitutional responsibility for the consequences. Thus even before 1957 and his controversial call for a drastic change in the political order—a "guided democracy"—Soekarno was already playing a major, if not the major, role in postrevolutionary Indonesian government and politics. This role has not been consistent with and far exceeds what is generally considered the proper function of a President in a constitutional parliamentary system. It might well have been much better, as Mohammad Hatta and Mohammad Natsir along with some of those still close to Soekarno have argued, to have endowed Indonesia with a presidential system explicitly providing much greater scope to the office but at the same time clearly locating responsibility.

Hatta and the Vice-Presidency

Article 45 of the 1950 constitution stipulates that the first appointment of a Vice-President in the new unitary state would be made by the President in accordance with recommendations of parliament. Mohammad Hatta, as the national leader second in stature only to Soekarno and a man who had filled this office during the revolution, was inevitably the unanimous choice. Coming from central Sumatra and regarded by most Sumatrans as their chief representative in government, Hatta was a fitting complement to the Javanese Soekarno. Since he is looked upon as a much more devout Muslim than Soekarno, his presence in the vice-presidential office tended to reconcile those Islamic leaders made uneasy by some of Soekarno's ideas. As heads of government, Soekarno and Hatta constituted a well-balanced team, supplementing one another in qualities of personality and leadership and functioning together in something like a co-presidency. While Soekarno has been weak in economics and in his capacity to work out practical economic policies for the country, this field has been Hatta's particular strength.[9] Thus Hatta brought to the vice-presidency a prestige and ability which lent the office a stature considerably beyond that suggested by the 1950 constitution.

[9] Hatta has, for instance, been the principal organizer and promoter of the co-operative movement in Indonesia, one of the few really significant economic achievements of the postrevolutionary period. See his *The Co-operative Movement in Indonesia* (Ithaca, N.Y.: Cornell University Press, 1956).

The constitution states merely that "in the exercise of his duties the President is assisted by the Vice-President" and that in the event of the President's death or disability the Vice-President will assume his functions. It does not permit the Vice-President to be Prime Minister. Therefore formation of a presidential cabinet such as existed over considerable periods during the revolution is not possible under the present constitution. Hatta did take over the reins of the presidency rather briefly during the summer of 1955 when Soekarno, coincident with an adverse political situation centering around a refusal of top army officers to agree with his selection of a chief of staff, departed on a pilgrimage to Mecca. In general, however, Hatta's role in the last few years has been primarily a symbolic one, symbolic particularly of national unity. This is in contrast to the active role he played in government during the revolution and the first year thereafter.

Since 1950 an increasing divergency of views has emerged between Hatta and Soekarno as to the basis for solving salient national problems and with regard to Soekarno's attitude toward the Communists and the Masjumi. Their estrangement, noticeable as early as 1952, became increasingly serious. It led to the deterioration of an important symbol of national unity and to Soekarno's becoming less and less receptive to Hatta's advice. By 1956, in the face of the evident inability of the Indonesian parliament and cabinet to meet the tremendous problems confronting the country, the possibility of Hatta's resigning the vice-presidency in order to receive an appointment by Soekarno as Prime Minister of a new and effective government was ruled out. The distance between the two men had become far too great, and this sort of teamwork was no longer possible. The completeness of Hatta's break with Soekarno was symbolized by his resignation in December 1956 from the office of Vice-President. Since then no new Vice President has been appointed, and Hatta has dissociated himself from the government.

Cabinet and Parliament

We have seen the extent to which the cabinet's functioning has been circumscribed by the vaguely defined, but important, role of the President. This has meant that harmony between the two has generally been dependent upon the relations between the Prime Minister and the President. When they have been cordial, as during the cabinets of Ali Sastroamidjojo and Dr. Sukiman Wirjosandjojo, co-operation has generally been smooth and has made the cabinet's work considerably easier. When they have not been cordial, as during those of Natsir, Wilopo, and Burhanuddin Harahap, the cabinet's task has been made extremely difficult and its governmental effectiveness decreased.

We have noted that the right to dissolve parliament lies explicitly with the President and that only implicitly does the cabinet share in this function. This has imposed a serious limitation upon the effectiveness of cabinet government in Indonesia, inasmuch as without presidential backing a cabinet has had no way to call parliament to account. In every case so far when a cabinet has felt inclined to press for dissolution, it has been on poor terms with the President. Moreover, dissolution would have had to be followed by elections, and not until April 4, 1953, was an election law passed. Even after this it was widely argued that parliament could not properly be dissolved in view of the constitution's prescription that elections be held within thirty days of a dissolution, a requirement widely regarded as impossible to fulfill because technical and administrative preparations for elections were seen as requiring ten to fourteen months. Indonesia's cabinets have thus been denied effective power to dissolve parliament, an attribute important to the viability of parliamentary government in most Western democracies. This has militated seriously against responsible conduct among many members of its parliament, allowing them to pursue their own personal courses, no matter how opportunistic, without being held accountable. The deficiency has been compounded because, except for a brief period prior to the elections in 1955, the party, too, has had little means of disciplining a member who sat in parliament. It has been obliged to be extremely circumspect and gentle in dealing with errant M.P.'s, since if pushed too hard they might leave the party (as a number have done), joining another or maintaining themselves as independents—sometimes available to the highest bidder. Party discipline was strengthened just before the 1955 elections, since a party's national headquarters had the right to determine whether or not an M.P. would be entered on its election list and whether he would stand near the top or bottom of the list. (Those at the top had first claim on the votes the party won.) Following the elections the situation gradually became similar to what it had been before, the only important sanction remaining in the hands of the party's leadership being patronage. Except for the Indonesian Communist Party and the now much smaller Indonesian Socialist Party, Indonesian political parties represented in parliament have never been able to exert party discipline over any considerable period of time.

The number of political parties represented in parliament has worked against efficient government. In the parliament that existed from August 1950 until early 1956, no party ever held more than 52 out of 236 seats, and even following the elections of 1955 none had more than 57 seats in the new 273-member parliament. Indonesia's multiparty system has thus always required a coalition government. This has introduced the same general difficulties as in France. The multiplicity of parties in combination with the fluctuating character of their relationships, a situation made all the more fluid and unpredictable in Indonesia as a result of the repeatedly shifting balances of power within the parties, has seriously undermined stability. The problem is made more serious and complicated because of the frequent divergence in attitude between those representing the party in the cabinet and the leaders at party headquarters as well as between both of these and the representatives in parliament. The general lack of party discipline makes all these relationships unpredictable.[10]

The effectiveness of parliamentary government has been further undermined, after as well as before the elections, because of the frequently irresponsible role of the parties not represented in the cabinet. Rarely has their opposition been constructive. Their frequent opportunism and lack of responsibilty undoubtedly derive in part from the previously mentioned residue of the colonial period, the posture of negativist obstructionism. And among the sizable ex-Federalist minority, most of whom attached themselves to one of the major Republican political parties, there are many whose conditioning during their period of collaboration with the Dutch undoubtedly helped to dispose them to opportunism and irresponsibility. There were strong hopes that national elections would result in greatly reducing irresponsibility among parliament members, but these expectations have been only very partially fulfilled. To some extent this is a consequence of the nature of the elec-

[10] Moreover, since a party is frequently not represented in the cabinet by its strongest leaders, cabinet members are generally obliged to refer back to party headquarters before making any important decisions. When this has not been done, party representatives in the cabinet have often been repudiated and denied backing by the party's top leadership. Since the party leadership itself is often divided, the requirement that cabinet members representing the party consult with the divided party leadership often means that they must wait a long time before discovering its position, thus delaying cabinet decisions on important matters longer than usual. And if the cabinet member feels he cannot wait for instructions from his party's high command and takes a position on his own responsibility in cabinet meetings, he may well find his position repudiated by his party afterward.

tions. The system involved multimember constituencies where the candidates were selected and ranked on the party election list by party headquarters in Jakarta, often with too little regard for local opinion. Dependent upon their party's national headquarters rather than on anything approximating a local primary, candidates usually tended to feel that their chief responsibility was to Jakarta headquarters and not to their local constituents. Since the elections most party representatives in parliament have not been closely related with their local party organizations or with their constituencies as a whole. This has undoubtedly contributed to the irresponsibility so many have shown in parliament.

Thus parliament has severely limited the cabinet's ability to act with dispatch and carry out a really efficient legislative role. Time and again it has held up or sidetracked the cabinet's legislative proposals or distorted them with amendments, sometimes refusing to pass even legislation advocated by cabinet representatives of parties holding a majority in parliament. Parliament has also slowed up the legislative process through its insistence upon time-consuming interpolations and the convening of meetings at which ministers are requested to attend and explain cabinet policies. All this has resulted in a tremendous backlog of government bills. In really pressing circumstances the cabinet has circumvented parliamentary obstructionism by promulgating emergency legislation. Emergency measures are valid unless rejected by the House of Representatives at its next session (Article 97 of the 1950 constitution), but such legislation is rarely annulled, so long as the cabinet which promulgated it is still in power when the House of Representatives reconvenes. Fortunately the cabinet's action potential has usually not been circumscribed by budgetary commitments. Indonesian cabinets, with the exception of those of Wilopo and Burhanuddin, have not presented their annual budgets to parliament until the years which they were designed to cover were well along.[11]

Political Parties

Indonesia's political parties have been built from the top down, the leader organizing the mass following rather than a mass movement thrusting up its own leader. The elections of 1955 showed that, except for the Communist Party and the very small Indonesian Socialist Party, the organization of political parties in Indonesia bears little resem-

[11] See Miriam S. Budiardjo, "The Provisional Parliament of Indonesia," *Far Eastern Survey*, XXV (Feb. 1956), 18.

blance to that of those presently operating in the Western democracies. With these exceptions they consist of loosely articulated aggre-
gates of political backing clustered about locally influential individuals
—to a major extent district officials, village headmen, and religious
leaders. The primary function of the generally nationally prominent
party elite has been to supply the political attraction, to find the funds
and patronage necessary to bring these local leaders into the party fold,
and to provide a skeletal nationwide organization attuned primarily
to the waging of the election struggle.[12] In the words of an able Indonesian political analyst:

The numerical strength of the political parties as shown by the election
results, or more precisely the political power of the particular elite groups
leading those parties is, therefore, not so much, and not only a reflection of
the measure of acceptance of either ideology or leadership, but also a reflection of such groups' ability to manipulate the traditional power relationships within the village.[13]

Not long after the national parliamentary elections of late 1955 and
the Constituent Assembly elections held in the months immediately
afterward there was a rapid loosening, and sometimes a dissolving, of
the bonds holding together the various nuclei of local leadership in the
major parties, only the Communists maintaining an integrated political organization. Moreover, even during elections the parties have
not incorporated all the major power factors in Indonesian society, the
most important lying outside the party organization (or only partially
effective through it) being the army, certain regional elites, and an
increasing proportion of secondary and college students.[14]

[12] No major party has financed its operations—particularly its election campaign
—solely from membership dues. The Communists have developed their own
unique system of raising money, but among the other important parties a major
source of funds has been contributions from those receiving the patronage which
the party is able to dispense because of its position in government. Probably an
equally important source has been a formula, applied particularly in the two years
before the elections, whereby those granted lucrative import licenses frequently
were expected to make a substantial contribution to the party's election chest.
With Indonesian society largely devoid of a middle-class or a wealthy upper
class upon which a party might draw for financial support, participation in the
government has been of particularly great importance in financing party activity.
Those in the opposition are at a much greater disadvantage in this respect than
they are in most other countries.

[13] Soedjatmoko, "The Role of Political Parties in Indonesia," in Philip W. Thayer,
ed., *Nationalism and Progress in Free Asia* (Baltimore: Johns Hopkins, 1956),
p. 131.

[14] In addition to the four major parties—the PNI, the Masjumi, the Nahdatul

Prior to mid-1952 the Islamic Masjumi (Madjelis Sjuro Muslimin Indonesia—Council of Indonesian Muslim Associations) was easily the largest political party in Indonesia. Since then, following the withdrawal of one of its major constituent organizations, the Nahdatul Ulama, it has been at least in second place. Although the Nahdatul Ulama's departure reduced the Masjumi's representation in the 236-member pre-election parliament from 52 to 44, it still held two more seats than any other party. In the elections of 1955 it won the second largest number of votes, 7,903,886 (21 per cent) and thereby 57 out of 273 parliamentary seats. It polled nearly 50 per cent of its vote outside Java (mostly in Sumatra and South Celebes), a little over 25 per cent in West Java and Jakarta, and only 25 per cent in East and Central Java combined. Its voting strength was much more evenly distributed throughout Indonesia than that of any other party, since it won the largest number of votes in 10 out of the 15 electoral districts.[15] Enrolling most of the nation's most prominent Muslim leaders, the Masjumi was able through its influence over district and village religious leaders to tap a wide reservoir of peasant support at election time. Although probably incorporating a majority of both the slender business element of the Indonesian middle class and of those Indonesian landowners owning in excess of the amount necessary to support their families (few could be called landlords in the usual Asian sense) and a relatively small proportion of the middle class's bureaucratic sector,

---

Ulama, and the Communist—there have been several minor parties. Primarily because no major party has ever commanded a majority, they have played a role in Indonesian government disproportionate to their size. The largest is the previously mentioned Partai Sarekat Islam Indonesia (PSII), which held 4 seats in the pre-election parliament and 8 thereafter thanks to an election poll of 1,091,160 (just under 3 per cent). Second largest is the Christian party, which garnered just over 1 million votes (2.6 per cent) in the 1955 elections and increased its number of seats in parliament from 5 to 8. It is a predominantly regional party, with strength primarily among the Lutheran Bataks of North Sumatra and Protestants in the Minahassa area of northern Celebes and in the South Moluccas. Next in size is the Catholic Party, polling 770,740 votes (2 per cent) and holding 6 seats in the present parliament as against 8 in the pre-election parliament, its major strength being in the eastern Lesser Sundas, especially Flores. With slightly fewer votes—753,191, in the 1955 elections—the Indonesian Socialist Party won 5 seats in the new parliament against 14 before elections. Despite its size this party has had a significant influence on the course of Indonesian politics because it numbers several able and influential intellectuals, including former Prime Minister Soetan Sjahrir. After the elections 27 political parties, organized into 17 parliamentary alignments, were represented in parliament.

[15] See Herbert Feith, *The Indonesian Elections of 1955* (Cornell Modern Indonesia Project, Interim Reports Series; Ithaca, N.Y., 1957).

the party's platform has nevertheless been predominantly socialist.[16] It is realized, however, that it will be a long time before Indonesians can run many sectors of the economy efficiently and that foreign capital will be badly needed for a considerable time to come. In general the Masjumi is more hospitable to foreign capital and has consistently taken a more hardheaded attitude toward nationalization than any other major party. In the words of the party's chairman, Mohammad Natsir: "Nationalization should not outrun the government's ability to accumulate sufficient capital and to train sufficient administrators and technicians; the government's initial efforts in the economic sphere should therefore be to invest in new enterprises rather than take over old ones." [17]

The fact that the Masjumi, despite its composition, has consistently been a proponent of socialist goals attests to the influence within the party of the Religious Socialist group. Led by Natsir and enrolling the support of such prominent men as Sjafruddin Prawiranegara, Mohammad Roem, and Burhanuddin Harahap, the Religious Socialists—all of them proponents of Modernist Islamic ideas and convinced of the necessity for Islamic leaders to know Western culture well—had come by the close of the revolution to be the most influential element in the direction of the party. They have not, however, dominated the party's thinking concerning the relationship of Islam to the constitutional basis of government (specifically concerning the nature of an Islamic state) to the same extent that they have its approach to socioeconomic questions. Nor have they fully controlled party organization. The Masjumi has never been a well-integrated party. Although it has enrolled a large number of individuals, it has also been heavily dependent upon its constituent "special members," a loose federation of semiautonomous Islamic social and educational organizations such as the Modernist Mohammadijah and until recently the more conservative Nahdatul Ulama.[18]

[16] Islam and socialism are seen as fully compatible, and socialism mixed with a system of co-operatives is regarded as the economic order best suited to Indonesian society. When, however, small-scale capitalist enterprise is controlled in conformity with the interests of Indonesian society, it is considered as socially healthy because it develops individual initiative and responsibility. Only when it is economically efficient to do so should such enterprises be integrated into co-operatives. The government's participation in the economy should be limited to sectors having a "social character," e.g., transportation, power, communication, mining, and heavy industries.

[17] Statement to the writer during talks in Jakarta, March 1955.

[18] Until 1948 it also included as one of these member organizations the

In mid-1952 the Masjumi was dealt a serious blow with the withdrawal of one of its two major component groups, the Nahdatul Ulama (Council of Ulemas)—a defection which removed its major basis of support in eastern and central Java. In leaving the party fold the Nahdatul Ulama (NU) carried off only 8 of the Masjumi's 52 parliamentary representatives, but in the 1955 elections it won 6,955,141 votes (18.4 per cent) and 45 out of 273 seats, polling 86.6 per cent of its vote in Java with nearly three-quarters of its total in East and Central Java. There were important political reasons for the NU's defection, but religion played a significant part. Its leadership is drawn primarily from predominantly rural areas of East Java, little influenced by Modernist political thinking. The NU was in fact founded as a nonpolitical organization in 1926 partly in protest against these ideas. Its leaders are wed to a conservative variant of Islam and at the same time are much more tolerant of and willing to compromise with the pre-Islamic Hindustic and Javanese mystical ideas, still strong in much of Java, than are adherents of Modernist doctrine. While Islamic Modernism encourages the study of Western learning, the usually locally rooted religious teachers prominent in the NU are probably less exposed to Western education than any other set of important political leaders in Indonesia.

Even after the NU's departure the Masjumi lacked cohesion. Personal as well as ideological differences militated against harmony and efficiency of effort among its leaders. Dr. Sukiman Wirjosandjojo, with a following primarily in Central Java and the only top party leader on close terms with Soekarno,[19] although ideologically much closer to the Modernist Islamic element than to the leaders of the Nahdatul Ulama, had enjoyed a leading position in party circles during the revolution in large part because of his ability to moderate between and straddle these groups. His strength in party circles became less after the revolution, in particular after the collapse of his cabinet in early 1952. Thereafter, especially following the NU's withdrawal, he was more and more eclipsed by Natsir, but he continued to command sufficient influence within the party to make him a significant factor in its internal politics.

residuum of a prewar nationalist party, the PSII. In July 1947, as a result of a political deal between Amir Sjarifuddin, who needed Islamic political support in the cabinet he was then trying to form (the Masjumi having refused to participate), several older-generation PSII leaders to whom he had promised cabinet posts defected from the Masjumi, bringing a rump PSII with them.

[19] Natsir and the other Religious Socialists have been much closer to Hatta.

The increasing influence of Isa Anshary, chairman of the Masjumi's West Java branch, which was noticeable as early as 1952, introduced the most incompatible element into the party's leadership. Dogmatic in his approach to Islam, he has been aggressively intolerant of what he considers to be the backsliding and religiously compromising conduct of many other members of the Islamic community, in particular of members of the Nahdatul Ulama. He regards as heretical their willingness to blend Islam with a considerable dose of Javanese mysticism and surviving elements of Hinduism. Although he was never able to challenge the dominant position of the Religious Socialists in the party, his strength in West Java was so substantial and his oratorical abilities so considerable that he could not be fully controlled. Indeed, his bitter public denunciations of "un-Islamic" Indonesians and "un-Islamic" activities earned him the sobriquet of "our Joe McCarthy" from his uncomfortable colleagues in the party's leadership. Whereas Natsir's approach to the place of Islam in politics was moderate and consistent with Indonesian realities—and if ever fully understood would probably not have alarmed Indonesian Christians, Soekarno, or the members of the Indonesian Nationalist Party [20]—this was not true of Isa Anshary. His demands concerning an Islamic state incorporated ideas that were much more dogmatic and extreme and which understandably caused them real concern. Ironically, the more the other major parties and Soekarno isolated the Masjumi politically—keeping it out of the government and pushing it to the opposition end of a political polarization—the more the position of Isa Anshary and his followers in the party was strengthened. After the elections, however, it was clear that his extremism had hurt the Masjumi's electoral appeal, especially in Java, and subsequently his influence declined. Despite this, the antagonism of Soekarno and parts of the Indonesian Nationalist Party toward Natsir and his group in the Masjumi has continued, and the struggle of these two groups for political ascendancy has been no less bitter.

Prior to the elections of 1955 when it held 42 parliamentary seats, the Indonesian Nationalist Party (Partai Nasionalis Indonesia, generally referred to as the PNI) was clearly at least the second largest party in the country. It emerged from the elections with the largest vote— 8,434,653 (22.3 per cent)—and 57 seats. The major base of its power is the bureaucracy. The PNI has been easily the most popular party

[20] This evaluation is based upon extensive talks with Mohammad Natsir in Jakarta, March–April 1955 and August 1956.

among the upper and middle strata of the bureaucrats, probably incorporating a sizable majority of them. Broadly speaking, the PNI is the party of the bureaucratic middle class and of the *pamong pradja* —the traditional Indonesian territorial civil service, the element with the strongest ties with the old Javanese aristocracy. It has found its widest following in Java, winning 86 per cent of its total vote there in the 1955 elections and more than 65 per cent of its total in East and Central Java.[21] With nearly all of its top leaders coming from Java, it has understandably been referred to as a "Javacentric" party. Through its strong position in government, both in Jakarta and through the regional civil service, the PNI has been able, particularly in Java, to muster substantial local support in elections through the powerful group of civil servants affiliated with it.[22]

The PNI has never possessed a really consistent and comprehensive ideology, particularly with regard to socioeconomic affairs. Its members are for the most part only nominal Muslims, many of them being both contemptuous and fearful of Islamic orthodoxy. The party's official credo, *Marhaenism* ("Proletarianism"—with as much rural as urban emphasis) is borrowed from President Soekarno, with whom the party has usually had a particularly close relationship. It has also been the most consistent of all parties in supporting his *Pantjasila*. The PNI in fact bears the name of Soekarno's prewar nationalist party, and although there is no organic connection between them many of its older-generation leaders were Soekarno's close associates in the prewar nationalist movement. All Indonesian political parties are strongly nationalistic, but the PNI's nationalism has a particularly strong emotional charge. Indeed, one of the party's major leaders has characterized its leadership as incorporating two major groups: the "irrational, emotional nationalists" and "the rational nationalist group." [23] There is also a third component; it is made up of many of the older civil servants, is not particularly dynamic, and is usually most influenced by the prewar nationalist leaders in the party. It has most frequently thrown its support to the "irrational" group, but since the 1955 elections its

[21] Feith, *Indonesian Elections.*

[22] Of the various ministries through which it has exerted influence, it has probably been able to achieve most through the Ministry of Information and its multitude of local branches. In this ministry PNI influence has been dominant throughout most of the postrevolutionary period. Until the fall of the Wilopo cabinet, the Masjumi could partially match this influence through its control of the Ministry of Religious Affairs; thereafter this ministry, along with its regional branches, came increasingly under the control of the Nahdatul Ulama.

[23] In a conversation with the writer in 1955.

members have become alarmed at the Communists' impressive show-ing in Central and East Java; it has therefore been less willing to follow such leadership and has shown more independence. Whereas Soekarno in the early postrevolutionary period appeared to stand about equally close to the "irrational" and to the older-generation groups, in recent years he has drawn closer to the former. The "rational nationalist group" has lately come to attract support from the largest proportion of educated, younger-generation party members, but with the possible exception of the first months of the Wilopo cabinet it has never quite been able to match the strength in party circles of the other two groups.[24]

The Indonesian Communist Party differs from the other major parties in that it is both well organized and able to maintain substantial party discipline. By the middle of 1957 it appeared to have become the big-gest political party in Indonesia, probably slightly larger in its following than the PNI, the Masjumi, or the NU and certainly larger in its active membership. Its attainment of major party status has been recent, the period of rapid growth not beginning until late 1952. With only 17 seats in the pre-election parliament, it increased its stature strikingly in the 1955 elections, winning 6,176,914 votes and 39 seats. Of its total vote in this national election 88.6 per cent came from Java, 75 per cent from East and Central Java alone. Whereas the organizations of the other three major parties were weakened after the 1955 elections, the Communists appear to have increased both the strength of their or-ganization and the size of their following, winning first place in the East Java and Central Java provincial elections of mid-1957.

During, and particularly in the first two years after, the revolution the Communists were poorly organized. They had been crippled by the Madiun rebellion—a taint which still, though diminishingly, em-barrasses them—and not until 1952 did they have much success in re-building their strength.[25]

---

[24] The strength of hypernationalism within the PNI is such that the party has been considerably less hospitable to foreign capital than the Masjumi has. Many influential members have not, however, been averse to building up Indonesian capitalists, especially if they were party members, through discriminatory govern-ment action, especially through the granting of import licenses and of privileged access to credit from government banks. This disposition has certainly not been absent among other parties wed to a socialist program, but after the fall of the Wilopo cabinet the PNI became the major practitioner of this art. Although this did not square with the party's socialism, it did with its nationalism, inasmuch as this process was regarded as an aspect of the Indonesianization of the economy.

[25] In August 1951 they received another setback, although much milder and

Early in 1951 D. N. Aidit—27 years old and reportedly just back from a year in Communist China and North Vietnam—with a group of other young men unsullied by any leading role in the Madiun rebellion, wrested control of the party from an older group, of which the intellectual leader was Tan Ling Djie, an Indonesian of Chinese descent. In the first half of 1952 Aidit apparently felt secure enough in control to announce a radical change in party policies—a switch from a small elite party to one with a mass organization and the inauguration of a National Front program calling for a largely constitutional role and cooperation with other "anti-imperialist parties." This entailed a policy of consistent enmity toward the Masjumi (which the Communists saw as their most dangerous rival) and support of the PNI and later the NU in an effort to drive a further wedge between them and the Masjumi—a strategy which was pursued with considerable success. After 1952 the Communist leaders seem to have realized more and more that their party's fortunes would largely be determined by their ability to clothe it in the symbols of Indonesian nationalism. They therefore not only ceased criticizing Soekarno but became vociferous exponents of his *Pantjasila,* backed up with vigor his every move to win Western New Guinea (West Irian), and did their best to excite his and PNI leaders' concern over the dangers of an Islamic state.

In late 1953 soon after the formation of Ali's cabinet the Communists radically altered their conduct in parliament. They now made a major

---

temporary. Reacting to an increasing level of terrorist activities which were aimed at disrupting the production of East Java estates and tying up port areas and which the Communists had been carrying out for more than a year, Prime Minister Sukiman, probably backed by Soekarno, ordered the arrest and temporary jailing of a large number of leaders. Following their release the Communists concentrated their previously scattered armed groups in an area in Central Java comprising the northern slopes of the Merapi volcano and Mt. Merbabu and the hills peripheral to it. Here they reinforced an older base and gave intensive military and political training to youths brought in from East and Central Java for short periods on a rotating basis. From this base, known as the "Merapi–Merbabu Complex" (MMC), they tied down between 3,000 and 4,000 government troops during 1952–1953. At the end of 1953, soon after the fall of the Wilopo cabinet (a PNI-Masjumi coalition) and the formation of the PNI-dominated cabinet under Ali Sastroamidjojo—incorporating the NU but with the Masjumi, the Socialist, and the Christian parties in opposition—the MMC troops suddenly ceased aggressive activities. It was reported that this had been ordered by Communist Party leaders as a result of an understanding which they had been able to reach with the new Ali government, one which they apparently considered made it worth while to cooperate with his government and concentrate on preparing for the coming elections. In 1954–1955 the pro-Socialist Party Governor of Middle Java, Budiono, initiated a vigorous military campaign which resulted in defeat of the MMC troops and elimination of their base.

effort to get along with the government in power. Communist deputies in parliament consistently supported Ali's coalition cabinet, whose majority was so slender and so dependent on several of the fickler minor parties that it welcomed the Communists' support—backing without which it could not have weathered a number of crises and without which it certainly could not have remained in office for as long as it did (from August 1, 1953, until August 12, 1955—longer than any other Indonesian cabinet before or since). One possible *quid pro quo,* either tacit or explicit, was the acquiescence of Ali and his cabinet to largely unrestricted Communist Party organizational drives and election preparations.

With solidarity re-established among the party's leaders, discipline could now be much greater, and the Communists were better able to capitalize on the influence which they were beginning to exert via a number of Communist-front and Communist-influenced organizations. Through the principal labor federation, the SOBSI (Sentral Organisasi Buruh Seluru Indonesia), they controlled or at least strongly influenced about 1.5 million trade unionists, well over half of those in Indonesia. In addition through the Barisan Tani Indonesia (Indonesian Peasant Front), an organization which they tightly controlled, they developed considerable peasant backing, particularly in plantation areas. In some of the poorer districts of East and Central Java, where in the 1955 national elections the Nahdatul Ulama and Masjumi were competing for peasant support, the Communists frequently offered an agreeable alternative to peasants who were only nominally Muslim. In some parts of Java the Communist Party was much more successful than the PNI, and it was particularly in these districts that, thanks to its continuing organization, it captured many of the votes in the provincial elections of 1957 which had gone to the PNI in 1955.

The Communist Party's spectacular growth during 1954–1957 is explainable in part by the ability of its top- and middle-rank leaders and by their dedication to the party cause, but there are other important reasons for its success. One was the continuing belief of President Soekarno and some of the most influential leaders of the PNI that the Communists posed less of a threat, at least in an immediate sense, to Indonesia and their own political fortunes than the Masjumi. They felt that the Masjumi had a real chance of emerging victorious from the elections and that the Communists did not. This made it easier for the Communists to promote a political polarization which served to isolate the Masjumi.

Another important reason for the Communists' success has been financial: their party has undoubtedly become the wealthiest in Indonesia. Their financial resources derive only partially from membership fees. They have been able to tap the Chinese business community in Indonesia for substantial funds, which have been utilized not only to fill party coffers and pay for organizational and election expenses, but also to purchase indirectly the good will of the peasantry. In doing this they have had important support from the Chinese Communist government's embassy and consulates in Indonesia. While many Chinese businessmen are undoubtedly far from eager to make these contributions, they do so because of the difficulties which might otherwise result.[26]

Political Developments, 1950–1958

From September 1950 until April 1957 Indonesia has had six parliament-based cabinets. The first of these, lasting from September 6, 1950, to April 27, 1951, and led by the Masjumi's Mohammed Natsir, was formed following an unsuccessful attempt to establish a Masjumi-PNI coalition cabinet, attempts to do so having broken down over disagreement on the apportionment of cabinet seats. Natsir's cabinet was based upon a coalition of the Masjumi and several of the smaller parties, including the Socialist and Christian parties but excluding the PNI and the then small Communist Party. Lack of PNI support was a major weakness, and PNI opposition in conjunction with increasing friction between Natsir and Soekarno finally forced the cabinet to resign. A major reason for Soekarno's opposition was his impatience with what he considered Natsir's lack of vigorous action in dealing with the West Irian problem. Further friction arose over their differing views as to the President's proper role in the government.

With the fall of the Natsir cabinet Soekarno selected two formateurs,

---

[26] They may sometimes make funds available because of the economic advantage involved, but undoubtedly they usually do so because of persuasion or pressure from the Chinese embassy or pressure from the Communist-controlled labor unions and the threat of retaliatory action in case of noncompliance. With regard to Communist-peasant relations, the principal formula is reported to be as follows: Chinese businessmen are induced to lend capital to Communist Party members who use it, particularly in Java, to buy up crops from peasants at rates above the going market price, thereby winning their good will. The crops are then turned over to the Chinese businessman who advanced the funds. He sells the crop, in some cases making a profit, though not necessarily so. Thus in many districts Indonesian Communist Party members have, at no cost to themselves, won the peasants' support.

one from the Masjumi and one from the PNI. Dr. Sukiman, the Masjumi formateur, accepted Soekarno's appointment without first securing authorization from the Masjumi executive council. Being relatively close to Soekarno and the PNI, Sukiman was able to form a coalition cabinet, based upon the Masjumi, the PNI, and several of the smaller parties, which lasted from April 27, 1951, to April 3, 1952. Sukiman's cabinet is the only one that has fallen over a foreign policy issue. The crisis was precipitated by an agreement negotiated with the United States for economic assistance. The American ambassador exceeded his instructions from Washington and, quite unnecessarily, prevailed upon the Indonesian Foreign Minister to subscribe to a statement widely interpreted by Indonesians as signifying their country's abandonment of an independent foreign policy and committing it to alignment with the United States. (Foreign Minister Achmad Subardjo had been led to believe by Ambassador Merle Cochran—quite at variance with Washington's intent—that refusal to subscribe to this statement would result in cessation of American economic assistance to Indonesia.) In this case both major political parties strongly condemned the agreement, and this in conjunction with a vociferous popular protest brought the cabinet down.[27]

Formateurs appointed by the President from each of the two major parties unsuccessfully attempted to put together a new cabinet. Following their failure, Soekarno appointed Wilopo, a leader of the more "rational" element in the PNI. He was successful in drawing support from the younger leaders within his party as well as from the Masjumi, Socialist, Christian, and Catholic parties. In the caliber of its members the Wilopo cabinet (April 3, 1952 to August 1, 1953) was probably the strongest of all cabinets in postrevolutionary Indonesia. Within a few months, however, its position was weakened by increasing friction with President Soekarno over control of the armed forces and by dissension among the army's officers—dissension that was rendered acute by cabinet attempts to rationalize and modernize the army. This process was envisaged by a number of officers and by Soekarno as leading to the ultimate dismissal of a substantial proportion of the less-well-educated men who had been trained initially during the Japanese period, the group which, on the whole, stood closest to

[27] A somewhat more substantial account of political developments during the Natsir and Sukiman cabinets can be found in the writer's "Indonesian Politics and Nationalism" in *Asian Nationalism and the West,* ed. by William L. Holland (New York: Macmillan, 1953), pp. 134–178 and 188–194.

Soekarno. Indications that efforts at rationalization were being frustrated by parliament members led by older-generation PNI members close to Soekarno provoked an attempted coup (the October 17 Affair) by anti-Soekarno officers aimed at forcing him to dismiss parliament. This move was actually directed against Soekarno and officers close to him more than it was against parliament itself. There was a sufficient rallying to Soekarno of officers opposing rationalization to enable him to stand up to the proponents of parliamentary dissolution and refuse. With division in the army and continued pressure from Soekarno and the strongly pro-Soekarno wing of the PNI, the cabinet finally fell over the refusal of parliament, including most of the PNI members, to support it in its attempt to remove peasant squatters from foreign-owned tobacco estates in North Sumatra.[28]

The fall of the Wilopo cabinet was symptomatic of the widening split which was developing between the Masjumi and the PNI. Attempts to form a new cabinet based upon a PNI-Masjumi coalition were unsuccessful, and only after two months was one finally formed by a leader of one of the minor parties, Wongsonegoro of the PIR (Persatuan Indonesia Raja). This cabinet centered on the PNI—with one of its leaders, Ali Sastroamidjojo, as Prime Minister—and included the Nahdatul Ulama and several of the smaller parties. The Masjumi, Socialist, and Christian parties were now in the opposition. Despite mounting criticism of the government's ineffectiveness in promoting economic reconstruction and development, of increased governmental corruption—relating in particular to activities of the cabinet's Minister of Economic Affairs, Iskaq Tjokrohadisurjo—and a serious revolt of the strongly Muslim Atjenese of northern Sumatra which broke out almost immediately after it took office, Ali's government managed to remain in power from August 1, 1953, until August 12, 1955. Soekarno's influence in government increased greatly during this period, and one reason for the longevity of Ali's cabinet was the consistent support which he gave it. Other reasons were its ability to hold its members and supporting M.P.'s in line due to a more lavish dispensation of patronage than had ever before occurred and the previously mentioned change in Communist tactics giving the Ali cabinet sustained support.

[28] For a comprehensive and scholarly account of the politics of the period immediately prior to and during the Wilopo cabinet, see the forthcoming study by Herbert Feith, *The Wilopo Cabinet, 1952–1953: A Turning Point in Post-revolutionary Indonesia* (Cornell Modern Indonesia Project, Monograph Series; Ithaca, N.Y., 1958).

In addition Ali's initiative in holding the Asian-African Conference earned his cabinet helpful domestic prestige.

During the course of the Ali cabinet an increasing polarization emerged in Indonesian politics. This resulted primarily from the maneuvering for elections and produced an increasing tendency for the President, the PNI, the Nahdatul Ulama, and the Communist party to work together for defeat of the Masjumi. In this situation the Nahdatul Ulama held a pivotal position, being courted by both the President and the PNI on the one hand and by the Masjumi on the other. Throughout this period President Soekarno, backed by the cabinet, made a sustained effort to strengthen his position in the army. It was in fact the attempt of the pro-Soekarno Minister of Defense, Iwa Kusumasumantri, to install a chief of staff desired by Soekarno but not acceptable to the majority of top-ranking army officers that precipitated the cabinet's fall.

The last cabinet to be formed prior to the 1955 elections was one whose formateur was designated by Vice-President Hatta, because President Soekarno had left the country on a pilgrimage to Mecca after meeting defeat over the army issue. This cabinet led by Burhanuddin Harahap of the Masjumi's Religious Socialist group lasted from August 13, 1955, until March 24, 1956. It was based upon a coalition of the Masjumi, the Nahdatul Ulama, the Socialists, and some of the smaller parties. However, the NU's support was generally either apathetic or unreliable. With the PNI in opposition and President Soekarno upon his return clearly hostile, the cabinet had a difficult time from the outset. It picked up some popular support because of a vigorous anti-corruption drive, but it lost prestige over its unsuccessful attempt to control the air force, whose commander-in-chief—clearly backed by Soekarno—refused to countenance the installation of a deputy chief sponsored by the cabinet. When the outcome of the elections became known in December and it was clear that the PNI had received more votes than the Masjumi, its position became even weaker. Because of this and a continuing lack of support from Soekarno, its effectiveness during its last months as a caretaker government pending the formation of a new cabinet based upon the results of the elections was less than that of any previous cabinet.

Following the elections the Masjumi and the "rational" and older groups in the PNI, all alarmed over the unexpectedly large vote won by the Communists, worked to re-establish sufficient co-operation to permit their joining together in a cabinet which would exclude the Communists. At the end of March 1956 such a cabinet was formed, under the prime ministership of the PNI's Ali Sastroamidjojo. In addition to the PNI and Masjumi the cabinet incorporated the NU and representatives of several of the smaller parties.[29] Thereby it could look to a wide base of support in parliament, but from the outset it never commanded strong backing from Soekarno. Moreover, party differences that had become more rigid during the course of the election campaigns were ineffectively bridged in the cabinet, and one could hardly say that it functioned as a harmonious team. Patronage continued to be dispensed on a large scale, a process which nourished governmental corruption. An attempt by Natsir to induce Prime Minister Ali to undertake a vigorous anticorruption cleanup, regardless of who in the Masjumi or the PNI suffered, was turned down. The Prime Minister was widely criticized for being more concerned with foreign affairs and the welfare of his party than in addressing himself to the country's pressing domestic problems. Continuing indications of corruption in high places, mounting inflation, and the government's ineffectiveness in dealing with Indonesia's major economic and administrative problems brought keen disappointment to the many Indonesians who had expected that elections would provide some sort of political panacea and bring effective government. As a consequence, disillusionment with parliamentary democracy became increasingly widespread. Understandably the Communist Party benefited from this situation. As the only major party not represented in the government, it could avoid responsibility for the discouraging situation while growing in strength through its effective organization. Although criticizing the government, it generally remained careful not to antagonize the PNI, directing its major barbs against the Masjumi.

The second half of 1956 was marked by growing regional dissatisfaction and a coincident decrease in the cabinet's control over military leaders, who were playing an increasingly important political role.[30]

[29] Soekarno had appointed Ali as formateur rather than Wilopo, whose name had been offered by the PNI along with that of Ali. Soekarno criticized Ali's cabinet list for incorporating no Communist Party supporters and urged that they be included, arguing that since the Communist Party had emerged as fourth largest in the elections national unity would best be served by including them. The PNI refused to go along with this suggestion.

[30] One of the first open indications of the army's increasing political role was the narrowly averted attempt in August 1956 by Colonel Kawilarang, commander in West Java, to arrest Foreign Minister Abdulgani on charges of corruption just as he was about to depart for the London conference on Suez. In the middle of November, Colonel Zulkifli Lubis, former deputy chief of staff, launched an abortive coup against the government. His plot was discovered before he could move certain army units from Bandung to Jakarta.

The regions outside Java were becoming intensely dissatisfied with the
government's failure to take effective action to further their economic development and to meet even their most immediate economic
problems or—alternatively—to provide sufficient administrative and
fiscal decentralization to allow them to undertake this themselves. The
conviction that Jakarta was utilizing for the benefit of Java a disproportionate amount of the country's foreign exchange, approximately
three-fourths of which was earned by areas outside Java, heightened
this dissatisfaction. The government's failure to allocate to army commanders sufficient funds to pay their men and provide them with adequate food and housing led regional commanders in Celebes and North
Sumatra as early as mid-1956 to enter into illegal barter trade in copra
and rubber. Thereby they took over directly foreign exchange which
would otherwise have been channeled through Jakarta.

Differences among political parties and between Soekarno and Hatta
continued to grow. Because the Masjumi had emerged from the elections as definitely the major party outside Java—particularly in Sumatra
—and because its representatives in the Ali cabinet held a clearly subordinate position in which they were able to accomplish very little
toward promoting measures calculated to assuage the mounting regional restiveness, the party's central leadership found itself under
great pressure from regional leaders as well as from Isa Anshary to pull
out of the cabinet and go into opposition. Natsir, however, argued that
to do so would further weaken national unity and benefit only the Communists, and he managed to keep the Masjumi in the government until
January 9, 1957, when the Sumatran coups, Soekarno's continuing call
for a new governmental system, and the withdrawal of one of the
smaller parties made the cabinet's position completely untenable.

Soekarno, never enthusiastic about Ali's second cabinet, increased
his criticism of it and eventually of the whole system of parliamentary
government. Those who knew him believed that his admiration for
the monolithic political solidarity of Communist China served to increase his critical attitude toward the ineffectiveness of parliamentary
government in Indonesia and made him all the more insistent that
the cabinet should include the Communist Party so that no major
political group would be outside the government. Late in October
1956 Soekarno remarked that political parties might best be "buried"
in order that national unity be advanced. On November 10 in his
opening address to the Constituent Assembly [31] he stated that "the

[31] In the elections for the Constituent Assembly, held in December 1955 just
after the elections for parliament had been concluded, the PNI received 9,070,218

freedom to set up political parties does not constitute the only means
to keep the democratic system going" and that Indonesian democracy
should be unique and not a copy of imported systems. The weaker
groups in Indonesian society should be protected from the stronger,
he argued, this necessitating that Indonesia's system of democracy
should "see to it that one group should not be exploited by another;
this means that for the time being, our democracy must be a guided
democracy." Soekarno's call for a guided democracy incorporating all
major political groups, including the Communists, and his attacks upon
the system of parliamentary democracy widened the breach with
Hatta, a separation which was formalized with Hatta's resignation as
Vice-President on December 1, 1956. Hatta's departure from the government was seen by the outer regions, particularly Sumatra, as de-
priving them of their principal representative in the government, and
their discontent with Jakarta increased. During December three successive bloodless coups by army commanders in North, Central, and
South Sumatra resulted in their administrations' being taken over by
army-led councils which announced that they no longer recognized
the Ali cabinet. Jakarta was able to manage a countercoup in North
Sumatra that ended in a progovernment commander's regaining control of Medan and some other parts of that province. The regional
councils of Central Sumatra and South Sumatra led by Lieutenant
Colonel Achmad Hussein and Lieutenant Colonel Barlian respectively
remained in power.

Following mounting indications of regional dissatisfaction with the
Jakarta government and the cabinet's continuing inability to control
regional military and civilian leaders in their arrogation of more local
powers, Soekarno on Feb. 21, 1957, made a major address in which
he set forth his recommendations for a drastic change in Indonesia's political system. The whole structure of government, he stated, "must be
rebuilt, renewed right to the very foundation, and a new, completely
new edifice constructed." Noting that every cabinet had had to cope
with recurrent crises arising because of a lack of authority and because
of sustained opposition from various groups in parliament, Soekarno
concluded:

I have finally come to the conclusion that the cause lies in our practicing a
system not suited to our specific requirements, in our indiscriminate adop-

---

votes and 119 seats (out of 514 elected seats for the whole assembly), the Masjumi
7,789,619 votes and 112 seats, the Nahdatul Ulama 6,989,333 votes and 91 seats,
and the Communist Party 6,232,512 votes and 80 seats (Feith, *The Indonesian
Elections of 1955*, p. 65).

tion of every feature of the system that is known as western democracy.
. . . The more I look back on our experiences of the last eleven years the
more I am convinced that the system of democracy that we have taken over is,
in fact, incompatible with the Indonesian outlook. . . . The principles of
western democracy, the parliamentary democracy of the western countries,
incorporate the concept of an active opposition, and it is precisely the
adoption of this concept that has given rise to the difficulties we have experienced over the last eleven years. By accepting this concept we have
come to think in a manner that is alien to the Indonesian way of life.

As a remedy Soekarno suggested that a new kind of cabinet be created in which the ministers would be drawn from all major parties
represented in parliament, making clear that this should include the
Communist Party. In addition he proposed that there be created a
National Council which would be "representative of every section of
the Indonesian people without exception . . . [with a] membership
drawn from all groups in the community—occupational, social, religious, cultural—along with the chiefs of the armed forces and of the
police, the Attorney General," and "those ministers of the cabinet holding key portfolios." Soekarno himself would be chairman. Its function,
he said, "will be to advise the cabinet, to submit recommendations to
the cabinet at the request of the cabinet or without a request of the
cabinet." Just as the cabinet would be a "concentrated reflection of the
composition of parliament," the National Council would be a "concentrated reflection of the Indonesian nation." Cabinet and council
would be closely linked, and by reason of their composition "a firmly
established bridge would be created between the parliament and the
dynamic forces of society."
    Although there have been many criticisms of Soekarno's proposal,
it should be observed that the system toward which he seemed to be
groping reflected a very real and widespread disillusionment among
Indonesians with parliamentary democracy (at least as they have experienced it), and also that it sought to incorporate some traditional
Indonesian political values—social solidarity, harmony, and the *mufakat* system of decision making—which hold considerable appeal. Moreover, the idea of an advisory National Council was, as we have seen,
not new, although its precursor in the revolutionary period—the High
Advisory Council—had far less influence on governmental policy and
was smaller than the organ of government Soekarno was now pro-
posing.
    Hatta's public criticism of Soekarno's proposal was prompt and

trenchant. Incorporation of the Communists into the cabinet, he said, would not promote political solidarity but would introduce a disruptive element inasmuch as the Communists were dedicated to quite different objectives from the other parties. "If co-operation with the Communists were to be imposed on the other parties, the existing antagonisms would only be heightened and the prospect of national unity would become even more remote." Moreover, being "a segment of an international movement dedicated to world revolution . . . and a dictatorship of the proletariat," the Communists, if represented in the cabinet, would make it impossible for Indonesia to follow an independent foreign policy since they would subordinate Indonesia's interests to those of Soviet Russia. To include the Communists in the cabinet would be as futile as "to try to mix water and oil"; their proper place was in the opposition:

These faults and the malpractice of allocating appointments on the basis of party affiliation will not be corrected by the installation of a composite cabinet and the elimination of opposition in the chamber of representatives. The situation can only be remedied by an efficient government comprised of honest and capable ministers under the leadership of the President.

Establishment of a National Council, Hatta added, would be unconstitutional and would in effect be a duplication of parliament; the attainment of a stable government with unquestioned authority could best come by formation of a presidential cabinet headed by Soekarno himself, with the President assuming clear responsibility. Whenever useful the President could hold regular meetings with cabinet members, party leaders, and nonparty experts to discuss urgent political issues. Consequently there would be no need for a National Council.

Soekarno's proposals were accepted by the PNI and the Communist Party, also, in somewhat altered and watered-down form, by the reluctant Nahdatul Ulama; but they were never accepted by the Masjumi. They provoked more dissatisfaction in the major islands outside Java, precipitating during the first week of March 1957 coups by the military commanders in Celebes and Indonesian Borneo, who established army-led councils similar to that set up in Central Sumatra. The rump Ali cabinet on March 14 signed an emergency decree declaring a state of martial law ("War and Siege") for all Indonesia and then promptly resigned. This had the immediate effect of strengthening the positions of Soekarno and the army, making both of them even less dependent than before upon the support of the political parties. While this regulation merely confirmed the existing arrogation of civil powers by commanders in the areas outside Java, it initiated the transfer of a wide range of these powers to army commanders in Java, and it clearly enhanced the authority of the army chief of staff, Major General A. H. Nasution, an officer who now apparently stood close to Soekarno.

Despite widespread demand, particularly from areas outside Java, that he appoint Hatta as formateur of the new cabinet, Soekarno on March 15 gave this mandate to Suwirjo, chairman of the PNI, instructing him to form a coalition cabinet incorporating all major parties and to establish a National Council. Unable to bring the major parties —including his own—to accept inclusion of the Communists in the cabinet, Suwirjo returned his mandate a week later. Soekarno then gave him a second mandate, this time instructing him to form a cabinet of experts, whose selection would not necessarily be in conformity with party strength. Again Suwirjo failed. Thereupon Soekarno undertook the unprecedented action of appointing himself, "Citizen Soekarno," as formateur for the purpose of establishing an "emergency extra-parliamentary cabinet of experts." Within a week's time he had succeeded in lining up a group, it could not well be called a team, of 23 heterogeneous men—some very able and some less so. This cabinet, still functioning as of April 1958, is headed by Djuanda Kartawidjaja, an able and respected nonparty man with considerable experience in earlier cabinets as Minister of Communications or of Economic Planning. His cabinet incorporates members of the PNI, the NU, and a few of the small parties, as well as several nonparty people. It contains no member of the Communist Party, but two ministers (Agriculture and Mobilization of National Strength for Reconstruction) are widely regarded as having connections with it. Although not represented in this cabinet (at least not formally), the Communist Party has given it strong support in parliament. The Masjumi refused to enter the government, labeling it unconstitutional. Djuanda stated that he considered his cabinet to be responsible to parliament and that he would conduct his government on that premise. Whether or not it is responsible, the inauguration of this cabinet has diminished the role of both parliament and the political parties in approximate proportion to the considerably increased role of the President and the army.

Soekarno insisted upon going ahead with his plan for the establishment of a National Council—a body that was designed to weld greater national unity but that appears to have resulted in greater dissension.

He and Djuanda signed the emergency decree establishing the council on May 6, 1957.[32] In installing the 43-member council on July 12, Soekarno stated, "The cabinet continues to be responsible to parliament and its position is exactly the same as in the past. . . . The council should not impair the position of the cabinet." It is as yet not possible to assess the importance to Indonesia's government of the National Council, but there seems to be little doubt that it speaks primarily for Soekarno.

The summer of 1957 was marked by continuing conflicts within the army and between the political parties. Although Soekarno and Nasution appeared to have been able to promote a greater degree of army unity in Java, where most of the troops are stationed, they were encountering great difficulty in their attempts to re-establish that unity among, and their control over, the military leaders outside Java. Army commanders, particularly those in the outer islands, continued to insist that unity was dependent upon a reconciliation between Hatta and Soekarno and installation of Hatta in a leading governmental position. Differences between the political parties remained wide, although the success of the Communists in the Java provincial elections of mid-1957 alarmed the other three major parties sufficiently to bring them at least to talk of the necessity of co-operation against the Communists. But the breach between Soekarno and the Masjumi became broader rather than narrower. Despite much larger subventions (far in excess of what had been allocated in the central government's budget) to the regions outside Java and genuine—though woefully belated—progress in the drafting of legislation providing for much greater administrative and fiscal autonomy, the Jakarta government was unsuccessful in re-establishing political unity. Moreover, it was now faced by the dissident areas' increasing arrogation of control over foreign-exchange-earning exports, a development that aggravated the already serious economic situation confronting the central government. This lack of success may have stemmed in part from the regions' further mistrust of Jakarta en-

[32] It was provided that all appointments and removals of council members would be the prerogative of the President, that the President would be its chairman, and that "members of the council shall be appointed from functional groups within the society, persons who can bring regional problems to the fore, the holders of military and civilian posts as necessary and ministers as necessary." In the official explanation attached to the decree it was stated, "In our further constitutional development it is clear that other efforts are necessary to accommodate the growth of active forces in our society which are not channeled effectively by existing institutions."

gendered by its efforts to reassert its control through exploiting and fomenting divisions within particular disaffected regions and their army commands.

In an effort to deal with these increasingly grave problems, to reconcile Soekarno and Hatta, and to bridge the divisions within the army and in the political community, Prime Minister Djuanda in early September 1957 organized a national conference, whose membership included most of the prominent regional, military, and civilian leaders. Through it Soekarno and Hatta were brought together for talks and promised to try to work together for solution of the nation's problems. The two men, however, continued to be divided on several key issues and were unable to agree on the scope of Hatta's role in any new cabinet that might replace Djuanda's or whether the Communists would be included in such a cabinet. Clearly Soekarno remained unwilling to meet Hatta's minimum terms as to the degree of real authority the latter would exercise in any such cabinet. The conference did result in the establishment of a committee of seven of the country's top leaders, whom it charged with the task of restoring unity within the army. Its members were Soekarno, Hatta, Djuanda, Dr. Johannes Leimena, the Sultan of Jogjakarta, Dr. Aziz Saleh, and General Nasution. On November 30, however, amid rumors that the committee was moving in a direction not entirely acceptable to him, an attempt was made to assassinate Soekarno. Although escaping unscathed, Soekarno was reported to be severely shaken; soon thereafter the committee of seven ceased to function, and prospects for an over-all military and political settlement looked dimmer than ever.

The day before this incident a vote in the United Nations General Assembly had fallen short of the two-thirds majority necessary for endorsement of Indonesia's petition that the Netherlands be called upon to negotiate over the status of West Irian. Soekarno had warned of the serious reaction which such a refusal would provoke in Indonesia, and during the first weeks of December there was a wide-scale seizure of Dutch properties and a campaign calling upon the some 46,000 Netherlanders still resident in Indonesia to leave. Apparently this was a move of which Soekarno was one of the major promoters, but labor unions, prominent among which were elements of the Communist-dominated SOBSI, took the major role in the seizures. These moves indicated a lack of planning and central co-ordination and resulted in considerable economic disruption until the Djuanda government ordered the army to move in and take over establishments from the squads sent in by the labor unions. The army was able to keep most of these enterprises going, but the efficiency of many was certainly decreased as a result of the departure of a sizable proportion of the Netherlanders who had been key personnel in their operation. The attempt to take over Dutch interisland shipping backfired, with the Dutch ultimately withdrawing their ships from Indonesia and leaving the country far short of needed shipping for interisland commerce.

The shortsightedness of this move, and the lack of proper planning behind it, brought criticism from Hatta and vigorous criticism from several of the Masjumi leaders. The stand of the Masjumi leaders was quickly exploited by their opponents, the Communists in particular, who accused them of being pro-Dutch and of lacking proper patriotism. Among those most vigorously attacked was one of the top Masjumi leaders, Sjafruddin Prawiranegara, governor of the Bank of Indonesia. He resigned his position in the bank and with a number of other Masjumi leaders, including Natsir, was reported to have been plagued by an increasing number of threats by politically motivated youth groups. These groups were alleged to have kidnaped and beaten a number of lesser party leaders, in some cases turning them over thereafter to Jakarta army authorities for arrest and confinement. Whether or not these allegations were true, several of the top Masjumi leaders, including Natsir, Sjafruddin, and Burhanuddin Harahap, stated that the practice of democratic government was no longer possible in Jakarta and they removed to Padang, capital of the already virtually autonomous central Sumatran regime headed by Lieutenant Colonel Achmad Hussein.

On February 10, 1958, Hussein issued an ultimatum to the Djuanda government calling upon it to resign within five days to pave the way for a governmental reorganization that would exclude the Communists and answer regional needs; the West Sumatran regime would take further steps if this demand should not be met. A week earlier a similar demand had been served upon Soekarno in Tokyo, his last stop on a six-week rest cure abroad, by Colonel Warouw, a north Celebes member of the Padang group. No reply was forthcoming, and on February 15, one day before Soekarno's return to Jakarta, Sjafruddin Prawiranegara was installed in Padang as Prime Minister of a newly proclaimed revolutionary government. Apparently the revolutionaries hoped to establish a dissident nucleus which would attract support from other Sumatran areas, Celebes, and Borneo and exert sufficient influence to weaken Soekarno's position, topple the Djuanda government, and make possible establishment of a new government from which pro-Communists as well as Communist Party members would be excluded and from which more attention to regional needs might be expected. Jakarta is taking vigorous military action to suppress the dissidents, who, though urged on and openly supported by the military-civilian council on north Celebes, have thus far (April 1958) been able to secure little more than sympathy from most other Sumatran areas.[33]

Anyone who would attempt at the present time to predict the course of Indonesia's politics would be rash indeed, but it is clear that military measures, even if completely successful, cannot alone ensure the country's unity. As many Indonesians clearly appreciate, no lasting unity will be achieved unless the very real political and economic grievances which have generated the existing dissension are significantly reduced. While the current situation remains complex and confused, one factor does seem to be emerging with some clarity; this is that at least for the present the positions of Soekarno and the army are relatively strong. The major power axis appears to lie between Soekarno, General Nasution, and the apparently substantial number of army officers (particularly on Java) who now give them varying degrees of support. The Communists, while stronger than any other political party, are still quite inferior in power to this Soekarno-army alliance. It would appear that if the Communists are to play a dominant political role, they will have to be more successful than they have been in infiltrating or influencing the ranks of army officers.

[33] By early May the central government's forces had driven the rebels from all major towns in Central Sumatra.

· XXIII ·

Some Major Problems

INDONESIA'S major problems are implicit, if not explicit, in the foregoing discussion. Currently the nation is at a confusing stage of transition: the momentum and unifying political dynamic of its struggle for independence are spent, and a new and positive political ethos must be developed. Although there is a reasonable measure of agreement concerning the socioeconomic role of the new state, there is no such consensus as to the proper nature of its political organization. A solution must be worked out which will be satisfactory to both Muslims and non-Muslims, and it must be a system of governmental organization in which the boundaries of authority and responsibility are clearly defined.

Representative Government

What has emerged thus far has been neither a reasonable copy of Western democratic systems nor an adequate synthesis of Western and traditional elements. No fair test of Western parliamentary democracy has yet been made. Responsibility for its waning attractiveness to Indonesians stems to some extent from unresolved conflicting ideologies and from their belief that its operation tends to exacerbate rather than bridge such differences. But the ineffectiveness of Indonesia's parliamentary system has been much more a consequence of irresponsible conduct by political parties having too little rapport with and

573

responsibility toward the population. It has also stemmed from the failure to provide Soekarno with a clearly defined constitutional role approximately equivalent to his stature as a national leader, while nevertheless allowing him to exercise substantial power without responsibility. One source of these troubles has been Indonesia's vague and ambiguous constitution—one which could confuse and frustrate the best-intentioned men in the world. Clearly, however, the dismal record of Indonesia's quasi-parliamentary system derives to a major extent from the conditioning of a colonial order which did so little to prepare Indonesians for self-government, much less for the practice of parliamentary democracy. It will undoubtedly take considerable time to overcome the limitations which this imposes. Moreover, some traditional, precolonial political concepts still have considerable vitality in Indonesia, and it may well be that no effective governmental system will emerge which does not give considerably greater attention to them than has the system based upon the 1950 constitution. It might be argued that Indonesian government is more apt to develop in a democratic direction and more likely to have a genuinely representative character if the traditional *mufakat* procedure can in some degree be adapted to and incorporated into the nation's representative institutions.

National Unity and Decentralization

Establishment of a strong central government capable of making major decisions which reflect a broadly based consensus and of carrying them out effectively is obviously dependent upon restoration of national unity. It has become increasingly clear that the attempt to control the details of local administration from Jakarta is wholly out of tune with Indonesia's geography and persisting regional economic and cultural differences and needs. The provinces' reaction against Jakarta's paternalism has been profound. Local dissatisfaction with the central government and the belief that a decentralization of authority and fiscal power would allow the regions to promote their welfare more effectively are not confined to that one-third of the Indonesian population which inhabits 90 per cent of the country's area lying outside of Java; these are found in Java as well, particularly West Java. Even if it possessed much larger military forces and a better-trained and more experienced bureaucracy than it does, the national government would not be able to impose unity in this situation and have it result in any lasting political equilibrium unless it also took measures to diminish outstanding regional grievances. A law passed at the end of 1956 will, when fully carried out, greatly decentralize governmental administration and give the provinces control over most of the government personnel working in them and a greater share of locally raised funds.[1] The seizures of power by regional groups have apparently persuaded the Jakarta government of the necessity for proceeding as rapidly as possible in implementing this legislation and supplementing it with other measures designed to increase the administrative and fiscal autonomy of the provinces.

The ideological aspect of the problem, however, cannot be fully resolved through this means alone. So long as the Communist Party is strong in Java and influential in Jakarta, the predominantly non-Communist regions outside of Java are likely to remain restive. Similarly, should proponents of an Islamic state wield too much influence in Jakarta, predominantly Christian areas in the outer islands would feel uneasy. This superimposition of ideological differences upon regional economic and cultural differences presents a very knotty political problem. For Jakarta, at least under the existing constitutional system, is likely to be particularly sensitive to those areas having the most votes and the widest access to means of more direct political influence—and this means Java. But it is upon the areas outside of Java that the government is particularly dependent for domestically raised finances and foreign exchange. While the present situation exists (and it is likely to exist for some time), with Java having most of the population and the outer islands the major sources of revenue, political stability will be difficult to attain via the existing formula of government. Clearly Indonesia is a country peculiarly suited to a highly decentralized political system. Unhappily the Dutch with their efforts to promote a spurious federalism have so tarnished this word that whatever formula is adopted must have some other label; federalism by any other name would be sweeter. What may emerge is a system of decentralized government not called "federal" by Indonesians, but having the basic properties of federalism.

The Army

Whatever course of political reorganization is undertaken, the problem of the army will have to be confronted. The longer the present state of martial law (war and siege) endures, the more accustomed

---

[1] For a discussion of this law see John D. Legge, *Problems of Regional Autonomy in Contemporary Indonesia* (Cornell Modern Indonesia Project, Interim Reports Series; Ithaca, N.Y., July 1957), pp. 50–62. Concerning earlier legislation see Gerald Maryanov, *Decentralization in Indonesia: Legislative Aspects* (Cornell Modern Indonesia Project, Interim Reports Series; Ithaca, N.Y., March 1957).

many army officers are likely to become to the idea that it is in the natural order of things for them to exercise extensive civil powers and have a significant political role. This could militate against the chances for achieving a solidly based army unity; and it means that if such unity is achieved it will be difficult to establish the civilian arm of government in a position of substantial authority over the army. In any case the problem of army unification is inextricably intertwined with the problem of political harmony and national unity.

Economic Development

Closely associated with the problem of regionalism is that of economic development. It is here that the government has been under great pressure from the heightened expectations born of the revolution, and it is here that in the eyes of so many Indonesians it has fallen down so discouragingly. The government has failed to provide any sizable amount of new economic development, and in a number of areas, particularly outside of Java, it has been unable even to restore prewar production or repair fully the communications and transportation facilities destroyed or badly damaged during the Japanese occupation and the revolution. Although Jarkarta has worked out a Five Year Plan for economic development which incorporates many good projects, it has lacked adequate finances and administrative resources for undertaking this.[2] The argument that governmental decentralization could increase prospects for economic development is undoubtedly cogent. More direct local participation in planning and carrying out projects would almost certainly excite greater local interest and bring more active local participation. Moreover, if a fiscal decentralization were effected, the way would be open for locally levied and collected income taxes which would undoubtedly net considerably more than the existing system of a centrally administered income tax destined for the Jakarta treasury. Local personnel charged with such tax collection cannot be expected to be zealous in the discharge of a task locally considered to benefit Jakarta rather than the region. Their efforts would probably yield much more if the taxes collected remained in the locality for application to projects planned by (with or without central government co-operation) and executed in the local area.[3]

[2] For a comprehensive discussion of the Five Year Plan and the problem of economic development in general see Benjamin Higgins, *Indonesia's Economic Stabilization and Development* (New York: Institute of Pacific Relations, 1957).

[3] See the excellent studies of Professor Douglas Paauw regarding this subject, in particular his "The Case for Decentralized Financing of Economic Development

The pace of economic growth has been hamstrung by the rapid growth of population which has tended to keep up with if not ahead of increased output in the agrarian sphere, wherein 80 per cent of the population make their living. On Java this rapidly mounting population results in an increasingly unsatisfactory ratio of arable land to the peasant population—a situation begetting a dangerous political potential, one which the Communists have thus far exploited most effectively. Given the slight prospects for any early establishment of birth control, this problem can probably be resolved only if industrialization is undertaken along with measures to increase food production. The transplanting of Javanese peasants to the outer islands where there is sufficient land can augment food production, but so far has proven to be extremely expensive. Small-scale industries in Java could probably absorb more of the island's excess peasants with less expenditure.

The rate of investment in Indonesia has been very low, even by contemporary Asian standards. In part this has derived from governmental policy wherein importers (many of them favorites of the political parties in control of the cabinet) have received a major share of government credit. The credit granted by the principal Indonesian banks to import trade was in 1956 more than three times as large as that granted to industries.[4] The central government's investment role has been minor; thus during the period 1951–1954 the average ratio of government investments, including loans and advances, to total budgeted government expenditure was reported to be under 4.2 per cent. During the same period in India, Pakistan, and Japan, the proportions were reported as averaging 38, 27.1, and 43.4 per cent respectively.[5] This assumes particular importance in view of the fact that Indonesians themselves play such a minor entrepreneurial role and that, except from American oil companies, so little capital is being attracted from outside. Unsettled political conditions and the inability of the government to pass bills governing foreign investment and mining rights have made the status of existing foreign investments un-

in Indonesia," *Far Eastern Quarterly*, November 1955, pp. 77–95. Paauw also concludes that "Central Government policy tends to stifle rather than promote local initiative in undertaking and financing small-scale government projects" (*ibid.*, p. 86).

[4] See *Report of the Bank of Indonesia, 1956–1957*, p. 88, cited in Stanislas Swianiewicz, "Tendencies to Development and Stagnation in the Indonesian Economy," *Ekonomi dan Keuangan Indonesia* (Economics and Finance in Indonesia), February 1958, p. 91.

[5] These percentages are based upon figures appearing in *Economic Survey of Asia and the Far East, 1955* (Bangkok: United Nations, 1956), p. 42.

predictable and have discouraged new outside capital from entering Indonesia. In all probability this reluctance has increased as the result of the seizure of Dutch properties in December 1957.

Another major obstacle to economic development in Indonesia, one related to the absence of strong and effective government, has been the country's increasing inflation. From 1951 to 1957 the increase in the supply of money in Indonesia was reported to be greater than in any other country whose monetary statistics have been covered by ECAFE economic surveys except South Korea and Formosa—both of which are particularly burdened by heavy defense expenditures (but which are also recipients of large American economic aid).[6] A governmental budget which has been heavily in deficit except for the one year 1951 (made possible by the high price of rubber and tin attendant upon the Korean War) has been an important stimulus to this inflation.

Expansion of educational facilities has been one of the signal accomplishments of the postrevolutionary government, but unfortunately it has not been possible to maintain prewar standards, particularly at the secondary level. The greatly increasing number of people possessing an education does contribute in many ways to the welfare of the country, but too many of them are neither sufficiently trained to fill business or technical positions competently nor well enough educated to be of real benefit to the bureaucracy—whose standards still are greatly in need of improvement. Moreover, if development of the economy continues to lag as far behind as it has, educational expansion may result in producing a large number of dissatisfied individuals who can find no place in Indonesian society where their education can be properly utilized. As in India, this situation could produce dangerous political possibilities.

Foreign Relations

Although geography shields Indonesia from some of the realities of international power politics which the other major Asian states must more directly confront, foreign relations are, and have been from the beginning of the revolution, one of its important problem areas. Probably more than any other Asian state, Indonesia's posture in foreign relations is conditioned by its colonial experience, in particular the arduous fight for independence. As with other ex-colonial countries, long

---

[6] The supply of currency plus deposits in Indonesia rose from 5.03 billion rupiahs at the end of 1951 to 15.1 billion in June 1957 (Swianiewicz, "Indonesian Economy," p. 91).

subjection to colonial rule has engendered an extreme aversion to anything that can be interpreted as subservience to any foreign power. But among Indonesians this concern is heightened as a result of their revolutionary experience, in particular their interpretation of the roles of the United States and Soviet Russia during that period. Indeed, one cannot fully understand the insistence of every Indonesian government to date upon an independent foreign policy without reference to this. Indonesian leaders tend to view the records of both the United States and Soviet Russia during 1945–1949 as having been actuated much more by calculations of narrow self-interest than by the principle of self-determination for Indonesia.[7] They believe that during the first three and a half years of their struggle for independence both the United States and Soviet Russia, whatever may have been the public statements issued, either left the Republic of Indonesia to fend for itself against heavy odds or gave indirect help or encouragement to its enemies, the Dutch or the Communists.[8] This fear of outside control or influence has been largely instrumental in making Indonesians so suspicious of foreign capital and reluctant to agree to the conditions that would attract it to their country.

As with India, Indonesia's "neutrality" is not one of isolation from world affairs, but rather a refusal to commit itself to either of the two great power blocs. Its leaders have been jealous guardians of an independence of action brooking no advance commitments—what they have termed "an independent and active foreign policy." Their conduct of foreign policy has been closer to that of India than to any other major state, and on most international issues Indonesia and India have taken similar stands, though not always for exactly the same reasons. In part, too, insistence upon an independent and active foreign policy is symptomatic of the protest of Indonesian leaders against the failure of the major powers to consult sufficiently with them (and other Asian

[7] For an excellent account of Soviet Russia's attitude toward and relations with Indonesia during the revolution see Ruth T. McVey, *The Soviet View of the Indonesian Revolution* (Cornell Modern Indonesia Project, Interim Reports Series; Ithaca, N.Y., 1957).

[8] The United States is generally regarded as having enabled the Netherlands to mount its military offensives in Indonesia by giving major financial assistance to its home economy and thus making possible the Netherlands government's utilization of a large part of the country's domestic economic substance for support of its costly military effort in Indonesia. Many Indonesians regard Soviet Russia as having encouraged, if not instigated, the attempted *coup d'état* of the Communists at Madiun in 1948, a revolt which, though effectively suppressed, certainly weakened the Republic's military strength on the eve of the second Dutch offensive.

leaders) in matters concerning Asia. This feeling was important in bringing them to sponsor the Asian-African Conference at Bandung in 1955.

Indonesia's foreign policy cannot be divorced from its domestic politics. Most of its leaders are convinced that a genuinely independent foreign policy contributes much to easing internal tensions, particularly in offsetting Communist propaganda that the government is a puppet of the United States and in answering the weaker voices which allege that its policies are too close to those of Moscow or Peking.

Of all foreign policy issues that of West Irian (Western New Guinea) is by far the most important to Indonesians, and it is one which has particularly strong domestic political overtones. There may well be some basis to the allegation that this issue has sometimes been used to promote a psychological atmosphere conducive to national consciousness and unity and that on occasion it has served to divert attention from a government's shortcomings in domestic matters. Regardless of this, the issue has a deep intrinsic reality for most politically conscious Indonesians. They believe that West Irian is an integral part of their nation and that their government's claim to it is just and legitimate. There is no doubt that Australia's outspoken support of the Netherlands' claim to West Irian has antagonized those Indonesians who are most concerned over this issue—and Soekarno is among them. On the other hand they have generally appreciated Soviet Russia's and Communist China's sedulous support of the Indonesian position. The neutrality of the United States in the dispute is usually interpreted by these Indonesians as in fact favoring the Netherlands (a neutral position being regarded as acquiescence to the *status quo*) and consequently is displeasing to them. Even before the Indonesian Communist Party threw its propaganda campaign into high gear, moderate Indonesian leaders, including those of the Catholic Party and the Masjumi, were in agreement with Mohammad Hatta that the neutral position of the United States constituted, in fact, support of the Netherlands. Later there was wide agreement with his view that because of the United States stand and influence in the United Nations the request of Indonesia to the General Assembly in 1957 for the opening of discussions with the Netherlands concerning West Irian fell short of securing the two-thirds vote required to pass.[9]

The Communist Party has demonstrated great skill in its efforts to convert the West Irian issue into domestic political capital. Mohammad

[9] See Mohammad Hatta, "Indonesia between the Power Blocs," *Foreign Affairs*, XXXVI, no. 3 (April 1958), 486.

Hatta speaks for probably an overwhelming majority of those Indonesian leaders who stand in opposition to communism when he argues:

To permit West Irian to continue indefinitely as a bone of contention between Indonesia and the Netherlands is to afford Communism an opportunity to spread in Indonesia. . . . So long as West Irian is in Dutch hands, that long will the Communist Party of Indonesia be able to carry on a violent agitation, using nationalism as an excuse, to oppose colonialism and thereby touch the soul of the Indonesian people whose memories are still fresh with the struggle for freedom against colonialism. . . . Indeed, till the question of West Irian is settled Indonesian politics will be more irrational than rational.[10]

Primarily because of the breakdown in the negotiations over West Irian the relationship between Indonesia and the Netherlands has deteriorated drastically.[11] With the increasing evidence that the Dutch intended to hold New Guinea and give no further consideration to negotiations, anti-Netherlands sentiment in Indonesia grew deeper and more widespread. This resulted in 1956 in Indonesia's unilateral abrogation of the Round Table Conference Agreement of 1949 and its repudiation of that major part of its indebtedness to the Netherlands then assumed which Indonesians calculate to have been incurred through Dutch military operations against the Republic. And in December of 1957, with the Netherlands' continuing refusal to negotiate, Dutch properties in Indonesia were seized and strong and effective pressure was exerted upon the Dutch community of some 46,000 still resident there to evacuate to the Netherlands. As a consequence any prospect of agreement by the Netherlands to a negotiated settlement of the West Irian issue is understandably even dimmer than before. Whereas in 1957 a considerable majority in the United Nations General Assembly backed Indonesia's demand for negotiations (though less than the two-thirds necessary to pass a motion calling upon the Netherlands to negotiate), it is probable that today such support has diminished.

With a Chinese minority of two and a half to three million, a substantial proportion of which feel their primary loyalty to China, Indonesia has particularly good cause to maintain cordial relations

---

[10] *Ibid.*, pp. 486–487, 489.

[11] For a comprehensive and scholarly account of the dispute between Indonesia and the Netherlands over West Irian see *The Dynamics of the Western New Guinea (Irian Barat) Problem,* a study by Professor Robert C. Bone to be published by the Cornell Modern Indonesia Project in October 1958.

with a powerful China. Diplomatic recognition was exchanged with Communist China in 1950, and its claim to represent China in the United Nations has been consistently backed by Indonesia. Since at least 1953 the Peking government has made a persistent effort to win Indonesian friendship, its able Foreign Minister, Chou En-lai, attaining considerable success. The relationship is, however, not necessarily a stable one. Although Soekarno is at present favorably impressed with Mao Tse-tung and his government, his attitude and that of other influential Indonesians might quickly change should Peking's posture become less friendly, particularly if it should attempt to exert too much influence upon the Indonesian Chinese community or upon Jakarta in its relationship with this community. Given the widespread anti-Chinese sentiment among the mass of the Indonesian population, a situation might then arise which could produce explosive consequences in Indonesia and bring misfortune to much of its Chinese population.[12]

Although during the first few years after the revolution the Indonesian government showed a reluctance to develop close relations with Soviet Russia, even at the diplomatic level (embassies were not exchanged until 1954), this is no longer the case, and toward the end of 1957 parliament approved acceptance of a Russian loan amounting to $100 million. This and small credits currently being extended from East European Communist countries and Communist China will bring the total of Communist assistance to Indonesia close to the amount extended by the United States—a balance which the present Indonesian government maintains is indicative of its pursuit of an independent foreign policy.

[12] The relationship between the two countries is bound to be affected by the way in which the national status of Indonesia's Chinese minority is settled. Chou En-lai and the Indonesian Foreign Minister, Sunario, in 1955 laid the basis for a treaty between China and Indonesia which was to end Peking's claim to double citizenship for Chinese living in Indonesia and provide for their holding only one nationality—Indonesian or Chinese. Upon closer inspection, however, of the document which their government had initiated, Indonesians discovered that it contained several features disadvantageous to Indonesia and that under its provisions many more Indonesia-domiciled Chinese than had been expected might end up with Chinese rather than Indonesian citizenship. (For the text of this agreement see Donald Willmott, *The National Status of the Chinese in Indonesia* [Cornell Modern Indonesia Project, Interim Reports Series; Ithaca, N.Y., 1956], pp. 82–86.) As a consequence the Indonesian parliament delayed ratification of the agreement until late 1957. The future of Indonesia's relations with China may well hinge upon the willingness of Peking to acquiesce to Jakarta's interpreting some of the ambiguous provisions of the treaty more in conformance with what Indonesians consider to be their own national interests than the actual text would appear to warrant.

SUGGESTED READING

XIX: *Historical Background*

Allen, G. C., and Audrey G. Donnithorne. *Western Enterprise in Indonesia and Malaya*. London and New York: Macmillan, 1957. Useful for its account of the colonial period, but not a well-balanced treatment.

Bastin, John. *The Native Policies of Sir Stamford Raffles*. Oxford: Clarendon Press, 1957. A scholarly and useful study.

Benda, Harry J. "The Communist Rebellions of 1926–1927 in Indonesia," *Pacific Historical Review*, May 1955, pp. 139–152.

———. *The Crescent and the Rising Sun: Indonesian Islam under the Japanese Occupation*. The Hague and Bandung: van Hoeve, 1958. Contains a good account of Dutch Islamic policy.

Boeke, J. H. *The Evolution of the Netherlands Economy*. New York: Institute of Pacific Relations, 1946.

———. *The Structure of Netherlands Indian Economy*. New York: Institute of Pacific Relations, 1942. Tendentious, but useful.

Bousquet, G. H. *A French View of the Netherlands Indies*. Trans. by Philip E. Lilienthal. London and New York: Oxford University Press, 1940. An imaginative and provocative critique of Dutch colonial policy, particularly of Dutch Islamic policy and attitudes toward Indonesian nationalism, by a distinguished French Islamic specialist and colonial civil servant.

Broek, Jan O. M. *Economic Development in the Netherlands Indies*. New York: Institute of Pacific Relations, 1942.

Burger, D. H. *Structural Changes in Javanese Society: The Village Sphere and The Supra-Village Sphere*. Trans. by Leslie Palmier. (Cornell Modern Indonesia Project, Translation Series.) Ithaca, N.Y., 1957. A useful analysis of Indonesian society by an established Dutch scholar.

Cator, W. L. *The Economic Position of the Chinese in the Netherlands Indies*. Chicago: University of Chicago Press, 1936. A scholarly and valuable study.

Cole, Fay-Cooper. *The Peoples of Malaysia*. New York: Van Nostrand, 1945.

Coolie Budget Commission. *Living Conditions of Plantation Workers and Peasants on Java in 1939–1940*. Trans. by Robert Van Niel. (Cornell Modern Indonesia Project, Translation Series.) Ithaca, N.Y., 1956. An important, but hitherto classified and unpublished, report of the Netherlands Indies government.

Day, Clive. *The Policy and Administration of the Dutch in Java*. New York: Macmillan, 1904. A useful, though somewhat uncritical, historical study.

Dobby, E. H. G. *South East Asia*. London: University of London Press, 1950. Contains useful geographic data on Indonesia; the last chapter, dealing with political aspects, is weak.

Emerson, Rupert. *Malaysia: A Study in Indirect Rule.* New York: Macmillan, 1937. An imaginative, but sound and scholarly analysis of colonial rule in Indonesia and Malaya—a classic, but unfortunately out of print.

——, Lennox A. Mills, and Virginia Thompson. *Government and Nationalism in Southeast Asia.* New York: Institute of Pacific Relations, 1942. Contains a brief and useful description of the colonial government.

Furnivall, J. S. *Colonial Policy and Practice: A Comparative Study of Burma and Netherlands India.* New York: New York University Press, 1956. The treatment of Indonesia is less full than in the author's *Netherlands India,* but is nevertheless very useful; contains a full exposition of his theory of plural economy.

——. *Educational Progress in Southeast Asia.* (Institute of Pacific Relations, Inquiry Series.) New York: Institute of Pacific Relations, 1943.

——. *Netherlands India: A Study of Plural Economy.* New York: Macmillan; Cambridge, Eng.: Cambridge University Press, 1944. The best treatment of colonial rule in Indonesia; an excellent general history.

Haar, B. ter. *Adat Law in Indonesia.* Ed. and with an introduction by E. Adamson Hoebel and A. Arthur Schiller. New York: Institute of Pacific Relations, 1948. A good description of the customary law of the principal indigenous communities.

Hall, D. G. E. *A History of South East Asia.* London: Macmillan; New York: St. Martin's Press, 1955. The most comprehensive and scholarly general history of the area; almost exclusively concerned with events prior to World War II. Its coverage of Indonesia is excellent.

Harrison, B. *A Short History of South East Asia.* London: Macmillan; New York: St. Martin's Press, 1954. A much shorter survey than that by Hall, but nonetheless very useful.

Heine-Geldern, Robert. *Conceptions of State and Kingship in Southeast Asia.* (Southeast Asia Program, Cornell University, Data Paper no. 18.) Ithaca, N.Y., 1956. Useful to an understanding of the traditional (precolonial) political ethos.

Higgins, Benjamin. "The 'Dualistic Theory' of Underdeveloped Areas," *Economic Development and Cultural Change,* IV (Jan. 1956), 99–115. A substantial answer to Dr. Boeke's controversial theory, with particular relevance to Indonesia.

Kat Angelino, A. D. A. de. *Colonial Policy,* vol. II. Trans. from the Dutch by G. J. Renier. The Hague: M. Nijhoff, 1931. Comprehensive and solid description of the colonial government and of Dutch colonial policy.

Kennedy, Raymond. *The Ageless Indies.* New York: John Day, 1942. A well-written, though rather skimpy, survey.

Klerck, Edward S. de. *History of the Netherlands East Indies.* 2 vols. Rotterdam: W. L. and J. Brusse, 1938. A comprehensive and detailed coverage, rather turgid.

McVey, Ruth T. *Comintern Colonial Policy, 1920–1927, and Its Effect on the Development of Indonesian Communism.* (Cornell Modern Indonesia Project, Monograph Series.) Ithaca, N.Y., 1958.

Pelzer, Karl J. *Pioneer Settlement in the Asiatic Tropics.* New York: American Geographical Society, 1945. Contains an excellent description of prewar agrarian conditions in Java and of Dutch-sponsored efforts to transplant Javanese peasants in the outer islands.

Purcell, Victor. *The Chinese in Southeast Asia.* London: Oxford University Press, 1951. Contains a useful history of the Chinese minority in Indonesia prior to the revolution.

Raffles, Sir Thomas Stamford. *History of Java.* London: Black, Parbury, and Allen, 1817.

Schrieke, B. *The Effect of Western Influence on Native Civilizations of the Malay Archipelago.* Batavia: G. Kolf and Co., 1929. Contains several excellent essays. See particularly those by G. H. Van der Kolff and J. W. Meyer Ranneft.

——. *Indonesian Sociological Studies,* part I. The Hague and Bandung: van Hoeve, 1955. *Ruler and Realm in Early Java,* part II. The Hague and Bandung: van Hoeve, 1957. Recently translated selections from the works of an outstanding Dutch scholar. These are important studies of aspects of precolonial and colonial society.

Snouck-Hurgronje, C. *The Atjehnese.* Leyden: late E. J. Brill; London: Luzac and Co., 1906.

Vandenbosch, Amry. *The Dutch East Indies: Its Government, Problems, and Politics.* Berkeley and Los Angeles: University of California Press, 1944. The fullest account in English of government organization in the prewar period.

Van Leur, J. C. *Indonesian Trade and Society.* The Hague and Bandung: van Hoeve, 1955. Translation of the principal work of one of the most imaginative and provocative of Dutch scholars, who marshals convincing data to challenge the previously dominant European-centered view of Indonesian history.

Vlekke, Bernard H. M. *Nusantara: A History of the East Indian Archipelago.* Cambridge, Mass.: Harvard University Press, 1945. A useful history, especially with regard to the precolonial period; a new and revised edition is to be published in 1958.

XX: *The Revolution and the Revolutionary Government*

Alisjahbana, Takdir. "The Indonesian Language—By-Product of Nationalism," *Pacific Affairs,* XXII (Dec. 1949), 388–392.

Benda, Harry J. "The Beginnings of the Japanese Occupation of Java," *Far Eastern Quarterly,* XV (Aug. 1956), 541–560.

——. *The Crescent and the Rising Sun: Indonesian Islam under the Japanese*

Occupation. The Hague and Bandung: van Hoeve, 1958. By far the most scholarly and valuable study of the Japanese occupation.

Coast, John. *Recruit to Revolution.* London: Christopers, 1952. An exciting, somewhat flamboyant account incorporating considerable significant data by a Britisher who worked closely with the Foreign Ministry of the Republican government in London, Bangkok, and Jogjakarta during the period 1945–1948.

Gandasubrata, S. M. *An Account of the Japanese Occupation of Banjumas Residency, Java, March 1942 to August 1945.* Trans. by Leslie Palmier. (Southeast Asia Program, Cornell University, Data Paper no. 10.) Ithaca, N.Y., 1953. Firsthand observations by the Resident of Banjumas.

Kahin, George McT. *Nationalism and Revolution in Indonesia,* Ithaca, N.Y.: Cornell University Press, 1952.

Schiller, A. Arthur. *The Formation of Federal Indonesia.* The Hague and Bandung: van Hoeve, 1955. A scholarly, highly legalistic account concerned with the formal documents describing the Dutch-sponsored federal order of 1946–1949, but eschewing consideration of its political context or objectives.

Sjahrir, S. *Out of Exile.* Trans. by Charles Wolf, Jr. New York: John Day, 1949. The very readable personal journal of a leading Indonesian intellectual who was later to become Prime Minister of the Republic. All but the first chapter, dealing with the 1945 period, were written while he was in exile during the 1930s.

Soekarno. *The Birth of the Pantja Sila.* Jakarta: Ministry of Information, 1952. The original formulation by the future President of the Republic of his Five Principles of State.

Soemardjan, Selo. "Bureaucratic Organization in a Time of Revolution," *Administrative Science Quarterly,* II (Sept. 1957), 182–199. A keen piece of sociopolitical analysis by an Indonesian who was in a key position to observe.

van Mook, H. J. *The Stakes of Democracy in South East Asia.* New York: Norton, 1950. The personal views of the last Dutch Governor-General.

Wehl, David. *The Birth of Indonesia.* London: George Allen and Unwin, 1948. An interesting and useful account of the 1945–1947 period by a writer who was apparently an officer in the British occupation forces. Although this is not a balanced account, it contains considerable important information and a useful appendix of documents relating to the Dutch-Indonesian negotiations.

Wolf, Charles, Jr. *The Indonesian Story.* New York: John Day, 1948. An account of the 1945–1949 period containing by far the most reliable coverage of the Indonesian-Dutch negotiations culminating in the Linggadjati Agreement.

XXI: *The Postrevolutionary Setting*

Geertz, Clifford. "Religious Belief and Economic Behaviour in a Central Javanese Town: Some Preliminary Considerations," *Economic Development and Cultural Change,* IV (Jan. 1956), 134–158. A keen and deeply probing analysis of social and economic factors in rural central Java which also gives important insights into an understanding of developments during the elections.

———. *The Social Context of Economic Change: An Indonesian Case Study.* Cambridge: Massachusetts Institute of Technology, Center for International Studies, 1956. Mimeograph. A study of the sugar industry in Java and of its social context and impact.

Grader, Charles J. *Rural Organization and Village Revival in Indonesia.* (Southeast Asia Program, Cornell University, Data Paper no. 5.) Ithaca, N.Y., 1952.

Human Relations Area File. *Indonesia.* Subcontractor's Monograph. 3 vols. New Haven, 1957. Of uneven quality, but useful for reference on a variety of subjects.

Jay, Robert R. "Local Government in Rural Central Java," *Far Eastern Quarterly* XV (Feb. 1956), 215–227. A very useful study.

Kattenburg, Paul M. *A Central Javanese Village in 1950.* (Southeast Asia Program, Cornell University, Data Paper no. 2.) Ithaca, N.Y., 1951.

Kennedy, Raymond. *Field Notes on Indonesia: South Celebes, 1949–1950.* Ed. by Harold C. Conklin. New Haven: Human Relations Area Files, 1953. Useful, though not completely digested, data on rural life.

Metcalf, John E. *The Agricultural Economy of Indonesia.* Washington, D.C.: U.S. Department of Agriculture, Office of Agricultural Relations, 1952.

Palmier, Leslie H. "Aspects of Indonesia's Social Structure," *Pacific Affairs,* XXVIII (June 1955), 117–131. A discussion of changes in social stratification and the role of education in bringing these about.

———. "Modern Islam in Indonesia: The Muhammadiyah after Independence," *Pacific Affairs,* XXVII (Sept. 1954), 255–263.

Soeleman Soemardi. "Some Aspects of the Social Origins of the Indonesian Political Decision-Makers," in *Transactions of the Third World Congress of Sociology.* London, 1956. Interesting and useful data based on biographical research.

Supomo. "The Future of Adat Law in the Reconstruction of Indonesia," in Philip Thayer, ed., *South East Asia in the Coming World.* Baltimore: Johns Hopkins University Press, 1953. Pages 217–236.

van der Kroef, J. M. "Economic Development in Indonesia: Some Social and Cultural Impediments," *Economic Development and Cultural Change,* IV (Jan. 1956), 116–133.

———. *Indonesia in the Modern World*. 2 vols. Bandung: Masa Baru, 1954, 1956. A collection of essays of rather uneven quality, incorporating some useful (though not always completely reliable) data and stimulating (though not always soundly based) ideas.

van der Veur, Paul. "The Eurasians of Indonesia: Castaways of Colonialism," *Pacific Affairs*, XXVII (June 1954), 124–137. A solid treatment based upon substantial research.

van Nieuwenhuijze, C. A. O. *Aspects of Islam in Post-Revolutionary Indonesia*. The Hague and Bandung: van Hoeve, 1958. A series of essays based primarily on the author's experience in Indonesia before 1950.

Wertheim, W. F. "Changes in Indonesia's Social Stratification," *Pacific Affairs*, XXVIII (March 1955), 41–52. A discussion of individualist and collectivist tendencies in contemporary society.

———. *Indonesian Society in Transition*, The Hague and Bandung: van Hoeve, 1956. An analysis of past and present Indonesian society by a leading Dutch sociologist which is very useful for its account of pre-war society but has serious limitations in its treatment of the subsequent period.

Willmott, D. E. *The Status of the Chinese in Indonesia*. (Cornell Modern Indonesia Project, Interim Reports Series.) Ithaca, N.Y., 1956. A very useful report by a sociologist who has done intensive field research among the Chinese in Indonesia.

Woodman, Dorothy. *The Republic of Indonesia*. New York: Philosophical Library, 1955. A good introduction, but uneven in quality. The best chapters deal with the British occupation and the role of the United Nations in the Indonesian-Netherlands dispute.

XXII: *Postrevolutionary Government and Politics*

Bone, Robert C. "The Future of Indonesian Political Parties," *Far Eastern Survey*, XXIII (Feb. 1954), 17–24.

Budiardjo, Miriam S. "The Provisional Parliament of Indonesia," *Far Eastern Survey*, XXV (Feb. 1956), 17–23. A good discussion of an important aspect of governmental weakness in the postrevolutionary period.

Dohrenwend, Barbara S. *Some Factors Related to Autonomy and Dependence in Twelve Javanese Villages*. (Cornell Modern Indonesia Project, Interim Reports Series.) Ithaca, N.Y., 1957. An analysis by a social-psychologist based on research undertaken by Indonesian graduate students during 1955–1956.

Emerson, Rupert. *Representative Government in Southeast Asia*. Cambridge, Mass.: Harvard University Press, 1955. Parts of the excellent introduction and conclusion are relevant to Indonesia.

Feith, Herbert. *The Indonesian Elections of 1955*. (Cornell Modern Indonesia Project, Interim Reports Series.) Ithaca, N.Y., 1957. The most comprehensive and reliable account. The author is at work on a more substantial study which is due for publication in 1960.

——. *The Wilopo Cabinet, 1952–1953: Turning Point in Post-Revolutionary Indonesia*. (Cornell Modern Indonesia Project, Monograph Series.) Ithaca, N.Y., 1958. A full description of a key period in postrevolutionary politics, incorporating keen and illuminating political analysis.

Kahin, George McT. "Indonesian Politics and Nationalism," in W. L. Holland, ed., *Asian Nationalism and the West*. New York: Macmillan, 1953. Pages 65–196. Includes a brief account of developments in government and politics in 1950 and 1951.

Natsir, Mohammad. *Some Observations concerning the Role of Islam in National and International Affairs*. (Southeast Asia Program, Cornell University, Data Paper no. 16.) Ithaca, N.Y., 1954. Important insights into the thinking of the chairman of the Masjumi Party.

Pringgodigdo, A. K. *The Office of President in Indonesia as Defined in the Three Constitutions in Theory and Practice*. Trans. by Alexander Brotherton. (Cornell Modern Indonesia Project, Translation Series.) Ithaca, N.Y., 1957. The author is a distinguished scholar who served until recently as director of the cabinet of the President.

Soedjatmoko. "The Role of Political Parties in Indonesia," in P. W. Thayer, ed., *Nationalism and Progress in Free Asia*. Baltimore: Johns Hopkins Press, 1956. Pages 128–140. A keen analysis of the role of political parties in the 1955 elections.

van Marle, A. "The First Indonesian Parliamentary Elections," *Indonesië* (The Hague and Bandung), IX (June 1956), 257–264.

XXIII: *Some Major Problems*

de Meel, H. "Demographic Dilemma in Indonesia," *Pacific Affairs*, XXIV (Sept. 1951), 266–283. A pessimistic view of Indonesia's population problem.

Ekonomi dan Keuangan Indonesia (Economics and Finance in Indonesia). Published monthly or bimonthly beginning in 1953 by Pembangunan, Jakarta. This is a scholarly journal edited by a group of Indonesia's leading economists, with contributions by foreign economists concerned with Indonesia as well as by Indonesians. Usually each issue has at least one article in English. In general a high standard has been maintained, many of the contributions being unique in coverage and extremely useful.

Finkelstein, Lawrence S. "The Indonesian Federal Problem," *Pacific Affairs*, XXIV (Sept. 1951), 284–295.

Fryer, D. W. "Economic Aspects of Indonesian Disunity," *Pacific Affairs*, XXX (Sept. 1957), 195–208.

Hatta, Mohammad. *The Co-operative Movement in Indonesia.* Ithaca, N.Y.: Cornell University Press, 1957. The only full account of the development and present condition of co-operatives. Also gives considerable insight into the economic and political views of the still-influential former Vice-President.

Hawkins, Everett H. D. "Prospects for Economic Development in Indonesia," *World Politics,* VIII (Oct. 1955), 91–111. One of the best brief surveys.

Higgins, Benjamin. "Indonesia's Development Plans and Problems," *Pacific Affairs,* XXIX (June 1956), 107–125.

———. *Indonesia's Economic Stabilization and Development.* New York: Institute of Pacific Relations, 1957. The fullest account of contemporary economic problems and of plans for economic development. It incorporates significant observations by Guy Pauker on political aspects of these problems.

Hollinger, William C. "The Trade and Payments Agreements Program of Indonesia, 1950–1955," *Economic Development and Cultural Change,* IV (Jan. 1956), 186–199.

Hutasoit, M. *Compulsory Education in Indonesia.* UNESCO, 1954. An account of Indonesia's rapid and substantial expansion of its educational system by the secretary-general of its Ministry of Education.

Legge, John D. *Problems of Regional Autonomy in Contemporary Indonesia.* (Cornell Modern Indonesia Project, Interim Reports Series.) Ithaca, N.Y., 1957. An excellent account of the decentralization program in its administrative and political context.

Maryanov, Gerald S. *Decentralization in Indonesia: Legislative Aspects.* (Cornell Modern Indonesia Project, Interim Reports Series.) Ithaca, N.Y., 1957. A useful and full account of the earlier legislation.

Massachusetts Institute of Technology, Center for International Studies, Indonesia Project. *Stanvac in Indonesia.* New York: National Planning Association, 1957. A critical evaluation of the operations of the major U.S. business enterprise in Indonesia.

Paauw, Douglas S. "The Case for Decentralized Financing of Economic Development in Indonesia," *Far Eastern Quarterly,* XV (Nov. 1955), 77–95. A very valuable study.

———. "Financing Economic Development in Indonesia," *Economic Development and Cultural Change,* IV (Jan. 1956), 171–185. Discusses the problems of taxation, based on extensive investigations in the field.

Palmier, Leslie. "Occupational Distribution of Parents of Pupils in Certain Indonesian Educational Institutions," *Indonesië* (The Hague and Bandung) X (Aug. and Oct. 1957), 320–348, 349–376.

Pelzer, Karl J. "The Agrarian Conflict in East Sumatra," *Pacific Affairs*, XXX (June 1957), 151–159. An important article based on thorough and extensive research.

Soedjatmoko. *Economic Development as a Cultural Problem.* (Cornell Modern Indonesia Project, Translation Series.) Ithaca, N.Y., 1958. A brief but useful analysis.

United States Department of Commerce, *Investment in Indonesia.* Washington, D.C., U.S. Government Printing Office, 1956. Uneven in quality, but useful.

University of Indonesia, Institute for Economic and Social Research. *The Government's Program on Industries: A Progress Report.* Jakarta, Nov. 1954.

FOREIGN RELATIONS

Bone, Robert C. *The Dynamics of the Western New Guinea (Irian-Barat) Problem.* (Cornell Modern Indonesia Project, Interim Reports Series.) Ithaca, N.Y., 1958. Based upon several years of intensive research in Indonesia and the Netherlands and precursor of a more comprehensive monograph due for publication in late 1959.

Collins, J. Foster. "The United States and Indonesia," *International Conciliation,* March 1950.

Djajadiningrat, Idrus Nasir. *The Beginnings of the Indonesian-Dutch Negotiations and the Hoge Veluwe Talks.* (Cornell Modern Indonesia Project, Monograph Series.) Ithaca, N.Y., 1958. A deep and searching analysis of the early period of negotiations—one that was of great importance in establishing attitudes which dominated the later and better-known periods of negotiation.

Emerson, Rupert. "Reflections on the Indonesian Case," *World Politics,* I (Oct. 1948), 59–81.

Finkelstein, Lawrence S. "Indonesia's Record in the United Nations," *International Conciliation,* no. 475 (Nov. 1951), pp. 513–546. A good survey of 1950 and the first half of 1951.

Hatta, Mohammad. "Indonesia between the Power Blocs," *Foreign Affairs,* XXXVI (April 1958), 480–490.

——. "Indonesia's Foreign Policy," *Foreign Affairs,* XXXI (April 1953), 441–452.

Henderson, William. *Pacific Settlement of Disputes: The Indonesian Question, 1946–1949.* New York: Woodrow Wilson Foundation, 1954.

Kahin, George McT. *The Asian-African Conference, Bandung, Indonesia, April 1955.* Ithaca, N.Y.: Cornell University Press, 1956.

McVey, Ruth T. *The Calcutta Conference and the Southeast Asian Uprisings.* (Cornell Modern Indonesia Project, Interim Reports Series.)

Ithaca, N.Y., 1958. A useful supplement to previously much oversimplified accounts.

———. *The Soviet View of the Indonesian Revolution.* (Cornell Modern Indonesia Project, Interim Reports Series.) Ithaca, N.Y., 1957. A scholarly and pioneering study of high quality, precursor to a more comprehensive treatment of Soviet-Indonesian relations due for publication in 1960.

Sastroamidjojo, Ali, and Robert Delson. "The Status of the Republic of Indonesia in International Law," *Columbia Law Review,* XLIX (March 1949), 344–361.

INDEX

Index

(C=China; I=India; Is=Indonesia; J=Japan; P=Pakistan)

595

Date Due